Advanced Financial Accounting

Fifth Edition

Advanced
Financial
Accounting

Fifth Edition

Thomas H. Beechy
Schulich School of Business, York University

Toronto

Elizabeth Farrell
Schulich School of Business, York University

Library and Archives Canada Cataloguing in Publication

Beechy, Thomas H., 1937-
Advanced financial accounting / Thomas H. Beechy, Elizabeth Farrell. — 5th ed.

Includes index.
First-3rd eds. published under title: Canadian advanced financial accounting.
ISBN 0-13-123699-7

1. Accounting—Textbooks. I. Farrell, Elizabeth II. Beechy, Thomas H., 1937- .
Canadian advanced financial accounting. III. Title. IV. Title: Canadian
advanced financial accounting.

HF5635.B465 2006   657'.046   C2005-900655-2

Vice President, Editorial Director: Michael J. Young
Editor in Chief, Business and Economics: Gary Bennett
Executive Marketing Manager: Cas Shields
Associate Editor: Stephen Broadbent
Production Editor: Judith Scott
Copy Editor: Laurel Sparrow
Production Coordinator: Debroah Starks
Manufacturing Coordinator: Susan Johnson
Permissions Researcher: Sandy Cooke
Composition Specialist: Gerry Dunn
Art Director: Julia Hall
Interior and Cover Design: Anthony Leung
Cover Image: PhotoDisc

2 3 4 5   10 09 08 07 06

Printed and bound in the United States.

Materials from the Canadian Institute of Chartered Accountants, the Society of
Management Accountants of Canada, the Certified General Accountants
Association of Canada, and the Institute of Chartered Accountants of Ontario are
reprinted with permission.

Problem P6–20 on page 319 copyright ©1984 by the American Institute of
Certified Public Accountants, Inc. Reprinted with permission.

Brief Contents

Contents

Chapter 4:
Wholly Owned Subsidiaries: Reporting Subsequent to Acquisition

Chapter 5:
Consolidation of Non-Wholly Owned Subsidiaries

Contents

x

About the Authors

Thomas H. Beechy, DBA, CPA (Illinois)

Thomas H. Beechy (Tom) is Professor Emeritus of Accounting at the Schulich School of Business, York University. He has been an active accounting textbook author since the early 1980s, when he wrote the first edition of *Canadian Advanced Financial Accounting*, the first completely Canadian textbook above the introductory level. Tom was born, raised, and educated in the USA, but came to Canada in 1971. He holds degrees from The George Washington University (BA), Northwestern University (MBA), and Washington University (DBA). He also is a Certified Public Accountant in the state of Illinois. Prior to migrating to Canada, he taught at Northwestern University, Illinois Institute of Technology, and Washington University. At the Schulich School of Business, Professor Beechy was Associate Dean for 12 years and has served in a variety of other capacities including BBA Program Director, Executive Director of International Relations, and Executive Director of the York-CGA International Business Research Program. Tom loves to travel, and often can be found in Asia or Europe. He is a classical music fanatic, but he also likes piano jazz and live theatre.

Elizabeth Farrell, CA

Elizabeth Farrell is Adjunct Professor of Accounting at the Schulich School of Business, York University. In recognition of her excellence in teaching, she was selected as the winner of the 1999 Seymour Schulich Award for Teaching Excellence. Professor Farrell holds degrees from Queen's University (BA/BPHE) and York University (MBA). Elizabeth is actively involved in professional accounting education. She has served as a member of the Education, Program, Administration and Examination Committee for the Institute of Chartered Accountants of Ontario. In addition, she was their representative for the Ontario government of mathematics expert panel for secondary curriculum reform. Her other publications include an accounting case analysis software package, study guide, professional development courses, a variety of case material, and other publications. She also enjoys snowboarding.

Preface

This edition of *Advanced Financial Accounting* continues the book's tradition of providing comprehensive yet readable coverage of the topics normally included in advanced accounting courses. Not only have we updated the book for the latest changes in accounting standards, we also explain the changes that come into effect in late 2006. The topics are:

- The environment of financial reporting, including objectives of financial reporting and the basis for exercising professional judgement
- An overview of accounting for intercorporate investments, including new reporting requirements for investments in financial instruments
- Business combinations and consolidated financial reporting
- Foreign currency transactions and hedging, including new reporting requirements for hedges
- Foreign operations, including the new shareholders' equity classification of *other comprehensive income*
- Non-business organizations—non-profit organizations and public sector reporting

The principal focus of the book continues to be on business combinations and consolidations. Consolidation of an acquired subsidiary is a complex and demanding topic. Some books treat the topic lightly, looking only at the simplest situations and only at consolidation at the date of acquisition. In fact, consolidated financial statements are not prepared at the date of acquisition, except possibly for internal purposes. Any meaningful study of consolidations must be reasonably realistic by carrying examples (and problem material) into successive years. Students need practice at more than date-of-acquisition consolidations in order to understand the topic.

On the other hand, consolidation accounting is a topic that lends itself to endless "what if?" speculation. It is easy to envision situations that could conceivably arise, but which are actually very uncommon or even unknown in practice. The limited and valuable time of instructors and students should not be wasted on uncommon complexities. This view is reflected in professional examinations, which increasingly are focusing only on main issues.

For that reason, we have reduced the number of chapters devoted to intercorporate investments from six to five. The material on restricted shares and on step purchases has been placed in appendices. While this material may be interesting to some readers, it is not crucial for understanding the core issues of consolidated financial reporting.

The second most important topic in the book is foreign currency. In this edition, we have included the new Canadian standards on financial instruments, hedging, and comprehensive income. These new standards come into effect for fiscal years beginning on or after October 1, 2006. The new standards are harmonized with International Accounting Standards and convergent with (but not the same as) U.S. standards. Given the wide-spread acceptance and use of international standards around the world, students should be aware of these standards even before they officially go into effect in Canada.

The concept of comprehensive income will be new to many students taking an advanced accounting course, and therefore we have included a brief appendix to explain that concept, including the new shareholders' equity classification of *accumulated other comprehensive income*. This appendix can be ignored in later years (after 2005–2006), when students will have studied comprehensive income in intermediate courses prior to taking advanced accounting.

We have eliminated the defer-and-amortize approach to gains and losses on long-term monetary items because it no longer is accepted practice. We also have eliminated discussion of the current/noncurrent approach to foreign operations which is no longer discussed in the accounting community.

The new financial instruments and hedging standards are quite complex. We have focused on those aspects of the standards that are most meaningful for general practice. We believe that the material is presented in a way that is realistic but comprehensible.

The last two chapters are devoted to non-business financial reporting. Chapter 10 discusses and illustrates the reporting for non-profit (or not-for-profit) organizations, incorporating the current recommendations of the *CICA Handbook*. The main chapter focuses on *reporting* issues; the procedural detail of fund accounting is covered in an appendix to that chapter.

Chapter 11 discusses financial reporting for governments. Governmental and non-profit reporting are *not* the same thing. The reporting constraints of governments and non-profit organizations are quite distinct. Our discussion of public sector reporting incorporates the reporting recommendations of the *CICA Handbook*, as well as the recommendations of the CICA's 2003 *New Government Reporting Model*.

Assignment Material

The end-of-chapter assignment material consists of questions, cases, and problems. The book has always included a large number of cases, which are not problems-in-disguise; they really require the exercise of professional judgement. Practice in developing judgement is crucial for students at the advanced stages of their study. Professional examinations increasingly are testing judgement rather than bookkeeping techniques.

An important recent development in professional examinations is the emergence of competency-based testing. Students are examined on their ability to apply their knowledge and judgement in a consistent way to multi-faceted case situations.

This edition includes 13 new cases, three of which are in the first chapter. Most of the other chapters also have a new case. They are competency-based, and we have also revised many of the cases carried over from the previous edition to include multiple competencies. The competencies included are:

■ financial accounting and reporting
■ finance

- performance measurement
- organizational effectiveness, control, and risk management
- assurance
- information and information technology

Instructors may focus only on financial accounting competencies by excluding parts of the "required" for each case. Overall, the cases provide a variety of breadth and depth, and instructors have a great deal of flexibility in their use.

The problem material is extensively revised and enhanced for this edition. The changes provide comprehensive coverage of new and changed standards, as well as practice on practical application.

Self-Study Problems

Chapters 2 to 6, plus 8 and 9, each contains at least one self-study problem. These problems give students practice at applying the concepts and techniques that are explained in the chapters. The solutions are included in the back of the book, following chapter 11. Students are encouraged to solve these problems on their own, without referring to the solutions right away.

Student Resource CD-ROM

New with this edition is a CD-ROM that contains **Problem Templates** in **Excel®** for many of the consolidation problems. Students often spend a great deal of time on simply setting up the framework for the solution, whether by the direct approach or the spreadsheet (worksheet) approach. The CD-ROM will save the student a lot of the set-up time, and permit her or him to focus on the learning experience rather than the procedural detail.

The **Weblinks** section adds a comprehensive list of online resources that allow students to further explore financial accounting topics and issues presented in the text.

Finally, the Student Resource CD contains a link to **Online Learning Problems** placed on the text's website. This section provides additional practice to the self-study problems in the text, where the keen student can continue applying the concepts and techniques explained in the chapters.

Other Supplements

This book includes all revised accounting standards (and exposure drafts) through 2004; however, the pace of accounting standards revision has accelerated due to the pressures for harmonization and convergence with international and U.S. standards. As standards continue to develop, we will post updates on the book's website: **www.pearsoned.ca/beechyfarrell**.

In addition to the website, we offer to instructors a comprehensive **Instructor's Resource Manual** that contains solutions for all of the questions, cases, and problems. As well, we are providing instructors with a new **Test Item File** that contains additional materials for tests and for extra student practice.

Acknowledgements

As in the previous editions, much of the assignment material was drawn from the professional examination of Canada's three professional accounting bodies: CGA-Canada, CICA, and SMA Canada. A few cases have also been included by the kind permission of the Institute of Chartered Accountants of Ontario. We are deeply indebted to all of these organizations for their cooperation and support in permitting us to use their copyrighted material. An acknowledgement appears at the end of each case or problem that was obtained from one of these four professional sources.

We also are deeply indebted to the individuals who reviewed and provided valuable suggestions on the revision plan and the manuscript, including Christopher Wright, Lakehead University; Robin G. Dalziel, British Columbia Institute of Technology; Nola Buhr, University of Saskatchewan; Joan Conrod, Dalhousie University; Pauline Downer, Memorial University; Talal Hayale, University of Windsor; Marg Forbes, University of Saskatchewan; Valorie Leonard, Laurentian University; and David Hiscock, McMaster University.

We are grateful for the enthusiastic support and encouragement of the people at Pearson Education Canada for bringing this project to fruition. In particular, we would like to thank Gary Bennett, Editor in Chief of Business and Economics; Stephen Broadbent, Associate Editor; Laurel Sparrow, Copy Editor; Michelle Hodgson, Technical Checker; Shari Mann, for her excellent work in creating the problem templates in Excel on the CD-ROM; Judith Scott, Production Editor; and Deborah Starks, Production Manager.

On a personal level, we would like to thank our friends and family for their support and encouragement throughout the lengthy process of bringing this book to a close.

Despite the efforts of many people and many sets of eyes, errors have a nasty habit of creeping into all books. Of course, we authors bear the responsibility for any errors that you may find. We would greatly appreciate your bringing any and all errors to our attention, no matter how minor. We will forward these corrections to other students and instructors and will then be able to correct them before the next printing of the book.

Please report any errors by email to **tbeechy@schulich.yorku.ca**.

Thank you for using *Advanced Financial Accounting*, Fifth Edition. We hope you will find it an enjoyable book to use.

Thomas H. Beechy
Elizabeth Farrell

Chapter 1

Setting the Stage

Introduction to Advanced Accounting

What is *advanced financial accounting*? Essentially, advanced accounting is the detailed study of three broad topics that you may have studied at a more basic level in intermediate accounting:

- accounting for intercorporate investments
- accounting for foreign currency transactions and foreign operations, and
- financial reporting by non-business organizations—non-profit organizations and governments.

It is not difficult to understand the basic concepts underlying these broad topics. However, it can be quite complex and difficult to apply these topics in practice.

In this book, we will emphasize the "big picture." It is easy to get tangled in the detailed numbers and to lose sight of the ultimate financial reporting objective. Therefore, we will begin by reviewing the broader context of financial reporting. In this chapter, we will:

- review the meaning of *professional judgment* in accounting
- discuss the various major *financial reporting objectives* and how the presence of these objectives in a specific business will affect the exercise of professional judgment
- review the forms of *business organization*
- discuss *GAAP* and the alternatives to GAAP reporting, including the circumstances in which each is appropriate, and
- introduce *international accounting standards* and their impact on the world of financial reporting.

The Context—Overview

Accounting is not a matter of simply following rules; a professional accountant must continually exercise professional judgment in the exercise of her or his responsibilities.

Judgment depends on context. A professional accountant must understand the context within which judgmental issues arise; otherwise, there is no difference between professional judgment and non-professional judgment—anyone's guess would be as valid as the accountant's! Therefore, this chapter will deal first with the meaning of professional judgment and how it comes into play in the topics covered in this book.

Next, the chapter briefly reviews the applicability of generally accepted accounting principles, or GAAP. GAAP is not *always* the appropriate basis of reporting, and every accountant must be capable of recognizing the situations in which some elements of GAAP may not be appropriate. In private companies, *differential reporting* alternatives may be chosen. Sometimes, a *disclosed basis of accounting* should be used. We will discuss these options a little later in the chapter.

The chapter also reviews financial reporting objectives. Many judgments affecting accounting numbers are shaped by management's financial reporting objectives. Is management seeking to satisfy users' needs, such as facilitating cash flow prediction or performance evaluation, or does management want to maximize reported earnings, minimize current income taxes, or meet debt covenants? Understanding management's financial reporting objectives (which are implicit rather than explicitly stated) is crucial to the exercise of professional judgment.

Much of what follows in this chapter may already be familiar to you. Nevertheless, it may well be useful to review this material. It never hurts to refresh your awareness of the factors that affect the exercise of professional judgment.

Professional Judgment

The accountant functions in a world of conflicting demands and multiple alternatives. Professional judgment is essential in choosing from among alternative valid approaches to solving a problem. But the exercise of judgment requires benchmarks or explicit criteria by which to evaluate alternative approaches and alternative results. The use of professional judgment is not an application of arbitrariness. If choices were purely arbitrary, then there would be no difference between professional judgment and non-professional judgment; the professional would be in no better position to make a decision than would someone with no accounting background.

Judgment is required whenever there are choices to be made. Three types of choices are pervasive in accounting:

1. accounting policy choices

2. accounting estimates, and

3. disclosure decisions.

Accounting policy choices arise whenever more than one acceptable accounting policy can be used in a particular situation. An obvious example is the choice of depreciation method. Several different policies are equally acceptable under GAAP—which one to choose?

Accounting policies such as inventory valuation, revenue recognition, intangible asset recognition and amortization, tangible capital asset depreciation, and various other types of expense recognition policies all have a significant impact on both the balance sheet and the income statement. Some also affect the way in which transactions are reported on the cash flow statement. Accounting policy choices have a more or less permanent impact on financial reporting because they cannot easily be changed.

The use of *accounting estimates* is at least as important as the choice of accounting policy. Significant accounting policies should be disclosed, but accounting estimates very rarely are disclosed. Accounting estimates are the unseen factor that management can use to shape reported accounting numbers.

For example, accounting policies for inventory valuation (e.g., first-in first-out, average cost, or lower of cost or market (LCM)) usually are disclosed, but companies never disclose the methods used to estimate these amounts. What cost components are included in acquisition cost? How much overhead is included in inventory cost? What measures of "market" are used in LCM valuation? How long does it take for a company to decide that inventory should be written down? All of these decisions affect reported results, but we will look in vain for any description of these estimates in the financial statements or the notes thereto.

Disclosure decisions are the third area in which accounting judgments must be made. What should be disclosed, and in how much detail? The *CICA Handbook* suggests quite a lot of disclosure, but much of it is "advisable" rather than obligatory. Even the "recommended" disclosures are subject to a great deal of judgment about the extent of clarity and detail.

Disclosures beyond the *CICA Handbook*'s specific disclosure recommendations are purely judgmental. Many companies are quite vague (in their financial statement notes) about the extent of non-arm's-length transactions, about their relationships with other companies, about who controls the company, or about how significant accounting policies (such as revenue recognition) are applied. Some companies seem to prefer favourable disclosures to unfavourable disclosures—it is common for the sources and nature of unusual losses to be disclosed, but unusual gains often seem to end up in income without being separately disclosed!

It is management's responsibility to make decisions about accounting policies, accounting estimates, and disclosure. However, a professional accountant must be able to advise management on acceptable accounting practices—on the range of feasible and ethical alternatives. As well, an auditor must use her or his professional judgment to determine whether management's choices are suitable within the context of the company—the company's form of organization, the applicability of GAAP, the financial reporting objectives, and the reasonableness of business estimates and measurements.

Professional Judgment in Advanced Accounting Topics

As we go through the topics in this book, it may appear that the *CICA Handbook* severely constrains the possible accounting alternatives. In particular, the accounting choices related to intercorporate investments may seem to be sharply limited. However, a number of choices still exist, some of which are quite significant. These are summarized in Exhibit 1–1.

Notice that there is not a lot of policy choice in some areas, particularly those connected with business combinations and consolidations, but there can be substantial measurement issues that require many accounting estimates. The detail in this table may not mean much at first, but you should refer to it as you make your way through the book. The table will be a useful reminder of the importance of professional judgment in the areas of financial reporting that are discussed in this book.

EXHIBIT 1–1 ACCOUNTING POLICY CHOICES AND ACCOUNTING ESTIMATES—EXAMPLES WITHIN GAAP

	Extent of Choice	
	Policy	Estimates
Consolidations:		
Which subsidiaries to consolidate	None	None
Amount of unrealized profit	None	Large
Joint ventures	None	Medium
Business combinations:		
Cost of acquisition—cash purchase	None	Small
Cost of acquisition—share exchange	Small	Large
Method of consolidation	None	None
Allocation of purchase price	None	Large
Amortization of fair value increments/decrements	None	Medium
Write-down of goodwill	None	Large
Foreign operations:		
Foreign-currency denominated transactions	None	Small
Designation of each foreign operation (integrated vs. self-sustaining)	Large	Medium
Non-business organizations:		
Non-profit organizations	Large	Large
Governments	Large	Large

Financial Reporting Objectives

The most fundamental set of criteria governing the application of professional judgment is the **financial reporting objectives** that are being used by the reporting enterprise. Accounting policy choices, accounting measurements and estimates, and disclosure policies are all affected by the specific reporting objectives of management.

Reporting objectives are not vague and unmeasurable like "to serve the general reader" or "to provide fair presentation"; general objectives like these are of no help at all to the practising professional accountant. If several choices are available within GAAP (or an alternative framework, if appropriate), how can an objective like *fair presentation* provide any guidance? Obviously, fair presentation is much better than unfair presentation, but unfair presentation basically is unethical and/or fraudulent reporting.

The *CICA Handbook* is not much help for setting objectives. It states that the general financial reporting objective "is to communicate information that is useful"—not, to be sure, information that is useless—for the purpose of making the users' "resource allocation decisions and/or assessing management stewardship."[1] What users? What types of resource allocation decisions? How is management performance to be assessed? Not only is the meaning unclear, but also there is

---

1. *CICA Handbook*, paragraph 1000.15.

conflict among the various types of decisions implied by this broadly stated objective.

We will not discuss financial reporting objectives at length, you will be glad to know. But we will make a quick review. The importance of financial reporting objectives will become apparent in subsequent chapters when we discuss circumstances in which there is a choice of accounting policies or accounting estimates.

User objectives

Financial statement readers use the statements as a basis for decisions. Users often want information that will help them to:

1. predict cash flows

2. ascertain whether the company has complied with contractual requirements, and

3. evaluate the performance of management.

Cash flow prediction Investors and creditors often are concerned about the cash flow of a company. On a continuing basis they are particularly interested in the cash flow from operations, because it is the operating cash flow that provides the cash for paying bills, paying dividends, and expansion. Users, therefore, often want accounting decisions made in a way that facilitates their *cash flow prediction*.

The cash flow prediction objective is that the financial statements should convey information to users that will help them to predict future cash flows of the company based on past and current data. The statements should describe the current pattern of cash flows, and should indicate any expected alteration of those flows.

One important aspect of this objective is that the phrase "cash flow" should not be taken too literally. Cash flow from operations does not really mean just the net cash received for a specific period of time. The concept is really more of a longer-term view of how much cash will be returned to the enterprise as the result of current operations. Thus cash flow should be viewed within the context of accrual accounting to include prepaid and accrued items:

> [Users'] interest in an enterprise's future cash flows... leads primarily to an interest in information about its earnings rather than information directly about its cash flows.... Information about enterprise earnings and its components measured by accrual accounting generally provides a better indication of enterprise performance than information about current cash receipts and payments.[2]

There are two principal accounting impacts when a cash flow prediction objective is adopted as the primary reporting objective:

1. net income will tend to be measured in a way that indicates long-run cash flow from operations, and

2. notes will be used to describe future cash flows not indicated in the body of the statements themselves, including expected changes in those flows that are reported.

2. *Statement of Financial Accounting Concepts No. 1: Objectives of Financial Reporting by Business Enterprises* (Stamford, Connecticut: Financial Accounting Standards Board, 1978), paragraphs 43–44.

The dominant impact of the cash flow prediction objective is that accounting choices will measure revenue and expenses in a way that most closely corresponds to accrual-basis cash flows. If a company uses many interperiod allocations of past costs and estimates of future costs in measuring earnings, the relationship between earnings and cash flow is unclear. When earnings relate closely to cash flows, prediction of future cash flows is easier than when earnings do not relate closely to cash flows.

Accountants are accustomed to the fact that periodic earnings measurement is different from cash flow measurement. Cash flow and net income are two different measures. In the long run, however, they are equal. An enterprise's lifetime net income is the net cash return on the investment. There is a clear relationship between cash flow and earnings, and earnings cannot be measured without direct reference to past, present, and future cash flows.

Financial analysts refer to earnings that correspond closely to cash flows as **high-quality earnings**. *Low-quality* earnings, on the other hand, are those that are not reflected in cash flows from operations. Since investors tend to be interested in cash flows, high-quality earnings are preferred to low-quality earnings, and this preference may show up in the market as higher share prices or a greater willingness of a bank to lend money.

Under the cash flow prediction objective, then, companies will opt for immediate recognition of costs rather than deferral and amortization. For example, retail chains regularly open and close stores as they adjust to changing markets. The costs of opening new stores can either be expensed immediately or deferred and amortized. Using a cash flow prediction objective, the costs would be expensed immediately because that treatment reflects the fact that the cash has been spent on an activity that is a normal, recurring business activity in the industry. Similarly, interest costs incurred on new development activities would be expensed rather than being capitalized as part of the costs of the project.

A secondary impact of the cash flow prediction objective is that the notes to the financial statements may be used to disclose supplementary information about future cash flows. Some of the disclosures that are currently recommended in the *CICA Handbook* reflect the need for information about future flows. Examples include the detailed information on amounts due for debt repayments and lease payments over the next five years. In addition, however, a company could also disclose information such as major expected changes in cost structure, the size of the order backlog, or the current value of inventories.

Contract compliance Both *shareholders' agreements* and *loan agreements* (including bond indentures) usually contain specific requirements that involve accounting measurements. A **shareholders' agreement** is a contract among the shareholders. Shareholders' agreements are normal in a private company, but sometimes exist in a public company (primarily to limit voting power).

Shareholders' agreements in private corporations often contain provisions such as dividend entitlements, limitations on cash withdrawals, and valuation. Valuation is a particularly important issue in private companies because valuation provisions govern the way shares are valued if an investor wishes to buy additional shares or sell her or his shares. Valuation is determined on the basis of accounting measurements, usually book value per share, since there is no public market for the shares of private companies. Asset valuation and income measurement policies obviously have a significant impact on book values.

A **loan agreement** is the contract between a borrower and a lender. Lenders usually include **covenants** or **maintenance tests** in loan agreements, which are requirements that the borrower must meet in order to keep the loan in good standing. Examples of covenants or maintenance tests are:

- a minimum level of the current ratio
- a maximum age of receivables
- a minimum turnover of inventory
- a maximum debt–equity ratio
- a minimum times-interest-earned ratio, and
- limitations on dividend payout.

Failure to meet the requirements of the loan agreement could result in the lender's calling the loan or refusing to renew or extend loans. A lender will use the financial statements of the borrower to determine whether or not the maintenance tests have been met. The level of the maintenance tests is (or should be) determined by the lender after taking into consideration the accounting policies used by the borrower. Therefore, the lender is concerned not only with the level of the ratios but also whether consistent accounting policies have been used as the basis for their calculation.

Performance evaluation Frequently, financial statement readers want to know how well management is running the business. Indeed, managers themselves usually need a report card to see how they are doing. In a small business, the managers may have a good idea of the success of their management, but may need the financial statements in order to show creditors or silent partners how the business is going. On the other hand, managers may think they are doing alright, but need the statements in order to verify their perceptions.

In larger businesses, financial statements are essential for determining how well the company is managed. Investors and creditors are concerned, as are the directors and the managers themselves. In a diversified corporation, the separate-entity financial statements of the individual operating companies may form the primary basis by which the corporation's top management evaluates the performance of the component companies and their managers.

It is very difficult to separate good management from the benefits of a good economy or from simple good luck. Nevertheless, financial statements can be of some assistance in performance appraisal, especially when used in conjunction with the statements of similar businesses and with more general economic information.

When performance appraisal is the primary objective of the financial statements, the accounting policies should, as much as possible, reflect the way in which decisions are made.

For example, suppose that the management of a chain of hotels wants to issue financial statements that show investors how well management is doing its job. The chain opens new hotels fairly regularly, and it has a policy of renovating older hotels. Suppose that management decides to build a new hotel based on an analysis of the future market in the area, and on the potential net cash flow and present value of the project. Start-up costs will be substantial, but management believes that future revenues will recover these costs. Since the decision was made by offsetting the start-up costs against revenues in future periods, the performance evaluation objective would call for capitalizing the costs and amortizing them against the future revenues.

The treatment of hotel start-up costs would be quite different under the cash flow prediction alternative. For cash flow prediction, it would be better to expense the costs immediately because the cash outflow occurred immediately and because start-up costs are a routine part of doing business and opening new hotels.

One problem with the performance evaluation objective is that it is sometimes indistinguishable from an approach that seeks simply to maximize reported earnings. Statement users who are close to the company (such as managers, directors, owners of private corporations, or controlling shareholders of public companies) are frequently in a position to know which objective is being followed. But for an external user, it is sometimes hard to tell the two apart. Clues may be gained by closely scrutinizing the accounting policies relating to revenue and expense recognition in the notes to the financial statements.

Preparer objectives

The preceding objectives relate to users' decision needs. The preparers of the statements are likely to have their own set of priorities when they select accounting policies. **Preparers** refers to the *managers*, not to their accounting staff. Remember that the financial statements are the responsibility of management. The accountant provides the expertise to assist the managers in meeting their reporting objectives, but the statements are management's.

The policies that management chooses will have an impact on the reported results and therefore may affect users' perceptions. The policies may also have a more direct impact on the managers themselves—compensation levels often are tied to accounting measurements, and the managers' future job prospects may be enhanced by reporting the "right" results.

In the following sections, we will discuss four major reporting objectives of the preparers. These are:

1. income tax deferral

2. net income maximization or minimization

3. income smoothing, and

4. minimum disclosure and contract compliance.

Some accountants would prefer to refer to these preparer reporting objectives as preparer **motivations** rather than as objectives, reserving the term "objectives" to relate to the legitimate decision needs of the users.

Income tax deferral One of the responsibilities of management is to maximize the discounted net present value of the enterprise's future cash flow. One way of doing this is to delay the liability for income taxes. There is a time value of money, and a dollar of taxes paid in the future has a smaller present value than a dollar of taxes paid currently. Thus the deferral of tax payments will increase the present value of the company.

To some extent, adopting accounting policies and accounting measures that reduce revenue and/or increase current expense recognition can reduce current income taxes. In particular, revenue recognition policies can have a significant impact on the amount of taxes due. If tax deferral is the objective, revenue recognition is delayed as long as is feasible. In contrast, a performance evaluation objective often leads to early revenue recognition. Some companies may have little flexibility in this regard. A retail business with a high proportion of cash sales, for instance, has little option in revenue recognition.

Expense recognition also offers some flexibility for tax deferral, particularly in inventory valuation—minimizing the amount of overhead included in inventory has the effect of recognizing overhead expenses as soon as possible. However, interperiod cost allocations seldom have much impact on income taxes. Development costs, for example, are tax-deductible when incurred, regardless of whether the company chooses to defer and amortize those expenditures.

Bear in mind that shifting relatively small amounts of revenue or expense from one period to another can have a substantial impact on *net* income. If net income is 10% of revenue, delaying recognition of 2% of revenue will have an impact of up to 20% of net income.

In general, an objective of tax deferral (sometimes cited as *tax minimization*) leads to accounting policies that delay revenue recognition and speed up expense recognition. The result is net income that is lower than would be reported under alternative acceptable accounting policies. The policies must be long-term in scope; the accounting treatment cannot be changed from year to year.

For some companies, particularly small private corporations, tax deferral may be the dominant (or only) objective of financial reporting. The managers know that net income is on the low side of the permissible range of accounting net income figures, and they can explain the situation to bankers or other major creditors who might be using the statements. Since tax deferral reduces the current cash flow drain on the company, bankers may welcome the astute tax management and may evaluate the company's reported performance more favourably.

Tax deferral might seem to be a desirable objective for all companies. But, for many enterprises, the low net income that would be reported is incompatible with other objectives of the financial statements. If the company is trying to attract investors, for example, a low reported net income will not help. Bear in mind that the company cannot say in its annual report that the accounting figures should be taken with a grain of salt because they are tax-influenced amounts. The company must live with the results of its accounting policy decisions because they are chosen from an array of acceptable alternatives. Therefore, many companies choose not to emphasize tax deferral as an objective of financial reporting, but rather adopt other objectives that are more important to the overall corporate goals.

Maximization or minimization of earnings Sometimes management's objective of financial reporting is simply to *maximize* or *minimize* the enterprise's reported net income. Management may wish to maximize earnings in order to attract new investors or to allay the fears of present investors.

Companies that are having a difficult time have been known to adopt accounting policies that increase earnings by recognizing revenue earlier or expenses later. If bond indentures or loan agreements contain covenants concerning dividend payout ratios, times-interest-earned ratios, etc., a high level of earnings will make it easier to comply with the restrictions. Other companies may be in satisfactory financial health, but wish to look even better in order to be well perceived in a competitive financial and business market. In addition, management bonuses or salaries may be tied to reported earnings, so that the managers benefit directly by maximizing reported earnings.

On the other hand, management may wish to minimize reported earnings (for reasons other than tax deferral). Management may feel that the company's earnings are embarrassingly high and may wish to discourage the entry of new competitors or to avoid attracting public or political attention, or higher wage demands by employees. Management may hope to discourage takeover bids if control is not firmly held by friendly shareholders. Earnings can be minimized by delaying revenue recognition as long as possible and by expensing (rather than deferring) as many costs as possible.

Such tactics should not fool an efficient market. Indeed, research suggests that the stock market reacts adversely to changes in accounting policies that would tend to increase earnings, because the change is interpreted as a signal that management expects real earnings to decline.

Similarly, minimization of earnings may not be expected to mislead an efficient market. There is ample empirical evidence that the stock market will adjust for different accounting policies in assigning a value to shares. And understated earnings surely would not lead astray any acquisition-minded managers of another company. If anything, reduced reported earnings would only depress the potential price that the acquiree's shareholders would receive.

But management may not be trying to influence the reactions of the market as a whole. It may be more concerned with the perceptions of individual shareholders or outsiders, and individual users are not necessarily efficient and unbiased processors of information. Indeed, managers may believe that it is more important to cater to the biases and perceptions of a single large shareholder or shareholder group (such as a controlling family) than to recognize the efficiency of the public securities markets.

Earnings management—the "big bath" One aspect of earnings management that merits special mention is the practice of taking a "big bath" or "big hit" in a loss year. This is an observed tendency of companies to load all possible losses and write-downs into a year that is going to be a low-earnings or loss year anyway. Management's view is that if they're going to report a loss, they might as well report a large one and "clean up the balance sheet."

Companies often take the opportunity offered by a loss year to write down assets of doubtful future benefit, especially intangible assets. Sometimes, the write-down is very substantial, and there have been cases in which the auditors have objected that the company is writing its assets down to an amount that is well below recoverable cost. Another strategy is to make substantial provisions for future costs related to current decisions and actions, such as restructuring costs or reclamation costs.

The earnings management objective of the big bath is that, by writing down assets, the company has less amortization in future years. Hence, future earnings are enhanced. This is why the big bath strategy can be part of an earnings maximization objective. Similarly, when a company makes provisions for future costs that are at the high end of the feasible range of estimates, the current provision reduces the amount of expense that is charged in future years. Indeed, if the current charge turns out to be excessive, the company can recognize a gain in future years when it reduces the recorded liability.

The big bath approach is an aggressive use of accounting estimates. Not only can estimates be used to write down assets and to charge large future cost provisions against current earnings, but estimates relating to routine accounting measurements can be adjusted. For example, pension cost estimates are subject to a wide range of very future-oriented estimates. A relatively minor adjustment to an estimate (such as the future earnings rate of the pension plan) can contribute significantly to the big bath.

The big bath philosophy treads very close to the line of ethical reporting. The intent, either conscious or unconscious, is to increase future earnings by stretching the limits of accounting estimates. Taken far enough, a big bath can result in deliberate misstatement of accounting results, in both the current and future periods. If all of the charges in a big bath are legitimate, then one wonders whether the prior years' financial statements were misstated because they included assets that had no future benefit.

Income smoothing Investors and creditors are concerned not only with the level of earnings, but also with the business risk of a company. The level of risk is equated with the volatility of earnings and cash flows. In attempting to influence users' perceptions about the company, managers may wish to select accounting policies that not only increase the apparent *level* of earnings but also decrease the apparent *volatility* of earnings. Accounting policies can have the effect of smoothing earnings.

Smoothing may be accomplished through either revenue or expense recognition policies, or both. Revenue can be smoothed by spreading its recognition over an earnings cycle, such as by using percentage-of-completion rather than completed contract, or by timing the recognition of irregular lumps of revenue to fall into periods of low economic activity. Expenses can be smoothed by amortizing costs over a period of years rather than by recognizing them at inception; examples include development costs and start-up costs.

Smoothing can also be accomplished through the recognition of significant future-oriented cost estimates. A great deal of flexibility is associated with such estimates as future restructuring costs, reclamation costs, costs/benefits of discontinued operations, and so forth. Indeed, accounting pronouncements in recent years have tended to increase the ability of management to "manage" the recognition of major future-related cost estimates.

The smoothing of expenses is most effective if the expenses can be related to levels of revenue, since smoothing of expenses will not in itself necessarily lead to the smoothing of net income. For example, if net revenue fluctuates substantially, the smoothing of an expense will tend to lower the entire level of earnings over a period of years but will not decrease the fluctuation. Indeed, if the same volatility exists but at a lower overall level of earnings, the relative risk will appear to increase rather than to decrease.

As with the maximization or minimization of earnings, one might assume that smoothing tendencies would not fool an efficient market. Discerning the impacts of interperiod allocations is easier said than done, however, since smoothing is often accomplished through the adroit use of accounting estimates.

Minimum compliance and contract compliance Sometimes management wishes to report the least possible amount of information to external stakeholders. This practice is known as **minimum compliance**.

In a public company, minimum compliance takes the form of compliance with all of the reporting requirements of the *Securities Act* and the *Corporations Act* and with the "required" recommendations of the *CICA Handbook*; the reporting company provides none of the "desirable" disclosures recommended by the *CICA Handbook*. Managers may be motivated to use minimum disclosure because they do not wish to reveal what they consider to be confidential information to competitors, labour unions, etc. Often, the practice of minimum compliance derives from a somewhat secretive attitude on the part of managers—the "it's none of your business" approach to financial reporting.

The managers of private companies commonly follow the practice of minimum compliance. As the number of external stakeholders is limited, the managers need only provide the minimum information required to satisfy their external reporting requirements.

Related to the practice of minimum compliance (especially, but not exclusively, in a private company) is financial reporting that is based on the goal of optimizing compliance with the terms of contracts. This objective of **contract compliance** may be observed when managers choose accounting policies that will most readily enable the company to meet covenants imposed by major lenders in loan agreements. Often, the desire to meet (or, when the provisions are restrictive, to avoid) contract provisions translates to other reporting objectives such as income maximization or smoothing. The real motivation may be the contract provisions, however.

Other objectives

The user and preparer objectives discussed above are only some of the most common objectives. There can be a wide array of other objectives, depending on the nature of the enterprise and its reporting environment.

Regulated companies, for example, normally are permitted to earn a maximum percentage return on their invested capital. As a result, a regulated company will tend to use accounting policies that maximize the book value of the asset base in order to maximize the permitted dollar return on investment (and, after financial leverage, on the shareholders' equity).

Similarly, a company that is subsidized by some level of government is apt to use accounting policies that maximize the amount of subsidy to which the company is legally and ethically entitled.

Canadian companies that are wholly-owned subsidiaries of foreign parents usually must comply with the accounting mandates of their parents. Generally, that means complying with U.S. GAAP or with International Accounting Standards (IAS). About 65% of the wholly-owned foreign subsidiaries in the *Financial Post 500* have U.S. parents, and U.S. GAAP will prevail in those subsidiaries.

For subsidiaries of non-U.S. parent companies, IAS usually is used. IAS is accepted as the reporting standard on the vast majority of stock exchanges worldwide. Even in Europe, where separate-entity reporting must comply with local law, consolidated statements are prepared in accordance with IAS. For the topics covered in this book, there is little difference between IAS and the *CICA Handbook* recommendations, but in a broader accounting context there are significant differences.

In addition to ignoring Canadian GAAP, however, a wholly-owned subsidiary of a foreign parent derives its reporting objectives from its parent, and the parent's reporting objectives may be driven by factors that are quite different from anything encountered in Canada. Therefore, an accountant who is working for such a subsidiary must be sensitive to and familiar with its different reporting context.

Resolving conflicts among objectives

In any financial reporting situation, there is a potential conflict between user objectives and preparer motivations. Since the managers are preparing the statements, it would appear that preparer motivations would dominate the selection of objectives.

However, users are not without power. The Canada Revenue Agency (CRA) clearly has the power to assess taxes on taxable income determined independently of reported accounting income. Major shareholders can, through the board of directors and its audit committee, have an influence on reporting objectives. Public shareholders have little direct influence, but security analysts and the financial press can put pressure on corporations to provide financial information that is most useful to outsiders rather than self-serving to managers. Major lenders certainly have more direct power to demand attention to their reporting needs, although competitive forces temper this power—bankers sometimes worry that if they are too insistent, the customer will go to another bank.

All financial reporting situations therefore involve a trade-off between users and preparers in determining the reporting objectives. The relative strength of the two groups will influence the selection of accounting policies.

In some companies, there may be only one significant reporting objective, either a user objective or a preparer objective. In most cases, however, there will be several objectives, and the objectives may not be compatible with each other. For example, a corporation's management (1) may need to satisfy covenants in a loan agreement, (2) may wish to defer income taxes, and (3) may want to maximize reported earnings in order to maximize executive compensation.

When choosing from among alternative accounting policies, management will not be able to select policies that satisfy all of these objectives simultaneously. Therefore it is necessary to prioritize the objectives by deciding which is the most important, which is the next most important, and so forth.

The prioritizing of reporting objectives involves making a **hierarchy** of objectives. A hierarchy of objectives must be tailored to each reporting enterprise; there is no generalized hierarchy. When there is a conflict in the accounting policies indicated by the various objectives, the objective(s) at the top of the hierarchy will win out over those further down.

Applicability of GAAP

You undoubtedly will have studied the origins and meaning of GAAP in your earlier accounting courses. We will not belabour the issue here. But it is worth remembering that GAAP is defined partially by the *CICA Handbook* and partially by existing (and therefore "generally accepted") practices. For the topics covered in this book, the *CICA Handbook* is particularly important.

Who must comply with GAAP? The easy answer is, "everyone." But the easy answer is seldom the correct answer. There are important exceptions to the GAAP requirement. If GAAP is not necessarily applicable to a specific reporting entity, a broader range of possible accounting options are available. Any entity is likely to conform to GAAP for the vast majority of its accounting practices, simply because GAAP is derived largely from existing practices (rather than from the *CICA Handbook*) and existing practices evolved to satisfy reporting needs.

When management of a reporting entity chooses to deviate from GAAP, it does not throw the entire structure of GAAP out the window. Instead, deviation from GAAP usually is on one or two specific accounting issues. For example, a small business may decide not to capitalize its lease obligations, in order to clarify the cash flow aspects of its operations in the income statement.

The applicability of GAAP depends on the nature of the business. Therefore, we must look at the different possible types of business organization. The form of business organization shapes the nature of financial reporting.

Form of Business Organization

Proprietorship

The most basic form of business organization is the **proprietorship**, often known as the **sole proprietorship**. A proprietorship has one owner (i.e., the proprietor), and the business is not legally separate from the owner. Legally, a proprietorship is indistinguishable from its owner. To prepare financial statements for a proprietorship, we must be able to separate the business activities from the owner's personal affairs.

The users of a proprietorship's financial statements are very few. Usually, the only users are the owner and the federal and provincial tax authorities. In some cases, a bank may extend a loan, but the loan really is to the owner and not to the "business." The bank will be interested in the financial statements of the proprietorship because the proprietorship's cash flow affects the owner's ability to repay the loan.

A proprietorship cannot be audited. An audit is impossible because there is no clear distinction between the business and its owner. Therefore, GAAP is not a constraint. When a proprietorship prepares a full set of financial statements, a disclosed basis of accounting is used. The notes to the financial statements disclose the accounting policies, which usually are quite simple. The most common objective of financial reporting is *tax compliance*, with *cash flow prediction* as a secondary objective.

Partnership

In a partnership, two or more individuals come together to operate a business jointly. The partners sign a **partnership agreement**, a legal contract that defines the rights and responsibilities of each partner. The partnership agreement specifies the amount and type of investment by each partner, defines the profit sharing arrangements, and describes how partners can leave the partnership or new partners can join it.

A partnership is not a separate legal entity. A partnership is not subject to income tax. Instead, the profits of a partnership are taxed to the individual partners. In effect, a partnership is a joint proprietorship—two or more proprietors joining for a common purpose. For accounting purposes, the primary distinction between a proprietorship and a partnership is that a partnership is more clearly defined (by the partnership agreement). The business affairs of a partnership are less likely to be confused with the partner's personal affairs than is the case with a proprietorship.

Private corporation

A corporation is an "individual" in the eyes of the law: it has a clear legal status as a separate entity. A private corporation is one that is held by one person or by a small group of shareholders. The shares of a private corporation cannot be bought or sold on the open market.

Most corporations are private, and most private corporations are small businesses. But a private corporation can be very large, too. Examples of large Canadian private corporations include Bata Shoe (the world's largest shoe maker), McCain Foods (maker of one-third of all the frozen french fries in the world), and Katz Group Canada (operator of 1,700 drug stores, including PharmaPlus).

By definition, a private corporation has no public shareholders. Therefore, the financial statements are not subject to public scrutiny. The financial statement users will include the managers, private shareholders, tax authorities, bankers, and creditors.

Public corporation

A public corporation is one that has registered with a securities commission and is permitted to sell its securities to the public. Since the shares may be publicly traded, the financial statements of a public company are available to the public. The financial statements of all Canadian public corporations are available on the Internet at www.sedar.com. The financial reporting of public companies must comply with the requirements of the securities commissions. Also, if the company's shares are listed on a stock exchange, the company must comply with the exchange's rules and regulations.

Some public corporations are widely held—no one person or one group owns a majority of the shares. Other corporations are closely held, even though the shares are publicly traded. It is very common for Canadian corporations to have controlling shareholders who own a majority of the shares, including companies such as Canadian Tire and Bombardier. George Weston Limited, Canada's second-largest corporation (and parent of Loblaws, Provigo, etc.), is 62% owned by its chairman, George Weston. Of the largest 500 Canadian corporations, only about 20% are widely held.

Public corporations that have controlling shareholders usually have more than one class of common shares, each of which has different voting rights. One class of common shares has reduced voting power (or no voting power); it is called a **restricted share**. The controlling shareholders may not own a majority of the total common shares, but they generally own most or all of the share class that has maximum voting power.

There is no technical or legal distinction between a *widely held* public corporation and a *controlled* public corporation. However, there can be implications for financial reporting.

GAAP and Public Corporations

Public companies are subject to scrutiny by the securities commissions, and questionable accounting practices can lead to a suspension of trading. The securities commissions therefore have an effective tool by which they can force compliance with the GAAP reporting requirements. Companies with securities traded on major exchanges will restrict their accounting policies to GAAP.

Although GAAP is required for public companies, this does not mean that everything is prescribed. The *CICA Handbook*'s "Introduction to Accounting Recommendations" states that

> Accounting Handbook Sections emphasize principles rather than detailed rules and, therefore, cannot be phrased to suit all circumstances or combinations of circumstances that may arise [paragraph .03].

The clear implication, therefore, is that although GAAP is mandatory for public companies, there is still a lot of room for judgement in the application of accounting standards through the choice of accounting policies, estimates, and disclosures.

GAAP and Alternatives for Private Corporations

Private corporations have a much wider range of possible accounting practices. In general, they can choose from among three bases of accounting:

- full GAAP, following all of the recommendations in the *CICA Handbook*
- *differential reporting*, which is within GAAP but permits private companies to use simplified accounting in some areas of accounting, and
- *disclosed basis of accounting*, wherein a company deviates from GAAP in one or more ways but discloses the basis of accounting in an accounting policy note.

The following sections will discuss the reasons that GAAP is not a binding constraint on private corporations, and then explain differential reporting and the disclosed basis of reporting.

GAAP

According to federal and provincial law (that is, the corporations acts), each corporation is required to give *audited* financial statements to its shareholders every year.

However, the shareholders of a private company can waive the audit by unanimous consent. For example, the *Canada Business Corporations Act* (*CBCA*) states that "if all the members of a company that is not a reporting company [i.e., a public company] consent in writing to a resolution waiving the appointment of an auditor, the company is not required to appoint an auditor."

Some of the acts limit the availability of a waiver to companies that are below certain size thresholds. The thresholds under the *CBCA* are gross revenues of $10 million *or* total assets of $5 million. The other provincial limits are lower—for example, Ontario limits are half of the *CBCA* amounts. In provinces where *size tests* exist, companies that are larger than these size limits should, in theory, submit their financial statements to audit and should comply with GAAP.

In fact, private companies may have little concern about the statutory requirements. Quite a few corporations that exceed the size tests do not have an audit, and many of those that do have an audit do not comply strictly with GAAP. The reason for the apparent non-compliance is that there is little basis for enforcing the statutory provisions on private companies of limited ownership. Since an audit is waived by consent of the shareholders, the shareholders cannot complain if it turns out later that the financial statements were incorrect or the system of internal control was not operating properly.

The vast majority of corporations in Canada are private corporations. Many are quite small. But even among large companies, very many are private. In the annual *Financial Post* listing of Canada's largest 500 corporations, 40% are private. Many of those are subsidiaries of foreign parents, and Canadian GAAP is largely irrelevant for those subsidiaries. At least half of the economic activity in Canada is through private companies.[3]

---

3. Relatively few public companies in Canada are widely held. Most have a control block held by an individual, a family, or another corporation. In the *Financial Post* 2003 listing, only about 20% of the 500 largest public companies are designated as being "widely held" by the investing public.

Private companies obtain external financing through bank loans or through private placements of securities.[4] Bankers and the purchasers of private placements are assumed to be sophisticated users of financial information. If they rely on unaudited statements or on non-GAAP statements, they are presumed to know what they are doing and to have consented to receive such statements.

Differential reporting

When compared to accounting standards in other countries, Canadian GAAP is rather unusual because the recommendations of the *CICA Handbook* apply to all corporations, public or private. An auditor must report in accordance with GAAP, according to the business corporations acts across the country. This is not the case in most other countries. In the U.S.A., for example, FASB pronouncements apply only to corporations that issue securities to the public and therefore must report to the U.S. Securities and Exchange Commission (SEC). U.S. private companies may (and often do) use a disclosed basis of reporting.

To ease some of the reporting complexities imposed by the recommendations of the *CICA Handbook*, the AcSB permits *differential reporting*. Differential reporting enables private companies to choose simpler accounting policies for a few selected reporting issues. A company may choose differential reporting only if [CICA 1300.06]:

- the company has no shares or other securities that are publicly traded, *and*
- the company is not otherwise accountable to the public, such as financial institutions or rate-regulated enterprises, *and*
- *all* of its shareholders agree unanimously with the use of the simplified or alternative differential accounting policies.

The use of differential accounting is not a deviation from GAAP, because this alternative is explicitly permitted by the recommendations of the *CICA Handbook*. Therefore, differential reporting is a part of GAAP.

As we write this book, differential reporting can be applied to recommendations in seven sections of the *CICA Handbook*. Four applications pertain to topics normally covered in intermediate accounting courses:

- the taxes payable method of accounting can be used for reporting income tax
- less detailed disclosure can be provided for share capital
- the company does not have to provide some of the fair value disclosures that generally are required for financial instruments, and
- certain types of redeemable preferred shares that otherwise would be classified as a liability can, instead, be reported as shareholders' equity.

The remaining applications of differential reporting—reporting of subsidiaries, significantly-influenced investees, joint ventures, and goodwill impairment tests—will be discussed later in this book.

It is not necessary to use an all-or-nothing approach to differential reporting. A corporation can choose to apply one or more of these alternative treatments. The choice of alternatives is up to management. An audit opinion need not be qualified, since use of these alternatives is permitted by the recommendations of the *CICA Handbook* and thus is within Canadian GAAP.

---

4. Any issuance of securities over a specified lower limit is exempt from the *Securities Acts'* reporting requirements. The minimum amount is $97,000 or $150,000, depending on the province.

Disclosed basis of accounting

Occasionally, it is necessary or desirable for a reporting organization to use specific accounting policies that are outside the body of generally accepted accounting policies. The notes to financial statements normally include an accounting policy note that explains the choices made by the reporting entity when alternatives are available. The *CICA Handbook* recommends that:

> A clear and concise description of the significant accounting policies of an enterprise should be included as an integral part of the financial statements. [CICA 1505.04]

For example, the accounting policy note should describe the entity's revenue recognition policy, depreciation policies, policies relating to inventory valuation, and so forth.

When the policies described in the policy note are outside GAAP, the organization is then using a *disclosed basis of accounting* (*DBA*) in lieu of GAAP.

DBA may be used when the statements are prepared in accordance with contractual requirements. Examples of such contractual requirements include borrowing contracts and buy/sell agreements in shareholders' agreements. If the contractual requirements are those of a *public* company, then statements prepared in accordance with the contract are **special purpose reports** rather than general purpose reports.

In *private* corporations, the external contracting parties may well be the only significant external users of the entity's financial statements, and the special purpose report in effect becomes the general purpose report. In such cases, there is no reason to prepare separate general purpose statements in addition to those prepared in accordance with the contractual requirements.

Disclosed basis of accounting is sometimes given other names that more clearly identify the reason behind the departure from GAAP. These include **regulatory accounting policies (RAP)** for regulated entities (including banks) and **tailored accounting policies (TAP)** to describe accounting policies that are "tailored" to satisfy the needs of contractual arrangements. However, DBA remains the broader term.

Partnerships

The accounting policies used by partnerships vary widely due to the nature of the partnership agreement, the services provided, the asset base, and the funding sources. For that reason GAAP is often not an appropriate basis of accounting for their specific needs. The disclosed basis of accounting is widely used for reporting by partnerships.

The basic accounting for partnerships is relatively easy and is covered in most introductory financial accounting textbooks. However, the reporting issue can be explored in the context of the disclosed basis of reporting. Using an example, we will explore this issue a little further.

The partnership agreement is often the driving force behind the accounting policies chosen by a partnership. One thing that needs to be addressed in the partnership agreement is how partners enter and leave the partnership. The financial issue is (1) how much capital a new partner should invest and (2) how much capital a partner who is leaving the partnership should receive.

One alternative is for the partnership to use market values for its asset and liability valuation, and to accrue earnings on a performance basis (rather than on a completion basis). GAAP does not generally embrace market values, and therefore market values can be used only under a disclosed basis of accounting. Of course, the partnership agreement (and the DBA) needs to further define *market* to avoid future disagreements.

Another alternative is to use historical cost. If GAAP historical cost accounting is used, problems arise—e.g., the appreciation in the value of assets over time and the value of work in progress will not be shown. This will result in entering partners paying too little and exiting partners not receiving their fair share. Of course, there are other valid reasons why a partner entering would pay below market. For example, a partnership may need the entering person's unique talents or services. Or an exiting partner may receive a lower amount to be able to get cash out quickly. Using historical cost will require a special revaluation of assets and liabilities when partners enter or leave the partnership. This annual valuation will then be the DBA.

Therefore, partnerships usually declare their financial reporting policies in a note and the auditor's opinion (if any) states that "the financial statements have been prepared in accordance with the accounting policies described in Note 1," or some similar wording.

A DBA is particularly useful in this type of situation where there is a limited group of users (the partners) who have a specific need (e.g. determining the amount to enter or exit the partnership).

Proprietorships

A proprietorship will generally use a disclosed basis of accounting. The primary external user of a proprietorship's financial statements will probably be the income tax authorities (e.g., Canada Revenue Agency (CRA)) and possibly a bank. The tax authorities will be interested in taxable income, and the bank will be interested in earnings supported by cash flows. Of course, income tax is an important component of cash flows.

Therefore, a proprietorship will often prepare its financial statements by using accounting policies that minimize the difference between taxable income and reported earnings. Revenue and expenses will be recognized on a basis that is acceptable to CRA. Amortization will be based on CCA rates. Other interperiod allocations will be minimized, except when they are required for determining taxable income.

For proprietorships, GAAP is essentially irrelevant. Nevertheless, certain underlying concepts of GAAP will continue to be used, including historical cost, revenue recognition, and matching.

International Accounting Standards

One of the more pressing issues on the world accounting scene is the *harmonization* of accounting standards. **Harmonization** means achieving a high level of consistency among different countries' accounting standards. Standards will never become completely the same around the world, however, because economic factors vary significantly between nations. Each nation's accounting standards must, to some extent, reflect the unique characteristics of doing business in that country.

International Accounting Standards Board

The International Accounting Standards Board (IASB) has been striving to achieve harmonization for over 30 years. The current IASB is a reorganized form of the original International Accounting Standards Committee (IASC), a London-based organization formed in 1973 by members from nine countries: Australia, Canada, France, Germany, Japan, Mexico, the Netherlands, the U.K. (plus Ireland), and the U.S.A. The IASC members did not actually represent *countries*; instead, the members represented professional accountancy bodies in their countries. For example, the member from Canada was from the CICA; the member from the U.S.A. was from the American Institute of Certified Public Accountants.

By 2001, the IASC had grown to over 200 members, but the business of the IASC was conducted by a smaller Board consisting of 13 members. Although the Board membership varied, it always included a group of seven countries: Australia, Canada, France, Germany, Japan, U.K., and U.S.A. In other words, all of the original members except Mexico and the Netherlands continued as the core members throughout the history of the IASC.

For almost 30 years, the IASC Board strove to establish accounting standards for international use. That objective gained momentum in the 1990s when the International Organization of Securities Commissions (IOSCO) challenged the IASC to develop a set of high-quality accounting standards that reduced the range of accounting policy choices. The objective of IOSCO was to recommend the acceptance of international accounting standards to the securities regulators in its member countries.

In 2001, the IASC adopted a new constitution that changed the organization structure. The main aspects of the new structure are:

- the International Accounting Standards Committee Foundation, a new not-for-profit foundation incorporated in the state of Delaware, U.S.A. The foundation has 19 trustees, of which 10 are from English-speaking countries. The U.S. has five members, Japan has two, and 12 countries have one representative each. The chairman is Paul Volcker, a well-respected former chairman of the U.S. Federal Reserve System. The primary responsibility of the trustees is to select the members of the Board.

- the International Accounting Standards Board (IASB), which is based in London. The Board's responsibility is to establish international accounting standards. The Board has 14 members, including a permanent chairman (Sir David Tweedie, formerly the chairman of the accounting standard-setting board of the U.K.). The 13 other Board members include direct representatives of the standard-setters of the group of seven countries that have always been represented on the Board.

- a Standards Advisory Council, which makes agenda suggestions to the IASB. The IASB is under no obligation to accept the Council's recommendations. The Council may have up to 45 members, who are drawn from a broader constituency group of preparers and users of financial information.

One of the primary advantages of the new structure is that, for the first time, the IASB has a direct and official link with the standard-setters in the group of seven countries. Prior to the change in structure, the IASC had worked in cooperation with the major English-speaking standard-setters such as the AcSB and the FASB, but the new structure formalized the link and helps to coordinate activities between the IASB and the national standard setters.

Canada has always been a major participant in the work of the IASC/IASB. In fact, IASB standards are probably more similar to those of Canada than to those of any other single country that has a national standard-setter. Because the IASC and the CICA worked together on many issues, some of the IASB standards are virtually identical to the CICA standards, word-for-word.

Acceptance of international standards

There is nothing "theoretical" about international accounting standards. International standards are accepted for reporting on the vast majority of stock exchanges around the world. In some countries, international standards are acceptable only for foreign-based companies, such as for Japanese companies reporting on the Hong Kong exchange or for U.S. companies reporting on the London exchange.

In Europe, however, international standards are mandated as the reporting basis for both international and domestic companies' *consolidated* financial statements. Separate-entity (that is, unconsolidated) financial statements generally must be prepared using home-country GAAP, due to legal constraints.

Some countries permit (or require) international GAAP even for their own domestic public companies. Examples include Hungary, Peru, the Netherlands, the Czech Republic, and China (except for "A" shares, which are traded in Chinese currency in China only).

In Canada and the U.S., foreign companies can report on the basis of home-country GAAP or international GAAP, but they must provide a reconciliation to host-country GAAP.

Implications for Canadian standards

Since the IASB was restructured, Sir David Tweedie has been a very strong leader pushing for harmonization of international standards and national standards. In September 2002, the IASB and the FASB reached agreement for a convergence program. Under this agreement, the two standard-setters agree to:

- establish a short-term project to reduce differences between U.S. GAAP and IAS,
- identify areas in which convergence can best be achieved by joint major projects, and
- coordinate future work programs.

This agreement, known as the *Norwalk Agreement*, commits both organizations to work together for harmonization. The policy of the CICA Accounting Standards Board is to reduce differences between Canadian GAAP and both U.S. and international GAAP. Therefore, all of the proposals and changes that are emerging from this agreement are quickly being reflected in Canadian GAAP.

From now on, it will be impossible for Canadian accountants to ignore international developments. Therefore, we often will refer to international standards as we discuss the topics in this book. International standards are the future—Canadian GAAP will converge with international GAAP, although with some modifications that recognize the differences in Canada's accounting environment.

SUMMARY OF KEY POINTS

1. *Professional judgment* is the use of criteria for deciding from among acceptable accounting policies, accounting estimates, and disclosures. Professional judgment is what distinguishes an accountant from a bookkeeper.

2. Accounting choices are the responsibility of management. The accountant's role is to advise management on acceptable and ethical alternatives, or, as an auditor, to verify that management's choices are appropriate within the company's reporting context. Many aspects of the topics covered within this book are highly constrained by the recommendations of the *CICA Handbook*. However, choices still remain, especially in the broad area of *accounting estimates*.

3. The most important single set of criteria by which accounting judgments are made is that of *financial reporting objectives*. Financial reporting objectives must be determined for each enterprise individually. There are two general types of objectives: (1) user objectives, and (2) preparer (i.e., management's) objectives. Common user objectives are cash flow prediction, contract compliance, and management performance evaluation. Common preparer objectives are income tax deferral, earnings maximization, income smoothing, and influencing contract compliance criteria.

    There usually are several relevant objectives for a single enterprise, and the objectives often conflict with each other. In order for the accountant (and management) to choose from among alternative accounting policies and estimates, conflicting objectives must be prioritized. The objectives at the top of the hierarchy (with higher priority) take precedence over those further down the list.

4. Public companies must comply with generally accepted accounting principles (GAAP) in order to satisfy the requirements of securities commissions. However, only about 60% of Canada's 500 largest corporations are public; the other 40% are private corporations.

5. Technically, private corporations are required by the provincial and federal corporations acts to have an audit. But an audit can be waived by unanimous consent of the shareholders. Therefore, the technical requirement to report in accordance with GAAP has little effect on private corporations.

6. Private corporations may elect to use one or more of the provisions for *differential reporting*, as permitted by the *CICA Handbook*. Differential reporting allows private corporations to be exempted from certain accounting recommendations that apply to public companies. Since differential reporting is part of the accounting recommendations in the *CICA Handbook*, differential reporting still is part of GAAP.

7. If differential reporting does not meet a private corporation's reporting needs, the company may choose to use a *disclosed basis of accounting* (DBA), which is sometimes known as tailored accounting policies (TAP). DBA also is used by partnerships and proprietorships.

8. International Accounting Standards (IAS) are in wide use around the world. The principal use is by international companies that are listed on stock exchanges outside of their home countries. As well, many countries require IAS for consolidated reporting, even if publicly-released separate entity state-

ments are prepared by local GAAP. IAS is not acceptable for reporting in Canada at the present time, but this may change before long.

The London-based International Accounting Standards Board (IASB) is responsible for international standards. The IASB and the U.S. FASB have a *convergence agreement* to reduce the differences between U.S. and international GAAP. That drive for convergence is causing rapid changes in Canadian GAAP, since the AcSB's objective is to harmonize Canadian GAAP with both U.S. and international GAAP.

REVIEW QUESTIONS

1–1 What distinguishes *professional judgment* from non-professional judgment?

1–2 When is professional judgment required? What are three types of choices in accounting that require the use of professional judgment?

1–3 Why is it necessary for the accountant to define the objectives of financial reporting for the enterprise for which he or she is preparing financial statements?

1–4 Since most externally reported financial statements are required to be in accordance with GAAP, how can the existence of specific objectives of financial reporting affect the preparation of the statements?

1–5 If externally reported financial statements are *general purpose* statements, how can specific objectives influence their content?

1–6 What is the long-term relationship between cash flow and earnings?

1–7 How does the accrual method of accounting fit into the concept of a cash flow prediction emphasis for financial reporting?

1–8 Explain what is meant by *high-quality earnings*.

1–9 In what general ways would a *cash flow prediction* objective influence the selection of accounting policies?

1–10 What is a *shareholders' agreement*?

1–11 What is a *covenant*? Give five examples.

1–12 Why is it usually difficult to separate the results of good management from good luck?

1–13 In what general way will the adoption of a *performance evaluation* objective influence the selection of accounting policies?

1–14 How can the accounting policies adopted for financial reporting affect the assessment of income tax?

1–15 In what general ways would an objective of *income tax deferral* affect the financial statements?

1–16 Why would management adopt an *earnings maximization* objective?

1–17 Why would management adopt an *earnings minimization* objective?

1–18 What is a "big bath" and when would a company have this objective?

1–19 Why might a manager be tempted to adopt *income smoothing* as a financial reporting objective?

1–20 How would the practice of *minimum compliance* differ with a public company compared to a private company?

1–21 What users are served by each of the following objectives of financial reporting?

    a. Contract compliance

    b. Cash flow prediction

    c. Performance appraisal

1–22 Explain the difference between user objectives and preparer objectives.

1–23 How can a manager be both a *preparer* and a *user* of financial statements?

1–24 When would the use of GAAP not be appropriate?

1–25 How do the form of the business organization and financial reporting objectives affect whether GAAP is a constraint?

1–26 What are the three bases of accounting for a private corporation?

1–27 What is meant by a *size threshold*?

1–28 What are the three requirements to be eligible for *differential reporting*?

1–29 Would an audit opinion be qualified if *differential reporting* is selected by a private corporation?

1–30 What is a *disclosed basis of accounting*? When is it appropriate?

1–31 Provide a specific example of why a partnership may want to use a disclosed basis of accounting instead of GAAP.

1–32 What will be achieved with *harmonization* of accounting standards? Why will standards never be completely the same around the world?

CASES

CASE 1–1   W&K Gardens

Lindsay Kay approached her friend Michael Wait about going into business together as co-owners of a gardening centre. Lindsay loved gardening and had some skills as an accountant. Michael was a landscape architect. Lindsay and Michael agreed to become business partners and open a new garden centre to be called W&K Gardens (W&K). There were only two existing nurseries in the ever-expanding local area, and Lindsay and Michael felt that that there would be sufficient customer demand to support another gardening centre.

The pair decided that Lindsay would assume responsibility for the accounting and Michael would complete gardening layouts for customers. In addition, Michael would design a website where customers could order plants for pick-up or delivery, and on which Lindsay could eventually provide on-line gardening tips and advice. Michael suggested that they initially pay a flat fee to an Internet service provider for hosting their website. Michael would register their Internet domain name, develop the web page and create the initial graphics.

They developed a business plan for the gardening centre and Lindsay applied for a loan from the provincial Ministry of Agriculture and Education, which was offering forgivable loans for up to $500,000 to promote small businesses in the province. Lindsay and Michael soon received a letter from the provincial government that started with the words, "Congratulations—you have met all the criteria to receive a forgivable loan of $500,000." (Further details on the loan are provided in Exhibit A.)

Although there were many details to work out, they felt that they could be open for business by the first week of June. They already had start-up funds from the forgivable loan, and a business plan. Michael knew of a large plot of land (20 hectares) with a small but suitable building in a nearby location that was available for lease. Lindsay and Michael reviewed the terms of the lease (Exhibit B) received from a real estate agent and agreed that although the payments were considerable, the location would be well worth it and they would have plenty of space to carry a full assortment of annuals, perennials, shrubs, trees, and garden accessories. They were willing to pay a higher fee for the ability to expand in the future. Lindsay's notes concerning the inventory of plants and care that would be needed are included in Exhibit C.

The old building would have to be renovated before it could be used as a storefront and they agreed to hire someone to complete the necessary work on time. They estimated the cost of the renovation to be about $125,000 but realized that they would have to meet with a contractor to get a formal estimate for the work to be done.

Lindsay also noted that they would need an operating loan for approximately $100,000 in addition to the government loan. Lindsay arranged to meet with her bank manager as soon as possible. With her business plan in hand, she was going to approach the bank for additional financing for the initial costs and purchase of inventory. Lindsay's personal borrowing rate was currently 11%. However, she had been advised that the new business would be able to borrow at 2% below this rate, assuming that W&K would be able to maintain an adequate amount of assets to cover liabilities by the second year of operation. Lindsay now began to gather the details needed to finalize the business plan for the bank.

Michael determined that they would have to purchase a small truck and some equipment to carry out the landscape design service. Since he had been in charge of purchasing at Green Thumb Landscapers, he had a good idea of the type and cost of this equipment (Exhibit D).

To provide income during the off-season, Michael suggested they submit a bid for a tender that he had seen advertised in the paper. The town was accepting bids for snow removal from municipal parking lots and storage of snow from street removal. Last year, the town had had difficulty finding contractors for the snow removal since it was a small job. The town also needed space to "store" the removed snow and, with this new location, Michael and Lindsay would certainly have the capability to store snow. Michael was concerned, though, that the snow would contain chemical contaminants acquired from the town's roads. Michael believed that they could win the snow removal contract for a flat fee of $30,000 and an additional flat fee of $50,000 for storage of snow for one "snow season."

Michael suggested that they should discuss the details of the business partnership at a meeting the following morning to avoid future disputes. They had already agreed that Michael would contribute his personally owned landscaping equipment (fair value $18,000), a small used truck (fair value $12,000) and cash of $5,000. Lindsay would contribute computer equipment (fair value $8,500), office furniture (fair value $6,500) and cash of $20,000. Each partner would receive an equal interest in both capital and income. Michael also stated that he wanted Lindsay's opinion on the appropriate accounting policies that should be selected so he could anticipate earnings. He also wanted an outline of any matters related to the set-up of the business and Lindsay's opinion about whether a partnership would be the best structure for their business.

Required:

Assume the role of Lindsay Kay. Prepare notes to summarize your analysis in preparation for a meeting between Lindsay and Michael.

EXHIBIT A

FORGIVABLE LOAN FROM MINISTRY OF AGRICULTURE AND EDUCATION

Clause 1: Lindsay Kay will receive a forgivable loan of $500,000 for the development and operation of W&K Gardens as described in the attached business plan.

Clause 2: The government will provide $500,000 on May 20, 2006, which is forgivable on May 20th, 2011, if the following conditions are met:

– three university students are hired for the period June 1 to August 31 each year;

– all produce is grown on-site or purchased from Ontario growers; and

– audited financial statements are provided to the government three months after year-end.

Clause 3: If any of the above terms is not met, the loan is repayable with interest of 10% by the end of the fiscal year in which the term is broken.

Clause 4: The government has the right to inspect the premises and financial records to ensure that all conditions of the loan have been met at any time.

EXHIBIT B

TERMS OF THE LEASE

Addison Ltd. agrees to rent to W&K the land site and building that it requires in starting up its new business. The lease agreement calls for five annual lease payments of $300,000 (including executory costs of $19,506) at the beginning of each year; the details surrounding the agreement are as follows:

Commissions and legal fees (incurred by Addison)	$60,000
Building:	
Addison's carrying value of building	$340,000
Fair value of the building	$400,000
Economic life of building	6 years
Guaranteed residual value at end of lease term	$75,000
Land:	
Addison's carrying value of land	$375,000
Fair value of the land	$1,000,000
Residual value at end of lease term	$1,000,000
Rate implicit in the lease (known by W&K)	10%

Addison contacted its building contractor, who promised to have the renovations completed on time at a price very close to the estimated amount of $125,000. The renovation work would have a useful life of approximately eight years.

Addison stated that the lease will be non-cancellable but is willing to provide an option to renew the lease at the end of the five-year term.

EXHIBIT C

INVENTORY REQUIREMENTS

W&K would be open for business all year but the amount and type of inventory would fluctuate depending on the time of the year. The garden centre would consist of a greenhouse, outdoor tents, a store, and a small outdoor nursery. The storefront would be open year-round and would sell fertilizers, planters, garden tools, and accessories. Gift baskets would be brought in for special occasions such as Mother's Day, Halloween, Thanksgiving, and Christmas.

To attract customers to the store, Michael would provide customized landscape designs for a flat fee of $500. The customer would then receive a credit for the same amount at the store. The credit would have no cash value, but could be used for the purchase of shrubs, flowers, etc., at the store over the next two years.

Annual plants (such as geraniums, petunias, and many more varieties) would be purchased from local growing farms each spring. These plants would all have to be sold before the end of summer. Perennial plants (including bellflowers, day lilies, and hostas) would be grown in W&K's greenhouse and transferred to the outdoor store protected by large tents. Those plants not sold by September 30 would be returned to the greenhouse for winter storage and care. It was expected that most perennial plants would be sold, especially if Lindsay discounted the price to encourage customers to buy and plant in the fall instead of waiting for the following spring.

Shrubs and trees would be purchased from local nurseries early in the spring. It was expected that about 80% of these purchases would be sold during the growing season. The remaining 20% would be transferred to the outdoor nursery to be replanted and would remain there until the next season. To be competitive with the other two garden centres, Lindsay thought that they should offer a one-year warranty on all shrubs and trees returned by customers with a valid sales receipt.

The outdoor nursery would be used primarily for Christmas trees, which would be grown from seedling stock and could remain in the ground for a number of years. In the initial years, mature trees would be bought from a local supplier.

EXHIBIT D

CAPITAL ASSET REQUIREMENTS

Michael estimated that the following capital assets would be required for the first year of operation. Part of the government loan would be used to purchase these items.

Three small used trucks (in addition to the one contributed by Michael)	$40,000
Landscaping equipment (backhoe, rototiller, etc.)	$60,000
Small power tools	$15,000
Display shelves for the store	$12,000

[ICAO, adapted]

CASE 1–2   TripleB Security

TripleB Security (TripleB) is a general partnership that was formed and is operating in a Canadian city. Three brothers—George, Henry, and Gordon Bishop—have owned and operated TripleB since 1994, when they opened a centre to monitor security systems. TripleB provides the initial response when an alarm goes off at customers' business premises or homes, throughout the city.

TripleB follows an aggressive expansion strategy that includes acquiring customer contracts from competing monitoring services. The customers are immediately converted to TripleB's trademark and operating name.

Henry Bishop has an avid interest in e-commerce, and recently persuaded his brothers to enter the Internet service sector through an Internet business, SecurNet, which will be operated as a division of TripleB. SecurNet is to be a business-to-consumer Internet-based business that will use Henry's "SecurPay" system for processing Internet-based transactions between vendors and consumers to enable payments to be made and received through an independent and secure third-party verification system.

As a condition of a refinancing agreement, TripleB is required to provide annual audited financial statements within 60 days of the fiscal year-end. TripleB has never previously been audited. Its prior-year financial statements were prepared by TripleB's accountant, Todd Cook, for tax purposes only.

You, CA, are a senior with Stavness and Folk Chartered Accountants (SF). You and a partner in your firm recently met with the three Bishop brothers and Todd Cook to discuss the changes to TripleB's financial reporting requirements in light of recent developments. At the meeting, it was agreed that SF would be appointed auditor for the January 31, 2007, audit. George has provided you with the unaudited financial statements for the year ended January 31, 2006, and for the nine months ended October 31, 2006. These statements are shown in Exhibit E and notes related to financial statement items are in Exhibit F.

At the meeting, the brothers voiced their excitement about the upcoming launch of SecurNet. Henry mentioned that he had hoped to have the time to document the controls he has built into and around the SecurNet system but that he has been too busy. Everyone agreed to have SF prepare the documentation required by TripleB, which includes an identification of each control, an explanation of what each control achieves, and some procedures Henry could use to test the controls to ensure that they work properly.

It is now November 15, 2006. You have received information from Henry summarizing how SecurPay functions. This information is presented in Exhibit G. The partner has asked you to prepare a draft report for the client on SecurNet's controls and a planning memorandum for him discussing the audit and accounting issues related to the 2007 audit engagement.

Required:

Prepare the report and the memo.

BALANCE SHEET AND INCOME AND PARTNERS' EQUITY STATEMENT

TripleB Security
Balance Sheet
as at (unaudited)

	October 31, 2006	January 31, 2006
Assets		
Current Assets		
Cash	$ 395,427	$ —
Trade accounts receivable	254,148	271,976
Current portion of notes and advances	76,000	30,148
Prepaid expenses	51,810	47,713
	777,385	349,837
Notes and advances	—	76,000
Investment in customer contracts	2,675,356	2,447,126
Capital assets	851,159	558,466
	$4,303,900	$3,431,429
Liabilities		
Current Liabilities		
Bank advance	$ —	$ 87,433
Accounts payable and accrued liabilities	252,002	283,504
Current portion of obligations capital leases	110,148	106,814
Current portion of long-term debt	536,000	505,990
	898,150	983,741
Obligations under capital lease	248,399	334,014
Long-term debt	1,081,524	1,066,996
	2,228,073	2,384,751
Partners' Equity		
Partners' Equity	2,075,827	1,046,678
	$4,303,900	$3,431,429

TripleB Security
Income and Partners' Equity Statement
(unaudited)

	For the nine months ended October 31, 2006	For the year ended January 31, 2006
Revenue	$2,992,466	$2,627,227
Direct expenses:		
Monitoring costs	1,737,953	1,497,699
Amortization investment customer contract	112,630	136,520
	1,141,883	993,008
Administrative and general expenses	630,826	514,417
Interest on long-term debt	106,763	65,397
Amortization of capital assets	65,145	42,552
Net income	339,149	370,642
Partners' equity, beginning period	1,046,678	676,036
Partners' contributions	690,000	—
Partners' equity, end of period	$2,075,827	$1,046,678

NOTES RELATED TO FINANCIAL STATEMENT ITEMS

1. Lawsuits

TripleB is being sued by several of its larger customers because of a system failure that occurred on April 28, 2005. TripleB's customers are claiming that other private security systems were required during the period when TripleB's security system failed. Management's position is that the system failure was caused by a lightning storm and therefore TripleB is not responsible. TripleB has not accrued any amount for these lawsuits because management believes it can defend its position.

2. Revenue

Large business and wholesale customers are billed in advance monthly or quarterly for monitoring services. Revenue is recognized when billed. Experience has shown that bad debt expense is low for these customers because they view security monitoring as an essential service.

TripleB's residential customers pay by one of two methods: pre-authorized debit from their bank account, or prepayment of an annual amount. When customers prepay their annual fee, TripleB allows a 5% discount on the fee. Upon receiving payment, TripleB recognizes revenue for the amount received. The contract terms range from one to three years.

TripleB issues a refund cheque to customers who cancel their monitoring service partway through the prepaid period. These payments are debited to revenue when paid. Customer refunds are approximately $375,000 for the nine months ended October 31, 2006.

3. Investment in customer contracts

TripleB's aggressive expansion strategy has led management to acquire competing monitoring customer contracts at a premium. The purchase amount is booked to the Investment in Customer Contracts account.

Historically, TripleB has amortized its investment on the same basis for tax and accounting purposes. TripleB commissioned a market research study that concluded that the average customer stays with TripleB for seven years.

EXHIBIT G

NOTES FROM HENRY BISHOP

Overview

SecurNet certifies a business to accept payments through its system, and then allows the business to provide a link to SecurPay on its website. The link creates a secure environment in which on-line shoppers can enter payment information for products and services purchased over the Internet. The payment information is processed and accepted by SecurPay. If the credit card information is valid, SecurPay informs the shopper that the transaction will proceed and charges the payment against the credit card used by the shopper in the transaction. The payment is then forwarded to the business by the financial institution whose credit card is being used by the shopper. Certified businesses pay a transaction fee to SecurNet for each transaction that is processed through the SecurPay system, as well as a monthly fee for the right to use the system.

Particulars

The SecurPay system is activated when the shopper clicks on the business website's "buy" button. The shopper is then prompted to accept the list of items in his or her "shopping cart." The verification of the list of items is important because the shopper has the opportunity to cancel the transaction by clicking on the "cancel" button, thus leaving SecurPay and being linked back to the business website. If the shopper clicks on SecurPay's "buy" button, the shopper is informed that he or she has confirmed the purchase, but still has the option of cancelling the transaction.

The shopper is then asked to self-identify as a "first-time SecurPay user" or a "registered SecurPay user." If the shopper is a first-time user, he or she is asked to enter personal information, including name, shipping address, credit card information, e-mail address, and password (which is then confirmed through a second password request). If the shopper is a registered user, the personal information appears on the page and the shopper is asked to confirm the information and enter his or her password. At that point the order goes forward to the business to be filed and delivered.

The SecurPay system uses the most advanced encryption technology available to process the personal information.

The personal information is transferred hourly from SecurNet's Internet server to a separate storage server. Firewall protection is used for transfers to the storage server and for confirmation of information from this server when registered users make subsequent purchases.

SecurNet carries out procedures to certify businesses that are allowed to provide access to its SecurPay system. The certification process includes ensuring that the vendor is registered with one or more major credit card companies to receive payments. SecurNet also requires the vendor to sign a waiver holding SecurNet harmless from any false advertising or failure to deliver goods to the shopper. SecurNet maintains the right to suspend any business or terminate its use of SecurPay without notice or cause.

SecurNet has certified three businesses to use its SecurPay system and expects it to be up and running in the next fiscal year.

CASE 1–3   Smith and Stewart

Smith and Stewart (Stewart) is a partnership of lawyers. It was recently formed from a merger of Becker and Brackman (Becker) and Copp and Copp (Copp). Stewart has 38 partners—including 6 from Becker and 32 from Copp—and 75 employees. At the date of the merger, Stewart purchased land and an office building for $2 million, and fully computerized its offices. The partners have agreed to have the annual financial statements audited even though this was not done in the past.

The partnership agreement requires an annual valuation of the assets and liabilities of the firm. This valuation will be used to determine the amount an existing partner will receive from the partnership when exiting the partnership, and the amount a new partner will pay to enter the partnership.

The partners have been busy getting the new partnership up and running and have paid little attention to accounting policies.

Prior to the merger, Becker recorded revenue when it invoiced the client. Daily time reports were used to keep track of the number of hours worked for each client. This information was not recorded in the accounting system and in general the accounting records were not kept up-to-date.

Copp also recorded revenue at the time the client was invoiced. This was based on partner hours, which were determined based on work in progress and recorded for employees at their regular billing rate, based on the hours worked. At year-end, an adjustment was made to reduce work in progress to reflect the actual costs incurred by Copp.

The new partnership agreement requires a valuation of work in progress at the merger date. This amount, which has yet to be determined, will be recorded as goodwill.

Stewart has arranged a line of credit with a bank that allows the partnership to borrow up to 75% of the carrying value of accounts receivable and 40% of the carrying value of work in progress based on the partnership's monthly financial statements. The bank has also provided mortgage financing of $950,000 for Stewart's land and building. The bank requires unaudited monthly financial statements as well as the annual audited financial statements.

As at the date of the merger, capital assets owned by the predecessor firms were transferred to the new partnership.

Each partner receives a monthly "draw" payment, which is an advance on his or her share of annual profit.

Your auditing firm has been hired by Stewart to prepare a report advising the partnership on accounting policies—identifying alternatives and making specific supported recommendations. A partner in your auditing firm has asked you to prepare the report. In addition, the partner has asked you to prepare a memo detailing the important auditing issues that are likely to arise and how they could be resolved.

Required:

Prepare the requested report and the memo.

[CICA]

CASE 1–4   Miltonics Potions Ltd.

Miltonics Potions Ltd. (MPL) is a privately held Ontario corporation engaged in the development and marketing of patent medicines. In early 2001, the company's research chemists began working on a project to develop a patent remedy for colitis (a disease that causes inflammation of the bowel). During the year, $200,000 was spent in research on this project without developing a useful product.

Work continued in 2002, with an additional $100,000 being spent. By the end of 2002, an apparently feasible product had been developed and was being considered by MPL's top management for further development and exploitation. On February 14, 2003 (prior to completion and issuance of the 2002 financial statements), the managers reached the decision to proceed with further development, production, and marketing of the product, barring adverse medical results (i.e., unacceptable side effects) from tests then underway. Such adverse results were possible, but were considered unlikely since nothing untoward had occurred to date in the testing program.

During 2003, the product was refined and the mass production formulation was developed (at a cost of $150,000). Production facilities were prepared (at a cost of $300,000), and patent number 381–1003-86 was obtained on the product. Legal expenses totalled $32,000.

In early 2004, production and distribution began. Sales in the first year were modest, totalling only $450,000. However, $500,000 was spent on promotion, mainly in print media advertising and in sending free samples to doctors and clinics. Only in 2005 did the sales reach forecast levels, thereby indicating that MPL had a successful product.

However, the success of the product spawned an imitator and, in 2005, MPL sued a competitor for patent infringement. MPL demanded that the competitor cease production and marketing of the competing product and requested $2,000,000 in damages. Legal costs of $50,000 were incurred in this action in 2005; the case was still pending at the end of the year.

In July 2006, after MPL had spent an additional $20,000 in legal fees, the case was dismissed in court, thereby rendering MPL's patent indefensible. Since the competitor was a well-known pharmaceutical firm, MPL's sales suffered considerably from the competition.

Required:

a. On a year-by-year basis, describe the alternative accounting methods that MPL could use for the costs incurred in developing, patenting, and defending the new product. Do not use hindsight in arriving at your alternatives.
b. Explain what additional information you would need and what criteria you would use to make a decision on the alternative to adopt for each year.

CASE 1–5   Time-Lice Books, Ltd.

Time-Lice Books, Ltd. (TLBL) is a well-established company that publishes a wide variety of general interest non-fiction books. The company is incorporated under the *Canada Business Corporations Act*, and the heirs of Harold Lice, the firm's founder, hold 30% of the shares. The heirs do not take any active interest in the affairs of the company, but rely on the advice of their professional financial advisor, Mr. Hornblower Weeks, in voting their shares. The remaining 70% of the shares are widely distributed and are traded on the Toronto Stock Exchange.

TLBL distributes some of its books (about 25%) through retail bookstores, but the bulk of the sales (75%) are made directly to customers by direct mail advertising. About half of the direct mail sales are for series of books, and the company has decided to review its accounting policy for this segment of the business. TLBL is also exploring the alternative of selling its books through the Internet in the future.

A book series is a set of books on a particular topic. Rather than publishing all of the books at once, the approach is to issue one book at a time, at two- to four-month intervals. Topics of some series that have recently begun are Great Impressionist Artists, Time-Lice Guides to Home Maintenance, and Lives of Great Accountants (a particularly popular series).

When TLBL decides to begin a new series, the first step is to design an elaborate and expensive full-colour advertising brochure for the series, in which the first book is offered free of charge to those who return a postage-paid card. This brochure is then mailed to about two million homes in Canada, using TLBL's own mailing list plus purchased mailing lists. While the mail campaign is going on, TLBL contracts writers to prepare the text of the first book in the series, and begins design of the book. However, actual production of the book does not occur until the mail campaign has ended and the number of copies needed has been determined from the returned postal cards.

The second book is produced about two months after the first has been mailed out, and it is sent to all those customers who received the first (free) volume. However, customers are then asked either to subscribe to the entire series at a fixed price or to return the second volume without charge. Company experience has been that, on average, 80% of the customers elect to subscribe and about 15% return the second book. The other 5% neither subscribe nor return the book, and TLBL takes no action against these subscribers except to send them a letter and to delete their names from its mailing lists. While 80% is the average subscription rate, the rate for specific series may vary anywhere from 70% to 85%.

Customers who do subscribe have a choice of paying for the entire series all at once, or paying for each book (at a higher price) as it is sent. Roughly half of the customers elect each alternative, although there has been a trend towards advance payment since TLBL began accepting Visa and MasterCard (for advance payments only) two years ago.

The advertising brochure and direct mail campaign is the largest single cost incurred. The writers of the books are under a fixed-fee contract with TLBL and do not receive royalties. The layout and design work on each volume is performed by TLBL's salaried designers. Although printing costs have been escalating sharply, the cost to print and bind each book has lately been about $5.00. The books are sold to customers at about $30.00 per copy. All customers may cancel their subscriptions at any time. The advance-payment subscribers must send a letter of cancellation, but few do so. The installment subscribers may cancel simply by returning one of the volumes within 15 days of receipt, whereupon they are sent no more volumes in the series. At some point before the conclusion of the series, 20 to 30% of installment subscribers cancel.

Required:

Evaluate the revenue and expense recognition alternatives for TLBL for the book series.

CASE 1–6   Bay and Eastern Corp.; Harbinger Ltd.

Helen Hook is president and chief executive officer of Bay and Eastern Corp., a large, diversified corporation with its head office in Halifax and its executive offices in Toronto. The corporation controls 27 other corporations, mainly in North America but also in Europe. Bay and Eastern's common shares are traded on both the Toronto Stock Exchange and the New York Stock Exchange. Its preferred shares are held exclusively by a group of life insurance companies that purchased the shares in a private offering several years ago. The same insurance companies hold about half of Bay and Eastern's bonds, while the rest are publicly traded.

Helen's brother, Harvey, is president of Harbinger Ltd., a small chain of employment offices operating in and around Vancouver. The company was founded by Harvey Hook in 1981, when he left the personnel services division of a national consulting firm. Harvey owns 67% of the shares of Harbinger. His father, Henry, owns the other 33%. Henry has been an important source of capital for Harvey, lending Harbinger $175,000 at its inception and in 1986 accepting a 33% ownership interest in lieu of repayment of the debt. Harbinger has no other major creditors, although a line of credit has just been negotiated with a branch of the Royal Bank.

Required:

Explain how the objectives of financial reporting would differ between Bay and Eastern Corp. and Harbinger Ltd. Be as specific as possible.

CASE 1–7   Wraps Inc.

Wraps Inc. is a franchisor of fast-food restaurants that specialize in providing a variety of wraps filled with healthy food, the most popular of which is the sun-dried tomato wrap filled with fresh vegetables and a special California sauce. The restaurants all do business under the name of Wraps, but all are owned and oper-ated by independent entrepreneurs; the original Wraps outlets are separately owned by the founding shareholders of Wraps Inc., and not by the franchisor corporation itself.

Wraps Inc. sells franchises for $400,000. Of the total amount, $50,000 is due when the franchise agreement is signed, another $60,000 is due when the outlet opens, and the remainder is due 18 months after the opening. All payments are non-refundable. Wraps Inc. also receives a royalty of 3% of the invoice cost of the special supplies that the outlets are required to use (such as the special California sauce and the paper goods and other supplies that are imprinted with the Wraps logo). Wraps Inc. does not produce any of these goods; special arrangements are made with suppliers in each region of the country, and the royalties are forwarded to Wraps directly by the suppliers rather than by the franchisees.

Before the franchise agreement is signed, there is a period of discussion and exploration that can last from one to six months. During this time, the general feasibility of establishing a new outlet is examined. Market surveys are conducted to determine whether the local market could support another fast-food outlet, and the financial strength and backing of the prospective franchisee are exam-ined. The costs incurred during the pre-signing stage are borne by Wraps Inc.

Once the franchise agreement is signed, Wraps Inc. actively assists the fran-chisee in selecting a site, planning the restaurant, gaining building permits, equipping the restaurant, and selecting and training the staff. All of the direct costs of establishing the outlet are paid by the franchisee, but Wraps Inc. con-tributes substantial assistance in the form of legal, architectural, planning, and management experts. The experts are retained by Wraps Inc. as regular staff con-sultants, and they are paid a fixed-fee retainer each month, regardless of the amount of service that they provide to Wraps or its franchisees in that month. A supporting staff is employed directly by the franchisee.

Some of the expert assistance is delivered on-site, with Wraps Inc. paying the travel and other incidental costs. Head office provides other assistance—such as drafting construction blueprints (based on master plans kept at Wraps Inc. head office) and preparing supporting documents for city council site-zoning bylaws—and Wraps Inc. absorbs those costs as well. The period of time between the sign-ing of the franchise agreement and the opening of the outlet can vary from six months to two years. On average, though, it is approximately one year.

The direct involvement of Wraps Inc. largely ends when the outlet opens. Some additional management and employee training assistance is sometimes offered, but any significant additional services must be paid for by the franchisee.

Required:

Assume that you are an accounting advisor to Wraps Inc. Recommend an accounting and reporting policy for revenue and expense recognition for Wraps Inc. under each of the three following separate cases. Be sure to evaluate all of the alternative policies in light of the objectives of financial reporting in each case.

Case A: Wraps Inc. is a well-established franchisor that has franchised hundreds of successful outlets throughout North America. The corporation is controlled by the original founders, who own 54% of the outstanding common shares. The remaining shares are publicly traded on the Toronto Stock Exchange. The success rate is very high for the franchisees; only 3% of the licensed franchisees have failed to open during the history of Wraps Inc., and only 8% have failed before payment of the final installment of the franchise fee.

Case B: Wraps Inc. is privately owned by its three founders; each owns one-third of the common shares. There is no long-term debt, and few current liabilities. The company is well established, and has a good record of successful openings, similar to the success rate described in Case A, above.

Case C: Wraps Inc. is a relatively new company, having been founded only three years previously. Only five franchised restaurants have been opened (in addition to the three owned by Wraps Inc.'s founders) and all have been successful. Eight more franchise agreements have been signed and good progress is being made towards opening all of the new outlets. Wraps Inc. is planning to offer shares to the public in the near future. In the meantime, the corporation has been borrowing substantial sums from the bank in order to meet the upfront costs of opening new franchises.

CASE 1–8   Capreol Carpet Corporation

Capreol Carpet Corporation (CCC) is a manufacturer of broadloom carpeting, located in Winnipeg, Manitoba. The company enjoys a good reputation for its product, but unfortunately has not been very profitable in recent years owing to increasing imports of cheaper carpeting. In order to combat this threat, CCC has invested substantial sums of money in new equipment to improve efficiency. Although efficiency picked up as a result, the improvement seemed only to keep the profit picture from getting any worse, rather than to actually increase net income.

CCC is a public company, but control was held by Bay and Eastern Corporation, a large conglomerate. Three months ago, Bay and Eastern sold its 70% interest in CCC to Upper Lip Enterprises Ltd., a British carpet manufacturer. Upper Lip planned to integrate CCC into its own operations, such that CCC would be the manufacturer of certain carpets sold by all of Upper Lip's distributors and would be the North American distributor of Upper Lip's British-made carpets.

Last week, the financial vice-president of Upper Lip sent a letter to David Blase, the controller of CCC, in which he detailed certain changes in accounting policy that CCC should institute in order to make its reporting practices consistent with those of Upper Lip, for purposes of consolidation and divisional performance appraisal. Included in the letter were the following:

1. Inventories, both of raw materials and finished goods, should be valued on the LIFO basis rather than on the average-cost basis previously used by CCC.

2. Carpeting sold to Upper Lip and its other subsidiaries should be billed at standard cost plus 10%, rather than at full list price less 15%, as is now the case. In effect, the gross margin on the intercompany transfers would be reduced from 35% of cost to 10% of cost. Carpet purchased by CCC from the Upper Lip group of companies would also be invoiced to CCC at cost plus 10%.

3. Depreciation on the new equipment should be increased from 8% per year (straight-line) to 12.5% per year. Standard costs would be adjusted to reflect the higher rate.

The financial vice-president, in his letter to David, has asked for a report specifically identifying and describing any problems in implementing the suggested changes in accounting policies, and giving solutions to any problems that exist.

Required:

Assume that you are David Blase. Draft the report for the vice-president on the suggested changes to the accounting policies.

CASE 1–9   Madayag Development Corporation

Madayag Development Corporation (MDC) is a real estate development company that is 60% owned by Thomas Madayag. Seaton's Inc., a privately owned Canadian department store chain, owns 30%, and 10% is owned by a Canadian bank. MDC engages in two types of development: residential land sites, and commercial retail space.

Mr. Madayag has been considering issuing a new class of MDC non-voting common shares to a small group of private investors. The purpose would be to provide a larger equity base so that MDC could be more aggressive in its commercial division. Like all real estate development companies, MDC is very highly leveraged; about 90% of the assets are financed by debt, most of which is provided by or through the shareholder bank. The issue price of the new share would be determined on the basis of the net market value equity of the company's properties (that is, the total appraised values minus the company's outstanding debt). Since the company will continue to be private, a shareholders' agreement will govern the company's buy-back of the new shares should any investor decide in the future to sell his or her shares. The buy-back price of the non-voting shares is to be determined as the original issue price of the shares plus a proportionate share in the increase in the net book value of the common share equity from the date of issue to the date of repurchase, based on the most recent audited financial statements.

The shareholders' agreement places no restrictions on the potential resale price of the voting shares held by Mr. Madayag, Seaton's Inc., and the bank; should any of these shares be sold, they would be sold at their fair market value (which, for real estate developments, is normally based on the present value of future cash flows).

Mr. Madayag is interested in the implications of the proposed non-voting share issue for financial reporting. Therefore he has engaged an accounting advisor to offer advice on the most desirable accounting policies. A description of the business of the company follows.

Residential development

In the residential division, MDC buys large tracts of land near major Canadian cities and holds the land for a few years until the growth of the city makes the land attractive for residential development. The purchase of the land is financed at least 90% by bank loans, and the loans provide for a line of credit to enable the company to borrow from the bank to pay the interest on the loans for up to five years after the land purchase; this holding period is considered by the bank to be the development period. When the time seems right (but usually within five years), MDC develops the land by providing services (e.g., sewer, water, electrical, and telephone mains and connections), laying out roads, and subdividing the land into home sites. The development process takes less than a year.

The sites are then advertised and sold to customers; about 25% of the sales are for cash, but most often they are for a 10–20% down payment with MDC accepting a mortgage for the remainder. The mortgages are usually for a five-year term and a 20-year amortization and bear interest at a fixed rate that is one or two percentage points below the market rate of mortgage interest (but above the cost of MDC's borrowing). The prices charged to customers for the land vary within an individual tract. Some locations are considered more desirable than others and may therefore carry a price that is as much as double that of the less desirable locations within the same development.

MDC does no residential building; the company only sells the sites. Purchasers must arrange for construction of the houses themselves. Usually, however, MDC enters into an exclusive contract with one (or sometimes two) house builder(s) to perform the construction on the sites. The builders erect model homes on the front sites (i.e., on the major access road), and then negotiate individually with the customers for construction of their homes. MDC charges the builders rent for the properties occupied by the model homes. When sales of the sites are complete, MDC sells the property under the model homes to the purchasers of the model homes or to the builder.

MDC has been quite successful in its residential land development business. However, there is one land tract outside of Calgary that it has been unable to sell as quickly as desired. Purchased eight years ago and developed three years ago, only about 30% of the tract has been sold. Defaults by purchasers have been high, and the proceeds from the land sales have not been sufficient to pay the interest on the bank loan; the company has had to use cash from other developments to service the loan.

Commercial development

The commercial division builds and leases retail developments in urban and suburban locations. Sometimes the shopping centres are built on a part of the residential development areas described above, but usually the sites are completely independent of the residential division. There is little lag between acquisition and development of a retail site, although the project can take up to six years from land assembly to final grand opening. The acquisition and development costs are financed by the bank, although in very large developments the bank will syndicate its participation (that is, bring in other banks to share the cost and the risk). Syndicate members demand audited financial statements from MDC.

MDC's general policy is to hold and operate the properties, although the company will sell if the price is right. Each property usually has a Seaton's store as an "anchor" store (a major retailer that occupies a large space and provides much of the attractiveness of the development to shoppers and thereby to smaller retail lessees). There is a long-term lease agreement between the Seaton's store and MDC that locks the store into the development for at least 30 years. Similar leases bind other major anchor stores, but smaller retailers usually sign five-year leases that are cancellable by either party at the end of the lease term.

The long-term leases are for fixed lease payments, with provision for increases due to inflation and due to increases in operating costs. Shorter-term (e.g., five-year) leases are for a minimum monthly amount plus a percentage of the gross sales of the store. Smaller lessees also pay a large amount, equivalent to 50% of one year's minimum lease payments, at the inception of the lease; this payment is not repeated for lease renewals. MDC's cash flow from the lease payments is used to operate the developments and to service the bank debt that financed them.

MDC has not had to pay any income taxes in the commercial division because capital cost allowance on the properties is more than enough to offset lease income. Excess CCA from the commercial division cannot be used to offset profits in the residential division, however, for income tax purposes.

Most of the retail developments have been very successful; the insurable value of the properties is, in aggregate, four times the depreciated historical cost of the properties. There are three recently built shopping centres that have not yet reached their full potential but are expected to do so within the next two years. Four other developments were built in the early 2000s in parts of the country that were hit hard by the economic recession in those years and they have never fully recovered; these properties are unable to recover their full operating and carrying costs.

Required:

Outline the accounting policies that would seem to best serve the reporting objectives of MDC, assuming that the new share issue is to occur. Your recommendations should include (but not be limited to) recognition of the revenues for each division, treatment of costs (including development costs and interest), and valuation of properties under development and after development.

[ICAO]

Chapter 2

Intercorporate Investments: An Introduction

Introduction

Most economic activity is conducted not by individual corporations, but by groups of corporations in which one company directly or indirectly owns shares in a series of other companies. The objective of financial reporting is to show the assets and liabilities that are under the control of the shareholders of a corporation. When the reporting entity owns shares in other companies, the reporting entity may control not only the assets it legally owns, but also the assets that are owned by other companies in the group. How can financial statements reflect this economic reality underlying intercorporate share ownership? That is the main focus of this book. The saga begins here and continues through Chapter 6.

This chapter takes a broad view of intercorporate investments, including the types of investments and the underlying strategies for those investments, as well as the financial reporting implications. We will discuss:

- the definition of intercorporate investments, both passive and strategic
- accounting for passive portfolio investments
- the different strategic approaches to investing in other corporations' shares— (1) controlled subsidiaries, (2) special purpose entities, (3) significantly influenced affiliates, and (4) joint ventures, and
- the four basic accounting approaches to accounting for intercorporate investments—(1) cost method, (2) equity method, (3) consolidation, and (4) proportionate consolidation.

At the end of the chapter, we will discuss the basic approach to preparing consolidated financial statements. We will demonstrate two different preparation methods: the direct method and the worksheet method.

Chapter 2 lays the foundation for reporting intercorporate investments. Looking ahead, Chapter 3 discusses business combinations. Chapters 4 through 6 then discuss various facets of preparing consolidated financial statements, adding more complications as we go along. The concept of consolidated statements is fairly simple, but the execution of this simple concept can get very complicated very quickly!

But first, we will look very briefly at branch accounting, drawing a clear distinction between branch accounting and consolidation.

Branch Accounting

Before plunging into our discussion of intercorporate investments, we should point out the difference between branch accounting and consolidated financial statements. Branch accounting is an application of control account procedures for keeping track of operating results of individual branches that are *not* separate corporations. When operations are carried out through separate corporations that are controlled by the parent, a parent–subsidiary relationship exists. Subsidiaries may function like branches of the parent corporation in a substantive sense, but they are not branches in an accounting sense.

In traditional practice, each branch has its own set of operating accounts. These are supporting accounts to a general ledger control account at head office. The extent of the branch account structure depends on whether the branch is a cost centre, revenue centre, profit centre, or investment centre. When the head office prepares financial statements for the company as a whole, the control account for each branch must be disaggregated—the revenues and expenses for the branch are included in the company's overall revenues and expenses rather than being reported as a single, net amount. The process of disaggregation has much in common with the process of preparing consolidated financial statements, which is the focus of Chapters 2 to 6, but without the completeness and much of the complexity of consolidation.

In modern, computerized accounting systems, branch accounts are usually integrated into the head office reporting structure rather than being tied into a control account. The account numbering system classifies each account by both branch and type (and perhaps by other dimensions, such as by product line), thereby permitting a matrix approach to reporting. The operating results of each branch can easily be drawn from the system, and the combined results can equally easily be reported. Since the branch and head office account systems are integrated, there is no need for control accounts and there is no need for quasi-consolidation procedures to disaggregate the control accounts.

In contrast, "branches" that are separate legal corporations *must* have separate accounts and separate financial statements for legal and tax reasons. The parent keeps track of the subsidiaries through a single investment account for each subsidiary. In modern practice, therefore, there is a fundamental procedural difference between accounting for a branch (as a responsibility centre) and accounting for a corporate subsidiary. Management accounting systems are designed to report on responsibility centres, including branches. In this book, our focus is on financial reporting, whether internal or external, of corporate entities.

Definition of Intercorporate Investments

An **intercorporate investment** is any purchase by one corporation of the securities of another corporation. Broadly speaking, the investment may be in bonds, preferred shares, or common shares.

Many intercorporate investments are made simply as uses of excess cash or as investments to yield interest, dividend income, or capital gains. These investments do not give the investor any ability to control or influence the operations of the investee corporation.

A substantively different type of intercorporate investment is an investor corporation's purchase of enough of the voting shares of an investee corporation to give the investor the ability to *control* or *significantly influence* the affairs of the investee corporation. These types of intercorporate investments enable the investor corporation to control or influence the investee's strategic operating, financing, and investing activities, and are therefore called **strategic investments**. Accounting for strategic investments must reflect the ability of the investor to affect the investee's operations. The reporting and accounting practices for strategic investments will be explained in depth in the following chapters. First, however, we will take a brief look at the accounting for non-strategic investments.

Non-strategic investments

The accounting for non-strategic investments has undergone significant change. For close to 10 years, the FASB, AcSB, and IASB have been struggling to better define the reporting for financial instruments, which include both debt and equity investments. Historically, non-strategic investments were reported at historical cost—changes in market values were ignored until an investment was sold. Effective in 2006, however, Canadian standards for non-strategic investments will be harmonized with international standards (IAS 39) and with FASB requirements.

Intermediate accounting textbooks deal extensively with accounting for non-strategic investments. Here, we will only give a quick overview in order to clearly differentiate strategic from non-strategic investments. Non-strategic investments are sometimes called *portfolio investments* or *passive investments*. They can be either short-term or long-term.

Non-strategic share investments fall into three categories:

- held-to-maturity securities
- trading securities, and
- available-for-sale securities.

We will briefly discuss these three categories in the following sections. In general, the underlying presumption is that fair value is more appropriate than historical cost as the basis for valuing non-strategic investments [CICA 3855.66(a)]. The only exception to this general rule is for held-to-maturity investments.

Held-to-maturity investments To qualify as a held-to-maturity investment, an investment must have three essential characteristics:

- it must have a fixed maturity date
- it must have fixed or determinable payments, and
- the investor must have the intent and ability to hold the investment to maturity.

These three characteristics fit debt instruments only, or equity instruments that are debt instruments in substance, such as some retractable preferred shares. Common shares cannot be classified as held-to-maturity instruments because they have no maturity and no fixed payments.

Held-to-maturity investments are accounted for on an amortized cost basis. The carrying value of the investment reflects historical values only—never fair value or market value. If there is a difference between the purchase cost of the security and its maturity value, the difference must be accounted for by using the effective interest method of amortization [CICA 3855.17(l)].

Since investments in equity securities cannot be held-to-maturity investments, we will not deal further with this type of investment.

Financial assets held for trading Brokers, banks, pension funds, and other financial institutions make some of their money by actively trading securities on the open market. In substance, trading securities are a financial institution's inventory. When an investor first makes an investment, the investment may be designated as a trading investment. Once designated for trading, the investor cannot reclassify the investment later.

Trading securities are reported at *market value* on the balance sheet [CICA 3855.59]. Gains and losses that occur during the reporting period, *both realized and unrealized*, are included in net income [CICA 3855.67(a)]. Unrealized gains and losses are recognized because it is a fairly simple process to sell a trading security at any time—all it takes is a phone call or a few clicks of a computer mouse to make a sale at the going price.

The only exception to market value reporting for trading securities pertains to equities that "do not have a quoted market price in an active market" [CICA 3855.59(c)]. Although a direct market value is not available, the investor still must use fair value, not historical cost. The investor must use an indirect method to determine a fair value for such an investment. Indirect methods include using the current market value of a similar security or using "a valuation technique" such as an option pricing model.

Bear in mind that trading in securities is something that financial institutions do—the vast majority of other corporations do not have trading securities. Instead, they hold available-for-sale securities.

Available-for-sale securities This category is a catch-all. If an investment is not designated as hold-to-maturity, and it is not a trading security, then it is available-for-sale. The definition in the *CICA Handbook* is a negative definition:

> Available-for-sale financial assets are those financial assets that are not classified as loans and receivables, held-to-maturity investments, or held for trading. [CICA 3855.17(i)]

The vast majority of non-strategic investments by non-financial corporations fall into this category.

Accounting for available-for-sale securities is based on fair value:

- the investment is reported at fair value on the balance sheet
- realized gains or losses are recognized in net income, and
- unrealized gains and losses are recognized as a component of *other comprehensive income*.

It is this last part that is new for the majority of Canadian companies. Historically, gains were to be recognized on the income statement only when an investment was sold, although losses could be recognized in both the balance sheet and the income statement if the investment's value declined. Now, however, all changes in fair value are recognized, but *not included in net income until realized*.

Other comprehensive income (OCI) is a concept that originated in the U.S. and also is included (in a slightly different form) in international standards. The idea is to have a summary means of reporting items that are not recognized in net income but that also do not reflect capital flows between the corporation and its shareholders. U.S. standards require that public companies present a "statement of comprehensive income" either as a separate statement or as a continuation of the income statement—determining net income first, and then adding and subtracting the items of other comprehensive income. The total OCI is then included in retained earnings.

The OCI term is not mandatory, by the way; some companies use a different title, such as "other changes in owners' equity," to help financial statement readers distinguish between items of net income and OCI items.

Balance sheet recognition of unrealized gains is not completely new in Canadian or international accounting standards. Mutual funds have been required by law to report their investments at market value for many decades. Mutual funds' unit prices are based on market value, and the market value per unit must be calculated and reported on a daily basis. Mutual funds do not recognize unrealized gains and losses in net income because they can make dividend distributions only from realized gains, not from unrealized gains. Thus, this "new" accounting is just an extension of a long-standing practice in certain industries.

Example

Suppose that Regina Ltd. purchases 10,000 shares of Dartmouth Corporation for $500,000 on September 21, 2007:

Investment in Dartmouth Corp. shares	500,000	
Cash		500,000

At December 31, 2007, Regina still holds the Dartmouth shares. The year-end market value is $65 per share, for a total value of $650,000. Regina's investment has increased by an unrealized amount of $150,000. Regina will make the following entry on its books:

Investment in Dartmouth Corp. shares	150,000	
OCI—unrealized gain on Dartmouth Corp. shares		150,000

This entry will bring the investment account up to the year-end market value of $650,000. The OCI credit of $150,000 will be included in Regina Ltd.'s share equity at December 31, 2007.

On July 16, 2008, Regina sells the Dartmouth Corporation shares for $600,000. Regina Ltd. will record the sale as follows:

Cash	600,000	
OIC—Unrealized gain on Dartmouth Corp. shares	150,000	
Investment in Dartmouth Corp. shares		650,000
Gain on sale of Dartmouth Corp. shares		100,000

In this entry, Regina Ltd. removes the unrealized gain from OCI and recognizes a total gain (since the purchase date) of $100,000.

The only exception to fair value reporting for available-for-sale securities pertains to investments in shares that are not actively traded. Untraded (or thinly traded) securities should be reported at cost [CICA 3855.59(c)].

Strategic Intercorporate Investments

Many intercorporate investments are made for the explicit purpose of controlling or significantly influencing the operations of the investee corporation. When the effect of an intercorporate investment is to enable the investor to affect the operations of the investee, the cost basis of reporting is not appropriate because it does not reflect the substance of the relationship between the two corporations. Instead, other financial reporting approaches must be used.

Controlled subsidiaries

The meaning of control The term *control* is commonly used in its dictionary sense to describe one company's ability to exercise authority over another company. Often, control in this loose sense can be exercised by a company that holds only a relatively small proportion of the shares of another. While it is tempting to use the term in this broader sense, *control* in fact has a much more precise meaning in financial reporting and in law.

The *CICA Handbook* defines *control* as follows:

> **Control** of an enterprise is the continuing power to determine its strategic operating, investing and financing policies without the co-operation of others. [CICA 1590.03(b)]

When one corporation controls another, the controlled corporation is a *subsidiary* of the investor or *parent* corporation. The *CICA Handbook* defines this relationship as follows:

> A **subsidiary** is an enterprise controlled by another enterprise (the **parent**) that has the right and ability to obtain future economic benefits from the resources of the enterprise and is exposed to the related risks. [CICA 1590.03(a)]

In the *CICA Handbook* definitions, a subsidiary is defined by the existence of control; an investee that is not controlled by the investor is not a subsidiary of the investor.

Normally, control exists when one corporation has the ability to elect a majority of the board of directors of another corporation. Such control is usually obtained by owning sufficient voting shares (or "equity interest," in *CICA Handbook* terminology[1]) to ensure a majority of the votes for the board of directors of the controlled corporation.

Some corporations have more than one class of voting shares, with different voting rights. Bombardier Inc., for example, has two classes of shares that participate equally in dividends but that vary significantly in voting rights; Class A has 10 votes per share, while Class B has one vote per share. Control is obtained by having a majority of the *votes* rather than a majority of the shares outstanding.

In some cases, one corporation may control another without owning a sufficient equity interest to have a majority of the votes. Examples include the following.

- The parent corporation holds convertible securities or stock options that, if converted or exercised, would give the parent a majority of the seats on the board of directors.

- In a private corporation, a *shareholders' agreement* gives control to a shareholder who owns 50% or less of the shares.

- A major creditor (who also has an equity interest in the debtor) has the right to select a majority of the board of directors as a result of a debt agreement.

Regardless of the means by which control is obtained, control can exist only if there is an existing or attainable right to elect a majority of the board of directors *without the co-operation of other shareholders*.

Control is presumed to exist as long as the parent corporation has the ability to determine the subsidiary's strategic policies, and it ceases to exist when the parent

---

1. "A parent's control over a subsidiary... [is] normally acquired through an equity interest in the subsidiary" [CICA 1590.06].

loses that power. A parent can lose control voluntarily, (1) by selling enough of its interest to lose its vote majority, or (2) by permitting the subsidiary to issue sufficient voting shares to reduce the parent's interest to a non-controlling interest.[2]

A parent can also lose control involuntarily, such as when a subsidiary enters receivership and control passes to a trustee. Similarly, some loan agreements may give a major creditor voting shares as collateral, or non-voting common or preferred shares may automatically become voting shares in specified circumstances of financial distress. A foreign country may restrict a parent's control of a subsidiary. In these cases, the investee corporation ceases to be a subsidiary once control has passed from the parent. Until control ceases, however, the investee remains a subsidiary. The *possibility* of losing control does not affect the parent–subsidiary relationship (or the financial reporting thereof). Only when control is lost *in fact* does the parent–subsidiary relationship cease to exist.

A key phrase in the *CICA Handbook* definition of control is "without the co-operation of others." One corporation may appear to control another because it owns a relatively small block of shares and the remainder of the shares are widely held. In this case the corporation relies on the co-operation of the other shareholders, either by their active allegiance or by their passive disinterest, to exert control. However, the other shareholders may at any time decide not to co-operate or may rebel, and thus control does not truly exist. When the investor corporation owns a small block of shares but nevertheless can influence the strategic policies of the investee, the investor is said to have **significant influence** over the affairs of the investee, *but not control*. Significant influence is discussed more fully later in this chapter.

Indirect control Control need not be direct. **Indirect control** exists when a subsidiary is controlled by another subsidiary rather than by the parent company. Exhibit 2–1 shows three examples of indirect control.

In Case 1, the parent (**P**) controls subsidiary **A** by owning 70% of **A**'s voting shares, and **A** controls **C** by owning 60% of **C**'s voting shares. Since **P** controls **A**, **P** can control **A**'s votes for **C**'s board of directors. Therefore, **P** has indirect control of **C**. **C** is a subsidiary of **A**, and both **C** and **A** are subsidiaries of **P**.

Voting control is a yes–no matter, not multiplicative. **P** controls 60% of the votes for **C**'s board of directors, not just 42% (70% × 60%). **P** controls **A**, and **A** controls **C**; therefore **P** controls **C**. Ownership of 60%, whether direct or indirect, gives **P** virtually complete control over the strategic policies of **C**.

In Case 2, control of **P** over **C** is achieved indirectly through two direct subsidiaries of **P**: **A** and **B**. Neither **A** nor **B** has control of **C** because each has less than a majority of **C**'s voting shares. However, **P** can control **C** because **P** controls 70% of the votes in **C** through its control of **A** and **B** (40% + 30%). In this

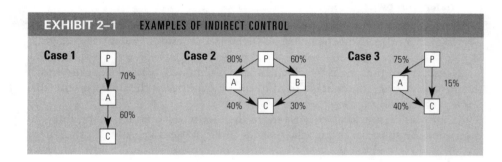

| EXHIBIT 2–1 | EXAMPLES OF INDIRECT CONTROL |

2. Reduction of the parent's ownership interest is discussed in an appendix to Chapter 6.

example, **A**, **B**, and **C** are all subsidiaries of **P**, but **C** is *not* a subsidiary of either **A** or **B**.

In Case 3, **P** has both direct and indirect ownership interests in **C**. Control is achieved only by virtue of the shares of **C** that are owned by both **P** and **A**, and thus **P**'s control of **C** is still indirect, despite **P**'s direct ownership of 15% of **C**'s voting shares. The sum of one corporation's direct and indirect interest in another corporation is known as the **beneficial interest**. **P** has a 55% beneficial interest in **C**. **A** and **C** are subsidiaries of **P**; **C** is *not* a subsidiary of **A**.

Other types of ownership arrangements can exist; these three examples are merely illustrative. Some intercorporate ownerships are very complex, and require careful analysis in order to determine who controls whom.

Limitations on control The ownership of a majority of votes of another corporation gives the parent control over the strategic policies of the subsidiary, but not necessarily *absolute* control. Legislation generally requires that *special resolutions* be approved by at least two-thirds of the votes of the shareholders. **Special resolutions** include proposals to change a corporation's charter or bylaws, including any changes to the structure of the share ownership. Thus a parent cannot be completely assured of the ability to restructure a subsidiary, to amalgamate it, or to change the broad business purposes stated in its charter (which is called the **letters patent**) unless the parent owns at least two-thirds of the voting shares.

While two-thirds ownership can guarantee the approval of special resolutions, it still does not give absolute control. As long as there are outside shareholders, the parent corporation cannot require the subsidiary to follow any policies that are detrimental to the interests of the non-controlling shareholders. Parent action that is detrimental to the interests of non-controlling shareholders is called **oppression of minority shareholders**.

For example, assume that ParentCorp owns controlling interest in SubLtd, and that SubLtd is the major source of supply for the primary raw material that is used by ParentCorp. The board of directors of ParentCorp may want SubLtd to sell the raw material to ParentCorp at less than market value. If ParentCorp owns 100% of SubLtd, then SubLtd can do so without harming any shareholders. The reduced profit in SubLtd is offset by increased profit in ParentCorp. But if ParentCorp owns only 70% of SubLtd, then the shifting of profits from SubLtd to ParentCorp will harm the 30% minority shareholders in SubLtd. Their equity, their potential dividends, and the market value of their shares will all be reduced.

Therefore, many corporations prefer to own 100% of their subsidiaries; this is particularly common when there is a close working relationship between the parent and the subsidiary, or among the various subsidiaries.

Because of the relatively unfettered ability of a parent to control the affairs of a wholly owned subsidiary, creditors of such a subsidiary frequently take steps to protect their own interests. Creditors may insist that the parent guarantee the subsidiary's debts, may require fairly liquid collateral (such as assignment of accounts receivable), or may include restrictive covenants in bond indentures.

A parent corporation can acquire a subsidiary in either of two ways: (1) by founding (or creating) a new corporation, or (2) by buying a controlling interest in an existing corporation.

Parent-founded subsidiaries The vast majority of subsidiaries are founded by the parent corporation in order to carry out some segment of the parent's business. Subsidiaries are formed for a variety of legal, regulatory, and tax reasons. For example, if a corporation is subject to taxation in several countries or provinces, it usually simplifies tax reporting if there is a separate legal entity in each taxation jurisdiction.

Similarly, lines of business that are subject to regulation are usually carried out in separate legal entities. The intercorporate organization of BCE is an example of a regulatory-inspired organization—Bell Canada and certain other subsidiaries are subject to regulation, while other subsidiaries are not. Maintaining distinct legal separation between regulated and non-regulated lines of business prevents the non-regulated businesses from unnecessarily falling under regulation.

Financing arrangements may also be facilitated by having subsidiaries rather than a single legal entity conducting all of the corporation's business. A separate corporation is frequently established to conduct customer financing activities. Finance companies have quite different financial structures than do product or service organizations. It may be easier to arrange the secondary financing of customers' installment debt or leases if the receivables from customers are assets of a distinct corporate finance company. Also, there can be tax advantages to creating a separate legal entity to carry out specialized finance services such as leasing.

The vast majority of parent-founded subsidiaries are wholly owned by the parent, although sometimes the parent will reduce its ownership below 100% once the subsidiary is established. There are two ways by which the parent can dilute its ownership interest. One is by selling part of its holding of the subsidiary shares to the public or to a private buyer. The other is by having the subsidiary issue new shares to public or private buyers. Both approaches reduce the parent's ownership share, but the first approach also reduces the parent's investment in the subsidiary. The second approach maintains the parent's share investment and raises new capital for the subsidiary.[3]

The sale of Air Canada shares to the public illustrates both approaches. The initial public share offer, in 1988, was an issuance of new shares by the corporation, while the second share offer in 1989 was a sale of the government's shares. The 1988 proceeds went to Air Canada, while the 1989 proceeds went to the federal government.

When a parent establishes a subsidiary in a foreign country, the parent may decide not to own 100% of the subsidiary's shares. The decision may be to include host-country shareholders for business reasons. In some countries, the parent has little choice. The host country may encourage or require local participation in the ownership of subsidiaries of foreign-owned parents in order to improve the subsidiary's responsiveness to economic conditions in the host country and to establish a basis for accountability to the host country's citizens or government.

Despite the exceptions, most subsidiaries are wholly owned. This fact greatly simplifies the preparation of consolidated statements, as we shall see when we get into the actual process of consolidation.

Purchasing a subsidiary—business combinations Instead of founding a subsidiary, a corporation can purchase a controlling interest in an existing corporation as a going concern. There are many reasons for acquiring a going concern instead of starting up a new subsidiary. For example:

- The acquired subsidiary may remove a competitor from the marketplace.
- The acquired company may provide a product or service that fills a void in the purchaser's existing product line.

---

3. The accounting and reporting implications of changes in the parent's ownership share are discussed in an appendix to Chapter 6.

- The acquired company may have licences or geographic rights that complement those of the purchaser.

- The new subsidiary may enable the acquirer to pursue a new strategic direction without having to start from scratch in a highly competitive environment.

- The new subsidiary may ensure sources of supply or provide direct access to the industrial, retail, or Internet market.

- The newly acquired company may have a business that is counter-cyclical to the parent's, thereby increasing the parent's overall stability and reducing investors' and creditors' perceptions of the financial risk of the total entity.

- The subsidiary may generate a large cash flow that is needed by the parent to fund its operations or product development.

Whenever one corporation buys a controlling interest in another, and thereby obtains control over the net assets of the acquired company, a **business combination** has occurred. A business combination can be accomplished in a variety of ways, and the accounting problem is to report the substance of the combination regardless of the legal form of the transaction. This topic is discussed at length in Chapter 3.

Non-controlling and minority interests: A terminology note Prior to the introduction of Section 1590 in 1992, the CICA Handbook used the phrase "minority interest" to designate the interest of those shareholders who did not have a controlling interest. Section 1590 explicitly recognized that it may be possible to have a controlling interest while owning less than 50% of the investee's shares, and thus a controlling interest could also be a minority interest. As a result, the terminology in the CICA Handbook was altered; "minority interest" was consistently replaced by "non-controlling interest."

Non-controlling interest is the broader, all-inclusive phrase. In practice, however, the vast majority of non-controlling interests really are minority interests. Indeed, it will be a very rare thing for a *majority* non-controlling interest to exist (although it is possible). As a result, consolidated financial statements continue to use the phrase *minority interest*. Just because the phrase has disappeared from the *CICA Handbook* does not mean it will disappear from financial statements.

Variable interest entities (VIEs)

A **variable interest entity (VIE)** is an entity that is created apart from the reporting enterprise in order to carry out or facilitate a specific aspect of the enterprise's business, but that is not a subsidiary. A VIE is not a subsidiary because the corporation that created the VIE does not own a majority of the votes for the VIE's board of directors. Nevertheless, the corporation does receive some sort of benefit from the VIE. The following two examples illustrate the legitimate use of VIEs,

- Many companies have one or more registered pension plans for their employees. Each company also has a separate, trusteed pension fund that invests and manages the pension fund on behalf of the employer, the employees, and the retirees. A pension fund VIE (1) removes the funds in the plan from the reach of the company's management, (2) enables the trustee to fulfill the trustee's obligations for wise investment of the funds, and (3) makes sure that the plan is administered in keeping with the pension agreement and provincial law. The company benefits from a pension fund VIE because proper pension fund administration is in the best interests of the company. However, the company does not control the pension plan either directly or indirectly. Therefore, pension plans are not included in the company's consolidated financial statements.

- Similarly, a separate corporation (i.e., a VIE) may be established in order to *securitize* a company's receivables. Securitization is the process of transferring receivables into a VIE and then issuing securities to private or public investors as a means of financing those receivables. That is, the company sells the receivables to a VIE, and the VIE gets the money (or the vast majority of the money) to pay for the receivables by selling bonds or similar financial instruments to other investors.

On the other hand, corporations sometimes use VIEs to manipulate their financial reporting and to keep liabilities off the balance sheet. Manipulation is unethical because it is an attempt to mislead financial statement readers by understating liabilities, hiding assets, or concealing certain operating activities. Enron Corporation made this unethical use of VIEs famous, but it is a manipulative technique that has been used for many years and by many corporations.

For example, a reporting enterprise may establish a VIE and use it to acquire tangible capital assets under a *capital* lease. The VIE then leases those assets to the reporting enterprise under an *operating* lease. The purpose of the VIE is to circumvent the *CICA Handbook* requirement to capitalize capital leases. If the reporting enterprise does not control the VIE through share ownership, then the VIE escapes the *CICA Handbook* definition of control and is not consolidated. The capital lease liabilities (and the related assets) do not appear on the consolidated financial statements.

Despite the lack of substantial equity interest, the reporting corporation controls the VIE through contractual arrangements and/or by having its corporate executives or board members as officers and board members of the VIE. The definition of *control* in Section 1590 of the *CICA Handbook* relies only on voting control, and not on other methods of control.

It was the use of VIEs that enabled Enron to avoid reporting significant financial and operating activities in its consolidated financial statements without running afoul of GAAP. Historically, GAAP implicitly condoned the practice of corporations not reporting their VIEs, except through the very limited disclosure requirements for related party transactions.

The Enron affair focused a lot of attention on the accounting shortcomings related to VIEs, and since then both the FASB and the AcSB have issued recommendations on accounting for VIEs.

The AcSB issued updated Accounting Guideline 15, "Consolidation of Variable Interest Entities," in June 2003 as a temporary measure until the *CICA Handbook* is revised to include a single internationally accepted standard on consolidation that includes guidance on VIEs. The purpose of the guideline is to expand the requirements for consolidation beyond those in Section 1590 to include VIEs. Under the guideline, a corporation should consolidate a VIE if the corporation is the *primary beneficiary* of the VIE's activities. A **primary beneficiary** is the party that stands to gain most from the variable interests. A **variable interest** is any participation in a VIE that stands to gain or lose through changes in the values of the VIE's assets and liabilities. We will illustrate both a non-variable interest and a variable interest as follows.

- In the case of a *non-variable interest*, a VIE borrows money from a bank at a fixed rate or at a rate that varies only in response to market interest rates. The bank has an interest in the VIE, but only to the extent that the bank wishes to recover its loan plus interest. The bank will not benefit from increases in the VIE's asset value.

- In the case of a *variable interest*, a corporation establishes a VIE and extends a loan to the VIE. The loan is the VIE's primary source of financing, and can be repaid either in dollars or by transferring the VIE's assets to the corporation at maturity, at the corporation's option. The corporation does not *control* the VIE, as defined in Section 1590 of the *CICA Handbook*, because the corporation does not control a majority of the votes. However, the corporation stands to benefit substantially from changes in the value of the VIE's assets.

There may be more than one party with a variable interest in a VIE. The primary beneficiary is the party that has the highest exposure to future *losses*. The primary beneficiary must consolidate the VIE, regardless of the proportion of shares in the VIE that is held by the beneficiary. There can be only one *primary* beneficiary, and thus only one company can consolidate a VIE.

The consolidation procedure is no different for a VIE than it is for a subsidiary. The consolidation illustration later in this chapter deals with a subsidiary, but the procedure is the same for a VIE.

Significantly influenced affiliates

Frequently, one corporation will purchase less than a controlling equity interest in another corporation. However, the investor may nevertheless be able to have a substantial impact on the strategic operating, investing, and financing policies of the investee. Such substantial impact is known as **significant influence**.

Significant influence can be achieved if the investee corporation's shares are widely distributed and there is no effective opposition to the investor's active involvement. However, *control* does not exist in such situations. It is possible for another investor or group of investors to acquire control over a majority of the shares of the investee, and then to wrest influence from the hands of the minority investor. When such a change in control takes place against the wishes of the previously dominant shareholder (and, usually, against the wishes of the board of directors), the change is known as a **hostile takeover**.

It usually is clear when control exists: the investor either can or cannot elect a majority of the board of directors (without the co-operation of other shareholders). In contrast, the presence of significant influence is not so clearly determinable. The general numerical guideline cited in the *CICA Handbook* [CICA 3050.04] is that significant influence is presumed to exist if the investor corporation owns 20% or more of the voting shares of the investee and does not have a controlling interest.

The percentage of ownership is only a guideline; it is the *substance* of the relationship between the two companies that must be examined. The issue is important because investments in significantly influenced companies are reported on a different basis than are subsidiaries or portfolio investments. Subsidiaries are consolidated, while portfolio investments are reported on the cost basis. In contrast, significantly influenced affiliates are reported on the *equity basis*.

On the cost basis, income is recorded only when dividends are declared by the investee. If the investor has the ability to significantly influence the strategic policies of the investee, then reporting the investment on the cost basis gives the investor the ability to manipulate its own income by influencing the affiliate's dividend policy. If the investor wanted to smooth its reported net income, the affiliate could be "influenced" to declare small dividends in years in which the investor had high operating income, and to declare large dividends in years of low investor operating income.

Significant influence gives the investor the power to play a major role in the investee's earnings process. Since the investor is a participant in the investee's earnings process, the investor's proportionate share of the investee's earnings should be reported in the investor's income statement. This is known as the *equity method of reporting*. We will discuss the equity method a little later in this chapter.

When does significant influence exist? The size of the investor's ownership share gives us a clue, but only a clue. The presence of significant influence is a matter of operating substance, not of proportionate share investment.

Several factors must be examined in order to determine whether significant influence exists. The composition of the board of directors is one important factor. If the board contains representatives of the investor, these representatives may be able to influence corporate policies significantly in the boardroom. This is particularly true when the investor's non-controlling shareholding is the largest single block of shares. In that case, a majority of the investee's board may be representatives of the investor. Significant influence may exist, however, when other investors also have significant influence over the investee corporation and even when another investor holds controlling interest in the investee.

The existence of significant influence is determined by more than just the extent of share ownership. A voting interest of less than 20% can carry significant influence if there are other important relationships between the two companies, or if the affiliate's shares are widely held and all other owners are passive, or if the investor corporation has the active support of other shareholders. Conversely, a voting interest of up to 50% may not give significant influence if the management and controlling shareholders of the investee corporation are hostile to the investor corporation, and will not accede to the investor's demands or permit the investor's nominees to sit on the investee's board.

Significant influence may also be indicated by the extent of intercorporate transactions. If the investor is a major supplier or major customer of the investee, significant influence can be exercised not only by the ownership of shares but also by means of the supplier–customer relationship.

Other indications of significant influence include substantial debt financing provided by the investor, the investor's ownership of patents, trademarks, or processes upon which the affiliate's business depends, and the provision of managerial or technical assistance to the affiliate.

There is a larger grey area for the existence of significant influence than there is for the existence of control. Nevertheless, it is reasonably clear in most situations whether or not significant influence does exist. If there is doubt, then significant influence probably does not exist. But the doubt must arise as a result of examining the substance of the operating situation, and not merely by looking at the percentage of ownership of the voting shares.

Joint ventures

A particular instance in which significant influence is a matter of contractual right is when the investor corporation is part-owner of a *joint venture*. A **joint venture** is an arrangement whereby two or more parties jointly control a specific business undertaking and contribute resources towards its accomplishment. Joint ventures are common in certain industries (such as resource exploration), and are common in global competition when two otherwise competing companies join forces to establish operations in another country or when one company joins with the host country's government in establishing a new venture. For example, Nortel established joint ventures with Motorola in the U.S. and the Matra Group in France to jointly develop the market for cordless digital telephones by shared technologies.

An essential and distinguishing characteristic of a joint venture is that the investors or *co-venturers* enter into an agreement that governs each co-venturer's involvement in the joint venture. The joint venture agreement specifies each co-venturer's capital contribution, representation on the board of directors, and involvement in management, plus other relevant matters. No one investor can make major strategic decisions unilaterally; major decisions require the consent of all of the co-venturers. This is known as **joint control**.

Joint ventures are always established by a very limited number of co-venturers. Joint ventures are always private companies. The joint venture agreement is similar to the **shareholders' agreement** in private corporations that clarifies the rights and responsibilities of the various shareholders. The difference is that, in private corporations, a single shareholder or a small group may exercise control. In a joint venture, in contrast, no one investor (or subgroup of investors) can control the joint venture even though that investor may contribute a majority of the capital. Joint ventures require agreement amongst the co-venturers, not voting power.

Joint control should not be confused with *profit sharing*. Control is joint, but profit sharing is not necessarily equal. The joint venture stipulates how the risks and benefits of the venture will be shared, including the distribution of profits and dividends.

Since each investor in a joint venture has participation rights, each investor has significant influence in the joint venture. Significant influence in a joint venture is a matter of fact, not professional judgment.

Reporting Investments in Affiliates and Subsidiaries

When an investor corporation prepares its financial statements, there are four basic ways in which share investments can be reported: (1) the *cost method*, (2) the *equity method*, (3) *consolidation*, and (4) *proportionate consolidation*.

Cost method

The **cost method** or **cost basis** is the approach that is used for investments in the shares of companies over which the investor does not have significant influence. The investment is shown in the balance sheet at cost, and dividends are reported in the investor's income when declared by the investee. The cost method is also used for all investments in fixed-income securities, including nonparticipating preferred shares, regardless of whether the investee corporation is significantly influenced or not.

The cost method is used for subsidiaries and significantly influenced affiliates only if the parent is prevented from exercising its control or influence. The exercise of control or significant influence can be blocked by foreign governments (for affiliates in foreign countries). If the affiliate enters receivership, control or influence also is lost, at least temporarily. Loss of control or significant influence may be an indication that the investment has been impaired. A write-down of the investment may be advisable if there is a decline in value "that is other than a temporary decline" [CICA 3051.18].

For external reporting by public companies, the cost method is used only for portfolio investments and for subsidiaries over which control is impaired, as described just above. However, the cost basis is commonly used in two other circumstances, as follows.

- The cost basis almost always is used internally, as the *recording* method, for *all* investments in other companies. This is a bookkeeping matter, not an external reporting matter. As we will demonstrate in the following chapters, it is easier to consolidate the subsidiaries if the cost method is used on the books.

- Under the differential reporting provisions of the *CICA Handbook*, private corporations do not have to report on a consolidated basis if the shareholders unanimously agree to non-consolidated reporting. In its non-consolidated financial statements, a private parent company may use either the cost or the equity basis to report investments in subsidiaries, joint ventures, and significantly influenced affiliates.

Equity method

The **equity method** or **equity basis** is the method that is used for reporting investments in income-participating shares of significantly influenced investee corporations. Income-participating shares include all unrestricted and restricted common shares and cumulative participating preferred shares, regardless of whether the shares are voting or non-voting. Since the investor has the ability to significantly influence the operations of the investee, the investee's economic performance is closely bound to that of the investor.

To give the investor's stakeholders a fair presentation of the corporation's overall economic performance, the investor's earnings must include its proportionate share of (or equity in) the *investee's earnings*, rather than just the dividends declared. The financial reporting objective of performance evaluation is thereby better served. The cash flow prediction objective is also better served—since the investor can control the dividend policy of the investee, the equity method requires that the proportionate share of the full amount of earnings available as dividends (and thus hypothetically transferable in cash) be reported in the investor's income statement.

Historically, the manipulative possibilities inherent in reporting income on a dividend-only basis from controlled or significantly influenced investee corporations led to accounting standards that recommend the equity method. Section 3050, "Long-Term Investments," of the *CICA Handbook* is a good example of an accounting standard that gives precedence to user objectives over preparer objectives; it removes the ability of the investor to manipulate its own net income by regulating the dividend flow from the affiliate.

On the financial statements, share investments are accounted for as follows under the equity method.

- The investor's income statement shows the investor's proportionate share of the investee's net income as "equity in earnings of affiliates" (or a similar title). Also, the income statement will show the investor's proportionate share of any discontinued operations and extraordinary items.

- The balance sheet shows the balance of the investment account as follows:

Cost of the investment
+ The investor's share of the investee's earnings to date
– Dividends paid by the investee to the investor, to date
= Investment balance at the reporting date.

- The cash flow statement shows dividends received for the year as an inflow of cash from investing activities; if the investor uses the indirect method of reporting cash from operations, then the investor's "equity in earnings" is subtracted from net income as a non-cash flow.

The net result is that, at any point in time, the investment account shows the historical cost of the investment plus the investor's proportionate share of the increase (or decrease) in the investee's net asset value since the date of the initial investment. A simple illustration is given later in this chapter.

Usually, we must make several adjustments to the reported earnings of the affiliate before the investor's share of the earnings is reported on the investor's income statement. Chapter 4 contains a numerical illustration of the equity method that includes adjustments.

Consolidation

Consolidation is the process of reporting on one set of financial statements the total amount of assets, liabilities, revenues, and expenses of an economic entity comprising a parent corporation and its subsidiaries. Consolidated statements will show the *total* economic activity of the parent and its subsidiaries. All of the resources and obligations under the control of the parent corporation are reported on consolidated statements.

Canadian practice calls for consolidation of *all* of a parent company's subsidiaries [CICA 1590.16]. Non-consolidated reporting is permitted in certain reporting situations; these will be discussed toward the end of this chapter.

Consolidated statements are prepared from the point of view of the shareholders of the parent company. Consolidation adds the elements in the financial statements of subsidiaries to those of the parent. On the balance sheet, there will be no investment account for the consolidated subsidiaries. Instead, the assets and liabilities of the subsidiaries will be added to those of the parent in order to show the economic resources of the entire economic entity comprising the parent and its subsidiaries. On the income statement, the revenues and expenses will be the totals for each item for the parent plus the subsidiaries. The effects of any intercompany transactions will be eliminated in order to avoid double-counting.

When there are several layers of subsidiaries, consolidated statements will normally be prepared at each level, particularly when there are non-controlling shareholders in the intermediate layers. For example, assume that Corporation A owns 70% of Corporation B, and Corporation B owns 60% of C. The following financial statements will be prepared.

- C will prepare its own separate-entity financial statements, which will be used by C's minority shareholders and for income tax purposes.
- B will prepare separate-entity (i.e., non-consolidated) statements for tax purposes, internal purposes, and perhaps for specific users, such as the bank. In the non-consolidated statements, the investment in C will be shown as an asset.
- For issuance to the general public, B will also prepare consolidated statements that include the assets, liabilities, revenue, expenses, and cash flows of C. These statements are relevant for B's non-controlling shareholders.
- A will prepare consolidated statements that include all of the assets, liabilities, revenues, expenses, and cash flows of the consolidated statements of B, which includes C. A's consolidated statements are relevant to the shareholders of A, and of A *only*. A will also prepare non-consolidated statements for tax purposes and perhaps as special-purpose statements for bankers and creditors.

Non-controlling or minority shareholders are interested only in the statements of the company in which they own shares. B's non-controlling shareholders are not entitled to the statements of A, even though B is controlled by A, because they are not shareholders of A.

Proportionate consolidation

In Canada, proportionate consolidation is required by the *CICA Handbook* for reporting joint ventures [CICA 3055.17]. In **proportionate consolidation**, only the investor's proportionate share of the joint venture assets, liabilities, revenues, and expenses is added to the investee's consolidated financial statements. If the investor has a 30% share in a joint venture, then only 30% of the joint venture's financial statement amounts are consolidated in the parent's statements. As well, the co-venturer should disclose the total amounts and the major components of the joint venture's balance sheet, income statement, and cash flow [CICA 3055.41].

Canada is unique in its requirement for proportionate consolidation. International accounting standards, as well as the accounting standards of all other countries, require that joint ventures be reported on the equity basis. The move towards harmonization may cause the AcSB to change its recommendation in order to be in harmony with international standards.

Canada uses the proportionate consolidation method because of the high level of joint venture activity in the resource industry. Joint ventures often involve large public companies. Since joint ventures are always private companies, there would be no public reporting of joint venture assets and liabilities were it not for proportionate consolidation.

Although other countries do not permit proportionate consolidation, there is some empirical evidence suggesting that proportionate consolidation provides useful information to investors that is lost with equity reporting. For example, one study examined 78 public companies that use proportionate consolidation. The researchers found that "financial statements prepared under proportionate consolidation provide better predictions of future return on shareholders' equity than do financial statements prepared under the equity method."[4]

Reporting versus *recording* methods

The next section gives an introductory illustration of consolidation. Before turning our attention to the preparation of consolidated statements, however, it is important to point out that the *reporting* of intercorporate investments is not the same as the *recording* of the investments in the books of the investor.

Investments in significantly influenced affiliates are normally *reported* in the investor's financial statements on the equity basis, but the investment account on the books of the investor corporation may be *recorded in the investor's books* on the cost basis. The adjustments to convert from the cost to the equity basis for reporting purposes are then made on working papers and are not necessarily recorded on the books of the investor. Therefore, the reporting method for the investment in significantly influenced affiliates *may* be different from the recording method used in the investor's books.

Consolidation is a different story. Consolidated statements are prepared by means of a series of adjustments and eliminations that are *always* made only on working papers and are *never* recorded on the books of the parent company. An investor corporation's recording procedures for investments in affiliates and sub-

---

4. R. C. Graham, R. D. King, and C. K. J. Morrill, "Decision usefulness of alternative joint venture reporting methods." *Accounting Horizons* 17:2 (June 2003), p. 123.

sidiaries are frequently based on ease of recordkeeping. The reported amounts on the investor's consolidated financial statements are derived from schedules and worksheets that are prepared only for reporting purposes. The adjustments are not recorded on anyone's books, because there is no legal or bookkeeping entity that corresponds to the consolidated statements. Consolidated statements are reports intended to reflect an economic concept, rather than a practical or legal reality.

Remember the rules:

- Investments in significantly influenced affiliates *may* be recorded in the investor's books on the cost basis, even when reporting is on the equity basis. In that case, adjustments to convert from cost to equity for reporting purposes are on worksheets and working papers only.

- Consolidations *must* occur on worksheets only. The adjustments made for consolidation are *never* recorded on any company's books. There are no journal entries recorded anywhere except on the accountant's working papers.

Example of Accounting for Strategic Investments

We will begin our illustration by preparing consolidated statements under the assumption that the cost method of recording is used on the parent's books. We will then use the same example to illustrate the use of the equity basis of reporting in unconsolidated statements. Finally, we will prepare consolidated statements assuming that the equity method of recording is used on the parent's books.

Consolidation when the cost method is used

Assume that Parco established a subsidiary in 2000 by creating a new corporation named Subco. Subco issued 100 common shares to Parco in return for $80,000 cash paid by Parco for the shares. Parco has remained the sole shareholder of Subco in succeeding years.

On December 31, 2008, several years after the incorporation of Subco, the trial balances for the two companies are as shown in Exhibit 2–2. The 2008 separate-entity financial statements of the two companies (derived from the trial balances) are presented in Exhibit 2–3, prior to any adjustments related to Parco's investment in Subco. In Exhibit 2–3, we have boldfaced those elements that are of particular interest for consolidation purposes.

In order to prepare the consolidated statements, we first need to know the nature and extent of financial interactions between the two. Important facts relating to the 2008 statements are as follows:

1. Parco's investment in Subco is carried on Parco's books at cost ($80,000).

2. The two balance sheets include $60,000 that is owed by Subco to Parco. The amount is a current asset for Parco and a current liability for Subco.

3. Dividends received from Subco during the year are shown as dividend income on Parco's income statement.

4. The sales of Parco include $100,000 of merchandise sold to Subco, all of which was sold by Subco to outside customers during the year.

EXHIBIT 2-2   SEPARATE-ENTITY TRIAL BALANCES

December 31, 2008

	Parco Dr	Parco Cr	Subco Dr	Subco Cr
Cash	$ 70,000		$ 40,000	
Accounts receivable	200,000		110,000	
Receivable from Subco	60,000		—	
Inventories	150,000		120,000	
Land	100,000		—	
Buildings and equipment	1,000,000		450,000	
Accumulated depreciation		$ 300,000		$ 100,000
Investment in Subco (at cost)	80,000			
Accounts payable		120,000		80,000
Due to Parco		—		60,000
Long-term notes payable		—		300,000
Future income taxes		140,000		30,000
Common shares		300,000		80,000
Dividends declared	30,000		20,000	
Retained earnings, December 31, 2007		762,000		60,000
Sales revenue		800,000		400,000
Dividend income		20,000		—
Cost of sales	480,000		280,000	
Depreciation expense	130,000		30,000	
Income tax expense	32,000		20,000	
Other expenses	110,000		40,000	
	$ 2,442,000	$ 2,442,000	$ 1,110,000	$ 1,110,000

When a subsidiary's financial statements are consolidated with those of the parent, the parent and the subsidiary are viewed as a single economic entity. The objective of consolidation is to show on the consolidated statements of the parent all of the assets, liabilities, revenues, and expenses over which the parent company has control.

To prepare its consolidated financial statements, Parco will add together the financial statement amounts for Parco and Subco. In the process, however, some changes to the pre-consolidation reported balances must be made. There are two types of changes that are made when statements are consolidated: (1) *eliminations* and (2) *adjustments*:

- **Eliminations** are changes that prevent certain amounts on the separate-entity statements from appearing on the consolidated statements. Eliminations are necessary to avoid double-counting (such as intercompany sales) and to cancel out offsetting balances (such as intercompany receivables and payables).

- **Adjustments**, on the other hand, are made to alter reported amounts in order to reflect the economic substance of transactions rather than their nominal amount.

EXHIBIT 2–3   SEPARATE-ENTITY FINANCIAL STATEMENTS

Balance Sheets
December 31, 2008

Assets	Parco	Subco
Current assets:		
Cash	$ 70,000	$ 40,000
Accounts receivable	200,000	110,000
Receivable from Subco	**60,000**	—
Inventories	150,000	120,000
	480,000	270,000
Property, plant, and equipment:		
Land	100,000	—
Buildings and equipment	1,000,000	450,000
Accumulated depreciation	(300,000)	(100,000)
	800,000	350,000
Other assets:		
Investment in Subco (at cost)	**80,000**	—
Total assets	$1,360,000	$ 620,000
Liabilities and shareholders' equity		
Current liabilities:		
Accounts payable	$ 120,000	$ 80,000
Due to Parco	—	**60,000**
	120,000	140,000
Long-term notes payable	—	300,000
Future income taxes	140,000	30,000
Total liabilities	260,000	470,000
Shareholders' equity:		
Common shares	300,000	**80,000**
Retained earnings	800,000	70,000
Total shareholders' equity	1,100,000	150,000
Total liabilities and shareholders' equity	$1,360,000	$ 620,000

Statements of Income and Retained Earnings
Year Ended December 31, 2008

	Parco	Subco
Sales revenue	$ 800,000	$ 400,000
Dividend income	**20,000**	—
	820,000	400,000
Operating expenses:		
Cost of sales	480,000	280,000
Depreciation expense	130,000	30,000
Income tax expense	32,000	20,000
Other expenses	110,000	40,000
	752,000	370,000
Net income	68,000	30,000
Retained earnings, December 31, 2007	762,000	60,000
Dividends declared	(30,000)	**(20,000)**
Retained earnings, December 31, 2008	$ 800,000	$ 70,000

There are two general approaches to preparing consolidated financial statements. One is called the *direct approach*. The **direct approach** prepares the consolidated statements by setting up the balance sheet and income statement formats and computing each consolidated balance directly. Each asset, liability, revenue, and expense is separately calculated and entered into the consolidated statement. The direct approach works from the separate-entity financial statements (that is, by using Exhibit 2–3).

The alternative method is the *worksheet approach*. The **worksheet (or spreadsheet) approach** uses a multi-columnar worksheet to enter the trial balances of the parent and each subsidiary. Then, eliminations and adjustments are entered onto the worksheet, and the accounts are cross-added to determine the consolidated balances. The finished consolidated statements are then prepared from the consolidated trial balance.

The direct approach is intuitively appealing because we are working directly with the statements and can see clearly what is happening to the consolidated statements as we make eliminations and adjustments.

The worksheet approach is more methodical and is the technique that is used in practice (usually computerized). A worksheet is less intuitive, but its use enables us to keep better track of the eliminations and adjustments, some of which get very complicated.

In this book, we will illustrate both approaches. The direct approach will be presented first, and the worksheet approach second. Both approaches yield the same result. It doesn't matter which approach is used—what is important is the result, not the method used to derive the result.

Direct approach to consolidation The Parco consolidated financial statements for 2008 are shown in Exhibit 2–4. In this exhibit, the statements have been prepared by using the direct method. The consolidated financial statements are obtained by: (1) adding together the individual amounts on the parent and subsidiaries' financial statements and (2) subtracting amounts as necessary for adjustments and eliminations, and then (3) entering the resulting amounts *directly* into consolidated financial statements.

An important point is that the consolidated statements are being prepared by Parco for submission to its shareholders. The net assets and shareholders' equity that will be shown in Parco's consolidated balance sheet will be *the net assets* (equal to shareholders' equity) *from the point of view of the Parco shareholders*. The common shares that are outstanding for Parco are the $300,000 shown in Parco's balance sheet, not the total of $300,000 + $80,000 that would be obtained by adding the two separate-entity balances together.

Therefore, the first elimination in preparing the consolidated balance sheet is the $80,000 common share amount for Subco. The common share line in Exhibit 2–4 shows $300,000 + $80,000 – $80,000, the amount in bold being the elimination of Subco's share equity.

Since a credit balance of $80,000 is being eliminated, there must be an offsetting elimination in order to preserve the equality of debits and credits on the balance sheet. The offset is the $80,000 debit shown as "Investment in Subco" on the Parco balance sheet. The investment account is really just an aggregate that represents the net assets of the subsidiary; instead of showing the *net* investment in the subsidiary as an asset, the consolidated statements show all of the assets and liabilities of the subsidiary that underlie the investment. Thus neither the $80,000 debit for Parco's investment nor the $80,000 credit for the common shares of Subco will appear on the consolidated balance sheet; both amounts are eliminated.

EXHIBIT 2–4   PARCO CONSOLIDATED FINANCIAL STATEMENTS

Consolidated Balance Sheet
December 31, 2008

Assets

Current assets:

Cash [70,000 + 40,000]	$ 110,000
Accounts receivable [200,000 + 110,000]	310,000
Receivable from Subco [60,000 + 0 – **60,000**]	—
Inventories [150,000 + 120,000]	270,000
	690,000

Property, plant, and equipment:

Land [100,000 + 0]	100,000
Buildings and equipment [1,000,000 + 450,000]	1,450,000
Accumulated depreciation [300,000 + 100,000]	(400,000)
	1,150,000

Other assets:

Investment in Subco, at cost [80,000 + 0 – **80,000**]	—
Total assets	$1,840,000

Liabilities and shareholders' equity

Current liabilities:

Accounts payable [120,000 + 80,000]	$ 200,000
Due to Parco [0 + 60,000 – **60,000**]	—
	200,000

Long-term notes payable [0 + 300,000]	300,000
Future income taxes [140,000 + 30,000]	170,000
Total liabilities	670,000

Shareholders' equity:

Common shares [300,000 + 80,000 – **80,000**]	300,000
Retained earnings [800,000 + 70,000]	870,000
Total shareholders' equity	1,170,000
Total liabilities and shareholders' equity	$1,840,000

Consolidated Statement of Income and Retained Earnings
Year Ended December 31, 2008

Revenue:

Sales revenue [800,000 + 400,000 – **100,000**]	$1,100,000
Dividend income [20,000 + 0 – **20,000**]	—
	1,100,000

Operating expenses:

Cost of sales [480,000 + 280,000 – **100,000**]	660,000
Depreciation expense [130,000 + 30,000]	160,000
Income tax expense [32,000 + 20,000]	52,000
Other expenses [110,000 + 40,000]	150,000
	1,022,000

Net income	$78,000
Retained earnings, December 31, 2007 [762,000 + 60,000]	822,000
Dividends declared [30,000 + 20,000 – **20,000**]	(30,000)
Retained earnings, December 31, 2008	$ 870,000

Notice that Subco's accumulated retained earnings is *not* eliminated. Since Subco is a wholly owned, parent-founded subsidiary, the amount of retained earnings shown by Subco represents Parco's earnings on its investment that have not been distributed to Parco in the form of dividends. In other scenarios later in the book, some or all of the subsidiary's retained earnings may be eliminated, depending on (1) the degree of ownership and (2) whether the subsidiary was purchased or parent-founded. Stay tuned for further developments!

Second, the amount owed by Subco to Parco must be eliminated. The current assets of Parco ("Receivable from Subco") are reduced by $60,000 and the current liabilities of Subco ("Due to Parco") are reduced by an equal amount.

Third, the intercompany sales of $100,000 have to be eliminated. Sales are reduced by $100,000 to eliminate the amount from consolidated sales. On Subco's books, the cost of the merchandise purchased from Parco was recorded as $100,000. When Subco subsequently sold the merchandise to outsiders, the cost of sales would be recorded as $100,000. Therefore, the offsetting account for elimination of the sales amount is the cost of sales.

Similarly, an elimination must be made to offset the dividends paid by Subco against the dividend income recorded by Parco. The consolidated statements must only reflect the results of transactions between the consolidated entity and outsiders. Since the payment of dividends by a subsidiary to its parent is an intercompany transaction, the dividend flow must not be reported on the consolidated statements.

Worksheet approach to consolidation When the statements to be consolidated are fairly simple, it is quite feasible to compile the consolidated statements by the direct method. In more complex situations, it becomes difficult to keep track of the many adjustments, with the frustrating result that the financial statements won't balance! In complex situations, therefore, accountants usually find it easier to use a worksheet to summarize the necessary eliminations and adjustments. The worksheet also provides the management trail (or audit trail) that explains how the consolidated statements were derived.

Exhibit 2–5 illustrates a worksheet based on the separate-entity trial balances for each company. The trial balances of the parent and the subsidiary (or subsidiaries) are listed in the first columns of the worksheet, and the eliminations and adjustments are inserted in the next column. Cross-adding the rows yields the amounts that will be used to prepare the consolidated statements.

The eliminations that were made in preparing Parco's consolidated statements can be summarized as follows, in general journal format. The parentheses indicate the company on whose statements the accounts being adjusted appear:

(a) Common shares (of Subco)	80,000	
Investment in Subco (by Parco)		80,000
(b) Due to Parco (Subco)	60,000	
Receivable from Subco (Parco)		60,000
(c) Sales (Parco)	100,000	
Cost of sales (Subco)		100,000
(d) Dividend income (Parco)	20,000	
Dividends declared (Subco)		20,000

In each of the eliminations, one side eliminates an amount on Subco's financial statements, while the other side of the entry eliminates an amount on Parco's statements. There is no way that these entries can or should be recorded on either company's books. Consolidation elimination "entries" are entered only on work-

December 31, 2008

	Parco Dr/(Cr)	Subco Dr/(Cr)	Adjustments Dr/(Cr)	Parco consolidated trial balance
	Trial balances			
Cash	$ 70,000	$ 40,000		$ 110,000
Accounts receivable	200,000	110,000		310,000
Receivable from Subco	60,000	—	$ (60,000) **b**	—
Inventories	150,000	120,000		270,000
Land	100,000	—		100,000
Buildings and equipment	1,000,000	450,000		1,450,000
Accumulated depreciation	(300,000)	(100,000)		(400,000)
Investment in Subco (at cost)	80,000	—	(80,000) **a**	—
				—
Accounts payable	(120,000)	(80,000)		(200,000)
Due to Parco	—	(60,000)	60,000 **b**	—
Long-term notes payable	—	(300,000)		(300,000)
Future income taxes	(140,000)	(30,000)		(170,000)
Common shares	(300,000)	(80,000)	80,000 **a**	(300,000)
Dividends declared	30,000	20,000	(20,000) **d**	30,000
Retained earnings, December 31, 2007	(762,000)	(60,000)		(822,000)
Sales revenue	(800,000)	(400,000)	100,000 **c**	(1,100,000)
Dividend income	(20,000)		20,000 **d**	—
Cost of sales	480,000	280,000	(100,000) **c**	660,000
Depreciation expense	130,000	30,000		160,000
Income tax expense	32,000	20,000		52,000
Other expenses	110,000	40,000		150,000
	$ —	$ —	$ —	$ —

ing papers in order to prepare the consolidated statements, and they are never entered on the formal books of account of either the parent or the subsidiary.

The equity method

Separate-entity financial statements The preparation of consolidated financial statements does not eliminate the need for each separate legal entity to prepare its own financial statements. Each corporation is taxed individually, and unconsolidated statements are necessary for income tax reporting if for no other purpose.

Consolidated statements may not be adequate for the needs of creditors or other users of financial statements. Creditors have claims on the resources of specific corporations, not on the resources of other corporations within a consolidated group of companies. Therefore it may be of little benefit to a creditor to see the consolidated assets and liabilities when the credit risk is associated with the financial position of a single company.

When separate-entity statements are prepared for the parent corporation, the investment in the unconsolidated subsidiaries often is reported on the equity basis. This is especially true when the separate-entity statements are for an external user, such as a bank or other major lender, who is interested in the net assets, earnings, and cash flow of the individual corporation. The equity basis permits the financial statement user to discern the full economic impact of the operations of the overall economic entity (i.e., the parent corporation and its subsidiaries) and yet still see the assets, liabilities, results of operations, and cash flows for the parent company alone.

On Parco's books, the investment in Subco is being carried at cost. Therefore, preparation of Parco's equity-basis financial statements requires the conversion of the accounts relating to the investment in Subco to the equity basis for external reporting purposes.

The adjustments to convert the investment account from the cost to the equity basis *can* be formally recorded on Parco's books, but do not need to be. Indeed, it is likely that Parco will not record the adjustments, but will continue to carry the investment account on the cost basis for ease of bookkeeping. In that case, the adjustments will appear only on the working papers used to prepare the equity-basis unconsolidated financial statements for Parco as a separate entity.

We explained earlier that, under the equity method, the parent's share of the earnings of the subsidiary or affiliate is reported on the parent's income statement. On Parco's 2008 unconsolidated income statement, the dividend income is eliminated and is replaced by a line for *equity in earnings of subsidiary.*

Since Parco is the sole owner of Subco, 100% of Subco's 2008 earnings will be reported on Parco's income statement. On Parco's income statement, the $20,000 dividend income is replaced by $30,000 "equity in earnings of Subco." As a result, Parco's earnings increase by $10,000. The adjustments can be illustrated in debit/credit form as follows:

Dividend income	20,000	
Investment in Subco		20,000
Investment in Subco	30,000	
Equity in earnings of Subco		30,000

The difference between Parco's share of Subco earnings ($30,000) and the dividends received from Subco ($20,000) is known as **unremitted earnings**. Each period, the investment account increases by the amount of unremitted earnings.

In addition to the unremitted earnings of $10,000 for Subco for 2008, the investment account should also include the unremitted earnings for the years between the creation of Subco by Parco and the beginning of the 2008 fiscal year. The amount of unremitted earnings from prior years is equal to the amount of the retained earnings of Subco at the beginning of 2008, $60,000. Therefore, the investment account and Parco's prior years' earnings must be adjusted before the unconsolidated statements for Parco are prepared:

Investment in Subco	60,000	
Retained earnings		60,000

These two adjustments increase the balance of the investment account from $80,000 under the cost method to $150,000 under the equity method of reporting. The offsetting credits are a net increase of $10,000 in 2008 income and an increase of $60,000 in retained earnings for prior years' income.

Note that under the equity method, it is *not* necessary to eliminate intercompany transactions such as the $100,000 sales by Parco to Subco. The necessary adjustments are only for items that affect net income—the intercompany transaction washes out in its effect on net income.[5]

Exhibit 2–6 provides a comparison of the financial statements of Parco under the three different policies for reporting the investment in Subco. The first column shows Parco's separate-entity financial statements with the investment in Subco reported on the cost basis. These financial statements are derived from the first column of Exhibit 2–3.

The second column shows Parco's separate-entity financial statements prepared on the equity basis. Note that the first two columns are identical except for the investment in Subco and reported earnings from Subco. As a result, the reported net income and retained earnings of Parco differ significantly between the first and second columns.

The third column of Exhibit 2–6 shows Parco's consolidated financial statements. Almost all of the amounts in the third column are different from those in the first two columns. The assets, liabilities, revenues, and expenses include those of both Parco and Subco, while the investment account and the related earnings accounts have disappeared.

It is impossible to tell from the third column which of the assets and liabilities are those of Parco, since the two corporations are reported as a single economic entity. If a lender were to extend a line of credit to Parco based on (for example) 75% of Parco's accounts receivable, the lender would not be able to tell from the consolidated statements just how much of the $310,000 reported accounts receivable is an asset of Parco.

While most of the consolidated amounts differ from those in the first two columns of Exhibit 2–6, two items are the same in the second and third columns but different from the first column: *Retained Earnings* and *Net Income*. A basic and important attribute of the equity method is that the parent's reported net income and net assets (shareholders' equity) will be the same as when the subsidiaries are consolidated. The effect of consolidation is to disaggregate the net investment in the subsidiary into the component assets and liabilities, and to disaggregate the parent's equity in the earnings of the subsidiary into its components of revenue and expense.

The equity method is frequently referred to as **one-line consolidation** because the equity method and consolidation both result in the same net income and shareholders' equity for the parent. There is one line on the balance sheet that shows the net asset value of the subsidiary, and one line on the income statement that shows the net earnings derived from the subsidiary.[6]

The one-line adjustment to the parent's earnings is commonly known as the **equity pick-up** of the subsidiary's earnings.

Consolidation: Equity *recording* In our earlier illustration of direct consolidation and of the consolidation worksheet, we assumed that the parent company carried the investment in Subco at cost. While the cost method is most commonly used for internal recordkeeping, the equity method may also be used.

---

5. If some of the intercompany merchandise remains in inventory at year-end, an additional complication arises. We will deal with the necessary adjustment in later chapters. But there never is a need to eliminate the intercompany sale transaction itself for equity-basis reporting.

6. An exception arises for the investor's share of any discontinued operations or extraordinary items of the investee. The investor's proportionate share of discontinued operations and extraordinary items will be reported net of related taxes on the investor's income statement after net income from continuing operations.

EXHIBIT 2–6   PARCO FINANCIAL STATEMENTS USING DIFFERENT REPORTING PRACTICES

Balance Sheet, December 31, 2008

	Cost basis	Equity basis	Consolidated
Assets			
Current assets:			
Cash	$ 70,000	$ 70,000	$ 110,000
Accounts receivable	200,000	200,000	310,000
Receivable from Subco	60,000	60,000	—
Inventories	150,000	150,000	270,000
	480,000	480,000	690,000
Property, plant, and equipment:			
Land	100,000	100,000	100,000
Buildings and equipment	1,000,000	1,000,000	1,450,000
Accumulated depreciation	(300,000)	(300,000)	(400,000)
	800,000	800,000	1,150,000
Other assets:			
Investment in Subco	80,000	150,000	—
Total assets	$1,360,000	$1,430,000	$1,840,000
Liabilities and shareholders' equity			
Liabilities:			
Current accounts payable	$ 120,000	$ 120,000	$ 200,000
Long-term notes payable	—	—	300,000
Future income taxes	140,000	140,000	170,000
Total liabilities	260,000	260,000	670,000
Shareholders' equity:			
Common shares	300,000	300,000	300,000
Retained earnings	800,000	870,000	870,000
Total shareholders' equity	1,100,000	1,170,000	1,170,000
Total liabilities and shareholders' equity	$1,360,000	$1,430,000	$1,840,000

Statement of Income and Retained Earnings
Year Ended December 31, 2008

	Cost basis	Equity basis	Consolidated
Sales revenue	$ 800,000	$ 800,000	$1,100,000
Operating expenses:			
Cost of sales	480,000	480,000	660,000
Depreciation expense	130,000	130,000	160,000
Income tax expense	32,000	32,000	52,000
Other expenses	110,000	110,000	150,000
	752,000	752,000	1,022,000
Net income from operations	48,000	48,000	78,000
Dividend income	20,000		
Equity in earnings of Subco		30,000	
Net income	$ 68,000	$ 78,000	$ 78,000
Retained earnings, December 31, 2007	762,000	822,000	822,000
Dividends declared	(30,000)	(30,000)	(30,000)
Retained earnings, December 31, 2008	$ 800,000	$ 870,000	$ 870,000

If Parco had been using the equity method, then the investment account would be $150,000 at the end of 2008, Parco's opening retained earnings would be $822,000 instead of $762,000, and the income statement accounts would include the $30,000 equity in the earnings of Subco rather than dividend income of $20,000. All of these amounts are explained in the immediately preceding section.

The first column of Exhibit 2–7 shows the condensed financial statements for Parco, assuming that the investment has been recorded by use of the equity method. The accounts and amounts that are affected by using the equity method rather than the cost method are highlighted in bold. When the eliminating entries are prepared, the two entries to eliminate the balance of the investment account differ from those shown in Exhibit 2–4 because the composition of the balance in the investment account is different.

Under the cost method, only the original cost of the investment is included in the investment account, and the only elimination necessary is to offset the cost of the investment against the common share account of the subsidiary.

Under the equity method, however, the investment account includes both the original cost of the investment and the unremitted earnings of the subsidiary.

EXHIBIT 2–7   PARCO CONSOLIDATION WORKSHEET—EQUITY BASIS OF RECORDING

December 31, 2008

	Parco Dr/(Cr)	Subco Dr/(Cr)	Elimination & adjustments Dr/(Cr)	Parco consolidated trial balance
	Trial balances			
Cash	$ 70,000	$ 40,000		$ 110,000
Accounts receivable	200,000	110,000		310,000
Receivable from Subco	60,000	—	$ (60,000) c	—
Inventories	150,000	120,000		270,000
Land	100,000	—		100,000
Buildings and equipment	1,000,000	450,000		1,450,000
Accumulated depreciation	(300,000)	(100,000)		(400,000)
Investment in Subco (at equity)	**150,000**	0	(140,000) a / (10,000) b	
Accounts payable	(120,000)	(80,000)		(200,000)
Due to Parco	—	(60,000)	60,000 c	—
Long-term notes payable	—	(300,000)		(300,000)
Future income taxes	(140,000)	(30,000)		(170,000)
Common shares	(300,000)	(80,000)	80,000 a	(300,000)
Dividends declared	30,000	20,000	(20,000) b	30,000
Retained earnings, December 31, 2007	**(822,000)**	(60,000)	**60,000 a**	(822,000)
Sales revenue	(800,000)	(400,000)	100,000 d	(1,100,000)
Equity in earnings of Subco	**(30,000)**		**30,000 b**	—
Cost of sales	480,000	280,000	(100,000) d	660,000
Depreciation expense	130,000	30,000		160,000
Income tax expense	32,000	20,000		52,000
Other expenses	110,000	40,000		150,000
	$ —	$ —	$ —	$ —

Both of these amounts must be eliminated. The parent's retained earnings also include the earnings of the subsidiary, since the subsidiary's earnings are taken into the parent's income each year. If we add the retained earnings of Subco to the retained earnings of Parco, as we did under the cost method, we would be double-counting Subco's retained earnings. Therefore, the worksheet entries to eliminate the investment account are shown as follows when the equity method of recording the investment has been used:

(a)	Common shares (Subco)	80,000	
	Retained earnings (Subco)	60,000	
	Investment in Subco (Parco)		140,000
(b)	Equity in earnings of subsidiary (Parco)	30,000	
	Dividends declared (Subco)		20,000
	Investment in Subco (Parco)		10,000

Worksheet entry (**a**) eliminates the original investment and the accumulated retained (and unremitted) earnings of Subco of prior years. Entry (**b**) eliminates the dividends and the double-counting of Subco's earnings for the current year. In effect, the two adjustments reverse the entries that were originally made by Parco to record its interest in the earnings of Subco and to record the original investment.

The process of consolidation cancels out entries made for the equity pick-up of the subsidiaries' earnings. Since the process of consolidation eliminates the equity adjustments, most companies simply record the investment on the cost basis instead of the equity basis. It is simpler *not* to use the equity method for *recording* the investment.

The remaining two eliminations, for the intercompany debt and the intercompany sales, are unaffected by the method of recording the investment.

The net effect of the eliminations to the statement of income and retained earnings is to reduce the combined ending retained earnings by $70,000, thereby preventing the double-counting of Subco's ending retained earnings. This net change of $70,000 is transferred to the balance sheet to complete the worksheet.

Unconsolidated Statements

Limitations of consolidated statements

The theory underlying consolidated financial statements is that financial statements should disclose the resources and obligations of the entire economic entity. This is a straightforward application of the entity concept in accounting. When one corporation can control the resources of another, the economic entity includes the combined assets of both companies over which the directors of the parent corporation have control. Since the parent is assumed to be able to control the resources of the subsidiary, unconsolidated statements are frequently viewed as potentially misleading because they do not reflect the total economic resources that are at the disposal of the parent.

For example, a parent company may have little cash available within its own accounts, but a subsidiary may have surplus cash balances. The parent can obtain access to the subsidiary's cash, such as by instructing the subsidiary to declare dividends, by charging management fees to the subsidiary, or by borrowing. Since the parent controls the subsidiary, a loan need not be repaid at any specific date, if ever.

Similarly, a parent corporation has the ability to control the operations of a subsidiary, particularly if there are substantial intercompany transactions. For example, the parent could improve its apparent sales level by requiring the subsidiary to purchase unneeded quantities of goods from the parent, or it could generate other revenue by charging high management fees or royalties to the subsidiary. Consolidated statements eliminate the potential benefit of such intercompany activities.

But there also are problems with relying only on consolidated statements. While it is true that the parent and its subsidiaries are an *economic* entity, they are still separate *legal* entities. The title to assets and the obligation for liabilities attaches to the legal entity and not to the economic entity. A parent can go bankrupt while the subsidiaries remain healthy (or vice versa). Consolidated statements may hide the precarious financial position of a parent corporation because the stronger net asset position of the subsidiaries cloaks the shaky structure of the parent.

Creditors of the parent have no claim on the assets of the subsidiaries, unless the parent has deliberately (and unethically) been transferring assets to the subsidiaries in order to get them out of reach of the creditors in anticipation of bankruptcy. The share investment in the subsidiaries is, of course, an asset of the parent that can be sold in order to satisfy creditors' claims. But the assets of the subsidiaries are beyond the reach of the parent's creditors.

For example, PLC Industries Ltd. was delisted from the Toronto Stock Exchange and was in very precarious financial health. However, its major operating subsidiaries remained healthy. One wholly owned subsidiary, PLC Plastics, turned its back totally on its parent company, keeping its cash and other resources to itself and pledging its own assets for bank credit. Anyone reading consolidated statements of PLC Industries (the parent) would be led to believe that the parent was healthy because of the consolidated cash flows and net assets of its subsidiaries, and yet the parent itself was in bad shape.

It is an unwise lender who relies exclusively on consolidated financial statements.

Differential reporting for strategic investments

Most private companies can use *differential reporting*. **Differential reporting** permits private companies to use simpler accounting methods than those required for public companies. For example, differential reporting permits companies to use the taxes payable method of accounting for income taxes instead of the greatly more complex tax allocation procedures (i.e., accounting for temporary differences).

The qualifying conditions for using the differential reporting provisions are:

- the company must have no shares or other securities that are publicly traded, *and*

- the company is not otherwise accountable to the public, such as financial institutions or rate-regulated enterprises, *and*

- all of the company's shareholders agree unanimously with the use of alternative differential accounting policies.

Essentially, we can generalize by saying that the differential reporting provision applies to private companies exclusively. No public company can qualify for differential reporting. Note that *all* shareholders must agree—both voting and non-voting, common and preferred. Voting shareholders cannot override the interest of non-voting shareholders.

The use of differential reporting policies is not a deviation from GAAP because the alternatives are explicitly permitted by the recommendations of the *CICA Handbook* and therefore, by definition, are a part of GAAP.

The AcSB specifically identifies those areas in which differential reporting alternatives may be used. Differential reporting is not an all-or-nothing matter—a company can choose to use differential policies in one or more areas while not using them in other areas.

One of the permitted differential policies is that of strategic investments. The *CICA Handbook* states that "an enterprise that qualifies under Differential Reporting" need not prepare consolidated statements [CICA 1590.26].

The AcSB recognizes that the reporting needs of private companies do not always coincide with those of public companies in the area of strategic investments. Private companies do not issue their financial statements to the public. The readership of private company statements is restricted to a small set of users. Often, the only statement users are the limited number of shareholders and the company's bank. Private company shareholders can normally obtain access to whatever additional information they need, beyond what is provided in the financial statements. Bankers can also request that they be given statements prepared in ways that best suit their needs.

The users of private companies often prefer to see non-consolidated statements in order to evaluate the creditworthiness, management performance, or dividend-paying ability of the separate entity, as we discussed in the previous section. If consolidated statements are forced upon these users, the additional costs of consolidation will be pointless and will violate the basic concept that user benefits should exceed the preparation cost.

Either the cost or equity method may be used to account for the non-consolidated subsidiaries and variable interest entities (VIE). A company cannot choose to consolidate some subsidiaries and not others. "All subsidiaries should be accounted for using the same method" [CICA 1590.26].

Differential policies also apply to accounting for investments in significantly influenced companies and joint ventures. For significant-influence investments, it is not necessary to use the equity method. The cost method may be used instead [CICA 3050.39]. All investments in significantly influenced companies must be reported on the same basis, either all by the cost method or all by the equity method.

Similarly, joint ventures do not need to be reported by proportionate consolidation. The investor can use either cost- or equity-basis reporting [CICA 3055.47]. All joint ventures must be reported on the same basis, either cost or equity.

Summary of Accounting for Intercorporate Investments

Exhibit 2–8 summarizes the accounting approaches for intercorporate investments. In general, (1) significantly influenced affiliates are reported by the equity method, while (2) subsidiaries are consolidated.

Joint ventures are not included in the chart; they (at the time of writing) are reported by proportionate consolidation—a unique Canadian approach!

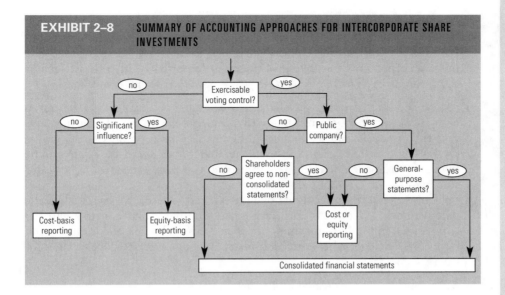

EXHIBIT 2–8   SUMMARY OF ACCOUNTING APPROACHES FOR INTERCORPORATE SHARE INVESTMENTS

VIEs also are not included in the chart. If the reporting enterprise is the primary beneficiary of any VIEs, those VIEs must be consolidated.

The appropriate reporting method for an investment may vary over time. An investment may start out as a portfolio investment (reported on the cost basis), and then become a significant-influence investment (reported on the equity basis) as a larger proportion of shares is acquired. If control is eventually acquired, consolidation will be required for general purpose financial statements.

Similarly, an investment may go from being a consolidated subsidiary to being a significantly influenced affiliate, finally becoming just a portfolio investment.

Non-consolidated statements may be prepared for specific users, and may also be prepared by private corporations if the shareholders all agree.

A basic assumption underlying Exhibit 2–8 is that the investment is in voting shares. Investments in non-voting shares are reported on the cost basis, unless the investor holds enough non-voting common shares in conjunction with voting shares to gain significant influence or control. Investments in debt securities are always reported as portfolio investments—there is no alternative.

SUMMARY OF KEY POINTS

1. Canadian businesses commonly operate through a multi-corporate structure, with a parent company controlling several subsidiaries. Each legal corporate entity must prepare its own separate-entity financial statements for tax and other special purposes. Corporations that issue general purpose financial statements must issue only consolidated financial statements to the general public.

2. Branch accounting is not the same as consolidation. Branch accounting is simply the use of control accounts or an account matrix to monitor and control the finances of branches.

3. An intercorporate investment is any investment by one corporation in the debt or equity securities of another.

4. A portfolio investment is an intercorporate investment in debt, non-voting shares, or a relatively small number of voting shares in another corporation. Portfolio investments do not carry the ability to influence the strategies of the investee corporation. Portfolio investments are reported as either held-to-maturity (at amortized cost) or available-for-sale (at market value) investments.

5. A strategic intercorporate investment is intended to enable the investor to control or significantly influence the strategic financing, operating, and investment policies of the investee. If the investor has the ability to determine the strategic policies of the investee *without the co-operation of others*, the investor controls the investee. The controlled company is deemed to be a subsidiary of the investor, or parent, corporation.

   Control can be either direct or indirect. Indirect control exists when the parent company controls an intermediate company that controls another company. *Control* does not imply *absolute* control. The parent company can have complete control over the subsidiary only by owning 100% of the subsidiary's shares.

6. Most subsidiaries are created by the parent company to carry on some aspect of the company's business. These are known as parent-founded subsidiaries. Other subsidiaries are acquired by buying voting control from the subsidiary's former shareholders. When a parent controls a subsidiary by owning less than 100% of the shares, a non-controlling interest exists.

7. A variable interest entity (VIE) is a business venture that is established by a corporation but that is not controlled by the corporation through share ownership. Nevertheless, if the corporation is the *primary beneficiary* of the VIE, the corporation must consolidate the VIE. The primary beneficiary is the party that stands to gain or lose the most from value changes in the VIE.

8. Significant influence may exist if the investor holds less than voting control, but more than a nominal amount. The general guideline is that ownership of between 20% and 50% of the voting shares gives the investor significant influence. Equity-basis reporting is normally used to report investments in significantly influenced companies. Equity-basis reporting is sometimes called one-line consolidation.

9. A joint venture is a co-operative venture undertaken together with one or more other investors. No one investor controls a joint venture. All of the co-venturers must agree on strategic policies. In Canada, joint ventures are reported by proportionate consolidation.

10. Parent companies should prepare consolidated statements that report on the total economic entity that is controlled by the parent. All subsidiaries should be consolidated. Joint ventures are reported by proportionate consolidation, wherein only the investor's share of the joint venture's revenues, expenses, assets, and liabilities is included in the consolidated statements.

11. The *recording* and *reporting* of strategic intercorporate investments are two different things. Intercorporate investments are usually recorded on the books of the investor on the cost basis. If the equity basis is used for reporting, the adjustments from cost to equity are entered on working papers and are not recorded in the investee's books. Consolidated financial statements are always prepared on working papers. The working papers may use either a direct approach or a spreadsheet approach. It is not possible to record the adjust-

ments needed for consolidation, because there is no set of books that corresponds to the consolidated economic entity.

12. Exceptions to the consolidation policy can occur when the reporting enterprise is a private corporation (and not otherwise accountable to the public) and all of the shareholders agree to waive the requirement for consolidated statements. This is an application of differential reporting.

SELF-STUDY PROBLEM 2–1[7]

Bunker Ltd. is a wholly owned subsidiary of Archie Corp. Bunker was formed by Archie with an initial investment of $1,000,000. Bunker produces some of the merchandise sold by Archie in its retail stores. Bunker also sells some of its output to other unrelated companies. The December 31, 2006, trial balances for Archie and Bunker are shown in Exhibit 2–9. The condensed balance sheets and income statements for both companies are shown in Exhibit 2–10. Additional information is as follows:

1. During 2006, Bunker sold goods with a production cost of $2,600,000 to Archie for $4,000,000. Archie subsequently sold the goods to its customers for $7,000,000.

2. Included in Archie's current receivables is $80,000 in dividends receivable from Bunker.

EXHIBIT 2–9 SEPARATE-ENTITY TRIAL BALANCES

December 31, 2006

	Archie Corp.		Bunker Ltd.	
	Dr	Cr	Dr	Cr
Cash and current receivables	$ 200,000		$ 400,000	
Inventories	900,000		500,000	
Furniture, fixtures, and equipment (net)	2,000,000		1,700,000	
Buildings under capital leases (net)	6,000,000		3,000,000	
Investment in Bunker Ltd. (at cost)	1,000,000			
Current liabilities		1,500,000		400,000
Long-term liabilities		4,000,000		2,000,000
Common shares		1,500,000		1,000,000
Retained earnings, December 31, 2005		2,100,000		1,600,000
Dividends declared	2,000,000		500,000	
Sales revenue		13,000,000		5,000,000
Dividend income		500,000		—
Cost of sales	7,000,000		3,200,000	
Other expenses	3,500,000		700,000	
	$22,600,000	$22,600,000	$10,000,000	$10,000,000

7. The solutions to all of the Self-Study Problems are at the end of the book, following Chapter 11.

EXHIBIT 2–10 SEPARATE-ENTITY FINANCIAL STATEMENTS

Balance Sheets
December 31, 2006

	Archie Corp.	Bunker Ltd.
Assets		
Cash and current receivables	$ 200,000	$ 400,000
Inventories	900,000	500,000
Furniture, fixtures, and equipment		
(net of accumulated depreciation)	2,000,000	1,700,000
Buildings under capital lease		
(net of related amortization)	6,000,000	3,000,000
Investment in Bunker Ltd. (at cost)	1,000,000	—
	$10,100,000	$5,600,000
Liabilities and shareholders' equity		
Current liabilities	$ 1,500,000	$ 400,000
Long-term liabilities	4,000,000	2,000,000
Common shares	1,500,000	1,000,000
Retained earnings	3,100,000	2,200,000
	$10,100,000	$5,600,000

Statements of Income and Retained Earnings
Year Ended December 31, 2006

	Archie Corp.	Bunker Ltd.
Revenue		
Sales	$13,000,000	$5,000,000
Dividend income	500,000	—
	13,500,000	5,000,000
Expenses		
Cost of sales	7,000,000	3,200,000
Other operating expenses	3,500,000	700,000
	10,500,000	3,900,000
Net income	$ 3,000,000	$1,100,000
Retained earnings, December 31, 2005	2,100,000	1,600,000
Dividends declared	(2,000,000)	(500,000)
Retained earnings, December 31, 2006	$ 3,100,000	$2,200,000

3. Included in Bunker's current receivables is $200,000 due from Archie for merchandise purchases.

4. During 2006, Archie declared dividends of $2,000,000 and Bunker declared dividends of $500,000.

Required:

Prepare a consolidated balance sheet and a consolidated statement of income and retained earnings for Bunker Ltd. for the year ended December 31, 2006. Use either the direct method or the worksheet method (or both!).

REVIEW QUESTIONS

2–1 Define the following terms:
  a. Intercorporate investment
  b. Subsidiary
  c. Significant influence
  d. Control
  e. Indirect control
  f. Joint control
  g. Variable interest enterprise (VIE)
  h. Primary beneficiary
  i. Variable interest
  j. Non-controlling interest
  k. Minority interest
  l. Business combination
  m. Consolidated statements
  n. Equity method
  o. Available-for-sale securities
  p. Portfolio investment
  q. Unremitted earnings
  r. Other comprehensive income

2–2 What distinguishes a *branch* from a *subsidiary*?

2–3 What is the difference between *trading securities* and *available-for-sale securities*?

2–4 What are the three types of non-strategic investments? What is the appropriate method of accounting for these investments?

2–5 What is the normal method by which one corporation obtains control over another corporation?

2–6 "The extent of share ownership does not necessarily coincide with the extent of control exercised." Explain.

2–7 Under what circumstance can one corporation control another without owning a majority of the controlled corporation's voting shares?

2–8 P Corporation owns 75% of S Corporation, and S Corporation owns 55% of T Corporation. Is T a subsidiary of P?

2–9 P Corporation owns 55% of Q Corp. and 58% of R Corp. Q and R each own 30% of W Ltd. Is W a subsidiary of one or more of the other three companies? If so, which one(s)?

2–10 Why do many parent corporations prefer to own 100% of the shares of their subsidiaries, rather than smaller proportions?

2–11 What advantages are there to a parent in owning *less* than 100% of its subsidiaries?

2–12 Why do many corporations carry out their operations through multiple subsidiaries?

2–13 Why would a company purchase a subsidiary rather than simply establish a new subsidiary of its own?

2–14 Why would a corporation want to keep a purchased subsidiary as a separate legal entity?

2–15 Explain one legitimate use for a *variable interest enterprise* (VIE).

2–16 How can a VIE escape the *CICA Handbook* definition of control?

2–17 What is the purpose of the accounting guideline on "Consolidation of Variable Interest Entities"?

2–18 What is the difference between a non-variable interest and a variable interest?

2–19 When should an investor corporation report its investment in the shares of another corporation on the equity basis?

2–20 ABC Corporation owns 12% of XYZ's common shares. Is the cost method of reporting the investment necessarily appropriate? Explain.

2–21 What factors should be examined to determine whether significant influence exists?

2–22 What is a *joint venture*?

2–23 Is profit sharing equal in a joint venture?

2–24 What method of accounting is used for a joint venture?

2–25 What are two circumstances when the cost method is used for strategic investments?

2–26 How are dividends received from an investee corporation reported by an investor corporation if the investor is using the equity method?

2–27 What is the objective of preparing consolidated financial statements?

2–28 What method do other countries use for reporting joint ventures? Why does Canada use a different method of accounting for joint ventures?

2–29 Distinguish between the *recording* and the *reporting* of intercorporate investments.

2–30 Why might a corporation use the cost method of recording while using the equity method or consolidation for reporting?

2–31 Explain the purpose of consolidation eliminating entries.

2–32 Explain the purpose of consolidation adjusting entries.

2–33 What are the two general approaches to preparing consolidated financial statements? Do the different approaches provide different results?

2–34 When intercompany sales are eliminated, why is cost of sales reduced by the amount of intercompany sales?

2–35 Are consolidation eliminating and adjusting entries entered on the books of the parent or of the subsidiary? Explain.

2–36 Why is the equity method often referred to as *one-line consolidation*?

2–37 Why might it be necessary for a parent company to prepare *unconsolidated* financial statements as well as consolidated statements?

2–38 How does the process of consolidation differ when the parent company has used the equity method of recording its investment in a subsidiary, as compared to consolidation when the cost method of recording has been used?

2–39 When might consolidated statements be misleading?

2–40 Is it possible for a parent company to go bankrupt while its operating subsidiaries stay healthy?

2–41 To what extent do the creditors of a subsidiary have a claim on the assets of the parent company?

2–42 What are the three conditions that a corporation must meet to qualify for *differential reporting*?

2–43 Why do users of private companies often prefer non-consolidated financial statements?

2–44 How does differential reporting impact on the accounting for strategic investments?

CASES

CASE 2–1   Multi-Corporation

Multi-Corporation has been on a growth and diversification strategy for the last two years. To accomplish this goal, it has been making a series of strategic investments. This growth has been financed through the bank and private investors. Next year, the company is going to issue shares to the public.

You have just finished a meeting with Catherine, the controller of Multi-Corporation. She has asked you to provide recommendations on how to report the following investments that were made in 2006.

1. Multi-Corporation purchased all of the 100,000 outstanding B shares of Suds Limited. Each share has one vote. The previous owner, Megan, retained all of the 80,000 outstanding A shares of Suds Limited. Each share also has one vote. In order to avoid sudden changes to the business, Megan stipulated in the sales agreement that she was to retain the right to refuse the appointment of management for Suds Limited and to approve any significant transactions of Suds Limited.

2. Multi-Corporation owns 37% of the voting common shares of Berry Corporation. The remaining 63% of the shares are held by members of the family of the company founder. To date, the family has elected all members of the board of directors, and Multi-Corporation has not been able to obtain a seat on the board. Multi-Corporation is hoping eventually to buy a block of shares from an elderly family member and eventually own 60% of the shares.

Required:

Provide a report to Catherine outlining the appropriate method of accounting for these investments.

[CICA, adapted]

CASE 2–2   Salieri Ltd.

Salieri Ltd. is a manufacturer of musical instruments that is controlled by Tony Antonio. Salieri Ltd. was originally a private company, but it became public in 1980 when a substantial public share issue occurred. The Antonio family now holds 68% of the shares of Salieri; the remaining 32% are widely distributed throughout Canada.

Although Salieri is an operating company, it also has substantial investments in a number of other Canadian corporations. One such investment is its ownership of 80% of the shares of Bach Burgers, Inc., a chain of fast-food outlets. Salieri acquired its shares in Bach from the original founder of the company, John Sebastian, in 1989. Bach Burgers is run completely independently; Teresa Antonio (Tony's wife) is one of the members of Bach Burgers' 12-person board of directors, but otherwise Salieri exercises no direction over the operations of Bach Burgers.

Another investment of Salieri Ltd. is its 45% interest in Pits Mining Corporation. This investment was the outcome of a takeover attempt by Salieri two years ago. Salieri was frustrated in its attempt by a coalition of other companies in the extraction industry, which effectively blocked Salieri's bid for control. Salieri was left with the 45% interest that it had managed to acquire. Although Salieri's block of Pits shares is by far the largest single block, Salieri has not been able to gain representation on the Pits board of directors. Salieri Ltd. has instituted court action against Pits Mining in order to force the other shareholders to admit Salieri nominees to the board.

Mozart Piano Corporation is a piano manufacturer that is 20% owned by Salieri Ltd. Although Salieri does manufacture musical instruments, it does not produce pianos, and Salieri and Mozart frequently conduct joint marketing efforts since their products are complementary and not competitive. Mozart is a private company; all of the other shares are held by the Amadeus family. Mozart has an 80%-owned subsidiary, Leopold Klaviers, Inc., which manufactures harpsichords and clavichords to be sold domestically through Mozart and internationally through other agents.

Salieri Ltd. also owns 15% of Frix Flutes, Ltd. The 15% share was acquired several years ago to provide Frix with some new financing at a time when the company was experiencing financial difficulties. Salieri also assisted Frix by licensing to Frix the rights to use patents owned by Salieri. The licensing agreement can be cancelled by Salieri upon six months' written notice.

The only other corporate share investment held by Salieri is its 100% ownership of Salieri Acceptance Corporation (SAC). SAC was formed by Salieri to aid its customers in purchasing Salieri instruments on an installment basis. Six of the nine SAC directors are also directors of Salieri Ltd. The other three are representatives of the financial institutions that finance SAC's operations.

Required:

Discuss the manner in which Salieri should account for its various investments when issuing its annual financial statements. Specify what additional information you would like to have, if any. Recommend an accounting approach for each investment, stating any assumptions that you make in arriving at your recommendations.

CASE 2–3   XYZ Ltd.

During 2005, XYZ Ltd. purchased for cash all of the 100,000 Class B shares of Sub Limited. Each share carries one vote. The previous owner, Mr. Bill, retained all 20,000 outstanding Class A shares of Sub Limited, each carrying four votes. In order to avoid sudden changes, Mr. Bill stipulated in the sale agreement that he was to retain the right to refuse the appointment of management for Sub Limited and to approve any significant transactions of Sub Limited.

Required:

Should XYZ Ltd. consolidate the operations of Sub Limited in its 2005 financial statements, which are to be issued in accordance with generally accepted accounting principles? Provide support for your recommendation.
[CICA]

CASE 2–4   Jackson Capital Inc.

Jackson Capital Inc. (JCI) is a new private investment company that provides capital to business ventures. JCI's business mission is to support companies to allow them to compete successfully in domestic and international markets. JCI aims to increase the value of its investments, thereby creating wealth for its shareholders.

Funds to finance the investments were obtained through a private offering of share capital, conventional long-term loans payable, and a bond issue that is indexed to the TSX Composite. Annual operating expenses are expected to be $1 million before bonuses, interest, and taxes.

Over the past year, JCI has accumulated a diversified investment portfolio. Depending on the needs of the borrower, JCI provides capital in many different forms, including demand loans, short-term equity investments, fixed-term loans, and loans convertible into share capital. JCI also purchases preferred and common shares in new business ventures where JCI management anticipates a significant return. Any excess funds not committed to a particular investment are held temporarily in money market funds.

JCI has hired three investment managers to review financing applications. These managers visit the applicant's premises to meet with management and review the operations and business plans. They then prepare a report stating their reasons for supporting or rejecting the application. JCI's senior executives review these reports at their monthly meetings and decide whether to invest and what types of investments to make.

Once the investments are made, the investment managers are expected to monitor the investments and review detailed monthly financial reports submitted by the investees. The investment managers' performance bonuses are based on the returns generated by the investments they have recommended.

It is now August 2006. JCI's first fiscal year ended on June 30, 2006. JCI's draft balance sheet and other financial information is included in Exhibits A, B, and C. An annual audit is required under the terms of the bond issue. Potter and Cook, Chartered Accountants, has been appointed auditor of JCI. You, CA, are the in-charge accountant on this engagement. Mr. Potter has asked you to prepare a memo discussing the significant accounting issues, audit risks, and related audit procedures for this engagement.

Required:

Prepare the memo requested by Mr. Potter.

EXHIBIT A

DRAFT BALANCE SHEET (JUNE 30, 2006) (THOUSANDS)

Assets

Cash and marketable securities	$ 1,670
Investments (at cost)	21,300
Interest receivable	60
Furniture and fixtures (net of amortization)	50
	$23,080

Liabilities

Accounts payable and accrued liabilities	$ 20
Accrued interest payable	180
Loans payable	12,000
	$12,200

Equity

Share capital	$12,000
Deficit	(1,120)
	$23,080

EXHIBIT B

SUMMARY OF INVESTMENT PORTFOLIO (JUNE 30, 2006)

The balance sheet for June 30, 2006, shows a total of $21.3 million in long-term investments. The breakdown of these investments is as follows:

Investments	**Cost**
15% common share investment in Fairex Resource Inc., a company listed on the TSX Venture Exchange. Management intends to monitor the performance of this mining company over the next six months and to make a hold/sell decision based on reported reserves and production costs.	$3.8 million
25% interest in common shares of Hellon Ltd., a private Canadian real estate company, plus 7.5% convertible debentures with a face value of $2 million acquired at 98% of maturity value. The debentures are convertible into common shares at the option of the holder.	$6.2 million
Five-year loan denominated in Brazilian currency (reals) to Ipanema Ltd., a Brazilian company formed to build a power generating station. Interest at 7% per annum is due semiannually. 75% of the loan balance is secured by the power generating station under construction. The balance is unsecured.	$8 million
50% interest in Western Gas, a jointly owned gas exploration project operating in Western Canada. One of JCI's investment managers sits on the three-member board of directors.	$2 million
50,000 stock warrants in Toronto Hydrocarbons Ltd., expiring March 22, 2008. The underlying common shares trade publicly.	$1.3 million

EXHIBIT C

CAPITAL STRUCTURE (JUNE 30, 2006)

The balance sheet for June 30, 2006, shows a total of $12 million in share capital and $12 million in loans payable.

Loans Payable

The Company has $2 million in demand loans payable with floating interest rates, and $4 million in loans due September 1, 2008, with fixed interest rates.

In addition, the Company has long-term 5% stock-indexed bonds payable. Interest at the stated rate is to be paid semiannually, commencing September 1, 2006. The principal repayment on March 1, 2009, is indexed to changes in the TSX Composite as follows: the $6 million original balance of the bonds at the issue date of March 1, 2006, is to be multiplied by the stock index at March 1, 2009, and then divided by the stock index as at March 1, 2006. The stock-indexed bonds are secured by the Company's investments.

Share Capital

Issued share capital consists of:

– 1 million 8% Class A (non-voting) shares redeemable at the holders' option $7 million
  on or after August 10, 2008

– 10,000 common shares $5 million

[CICA, adapted]

PROBLEMS

P2–1

Summer Corporation acquired a 45% interest in Winter Company on June 1, 2006, for $250,000. The controller for Summer Corporation is now preparing the first set of financial statements since the acquisition and is unsure about what method of accounting is most appropriate for the investment. She has come to you for advice.

Required:

a. Under what conditions would it be appropriate for Summer to report the investment in Winter using proportionate consolidation? Identify the extent of control that would be implied by the use of proportionate consolidation and specific factors that would determine the extent of control.

b. Under what conditions would it be appropriate for Summer to report the investment in Winter using the equity method of accounting? Identify the specific factors that would determine that the equity method would be appropriate. Describe the circumstances or factors in which Summer would use the cost method instead of the equity method.

c. Under what conditions would it be appropriate for Summer to prepare consolidated financial statements? Identify the extent of control that would be implied by the use of consolidation and examples of factors that would make consolidation appropriate.

[CGA, adapted]

P2–2

On January 1, 2006, LJ Corporation purchased 20% of the outstanding shares of XYZ Corporation at a cost of $150,000. During the next two fiscal years, XYZ reported net income and dividends as follows:

Year	Net Income	Dividends
2006	$45,000	$30,000
2007	20,000	50,000

Required:

a. If LJ uses the cost method to account for its investments in XYZ, what would be the balance in the investment account at the end of fiscal year 2007?

b. If LJ uses the equity method to account for its investment in XYZ, what would be the balance in LJ's account called "Investment in XYZ" at December 31, 2007?

[CGA]

P2–3

On April 30, 2004, Large Inc. established a subsidiary known as Small Inc. Large invested $500,000 in the shares of Small. Small has no other shares outstanding. Since its establishment, Small has had the following earnings and paid the following dividends:

Year	Net Income (Loss)	Dividends
2004	$(50,000)	—
2005	60,000	$16,000
2006	56,000	38,000
2007	104,000	44,000

Required:

a. Determine the amount of Small Inc.'s earnings that will be reported as investment income by Large Inc. in 2007, under the equity method.

b. Calculate the balance of the investment in the Small Inc. account on Large Inc.'s books at December 31, 2007, assuming that Large Inc. maintains the investment account on the equity basis.

P2–4

Max Corporation has a wholly owned subsidiary, Min Ltd., which was formed several years ago. Min's initial capital was provided by Max, which purchased all of Min's shares for $500,000. At December 31, 2006, the balance sheet accounts of Max and Min appeared as follows:

	Max	Min
Cash	$ 90,000	$ 30,000
Accounts receivable	200,000	130,000
Receivable from Min	80,000	—
Property, plant, and equipment	2,500,000	1,400,000
Accumulated depreciation	(670,000)	(360,000)
Investment in Min	500,000	—
Total assets	$2,700,000	$1,200,000
Accounts payable	$ 300,000	$ 200,000
Payable to Max	—	80,000
Bonds payable	1,000,000	—
Future income taxes	100,000	50,000
Common shares	400,000	500,000
Retained earnings	900,000	370,000
Total equities	$2,700,000	$1,200,000

During 2006, Min paid dividends of $80,000 to Max, and purchased goods from Max at a total price of $1,200,000. All of the purchases from Max were subsequently sold to third parties during the year.

Required:

Prepare a consolidated balance sheet for Max Corporation at December 31, 2006.

P2–5

Hook Corp. is a wholly owned, parent-founded subsidiary of Chappell Inc. The unconsolidated statements of income and retained earnings for the two companies for the year ended December 31, 2006, are as follows:

	Chappell	Hook
Revenues:		
Sales	$6,500,000	$2,100,000
Interest	200,000	60,000
Dividends	100,000	—
	6,800,000	2,160,000
Expenses:		
Cost of goods sold	3,300,000	1,300,000
Depreciation expense	600,000	160,000
Administrative expense	900,000	300,000
Income tax expense	780,000	170,000
Other expenses	290,000	40,000
	5,870,000	1,970,000
Net income	930,000	190,000
Retained earnings, January 1, 2006	1,920,000	520,000
Dividends declared	(330,000)	(100,000)
Retained earnings, December 31, 2006	$2,520,000	$ 610,000

Additional Information:

1. During the year, Hook acquired merchandise from Chappell at a total sale price of $900,000. None of the merchandise was in Hook's inventory at year-end.

2. At the beginning of the year, Hook borrowed $800,000 from Chappell at 10% interest per annum. The loan (and accrued interest) was still outstanding at the end of the year.

3. Chappell carries its investment in Hook at the cost basis in its accounts.

Required:

Prepare a consolidated statement of income and retained earnings for Chappell Inc., for the year ended December 31, 2006.

P2–6

Thorne Ltd. is a wholly owned subsidiary of Fellows Corporation. The balance sheets and statements of retained earnings for each company are shown below. Additional information is as follows:

1. Thorne sells most of its output to Fellows. During 2006, intercompany sales amounted to $3,500,000. Fellows has accounts payable to Thorne for $200,000.

2. Fellows owns the land on which Thorne's building is situated. Fellows leases the land to Thorne for $30,000 per month.

3. The long-term note payable on Thorne's books represents a loan from Fellows. The note bears interest at 10% per annum.

4. Both companies declare dividends quarterly. The last quarter's dividends were declared on December 31, 2006, payable on January 10, 2007.

Required:

Prepare a consolidated balance sheet and a consolidated statement of income and retained earnings for Fellows Corporation.

Separate-Entity Financial Statements
Statements of Income and Retained Earnings
Year ended December 31, 2006

	Fellows	Thorne
Revenues:		
Sales	$5,600,000	$4,700,000
Interest, dividend and lease	650,000	15,000
Equity in earnings Thorne	350,000	—
	6,600,000	4,715,000
Expenses:		
Cost of goods sold	4,400,000	2,500,000
Interest expense	—	70,000
Other expenses	1,300,000	1,795,000
	5,700,000	4,365,000
Net income	900,000	350,000
Retained earnings, January 1, 2006	1,430,000	100,000
Dividends declared	(700,000)	(200,000)
Retained earnings, December 31, 2006	$1,630,000	$ 250,000

Balance Sheets
December 31, 2006

	Fellows	Thorne
Assets		
Current assets:		
Cash	$ 180,000	$ 25,000
Accounts receivable	700,000	135,000
Temporary investments and		
accrued investment income	360,000	90,000
Inventories		330,000
	1,240,000	580,000
Property, plant, and equipment		
Land	900,000	—
Buildings and equipment	—	1,500,000
Accumulated depreciation	—	(500,000)
	900,000	1,000,000
Long-term note receivable	700,000	—
Investment in Thorne	750,000	—
Total assets	$3,590,000	$1,580,000
Equities		
Current liabilities:		
Accounts payable and accrued liabilities	$ 240,000	$ 80,000
Dividends payable	120,000	50,000
	360,000	130,000
Long-term note payable	—	700,000
Total liabilities	360,000	830,000
Shareholders' equity		
Common shares	1,600,000	500,000
Retained earnings	1,630,000	250,000
Total liabilities and shareholders' equity	$3,590,000	$1,580,000

P2–7

Empire Optical Co., Ltd., is a chain of eyeglass outlets. Empire owns 100% of Class Glass Ltd., a competing chain that Empire established in order to serve a different market segment. To obtain the best deal from suppliers, Empire buys most of the materials and frames for both chains, and resells to Class whatever that chain needs.

During 2006, Empire sold materials costing $2,000,000 to Class at cost. At the end of the year, Class still owed Empire $250,000 for purchases of the materials.

Empire records its investment in Class on the equity basis. During 2006, Class declared and paid dividends totalling $200,000. Empire has not yet recorded its equity in the earnings of Class for 2006. The pre-consolidation trial balances for the two companies are as shown below.

Required:

Prepare a consolidated balance sheet and income statement for Empire Optical Co., Ltd., for 2006.

Trial Balances
Dr (Cr)

	Empire	Class
Cash	$ 400,000	$ 50,000
Accounts receivable	300,000	150,000
Inventory	1,200,000	600,000
Fixtures and equipment (net)	5,000,000	1,400,000
Investment in Class Glass Ltd.	2,100,000	
Other investments	500,000	—
Accounts payable	(700,000)	(500,000)
Common shares	(1,600,000)	(1,000,000)
Retained earnings	(5,700,000)	(1,300,000)
Dividends paid	600,000	200,000
Sales	(16,000,000)	(7,100,000)
Cost of goods sold	11,000,000	5,000,000
Other operating expenses	3,000,000	2,500,000
Dividend and interest income	(100,000)	—
	$ 0	$ 0

Chapter 3

Business Combinations

Introduction

In the previous chapter, we pointed out that most subsidiaries have been established by the parent corporation in order to carry out some part of the parent's operations. We also illustrated how to prepare consolidated financial statements for a parent and its parent-founded subsidiary.

However, a parent corporation can buy an existing corporation in a *business combination*. The purchase can be for cash (or other assets), or can be via an *exchange of shares*. When a company buys a subsidiary, preparing consolidated financial statements becomes much more complicated than for a parent-founded subsidiary.

This chapter focuses on the meaning and the broad accounting implications of business combinations. The chapter covers the following issues:

- the definition of a business combination and the general accounting approach to business combinations
- the problems of measuring the cost of a business acquisition, and the allocation of that cost to the acquired assets and liabilities
- the alternative theoretical approaches to consolidating purchased subsidiaries, and
- consolidation procedures.

The consolidation procedures that we illustrate in this chapter are at the simplest level—a consolidated balance sheet at the date of acquisition. However, all consolidations after the acquisition date are much more complicated. Chapters 4, 5, and 6 will deal with these post-acquisition complexities.

Definition of a Business Combination

A **business combination** occurs when one corporation obtains control of a group of *net assets* that constitutes a *going concern*. A key word is *control*—**control** can be obtained either by:

1. buying the assets themselves (which automatically gives control to the buyer), or

2. buying enough shares in the corporation that owns the assets to enable the investor to control the investee corporation (which makes the purchased corporation a subsidiary).

A second key aspect of the definition of a business combination is that the purchaser acquires control over "net assets that constitute a business" [CICA 1581.06(a)]—i.e., a going concern. Purchasing a group of idle assets is not a business combination.

A third aspect is the phrase *net assets*—**net assets** means assets minus liabilities. Business combinations often (but not always) require the buyer to assume some or all of the seller's liabilities.

When the purchase is accomplished by buying control over another corporation, liabilities are automatically part of the package. But when the purchaser buys a group of assets separately, there may or may not be liabilities attached, such as when one corporation sells an operating division to another company. In any discussion of business combinations, remember that *net assets* includes any related liabilities.

Finally, observe that *business combination* is not synonymous with *consolidation*. As we discussed in the previous chapter, consolidated financial statements are prepared for a parent and its subsidiaries. The subsidiaries may be either parent-founded or purchased. A purchased subsidiary *usually* is the result of a business combination. But sometimes one corporation will buy control over a shell corporation or a defunct corporation. Since the acquired company is not an operating business, no business combination has occurred.

As well, not all business combinations result in a parent–subsidiary relationship. When a business combination is a direct purchase of net assets, the acquired assets and liabilities are recorded directly on the books of the acquirer, as we shall discuss shortly.

Accounting for Business Combinations— General Approach

The general approach to accounting for business combinations, whether (1) a direct purchase of net assets or (2) a purchase of control, is a three-step process:

1. Measure the cost of the purchase.

2. Determine the fair values of the assets and liabilities acquired.

3. Allocate the cost on the basis of the fair values.

The *mechanics* of accounting for the acquisition will depend on the nature of the purchase, particularly on whether the purchase was of the *net assets* directly or of *control* over the net assets through acquisition of shares of the company that owns the assets. Let's look at the general features that apply to all business combinations before we worry about the acquisition method used.

Measuring the cost

The acquirer may pay for the assets (1) in cash or other assets, (2) by issuing its own shares as consideration for the net assets acquired, or (3) by using a combination of cash and shares.

When the purchase is by cash, it is not difficult to determine the total cost of the net assets acquired. When the purchase is paid for with other assets, the cost is measured by the fair value of the assets surrendered in exchange or by the fair value of the assets acquired, whichever is more reliably measured [CICA 1581.22].

One of the most common methods of acquiring the net assets of another company is for the acquirer to issue its own shares in full or partial payment for the net assets acquired. When publicly traded shares are issued as consideration for the purchase, the cost of the purchase is based on the market value of the existing shares.

Note that although the valuation of the shares issued is *based* on the market value, the value assigned to the newly issued shares may not actually *be* the market price on the date of acquisition. The value assigned to the issued shares is more likely to reflect an average price for a period (e.g., 60 days) surrounding the public announcement of the business combination. The *CICA Handbook* suggests, for example, that the value of shares issued should be "based on their market price over a reasonable period before and after the date the terms of the business combination are agreed to and announced" [CICA 1581.25]. Notice the use of the words *based* and *reasonable*, both of which are subject to professional judgment.

The assigned value may be further decreased to allow for the underpricing that is necessary for a new issue of shares. Nevertheless, the value eventually assigned to shares issued by a public company normally will bear a proximate relationship to the value of the shares in the public marketplace.

Exceptions to the use of market values do still arise, even when a public market value exists. The *CICA Handbook* suggests that the fair value of the net assets acquired should be used instead of the value of the shares issued when the quoted market price is not representative of their fair value. Again, notice the use of the judgmental word *representative*.

Valuation of shares issued by a private company is even more judgmental. If it is not feasible to place a reliable value on the shares issued, it will instead be necessary to rely upon the fair value of the net assets acquired in order to measure the cost of the purchase. In practice, the fair values assigned to the acquired assets and liabilities in a purchase by a private corporation often are remarkably similar to their recorded book values on the books of the acquiree.

There is a lot of room for the exercise of professional judgment in determining the cost of an acquisition.

Contingent consideration A business combination, whether paid for by assets or by shares, may include a provision for **contingent consideration**. Contingent consideration is an add-on to the base price that is determined some time after the deal is finalized. The amount of contingent consideration can be based on a number of factors, such as:

- a fuller assessment of the finances and operations of the acquired company
- the outcome of renegotiating agreements with debt holders
- achievement of stated earnings objectives in accounting periods *following* the change of control, or
- achievement of a target market price for the acquirer's shares by a specified future date.

Contingent consideration that is paid in future periods usually is considered to be additional compensation. The treatment of additional compensation varies. If the additional future amount can be estimated beyond a reasonable doubt at the time that the business combination takes place, the estimate is included in the original calculation of the cost of the purchase [CICA 1581.29].

If the amount cannot be estimated at the date of the combination but additional compensation is paid in the future, the fair value of the net assets is adjusted (usually by increasing the amount of goodwill attributed to the purchase) [CICA 1581.31].

If additional shares are issued because the market price of the issued shares falls below a target price (or fails to reach a target price in the future), the additional shares do *not* represent an additional cost, but simply the issuance of more shares to maintain the same purchase price [CICA 1581.34].

Determining fair values

The cost of a business combination is not treated as a lump sum. The cost must be allocated to the assets and liabilities acquired. The basis for the allocation is the fair value of each asset and each liability that is included in the purchase. This is true regardless of whether the purchase was of a group of assets or of a subsidiary. Therefore, the second step in a business combination is to estimate the fair values of the assets and liabilities.

Note that the book values of the acquired assets and liabilities are completely irrelevant to the acquiring corporation's consolidated financial statements. Only current fair values at the date of the business combination are relevant.

Guidelines for determining fair values of net assets are outlined in the *CICA Handbook* [CICA 1581.43]. In general, the recommended approaches are:

1. Net realizable value for assets held for sale or conversion into cash.

2. Replacement cost for productive assets such as raw materials and tangible capital assets.

3. Appraisal values for intangible capital assets, land, natural resources, and non-marketable securities.

4. Present value for liabilities, discounted at the current market rate of interest.

These guidelines are completely consistent with both U.S. and International Accounting Standards. However, they are only guidelines. Furthermore, it should be apparent that fair value measurements are *accounting estimates*. The fair values are judgmental combinations of different methods of valuation—a bit of a hodgepodge, really. There is a great deal of latitude for management to exercise judgment in determining these values. As we shall explain in the next chapter, such judgment can have significant consequences for reporting in future periods.

Fair values must be assigned to all identifiable tangible and intangible assets that can be detached from the company and "sold, transferred, licensed, rented, or exchanged (regardless of whether there is an intent to do so)" [CICA 1581.48]. Often, the acquired company has intangible assets that are not reported on its balance sheet because the acquired company did not originally incur a cost to buy those assets. For example, suppose that Snowball Corporation has developed a valuable trademark over the course of its business. That trademark has not been reported as an asset on Snowball's balance sheet because the company did not incur any direct cost to acquire it. Subsequently, Icicle Limited buys Snowball. The trademark "Snowball" has been purchased by Icicle as part of the basket of Snowball's net assets. Icicle must estimate the fair value of the trademark, even though it does not appear on Snowball's books or balance sheet.

In addition to the trademarks, other separable intangible assets that often are not shown on the acquired company's balance sheet are patents and copyrights. Easily overlooked assets include customer lists, employment contracts, favourable lease agreements, secret formulas (e.g., Coca-Cola; KFC), Internet domain names, and order backlogs. Goodwill should not be used as a catch-all to include separable intangible assets. One type of asset and/or liability that is not given a fair value is any future income tax amounts that appear on the selling company's balance sheet.[1] These are not assets and liabilities from the standpoint of the buyer, since they relate solely to the differences between tax bases and accounting carrying values on the books of the *acquired company.*

We don't escape the complications of income tax allocation, however. Future income tax accounting is a factor in the purchaser's financial reporting for purchased subsidiaries. Acquiring companies must determine their own future income tax balances based on the difference between the asset and liability values they show on their consolidated financial statements and the tax bases. Future income tax considerations tend to confuse students who are trying to understand the sufficiently complex issues in business combinations and consolidations. Therefore, we have decided to treat future income tax aspects separately in Appendix 3A (as well as in Appendix 4B).

Allocating the cost

The third step in accounting for a business combination is to allocate the cost. It is a generally accepted principle of accounting that when a company acquires a group of assets for a single price, the total cost of the assets acquired is allocated to the individual assets on the basis of their fair market values. If a company buys land and a building for a lump sum, for example, the land and building are recorded at their proportionate cost, as determined by estimates of their fair values.

The same general principle applies to assets and liabilities acquired in a business combination. The total cost of the purchase is allocated on the basis of the fair market values of the assets and liabilities acquired.

However, the price paid for the operating unit will be determined in part by its earnings ability. The acquirer may or may not choose to continue to operate the unit in the same manner; but regardless of the acquirer's plans, the price to be paid will take into account the acquired unit's estimated future net revenue stream.

If the unit has been successful and has demonstrated an ability to generate above-average earnings, then the acquirer will have to pay a price that is higher than the aggregate fair value of the net assets. On the other hand, if the unit has not been successful, the price may be less than the fair value of the net assets (but not normally less than the liquidating value of the net assets including tax effects).

The difference between the fair value of the net assets (assets less liabilities assumed) and the acquisition cost is known as **goodwill** when the acquisition cost is higher than the fair value of the net assets, and as **negative goodwill** when the cost is less.

Goodwill acquired in a purchase of net assets is recorded on the acquirer's books, along with the fair values of the other assets and liabilities acquired. It is important to understand that goodwill *is* a purchased asset. The purchaser paid good money (or shares) for the goodwill just as surely as for buildings and

---

1. This refers to the results of the interperiod income tax allocation process, sometimes known as deferred income tax accounting. Any *current* taxes receivable or payable are assigned a fair value.

inventory. In some circles (and in some countries), goodwill is called a "nothing," which derives from the fact that it does not represent any specific asset, either tangible or intangible. But the fact that we can't point at an object (for a tangible asset) or a specific right (for an intangible or financial asset) does not make its cost any less real.

Negative goodwill, however, is not recorded as such. Instead, the costs assigned to the assets are reduced until the total of the costs allocated to the individual assets and liabilities is equal to the total purchase price of the acquired net assets.

Not all assets are adjusted to eliminate negative goodwill. Only non-financial assets are adjusted, and among that group, the following are also excluded from adjustment [CICA 1581.40(a)]:

- assets to be disposed of by sale
- future income tax assets, and
- current assets.

If there still is negative goodwill left over after the fair value of the non-financial assets has been written down to zero, the excess is reported as an extraordinary gain.[2]

The allocation process, therefore, is essentially a two-step process [CICA 1581.50]:

1. acquisition cost is allocated to the fair values of the net assets acquired, and

2. any excess of acquisition cost over the aggregate fair value is viewed as goodwill.

Illustration of Direct Purchase of Net Assets

To illustrate the accounting for a direct purchase of net assets, assume that on December 31, 2005, Purchase Ltd. acquires all of the assets and liabilities of Target Ltd. by issuing 40,000 Purchase Ltd. common shares to Target Ltd. Before the transaction, Purchase Ltd. had 160,000 common shares outstanding. After the transaction, 200,000 Purchase Ltd. shares are outstanding, of which Target Ltd. owns 20%. The pre-transaction balance sheets of both companies are shown in Exhibit 3–1.

The estimated fair values of Target Ltd.'s assets and liabilities are shown at the bottom of Exhibit 3–1. Their aggregate fair value is $1,100,000. If we assume that the market value of Purchase Ltd.'s shares is $30 each, then the total cost of the acquisition is $1,200,000. The transaction will be recorded *on the books of Purchase Ltd.* as follows:

Cash and receivables	200,000	
Inventory	50,000	
Land	400,000	
Buildings and equipment	550,000	
Goodwill	100,000	
Accounts payable		100,000
Common shares		1,200,000

[2] Negative goodwill is discussed more fully at the end of this chapter.

EXHIBIT 3-1   PRE-TRANSACTION BALANCE SHEETS

December 31, 2005

	Purchase Ltd.	Target Ltd.
Cash	$1,000,000	$ 50,000
Accounts receivable	2,000,000	150,000
Inventory	200,000	50,000
Land	1,000,000	300,000
Buildings and equipment	3,000,000	500,000
Accumulated depreciation	(1,200,000)	(150,000)
Total assets	$6,000,000	$ 900,000
Accounts payable	$1,000,000	$100,000
Long-term notes payable	400,000	—
Common shares*	2,600,000	200,000
Retained earnings	2,000,000	600,000
Total liabilities and shareholders' equity	$6,000,000	$ 900,000

* for Purchase Ltd.—160,000 shares outstanding

Fair values of Target Ltd.'s net assets:

Cash	$50,000
Accounts receivable	150,000
Inventory	50,000
Land	400,000
Buildings and equipment	550,000
Accounts payable	(100,000)
Total	$1,100,000

The selling company, Target Ltd., will record the transaction by writing off all of its assets and liabilities and entering the new asset of Purchase Ltd.'s shares, recognizing a gain of $400,000 on the transaction.

The post-transaction balance sheets for the two companies will appear as shown in Exhibit 3–2. Purchase Ltd.'s assets and liabilities increase by the amount of the fair values of the acquired assets and by the purchased goodwill, while Target Ltd.'s previous net assets have been replaced by its sole remaining asset, the shares in Purchase Ltd. If the transaction had been for cash instead of Purchase Ltd. shares, Target Ltd.'s sole remaining asset would have been the cash received.

The purchase of Target Ltd.'s net assets by Purchase Ltd. is a business combination, but it is not an intercorporate investment by Purchase Ltd. because Purchase Ltd. is not investing in the *shares* of Target Ltd. Since Purchase Ltd. is acquiring the assets and liabilities directly instead of indirectly through the purchase of Target Ltd. shares, Purchase Ltd. records the assets and liabilities directly on its books and there is no need for consolidated statements; Target Ltd. is *not* a subsidiary of Purchase Ltd.

After the net asset purchase has been recorded, Purchase Ltd. will account for the assets as it would any new assets. There is no special treatment required.

EXHIBIT 3–2   POST-TRANSACTION BALANCE SHEETS

December 31, 2005

	Purchase Ltd.	Target Ltd.
Cash	$1,050,000	$ —
Accounts receivable	2,150,000	—
Inventory	250,000	—
Land	1,400,000	—
Buildings and equipment	3,550,000	—
Accumulated depreciation	(1,200,000)	—
Goodwill	100,000	
Investment in Purchase Ltd. shares	—	1,200,000
Total assets	$7,300,000	$1,200,000
Accounts payable	$1,100,000	$ —
Long-term notes payable	400,000	—
Common shares*	3,800,000	200,000
Retained earnings	2,000,000	1,000,000
Total liabilities and shareholders' equity	$7,300,000	$1,200,000

* for Purchase Ltd.—200,000 shares outstanding

Purchase of Shares

Reasons for purchasing shares

Buying the *assets* (or *net assets*) of another company is one way to accomplish a business combination. However, a much more common method of acquiring control over the assets of another company is to buy the *voting shares* of the other business. If one company buys a controlling block of the shares of another company, then control over the assets has been achieved, and the acquirer has a new subsidiary.

An acquirer can obtain a controlling share interest by any one or a combination of three methods:

- buying sufficient shares on the open market
- entering into private sale agreements with major shareholders, or
- issuing a public tender offer to buy the shares.

Regardless of the purchase method used, the acquirer purchases shares already outstanding. The transaction is with the existing shareholders, not with the target company. The buyer does not need the co-operation of the acquired company itself. Sometimes the target company's board of directors opposes a takeover attempt and tries to persuade the shareholders not to sell their shares to the acquirer—this is known as a **hostile takeover**. Nevertheless, if the purchaser can convince enough of the target company's shareholders to sell their shares, a business combination will occur.

Unlike a direct purchase of assets, a business combination that is achieved by an acquisition of shares does not have any impact on the asset and equity structure of the acquired company.[3] The acquired company continues to carry its assets and liabilities on its own books. The purchaser has acquired *control* over the assets, but has not acquired the assets themselves.

Purchase of shares rather than assets has the obvious advantage that control can be obtained by buying considerably less than 100% of the shares. Control can be obtained at substantially less cost than if the acquirer purchased the assets directly.

There are several other advantages to buying shares rather than the net assets themselves:

- The shares may be selling at a price on the market that is less than the fair value per share (or even book value per share) of the net assets. The acquirer can therefore obtain control over the assets at a lower price than could be negotiated for the assets themselves.

- By buying shares rather than assets, the acquirer ends up with an asset that is more easily saleable than the assets themselves, in case the acquirer later decides to divest itself of the acquired business, or a portion thereof.

- The acquirer may prefer to retain the newly acquired business as a separate entity for legal, tax, and business reasons. The acquired business's liabilities need not be assumed directly, and there is no interruption of the business relationships built up by the acquired corporation.

- Income tax impacts can be a major factor in the choice between purchasing assets and purchasing shares. A purchase of shares may benefit the seller because any gain to the seller on a sale of shares will be taxed as a capital gain. However, if the assets are sold, gains may be subject to tax at full rates, such as (1) CCA (capital cost allowance) recapture, (2) a sale of inventory, or (3) a sale of intangibles that were fully deducted for tax purposes when paid for initially. Also, the acquired company may have substantial tax loss carryforwards, the benefits of which are unlikely to be realized. The purchaser may be able to take advantage of these carryforwards.

For the buyer, however, a purchase of assets may be more desirable than a purchase of shares from a tax viewpoint. When the assets are purchased directly, their cost to the acquiring company becomes the basis for their tax treatment. For example, depreciable assets are recorded on the acquiring company's books at fair values, and CCA will be based on those fair values. Similarly, goodwill purchased is treated as *eligible capital property* for tax purposes and 75% of the goodwill is subject to CCA (the other 25% is not deductible).

If control over the assets is obtained via a share purchase, on the other hand, there is no change in the tax basis for the assets because there is no change in the assets' ownership. Thus the buyer cannot take advantage of any increased tax shields if net assets are purchased at fair values that are greater than book values.

Another advantage of buying control over another company is that the acquirer does not automatically assume the contingent liabilities of the target company, such as lawsuits or environmental liabilities. If large unexpected liabilities arise, the controlling company can let the subsidiary go bankrupt—the parent loses its investment, but that's better than being pulled down by overwhelming liabilities.

Obviously, the decision on acquisition method is subject to many variables. In a friendly takeover, the method of purchase and the purchase price are subject

---

3. An exception occurs when "push-down" accounting is used. We will discuss this concept towards the end of the chapter.

to negotiation, taking into account the various factors affecting both parties, including income tax. If the takeover is hostile, then a purchase of shares is the only alternative.

The share acquisition can be accomplished by paying cash or other assets, or by issuing new shares of the acquirer, or by some combination thereof. When the acquirer issues new shares as consideration for the shares of an acquired business, the transaction is frequently called an **exchange of shares**. When there is an exchange of shares, it is important to keep track of who owns which shares, in order to determine who exercises control over whom.

Share exchanges

There are many different ways in which shares can be exchanged in order to accomplish a business combination. Some of the more common and straightforward methods include the following.

- The acquirer issues new shares to the shareholders of the acquired company in exchange for the shares of the target company (the acquiree).
- *Subsidiaries* of the acquirer issue shares in exchange for the acquiree's shares.
- A new corporation is formed; the new corporation issues shares to the shareholders of both the acquirer and the acquiree in exchange for the outstanding shares of both companies.
- The shareholders of the two corporations agree to a *statutory amalgamation*.
- The acquiree issues new shares to the shareholders of the acquirer in exchange for the acquirer's outstanding shares.

The first method listed above is the most common approach. What happens in this type of share exchange is:

- the acquirer issues new shares to the shareholders of the acquiree, and therefore has more shares outstanding after the acquisition than before the acquisition;
- the pre-acquisition shareholders of the acquiree become shareholders in the acquirer instead, so that the acquirer's post-acquisition shareholders consist of both its original shareholders *and* the former shareholders of the acquiree; and
- the acquiree's shares are now held by the acquiring *corporation* instead of external shareholders.

The second approach is similar to the first, except that the acquirer does not issue its own shares to acquire the company directly. Instead, the acquirer obtains indirect control by having its subsidiaries issue new shares to acquire the company. This approach is useful when the acquirer does not want to alter the ownership percentages of the existing shareholders by issuance of additional shares. For example, if the controlling shareholder of the acquirer owns 51% of the acquirer's shares, the issuance of additional shares would decrease the controlling shareholder's interest to below 50%, and control could be lost. But if the acquirer has a subsidiary that is, say, 70% owned, quite a number of additional shares could be issued by the subsidiary without jeopardizing the parent's control.

Under the third method, a new company is created that will hold the shares of both of the combining companies. The holding company issues its new shares in exchange for the shares of both the acquiree and the acquirer. After the exchange, the shares of both operating companies are held by the holding company, while the shares of the holding company are held by the former shareholders of both the acquiree and the acquirer.

The third method is not likely to be used by public companies. If the acquirer has a stock exchange listing, that listing would not automatically transfer to the newly formed company. The new company would have to apply for a new listing, which would disrupt trading in the acquirer's shares. The interruption in trading would likely have an adverse effect on the acquirer's share price.

Statutory amalgamation In a **statutory amalgamation**, the shareholders of the two corporations approve the combination or amalgamation of the two companies into a single surviving corporation. Statutory amalgamations are governed by the provincial or federal corporations acts under which the companies are incorporated. For two corporations to amalgamate, they must be incorporated under the same act. The shareholders of the combined company are the former shareholders of the two combining companies.

Statutory amalgamation is the only method of combination wherein the combining companies cease to exist as separate legal entities. It is also the only method of share exchange in which the assets of both companies end up being recorded on the books of one company, similar to the recording of assets in a direct purchase of net assets.

In all other forms of share exchange, there is no transfer of assets and thus no recording of the acquiree's assets on the acquirer's books—the results of the combination are reported by means of consolidated financial statements, as we discussed in the previous chapter. In contrast, consolidated statements are not needed for the combined companies after a statutory amalgamation because only one company survives. Of course, if either amalgamating company had subsidiaries, it would still be necessary to prepare consolidated statements that included those subsidiaries.

Reverse takeover The foregoing four methods of combination all specify one corporation as the acquirer. The acquirer is the corporation that obtains control over the other entity. It is possible to arrange the combination in such a way that the company that legally appears to be the acquirer is, in substance, the acquiree (the fifth method).

For example, suppose that LesserLimited has 100,000 shares outstanding before the combination, and issues 200,000 new shares to acquire all of GreaterCorp's shares. LesserLimited will own all of the shares of GreaterCorp and thus will legally control GreaterCorp. However, two-thirds of the shares of LesserLimited will be owned by the former shareholders of GreaterCorp, and the former shareholders of GreaterCorp will have voting control of LesserLimited after the combination. The substance of the combination is that control resides with GreaterCorp's shareholders even though the legal form of the combination is that LesserLimited acquired GreaterCorp. This form of business combination is called a **reverse takeover**.

After a reverse takeover occurs, the consolidated financial statements will be issued under the name of the legal parent (in this example, LesserLimited) but should reflect the substance of the combination as a continuation of the financial statements of the legal subsidiary (i.e., GreaterCorp). Pre-combination comparative statements and historical data should be those of the legal subsidiary (and in-substance acquirer) rather than of the legal parent (and in-substance acquiree).

Because of the potential confusion from reporting the substance of the activities of the legal subsidiary under the name of the legal parent, it is common for reverse takeovers to be accompanied by a company name change so that the name of the legal parent becomes almost indistinguishable from that of the legal subsidiary.

An example of a reverse takeover is the 1999 acquisition of Allied Hotel Properties by King George Development Corporation. King George acquired 100% of the shares of Allied by issuing King George shares. After the share exchange, the former shareholders of Allied owned a majority of the shares of King George. In the 1999 annual report, the consolidated financial statements after the acquisition reflected the fair values of King George and the book values of Allied. After the combination, the name of King George Development Corporation was changed to Allied Hotel Properties Inc.[4]

One of the main reasons for a reverse takeover is to acquire a stock exchange listing. If LesserLimited had a Toronto Stock Exchange (TSX) listing and GreaterCorp wanted one, a reverse takeover could be arranged instead of going to the trouble and expense of applying to the Ontario Securities Commission (OSC) and the TSX for a listing. In some instances, the legal acquirer (and in-substance acquiree) is just a shell company that has an exchange listing but no assets.

The accounting problem in any business combination is to report in accordance with the *substance* of the combination, and not to be misled by its legal form. Accountants must be sensitive to the objectives of managers and owners in arranging business combinations, and must examine the end result in order to determine who purchased what and for how much.[5]

Illustration of a share exchange

To illustrate the acquirer's accounting for a purchase of shares, assume that on December 31, 2005, Purchase Ltd. acquires all of the outstanding shares of Target Ltd. by issuing 40,000 Purchase Ltd. shares with a market value of $30, or $1,200,000 total, in exchange.[6] After the exchange of shares, all of the Target Ltd. shares will be held by the corporate entity of Purchase Ltd., while the newly issued shares of Purchase Ltd. will be held by the former shareholders of Target Ltd. and *not* by Target Ltd. as a corporate entity. Target Ltd. will have no shareholders external to the combined entity, while the shareholder base and the number of shares outstanding for Purchase Ltd. have increased.

When Purchase Ltd. acquires the shares, the entry to record the purchase on the books of Purchase Ltd. will be as follows:

Investment in Target Ltd.	1,200,000	
Common shares		1,200,000

There will be no entry on Target Ltd.'s books, because Target Ltd. is not a party to the transaction; the transaction is with the shareholders of Target Ltd. and not with the company itself. After the original purchase is recorded, the

4. For additional details, the post-consolidation financial statements of Allied Hotel Properties Inc. (i.e., the new name) can be accessed through SEDAR.com.

5. A detailed description of reverse takeover accounting is beyond the scope of this book. The Emerging Issues Committee issued abstract EIC-10 in January 1990, "Reverse Takeover Accounting," which deals with many of the issues that arise when attempting to account for reverse takeovers. EIC-10 was amended and updated in 2001 and 2003.

6. This transaction has the same value as the illustration used earlier in the chapter for a direct purchase of net assets.

investment is accounted for on Purchase Ltd.'s books by either the cost or equity method, as discussed in Chapter 2.

Exhibit 3–3 shows the balance sheets of Purchase Ltd. and Target Ltd. on December 31, 2005, both before and after the purchase of Target Ltd.'s shares by Purchase Ltd. The pre-transaction amounts are the same as were shown in Exhibit 3–1, when Purchase Ltd. purchased the net assets of Target Ltd.

The post-transaction amounts on Purchase Ltd.'s separate-entity balance sheet differ from the pre-transaction amounts only in one respect—Purchase Ltd. now has an account, "Investment in Target Ltd.," that reflects the cost of buying Target Ltd.'s shares, offset by an equal increase in Purchase Ltd.'s common share account. The purchase price was $1,200,000, determined by the value of the 40,000 Purchase Ltd. common shares given to Target Ltd.'s shareholders in exchange for their shares in Target Ltd.

Target Ltd.'s balance sheet is completely unaffected by the exchange of shares. Target Ltd.'s *owner* has changed, but nothing has changed in the company's accounts. Target Ltd.'s net asset book value was $800,000 prior to the change of ownership, and remains $800,000 after the change of ownership.

Target Ltd. is now a subsidiary of Purchase Ltd., and therefore Purchase Ltd. will prepare consolidated financial statements for public reporting purposes. The preparation of consolidated statements for a purchased subsidiary is somewhat more complex than for parent-founded subsidiaries, and involves choices from among several optional approaches. Consolidation of a purchased subsidiary at the date of acquisition will be illustrated shortly.

EXHIBIT 3–3	BALANCE SHEETS, DECEMBER 31, 2005			
	Before the exchange of shares		**After the exchange of shares**	
	Purchase Ltd.	**Target Ltd.**	**Purchase Ltd.**	**Target Ltd.**
Cash	$1,000,000	$ 50,000	$1,000,000	$ 50,000
Accounts receivable	2,000,000	150,000	2,000,000	150,000
Inventory	200,000	50,000	200,000	50,000
Land	1,000,000	300,000	1,000,000	300,000
Buildings and equipment	3,000,000	500,000	3,000,000	500,000
Accumulated depreciation	(1,200,000)	(150,000)	(1,200,000)	(150,000)
Investment in Target Ltd.	—	—	1,200,000	—
Total assets	$6,000,000	$900,000	$7,200,000	$900,000
Accounts payable	$1,000,000	$100,000	$1,000,000	$100,000
Long-term notes payable	400,000	—	400,000	—
Common shares*	2,600,000	200,000	3,800,000	200,000
Retained earnings	2,000,000	600,000	2,000,000	600,000
Total liabilities and share equity	$6,000,000	$900,000	$7,200,000	$900,000

*For Purchase Ltd., 160,000 shares before the exchange; 200,000 shares after the exchange.

Alternative Approaches to Reporting Business Combinations

Overview

In Chapter 2, we demonstrated the preparation of consolidated statements for Parco. To obtain the Parco consolidated balance sheet, we simply added the balances of Subco's assets and liabilities to those of Parco, after eliminating the intercompany balances. It might seem logical to use the same procedure to prepare Purchase Ltd.'s consolidated balance sheet, adding the book values of the two companies' assets and liabilities together to get the consolidated amounts.

However, in Chapter 2 we were demonstrating consolidation of a *parent-founded* subsidiary. In wholly owned parent-founded subsidiaries, the carrying values of the subsidiary's net assets represent the costs of the assets to the consolidated economic entity, because it was the parent's investment that provided the equity to purchase the assets. When a subsidiary is purchased, however, the purchase price of the net assets acquired will almost certainly be different from the carrying value of those assets on the subsidiary's books.

Target Ltd. has net assets with a book value of $800,000. Purchase Ltd. issued shares worth $1,200,000 to acquire control over Target Ltd.'s net assets. The $400,000 difference between the purchase price and the book value of the net assets acquired is known as the **purchase price discrepancy**. Any method of combining the balance sheets of the two companies must find a way of accounting for the $400,000 difference.

Three general alternative approaches are available for combining the balance sheets of Purchase Ltd. and Target Ltd. in order to obtain a consolidated balance sheet for Purchase Ltd.

These alternatives are:

1. Add together the book values of the assets and liabilities of the two companies (the **pooling-of-interests** method).

2. Add the fair values of Target Ltd.'s assets and liabilities at the date of acquisition to the book values of Purchase Ltd.'s assets and liabilities (the **purchase** method).

3. Add the fair values of Target Ltd.'s assets and liabilities to the fair values of Purchase Ltd.'s assets and liabilities (the **new-entity** method).

The two variables that determine the results are (1) the valuation of the parent's net assets and (2) the valuation of the subsidiary's net assets. The alternatives can be summarized as follows:

Method	Net Assets of Parent Company	Net Assets of Subsidiary
Pooling of interests	Book value	Book value
Purchase	Book value	Fair value
New entity	Fair value	Fair value

To demonstrate the alternatives, we need to know the fair values of the two companies' net assets. Exhibit 3–4 compares each company's book values with its assumed fair values. To keep this example simple, we assume that only the capital assets have fair values that are different from book values. The capital assets are highlighted in Exhibit 3–4.

EXHIBIT 3–4 BOOK VALUES AND FAIR VALUES, DECEMBER 31, 2005

	[Dr/(Cr)]			
	Purchase Ltd.		Target Ltd.	
	Book value	Fair value	Book value	Fair value
Cash	$ 1,000,000	$ 1,000,000	$ 50,000	$ 50,000
Accounts receivable	2,000,000	2,000,000	150,000	150,000
Inventory	200,000	200,000	50,000	50,000
Land	**1,000,000**	**2,000,000**	**300,000**	**400,000**
Buildings and equipment	**3,000,000**	**2,300,000**	**500,000**	**550,000**
Accumulated depreciation	**(1,200,000)**	**—**	**(150,000)**	**—**
Accounts payable	(1,000,000)	(1,000,000)	(100,000)	(100,000)
Long-term notes payable	(400,000)	(400,000)	—	—
Net assets	$ 4,600,000	$ 6,100,000	$ 800,000	$ 1,100,000

Pooling of interests

Pooling of interests certainly is the simplest method of consolidating a purchased subsidiary. Under this method, the book values of the parent and the subsidiary are added together and reported on the parent's consolidated balance sheet.

The assumption underlying the pooling method is that the combined economic entity is a continuation under common ownership of two previously separate going concerns, and that the operations of both companies will continue without substantial change. If the companies continue to function as separate entities—although now under common ownership—then it is presumed that there should be no change in the basis of accountability for the assets and liabilities as a result of the combination.

Notice that the pooling method completely ignores the fair value of both companies' assets and liabilities. It is a "business as usual" approach.

Pooling was permitted in Canada prior to 2001, but it was very seldom used in practice. Pooling was permitted only when an acquirer could not be identified—that is, when the two companies clearly were equals, and the post-acquisition shareholdings were about evenly split between the shareholders of the two pre-acquisition companies. But the concept of equality is illusory; merged companies do not end up with two CEOs, two boards of directors, and two separate shareholders' annual meetings. There always is one company that becomes the dominant company after the combination. Therefore, pooling is not now permitted by the AcSB.

Purchase method

The purpose of Purchase Ltd.'s purchase of Target Ltd.'s common shares was to obtain control over the net assets and the operations of Target Ltd. The control obtained by a purchase of shares is essentially the same as by purchasing Target Ltd.'s net assets directly. If Purchase Ltd. had purchased the net assets, Purchase Ltd. clearly would have recorded the acquired net assets at their fair values. If the price paid exceeded the total fair value, the excess would be assigned to goodwill.

The purchase of shares achieves the same result as does the direct purchase of assets. Therefore, the objective of the purchase method of consolidation is to report the results of the purchase of shares as though the assets had been acquired directly. The fair values of the subsidiary's assets and liabilities are added to those of the parent (at book value), because the fair value is considered to be the cost of the assets and liabilities to the acquirer. Any excess of the purchase price over the aggregate fair value is assigned to goodwill.

The allocation of the purchase price discrepancy was illustrated earlier, when we assumed that Purchase Ltd. bought Target Ltd.'s net assets directly. The same calculation applies when the method of combining is an exchange of shares. The fair value of Target Ltd.'s net assets is $1,100,000. The purchase price was $1,200,000. The difference of $100,000 between the purchase price and the net asset fair value is attributed to goodwill.

The second column of Exhibit 3–5 shows Purchase Ltd.'s consolidated balance sheet under the purchase method. Note that the purchase-method consolidated balance sheet is exactly the same as the post-transaction balance sheet for direct purchase of the assets as shown in Exhibit 3–2.

New-entity method

The purchase method has been criticized because the consolidated balance sheet contains a mixture of old book values (for Purchase Ltd.'s assets) and date-of-acquisition fair values (for Target Ltd.'s assets). One can argue that when a business combination occurs, a new economic entity is formed, and that a new basis of accountability should be established for *all* of the assets.

Under the new-entity approach, the assets and liabilities of Purchase Ltd. are revalued to fair value, so that the consolidated balance sheet will disclose the current fair values (on the date of the combination) of all of the assets for the com-

EXHIBIT 3–5	ALTERNATIVE APPROACHES TO CONSOLIDATED STATEMENTS FOR A BUSINESS COMBINATION

Purchase Ltd.
Consolidated Balance Sheet
December 31, 2005

	Pooling	Purchase	New Entity
Cash	$ 1,050,000	$ 1,050,000	$1,050,000
Accounts receivable	2,150,000	2,150,000	2,150,000
Inventory	250,000	250,000	250,000
Land	1,300,000	1,400,000	2,400,000
Buildings and equipment	3,500,000	3,550,000	2,850,000
Accumulated depreciation	(1,350,000)	(1,200,000)	—
Goodwill	—	100,000	100,000
Total assets	$ 6,900,000	$ 7,300,000	$8,800,000
Accounts payable	$ 1,100,000	$ 1,100,000	$1,100,000
Long-term notes payable	400,000	400,000	400,000
Common shares*	2,800,000	3,800,000	3,800,000
Add'l paid-in capital: Reappraisal surplus	—	—	1,500,000
Retained earnings	2,600,000	2,000,000	2,000,000
Total liabilities and share equity	$ 6,900,000	$ 7,300,000	$8,800,000

*200,000 shares issued and outstanding

bined entity. The third column of Exhibit 3–5 shows Purchase Ltd.'s consolidated balance sheet under the new-entity method.

Notice that a new account has appeared in the new-entity column: "reappraisal surplus." We have written up the carrying values of Purchase Ltd.'s assets, and we need an offsetting account to credit. Any upward asset revaluation is reflected in shareholders' equity, as a part of paid-in capital. This is true any time that an asset is written up, whether as a part of a business combination or because assets are carried at fair value instead of cost.

Under certain circumstances, there is merit in the arguments for the new-entity method. If the combining enterprises are of roughly comparable size, and if the operations of the newly combined enterprises are going to be substantially different from the predecessor operations, then a case can be made for establishing a new basis of accountability.

However, there are significant practical problems in implementing the method. Obtaining fair values for all of the assets is likely to be an expensive and time-consuming project, unless the acquiring company already uses current values for internal reporting purposes. In addition, a substantial degree of subjectivity would inevitably exist in the fair-value determination.

While subjective estimates are required to assign the purchase price of a subsidiary to the subsidiary's specific assets and liabilities, the total of the fair values assigned is limited by the total purchase price paid by the parent. But in revaluing the parent's assets for application of the new-entity method, there is no verifiable upper limit for the fair values because no transaction has occurred. In addition, the measurement of goodwill for the parent corporation would be highly subjective. Since it is not clear how the new-entity method would improve the decisions of users of the consolidated financial statements, it has not been accepted in practice.

Other approaches

In the past, approaches to consolidation other than the three discussed above have been used in practice. One of the more common was to value the transaction at the fair value of the consideration given, as in a purchase, but to consolidate the subsidiary's assets and liabilities at their book values, as under pooling. The difference between the book value and the purchase price would be assigned to goodwill on the consolidated statements.

This approach, sometimes called the *carrying-value purchase method*, has the same net impact on the acquirer's net assets as the fair-value purchase method. However, the assignment of the entire excess of the purchase price over net book value to goodwill can have a significant impact on consolidated earnings subsequent to the acquisition, because accounting for goodwill will be different in impact than would subsequent reporting of the fair values of specific assets and liabilities.

Purchase vs. pooling

Before leaving our discussion of the alternative methods of consolidation, we should consider further the use of the purchase method as opposed to the pooling-of-interests method.

In most business combinations, one company clearly is acquiring the other. The acquirer is the company whose pre-combination shareholders have a majority of the voting shares in the combined enterprise, regardless of which company is legally acquiring the shares of the other. If one company can be identified as the acquirer, then there is widespread agreement that the purchase method should be used.

An acquirer can *always* be identified when the purchase of shares is for cash, notes, or other assets of the acquirer. In such an acquisition, the former shareholders of the acquiree have no stake in the combined venture, and clearly they are not pooling their interests with those of the acquirer's shareholders. An exchange of shares must occur for the possibility of pooling even to arise.

Consolidated financial statements can be drastically affected by the choice of pooling or purchase accounting. The consolidated asset values usually will differ considerably, especially for tangible and intangible capital assets. Goodwill that is reported under the purchase method is not shown under pooling. The difference in the asset values will have a consequent impact on earnings measurement.

The difference in reporting can have an impact not only on the *size* of earnings, but also the comparative *direction* over time. Pooling could cause post-combination earnings per share (EPS) to increase, relative to pre-combination earnings, while purchase accounting could cause EPS to decrease. The reverse situation could also occur.

The difference in results is not something that external financial statement users can adjust for. If pooling is used, there is no way to know what the reported results would have been under purchase accounting—there is no information available to the public about the fair values of the net assets acquired. When information on measurements under different accounting methods does not exist, the market cannot adjust for the differences.

Due to the significant differences between reported results under the two methods, there has long been a controversy about the use of pooling versus purchase. This controversy has now been resolved firmly in favour of purchase, as we shall discuss in the next section.

Current Canadian practice

Purchase method The recommendation of AcSB is clear: "The purchase method of accounting should be used to account for all business combinations" [CICA 1581.09]. This recommendation is intended to slam the door on the use of pooling by public companies.

Pooling was never widespread in Canada. Indeed, around the world, pooling was in widespread use only in the United States. Other countries either prohibited pooling or restricted its use to very narrow circumstances. The *CICA Handbook*, for example, previously stated that pooling could be used only *when an acquirer could not be identified*. The change in Canada to prohibit pooling was basically part of a multicountry strategy to help the Financial Accounting Standards Board (FASB) prohibit pooling in the United States.

Identifying the acquirer The acquirer in a business combination is the corporation whose shareholders control the combined economic entity. When the purchase is for cash (or other assets), it is obvious that the acquirer is the company that pays to acquire the other (or the assets of the other). When the combination is effected by an exchange of shares, the acquirer may not be so obvious.

The corporation that issues the shares is usually, but not always, the acquirer. Earlier in this chapter, we discussed the issue of *control* and the fact that some business combinations are reverse takeovers. Therefore, it is necessary to examine which shareholder group has control of the combined economic entity in order to determine who is the acquirer.

Voting control may appear to be evenly split between the shareholders of the two combining companies. If that is the case, other factors must be examined to determine who is the acquirer [CICA 1581.14]. Examples of other factors include:

- the existence of major voting blocks
- special voting rights for some shareholders, or voting restrictions on others
- holdings of convertible debt securities and other options or derivatives
- the composition of the board of directors, and
- the composition of the senior management team.

Corporate restructurings—non–arm's-length pooling

The AcSB's purchase method recommendation does not apply to combinations of companies under common control [CICA 1581.03]. The *CICA Handbook* cites three examples that relate to transfers between subsidiaries or between a parent and its existing or newly formed subsidiaries. The exemption of transfers between entities under common control also would apply to corporations that are not in a parent–subsidiary relationship, but that have a common controlling shareholder.

A shifting of assets among companies under common control is often called a **corporate restructuring**. A parent company (or its owners) may decide to rearrange the intercorporate ownerships of the economic entity comprising the parent and its several subsidiaries. New subsidiaries may be formed, or parts of the economic entity may be combined or otherwise regrouped or redefined. When a corporate restructuring takes place, it is not an arm's-length transaction because all of the individual corporations are ultimately controlled by the same shareholders. Since there is no arm's-length transaction, the assets cannot be revalued for reporting on either the separate-entity or the consolidated financial statements.

Voluntary restructurings of corporate ownerships are quite common in both public and private companies in Canada. Since corporate ownership restructurings are accounted for as though they were poolings of interest, it is necessary to understand the pooling method even though it is not widely used for business combinations reported by public companies.

International Practices for Business Combinations

In general, countries around the world have required that the purchase method be used for business combinations. Pooling has been permitted in many countries, such as Canada and the U.K., if an acquirer cannot be determined. The one big exception to the general application of the purchase method has been the United States. The U.S.A. has been the most enthusiastic pooler in the world, by far.

In contrast, Australia and New Zealand banned the use of pooling altogether; only purchase accounting has been permitted. Although it may, in some instances, be difficult to establish which company among equals is the acquirer, "experience with the Australian standard suggests that any difficulties in identifying the acquirer are not insurmountable."[7]

Originally, there were absolutely no restrictions on the use of pooling in the United States. Pooling could be used for *any* business combination, regardless of the relative size and power of the combining companies. Pooling could even be used when the purchase was for cash, with no continuing share ownership by the previous shareholders of the target company.

In 1970, the AICPA's Accounting Principles Board tried to rein in the use of pooling by imposing a set of 12 criteria that would govern whether the transaction should be accounted for as a purchase or by pooling.[8] Given the radically different reported results that can be obtained under pooling, it was hardly surprising that many U.S. acquirers structured their purchase transactions in a way that would then "require" them to use their preferred method of accounting.[9]

The result of the use of pooling was that "two economically similar business combinations can be accounted for using different accounting methods that produce dramatically different financial results."[10] A further consequence was that companies that could not use pooling (such as Canadian companies that were competing for acquisitions) felt that they were severely disadvantaged by lower reported earnings that may be caused by their inability to use pooling. Some observers felt that companies that could use pooling were able to pay more for a target acquisition than a company that could not use pooling. Therefore, "having two accounting methods that produce dramatically different results affects competition in markets for mergers and acquisitions."[11]

In 1999, the standard-setters of Canada, Australia, New Zealand, the U.K., and the U.S. (i.e., the "G4+1" countries) co-operated on the issuance of new standards to eliminate the use of pooling. Effectively, the only country whose standards were seriously changed by the new proposals was the U.S.A. The new standards achieve international harmonization on a major issue in accounting.

International Accounting Standard 22, *Business Combinations*, is in agreement with the new harmonized standard of the G4. However, it does still permit the pooling of interests method, known as "uniting of interests."

New-entity revisited?

The new-entity method has become a topic of a joint project of the IASB and the FASB. The method is now being called *fresh-start accounting* or *new basis accounting*. The FASB describes the project as follows in *The FASB Report* for July 26, 2002:

> The objective of this research project is to develop a proposal for a project that would identify those situations in which fresh-start (a new basis at fair value) recognition and measurement of all of an entity's assets and liabilities would be appropriate. That proposal would define the scope of a potential project and proposed solution in the

---

7. *Methods of Accounting for Business Combinations: Recommendations of the G4+1 for Achieving Convergence*, paragraph 75. Published simultaneously by the standard-setting bodies of Canada, U.S.A., U.K., Australia, and New Zealand, December 1998.

8. *APB Opinion 16*, issued in 1970. The Accounting Principles Board, or APB, was the standard-setting body in the U.S. prior to establishment of the FASB in 1971.

9. This should be a familiar scenario. It is similar to companies' approach to lease transactions—decide how they want the lease to be reported (i.e., capital or operating), and then structure the lease contract accordingly.

10. Edmund L. Jenkins, FASB Chairman, in testimony before the U.S. Senate Committee on Banking, Housing, and Urban Affairs, March 2, 2000; quoted in the FASB *Status Report* of March 24, 2000.

11. *Ibid.*

form of a draft working principle. One commonly identified candidate for application of this approach is a multiparty business combination or other new entity formation in which no single preexisting entity obtains majority ownership and control of the resulting new entity. Similarly, joint venture formations also are candidates for this accounting treatment.

Notice that this is a *project* to develop a *proposal* for a *project* to *consider* a working *principle*—there are a lot of "ifs." Something may come from this project *if* it ever gets off the ground. Alternatively, the fresh start method could once again disappear without leaving a trace in professional pronouncements.

Consolidation Procedures

Exhibit 3–5 illustrated the purchase-method consolidated statements in the second column. We explained that the amounts in that column were obtained by adding the book value of each of Purchase Ltd.'s assets and liabilities to the fair values of the same items for Target Ltd.

Before plunging into the greater complexities of consolidation in the following chapters, we will more carefully illustrate the general procedure for consolidating subsidiaries that were acquired through a business combination. The key factor that differentiates the procedure is that, for business combinations, consolidation mechanics must adjust for fair values. Fair values are not an issue for parent-founded subsidiaries.

Direct method

After one company acquires control over another, each company will still continue to prepare its own separate-entity financial statements. Remember that each company is still a legal and operating entity. Consolidated statements are an artificial construct of the accounting profession—*artificial* in that there is no legal entity that corresponds to the economic entity of the parent and its subsidiaries.

But the reporting objective is *substance over form*. Although the parent and its subsidiaries are separate *legal* entities and prepare separate, individual financial statements, the overall *economic* entity is the group of companies. For that reason, consolidated statements are called **group accounts** in most parts of the world, even though there are no formal group accounts—just consolidation working papers and statements.

In theory, purchase accounting combines the book values of the parent with the fair values (*at date of acquisition*) of the purchased subsidiaries. In practice, consolidation actually begins with *book values* of both companies. At the date of acquisition, it is clear that the book values and the fair values relate to the same assets and liabilities. As time moves on, however, assets will enter and leave the balance sheet of the purchased subsidiary, and the asset base will change.

Therefore, consolidation takes the book values of both companies and adds the *fair-value increments* relating to the assets of Target Ltd. that existed when Target Ltd. was acquired. The fair-value increments (or decrements) are the differences between Target Ltd.'s book values and fair values at the date of acquisition.

An analysis of the purchase price is illustrated in Exhibit 3–6. Of the $1,200,000 purchase price, $800,000 is attributed to the book value of the net assets acquired, $300,000 is the total of the fair-value increments, and the

EXHIBIT 3–6   ALLOCATION OF PURCHASE PRICE

100% Purchase of Target Ltd., December 31, 2005

	Book value	Fair value	Fair value increment	% share	FVI acquired
Purchase price					**$1,200,000**
Cash	$50,000	$50,000	—		
Accounts receivable	150,000	150,000	—		
Inventory	50,000	50,000	—		
Land	300,000	400,000	$100,000 × 100% =		$100,000
Buildings and equipment	500,000	550,000	50,000 × 100% =		50,000
Accumulated depreciation	(150,000)	—	150,000 × 100% =		150,000
Accounts payable	(100,000)	(100,000)	—		
Total fair value increment					300,000
Net asset book value	$ 800,000			× 100% =	800,000
Fair value of assets acquired					1,100,000
Goodwill					$ 100,000

residual $100,000 is attributed to goodwill. On a continuing basis, consolidated net assets will be computed as:

- book value of each asset and liability,
- plus any fair-value increments (or minus any fair-value decrements) relating to assets still on Target Ltd.'s books from the date of consolidation,
- plus goodwill, if any.

Exhibit 3–7 shows the derivation of Purchase Ltd.'s consolidated balance sheet at December 31, 2005, using the direct method. For each item on the balance sheet, we take the book value for Purchase Ltd., add the book value of Target Ltd., and add the fair-value increment. The fair-value increment (and goodwill) adjustments are indicated with a "**b**." Also, we must eliminate Purchase Ltd.'s investment account and Target's shareholders' equity accounts (indicated with an "**a**"). The resulting balance amounts are identical to those shown in the second column of Exhibit 3–5.

There is one aspect of Exhibit 3–7 that merits explanation. You'll notice that *accumulated depreciation* is calculated by adding the two companies' amounts together, and then *subtracting Target Ltd.'s accumulated depreciation at the date of acquisition.* We subtract Target Ltd.'s accumulated depreciation because we want to show the fair value of Target Ltd.'s depreciable assets at the date of acquisition. This amount is included in the capital asset account itself. If we carried Target's accumulated depreciation forward, we would be reducing the fair value. In effect, we would be combining fair value in the asset account with written-off cost in the accumulated depreciation. To emphasize the point, the *CICA Handbook* explicitly points out that "the acquirer does not carry forward the accumulated depreciation of the acquired enterprise" [CICA 1581.43].

Although we have indicated which adjustments on Exhibit 3–7 are for fair-value increments and which are eliminations, bear in mind that these purchase adjustments and eliminations are not independent. Essentially, all of the adjustments shown in Exhibit 3–7 are allocations of the $1,200,000 purchase price. In

EXHIBIT 3–7   PURCHASE LTD. CONSOLIDATED BALANCE SHEET

Balance Sheet
December 31, 2005

Assets

Current assets:

Cash [1,000,000 + 50,000]	$ 1,050,000
Accounts receivable [2,000,000 + 150,000]	2,150,000
Inventory [200,000 + 50,000]	250,000
	3,450,000

Property, plant, and equipment:

Land [1,000,000 + 300,000 **+ 100,000b**]	1,400,000
Buildings and equipment [3,000,000 + 500,000 **+ 50,000b**]	3,550,000
Accumulated depreciation [1,200,000 + 150,000 **– 150,000b**]	(1,200,000)
	3,750,000

Other assets:

Investment in Target Ltd. [1,200,000 **– 800,000a – 400,000b**]	—
Goodwill [**+ 100,000b**]	100,000
Total assets	$ 7,300,000

Liabilities and shareholders' equity

Liabilities:

Current accounts payable [1,000,000 + 100,000]	$ 1,100,000
Long-term notes payable [400,000 + 0]	400,000
	1,500,000

Shareholders' equity:

Common shares [3,800,000 + 200,000 **– 200,000a**]	3,800,000
Retained earnings [2,000,000 + 600,000 **– 600,000a**]	2,000,000
	5,800,000
Total liabilities and shareholders' equity	$ 7,300,000

future years, all of the components of this purchase adjustment must be made simultaneously, as we will illustrate in the following chapters.

Worksheet method

Exhibit 3–8 shows the trial balance-based spreadsheet for Purchase Ltd.'s consolidated balance sheet. The separate-entity columns for the individual companies correspond to the post-transaction balance sheets shown in the last two columns of Exhibit 3–3.

The eliminations and adjustments that are necessary in order to prepare the consolidated trial balance are composed of two elements. First, it is necessary to eliminate the shareholders' equity accounts of Target Ltd. by offsetting the balances of these accounts against the investment account:

a	Common shares (Target)	200,000	
	Retained earnings (Target)	600,000	
	Investment in Target Ltd. (Purchase)		800,000

EXHIBIT 3–8   PURCHASE LTD. CONSOLIDATION WORKSHEET AT DATE OF ACQUISITION

December 31, 2005

	Trial balances		Adjustments Dr/(Cr)	Purchase consolidated trial balance
	Purchase Dr/(Cr)	Target Dr/(Cr)		
Cash	$ 1,000,000	$ 50,000		$ 1,050,000
Accounts receivable	2,000,000	150,000		2,150,000
Inventories	200,000	50,000		250,000
Land	1,000,000	300,000	100,000 **b**	1,400,000
Buildings and equipment	3,000,000	500,000	50,000 **b**	3,550,000
Accumulated depreciation	(1,200,000)	(150,000)	150,000 **b**	(1,200,000)
Investment in Target Ltd.	1,200,000	—	(800,000) **a** (400,000) **b**	—
Goodwill	—	—	100,000 **b**	100,000
Accounts payable	(1,000,000)	(100,000)		(1,100,000)
Long-term notes payable	(400,000)	—		(400,000)
Common shares	(3,800,000)	(200,000)	200,000 **a**	(3,800,000)
Retained earnings	(2,000,000)	(600,000)	600,000 **a**	(2,000,000)
	$ —	$ —	$ —	$ —

The names in parentheses indicate the company trial balance to which that particular elimination element refers. Again, we must emphasize that there is no actual journal entry on either company's books—this is purely a worksheet entry.

The second entry adjusts the asset accounts of the subsidiary from their carrying values on the subsidiary's books to the fair values at the date of acquisition:

b Land (Target)	100,000	
Buildings and equipment (Target)	50,000	
Accumulated depreciation (Target)	150,000	
Goodwill	100,000	
Investment in Target Ltd. (Purchase)		400,000

The net result of these two adjustments is to eliminate the investment account, eliminate the subsidiary's share equity accounts at the date of acquisition, and establish the fair values of the assets and liabilities acquired by Purchase Ltd. through purchase of Target Ltd.'s shares. These two adjustments will be made in every subsequent period when the consolidated statements are prepared.

Negative Goodwill

In the business combination used in the previous example, control over net assets with a fair value of $1,100,000 was acquired for $1,200,000. The difference between the purchase price and the fair value of the acquired net assets is treated as goodwill.

It is not unusual, however, for the total fair value of the assets and liabilities to be *greater* than the purchase price. This excess of fair values over the purchase price is commonly known as **negative goodwill**, although the title is not particularly indicative of the accounting treatment of the amount. The total of the net debits (to record the fair values) is greater than the credits (to record the consideration paid), and therefore there are more debits than credits in the consolidated statements—not a tolerable situation in a double-entry system. The task is to correct the balance by either increasing the credits or decreasing the debits.

Once upon a time, it was common practice to increase the credits by establishing an account to credit for the amount of negative goodwill. It was not normally called "negative goodwill," of course. Usually a more opaque title was chosen, such as "excess of fair value over cost of assets acquired." This is now a prohibited practice in Canada, and in most countries. Instead of creating a credit for negative goodwill, the balance of debits and credits must be achieved by reducing the total amount allocated to the net assets.

Negative goodwill is, in essence, an indication that the acquirer achieved a bargain purchase. A bargain purchase is possible for a variety of reasons. If the acquisition is by a purchase of shares, then the market price of the acquiree's shares may be well below the net asset value per share. Or if the acquiree is a private company, a bargain purchase may be possible if the present owners are anxious to sell because of the death of the founder–manager, divorce, changed family financial position, or simply an inability to manage effectively.

Regardless of the reason, negative goodwill should be viewed as a discount on the purchase and not as a special credit to be created and amortized. When any company buys an asset at a bargain price, the asset is recorded at its cost to the purchaser, and not at any list price or other fair value. For example, suppose that a company buys a large computer from a financially troubled distributor for only $80,000. The price of the computer from any other source would be $120,000. On the buyer's books, the computer obviously would be recorded at $80,000, not at $120,000 with an offsetting credit for $40,000.

The same general principle applies to bargain purchases in business combinations. The purchase price is allocated to the acquired assets and liabilities on the basis of fair values, but not necessarily *at* fair values if the total fair value exceeds the purchase price. A problem does arise, however, in deciding to which assets and liabilities the bargain prices or negative goodwill should be assigned.

A business combination involves the assets and liabilities of a going concern. The net assets acquired usually comprise a mixture of financial and non-financial, current and long-term assets and liabilities. Because the various assets and liabilities have varying impacts on reported earnings, the allocation of negative goodwill will affect the amount of future revenues and expenses.

For example, suppose that Purchase Ltd. acquired all of the shares of Target Ltd., as above, but at a cost of only $1,050,000. Since the fair value of Target's net assets is $1,100,000, negative goodwill of $50,000 exists. Target Ltd.'s assets and liabilities will be reported on Purchase Ltd.'s consolidated balance sheet at a total amount of $1,050,000, $50,000 less than their fair values. At least one of the Target Ltd. assets must be reported at an amount that is less than its fair value.

If the negative goodwill were assigned to inventory, Target Ltd.'s inventory would be consolidated at zero value, since the fair value of Target Ltd.'s inventory was assumed to be $50,000 (Exhibit 3–4). Reduction in the cost assigned to inventory will flow through to the income statement in the following year as a reduction in cost of goods sold and an increase in net income. If, on the other hand, the negative goodwill were assigned to buildings and equipment, then the effect of the bargain purchase would be recognized over several years in the form of reduced depreciation on the lower cost allocated to buildings and equipment. Allocation of the negative goodwill to land would result in no impact on earnings until the land was sold; allocation to monetary receivables would result in a gain when the receivables were collected.

If the purchase price allocations to the relevant non-financial assets have all been reduced to zero and there still is negative goodwill remaining, the remaining amount is recognized as an extraordinary gain, even though the normal conditions for recognizing an extraordinary gain have not been met.

Disclosure

Business combinations are significant events. They often change the nature of operations of a company and thus change the components of the earnings stream. All users' financial reporting objectives are affected by substantial business combinations. At a minimum, the asset and liability structure of the reporting enterprise is changed. Disclosure of business combinations therefore is quite important.

The AcSB recommends a long list of disclosures for business combinations completed during the period [CICA 1581.55–1581.57]. We will not reproduce the complete list here, but the acquirer should disclose essential aspects such as:

- a description of the acquired subsidiary, its business, the date of purchase, and the nature of the purchase transaction
- the cost of the acquisition and the nature and value of the consideration given
- a summary of the major classes of assets and liabilities acquired, including goodwill, and
- the nature of any contingent consideration.

For acquisitions that are individually immaterial, similar information should be disclosed in the aggregate [CICA 1581.57].

Also, the acquirer should disclose significant intangible assets that have been acquired as part of the business combination. The nature of the assets and the amortization basis should be described.

Exhibit 3–9 shows the 2002 disclosure note for Petro-Canada's acquisition of Veba Oil & Gas. You can see several pieces of information in this note:

- Veba is a private German company, a fact that is indicated by the "GmbH" where we would expect to see "Ltd." or "Inc." (Public companies in Germany are "A.G.") Petro-Canada did not buy Veba directly. Instead it bought the shares of other companies (undoubtedly private companies) that held the Veba shares.
- The purchase was accomplished in two steps, on May 2 and December 10, 2002.
- The purchase was for cash, and the total purchase price of $2,234 million includes acquisition costs. The cash was provided mainly by bank loans.
- Of the total cost, $709 million was allocated to goodwill, which is about 32% of the total purchase price. The fair value of the net assets was $1,912 million, excluding goodwill of $709 million and future income tax liability of $387 million: $2,234 − $709 + $387 = $1,912. [Appendix 3A explains future income taxes relating to business combinations, for optional reading.]
- The goodwill was assigned to Petro-Canada's "International business segment." As we shall explain in the following chapter, the mandatory goodwill impairment test requires that goodwill be assigned to specific operating units, and not just left as a residual for the company as a whole.

EXHIBIT 3–9   DISCLOSURE OF ACQUISITIONS

Petro-Canada

Note 3 – ACQUISITION OF OIL AND GAS OPERATIONS OF VEBA OIL & GAS GMBH

On May 2, 2002 the Company acquired the shares of companies holding the majority of the international oil and gas operations of Veba Oil & Gas GmbH and on December 10, 2002 the Company acquired certain of the remaining operations which were subject to rights of first refusal. The total acquisition cost, consisting of cash consideration and acquisition costs, was $2,234 million and the results of these operations have been included in the consolidated financial statements from the dates of acquisition. The remaining operations not yet acquired are in Venezuela and are subject to rights of first refusal.

The acquisition was accounted for by the purchase method of accounting and the estimated allocation of fair value to the assets acquired and liabilities assumed was:

Property, plant and equipment	$2,012
Goodwill	709
Current assets, excluding cash of $15 million	640
Deferred charges and other assets	6
Total assets acquired	3,367
Current liabilities	634
Future income taxes	387
Deferred credits and other liabilities	112
Total liabilities assumed	1,133
Net assets acquired	$2,234

Although the estimated allocation of fair value to the assets acquired and liabilities assumed is subject to changes as additional information becomes available, the final allocation is not expected to differ materially from the estimated allocation.

Goodwill, which is not tax deductible, was assigned to the Company's International business segment.

Funds for the acquisition were provided from credit facilities arranged with certain banks (Note 16) and from cash and short-term investments.

- There is no contingent consideration mentioned in the note. However, the note does indicate that the fair values are subject to modification as "additional information becomes available." A change in fair values will affect the *allocation* of the purchase price but will not affect the *amount* of the purchase price.

Recording Fair Values: Push-Down Accounting

We have emphasized that the fair values of the net assets of the acquiree are never recorded in the books of the acquirer; the full purchase price is simply recorded in an investment account on the acquirer's books. We have also stated that when a business combination is accomplished by a purchase of shares (rather than by a direct purchase of assets), the acquiree continues to exist as a separate legal and reporting entity. The carrying values of the acquiree's net assets are not affected by the acquisition or by the fair values attributed to the assets by the acquirer.

An exception to the general rule that the acquiree's carrying values are unaffected by the purchase may arise when substantially all of the acquiree's shares are purchased by the acquirer. In that case, the acquirer may direct the acquiree to restate its assets to fair value. This practice is known as **push-down accounting**, because the fair values are "pushed down" to the acquiree's books. The net effect is the same as though the acquirer had formed a new subsidiary, which then purchased all of the assets and liabilities of the acquiree.

There are two advantages to push-down accounting. The first is that the financial position and results of operations of the acquiree will be reported on the same economic basis in both the consolidated statements and its own separate-entity statements. Without push-down accounting, for example, it would be possible for the subsidiary to report a profit on its own and yet contribute an operating loss to the parent's consolidated results, if the consolidation adjustments are sufficient to tip the balance between profit and loss.

The second advantage is that the process of consolidation will be greatly simplified for the parent. Since the carrying values will be the same as the acquisition fair values, there will be no need for many of the consolidation adjustments that otherwise will be required every time consolidated statements are prepared.

Although push-down accounting is used in Canada, the practice is more prevalent in the United States, where the Securities and Exchange Commission *requires* its registrants to use the practice when an acquired subsidiary is "substantially" wholly owned and there is no publicly held debt or senior shares.

CICA Handbook Section 1625, "Comprehensive Revaluation of Assets and Liabilities," states that push-down accounting *may* be used when:

> All or virtually all of the equity interests in the enterprise have been acquired, in one or more transactions between non-related parties, by an acquirer who controls the enterprise after the transaction or transactions. [CICA 1625.04(a)]

A guideline of at least 90% ownership is provided for the phrase "virtually all of the equity interests" [CICA 1625.10]. Note that the recommendation provides for acquisitions that are accomplished by a series of smaller share purchases as well as by one large transaction—substantially complete ownership need not be achieved all at once.

Despite the permissibility of applying push-down accounting, acquirers may choose not to apply push-down accounting to subsidiaries that have outstanding public debt. The reason is that the basis for assessing contract compliance is disturbed by an asset revaluation. Reported results (e.g., earnings per share) will be discontinuous, and debt covenants may be violated or rendered less suitable if the reporting basis is changed. Indeed, debt agreements with banks may be based on accounting principles in effect on the date of the agreement, and thereby effectively constrain the application of push-down accounting.

A special case of push-down accounting arises in a reverse takeover. In a reverse takeover, it is the legal acquirer that is really the in-substance acquiree—the fair values reported on the consolidated statements will be those of the company issuing the statements (the legal parent but in-substance subsidiary). In that case, it makes little sense for the in-substance acquiree to be carrying its assets and liabilities at book values that will never be reported in its own financial statements. It is more logical simply to put the fair values on the books of the in-substance acquiree.

SUMMARY OF KEY POINTS

1. A business combination is the acquisition of net assets or *control* over net assets that constitute a functioning business. Control over net assets is usually obtained by buying a majority of the shares in the company that owns the assets. When control is acquired, the acquired net assets remain the property of the controlled subsidiary. Therefore, consolidated financial statements are necessary.

2. Accounting for a business combination requires three steps: (1) determine the cost of the acquisition, or purchase price, (2) determine the fair values of the acquired assets and liabilities, and (3) allocate the purchase price to the identifiable assets and liabilities, with any excess attributed to goodwill.

   The basis for the allocation of purchase price is the fair values of the acquired assets and liabilities. If the purchase price is less than the aggregate fair value of the net assets, negative goodwill arises. The value assigned to non-financial assets, starting with intangible assets with no observable market value, must be reduced until the total allocated amount equals the purchase price. If there is still negative goodwill left over after fair value of the non-financial assets has been written down to zero, the excess of fair value over the purchase price is recognized as an extraordinary item.

3. A purchase of net assets may be accomplished (1) by paying cash or other assets or (2) by issuing shares. A combination of cash and shares may be used. When shares are issued, the purchase price is based on the market value of the shares, if determinable. If the market value of issued shares is not determinable, the fair value of the net assets acquired may be used as the measure of the purchase price. Fair values are determined on various bases, depending on the type of asset or liability. Generally, fair values of assets are based on net realizable values, replacement costs, and appraised values. Liabilities are measured at their discounted present value, using the market rate of interest at the time of the combination.

4. If the net assets are purchased directly, the fair values of the acquired assets and liabilities are recorded on the books of the acquirer. There is no parent–subsidiary relationship because the acquirer did not buy another corporation; it bought the net assets instead.

5. Acquisition of majority control over another company enables the investor to obtain control over the assets without having to pay the full fair value of the assets. Shares can be purchased for cash or other assets. Alternatively, the purchaser can issue its own shares in exchange for the shares of the acquiree. If there is an exchange of shares, the acquirer does not have to give up any cash. The previous holders of the acquiree's shares now hold shares in the acquirer instead.

6. Theoretically, there are three approaches to reporting consolidated financial statements following purchase of control over another corporation: pooling of interests, purchase, and new entity.

   Under the pooling method, the book values of the parent and the subsidiary are simply added together and reported as the consolidated amounts.

   Under purchase accounting, the date-of-acquisition fair values of the subsidiary are added to the parent's book values. The purchase method of consolidation gives the same results as if the net assets had been purchased directly.

With the new-entity method, the fair values of the parent and the subsidiary are added together to form a new basis of accountability for the ongoing economic entity.

7. The pooling method is not permitted for arm's-length business combinations by the *CICA Handbook*, by FASB standards in the U.S.A., or by International Accounting Standards. However, the pooling method is applied to non–arm's-length corporate restructurings, including the combination of companies under common control.

8. Normally, fair values are not recorded on the books of the acquiree; adjustments are made solely on working papers to prepare consolidated financial statements. However, fair values may be recorded on the books of the acquired company if the investor corporation has acquired substantially all of the shares of the subsidiary. This practice is known as *push-down accounting*.

SELF-STUDY PROBLEM 3–1

Ace Corporation acquired Blue Corporation on August 31, 2006. Both corporations have fiscal years ending on August 31. Exhibit 3–10 shows the balance sheet for each corporation as of August 31, 2006, immediately *prior* to the combination, and net income amounts for each corporation for the fiscal year ended August 31, 2006.

The fair values of the assets and liabilities of the two companies at the date of acquisition are shown in Exhibit 3–11. The deferred development costs represent the unamortized amount of the companies' leading-edge products. There is no observable market value for this identifiable intangible asset, but Ace expects to fully recover the costs in future years.

Before the combination, Ace had 1,200,000 common shares issued and outstanding. Blue had 750,000 common shares issued and outstanding.

EXHIBIT 3–10 PRE-COMBINATION BALANCE SHEETS, AUGUST 31, 2006		
	Ace	**Blue**
Cash and cash equivalents	$ 2,350,000	$ 1,200,000
Accounts receivable	2,000,000	1,800,000
Land	5,000,000	—
Machinery and equipment, net	13,500,000	8,400,000
Deferred development costs	600,000	3,100,000
	$23,450,000	$14,500,000
Accounts payable	$ 650,000	$ 1,100,000
Notes payable, long-term	2,000,000	1,000,000
Common shares	15,000,000	6,950,000
Retained earnings	5,800,000	5,450,000
	$23,450,000	$14,500,000
Net income, year ended August 31, 2006	$ 2,450,000	$ 1,300,000

EXHIBIT 3–11   FAIR VALUES, AUGUST 31, 2006

	Ace	Blue
Cash and cash equivalents	$ 2,350,000	$ 1,200,000
Accounts receivable	2,000,000	1,800,000
Land	8,500,000	—
Machinery and equipment, net	11,000,000	11,000,000
Deferred development costs	750,000	4,000,000
Accounts payable	(650,000)	(1,100,000)
Notes payable, long-term	(2,000,000)	(900,000)
Net asset fair value	$21,950,000	$16,000,000

Required:

Prepare the Ace Corporation post-combination balance sheet under each of the following *independent* situations:

1. Ace Corporation purchased the assets and assumed the liabilities of Blue Corporation by paying $2,000,000 cash and issuing long-term installment notes payable of $18,000,000.

2. Ace issued 400,000 common shares for all of the outstanding common shares of Blue. The market value of Ace's shares was $50 per share.

3. Ace purchased 100% of Blue's outstanding common shares from Blue's previous shareholders. As consideration, Ace issued 270,000 common shares and paid $1,000,000 in cash. The market value of Ace's shares was $50 per share.

REVIEW QUESTIONS

3–1 Define the following terms:
   a. Business combination
   b. Control
   c. Net assets
   d. Contingent consideration
   e. Goodwill
   f. Negative goodwill
   g. Exchange of shares
   h. Hostile takeover
   i. Statutory amalgamation
   j. Reverse takeover
   k. Purchase price discrepancy
   l. Pooling-of-interests method
   m. Purchase method
   n. New-entity method
   o. Corporate restructuring
   p. Push-down accounting

3–2 Describe the two basic types of acquisitions that can result in a business combination.

3–3 What are the three steps in accounting for a business combination?

3–4 What are the forms of consideration that can be used in a business combination?

3–5 When one corporation buys the assets or assets and liabilities of another company, at what values are the acquired assets recorded on the buyer's books?

3–6 What are the alternative methods of accounting for a contingent consideration in a business combination?

3–7 In general, how would fair values be determined for productive assets?

3–8 In general, how would fair values be determined for liabilities?

3–9 What is the appropriate accounting for negative goodwill?

3–10 When an acquirer buys the net assets of another company by issuing shares, what is the relationship between the two companies after the transaction has taken place?

3–11 What are the advantages for the acquirer of obtaining control over assets by a purchase of shares rather than by a direct purchase of assets?

3–12 What are the disadvantages for the acquirer of obtaining control by a purchase of shares?

3–13 How can an acquirer obtain control if the management of the acquiree is hostile to the business combination?

3–14 For the acquirer, what is the difference in income tax treatment of goodwill acquired in a direct purchase of assets as compared to goodwill acquired in a purchase of shares?

3–15 From an income tax standpoint, what may be the disadvantages for an acquirer in obtaining control through a purchase of shares rather than by a direct purchase of net assets?

3–16 If an acquirer issues a tender offer, is it necessary for the offering company to buy all of the shares tendered?

3–17 Company P issues its shares in exchange for the shares of Company S. After the exchange, who owns the newly issued shares of P?

3–18 In an exchange of shares, how can the acquirer be identified?

3–19 What is the most common reason for a combination of a public company and a private company accomplished by means of a reverse takeover?

3–20 In consolidated statements following a reverse takeover, which company's net assets are reported at fair values: the legal acquirer or the legal subsidiary?

3–21 Why is a reverse takeover often immediately followed by a name change of the legal parent corporation?

3–22 In what form(s) of business combination do the combining companies cease to exist as separate legal entities?

3–23 When a business combination is executed via a purchase of shares, at what values are the assets and liabilities of the acquiree recorded on the books of the acquirer?

3–24 Briefly explain the difference between these three approaches to preparing consolidated financial statements:

  a. Pooling-of-interests method

  b. Purchase method

  c. New-entity method

3–25 What is the logic underlying the use of pooling-of-interests reporting for a business combination?

3–26 How prevalent is pooling-of-interests reporting in Canada?

3–27 What is a corporate restructuring? How are restructurings accounted for?

3–28 What is fresh-start accounting and when would it be appropriate?

3–29 Company P has 800,000 common shares outstanding. The shares are traded on the Toronto Stock Exchange. The founders and managers of Company P hold 200,000 shares, and another 250,000 are held by institutional investors as long-term investments. P's board of directors has approved issuance of an additional 300,000 shares to acquire the net assets of Company S. What difficulties may arise in attempting to set a value on the newly issued shares in order to determine the cost of the acquisition?

3–30 Under what circumstances would a corporation be able to obtain control over the net assets of another corporation for less than the fair value of those net assets? Explain.

3–31 If negative goodwill is still remaining after allocations, the remaining amount is recognized as an extraordinary gain. Does this meet the definition of an extraordinary item?

3–32 Define *push-down accounting*.

3–33 Under what circumstances is push-down accounting most likely to be used?

CASES

CASE 3–1   Ames Brothers Ltd.

Ames Brothers, Ltd. (ABL) is a relatively small producer of petrochemicals located in Sarnia. The common shares of the firm are publicly traded on the Toronto Stock Exchange, while the non-voting preferred shares are traded on the over-the-counter market. Because of the strategic competitive position of the firm, there was considerable recent interest in the shares of the company. During 2006, much active trading occurred, pushing the price of the common shares from less than $8 to more than $20 by the end of the year. Similarly, the trading interest in the preferred shares pushed the dividend yield from 12% to only 9%.

Shortly after the end of 2006, three other firms made public announcements about the extent of their holdings in ABL shares. Silverman Mines announced that it had acquired, on the open market, 32% of the common shares of ABL; Hislop Industries announced that it had acquired 24% of ABL's common shares in a private transaction with an individual who had previously been ABL's major shareholder; and Render Resources announced that it had accumulated a total of 58% of ABL's preferred shares.

However, Silverman Mines and Hislop Industries are related. The Patterson Power Corporation owns 72% of the voting shares of Silverman Mines and 38% of the voting shares of Hislop Mines. There are no other large holdings of stock of either Silverman or Hislop. Render Resources is not related to Silverman, Hislop, or Patterson.

Required:

a. Has a business combination occurred in 2006, with respect to ABL, as the term "business combination" is used in the context of the *CICA Handbook* recommendations? Explain fully.

b. What implications do the various accumulations of ABL shares have for the financial reporting (for 2006 and following years) for:

1. Silverman Mines
2. Hislop Industries
3. Render Resources
4. Patterson Power Corporation

CASE 3–2   Sudair Ltd.

On February 7, 2006, Sudair Ltd. and Albertair Ltd. jointly announced a merger of the two regional airlines. Sudair had assets totalling $500 million and had 1,000,000 common shares outstanding. Albertair had assets amounting to $400 million and 600,000 shares outstanding. Under the terms of the merger, Sudair will issue two new Sudair shares for each share of Albertair outstanding. The two companies will then merge their administrative and operating structures and will coordinate their routes and schedules to improve interchange between the two lines and to enable the combined fleet of nine jet aircraft to be more efficiently used. Both companies are publicly owned.

Required:

How should the merger of Sudair and Albertair be reported?

CASE 3–3   Pool Inc. and Spartin Ltd.

Pool Inc. and Spartin Ltd. are both public companies. The common shares of Pool have been selling in a range of $30 to $43 per share over the past year, with recent prices in the area of $33. Spartin's common shares have been selling at between $18 and $23; recently the price has been hovering around $20.

The two companies are in related lines of business. In view of the increasing exposure of the companies to world competition arising from the reduction in tariff barriers, the boards of directors have approved an agreement in principle to combine the two businesses. The boards have also agreed that the combination should take the form of a share exchange, with one share of Pool equivalent to two shares of Spartin in the exchange.

The manner of executing the combination has not yet been decided. Three possibilities are under consideration:

1. Pool could issue one new share in exchange for two of Spartin's shares.

2. Spartin could issue two new shares in exchange for each of Pool's shares.

3. A new corporation could be formed, PS Enterprises Inc., which would issue one share in exchange for each share of Spartin and two shares in exchange for each share of Pool.

The directors are uncertain as to the accounting implications of the three alternatives. They believe that the fair values of the assets and liabilities of both companies are approximately equal to their book values. They have asked you to prepare a report in which you explain how the accounting results would differ under the three share exchange alternatives. They have provided you with the condensed balance sheets of both companies. Pool Inc. currently has 1,600,000 common shares outstanding, and Spartin Ltd. has 1,200,000 shares outstanding.

Required:

Prepare the report requested by the boards of directors.

Condensed Balance Sheets

	Pool Inc.	Spartin Ltd.
Current assets	$ 7,000,000	$ 4,500,000
Capital assets	63,000,000	22,500,000
	$70,000,000	$27,000,000
Current liabilities	$ 6,000,000	$ 1,500,000
Long-term debt	14,000,000	5,500,000
Common shares	17,000,000	16,000,000
Retained earnings	33,000,000	4,000,000
	$70,000,000	$27,000,000

CASE 3–4 Boatsman Boats Limited

Boatsman Boats Limited (BBL) is a dealer in pleasure boats located in Kingston, Ontario. The company is incorporated under the *Ontario Business Corporations Act* and is wholly owned by its founder and president, Jim Boatsman. In 2005, BBL had revenues of $2,500,000 with total assets of about $1,000,000 at year-end.

Late in 2006, Jim Boatsman reached an agreement with Clyde Stickney for the combination of BBL and Stickney Skate Corporation (SSC). SSC is a manufacturer of ice skates and is located in Ottawa, Ontario. SSC's 2005 revenue totalled $2,000,000 and year-end assets totalled $1,500,000. Clyde Stickney is president and general manager of SSC, and he owns 65% of the SSC shares. The other 35% is owned by Clyde's former partner, who left the business several years previously because of a policy disagreement with Clyde.

Clyde and Jim decided to combine the two businesses because their seasonal business cycles were complementary. Common ownership would permit working capital to be shifted from one company to the other, and the larger asset base and more stable financial performance of the combined company would probably increase the total debt capacity.

Under the terms of the agreement, BBL would issue common shares to Clyde Stickney in exchange for Clyde's shares in SSC. As a result of the exchange, Jim's share of BBL would drop to 60% of the outstanding BBL shares, and Clyde would hold the remaining 40%. Clyde and Jim signed a shareholders' agreement that gave each of them equal representation on the BBL board of directors.

As the end of 2006 approached, Jim, Clyde, and CA (the BBL auditor) were discussing the appropriate treatment of the business combination on BBL's 2006 financial statements. Clyde was of the opinion that CA should simply add together the assets and liabilities of the two companies at their book values (after eliminating intercompany balances and transactions, of course). Jim, on the other hand, thought that the combination had resulted in a new, stronger entity, and that the financial statements should reflect that fact by revaluing the net assets of both BBL and SSC to reflect fair values at the date of the combination. CA, however, insisted that only SSC's net assets should be revalued, and then only to the extent of the 65% of the assets that were represented by BBL's shareholdings in SSC.

While Jim and Clyde disagreed with each other on the appropriate valuation of the assets, both disagreed with CA's proposal. Jim and Clyde clearly controlled SSC through BBL, they argued; that was the whole point of the combination. In their opinion it would be inappropriate to value the same assets on two different bases, 65% current value and 35% book value. If only SSC's assets were to be revalued, then they reasoned that the assets at least should be valued consistently, at 100% of fair value.

In an effort to resolve the impasse that was developing, Jim and Clyde hired an independent consultant to advise them. The consultant was asked (1) to advise the shareholders on the pros and cons of each alternative in BBL's specific case, and (2) to make a recommendation on a preferred approach. The consultant was supplied with the condensed balance sheets of BBL and SSC as shown in Exhibit A, and with CA's estimate of fair values (Exhibit B).

Required:

Prepare the consultant's report. Assume that the business combination took place on December 31, 2006.

EXHIBIT A

CONDENSED BALANCE SHEETS OF BBL AND SSC

Condensed Balance Sheets
December 31, 2006

	Boatsman Boats Ltd.	Stickney Skate Corp.
Current assets	$ 600,000	$ 350,000
Land	—	250,000
Buildings and equipment	—	2,500,000
Accumulated depreciation	—	(1,500,000)
Furniture and fixtures	800,000	300,000
Accumulated depreciation	(330,000)	(100,000)
Investment in Stickney Skate Corp.	1,300,000	—
Total assets	$2,370,000	$ 1,800,000
Current liabilities	$ 370,000	$ 400,000
Long-term liabilities	300,000	900,000
Common shares	1,500,000	200,000
Retained earnings	200,000	300,000
Total equities	$2,370,000	$ 1,800,000

ESTIMATED FAIR VALUES OF BBL AND SSC

Net Asset Fair Values
December 31, 2006

	Boatsman Boats Ltd.	Stickney Skate Corp.
Current assets	$ 600,000	$ 350,000
Land	—	700,000
Buildings and equipment:		
estimated replacement cost new	—	5,000,000
less depreciation	—	(3,000,000)
Furniture and fixtures:		
estimated replacement cost new	1,300,000	500,000
less depreciation	(520,000)	(240,000)
Current liabilities	(370,000)	(400,000)
Long-term liabilities*	(270,000)	(930,000)
Net asset fair value	$ 740,000	$ 1,980,000

* Discounted at current long-term interest rates.

[ICAO]

CASE 3–5   Growth Inc.

Growth Inc. has just acquired control of Minor Ltd. by buying 100% of Minor's outstanding shares for $6,500,000 cash. The condensed balance sheet for Minor on the date of acquisition is shown below.

Growth is a public company. Currently, it has two bank covenants. The first requires Growth to maintain a specific debt-to-equity ratio and the second requires a specific current ratio. If these covenants are violated, the bank loan will be payable on demand. Growth is in a very competitive business. To encourage its employees to stay, it has adopted a new business plan that provides managers a bonus based on a percentage of net income.

The president of Growth Inc., Teresa, has hired you, CA, to assist her with the accounting for Minor.

In order to account for the acquisition, Growth's management has had all of Minor's capital assets appraised by two separate, independent engineering consultants. One consultant appraised the capital assets at $7,800,000 in their present state. The other consultant arrived at a lower figure of $7,100,000, based on the assumption that imminent technological changes would soon decrease the value-in-use of Minor's capital assets by about 10%.

The asset amount for the leased building is the discounted present value of the remaining lease payments on a warehouse that Minor leased to Growth Inc. five years ago. The lease is non-cancellable and title to the building will transfer to Growth at the end of the lease term. The lease has 15 years yet to run, and the annual lease payments are $500,000 per year. The interest rate implicit in the lease was 9%.

Minor's debentures are thinly traded on the open market. Recent sales have indicated that these bonds are currently yielding about 14%. The bonds mature in 10 years.

The future income tax balance is the accumulated balance of CCA/depreciation temporary differences. The management of Minor sees no likelihood of the balance being reduced in the foreseeable future, because projected capital expenditures will enter the CCA classes in amounts that will more than offset the amount of depreciation for the older assets.

The book value of Minor's inventory appears to approximate replacement cost. However, an overstock of some items of finished goods may require temporary price reductions of about 10% in order to reduce inventory to more manageable levels.

Required:

Provide a report for Teresa outlining how the assets of Minor Ltd. should be valued for purposes of preparing consolidated financial statements. She wants you to identify alternatives and support your decision.

Minor Ltd.
Condensed Balance Sheet

Cash	$ 200,000
Accounts receivable	770,000
Inventories	1,000,000
Capital assets (net)	5,000,000
Leased building	4,030,000
	$11,000,000
Accounts payable	$ 300,000
8% debentures payable	7,000,000
Future income taxes	700,000
Common shares	1,000,000
Retained earnings	2,000,000
	$11,000,000

CASE 3–6   Wonder Amusements

Wonder Amusements Limited (WAL) was incorporated over 40 years ago as an amusement park and golf course. Over time, a nearby city has grown to the point where it borders on WAL's properties. In recent years WAL's owners, who are all members of one family, have seen WAL's land values increase significantly. WAL's majority shareholder, Howard Smith, owns 55% of the outstanding shares and is not active in WAL's day-to-day activities.

Last year, Howard hired a new chief executive officer, Leo Titan, who has a reputation for being an aggressive risk taker. Howard is committed, and has the personal financial resources required, to support Leo's plans.

Eight months ago, WAL became the successful bidder for a new sports franchise, in conjunction with a minority partner. Under the terms of the franchise agreement, WAL is required to build a sports arena, which is currently being constructed on a section of the amusement park. Another section of the amusement park is being relocated to ensure that the entrances to the arena are close to public transportation and parking. Consequently, some of the rides will be relocated. WAL is the sole owner of the arena at present.

The sports franchise is separately incorporated as Northern Sports Limited (NSL); WAL holds 75% of the shares in the company. Another bid is being prepared by NSL to obtain a second sports franchise so that the arena can be used more often. NSL will be required to lease space from WAL when the arena is completed in about 22 months.

For the first two sports seasons, NSL will have to lease arena space from Aggressive Limited (AL). During this time, NSL does not expect to be profitable because:

- it may take time to build a competitive team
- AL is charging a high rent, and is not giving NSL a share of concession revenue;
- AL cannot make the better dates (e.g., Saturday nights) available to NSL to attract sports fans, and
- as a newcomer to the league, NSL is restricted with regard to the players who are available to it and the days of the week it can play in its home city.

Consequently, NSL has arranged to borrow funds from WAL and from others to finance costs and losses.

Your employer, Fabio & Fox, Chartered Accountants, has conducted the audit of WAL for several years. WAL has tended to be marginally profitable one year and then have losses the next year. The company has continued to operate because the directors knew the real estate holdings were becoming increasingly valuable.

Leo is expected to oversee the expanded accounting and finance functions in the company. Leo has met with you and the partner in charge of the WAL audit and has discussed various issues related to the year ending September 30, 2006. His comments are provided in Exhibit C.

You have been asked by the partner to prepare for him a report, which will be used for the next meeting with Leo. He would like you to discuss the accounting and audit implications related to your discussion with Leo. The partner wants a thorough analysis of all important issues as well as support for your position.

In your review of documents, and as a result of various conversations, you have learned the following:

1. The arena will be mortgaged, but only for about 50% of its expected cost. Lenders are concerned about the special-use nature of the arena and whether it will be successfully rented for other events, such as concerts.

2. The mortgage lenders to WAL and the minority shareholders in NSL are both expected to want to see appraisals and financial statements before deciding to invest. Covenants will be required by the lenders to ensure that excessive expenditures are not undertaken and that cash is preserved.

3. Leo does not intend to consolidate NSL until it is profitable. The investment in NSL will be reported on WAL's financial statements at cost. Thus, the WAL financial statements will also be used for income tax purposes.

4. WAL's minority shareholders are not active in the business and want quarterly financial statements in order to monitor progress and assess Leo's performance. The minority shareholders have all expressed concern over Leo's growth strategy over the past year. Many are approaching their retirement years and are relying on WAL to supplement their retirement income.

Required:

Prepare the report.

EXHIBIT C

NOTES FROM DISCUSSIONS WITH LEO TITAN

1. In order to build a road to the arena's parking lot, two holes of the 18-hole golf course will be relocated next spring. Costs of $140,000 are expected to be incurred this year in design, tree planting, ground preparation, and grass seeding in order to have the arena ready for next spring. These costs are to be capitalized as part of the golf course lands, along with the related property taxes of $13,000 and interest of $15,000.

2. In May 2006, WAL acquired for $4.25 million all of the shares of an amusement park in a different city, when its land lease expired. The amusement park company was wound up and the equipment, rides, concessions, and other assets are being transported to WAL at a cost of $350,000. The estimated fair value of the assets and liabilities (according to Leo) is as follows:

Concession prizes (e.g., stuffed animals)	$ 22,500
Rides and games	4,200,000
Equipment and parts	1,650,000
Electrical supplies	75,000
Lighting and signs	100,000
Estimated present value of tax loss carryforward	700,000
	6,747,500
Liabilities	1,200,000
Net Assets	$5,547,500

WAL expects to spend approximately $400,000 in getting the assets in operating order and $500,000 on foundations and site preparations for the rides. Leo wants to "capitalize as much as possible."

3. Approximately $600,000 will be used to relocate rides that are currently on land that is needed for the arena. This amount is to be capitalized, net of scrap recovery on dismantled and redundant equipment of $60,000. Virtually all of the rides were fully depreciated years ago.

4. To assist in financing the new ventures, WAL sold excess land to developers who intend to construct a shopping centre, office buildings, and expensive homes that will be adjunct to the golf course and away from the amusement park. The developers and WAL agreed to these terms:

Paid to WAL on May 1, 2006	$ 6,000,000
To be paid to WAL on March 1, 2007	10,000,000
To be paid to WAL on March 1, 2008	8,000,000
	$24,000,000

The land is to be turned over to the developers on or about February 1, 2007, but the sale is to be reported in 2006.

5. An additional "contingent profit" will accrue to WAL if the developers earn a return on investment of more than 25% when they resell the newly constructed buildings. Leo wants a note to the 2006 financial statements that describes the potential of a contingent gain.

6. The excess land that was sold to the developers was carried on WAL's books at $1.35 million, on a pro rata cost basis. Leo would like to revalue the remaining land from $5.4 million to about $100 million in the 2006 financial statements.

7. The golf course has been unprofitable in recent years. However, green fees are to be raised and specific tee-off times will be allotted to a private club, which is currently being organized. Members of the private club will pay a non-refundable entrance fee of $2,000 per member plus $100 per month for five years. The $2,000 is to be recorded as revenue on receipt. Approximately $350,000 is to be spent to upgrade club facilities.

8. Leo wants to capitalize all costs of NSL on NSL's books until it has completed its first year of operations. In addition, to the franchise fee, $20 million will have to be spent on the following:

Acquisition of player contracts	$12,000,000
Advertising and promotion	1,500,000
Equipment	3,200,000
Wages, benefits and bonuses	6,800,000
Other operating costs	3,300,000
	26,800,000
Less:	
Revenue—ticket sales	(6,000,000)
Revenue—other	(800,000)
	$20,000,000

The value of players can change quickly, depending on their performance, injuries, and other factors.

9. The new sports arena will have private boxes in which a company can entertain groups of clients. The boxes are leased on a five-year contract basis, and they must be occupied for a minimum price per night. To date, 12 boxes have been leased for $15,000 per box for a five-year period, exclusive of nightly charges. A down payment of $3,000 was required; the payments have been recorded as revenue.

10. Three senior officers of WAL, including Leo, receive bonuses based on income before income taxes. The three have agreed to have their fiscal 2006 bonus accrued in 2007 along with their 2007 bonuses. Actual payments to them are scheduled for January 2008.

11. Insurance premiums on the construction activity that is taking place total $1.4 million in fiscal 2006, and to date they have been capitalized.

12. A $500,000 fee was paid to a mortgage broker to arrange financing for WAL. This amount has been recorded as "other assets." No financing has been arranged to date.

[CICA]

CASE 3–7   Aquatic Biotechnology

Aquatic Biotechnology Incorporated (ABI) is a medium-sized private company operating an aquaculture business in Eastern Canada. The company has been in operation since the late 1980s, and during the second half of the 1990s it grew at a rapid pace through increased sales and the acquisition of minor competitors.

ABI has an October 31 year-end. It is now November 15, 2006, and you, CA, are working on the 2006 audit. Your firm, Linkletter & Cormier Chartered Accountants, has conducted the audit of ABI for several years and has always considered it to be a routine audit engagement. The audit senior on the engagement recently resigned from the firm, and you have been asked to be the senior on the audit. All October 31 inventory counts and routine confirmations have been dealt with, and you have been provided with the audit planning files. These files are summarized in Exhibit D.

The corporate structure of ABI is based on management's philosophy that vertical integration will allow this growth-oriented business to achieve its objectives. ABI controls nearly all aspects of the supply chain, from growth of the product to processing and delivery to the customer. ABI operates the hatchery, where each of the three major products (salmon, trout, and scallops) are hatched, the fish farms where growth takes place, and the processing plant where smoking and packaging occur. ABI also owns Marine Tech Limited (MTL), a supplier of boats, nets, and gear to the Canadian market. MTL provides nearly all supplies, repairs, and maintenance for the corporate group.

Scallop farming is a relatively new area of aquaculture in which ABI has invested a substantial amount of capital for research and development. Scallops are grown in a "cage" that sits on the ocean floor in an area that does not experience problems such as strong tides and bacteria, which could destroy the crop. As with many aquaculture products, scallops can take from 24 to 30 months to reach a marketable size. ABI has yet to earn any money from scallop farming, but it is confident its new system will be successful.

ABI has been working on scallop farming technologies for about five years. Previous years' audit files indicate that the costs related to scallop farming had been expensed, as the company lost much of its stock during the winter months. ABI is confident that its new cage style, developed in 2005, will result in a tremendous crop ready for 2007. At year-end, the scallop stocks were checked by the company and by an aquaculture expert hired by your firm, and it was determined that the stock is at 75% of its marketable size. However, the aquaculture expert would not comment on the likelihood that the stock would reach full maturity. At maturity, it is estimated that the crop will be 500,000 kilograms. Costs to date related to the 2007 harvest have been $1.425 million, of which $1.2 million has been incurred in fiscal 2006.

Salmon and trout farming are major divisions of ABI. Both have been successful for a number of years, although the selling price of salmon decreased slightly in 2006. The salmon division has provided substantial cash flows to the company, due to the perfected method of growth and low marketing costs associated with the product. Trout farming is a relatively new division of the company and has been moderately successful for the past two years.

Despite the positive cash flows generated by the salmon division, ABI has had difficulty in managing its cash flows due to substantial investments in scallop farming. In August 2006, ABI decided to refinance much of its debt to consolidate loans. The Business Development Bank, a federal government agency, agreed to consolidate most of ABI's debt and lent ABI an additional $5 million for five years, with the first year to be interest-free. The bank further agreed to extend the interest-free period for each fiscal year that ABI is able to maintain net income at $1 million or more. A loan arrangement fee of $500,000 was paid in order to cover the bank's costs to consolidate the debt. The bank requires ABI to maintain a current ratio above 1, given the current level of debt. The new debt structure has allowed ABI to improve its cash position.

You have just reviewed the working papers and have met with ABI's controller, Jim Gibbons, to gather information related to the audit (Exhibit E) and a set of draft financial statements (Exhibit F). The engagement partner has asked you to prepare a memo summarizing the relevant accounting and audit planning issues in preparation for her meeting with ABI to discuss the ongoing audit.

Required:

Prepare this memo.

EXHIBIT D

EXTRACTS FROM THE AUDIT PLANNING FILES

1. Materiality has been set at $1.4 million since ABI is a continuing client and has always had low business risk and strong controls.

2. Preliminary tests of controls were performed in August during the audit planning, and no weaknesses were noted.

3. Bank confirmations have been sent to the appropriate financial institutions.

4. A signed engagement letter for the audit has been obtained from ABI.

5. Computer-assisted audit techniques have not been carried out in previous years due to difficulties in extracting data from ABI's database. Therefore, additional tests of controls and analytical procedures are necessary.

EXHIBIT E

INFORMATION OBTAINED FROM JIM GIBBONS

1. During the year, ABI acquired Bay Mussels Limited (BML), a large mussel grower in the area, to diversify its product lines. ABI paid $4.75 million to acquire 100% of the outstanding shares of BML. BML's net tangible assets were valued as follows on the date of acquisition:

	Book Value	Market Value
Current assets	$ 1,986,773	$ 1,986,773
Non-current assets	14,686,934	16,437,593
Current liabilities	2,089,657	2,089,657
Non-current liabilities	10,768,540	11,239,415

2. During September, ABI began the phase-in of its new information system. It is a resource planning software package for medium-scale enterprises that allows integration of all aspects of business, from production to sales to financial accounting. As of October 31, the financial accounting modules were fully implemented, and ABI was conducting its own testing while running the system in parallel with its old database. During testing, Jim Gibbons uncovered a number of unauthorized transactions in the database. Since their dollar amounts were insignificant, they have not been adjusted for. Jim believes the new system will allow ABI to better establish strategic direction and evaluate its profitability by product line.

3. Jim has not yet recorded revenue for the scallop production, but would like to record as much as possible in 2006, since the product is 75% of its marketable size and orders for the coming year are already being received. The price per kilogram can be reasonably estimated at approximately $20.00, although supply may affect the market price.

4. Since early November, ABI has been holding discussions with a major competitor to sell its trout division. ABI believes that, although the division has been relatively successful, scallop farming is much more attractive in the long run. The buyer has made a preliminary offer of $2.8 million for the trout division, and ABI management expects that the cash flow will assist the com-

pany in getting through the winter until the scallop sales begin. The buyer's offer expires on November 30, but the buyer may be open to further negotiations.

EXHIBIT F

EXTRACTS FROM BALANCE SHEET AND INCOME STATEMENT

Extracts from Balance Sheet
As of October 31 (in thousands)

	2006 (unaudited)	2005 (audited)
Assets		
Current		
Cash	$ 533	$ 555
Accounts receivable (net)	115	283
Inventory—salmon and other	1,650	1,030
Inventory—scallops	4,568	4,396
Prepaid expenses	1,435	—
	8,301	6,264
Property, plant and equipment (net)	67,913	64,423
Deferred costs (scallop cages)	3,007	500
Other	2,684	3,774
	$81,905	$ 74,961
Liabilities		
Current		
Bank indebtedness	$ 2,103	$ 1,131
Accounts payable and accruals	2,804	2,332
Current portion of long-term debt	3,145	2,365
	8,052	5,828
Long-term debt	61,500	58,243
Future income taxes	1,345	1,297
	70,897	65,368
Shareholders' Equity		
Share capital	10	10
Retained earnings	10,998	9,583
	11,008	9,593
	$81,905	$74,961

Extracts from Income Statement
For years ended October 31 (in thousands)

	2006 (unaudited)	2005 (audited)	2004 (audited)
Revenue			
Salmon	$ 27,345	$ 29,879	$ 26,567
Trout	13,588	10,673	9,453
Mussels	1,647	—	—
Fishing gear and other	32,486	30,788	29,765
	75,066	71,340	65,785
Cost of goods sold			
Salmon	15,714	15,917	13,359
Trout	6,280	5,140	7,860
Mussels	1,400	—	—
Scallops	—	1,310	1,260
Fishing gear and other	22,962	21,899	20,324
	46,356	44,266	42,803
Gross margin	28,710	27,074	22,982
Expenses			
Salaries and benefits	12,879	10,547	9,643
Selling and advertising	5,225	3,426	2,784
General, administrative and other	3,423	2,879	1,866
Interest on long-term debt	4,288	4,562	4,848
Research—scallop cages	—	5,250	3,078
Loan arrangement fee	500	—	—
Total expenses	26,315	26,664	22,219
Income from operations	2,395	410	763
Gain on acquisition of BML	345	—	—
Net income before income taxes	2,740	410	763
Income taxes	1,325	156	298
Net income	$ 1,415	$ 254	$ 465

[CICA]

PROBLEMS

P3–1

Company L and Company E have reached agreement in principle to combine their operations. However, the boards of directors are undecided as to the best way to accomplish the combination. Several alternatives are under consideration:

1. L acquires the net assets of E (including the liabilities) for $2,000,000 cash.

2. L acquires all of the assets of E (but not the liabilities) for $2,800,000 cash.

3. L acquires the net assets of E by issuing 120,000 shares in L, valued at $2,000,000.

4. L acquires all of the shares of E by exchanging them for 120,000 newly issued shares in L.

The current, condensed balance sheets of L and of E are shown below. Prior to the combination, L has 480,000 shares outstanding and E has 60,000 shares outstanding.

Required:

a. In a comparative, columnar format, show how the consolidated balance sheet of L would appear immediately after the combination under each of the four alternatives using the purchase method.

b. For each of the four alternatives, briefly state who owns the shares of each corporation and whether L and E are related companies.

Condensed Balance Sheets
(thousands of dollars)

	L Co.		E Co.	
	Balance sheet	Fair values	Balance sheet	Fair values
Current assets	$ 8,000	$ 8,000	$ 600	$ 600
Capital assets	12,000	16,000	800	1,400
Investments	—	—	600	400
	$20,000		$2,000	
Current liabilities	$ 4,000	6,000	200	200
Long-term liabilities	6,000	6,000	800	600
Future income taxes	2,000	2,000	200	—
Common shares	2,000	20,000	400	1,800
Retained earnings	6,000		400	
	$20,000		$2,000	

P3–2

North Ltd. acquired 100% of the voting shares of South Ltd. In exchange, North Ltd. issued 50,000 common shares, with a market value of $10 per share, to the common shareholders of South Ltd. Both companies have a December 31 year-end, and this transaction occurred on December 31, 2006. The outstanding pre-ferred shares of South Ltd. did not change hands. The call price of the South Ltd. preferred shares is equal to their book value.

Following are the balance sheets of the two companies at December 31, 2006, before the transactions took place:

Balance Sheets
As at December 31, 2006

	North Ltd.		South Ltd.	
	Book value	Fair value	Book value	Fair value
Current assets	$ 150,000	$200,000	$210,000	$260,000
Capital assets, net	950,000	820,000	780,000	860,000
Goodwill	110,000		—	
Total	$1,210,000		$990,000	
Current liabilities	$ 100,000	$ 90,000	$165,000	185,000
Long-term liabilities	500,000	520,000	200,000	230,000
Preferred shares	—		270,000	270,000
Common shares	300,000		100,000	
Retained earnings	310,000		255,000	
Total	$1,210,000		$990,000	

Required:

Prepare the consolidated balance sheet for the date of acquisition, December 31, 2006, under each of the following methods:

a. Pooling of interests

b. Purchase

c. New entity

[CGA–Canada, adapted]

P3–3

On December 31, 2006, the balance sheets of the Bee Company and the See Company are as follows:

	Bee Company	See Company
Cash	$ 400,000	$ 700,000
Accounts receivable	1,600,000	1,800,000
Inventories	1,000,000	500,000
Plant and equipment (net)	3,500,000	5,000,000
Total assets	$6,500,000	$8,000,000
Current liabilities	$ 600,000	$ 300,000
Long-term liabilities	900,000	600,000
Common shares	2,500,000	1,000,000
Retained earnings	2,500,000	6,100,000
Total equities	$6,500,000	$8,000,000

Bee Company has 100,000 common shares outstanding, and See Company has 45,000 shares outstanding. On January 1, 2007, Bee Company issues an additional 90,000 common shares to See Company at $90 per share in return for all of the assets and liabilities of that company. See Company distributes Bee

Company's common shares to its shareholders in return for their outstanding common shares, and ceases to exist as a separate legal entity. At the time of this transaction, the cash, accounts receivable, inventories, and current liabilities of both companies have fair values equal to their carrying values. The plant and equipment and long-term liabilities have fair values as follows:

	Bee Company	See Company
Plant and equipment (net)	$3,900,000	$5,300,000
Long-term liabilities	600,000	500,000

In addition, See Company has a patent worth $100,000.

Required:

1. What is the amount of goodwill that would be recorded for this business combination?

2. In completing the purchase price allocation, what other intangible assets could potentially exist that a value could be allocated to instead of (or in addition to) goodwill?

3. Prepare a balance sheet at January 1, 2007, for Bee Company after the purchase.

[SMA, adapted]

P3–4

On December 31, 2006, Retail Ltd. purchased 100% of the outstanding shares of Supply Corporation by issuing Retail Ltd. shares worth $960,000 at current market prices. Supply Corporation was a supplier of merchandise to Retail Ltd.; Retail had purchased over 80% of Supply's total output in 2006. Supply had experienced declining profitability for many years, and in 2004 began experiencing losses. By December 31, 2006, Supply had accumulated tax-loss carryforwards amounting to $140,000 after tax. In contrast, Retail Ltd. was quite profitable, and analysts predicted that Retail's positioning in the retail market was well suited to weather economic downturns without undue deterioration in profit levels.

The balance sheet for Supply Corporation at the date of acquisition is shown below, together with estimates of the fair values of Supply's recorded assets and liabilities. In addition, Supply held exclusive Canadian rights to certain production processes; the fair value of these rights was estimated to be $200,000.

Required:

Explain what values should be assigned to Supply Corporation's assets and liabilities when Retail Ltd. prepares its consolidated financial statements (including goodwill, if any).

Supply Corporation
Balance Sheet
December 31, 2006

			Fair values
Current assets:			
Cash	$ 20,000		$ 20,000
Accounts receivable (net)	40,000		40,000
Inventories	210,000		200,000
		$ 270,000	
Plant, property, and equipment:			
Buildings	$ 600,000		500,000
Machinery and equipment	500,000		370,000
Accumulated depreciation	(450,000)		
	$ 650,000		
Land	200,000		360,000
		850,000	
Investments in shares		100,000	110,000
Total assets		$1,220,000	
Current liabilities:			
Accounts payable	$ 60,000		60,000
Unearned revenue	170,000		150,000
Current portion of long-term debt	100,000		100,000
		$ 330,000	
Bonds payable		400,000	380,000
Shareholders' equity:			
Common shares	$ 150,000		
Retained earnings	340,000		
		490,000	
Total liabilities and shareholders' equity		$1,220,000	

P3–5

Askill Corporation (Askill), a public corporation, has concluded negotiations with Basket Corporation (Basket) for the purchase of all of Basket's net assets at fair market value, effective January 1, 2007. An examination at that date by independent experts disclosed that the fair market value of Basket's inventories was $300,000; the fair market value of its machinery and equipment was $320,000.

Additional Information:

- The fair value of the patent was $62,000. The value of the accounts receivable and of the current and long-term liabilities was equal to their book value.
- The purchase agreement stated that the purchase price of all the net assets will be $540,000 payable in cash.
- Both corporations have December 31 year-ends. The balance sheets of both corporations, as at the date of the implementation of the purchase agreement (January 1, 2007), are as follows:

	Askill Corp.	Basket Corp.
Cash	$ 700,000	$ —
Accounts receivable	288,000	224,000
Inventories at cost	270,000	248,000
Machinery and equipment—net	412,000	200,000
Patent	—	40,000
Total assets	$1,670,000	$712,000
Current liabilities	$ 60,000	$ 70,000
Long-term liabilities	520,000	300,000
Capital–common shares	200,000	100,000
Retained earnings	890,000	242,000
Total liabilities and shareholders' equity	$1,670,000	$712,000

Required:

1. What is the amount of goodwill that would be recorded for the business combination?

2. Prepare Askill's balance sheet at January 1, 2007.

[CICA, adapted]

P3–6

Par Ltd. purchased 100% of the voting shares of Sub Ltd. for $1,400,000 on October 1, 2006. The balance sheet of Sub Ltd. at that date was:

Sub Ltd.
Balance Sheet
October 1, 2006

	Net book value	Fair market value
Cash	$ 300,000	$300,000
Receivables	410,000	370,000
Inventory	560,000	750,000
Capital assets, net	1,220,000	920,000
	$2,490,000	
Current liabilities	$ 340,000	370,000
Long-term liability	700,000	700,000
Common shares	400,000	
Retained earnings	1,050,000	
	$2,490,000	

Required:

Prepare the eliminating entry (or entries) required *at the date of acquisition* that would be necessary to consolidate the financial statements of Sub Ltd. with those of Par Ltd.

[CGA–Canada, adapted]

P3–7

On December 31, 2006, Prager Limited acquired 100% of the outstanding voting shares of Sabre Limited for $2 million in cash; 75% of the cash was obtained by issuing a five-year note payable. The balance sheets of Prager and Sabre and the fair values of Sabre's identifiable assets and liabilities immediately before the acquisition transaction were as follows:

| | Prager Limited | Sabre Limited | |
		Book value	Fair value
Assets:			
Cash	$ 800,000	$ 100,000	$ 100,000
Accounts receivable	500,000	300,000	300,000
Inventory	600,000	600,000	662,500
Land	900,000	800,000	900,000
Buildings and equipment	6,000,000	1,400,000	1,200,000
Accumulated depreciation	(2,950,000)	(400,000)	
Patents	—	200,000	150,000
	$5,850,000	$3,000,000	
Liabilities and shareholders' equity:			
Accounts payable	$1,000,000	$ 500,000	500,000
Long-term debt	2,000,000	1,000,000	900,000
Common shares	1,500,000	950,000	
Retained earnings	1,350,000	550,000	
	$5,850,000	$3,000,000	

Required:

Prepare the consolidated balance sheet for Prager Limited immediately following the acquisition of Sabre Limited.

[SMA, adapted]

P3–8

On January 4, 2007, Practical Corp. acquired 100% of the outstanding common shares of Silly Inc. by a share-for-share exchange of its own shares valued at $1,000,000. The balance sheets of both companies just prior to the share exchange are shown below. Silly has patents that are not shown on the balance sheet, but that have an estimated fair value of $200,000 and an estimated remaining productive life of four years. Silly's buildings and equipment have an estimated fair value that is $300,000 in excess of book value, and the deferred charges are assumed to have a fair value of zero. Silly's buildings and equipment are being depreciated on the straight-line basis and have a remaining useful life of 10 years. The deferred charges are being amortized over the following three years.

Balance Sheets
December 31, 2006

	Practical	Silly
Cash	$ 110,000	$ 85,000
Accounts and other receivables	140,000	80,000
Inventories	110,000	55,000
Buildings and equipment	1,500,000	800,000
Accumulated depreciation	(700,000)	(400,000)
Deferred charges	—	120,000
	$1,160,000	$740,000
Accounts and other payables	$ 200,000	$100,000
Bonds payable	—	200,000
Future income taxes	60,000	40,000
Common shares*	600,000	150,000
Retained earnings	300,000	250,000
	$1,160,000	$740,000

*Practical = 300,000 shares; Silly = 150,000 shares.

Required:

Prepare a consolidated balance sheet for Practical Corp., immediately following the share exchange.

Appendix 3A Income Tax Allocation

Introduction

In your intermediate accounting course, you undoubtedly studied the topic of income tax allocation. The effects of income tax allocation show up as "future income taxes" on almost all balance sheets, as well as being a component of income tax expense. Future income taxes arise from two causes:

1. temporary differences between accounting income and taxable income, and

2. unrealized tax loss carryforwards.

In the main body of Chapter 3, we avoided any discussion of future income taxes as they relate to business combinations. However, they do play a part in the allocation of the purchase price and the calculation of goodwill. We have left this topic to an appendix because we did not want to obscure the principal issues of accounting for business combinations. Income taxes are not irrelevant, but they are not central to an understanding of business combinations and the reporting of strategic investments.

Temporary differences in business combinations

In general, temporary differences arise because the carrying values of assets (and liabilities) differ from their tax bases. The most common type of temporary difference relates to depreciable tangible capital assets—book depreciation methods *(accounting method)* are usually different from CCA *(tax method)*, and therefore an asset's carrying value is different from its tax basis.

A similar situation arises in business combinations. The cost allocated to an asset in a business combination is based on the asset's fair value. The fair value then becomes its carrying value on the consolidated balance sheet. However, the Canada Revenue Agency doesn't care about an asset's fair value—only its tax basis matters. Therefore, a temporary difference arises and must be dealt with.

For the purpose of consolidated statements, an asset's temporary difference is measured as the difference between its tax basis and the carrying value on the *parent's* consolidated financial statements—which is based on the asset's fair value at the date of acquisition. The relevant carrying value is ***not* its carrying value on the books of the subsidiary**.

Exhibit 3–12 attempts to clarify the situation. Suppose that a newly acquired subsidiary, S, has an asset with a tax basis of $70 and a carrying value *on S's books* of $100. The temporary difference is $30. If S's tax rate is 40%, the future income tax liability pertaining to that asset is $30 × 40% = $12 on *S's separate-entity balance sheet*.

However, the fair value of that asset is $150. P, the parent company, will show the asset on P's *consolidated* balance sheet at $150. For P's consolidated statements, the temporary difference is $150 − $70 = $80. At a 40% tax rate, the future income tax liability pertaining to that asset is $80 × 40% = $32 *on P's consolidated balance sheet*.

The amount shown as the future income tax liability on P's consolidated balance sheet does not affect the tax status of S. S and P are each taxed as a separate corporate entity.

Now, let's apply income tax allocation to the example in the main body of this chapter.

- Purchase Ltd. acquired 100% of the shares of Target Ltd. for $1,200,000.
- The carrying value of Target Ltd.'s net assets *on Target Ltd.'s books* was $800,000.
- Fair-value increments totalled $300,000: $100,000 for land plus $200,000 for buildings and equipment.
- Goodwill was $100,000.

Let's make some additional assumptions:

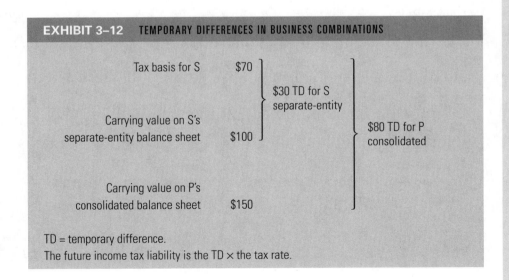

EXHIBIT 3–12   TEMPORARY DIFFERENCES IN BUSINESS COMBINATIONS

Tax basis for S $70

$30 TD for S separate-entity

Carrying value on S's separate-entity balance sheet $100

$80 TD for P consolidated

Carrying value on P's consolidated balance sheet $150

TD = temporary difference.
The future income tax liability is the TD × the tax rate.

- The tax basis for the land is equal to its carrying value on Target Ltd.'s books of $300,000.
- The tax basis of Target Ltd.'s buildings and equipment is $250,000.
- The tax basis for all other Target Ltd. assets and liabilities is equal to their carrying values.
- The tax rate for both Target Ltd. and Purchase Ltd. is 40%.

The relevant amounts can be summarized as follows.

	Land	Buildings & Equipment	Total
Tax basis	$300,000	$250,000	$550,000
Target Ltd.'s carrying value	300,000	350,000	650,000
Fair value to Purchase Ltd.	400,000	550,000	950,000

For Target Ltd., the total temporary difference is $650,000 − $550,000 = $100,000. The future income tax liability is $100,000 × 40% = $40,000. For simplicity's sake, we did not include this amount among the net assets shown in the main body of the chapter.

For Purchase Ltd.'s consolidated statements, the temporary difference is $400,000, and the future income tax liability (at 40%) is $160,000. Exhibit 3–13 shows the allocation of the purchase price with the future income tax liability included. We have fudged the original amounts a bit by subdividing accounts payable and shifting $40,000 to a future income tax liability account, to be consistent with our calculation of Target Ltd.'s temporary differences. This slight adjustment to the original numbers maintains the total amount of Target Ltd.'s net assets at $800,000. Thus we can clearly see what impact future income taxes have on the allocation of the purchase price.

Notice what happens to goodwill. Because we now are recognizing a liability that we did not recognize in Exhibit 3–6, the amount of the purchase price that is

---

EXHIBIT 3–13 ALLOCATION OF PURCHASE PRICE, INCLUDING FUTURE INCOME TAXES

100% purchase of Target Ltd., December 31, 2005

Purchase price	Book value	Fair value	Fair value increment	% share	FVI acquired	$1,200,000
Cash	$ 50,000	$ 50,000	—			
Accounts receivable	150,000	150,000	—			
Inventory	50,000	50,000	—			
Land	300,000	400,000	$ 100,000 × 100% =		$ 100,000	
Buildings and equipment	500,000	550,000	50,000 × 100% =		50,000	
Accumulated depreciation	(150,000)	—	150,000 × 100% =		150,000	
Accounts payable	(60,000)	(60,000)	—			
Future income tax liability	**(40,000)**	**(160,000)**	**(120,000)** × **100% =**		**(120,000)**	
Total fair value increment						180,000
Net asset book value	$ 800,000			× 100% =		800,000
Fair value of assets acquired		$980,000				$ 980,000
Goodwill						$ 220,000

allocated to the net assets goes down. This forces the difference between the purchase price and the net book value to go up, thereby increasing the residual. The residual is goodwill. Therefore, the net result of recognizing the future income taxes is to increase liabilities with an offsetting increase in goodwill.

The recognition of future income taxes based on consolidation fair values has been subject to some criticism. Prior to the effective date of Section 3465 (in 2000), fair-value increments were viewed as permanent differences because the fair-value increments never flow through to the income tax return. Fair-value increments are purely an accounting construct and are irrelevant for tax purposes.

Now, however, temporary differences are recognized in this situation because the current approach to income tax accounting requires a future tax liability to be recognized on the assumption that assets are sold *at their carrying values*, thereby attracting taxation [CICA 3465.02]. Since the carrying values for a purchased subsidiary are the fair values at date of acquisition, strict application of the concept results in the recognition of future income tax liabilities for what are sometimes called "phantom" values.

What happens to these amounts? We shall see in the following chapters that the fair-value increments must be amortized (except for land). As the fair values are amortized, the temporary difference goes down and the future income tax liability is comparably reduced. As well, goodwill (at its heightened amount) is subjected to an impairment test. Therefore, the recognition of future income tax liabilities based on fair values triggers three types of interperiod allocation in following years. Such complexity is the reason that we have chosen to put income tax allocation factors in appendices rather than in the main body of each chapter.

Unrecognized tax loss carryforwards

Some companies have tax loss carryforwards. Sometimes this is a target company's most attractive asset. When substantial amounts of unused tax loss carryforwards exist, a purchaser may be willing to pay quite a lot for those benefits even if the target company appears to be a real loser. To obtain the benefit of tax loss carryforwards, the business combination must be accomplished through an exchange of shares, not by paying cash (or other assets).

The target company may or may not have already recognized those benefits on its balance sheet. Recognition depends on the "more likely than not" criterion prior to acquisition. If the company has serious financial difficulties, the probability criterion won't have been met and therefore the tax losses would not be recorded as a future income tax asset. However, the acquisition may change the probabilities, so that the "more likely than not" criterion may have now been met. Therefore these losses now have value to the parent company. The losses will be recognized at their fair value in the purchase price allocation and be identified as a future income tax asset in the purchaser's consolidated balance sheet.

Using the following data we will consider what will happen in a business combination under two scenarios. XYZ Corporation purchased 100% of the shares of ABC Corporation for $2,000,000 and the fair value of the net assets (excluding tax losses) totalled $1,400,000. In addition, unused tax loss carryforwards that the target company had not recorded on the books have a fair value of $200,000.

If it is more than 50% likely that the benefit will occur, then the purchase price will be allocated as follows:

Purchase price		$2,000,000
Fair value of net assets acquired (excluding tax loss benefits)	$1,400,000	
Future income tax asset	200,000	1,600,000
Goodwill		$ 400,000

If the "more likely than not" criterion has not been met, the purchase price will be recorded as:

Purchase price		$2,000,000
Fair value of net assets acquired (excluding tax loss benefits)	$1,400,000	
Future income tax asset	0	1,400,000
Goodwill		$ 600,000

Note the difference in the goodwill amount depending on whether the "more likely than not" criterion has been met. If the future income tax asset is recognized, this will be considered a temporary difference.

Equity-basis reporting

The preceding brief discussion focused on business combinations. However, exactly the same process is followed for investments that are reported on the equity basis, whether they are unconsolidated subsidiaries or significantly influenced affiliates. Temporary differences and future tax loss carryforward benefits must enter the allocation of the purchase price exactly as illustrated above. The next chapter explains the adjustments that are necessary under the equity method.

Chapter 4

Wholly Owned Subsidiaries: Reporting Subsequent to Acquisition

The previous chapter discussed the conceptual foundations of accounting and financial reporting for business combinations. We saw that control can be acquired by either (1) a direct purchase of the assets or (2) buying voting control in the corporation that owns the assets. The purchase of voting control is the most common method. It also is the most challenging for the accountant.

In Chapter 3 we discussed the alternative approaches to the preparation of consolidated financial statements for an acquired subsidiary. We focused on consolidation at the date of acquisition in order to illustrate the essential characteristics of the different approaches.

Date-of-acquisition consolidation happens only once, and then only for internal reporting. The real issues are post-acquisition consolidation. In this chapter, things get more realistic—and more complex! This chapter explains the basics of consolidation for the income statement and balance sheet after acquisition. We illustrate the following aspects of consolidation for the first and second years after acquisition:

- eliminating transactions that occur between a parent and its subsidiaries
- eliminating unrealized profit on intercompany sales of inventory
- amortizing fair-value increments, and
- reporting non-consolidated subsidiaries on the equity basis.

Both the direct method and the worksheet method will be illustrated.

The two appendices to this chapter deal with issues that arise only from business combinations:

- future income tax calculations, and
- some details on goodwill impairment testing.

Bear in mind that the vast majority of subsidiaries are parent-founded. These two issues do not arise with parent-founded subsidiaries. In the main body of the chapter, we prefer to focus on the core issues of post-acquisition consolidation.

In this chapter, we deal only with wholly owned subsidiaries. Subsequent chapters will relax that simplifying assumption, thereby introducing further complexities.

Now, sit back, pay attention, and enjoy the ride!

Consolidation One Year After Acquisition

Before we begin, we must point out that each corporation—the parent and each of its subsidiaries—will prepare its own financial statements. These separate-entity financial statements will have no fair values, and will include all intercompany transactions that occur between the related companies.

When we talk about *consolidated* statements, we are referring to the set of statements that a parent company prepares for distribution to its shareholders in accordance with GAAP. These statements are based on the concept of the *economic entity*—there is no corresponding legal entity. Remember that consolidated statements comprise only one set of financial statements, intended for a specific purpose—every corporation still prepares its own individual statements for the tax authorities, for its bankers, for its own performance evaluation, and so forth.

Chapter 3 used an example of Purchase Ltd.'s acquisition of 100% of the shares of Target Ltd. To prepare Purchase Ltd.'s consolidated financial statements *after* the date of acquisition, we will need four types of information:

1. the details of the purchase transaction

2. the amortization or depreciation policy for capital assets

3. the nature and extent of intercompany transactions between the two companies, including intercompany receivables and payables, and

4. what happened to assets that were sold intercompany (including the assets in the original acquisition).

Over the next three chapters, we will add various types of transactions to our basic example of Purchase Ltd. and Target Ltd. We will not attempt to be exhaustive—this is an accounting textbook, not an all-inclusive consolidation handbook. By the time you finish with Chapter 6, however, you should have a thorough understanding of the consolidation process and of the types of interactions that must be accounted for.

Basic information

Assume that on December 31, 2005, Purchase Ltd. purchased all of the outstanding shares of Target Ltd. by issuing 40,000 new shares of Purchase Ltd. in exchange for the shares of Target Ltd. The newly issued Purchase Ltd. shares had a market value of $30 per share—a total purchase cost of $1,200,000. The total cost was apportioned to the fair values of Target Ltd.'s assets and liabilities and to goodwill *at the date of acquisition* as shown in Exhibit 4–1.[1] These fair values and goodwill are the same amounts used in the illustration in the previous chapter.

At every balance sheet date after December 31, 2005, Purchase Ltd. will have to include the fair-value increments (and/or decrements) and goodwill in its *consolidated* net assets. However:

- The carrying values of most fair-valued assets flow to income, either directly through cost of sales (for current assets such as inventories) or indirectly, through amortization or depreciation for tangible and intangible capital assets (except goodwill and other intangible assets with indefinite lives).

- Assets included in the purchase transaction may be sold or retired.

---

1. Exhibit 4–1 is identical to Exhibit 3-6. The same example is used throughout Chapters 3 to 6 in order to help readers with comparisons and to make it easier to see the impact of additional complexities.

EXHIBIT 4-1   ALLOCATION OF PURCHASE PRICE

100% Purchase of Target Ltd., December 31, 2005

Purchase price						$1,200,000
	Book value	**Fair value**	**Fair value increment**	**% share**	**FVI acquired**	
Cash	$50,000	$50,000	—			
Accounts receivable	150,000	150,000	—			
Inventory	50,000	50,000	—			
Land	300,000	400,000	$100,000 × 100% =		$100,000	
Buildings and equipment	500,000	550,000	50,000 × 100% =		50,000	
Accumulated depreciation	(150,000)	—	150,000 × 100% =		150,000	
Accounts payable	(100,000)	(100,000)	—			
Total fair value increment						300,000
Net asset book value	$ 800,000			× 100% =		800,000
Fair value of assets acquired						$1,100,000
Goodwill						$ 100,000

Wholly Owned

Subsidiaries:

Reporting

Subsequent to

Acquisition

145

When either of these events happens, we have to make periodic adjustments to the initial fair-value increments.

Other adjustments are needed to eliminate or "back out" intercompany transactions. For the year ended December 31, 2006, we will assume the following:

1. Target Ltd.'s buildings and equipment will be depreciated over 10 years after the date of acquisition, using straight-line depreciation.

2. During 2006, Target Ltd. sold goods of $55,000 to Purchase Ltd. Target Ltd.'s gross margin is 40% of sales.

3. On December 31, 2006, $20,000 of the goods acquired by Purchase Ltd. from Target Ltd. are still in Purchase Ltd.'s inventory.

4. During 2006, Target Ltd. paid dividends totalling $30,000 to Purchase Ltd., Target Ltd.'s sole shareholder. Purchase Ltd. maintains its Investment in Target Ltd. account on the cost basis, and therefore the dividends received were recorded as dividend income.

Chapter 2 illustrated the basic approach to eliminating intercompany transactions and balances. Chapter 3 explained the eliminations that are required when a subsidiary is purchased. The example in this chapter will combine these two types of adjustments, and will add three more issues that are essential to understanding consolidations:

1. amortization of fair-value increments

2. impairment testing for goodwill, and

3. elimination of unrealized profit on intercompany sales.

The next three sections will discuss these issues.

Amortization of fair-value increments

A large part of the purchase price in a business combination may be allocated to fair-value increments. A study of 756 U.S. business combinations revealed that the purchase price discrepancy—fair-value increments and goodwill—equalled, on average, almost 200% of book value. The aggregate purchase price was $404 billion, comprising $137 billion in book value and $267 billion in purchase price discrepancy.[2]

Therefore, fair-value increments (or decrements) most likely will significantly impact consolidated earnings subsequent to the purchase. Each of the major categories of assets is discussed below.

Inventory Fair-value increments for inventory will flow through cost of sales to decrease net income when the inventory is sold to third parties. In the period in which the inventory is sold, the fair-value increment is added to cost of sales instead of to inventory on the consolidation working papers.

Tangible capital assets Tangible capital assets are reported in accordance with the recommendations of Section 3061 of the *CICA Handbook*, "Property, Plant and Equipment." The recommendations apply to fair-value increments as well as to the carrying values shown on the subsidiary's books.

A purchased subsidiary will continue to amortize the depreciable capital assets that are recorded on its books. However, the subsidiary's depreciation will be based on the carrying value of the assets on its books. Unless push-down accounting is used, the depreciation on the *subsidiary's separate-entity* financial statements will not reflect the higher prices paid by the parent in the business combination.

When the *parent's consolidated statements* are prepared, the fair-value increments on depreciable assets must be amortized in accordance with the depreciation policy being used by the subsidiary. If, for example, a building has a 20-year estimated remaining useful life from the date of the business combination, the fair-value increment must be amortized over the 20-year remaining period.

For example, suppose a subsidiary has a four-year-old asset with an original cost of $100,000. This asset is being amortized on the subsidiary's books by the straight-line method over 20 years. At the date that the parent bought the subsidiary, the book value of the asset was:

Cost	$ 100,000
Accumulated amortization ($100,000 ÷ 20 × 4)	20,000
	$ 80,000

Fair value at the date of acquisition was $120,000. Therefore, the fair-value increment is $40,000. Following acquisition, the subsidiary will continue to amortize the asset at $5,000 per year: $100,000 ÷ 20 = $5,000. The fair-value increment will be amortized over the remaining expected useful life of the asset, which is 16 years after acquisition: ($120,000 − $80,000) ÷ 16 = $2,500 per year. Amortization of this asset on the *consolidated* income statement will be $7,500:

Subsidiary's amortization	$100,000 ÷ 20 =	$ 5,000
Fair-value increment	$40,000 ÷ 16 =	$ 2,500
Consolidated amortization		$ 7,500

---

2. Benjamin C. Ayers, Craig E. Lefanowicz, and John R. Robinson, "The Financial Statement Effects of Eliminating the Pooling-of-Interest Method of Acquisition Accounting," *Accounting Horizons*, March 2000, pp. 1–19.

Intangible capital assets Under GAAP, a company recognizes an intangible asset on its books only when the asset has been purchased or when capitalizable costs were incurred to develop the asset. As a result, a company often has intangible assets that are not reported on its books. Examples include trademarks, customer lists, franchises, and so forth. When one company is acquired by another in a business combination, the acquirer should identify any specific intangible assets that have not been reported on the acquiree's balance sheet. When intangible assets can be identified, *whether or not they appear on the acquired company's balance sheet*, they must be assigned a fair value.

Identifiable intangible assets are reported as recommended by Section 3062 of the *CICA Handbook*: an "intangible asset should be amortized over its useful life to an enterprise, unless the life is determined to be indefinite" [CICA 3062.10]. If the intangible asset's life is indefinite, then it is not amortized.

If the identifiable intangible asset is already reported on the subsidiary's balance sheet, the fair-value increment is accounted for in the same way. If the intangible asset is not already reported on the subsidiary's balance sheet, the asset's useful life must be determined. If the asset's life is not indefinite, the fair-value increment is amortized over its useful life.

If it becomes apparent that an intangible asset's value has declined to below its consolidated carrying value, fair value must be written down to the reduced value.

Goodwill Until very recently, acquiring companies were required to amortize any goodwill that they acquired in a business combination. Now, however, goodwill is not amortized (effective for fiscal years ending on or after December 31, 2002).

Since goodwill is not amortized, its continued existence must be re-evaluated periodically. This re-evaluation is known as an impairment test. An **impairment test** is an estimate of whether the reporting enterprise will be able to recover the carrying value of the asset that is reported on the company's balance sheet at the end of a reporting period.

To apply the impairment test, goodwill must be attributed to individual *reporting units*. A **reporting unit** is an operating division or segment that is accountable to senior management for its results. A reporting unit is not necessarily the same as a corporate entity. Therefore, when goodwill arises in a business combination, that goodwill must be allocated to individual reporting units, if there is more than one within the acquired corporation.

Once goodwill has been attributed to reporting units, a 2-step impairment test is applied by comparing the fair value of the reporting unit with its carrying amount, including goodwill. Any excess of carrying amount over fair value is the amount of impaired value that must be written off.

It is obvious that the impairment test involves a great amount of estimation and judgment on the part of management. Fair value of a reporting unit is a function of its future earnings, and there is a lot of subjectivity involved in estimating future earnings. The application of impairment tests for goodwill seems to give management a lot of opportunity for write-downs to contribute to a "big bath."

Reporting enterprises that qualify for differential reporting (i.e., companies without public accountability) do not need to apply an annual impairment test. Instead, such companies should apply an impairment test only when a specific event or circumstance indicates that an impairment might possibly have happened.

Appendix 4A explains the impairment test more extensively.

Wholly Owned
Subsidiaries:
Reporting
Subsequent to
Acquisition

147

Unrealized profits

One of the more challenging aspects of consolidated statements is that we must keep track of assets that were sold by one company in the group to another. In Chapter 2, we described intercompany sales of inventory; note that sales from a parent to a subsidiary are **downstream** sales, while sales from a subsidiary to a parent are called **upstream** sales. Sales between subsidiaries also are treated as upstream sales.

In Chapter 2, all of the inventory that was sold downstream was sold to third parties before the fiscal year-end. That is the easy scenario. A more difficult situation arises when some or all of the inventory is still on the receiving corporation's books at the balance sheet date. In that situation, we must deal with the problem of **unrealized profit**.

In the facts for Purchase Ltd. and Target Ltd. listed above, there are three points relating to the intercompany sales:

- Target Ltd. had sales to Purchase Ltd. (i.e., *upstream* sales) of $55,000
- $20,000 of those goods are still in Purchase Ltd.'s inventory at year-end, and
- Target Ltd.'s gross margin on sales is 40%.

The $20,000 of goods in Purchase Ltd.'s inventory are stated at their acquisition price to Purchase Ltd. However, they cost Target Ltd. less than that to produce. Target Ltd.'s gross margin is 40%, which means that the $20,000 inventory contains a gross profit margin of $20,000 × 40% = $8,000; the goods cost $12,000 to produce.

Consolidated statements must show only the results of transactions between the consolidated entity and those companies and individuals outside the combined economic entity. In substance, the $8,000 gross profit is only an internal transaction, not external. Therefore, consolidated inventory must be reduced by eliminating the $8,000 *unrealized profit* on intercompany sales.

Obviously, the consolidated inventory must be reduced by $8,000, but what happens to the offset? When we compute cost of sales, beginning inventory and purchases are added together, and ending inventory is subtracted. The income statement effect of an *overstated ending inventory* is to *understate cost of sales*. Therefore, we must not only reduce consolidated inventory by $8,000, but also we must increase cost of sales by $8,000. If this seems confusing, just remember that *increasing* a cost will *reduce* net income, thereby eliminating the unrealized profit.

In summary, two adjustments are necessary: (1) eliminate the intercompany sale transaction, and (2) eliminate the unrealized profit. We will illustrate these adjustments shortly.

Unrealized profit arises any time that one corporation sells assets to another, and those assets stay within the consolidated economic entity instead of being sold externally. Inventory is the most common type of intercompany sale, but capital assets or investments may also be sold. The same principles apply, regardless of the nature of the asset(s) involved.

Direct method

The unconsolidated financial statements for Purchase Ltd. and Target Ltd. are shown in Exhibit 4–2. We have assumed that Purchase Ltd. *records* its investment in Target Ltd. on the cost basis in its accounts, as is usually the case. Therefore, the separate-entity financial statements show (1) the investment at the purchase price of $1,200,000 and (2) the dividends of $30,000 received by Purchase from Target Ltd. as dividend income.

EXHIBIT 4–2 SEPARATE-ENTITY FINANCIAL STATEMENTS FOR 2006

Income Statements
Year Ended December 31, 2006

	Purchase Ltd.	Target Ltd.
Revenue:		
Sales	$2,400,000	$ 300,000
Dividend income	30,000	—
	2,430,000	300,000
Expenses:		
Cost of sales	1,750,000	180,000
Depreciation expense	100,000	35,000
Other expenses	250,000	20,000
	2,100,000	235,000
Net income	$ 330,000	$ 65,000
Retained earnings, December 31, 2005	2,000,000	600,000
Dividends declared	—	(30,000)
Retained earnings, December 31, 2006	$2,330,000	$ 635,000

Balance Sheets
December 31, 2006

	Purchase Ltd.	Target Ltd.
Assets		
Current assets:		
Cash	$ 980,000	$ 100,000
Accounts receivable	2,200,000	250,000
Inventory	250,000	70,000
	3,430,000	420,000
Property, plant, and equipment:		
Land	1,000,000	300,000
Buildings and equipment	3,000,000	500,000
Accumulated depreciation	(1,300,000)	(185,000)
	2,700,000	615,000
Other assets:		
Investments (at cost)	1,200,000	—
Total assets	$7,330,000	$1,035,000
Liabilities and shareholders' equity		
Liabilities:		
Accounts payable	$800,000	$200,000
Long-term notes payable	400,000	—
	1,200,000	200,000
Shareholders' equity:		
Common shares	3,800,000	200,000
Retained earnings	2,330,000	635,000
	6,130,000	835,000
Total liabilities and shareholders' equity	$7,330,000	$1,035,000

When using the direct method, we can go down the income statement and balance sheet and insert the correct amounts on a line-by-line basis. In Exhibit 4–3, we have added together the separate-entity amounts. For some items, we

EXHIBIT 4–3	PURCHASE LTD. CONSOLIDATED FINANCIAL STATEMENTS (DIRECT METHOD)

Statement of Income and Retained Earnings
Year Ended December 31, 2006

Sales revenue [2,400,000 + 300,000 – **55,000**]	$2,645,000
Dividend income [30,000 + 0 – **30,000**]	—
Operating expenses:	
Cost of sales [1,750,000 + 180,000 – **55,000** + **8,000**]	1,883,000
Depreciation expense [100,000 + 35,000 + **20,000**]	155,000
Other expenses [250,000 + 20,000]	270,000
	2,308,000
Net income	$ 337,000
Retained earnings, December 31, 2005 [2,000,000 + 600,000 – **600,000**]	2,000,000
Dividends declared [0 + 30,000 – **30,000**]	—
Retained earnings, December 31, 2006	$2,337,000

Balance Sheet
December 31, 2006

Assets

Current assets:	
Cash [980,000 + 100,000]	$1,080,000
Accounts receivable [2,200,000 + 250,000]	2,450,000
Inventory [250,000 + 70,000 – **8,000**]	312,000
	3,842,000
Property, plant, and equipment:	
Land [1,000,000 + 300,000 + **100,000**]	1,400,000
Buildings and equipment [3,000,000 + 500,000 + **50,000**]	3,550,000
Accumulated depreciation [1,300,000 + 185,000 – **150,000** + **20,000**]	(1,355,000)
	3,595,000
Other assets:	
Investments [1,200,000 + 0 – **1,200,000**]	—
Goodwill [100,000]	100,000
Total assets	$7,537,000

Liabilities and shareholders' equity

Liabilities:	
Current accounts payable [800,000 + 200,000]	$1,000,000
Long-term notes payable [400,000 + 0]	400,000
	1,400,000
Shareholders' equity:	
Common shares [**Purchase Ltd. shares only**]	3,800,000
Retained earnings	
[2,330,000 + 635,000 – **600,000** – **8,000** – **20,000**]	2,337,000
	6,137,000
Total liabilities and shareholders' equity	$7,537,000

will make additional adjustments and eliminations. The necessary adjustments and eliminations are listed below, starting with the income statement.

Statement of Income and Retained Earnings

- *Sales revenue.* The combined sales total is $2,700,000. We must eliminate the upstream intercompany sales of $55,000. The result is consolidated sales of $2,645,000.

- *Dividend income.* Since this income is Target Ltd.'s dividends paid to Purchase Ltd., the entire $30,000 must be eliminated.

- *Cost of sales.* The combined unadjusted cost of sales is $1,750,000 + $180,000 = $1,930,000. This amount must be decreased by the full amount of the intercompany sales ($55,000) and increased by the unrealized profit of $8,000 that is in Purchase Ltd.'s ending inventory.

- *Depreciation expense.* The net book value of Target Ltd.'s buildings and equipment *at the date of acquisition* was $350,000 net of depreciation: $500,000 − $150,000. The fair value was $550,000. The fair-value increment is $200,000. This fair-value increment must be amortized. The facts presented above state that the remaining useful life is 10 years. Therefore, we must add 1/10 of the fair-value increment to the depreciation account, or $20,000.

The combined, unadjusted, net incomes of the two companies is $330,000 + $65,000 = $395,000. After adjustment for amortization of fair-value increments, and after eliminating unrealized profit, consolidated net income drops to $337,000. The total reduction is $58,000. Remember this number—you will see it again shortly!

Balance sheet

- *Inventory.* Combined inventories must be reduced by the unrealized profit of $8,000.

- *Land.* The fair-value increment of $100,000 must be added.

- *Buildings and equipment.* The total fair-value increment for Target Ltd.'s buildings and equipment is $200,000. The increase is recognized in the consolidated statements by (1) eliminating Target Ltd.'s date-of-acquisition accumulated depreciation of $150,000, and (2) increasing the buildings and equipment asset account by $50,000. Therefore, only $50,000 is added to the asset account.

- *Accumulated depreciation.* Target Ltd.'s accumulated depreciation at December 31, 2006, is $185,000. This amount includes the $150,000 accumulated at the date of acquisition plus $35,000 additional depreciation expense for 2006. The $150,000 must be eliminated—the acquired company's accumulated depreciation at the date of acquisition should not be carried forward. The $35,000 remains, because it represents depreciation *after* the date of acquisition. But the $35,000 represents depreciation on Target Ltd.'s *book* value. To reflect depreciation on the *fair* value, the $20,000 amortization of the fair-value increment must be added.

- *Investments.* The investment account must be reduced by the cost of Purchase Ltd.'s investment in Target Ltd.[3] In this example, there are no other invest-

Wholly Owned
Subsidiaries:
Reporting
Subsequent to
Acquisition

151

---

3. If the investment account has been *recorded* on the equity basis, Purchase Ltd.'s equity in Target Ltd. will be eliminated, with offsetting eliminations in retained earnings. In Chapter 6, we will discuss the consolidation adjustments when equity-basis recording has been used.

ments. In many situations, however, there will be other investments that will *not* be eliminated.

- *Common shares*. Only Purchase Ltd.'s common shares are included.
- *Retained earnings* (at year-end). This is the challenging one! We start by adding the two companies' retained earnings together. Next, we must eliminate Target Ltd.'s date-of-acquisition retained earnings ($600,000). Then we make the adjustments that were necessary for the consolidated income statement:
  - eliminate the unrealized profit of $8,000, and
  - reduce retained earnings by the amount of additional fair-value amortization—$20,000.

There is one income statement adjustment that is missing from this little list: dividend income. The reason that it doesn't show up among our adjustments on the retained earnings line of the balance sheet is that the amount has already washed out. Dividend income has *increased* Purchase Ltd.'s net income and retained earnings, while dividends paid has *reduced* Target Ltd.'s retained earnings. When the retained earnings amounts for the two companies are added together, the reduction in Target Ltd.'s offsets the increase in Purchase Ltd.'s, and there is no need for an adjustment.

Remember the $58,000 decrease in net income from separate-entity to consolidated net income? That consists of two amounts: $30,000 dividend income shown as revenue to Purchase Ltd. but *not as an expense to Target Ltd.*, plus the $28,000 (i.e., $8,000 + $20,000) in other adjustments to consolidated net income. *When deriving consolidated retained earnings, all adjustments to consolidated net income are made* except *for intercompany dividends.*

You might ask why we simply don't take the consolidated retained earnings amount from the bottom of the statement of income and retained earnings and put that in the balance sheet. The answer is that we must be able to derive the retained earnings independently, to make sure that the statements balance and that we haven't overlooked anything.[4]

Worksheet approach

The general approach is to (1) start with the *pre-closing* separate-entity trial balances of the parent and its subsidiaries, (2) make the necessary eliminations and adjustments, and finally (3) cross-add the rows to determine the consolidated trial balance. The amounts in the consolidated trial balance are used to construct the income statement, statement of retained earnings, and the balance sheet. The final column of the worksheet does not, in itself, constitute consolidated financial statements. It does include all of the consolidated financial statement *elements* (assets, liabilities, revenues, and expenses), however.

Exhibit 4–4 shows a worksheet with the trial balances of the two companies in the first two numerical columns. These trial balances yield exactly the same amounts that are shown in the separate-entity financial statements in Exhibit 4–2.

To conserve space, our worksheets will have only one column for both debit and credit amounts. Double columns could be used just as well. An advantage of a single column (in addition to avoiding oversized worksheets) is that, in a computer spreadsheet, we can constantly see whether we are maintaining the zero

---

4. From a very practical student standpoint, it also is very useful to be able to derive consolidated retained earnings without having to work through a consolidated income statement. That is a favourite examination question, both in coursework and in professional examinations!

December 31, 2006

	Trial balances		Adjustments		Purchase consolidated trial balance
	Purchase Dr/(Cr)	Target Dr/(Cr)	Adjustments Dr/(Cr) – a	Operations Dr/(Cr) – c	
Cash	$ 980,000	$ 100,000			$1,080,000
Accounts receivable	2,200,000	250,000			2,450,000
Inventories	250,000	70,000		(8,000) c2	312,000
Land	1,000,000	300,000	100,000 a2		1,400,000
Buildings and equipment	3,000,000	500,000	50,000 a2		3,550,000
Accumulated depreciation	(1,300,000)	(185,000)	150,000 a2	(20,000) c4	(1,355,000)
Investments (at cost)	1,200,000	—	{ (800,000) a1 ⎰ (400,000) a2	}	—
Goodwill			100,000 a2		100,000
					—
Accounts payable	(800,000)	(200,000)			(1,000,000)
Long-term notes payable	(400,000)	—			(400,000)
Common shares	(3,800,000)	(200,000)	200,000 a1		(3,800,000)
Dividends declared	—	30,000		(30,000) c3	—
Retained earnings, December 31, 2005	(2,000,000)	(600,000)	600,000 a1		(2,000,000)
					—
Sales	(2,400,000)	(300,000)		55,000 c1	(2,645,000)
Dividend income	(30,000)	—		30,000 c3	—
Cost of sales	1,750,000	180,000		(55,000) c1	
				8,000 c2	1,883,000
Depreciation expense	100,000	35,000		20,000 c4	155,000
Other expenses	250,000	20,000			270,000
	$ —	$ —	$ —	$ —	$ —

Wholly Owned
Subsidiaries:
Reporting
Subsequent to
Acquisition

153

total of each column as we make adjustments and eliminations (i.e., that the debits equal the credits!).

An additional convention that we will follow is that we will strive for greater clarity by putting the eliminations and adjustments that arise from the acquisition adjustment in one column, while we enter post-combination adjustments in another. There is no need to follow this practice—one column can easily be used for all adjustments.

Acquisition adjustment The starting point of any consolidation must be to adjust the accounts to reflect the economic substance of the purchase transaction. As we already have stated several times, we (1) eliminate Target Ltd.'s shareholders' equity accounts at the date of acquisition, and (2) adjust the net assets for FVI and goodwill. The offset for both of these adjustments is to eliminate Purchase Ltd.'s investment account. We are indicating this set of adjustments with the letter **a**—it helps to keep track of which additions and subtractions on the financial statements belong to which others, in case we don't balance at the end and have to embark on a diagnostic investigation. In general journal form, the acquisition adjustments (**a**) are:

a1	Common shares	200,000	
	Retained earnings	600,000	
	Investments		800,000
a2	Land	100,000	
	Buildings and equipment	50,000	
	Accumulated depreciation	150,000	
	Goodwill	100,000	
	Investments		400,000

An important aspect of this adjustment is the debit to retained earnings. We add Target Ltd.'s year-end 2006 retained earnings of $635,000 to Purchase Ltd.'s, but we eliminate only $600,000. The goal is not to eliminate Target Ltd.'s retained earnings at the balance sheet date. Instead, the objective is to eliminate Target Ltd.'s retained earnings *as of the date of acquisition.*

The reason for eliminating only Target Ltd.'s date-of-acquisition retained earnings is that we are eliminating the shareholders' equity accounts that offset the acquired net assets. Additional earnings that accumulate in Target Ltd.'s retained earnings after acquisition represent part of consolidated retained earnings.

Operations adjustments We will label the adjustments and eliminations for post-acquisition activities and events the *operations adjustments*, just to keep them distinct from the acquisition adjustment. We will label all of the operations adjustments as **c**. (We will add another column for **b** later in the chapter.) The operations adjustments are as follows:

Intercompany sales: Target Ltd. sold $55,000 of goods to Purchase Ltd. during 2006, an *upstream* sale. If the entire inventory had been sold by Purchase Ltd. to third parties outside the consolidated enterprise for $80,000, the books of Target Ltd. and Purchase Ltd. would show the following (recall that Target sold the goods to Purchase Ltd. at a 40% gross margin on sales):

	Target Ltd.	**Purchase Ltd.**	**Total**
Sales	**$55,000**	$80,000	$135,000
Cost of sales	33,000	**55,000**	88,000
Gross margin	$22,000	$25,000	$47,000

In this example, we are assuming that $20,000 of the goods remain in Purchase Ltd.'s ending inventory. Goods sold by Target Ltd. to Purchase Ltd. for $20,000 would include a gross profit to Target Ltd. of 40% of that amount, or $8,000. Therefore, Purchase Ltd.'s ending inventory includes goods that cost $20,000 to Purchase Ltd. as a separate entity, but that cost only $12,000 to the consolidated entity. Unrealized profit of $8,000 must be eliminated from the consolidated ending inventory.

Since cost of goods sold is determined by subtracting the ending inventory from purchases plus beginning inventory, including $8,000 of unrealized profit in the ending inventory causes the cost of goods sold to be *understated* by $8,000. Therefore, in Exhibit 4–4, we have two steps: (1) eliminate the $55,000 inter-company sale, and (2) eliminate the unrealized profit by debiting cost of sales and crediting inventory by $8,000:

c1	Sales	55,000	
	Cost of sales		55,000
c2	Cost of sales	8,000	
	Inventory		8,000

Other intercompany transactions: The adjustment eliminates the intercompany payment of dividends. We eliminate $30,000 from both dividends declared and dividend income:

| **c3** | Dividend income | 30,000 | |
| | Dividends declared | | 30,000 |

This adjustment is based on the fact that, in our example, Purchase Ltd. is recording its investment in Target on the cost basis; the dividends received by Purchase Ltd. have been credited to dividend income and must be eliminated. Similarly, the credit to dividends declared is based on a scrutiny of the Target Ltd. accounts in Exhibit 4–4, which reveals that Target Ltd. debits that account when dividends are declared. If Target Ltd.'s debit had been directly to retained earnings, then the credit in the elimination entry would be to retained earnings.

If there had been any other intercompany transactions during the period, they would also have to be eliminated. For example, intercompany interest payments or accruals, lease payments, management fees, or royalty fees would be eliminated, along with any outstanding intercompany receivables and payables.

Fair-value increments: Target Ltd.'s depreciation expense is $35,000. This amount represents 2006 depreciation on Target Ltd.'s buildings and equipment. The depreciation is based on the $350,000 net book value (that is, $500,000 cost – $150,000 accumulated depreciation) and the 10-year remaining life of Target Ltd.'s assets beginning in 2006.

Consolidated depreciation expense must reflect depreciation on the *fair value* of Target Ltd.'s capital assets. The fair value was $550,000 at the beginning of 2006. Therefore, depreciation expense must be increased to $55,000, an increase of $20,000:

| **c4** | Depreciation expense | 20,000 | |
| | Accumulated depreciation | | 20,000 |

Completing the worksheet When all of the eliminations and adjustments have been entered on the worksheet (or computer spreadsheet), the rows can be added across. The final column shows the consolidated trial balance, from which the consolidated financial statements can be prepared. For Purchase Ltd., the consolidated statements will be the same as those shown in Exhibit 4–3.

Two important reminders:

1. Either the direct method or the worksheet method can be used to derive the consolidated amounts. The approach used is a matter of personal preference. It's only the result that matters.

2. The eliminations and adjustments shown in the worksheet (or in the direct approach financial statements) are *never* entered in any formal set of accounts. These are working paper adjustments only.

Wholly Owned
Subsidiaries:
Reporting
Subsequent to
Acquisition

155

Equity-Basis Reporting of Non-Consolidated Subsidiaries

A parent company that is also a public company will issue only consolidated statements as its general purpose financial statements. A private company may or may not choose to issue consolidated statements.

In addition to the consolidated statements, every parent company will also prepare non-consolidated statements. Non-consolidated statements are used for income tax reporting, for a bank's credit analysis, and for the shareholders of a private company when the shareholders agree to waive the normal requirement for consolidated statements.

In non-consolidated statements, the subsidiaries can be reported on either the cost or the equity basis. When the equity method of reporting is used, the parent corporation includes in its net income the parent's share of the subsidiary's earnings. Target Ltd.'s 2006 separate-entity net income is $65,000, as shown in Exhibit 4–2. Using the equity method, Target Ltd.'s net income (after adjustment) will be reported in Purchase Ltd.'s income statement as a single amount.

The Target Ltd. net income cannot be reported by Purchase Ltd. simply as $65,000, because to do so would ignore the substance of the purchase transaction. Since Purchase Ltd. has acquired control over the assets and liabilities of Target Ltd., the earnings of Target Ltd. must be reported in Purchase Ltd.'s statements *as though the net assets of Target Ltd. had been purchased directly by Purchase Ltd.*

If the assets and liabilities had been purchased directly, then they would have been recorded at their fair values, and goodwill of $100,000 would have been recorded. The fair values are amortized and any transactions between the Target Ltd. division and the rest of the company will not appear on the financial statements of Purchase Ltd. In other words, it is necessary to adjust the earnings of Target Ltd. to reflect *all of the same adjustments that would be made if Target Ltd. were consolidated.*

Part A of Exhibit 4–5 shows the computation of Target Ltd.'s adjusted earnings. Starting with the Target Ltd. reported net income of $65,000, deductions

EXHIBIT 4–5	EQUITY BASIS OF REPORTING PURCHASE LTD.'S INVESTMENT IN TARGET LTD.

Year Ended December 31, 2006

A. Equity in earnings of Target Ltd.:

Earnings as reported by Target	$ 65,000
Adjustments:	
1 Amortization of fair value increment on buildings & equipment: $200,000/10 years	(20,000)
2 Elimination of unrealized profit on upstream sales: $20,000 x 40% gross margin	(8,000)
Adjusted Target Ltd. earnings, equity basis	$ 37,000

B. Investment in Target Ltd.:

Balance, December 31, 2005	$1,200,000
Plus Purchase's share of Target's equity basis earnings: $37,000 × 100%	37,000
Less dividends received from Target	(30,000)
Balance, December 31, 2006	$1,207,000

are made for (1) depreciation of the fair-value increment on buildings and equipment and (2) elimination of the unrealized profit on intercompany sales.

The adjusted Target Ltd. earnings amount to $37,000. Purchase Ltd. owns 100% of the shares of Target Ltd.—Purchase Ltd. will report this entire amount on Purchase Ltd.'s income statement as equity in the earnings of Target Ltd. (the *equity pick-up*).

Part B of Exhibit 4–5 summarizes the impact of the equity method on the investment account. The year-end balance of $1,207,000 will be reported on Purchase Ltd.'s unconsolidated balance sheet. The investment account reflects (1) the cost of the investment plus (2) the cumulative amount of unremitted adjusted earnings since the date of acquisition.

The adjustments made to Target Ltd.'s net income are made only for *reporting* on Purchase Ltd.'s statements. Target Ltd. will report net income of $65,000 on its own separate-entity financial statements, even though Purchase Ltd.'s equity-basis income statement will report the lesser amount of $37,000 in earnings from Target Ltd.

Purchase Ltd. may choose to *record* the equity-basis earnings of Target in its accounts, in which case the adjustment will appear as follows:

Investment in Target Ltd.	37,000	
Equity in earnings of Target Ltd.		37,000

The credit to the income statement account is offset by a debit to increase the investment account. When Target Ltd. declares dividends, the declaration will be recorded as follows:

Dividends receivable	30,000	
Investment in Target Ltd.		30,000

When the dividends are paid, Purchase Ltd. will debit cash and credit the dividends receivable account.

It is not necessary for Purchase Ltd. to *record* its investment in Target Ltd. on the equity basis, even though it may *report* the investment on the equity basis. As a bookkeeping convenience, it is most common for the investor to maintain the investment account on the cost basis.

Comparison of consolidation vs. equity reporting Exhibit 4–6 shows the balance sheet and income statement for Purchase Ltd. for the year ended December 31, 2006. The first column shows the results of reporting Target on the equity basis, while the second column shows consolidated statements.

In the unconsolidated statements, the assets and liabilities are only those of Purchase Ltd., and the revenues and expenses are also only those generated or incurred by Purchase Ltd. One of the assets of Purchase Ltd. is the investment in Target Ltd., which appears as a non-current asset on the balance sheet. Similarly, the income statement shows Purchase Ltd.'s equity in the earnings of Target Ltd. as a separate item.

When we consolidate Purchase Ltd. and Target Ltd., however, we eliminate the investment in the Target Ltd. account on the balance sheet and instead show all of the individual assets and liabilities of Target Ltd. that the investment represents. The shareholders' equity accounts are exactly the same in both columns. The total net asset value of Purchase Ltd. is not altered by the process of consolidation; all that happens is that the investment account is disaggregated so that the readers of Purchase Ltd.'s financial statements can see the total resources (of both Purchase Ltd. and Target Ltd.) that are under the control of the management of Purchase Ltd.

Wholly Owned
Subsidiaries:
Reporting
Subsequent to
Acquisition

157

EXHIBIT 4–6 COMPARING EQUITY-BASIS REPORTING AND CONSOLIDATION

Purchase Ltd.
Statement of Income and Retained Earnings
Year Ended December 31, 2006

	Equity Basis	Consolidated
Sales revenue	$2,400,000	$2,645,000
Equity in earnings of Target Ltd.	37,000	—
	2,437,000	2,645,000
Operating expenses:		
Cost of sales	1,750,000	1,883,000
Depreciation expense	100,000	155,000
Other expenses	250,000	270,000
	2,100,000	2,308,000
Net income	$ 337,000	$ 337,000
Retained earnings, December 31, 2005	2,000,000	2,000,000
Dividends declared	—	—
Retained earnings, December 31, 2006	$2,337,000	$2,337,000

Purchase Ltd.
Balance Sheet, December 31, 2006

	Equity Basis	Consolidated
Assets		
Current assets:		
Cash	$ 980,000	$1,080,000
Accounts receivable	2,200,000	2,450,000
Inventory	250,000	312,000
	3,430,000	3,842,000
Property, plant, and equipment:		
Land	1,000,000	1,400,000
Buildings and equipment	3,000,000	3,550,000
Accumulated depreciation	(1,300,000)	(1,355,000)
	2,700,000	3,595,000
Other assets:		
Investments	1,207,000	—
Goodwill	—	100,000
Total assets	$7,337,000	$7,537,000
Liabilities and shareholders' equity		
Liabilities:		
Current accounts payable	$ 800,000	$1,000,000
Long-term notes payable	400,000	400,000
	1,200,000	1,400,000
Shareholders' equity:		
Common shares	3,800,000	3,800,000
Retained earnings	2,337,000	2,337,000
	6,137,000	6,137,000
Total liabilities and shareholders' equity	$7,337,000	$7,537,000

The unconsolidated income statement includes the net equity-basis earnings of Target Ltd. on a single line. Upon consolidation, that line disappears and the net amount thereof ($37,000) is disaggregated by including the revenues and expenses of Target Ltd. in the main body of the statement, along with those of Purchase Ltd. The consolidated net income is exactly the same as the unconsolidated net income of Purchase Ltd., since the investment in Target Ltd. has been reported on the equity basis.

The equity-basis investment account is increased by the $37,000 equity pick-up of Target Ltd.'s earnings, minus the $30,000 dividends received from Target Ltd. As a result, the investment account is shown at $1,207,000 in the equity basis column.

The equity-basis investment account and equity-in-earnings account summarize the investor's interest in the net assets and earnings from operations of the investee corporation in a single line on the financial statements of the investor. Therefore the equity method is sometimes referred to as **one-line consolidation** and is sometimes called the **consolidation method** of equity reporting. The net income and the shareholders' equity on the equity-basis unconsolidated statements are the same as they are on the consolidated statements.

Discontinued Operations and Extraordinary Items

Wholly Owned
Subsidiaries:
Reporting
Subsequent to
Acquisition

159

As a general rule, gains and losses from extraordinary items and discontinued operations that are shown on the income statement of an investee corporation retain their classification when that investee's financial results are consolidated or are reported on the equity basis.[5]

For example, suppose that Company P owns 40% of Company S. Company P reports its investment in S on the equity basis. In 2006, S reports an extraordinary item of $200,000 on its separate-entity income statement. When Company P prepares its 2006 consolidated income statement, P will report an extraordinary item of $80,000 (i.e., $200,000 × 40%).

There are exceptions, however.

Discontinued operations and extraordinary items of a subsidiary should be reported separately, net of non-controlling interest, *only if the items represent discontinued operations or are extraordinary to the parent* [CICA 1600.66].

There are three necessary conditions that gains or losses must satisfy in order to be classified as extraordinary [CICA 3480.02]:

1. They are not expected to occur frequently over several years.

2. They do not typify the normal business activities of the entity.

3. They do not depend primarily on decisions or determinations by management or owners.

To these three we can add the implicit fourth requirement, that they must be material in amount.

A transaction in a subsidiary or a significantly influenced company may meet these criteria and be properly classified as extraordinary. But when the transaction is considered from the viewpoint of the parent or investor corporation, it may fail to meet one or more of the criteria. The most obvious potential failing is on the

---

5. The AcSB's recommendations relating to equity-basis reporting can be found in CICA 3050.09.

dimension of materiality—what is material to a subsidiary may not be material to a much larger consolidated entity. An extraordinary item may fail to satisfy one of the other criteria instead of, or in addition to, the materiality criterion. In particular, transactions that are non-recurring in an individual company may actually be recurring in the consolidated entity.

Similar reasoning applies to discontinued operations. Suppose that a subsidiary discontinues its major line of business. The subsidiary will report the gain or loss as a discontinued operation in its own separate-entity income statement. However, suppose that the parent company has similar operations of its own or in other subsidiaries. From the point of view of the parent corporation, the subsidiary's discontinuance is just one of many similar lines of business. In that case, the parent would include the gain or loss as a normal operating activity.

For example, suppose that a parent company has several retail clothing subsidiaries. If one subsidiary ceases operations, that is big news for the subsidiary but not for the parent. The parent will still be in the retail clothing business, even though one subsidiary has left the business. The retail clothing business line continues for the parent and therefore is not a discontinued operation for consolidated financial reporting.

Thus the general rule of maintaining the status of a discontinued operation or an extraordinary item is, like many other recommendations in accounting, one that must be applied with professional judgment.

Consolidation in Second Subsequent Year

Basic information

Before we generalize the approach to preparing consolidated financial statements (which we do in Chapter 6), we will extend this example for one more year. The two companies' financial statements for the year ended December 31, 2007, are shown in Exhibit 4–7. Additional information is as follows:

1. Target Ltd. had sales of $60,000 to Purchase Ltd. (i.e., upstream); Target Ltd.'s 2007 gross margin was 45%; $10,000 (sales price) of the goods are in Purchase Ltd.'s inventory on December 31, 2007. Unrealized upstream profit therefore is $10,000 × 45% = $4,500.

2. Purchase had sales of $20,000 to Target Ltd. (i.e., downstream); Purchase Ltd.'s 2007 gross margin was 30%; $6,000 (sales price) of the goods sold to Target Ltd. are in Target Ltd.'s 2007 ending inventory. Unrealized downstream profit is $6,000 × 30% = $1,800.

3. Purchase Ltd. borrowed $500,000 from Target Ltd. on December 29, 2007. Both companies have reported this as a current item on their individual separate-entity balance sheets.

4. Target Ltd. sold its land to Purchase Ltd. for $450,000. The land originally cost Target Ltd. $300,000, and its fair value at the date of Purchase Ltd.'s acquisition of Target Ltd. was $400,000. The gain on the sale ($150,000) is separately disclosed on Target Ltd.'s income statement as an unusual item.

EXHIBIT 4–7   SEPARATE-ENTITY FINANCIAL STATEMENTS FOR 2007

Income Statements
Year Ended December 31, 2007

	Purchase Ltd.	Target Ltd.
Revenue:		
Sales	$3,000,000	$ 400,000
Dividend income	20,000	—
Gain on sale of land	—	150,000
	3,020,000	550,000
Expenses:		
Cost of sales	2,100,000	220,000
Depreciation expense	100,000	35,000
Other operating expenses	440,000	75,000
	2,640,000	330,000
Net income	$ 380,000	$ 220,000
Retained earnings, December 31, 2006	2,330,000	635,000
Dividends declared	(135,000)	(20,000)
Retained earnings, December 31, 2007	$2,575,000	$ 835,000

Balance Sheets
December 31, 2007

	Purchase Ltd.	Target Ltd.
Assets		
Current assets:		
Cash	$ 490,000	$ 70,000
Accounts receivable	1,900,000	775,000
Inventory	300,000	60,000
	2,690,000	905,000
Property, plant, and equipment:		
Land	1,450,000	—
Buildings and equipment	3,800,000	500,000
Accumulated depreciation	(1,400,000)	(220,000)
	3,850,000	280,000
Other assets:		
Investments (at cost)	1,200,000	—
Total assets	$7,740,000	$1,185,000
Liabilities and shareholders' equity		
Liabilities:		
Accounts payable	$ 865,000	$ 150,000
Long-term notes payable	500,000	—
	1,365,000	150,000
Shareholders' equity:		
Common shares	3,800,000	200,000
Retained earnings	2,575,000	835,000
	6,375,000	1,035,000
Total liabilities and shareholders' equity	$7,740,000	$1,185,000

Wholly Owned
Subsidiaries:
Reporting
Subsequent to
Acquisition

161

Direct method

Statement of income and retained earnings The consolidated statement of income and retained earnings is shown in Exhibit 4–8. The amounts that require adjustment are as follows:

- *Sales.* The two companies' combined sales of $3,400,000 must be adjusted for the intercompany sales. In 2007, there were upstream sales (Target Ltd. to Purchase Ltd.) of $60,000 and downstream sales (Purchase Ltd. to Target Ltd.) of $20,000. The sum of these amounts must be removed from sales revenue: $60,000 + $20,000 = $80,000.

- *Dividend income.* All of the dividend income shown on Purchase Ltd.'s income statement was received from Target Ltd. The intercompany dividends must be eliminated.

- *Gain on sale of land.* Target Ltd. sold its land to Purchase Ltd. during 2007 and recognized a gain of $150,000 on the transaction. However, the land is still owned within the consolidated entity. Therefore, the gain must be eliminated when we prepare the consolidated income statement.

- *Cost of sales.* Cost of sales must also be reduced by the $80,000 of intercompany sales. Some of the goods sold from one company to the other are still in inventory. Therefore, we must also adjust cost of sales by increasing it for the unrealized profit in the year-end inventory.

- *Upstream.* Target Ltd.'s gross profit margin for 2007 was 45%. Purchase Ltd.'s inventory contains $10,000 of goods purchased from Target Ltd. Therefore, we must increase cost of sales by $10,000 × 45% = $4,500.

- *Downstream.* Purchase Ltd.'s gross profit margin for 2007 was 30%. Target Ltd.'s inventory contains $6,000 of goods purchased from Target Ltd. The unrealized profit is $6,000 × 30% = $1,800. Cost of sales is increased by $1,800.

EXHIBIT 4–8 PURCHASE LTD. CONSOLIDATED INCOME STATEMENT (DIRECT METHOD)

Statement of Income and Retained Earnings
Year Ended December 31, 2007

Revenue:	
Sales revenue [3,000,000 + 400,000 – **60,000** – **20,000**]	$3,320,000
Dividend income [20,000 + 0 – **20,000**]	—
Gain on sale of land [0 + 150,000 – **150,000**]	—
	3,320,000
Operating expenses:	
Cost of sales	
[2,100,000 + 220,000 – **60,000** – **20,000** + **4,500** + **1,800** – **8,000**]	2,238,300
Depreciation expense [100,000 + 35,000 **+ 20,000**]	155,000
Other expenses [440,000 + 75,000]	515,000
	2,908,300
Net income	$ 411,700
Retained earnings, December 31, 2006	2,337,000
[2,330,000 + 635,000 – **600,000** – **20,000** – **8,000**]	
Dividends declared [135,000 + 20,000 – **20,000**]	(135,000)
Retained earnings, December 31, 2007	$2,613,700

Unrealized profit in the ending inventory is not the only thing we have to worry about. Remember that there was also $8,000 in unrealized profit in Purchase Ltd.'s ending inventory in 2006. The ending 2006 inventory is also the beginning 2007 inventory. If we include Purchase Ltd.'s beginning inventory in the consolidated cost of sales calculation, we will overstate the opening inventory by $8,000, and thereby *overstate* cost of sales by the same amount. Therefore, we must *reduce* consolidated cost of sales by $8,000.

- *Depreciation expense.* We must continue to amortize the fair-value increment on Target Ltd.'s buildings and equipment. As in 2006, the amortization is $200,000 ÷ 10 years, or $20,000. This amount is added to the depreciation expense.

- *Dividends declared.* Target Ltd.'s $20,000 in dividends paid to Purchase Ltd. must be eliminated.

- *Opening retained earnings.* The opening balances (i.e., the December 31, 2006, balances) must be adjusted for two things: (1) Target Ltd.'s retained earnings balance at the date of acquisition, and (2) adjustments to earnings since the date of acquisition. The 2006 earnings adjustments were for $20,000 amortization of the fair-value increment and for $8,000 unrealized profit on upstream inventory sales. Both of these amounts are subtracted from the opening retained earnings to get the correct, adjusted, beginning balance.

Balance sheet The consolidated balance sheet is shown in Exhibit 4–9. Adjustments are as follows:

- *Accounts receivable.* The intercompany receivable of $500,000 that is included on Target Ltd.'s books must be eliminated.

- *Inventory.* The unrealized profits from both the upstream and downstream sales must be eliminated. The upstream amount is $10,000 × 45% = $4,500; downstream is $6,000 × 30% = $1,800.

- *Land.* Target Ltd.'s land has been sold to Purchase Ltd. Target Ltd. recorded a gain of $150,000 on the sale. This is an intercompany unrealized profit that must be eliminated. However, there was a fair-value increment of $100,000 on the land at the date of purchase. This FVI still must be added on, even though legal title to the land has now been transferred from Target Ltd. to Purchase Ltd.

- *Buildings and equipment.* The date-of-acquisition FVI of $50,000 must be added, just as in 2006.

- *Accumulated depreciation.* Target Ltd.'s date-of-acquisition accumulated depreciation of $150,000 is eliminated; two years' worth of FVI amortization of $20,000 per year is added.

- *Current accounts payable.* Purchase Ltd.'s payables include the $500,000 owed to Target Ltd. This intercompany balance must be eliminated.

- *Common shares.* As usual, only the parent's shares are reported on the consolidated balance sheet.

- *Retained earnings.* Consolidated retained earnings is calculated by starting with the book balances of the two companies, and then:
  (1) subtracting Target Ltd.'s date-of-acquisition retained earnings,
  (2) subtracting year-end unrealized profits, and
  (3) subtracting the cumulative amount of FVI amortization since the date of acquisition (i.e., $20,000 × 2 years).

Wholly Owned

Subsidiaries:

Reporting

Subsequent to

Acquisition

163

EXHIBIT 4–9   PURCHASE LTD. CONSOLIDATED BALANCE SHEET (DIRECT METHOD)

Balance Sheet
December 31, 2007

Assets

Current assets:

Cash [490,000 + 70,000]	$ 560,000
Accounts receivable [1,900,000 + 775,000 – **500,000**]	2,175,000
Inventory [300,000 + 60,000 – **4,500 – 1,800**]	353,700
	3,088,700

Property, plant, and equipment:

Land [1,450,000 + 0 **+ 100,000 – 150,000**]	1,400,000
Buildings and equipment [3,800,000 + 500,000 **+ 50,000**]	4,350,000
Accumulated depreciation [1,400,000 + 220,000 – **150,000 + 40,000**]	(1,510,000)
	4,240,000

Other assets:

Investments [1,200,000 + 0 – **1,200,000**]	—
Goodwill	100,000
Total assets	$7,428,700

Liabilities and shareholders' equity

Liabilities:

Current accounts payable [865,000 + 150,000 – **500,000**]	$ 515,000
Long-term notes payable [500,000 + 0]	500,000
	1,015,000

Shareholders' equity:

Common shares [**Purchase Ltd. shares only**]	3,800,000
Retained earnings [2,575,000 + 835,000 – **600,000**	
– 150,000 – 4,500 – 1,800 – (20,000 × 2)]	2,613,700
	6,413,700
Total liabilities and shareholders' equity	$7,428,700

Notice that it is not necessary to adjust for the unrealized profit in the beginning inventory when we compute the ending consolidated retained earnings. Target Ltd.'s separate-entity retained earnings already includes the $8,000 previously unrealized profit from 2006, and by *not* making any adjustment, we permit it to flow through to consolidated retained earnings as a now-realized amount. Of course, we are assuming that the beginning inventory has been sold during the period. This is the normal assumption; we only need to be told how much of the intercompany sales is still in ending inventory each year (and the relevant gross margin percentage) in order to make the adjustments for unrealized year-end profit, regardless of which year the intercompany sales occurred.

The calculation for Purchase Ltd.'s consolidated retained earnings for December 31, 2007, is as follows:

Purchase Ltd. separate-entity retained earnings	$2,575,000
Target Ltd.'s separate-entity retained earnings	+ 835,000
Target Ltd.'s date-of-acquisition retained earnings	–600,000
Unrealized profit on sale of land	–150,000
Unrealized upstream profit in ending inventory	–4,500
Unrealized downstream profit in ending inventory	–1,800
Two years' amortization of FVI in buildings and equipment	–40,000
Purchase Ltd.'s consolidated retained earnings	**$2,613,700**

As we observed earlier in the chapter, we could have obtained the year-end consolidated retained earnings from the bottom of the statement of income and retained earnings, or simply by treating retained earnings as a "plug" once we had calculated all of the other balances. However, it is useful to be able to derive closing retained earnings directly from information given, rather than going through the whole process of constructing a consolidated income statement. And "plugs" are always dangerous—there is no way to tell if the balance sheet really is in balance.

Worksheet approach

The first two numerical columns of Exhibit 4–10 present the trial balances for Purchase Ltd. and Target Ltd. at December 31, 2007. We will make the adjustments and eliminations much as we did earlier in the chapter for 2006. Again, for greater clarity, we will use separate columns for the acquisition adjustment and the operations adjustments. As well, we will add yet another column, as we will explain in the following paragraphs. There is no real need to use separate columns—a single adjustment column can be used as long as you allow enough rows under each item to record all of the adjustments.

Acquisition and cumulative adjustments To consolidate financial statements at the date of acquisition, we make only two adjustments—to eliminate Target Ltd.'s date-of-acquisition shareholders' equity accounts and to allocate the purchase price discrepancy. When we consolidate the statements one year after acquisition, an additional group of adjustments is necessary to adjust the current year's operations for (1) amortization of the fair-value increments and (2) intercompany transactions and balances.

When we prepare consolidated financial statements more than one year after the acquisition, an additional type of adjustment is necessary. We must adjust the balance sheet accounts for unrealized earnings and fair-value amortization that occurred between the date of acquisition and the *beginning* of the year for which we are preparing consolidated financial statements.

For example, if we prepare consolidated statements for Purchase Ltd. for 2011, we will provide for $20,000 amortization of the fair-value increment of the buildings and equipment for 2011, just as we did in Exhibit 4–3 for 2006. However, the net amount of the fair-value increment that is included on the *balance sheet* on December 31, 2011, will only be $80,000: $200,000 original increment reduced by six years of amortization at $20,000 per year. Therefore, we first need to make an adjustment for the amortization in the five years *prior* to 2011, and then we can make the adjustment for the 2011 amortization to expense.

In Exhibit 4–10, the three different types of adjustments are shown in three separate columns for greater clarity. The first adjustment column (Acquisition) contains exactly the same adjustments as in Exhibit 4–4.

The second adjustment column (Cumulative) shows the adjustments that are necessary in order to restate the beginning balances (at January 1, 2007) correctly. The adjustments for pre-2007 amortization are as follows:

b1	Retained earnings	20,000	
	Accumulated depreciation		20,000

Recall that, at the end of 2006, there was unrealized profit of $8,000 in Purchase Ltd.'s inventory. As we explained above, unrealized profit causes the inventory balance to be overstated. When the overstated opening inventory is added to purchases, the goods available for sale are overstated. That, in turn, causes the cost of sales to be overstated. We adjust for this misstatement by

Wholly Owned
Subsidiaries:
Reporting
Subsequent to
Acquisition

165

EXHIBIT 4–10   PURCHASE LTD. CONSOLIDATION WORKSHEET, DECEMBER 31, 2007

December 31, 2007

	Trial balances		Adjustments Acquisition [a]	Operations Cumulative [b]	Current [c]	Purchase Ltd. consolidated trial balance
	Purchase	Target				
Cash	$ 490,000	$ 70,000				$ 560,000
Accounts receivable	1,900,000	775,000			(500,000) c6	2,175,000
Inventories	300,000	60,000			{ (4,500) c4 (1,800) c5 }	353,700
Land	1,450,000	—	100,000 a2		(150,000) c2	1,400,000
Buildings and equipment	3,800,000	500,000	50,000 a2			4,350,000
Accumulated depreciation	(1,400,000)	(220,000)	150,000 a2	(20,000) b1	(20,000) c1	(1,510,000)
Investments (at cost)	1,200,000	—	{ (800,000) a1 (400,000) a2		}	—
Goodwill			100,000 a2			100,000
						—
Accounts payable	(865,000)	(150,000)			500,000 c6	(515,000)
Long-term notes payable	(500,000)					(500,000)
Common shares	(3,800,000)	(200,000)	200,000 a1			(3,800,000)
Dividends declared	135,000	20,000			(20,000) c7	135,000
Retained earnings, December 31, 2006	(2,330,000)	(635,000)	600,000 a1	{ 20,000 b1 8,000 b2	}	(2,337,000)
Sales	(3,000,000)	(400,000)			80,000 c3	(3,320,000)
Dividend income	(20,000)	—			20,000 c7	—
Gain on sale of land	—	(150,000)			150,000 c2	—
Cost of sales	2,100,000	220,000		(8,000) b2	{ (80,000) c3 4,500 c4 1,800 c5 }	2,238,300
Depreciation expense	100,000	35,000			20,000 c1	155,000
Other expenses	440,000	75,000				515,000
	$ ——	$ ——	$ ——	$ ——	$ ——	$ ——

decreasing cost of sales and simultaneously decreasing opening retained earnings. We must decrease Target Ltd.'s beginning retained earnings by the amount of unrealized profit that is included therein:

b2	Retained earnings, December 31, 2006	8,000	
	Cost of sales		8,000

In effect, what we are doing is transferring the profit on unsold intercompany inventory from the period of Target Ltd.'s book recognition (in 2006) to the year that the inventory was sold externally (in 2007).

Current operations The third column of adjustments contains all the figures necessary to adjust the balance sheet at the end of the year and the income statement accounts for intercompany transactions during the year.

The first adjustment (1) is for the 2007 depreciation on the fair-value increment for buildings and equipment:

| **c1** | Depreciation expense | 20,000 | |
| | Accumulated depreciation | | 20,000 |

The second adjustment is to eliminate the gain that Target Ltd. recorded when it sold its land to Purchase Ltd. (i.e., upstream):

| **c2** | Gain on sale of land | 150,000 | |
| | Land | | 150,000 |

The third adjustment is for the intercompany sales during 2007. Total intercompany sales were $60,000 upstream plus $20,000 downstream, a total of $80,000:

| **c3** | Sales | 80,000 | |
| | Cost of sales | | 80,000 |

Of the upstream sales, $10,000 is still in Purchase Ltd.'s year-end 2007 inventory. Since Target Ltd. had a gross margin of 45%, unrealized gross profit is $4,500. The fourth adjustment is to increase cost of sales and reduce ending inventory by $4,500:

| **c4** | Cost of sales | 4,500 | |
| | Inventory | | 4,500 |

Of the $20,000 downstream sales, $6,000 is still in Target Ltd.'s year-end inventory. Purchase Ltd.'s gross margin is 30%, and therefore Target Ltd.'s ending inventory includes $1,800 of unrealized profit:

| **c5** | Cost of sales | 1,800 | |
| | Inventory | | 1,800 |

At the end of 2007, Purchase Ltd. borrowed $500,000 from Target Ltd. The offsetting receivable and payable must be eliminated before preparing the consolidated financial statements:

| **c6** | Accounts payable | 500,000 | |
| | Accounts receivable | | 500,000 |

The final adjustment that is made on Exhibit 4–10 is the elimination of the intercompany dividends paid by Target Ltd. to Purchase Ltd.:

| **c7** | Dividend income | 20,000 | |
| | Dividends declared | | 20,000 |

After all of the adjustments have been entered on the worksheet, we can cross-add the rows to find the 2007 consolidated trial balance amounts. The amounts in the last column are used to prepare the consolidated statements.

Completed consolidated financial statements

Exhibits 4–11 through 4–13 present the complete consolidated financial statements for Purchase Ltd. as of December 31, 2007. Since financial statements should be comparative statements, the 2007 statements also include the amounts for 2006. A complete set of financial statements must include a cash flow statement. Exhibit 4–13 illustrates a cash flow statement.

Wholly Owned
Subsidiaries:
Reporting
Subsequent to
Acquisition

167

EXHIBIT 4–11 PURCHASE LTD. CONSOLIDATED STATEMENT OF INCOME AND RETAINED EARNINGS

Years Ended December 31

	2007	2006
Sales revenue	$3,320,000	$2,645,000
Operating expenses:		
Cost of sales	2,238,300	1,883,000
Depreciation expense	155,000	155,000
Other expenses	515,000	270,000
	2,908,300	2,308,000
Net income	$ 411,700	$ 337,000
Retained earnings, January 1	2,337,000	2,000,000
Dividends declared	(135,000)	—
Retained earnings, December 31	$2,613,700	$2,337,000

EXHIBIT 4–12 PURCHASE LTD. CONSOLIDATED BALANCE SHEET

December 31

	2007	2006
Assets		
Current assets:		
Cash	$ 560,000	$ 1,080,000
Accounts receivable	2,175,000	2,450,000
Inventory	353,700	312,000
	3,088,700	3,842,000
Property, plant, and equipment:		
Land	1,400,000	1,400,000
Buildings and equipment	4,350,000	3,550,000
Accumulated depreciation	(1,510,000)	(1,355,000)
	4,240,000	3,595,000
Other assets:		
Goodwill	100,000	100,000
Total assets	$ 7,428,700	$ 7,537,000
Liabilities and shareholders' equity		
Liabilities:		
Current accounts payable	$ 515,000	$ 1,000,000
Long-term notes payable	500,000	400,000
	1,015,000	1,400,000
Shareholders' equity:		
Common shares	3,800,000	3,800,000
Retained earnings	2,613,700	2,337,000
	6,413,700	6,137,000
Total liabilities and shareholders' equity	$ 7,428,700	$ 7,537,000

EXHIBIT 4-13   CONSOLIDATED CASH FLOW STATEMENT

Years Ended December 31

	2007	2006
Operating activities		
Consolidated net income, as reported	$ 411,700	$ 337,000
Add expenses not requiring cash:		
Depreciation on capital assets	155,000	155,000
Changes in working capital items:		
Current accounts receivable	275,000	(300,000)
Inventory	(41,700)	(62,000)
Accounts payable	(485,000)	(100,000)
Net cash from operating activities	315,000	30,000
Financing activities		
Increase in long-term notes payable	100,000	—
Dividends declared and paid	(135,000)	—
	(35,000)	—
Investing activities		
Purchase of buildings and equipment	(800,000)	—
Increase (decrease) in cash	$(520,000)	$ 30,000

The preparation of a consolidated cash flow statement involves no particular challenges. The statement can be prepared by combining the cash flow statements of the separate entities and eliminating intercompany transactions. Alternatively, the statement can be prepared directly from the consolidated income statement, balance sheet, and statement of retained earnings in exactly the same manner as from any other set of financial statements.

Note disclosure

While Exhibits 4–11 through 4–13 do present the complete set of statements, they do not present the notes thereto. The notes should contain additional disclosure of Purchase Ltd.'s acquisition of Target Ltd., as we discussed at the end of the preceding chapter.

The 2003 edition of *Financial Reporting in Canada* reported that none of the business combinations in 2002 disclosed all of the *CICA Handbook*'s recommended information. Compliance ranged from 92% for the cost of the purchase down to 3% for a condensed balance sheet for the acquired company.[6] The report does not speculate on the reasons for non-compliance with the disclosure recommendations, but a lack of materiality may have been a factor in at least some instances.

Consolidating parent-founded subsidiaries

The example used throughout this chapter is that of a business combination.

Purchase Ltd. acquired control over the net assets of Target Ltd. at a price that included both fair-value increments and goodwill. By using a business combination as the basis for the example, we can fairly comprehensively illustrate the

Wholly Owned
Subsidiaries:
Reporting
Subsequent to
Acquisition

169

major types of adjustments that may be required when consolidated statements are prepared.

However, we pointed out in Chapter 2 that most subsidiaries are not the result of one corporation's acquiring another in a business combination. Instead, most subsidiaries are formed by their parent to conduct or facilitate some component of the parent's business. The process of consolidation for a subsidiary that was founded and wholly owned by its parent is much easier than for a subsidiary that was acquired as a going concern.

Since the investment by the parent was directly in the subsidiary (rather than by buying the subsidiary's shares from another shareholder), the paid-in capital accounts of the subsidiary directly offset the original investment in the investment account of the parent. There are no fair-value increments or goodwill to worry about. The lack of fair-value increments means that there is no periodic amortization of those amounts to adjust for. Consolidating a wholly owned, parent-founded subsidiary simply requires:

1. adjusting for intercompany transactions

2. eliminating any unrealized profits or losses, and

3. eliminating intercompany receivable and payable balances.

Indirect holdings

In Chapter 2, we pointed out that a parent company might control a subsidiary indirectly through other subsidiaries, rather than by direct ownership. When the parent prepares its consolidated financial statements, both the direct and the indirect subsidiaries are consolidated.

Procedurally, indirect subsidiaries can be consolidated in either of two ways. The first is to consolidate by steps, from the bottom up. If P controls A, and A controls B and C, then consolidated statements for A can be prepared that include its direct subsidiaries, B and C. A's *consolidated* statements will then include all of the assets and liabilities of B and C just as if A owned them directly, and the investment accounts will have been eliminated. The next step is then to consolidate A's *consolidated* statements with P's statements. If the consolidation is being performed by the direct approach without a worksheet, then the step method is almost certainly the best one to use.

The second approach is to perform the consolidation of all subsidiaries, direct and indirect, on a single worksheet. A single-step worksheet approach may be easiest for those who are performing the consolidation on a computer spreadsheet, since it is relatively easy to include all of the subsidiaries on the worksheet with adequate space for explanatory notes.

Whichever procedural approach is used, the elimination and adjustment process is no different from that illustrated in this chapter for directly owned subsidiaries.

The process of consolidation is simplified when all subsidiaries use the same accounting policies as the parent. This is fairly easily accomplished with wholly owned subsidiaries—the parent company's management can specify the subsidiaries' accounting policies. When the same accounting policies are used, there will be no need for the parent to adjust the accounts of the subsidiaries for accounting policy differences.

SUMMARY OF KEY POINTS

1. The parent company and each of its subsidiaries will prepare individual, separate-entity, financial statements. These statements are independent of the consolidated statements. Consolidated statements are prepared only for the shareholders of the parent company. The existence of consolidated statements does not eliminate the need for separate-entity statements.

2. Only a balance sheet is necessary when a parent and its purchased subsidiary are consolidated at the date of acquisition. At all subsequent reporting dates, consolidation involves a full set of financial statements.

3. At reporting dates following acquisition, consolidated net income must be adjusted for amortization of fair-value increments, adjustments to goodwill, and elimination of unrealized profits on intercompany sales. Amortization of fair-value increments on tangible and intangible assets should be based on the estimated remaining useful life of the asset. Goodwill must be written down if its value for generating future earnings is impaired.

4. Sales of current and non-current assets between a parent and its subsidiaries, or between subsidiaries, should be eliminated. Profits on intercompany sales of assets should be eliminated, unless the asset has been sold to outside third parties.

5. If consolidated statements are not prepared, the parent can report its investment in the subsidiary on either the cost or the equity basis. If the equity basis is used for reporting non-consolidated subsidiaries, the parent company's reported net income and retained earnings will be exactly the same as though the statements had been consolidated.

6. Discontinued operations and extraordinary items arising both in consolidated subsidiaries and in equity-reported subsidiaries are reported as such in the parent's income statement. However, a discontinued operation or an extraordinary item may change its status within the broader economic context of the consolidated entity.

7. A complete set of consolidated financial statements should include a cash flow statement. The cash flow statement can be prepared for consolidated statements in exactly the same manner as for separate-entity statements.

Wholly-Owned

Subsidiaries:

Reporting

Subsequent to

Acquisition

171

SELF-STUDY PROBLEM 4–1

Early in 2005, Parco acquired 100% of the shares of Subco by issuing Parco shares worth $10 million. The book value of Subco's net assets at the date of acquisition was $7,000,000. The fair values of Subco's assets were deemed to be equal to their carrying values on Subco's books with one exception: the aggregate fair value of Subco's buildings was $1,400,000 higher than their carrying value.

Parco and Subco enjoyed a trading relationship for many years prior to the combination. In 2004, for example, Subco had sold $1 million of goods to Parco (at a gross margin of 20% on sales), and Parco had billed Subco $300,000 for management services. However, the two companies had no common ownership interest and were not related companies prior to the 2005 business combination.

In 2005, following the business combination, Subco had sales of $1.2 million to Parco. Subco's gross margin remained at 20%. Of the amount sold, $200,000 remained in Parco's inventory at the end of 2005. Parco billed Subco $400,000 for management fees, of which $100,000 remained unpaid at the end of the year. Other information is as follows:

a. Subco reported separate-entity net income of $350,000 for 2005. Subco declared and paid dividends of $150,000 during the year.

b. Parco reported separate-entity net income of $680,000 for 2005, including the dividend income from Subco. Parco declared dividends of $200,000, of which one-quarter were unpaid at year-end.

c. Retained earnings at the date of acquisition were $3,450,000 for Parco and $1,250,000 for Subco.

d. Subco's buildings have an estimated remaining useful life of 14 years. Subco uses straight-line depreciation.

e. There has been no impairment of goodwill.

Required:

Determine the following amounts:

a. Parco's consolidated net income for the year ended December 31, 2005.

b. Parco's consolidated retained earnings at December 31, 2005.

c. Parco's equity-basis earnings from Subco for 2005.

SELF-STUDY PROBLEM 4–2

On January 1, 2008, Parent Ltd. (Par) bought 100% of the shares of Subsidiary Inc. (Sub) for $1,084,000 cash. Sub's balance sheet at the date of acquisition is shown in Exhibit 4–14, together with the estimated fair values of Sub's assets and liabilities.

Additional information is as follows:

a. Sub depreciates its tangible capital assets over 10 years on a straight-line basis, assuming zero residual value.

b. During 2009, Par sold goods with a cost of $300,000 to Sub for $390,000. At the end of 2009, 20% of those goods remain in Sub's inventory.

EXHIBIT 4–14 SUBSIDIARY INC. BALANCE SHEET		
January 1, 2008		
	Book values	**Fair values**
Cash	$ 80,000	$ 80,000
Accounts receivable	99,000	99,000
Inventory	178,000	195,000
Property, plant, and equipment	800,000	740,000
Accumulated depreciation	(200,000)	
Total assets	$ 957,000	
Accounts payable	$70,000	70,000
Long-term notes payable	200,000	200,000
Common shares	250,000	
Retained earnings	437,000	
Total liabilities and shareholders' equity	$ 957,000	

c. Sub sold goods costing $100,000 to Par for $150,000 in 2009. At the end of the year, 40% of these goods remain in Par's inventory.

d. Par sold land to Sub on January 1, 2009, for $710,000. The original cost of the land was $500,000 to Par. The gain was netted to "other expenses."

e. On January 1, 2009, Par had inventory on hand that it had bought from Sub for $45,000. Intercompany profit of $12,000 was included in that price.

The separate-entity financial statements for Par and Sub for the year ended December 31, 2009, are shown in Exhibit 4–15.

EXHIBIT 4–15 SEPARATE-ENTITY FINANCIAL STATEMENTS FOR 2009

Income Statements
Year Ended December 31, 2009

	Parent Ltd.	Subsidiary Inc.
Sales revenue	$1,200,000	$ 987,000
Cost of goods sold	(800,000)	(650,000)
	400,000	337,000
Other operating expenses	(235,000)	(147,000)
Net income	$ 165,000	$ 190,000
Retained earnings, December 31, 2008	1,153,000	330,000
Retained earnings, December 31, 2009	$1,318,000	$ 520,000

Balance Sheets
December 31, 2009

	Parent Ltd.	Subsidiary Inc.
Assets		
Current assets:		
Cash	$ 120,000	$ 110,000
Accounts receivable	150,000	135,000
Inventory	240,000	195,000
	510,000	440,000
Property, plant, and equipment	1,400,000	910,000
Accumulated depreciation	(510,000)	(320,000)
	890,000	590,000
Other assets:		
Investments (at cost)	1,084,000	
Goodwill	76,000	
	1,160,000	
Total assets	$2,560,000	$1,030,000
Liabilities and shareholders' equity		
Liabilities:		
Accounts payable	$ 142,000	$ 60,000
Long-term notes payable	600,000	200,000
	742,000	260,000
Shareholders' equity:		
Common shares	500,000	250,000
Retained earnings	1,318,000	520,000
	1,818,000	770,000
Total liabilities and shareholders' equity	$2,560,000	$1,030,000

Wholly-Owned
Subsidiaries:
Reporting
Subsequent to
Acquisition

173

Required:

Prepare the consolidated financial statements for 2009.

REVIEW QUESTIONS

4-1 Define the following terms:
   a. Unrealized profits
   b. Upstream sales
   c. Downstream sales
   d. One-line consolidation
   e. Equity pick-up of earnings
   f. Goodwill impairment test
   g. Reporting unit

4-2 What is accomplished by the acquisition adjustment when consolidated statements are prepared?

4-3 How would the acquisition adjustment for an acquired subsidiary differ from that for a parent-founded subsidiary?

4-4 How is goodwill arising from a business combination accounted for in years following the combination?

4-5 Why are the fair-value increments and decrements on depreciable capital assets amortized? What is the basis for determining the amount of amortization?

4-6 When is it necessary to eliminate the profit on intercompany transactions?

4-7 How does management judgment impact on the impairment test for goodwill?

4-8 What is the differential reporting option for the goodwill impairment test?

4-9 Explain why the adjustment for unrealized profit in ending inventories appears to *increase* cost of goods sold.

4-10 Explain the difference between the acquisition adjustment and the operations adjustments.

4-11 Why is the equity method of reporting sometimes called the consolidation method of equity reporting?

4-12 How does a parent company's total net assets differ under consolidated reporting as compared to equity reporting for a subsidiary?

4-13 Under equity reporting, how do discontinued operations or an extraordinary item of an investee corporation affect the income statement of the investor corporation?

4-14 How does unrealized profit in the beginning inventories affect the consolidated net income, if the inventories have been sold during the year?

4-15 What disclosure should be made in the financial statements of an acquirer as to the details of a business combination?

4–16 In what general ways will consolidation of a parent-founded subsidiary differ from consolidation of a purchased subsidiary?

4–17 Are consolidated statements required after one corporation directly acquires the net assets of another corporation?

CASES

CASE 4–1   Growth Limited

You are the CA appointed as the new auditor of Growth Limited (GL), a private company, for the next three years. The requirement for an audit is specified in GL's debt covenant with the bank. This is the first year that an audit will be completed.

As part of an ongoing expansion program, GL added two new sizes to its line of fish-crate products. The president of GL is pleased with the continuing expansion program. Annual sales are $1,800,000, the highest level in GL's history and a real achievement for a firm of its size. The president attributes the increase in sales to the exacting standards of quality incorporated in its new products.

"We have never amortized or tested goodwill for impairment since goodwill is being built up in our business, not used. In fact, I can never see it going down in value since our business is continuing to grow. This year for the first time we acquired another company that provides additional products to add to our line. That increased our goodwill even more than we have now."

"I have also been able to invest more funds and save taxes without impacting on the covenant through cumulative preferred shares. My friend, a tax whiz, thought of this option for me. The dividend rate is similar to our interest rate at the bank. These shares have a mandatory redemption or payment date five years from now. If there are dividends in arrears they must also be paid at that date. I cannot see that we will have any dividends in arrears at the rate we are growing. What's more, these shares have huge tax advantages."

"We also wrote off the future income tax balance this year because it doesn't mean anything. In fact, our banker adds the accumulated future income tax balance to retained earnings when he reviews our annual financing proposals. I just couldn't think of any reason why we should pay you to calculate future income taxes when no one uses them."

Required:

Discuss the president's comments.

[CICA, adapted]

CASE 4–2   Pelican Systems Inc.

Pelican Systems Inc. (PSI), a public company, develops and manufactures equipment that is sold to technology, communications, and airline enterprises, and designs and installs customized information networks for customers. The chief executive officer (CEO) of PSI retired on December 31, 2004, and Gerald Cinco was hired as his replacement. An executive search firm recommended Cinco and he signed a three-year employment contract with PSI that includes performance bonuses. At the annual shareholders' meeting held on March 6, 2005, Cinco predicted strong growth in revenue and in earnings per share, which would result in a healthy increase in the value of PSI's shares.

Wholly-Owned
Subsidiaries:
Reporting
Subsequent to
Acquisition

175

Cinco's predictions were validated by PSI's results as reflected in its audited financial statements for the fiscal year ended December 31, 2005, and a substantial increase in the share value from the preceding year-end share value.

Following its policy of appointing new auditors every five years, at the annual shareholders' meeting held on March 5, 2006, Sharp & Ipson, Chartered Accountants LLP (S&I), was appointed as auditor for the year ending December 31, 2006.

At the March 5 meeting, the board of directors agreed to adopt a conservative approach to financial reporting and has asked S&I to evaluate existing accounting policies with this in mind. The board stated that it wanted to be apprised of the cumulative effect of introducing more conservative policies in significant areas.

It is now March 17, 2006. You are a CA with S&I and have been assigned the responsibility for the PSI audit engagement. You have obtained the extracts from the consolidated financial statements for the year ended December 31, 2005 (Exhibit A), information pertaining to the operations and accounting policies of PSI gathered through interviews with company employees (Exhibit B), and extracts from the audit working papers prepared by the predecessor auditor (Exhibit C).

The partner responsible for the PSI audit will be attending a meeting of the board of directors on March 26, 2006, to report on S&I's evaluation of the accounting policies used to prepare the financial statements for the year ended December 31, 2005, and any significant considerations resulting from the use of these accounting policies, and to describe significant issues pertaining to the audit of the financial statements for the year ending December 31, 2006. In addition, the partner has been asked to provide advice about improvements to PSI's risk management and corporate governance systems. The partner has asked you to prepare a memo to help her to prepare for the board of directors meeting, and, to also include in the memo audit planning issues for her consideration.

Required:

Prepare the memo requested by the partner.

EXHIBIT A

EXTRACTS FROM CONSOLIDATED FINANCIAL STATEMENTS

Pelican Systems Inc.
Consolidated Balance Sheet
as at December 31
(in thousands of dollars)

	2005	2004
Assets		
Current Assets		
Cash	$ 2,080	$ 1,090
Accounts receivable	11,300	10,200
Inventory	8,400	7,350
Prepaids	720	690
	22,500	19,330
Property, plant and equipment (net)	40,400	44,800
Long-term investments	2,500	—
Deferred charges	2,604	870
Goodwill and other intangible assets	3,956	—
	$71,960	$65,000

Liabilities and Shareholders' Equity

Current Liabilities

Bank indebtedness	$ 8,850	$12,000
Accounts payable and accruals	3,110	3,160
Current portion of long-term debt	4,750	4,000
	16,710	19,160
Long-term debt	33,250	28,000
Future income taxes	1,090	980
	51,050	48,140
Common shares	12,000	12,000
Retained earnings	8,910	4,860
	20,910	16,860
	$71,960	$65,000

Pelican Systems Inc.
Consolidated Income Statement
for the years ended December 31
(in thousands of dollars)

	2005	2004
Revenues	$80,000	$73,000
Cost of generating revenues	49,600	44,100
Gross margin	30,400	28,900
Selling, general & administrative expenses	14,400	14,600
Interest and financing charges	2,650	2,380
Amortization expense	5,850	6,420
	22,900	23,400
Income before taxes	7,500	5,500
Income taxes	2,850	2,090
Net income	$ 4,650	$ 3,410

EXHIBIT B

INFORMATION PERTAINING TO THE OPERATIONS AND ACCOUNTING POLICIES OF PSI

Sales Leasing Program

To stimulate sales, PSI sells customized equipment on a leasing basis whereby an unrelated financial institution purchases the equipment from PSI and leases this equipment to PSI's customers. PSI arranges sales on this basis for higher credit-risk customers. This sales practice was adopted effective April 1, 2005, as directed by the CEO "to expand our customer base to meet our objective of sales and earnings growth."

PSI pays a financing arrangement fee of 10% of the selling price of the equipment to the financial institution as compensation for extending a lower interest rate to the customer than would be typical for the credit risk related to the customer. PSI guarantees the payments of the customers. The financial institution holds title to the equipment until the final lease payment is made, at which time title is transferred to the lessee. PSI has the right to purchase each of the lease receivables from the financial institution at any time for the amount of the outstanding balance. The financing arrangement fee is not refundable.

During the fiscal year ended December 31, 2005, sales totalling $12,000,000 were made under the terms of this leasing program, which provided PSI with a

Wholly-Owned
Subsidiaries:
Reporting
Subsequent to
Acquisition

177

cash flow of $10,800,000 net of the financing arrangement fee paid to the financial institution. PSI's gross margin on these sales, before the financing arrangement fee, was $5,400,000.

PSI's director of marketing stated that, in January 2006, the financial institution advised PSI that $1,600,000 of the $2,000,000 principal portion of the payments due by December 31, 2005, had been made by the lessees and requested compensation of $400,000 plus interest of $24,000 for payments in arrears.

Acquisition of Equipment

On July 1, 2005, PSI acquired state-of-the-art technology equipment that is being used to manufacture a new product line under a special financing arrangement. PSI is required to pay to the seller 15% of the profit, defined as gross margin, realized from sales of this product line during the three years ending August 31, 2008. PSI is required to remit the amount due annually no later than November 30 of each year, with the amount supported by "a certification by PSI's auditor that PSI has remitted in full the amount due under the terms of the financing arrangement."

According to PSI's director of procurements, the cost to PSI to purchase the equipment for cash would have been $3,000,000. Revenue from sales of the new product line is projected to total $65,000,000 for the three years ending August 31, 2008, as follows: first year, $19,500,000; second year, $27,300,000; third year, $18,200,000; and for the fourth and fifth years combined, $25,000,000. The life of the product line is estimated to be five years. The projected gross margin is 40%. Sales of the new product line commenced on September 1, 2005, and totalled $6,500,000 for the four months ended December 31, 2005, and generated a gross margin of $2,600,000. This product line is often included in a "bundle of equipment" sold to customers and a portion of the selling price of the "bundle" is allocated internally to this product line.

PSI's accounting policy is to recognize the amount payable to the seller annually on August 31 as a charge to the cost of generating revenues. No amount was accrued at December 31, 2005.

Sale of Subsidiary

On November 1, 2005, PSI sold a wholly owned subsidiary, Ersatz Technologies Inc. (ETI), and realized a gain of $1,600,000 on the sale. The gain was included in selling, general and administrative expense (SG&A) in PSI's income statement and was not separately disclosed. PSI's annual report for fiscal 2005 included a statement that the corporation had "achieved its goal of improvements in efficiency and cost control by reducing SG&A to 18% of sales revenue from its previous level of 20%."

Investment in H&P

In February 2005, PSI invested $2,500,000 in Hope & Pratt Ltd. (H&P), a publicly traded dot-com enterprise. This represented a 10% stake in the 25,000,000 shares issued. By May 2005, H&P's shares were trading at a market price of $60 per share. On December 31, 2005, H&P's shares were trading at $20 per share and had dropped to $5 per share by February 1, 2006, as a result of financial warnings issued by H&P. H&P's shares are currently trading at $4 per share. H&P reported a loss of $9,800,000 for the year ended December 31, 2005.

Acquisition of ATI

Effective September 1, 2005, PSI acquired 100% ownership of AvanTemps Inc. (ATI) at a cost of $6,000,000. PSI determined its offering price as follows:

- fair value of ATI's net tangible assets, $2,044,000

- $1,500,000 payment to Ethan Brodsky (who owned 51% of the shares of ATI, is the founder of ATI, and is responsible for the development of ATI's advanced technologies) for entering into a three-year employment contract with PSI

- $456,000 for unused non-capital losses totalling $1,200,000 at a tax rate of 38%, and

- $2,000,000 to reflect the value of ATI's business.

Brodsky was also granted stock options for shares of PSI.

Based on ATI's profitability in the first quarter of fiscal 2006 and on projected profitability in the future, the treasurer advised you that the benefit of the unused tax losses will be recognized as a reduction in income tax expense in fiscal 2006.

Other

The CEO's employment contract includes a bonus based on income before taxes and before special charges and credits.

PSI is subject to a debt covenant that specifies that PSI is not to exceed a debt to equity ratio of 2:1, with debt defined as consolidated long-term debt, including the current portion. If PSI is in violation of this covenant, the creditor has the right to demand repayment of all or a portion of the debt.

Your firm, S&I, is not engaged to review PSI's unaudited interim financial statements that are issued as required by regulatory authorities.

Wholly-Owned
Subsidiaries:
Reporting
Subsequent to
Acquisition

179

EXHIBIT C

EXTRACTS FROM WORKING PAPERS PREPARED BY PREDECESSOR AUDITOR

1. Materiality was set at $1,000,000 based on projected revenue for fiscal 2005.

2. Inherent risk was noted as "greater than in previous years for fiscal 2005 because of the new CEO's objective of reporting earnings growth and because of the risk of manipulation of earnings to maximize his bonus."

3. The working papers pertaining to the new sales leasing program include the following information:

- PSI's accounting policy is to recognize the profit on these sales at the date of sale to the financial institution that acts as a lessor to PSI's customers and to recognize the cost of the payment guarantees as paid to the financial institution. PSI accrued a $424,000 liability on December 31, 2005, and included this amount in accounts payable based on notification by the financial institution of customer payments in arrears. PSI remitted this amount, which includes interest of $24,000, to the financial institution on January 31, 2006. The CA concluded that PSI's accounting policy is acceptable because title to the equipment is transferred to the financial institution and the cost of the payment guarantee is reflected in PSI's financial statements.

- PSI's accounting policy is to defer and amortize the financing arrangement fee over the three-year term of the leases. Amortization of $200,000 of the $1,200,000 in fees incurred in fiscal 2005 is included in the "interest and financing charges" income statement account and the unamortized balance of $1,000,000 is included in the "deferred charges" balance sheet account.

4. A working paper noted that the determination of the gain on the sale of ETI had been verified and that PSI had received the full amount of the proceeds from the sale.

5. A working paper noted that the treasurer had informed the auditor that "it is too early to determine whether or not the loss in value of the H&P investment is other than a temporary decline." He is hopeful for a turnaround by H&P.

6. A working paper pertaining to the acquisition of ATI includes the following information:
    - An intangible asset in the amount of $1,500,000 has been recognized for the employment contract and is considered to have an indefinite life until such time as Brodsky announces his intention to leave PSI.

7. Deferred charges included the following (in thousands of dollars):

	2005	2004
Deferred development costs	$1,544	$870
Deferred financing arrangement fee	1,000	—
Deferred executive search fee	60	—
	$2,604	$870

The cost of the executive search for the new CEO was $90,000.

8. The bonus payable to the CEO for the year ended December 31, 2005 is $750,000 calculated as follows: income before bonus and income taxes of $8,250,000/1.10 = $7,500,000 × 10% bonus rate. The bonus is included in selling, general and administrative expenses.

9. Other information in the working papers includes:
    - the CEO, Gerald Cinco, is the chair of the audit committee
    - a reading of the minutes of the board of directors' meetings indicated that little attention was paid to financial accounting matters because the board relied on the audit committee to deal with these matters
    - internal audit was unable to meet its audit objectives because members were often called on to perform accounting functions and special projects for the treasurer, and
    - internal audit reports "in theory" to the CEO but, according to the director of internal audit, internal audit reports are usually not acted on.

10. A working paper concludes that the debt covenant has not been violated because the debt-to-equity ratio of 1.82:1 is below the limit of 2:1.

11. A working paper concludes that there are no matters to be communicated to the audit committee because "the committee has not requested us to specifically report any matters and because the CEO is a member of the audit committee."

[ICAO]

PROBLEMS

P4–1

Officeplus Corporation is a retailer of office supplies and equipment in Vancouver. On March 5, 2006, Officeplus formed a new corporation in Calgary in order to operate the same type of business. Officeplus invested $200,000 cash in exchange for 10,000 common shares in the new subsidiary, to be known as Plus Limited.

During 2006, Plus Limited commenced operations. Most of Plus's initial inventory came from Officeplus. In total, goods that had cost Officeplus $200,000 were sold to Plus at an assigned value of $250,000. These goods were repriced by Plus to sell for $500,000 at retail. At year-end, 30% of the merchandise acquired from Officeplus was still in Plus's inventory. 75K

Officeplus also extended a loan to Plus to finance the start-up costs. A total of $150,000 was lent during the year, of which $80,000 was still owing at year-end. Interest of $10,000 on the loan had been accrued by both companies, of which only $8,000 had actually been paid during 2006.

Condensed balance sheets and income statements of the two companies are presented below, as of December 31, 2006.

Required:

Prepare a consolidated balance sheet and income statement for Officeplus Corporation at December 31, 2006.

Balance Sheets
December 31, 2006

	Officeplus	Plus
Cash	$ 85,000	$ 10,000
Accounts and other receivables	275,000	130,000
Inventories	440,000	60,000
Capital assets	500,000	400,000
Accumulated amortization	(200,000)	(30,000)
Investment in Plus (at cost)	200,000	—
	$1,300,000	$570,000
Accounts and other payables	$ 300,000	$150,000
Long-term liabilities	270,000	200,000
Common shares	50,000	200,000
Retained earnings	680,000	20,000
	$1,300,000	$570,000

Statements of Income and Retained Earnings
Year Ended December 31, 2006

	Officeplus	Plus
Sales	$2,000,000	$600,000
Other income	70,000	—
	2,070,000	600,000
Expenses	1,700,000	540,000
Net income	370,000	60,000
Retained earnings, December 31, 2005	510,000	—
Dividends	(200,000)	(40,000)
Retained earnings, December 31, 2006	$ 680,000	$ 20,000

Wholly-Owned
Subsidiaries:
Reporting
Subsequent to
Acquisition

181

P4–2

At the end of 2007, the condensed balance sheets and income statements of Officeplus Corporation and Plus Limited were as they appear below. Intercompany activities were as follows:

1. Plus sold all of its opening (i.e., December 31, 2006) inventory including that acquired from Officeplus (see **P4–1**).

2. Plus purchased merchandise from Officeplus for $400,000. This price included a 25% markup over the cost to Officeplus. At year-end, 40% of these goods were still in Plus's inventory.

3. Plus sold to Officeplus some merchandise for $120,000. Plus had acquired the merchandise for $100,000. The merchandise was all in Officeplus's inventory at year-end, but is expected to sell for $150,000 in 2008.

4. Plus fully repaid Officeplus the $80,000 loan that had been outstanding at the beginning of the year, plus $7,000 in interest ($2,000 of the interest pertained to 2006).

5. Officeplus purchased a plot of land in Calgary for $100,000 and resold it to Plus for $140,000.

Required:

Prepare a consolidated statement of income and retained earnings and a consolidated balance sheet for Officeplus Corporation for 2007.

Balance Sheets
December 31, 2007

	Officeplus	Plus
Cash	$ 50,000	$ 10,000
Accounts and other receivables	230,000	60,000
Inventories	470,000	195,000
Capital assets	560,000	520,000
Accumulated depreciation	(230,000)	(60,000)
Investment in Plus	200,000	—
Other investments	140,000	—
	$1,420,000	$725,000
Accounts and other payables	$ 360,000	$250,000
Long-term liabilities	250,000	230,000
Common shares	50,000	200,000
Retained earnings	760,000	45,000
	$1,420,000	$725,000

Wholly-Owned

Subsidiaries:

Reporting

Subsequent to

Acquisition

183

Statements of Income and Retained Earnings
Year Ended December 31, 2007

Sales	$2,300,000	$720,000
Other income	100,000	—
	2,400,000	720,000
Expenses	2,100,000	650,000
Net income	300,000	70,000
Dividends	(220,000)	(45,000)
Retained earnings, December 31, 2006	680,000	20,000
Retained earnings, December 31, 2007	$ 760,000	$ 45,000

P4–3

On January 1, 2006, Big Inc. acquired 100% of the outstanding shares of Small Corp. for $10,000,000 cash. On this date, Small had shareholders' equity of $8,000,000, including $4,000,000 in retained earnings. Small had buildings and equipment that had a fair value of $1,200,000 less than book value, inventory that had a fair value of $300,000 greater than book value, and investments that had a fair value of $1,300,000 greater than book value.

The balance sheets of the two companies on December 31, 2006, are shown below.

Additional Information:

1. The goodwill on Small's books arose from the purchase of another company several years ago, a company that has since been amalgamated into Small. The goodwill was assumed to have a fair value of zero on January 1, 2006.

2. Small's plant and equipment has an estimated average remaining life of 10 years from January 1, 2006. The net book value of the plant and equipment was $10,000,000 on that date, after deducting $4,000,000 of accumulated depreciation.

3. On January 1, 2006, Big held inventory of $800,000 that had been purchased from Small. Small had sold the merchandise to Big at a 100% markup over cost.

4. On December 31, 2006, Big held inventory of $1,000,000 that had been purchased from Small during 2006 at 100% above Small's cost.

5. At the end of 2006, Big owed Small $400,000 for merchandise purchased on account.

6. During 2006, Small sold an investment for $800,000. The investment had cost Small $360,000, and had a fair value of $600,000 on January 1, 2006.

7. Big's retained earnings on December 31, 2006, include dividend income received from Small. Small declared dividends of $400,000 in 2006.

Required:

Prepare a consolidated balance sheet for Big Inc. at December 31, 2006.

Balance Sheet
December 31, 2006

	Big	Small
Cash	$ 2,000,000	$ 600,000
Accounts receivable	3,200,000	800,000
Inventories	4,800,000	1,400,000
Plant and equipment	42,000,000	14,000,000
Accumulated depreciation	(12,000,000)	(5,000,000)
Goodwill	—	800,000
Long-term investments (cost)	10,000,000	3,200,000
Total assets	$50,000,000	$15,800,000
Accounts payable	$ 6,000,000	$ 1,000,000
Bonds payable	10,000,000	6,000,000
Common shares	14,000,000	4,000,000
Retained earnings	20,000,000	4,800,000
	$50,000,000	$15,800,000

P4–4

On January 1, 2006, Parent Ltd. purchased 100% of the outstanding voting common shares of Sub Ltd. for $2,800,000. Any revaluation arising from the purchase of depreciable assets is to be amortized over 10 years.

During 2006, the following events occurred:

1. No dividends were paid on the shares by either company.

2. Sub Ltd. sold inventory costing $494,000 to Parent Ltd. for $682,000, 30% of which was not sold at year-end.

3. During 2006, all of the current assets that had a fair market value greater than book value were sold to outside parties or were collected.

4. On July 1, 2006, Parent Ltd. purchased 60% of the outstanding 10% bonds payable of Sub Ltd. for $129,000. These bonds have a 20-year total life with 15 years remaining at January 1, 2006.

5. Parent Ltd. has made no entries in the Investment in Sub Ltd. account following the acquisition.

Condensed trial balance information for Sub Ltd. and Parent Ltd. is shown below.

Required:

Prepare a consolidated statement of income and retained earnings and a consolidated balance sheet for Parent Ltd. for the year ended December 31, 2006.

[CGA–Canada, adapted]

Sub Limited

	Post-closing trial balance January 1, 2006	Fair market value January 1, 2006	Pre-closing trial balance December 31, 2006
Cash	$ 185,000	$185,000	$ 135,000
Accounts receivable, net	432,000	450,000	385,000
Inventory	690,000	730,000	730,000
Land	510,000	570,000	510,000
Buildings & equipment, net	974,000	850,000	963,000
Goodwill	110,000	0	110,000
	$2,901,000		$2,833,000
Current liabilities	$ 320,000	$320,000	$ 310,000
Bonds payable,10%	215,000	215,000	215,000
Common shares	400,000	—	400,000
Retained earnings	1,966,000	—	1,966,000
Sales	—	—	1,430,000
Cost of goods sold	—	—	(867,000)
Depreciation	—	—	(11,000)
Other expenses	—	—	(588,500)
Bond interest expense	—	—	(21,500)
	$2,901,000		$2,833,000

Parent Ltd.
Pre-closing Trial Balance
December 31, 2006

Cash	$ 275,000
Accounts receivable, net	384,000
Marketable securities *	129,000
Inventory	860,000
Land	730,000
Buildings & equipment, net	862,000
Goodwill **	140,000
Investment in Sub Ltd.	2,800,000
	$6,180,000
Current liabilities	$ 395,000
Bonds payable	685,000
Common shares	1,100,000
Retained earnings	3,757,000
Sales	1,930,000
Cost of goods sold	(1,463,000)
Depreciation	(27,000)
Other expenses	(203,450)
Bond interest income	6,450
	$6,180,000

* Bonds of Sub Ltd.
** Not related to Sub Ltd.

Wholly-Owned
Subsidiaries:
Reporting
Subsequent to
Acquisition

185

P4–5

Parent Ltd. acquired 100% of the voting shares of Sub Ltd. on January 1, 2006, for $1,255,000. The financial statement of Sub Ltd. on the date of acquisition was as follows:

Sub Ltd.
Balance Sheet
January 1, 2006

	Book value	Fair Market value
Cash	$ 40,000	$ 40,000
Accounts receivable	110,000	130,000
Inventory	280,000	320,000
Land	310,000	400,000
Depreciable capital assets, net	460,000	495,000
Total	$1,200,000	
Current liabilities	$ 250,000	250,000
Common shares	400,000	—
Retained earnings	550,000	—
Total	$1,200,000	

The inventory will be sold and the accounts receivable collected within seven months, and the depreciable capital assets will be depreciated over 10 years, straight-line, with no salvage value.

During 2006, Sub Ltd. sold inventory to Parent Ltd. for $150,000 with a 20% markup on retail. At the end of 2006, $30,000 (at retail) of these goods were still in the inventory. Parent Ltd. sold $200,000 of goods to Sub Ltd. during 2006, with a 25% markup on retail, and $40,000 (at retail) of these were still in inventory at the end of 2006. All of these goods remaining in inventory were sold during 2007.

During 2007, Parent Ltd. sold $180,000 of goods to Sub Ltd. with a 25% markup on retail, and $50,000 (at retail) of these goods were in inventory at the end of 2007. In addition, Sub Ltd. sold goods to Parent Ltd. for $220,000 with a 20% markup on retail, and $60,000 (at retail) of these were still in inventory at the end of 2007. All of these remaining goods were sold during 2008.

The following are the financial statements of the two companies at December 31, 2007:

Balance Sheets
December 31, 2007

	Parent Ltd.	Sub Ltd.
Cash	$ 55,000	$ 40,000
Accounts receivable	140,000	110,000
Inventory	400,000	320,000
Land	670,000	385,000
Depreciable capital assets, net	864,000	520,000
Investment in Sub Ltd.	1,255,000	—
Total	$3,384,000	$1,375,000
Current liabilities	$ 248,000	$ 180,000
Common shares	1,136,000	400,000
Retained earnings	2,000,000	795,000
Total	$3,384,000	$1,375,000

Income Statements
For the Year Ended December 31, 2007

	Parent Ltd.	Sub Ltd.
Sales	$900,000	$845,000
Cost of goods sold	542,000	479,000
Depreciation	120,000	110,000
Other expenses	128,000	126,000
	790,000	715,000
Net income	$110,000	$130,000

Neither company paid any dividends during 2006 or 2007.

Required:

Calculate the following, considering all dates carefully:

1. Investment income, under the equity method, for 2006.

2. Consolidated net income for 2007.

3. Consolidated balance of accounts receivable at December 31, 2007.

4. Consolidated balance of depreciable capital assets at December 31, 2007.

5. Consolidated balance of inventory at December 31, 2007.

[CGA–Canada, adapted]

P4–6

On January 4, 2007, Practical Corp. acquired 100% of the outstanding common shares of Silly Inc. by a share-for-share exchange of its own shares valued at $1,000,000 (**P3–8**). The balance sheets of both companies just prior to the share exchange are shown below. Silly had patents not shown on the balance sheet, but that had an estimated fair value of $200,000 and an estimated remaining productive life of four years. Silly's buildings and equipment had an estimated fair value $300,000 in excess of book value, and the deferred charges were assumed to have a fair value of zero. Silly's building and equipment are being depreciated on the straight-line basis and have a remaining useful life of 10 years. The deferred charges are being amortized over three years.

Balance Sheets
December 31, 2006

	Practical	Silly
Cash	$ 110,000	$ 85,000
Accounts and other receivables	140,000	80,000
Inventories	110,000	55,000
Buildings and equipment	1,500,000	800,000
Accumulated depreciation	(700,000)	(400,000)
Deferred charges	—	120,000
	$1,160,000	$740,000
Accounts and other payables	$ 200,000	$100,000
Bonds payable	—	200,000
Future income taxes	60,000	40,000
Common shares*	600,000	150,000
Retained earnings	300,000	250,000
	$1,160,000	$740,000

*Practical = 300,000 shares; Silly = 150,000 shares.

Wholly-Owned
Subsidiaries:
Reporting
Subsequent to
Acquisition

187

During 2007, the year following the acquisition, Silly borrowed $100,000 from Practical; $40,000 was repaid and $60,000 is still outstanding at year-end. No interest is being charged on the loan. Through the year, Silly sold goods to Practical totalling $400,000. Silly's gross margin is 40% of selling price, and its tax rate is 25%. Three-quarters of these goods were resold by Practical to its customers for $450,000. Dividend declarations amounted to $80,000 by Practical and $50,000 by Silly. There were no other intercompany transactions. The year-end 2007 balance sheets and income statements for Practical and Silly are shown below.

Required:

a. How would the income statement and balance sheet for Practical Corp. differ from those shown below if Practical reported its investment in Silly on the equity basis? Show all calculations.

b. Prepare a complete set of consolidated financial statements for Practical Corp. for 2007.

Balance Sheets
December 31, 2007

	Practical	Silly
Cash	$ 50,000	$ 25,000
Accounts and other receivables	240,000	90,000
Inventories	150,000	80,000
Buildings and equipment	1,300,000	900,000
Accumulated depreciation	(570,000)	(445,000)
Land	—	60,000
Investment in Silly (at cost)	1,000,000	—
Other investments	70,000	30,000
Deferred charges	—	80,000
	$2,240,000	$820,000
Accounts and other payables	$ 150,000	$180,000
Bonds payable	—	170,000
Future income taxes	70,000	45,000
Common shares	1,600,000	150,000
Retained earnings	420,000	275,000
	$2,240,000	$820,000

Statements of Income and Retained Earnings
Year Ended December 31, 2007

	Practical	Silly
Sales	$1,500,000	$900,000
Dividend income	50,000	—
	1,550,000	900,000
Cost of sales	1,000,000	540,000
Depreciation expense	70,000	45,000
Amortization expense	—	40,000
Income tax expense	50,000	25,000
Other expenses	230,000	175,000
	1,350,000	825,000
Net income	200,000	75,000
Retained earnings, December 31, 2006	300,000	250,000
Dividends declared	(80,000)	(50,000)
Retained earnings, December 31, 2007	$ 420,000	$275,000

Refer to **P4–6**. During 2008, the following events occurred:

1. Silly Inc. had sales of $800,000 to Practical Corp. Silly's gross margin was still 40% of selling price, and its income tax rate continued to be 25%. At year-end, $120,000 of these goods were still in Practical's inventory.

2. On October 1, 2008, Silly sold its land to Practical for $185,000 (on which income taxes were due for $20,000). Practical paid Silly $85,000 and gave a promissory note for $100,000 that was due in three years at 10% interest per year, simple interest to be paid at maturity.

3. $60,000 that Silly owed to Practical at the beginning of the year was repaid during 2008.

4. Practical paid dividends of $100,000 during the year; Silly paid dividends of $70,000.

The pre-closing trial balances of Practical and Silly at December 31, 2008, are shown below.

Required:

a. Determine Practical Corp.'s equity in the earnings of Silly Inc. for 2008. Determine the balance of the Investment in Silly account on Practical's books at December 31, 2008, assuming that Practical recorded its investment on the equity basis.

b. Prepare a comparative consolidated balance sheet and income statement for Practical Corp. for 2008.

Trial Balances
December 31, 2008

	Practical	Silly
Cash	$ 55,500	$ 45,000
Accounts and other receivables	160,000	116,000
Inventories	140,000	75,000
Buildings and equipment	1,700,000	900,000
Accumulated depreciation	(655,000)	(495,000)
Land	185,000	—
Investment in Silly	1,000,000	—
Due from Practical	—	102,500
Other investments	100,000	50,000
Deferred charges	—	40,000
Accounts and other payables	(225,000)	(215,000)
Payable to Silly	(102,500)	—
Future income taxes	(75,000)	(47,500)
Common shares	(1,800,000)	(150,000)
Retained earnings	(420,000)	(275,000)
Dividends paid	100,000	70,000
Sales	(1,680,000)	(1,200,000)
Cost of sales	1,120,000	720,000
Depreciation expense	85,000	50,000
Amortization expense	—	40,000
Income tax expense	31,000	57,000
Other expenses	351,000	244,500
Gain on sale of land	—	(125,000)
Other income	(70,000)	(2,500)
	$ 0	$ 0

P4-8

On January 1, 2005, Parent Ltd. purchased 100% of the shares of Sub Ltd. for $1,085,000. At that time Sub Ltd. had the following balance sheet:

Sub Ltd.
Balance Sheet
January 1, 2005

	Net book value	Fair value
Cash	$ 60,000	$ 60,000
Accounts receivable	120,000	150,000
Inventory—FIFO	180,000	230,000
Capital assets, net	1,500,000	1,350,000
Goodwill	100,000	—
	$1,960,000	
Current liabilities	$ 140,000	140,000
Bonds payable	800,000	850,000
Common shares	400,000	—
Retained earnings	620,000	—
	$1,960,000	

The bonds were issued at par and will mature in 10 years. Sub Ltd. has a receivables and inventory turnover of greater than six times per year. The capital assets have an average of 10 years of remaining life and are being amortized straight-line.

In 2005, Sub Ltd. sold inventory to Parent Ltd. for $260,000; the inventory had cost $320,000. At the end of 2005, 25% was still in Parent's inventory but was all sold in 2006.

In 2006, Parent Ltd. sold inventory to Sub Ltd. for $275,000; the inventory had cost $200,000. At the end of 2006, 35% was left in Sub's inventory.

During 2005, the subsidiary earned $875,000 and paid dividends of $50,000. During 2006, the subsidiary incurred a loss of $180,000 and paid dividends of $60,000.

The parent company uses the cost method for the investment in subsidiary and nets almost everything to "Other expenses."

At December 31, 2006, the following financial statements were available:

Balance Sheet
December 31, 2006

	Parent Ltd.	Sub Ltd.
Cash	$ 290,000	$ 75,000
Accounts receivable	850,000	179,000
Inventory	970,000	245,000
Capital assets, net	2,631,000	1,863,000
Goodwill	0	100,000
Investment in Sub Ltd.	1,085,000	0
	$5,826,000	$2,462,000
Current liabilities	$ 450,000	$ 49,000
Bonds payable	0	800,000
Common shares	1,000,000	400,000
Retained earnings	3,026,000	1,385,000
Net income (loss)	1,350,000	(172,000)
	$5,826,000	$2,462,000

Income Statement
Year Ended December 31, 2006

	Parent Ltd.	Sub Ltd.
Sales	$9,865,000	$1,650,000
Cost of sales	8,040,000	1,140,000
Gross profit	1,825,000	510,000
Depreciation	(106,000)	(96,000)
Other expenses	(369,000)	(816,000)
Gain on sale of building	0	230,000
Net income	$1,350,000	$ (172,000)

Required:

a. Prepare a consolidated income statement for 2006.

b. Calculate the amounts that would appear on the consolidated balance sheet at December 31, 2006 for:

   1. Capital assets, net

   2. Bonds payable

[CGA–Canada]

Appendix 4A

Wholly-Owned

Subsidiaries:

Reporting

Subsequent to

Acquisition

191

Goodwill Impairment Test

Allocation of goodwill to reporting units

When a corporation acquires goodwill through a business combination, the full amount of goodwill should be allocated to the corporation's *reporting units* [CICA 3062.36]. Basically, a reporting unit is defined by the internal reporting system of the corporation. A **reporting unit** is any part of the corporation that is evaluated regularly by the corporation's principal decision maker (normally the chief operating officer) for resource allocation decisions.

In order to allocate goodwill to reporting units, the corporation must first assign all of the assets and liabilities acquired in a business combination to reporting units. The assignment is made as though the corporation had purchased each reporting unit separately. Once the assets and liabilities are assigned, the fair value of each reporting unit is estimated, based on an allocation of the total purchase price of the business combination. Finally, each reporting unit's total fair value is compared to the fair value of the assets and liabilities assigned to that unit. The difference (if any) between the *fair value of the unit* and the *fair value of the assets and liabilities assigned to the unit* is the amount of goodwill allocated to that unit [CICA 3062.37].

Management must make many estimates in order to (1) assign the purchased assets and liabilities to reporting units and (2) estimate the hypothetical purchase price of each individual unit. It is possible that some reporting units of an acquired corporation may have a hypothetical purchase price that is less than the fair values of its assigned assets. To make things even more imprecise, the *CICA Handbook* states that goodwill should be assigned to units that "are expected to benefit from the synergies of the combination" even if none of the acquired assets and liabilities has been assigned to that unit [CICA 3062.37].

Relevant reporting units are those in the acquiring (i.e., buying) corporation, not the acquired corporation. Reporting units in the acquired corporation may either be built into a new reporting structure in the buying corporation, be combined with reporting units in the buyer, or be eliminated after the combination. It is only surviving reporting units in the reporting enterprise that matter.

The *CICA Handbook* states that the allocation of goodwill to reporting units should be completed within the same year as the purchase, if possible, or in the following year at the latest [CICA 3062.37]. This time constraint leaves relatively little time for a buying corporation to restructure its internal reporting structure after a major acquisition. If the acquirer's reporting structure is changed in a following year, then a "relative fair value allocation approach" is used to reallocate goodwill [CICA 3062.38].

Applying the impairment test

When fair value of a reporting unit is estimated at the date of acquisition, the overall acquisition price is known. The fair values allocated to individual reporting units should equal the total price paid for the business combination.

In years following the acquisition, the first step in applying the impairment test is to determine the *fair value of each reporting unit*. This fair value is a hypothetical "purchase price" that management estimates the reporting unit is worth.

When the fair value of a reporting unit is estimated at subsequent impairment test dates, there is no relatively objective value to serve as a guide. The *CICA Handbook* provides no guidance on estimating "fair value" of a reporting unit after the date of acquisition. Management seems to have considerable latitude. Since each reporting unit is part of the larger enterprise, it is not possible to use the market price of the unit's publicly traded securities as an estimate of fair value. Even if a reporting unit is a publicly traded subsidiary, the share market price may not be truly indicative of the future earning ability of the unit, which theoretically should be the basis of its fair value.

The second step is to compare the unit's estimated fair value with the carrying amount (including goodwill) of the unit's assets and liabilities. If the fair value is higher than the carrying value, then there is no impairment and the impairment test need not proceed further.

If the fair value is lower than carrying value, then impairment has occurred. The amount of impairment is measured by comparing the total estimated fair value with the total carrying value.

However, a complication arises because the impairment does not necessarily pertain to goodwill. It is possible that some other assets of the reporting unit are impaired. The other assets should be tested for impairment first [CICA 3062.30].

If other assets are impaired, those assets should be written down first. Only then should the impairment test be applied to goodwill, by comparing the hypothetical fair value of goodwill at the test date with the carrying value of goodwill. Any excess of carrying value over fair value is the amount of impairment.

The amount of any goodwill impairment should be reported as a separate line on the corporation's income statement, before extraordinary items and discontinued operations. Any impairment associated with a discontinued operation should be reported (net of tax) in the discontinued operations section [CICA 3062.49].

Timing of impairment tests

Normally, goodwill should be tested for impairment every year, at approximately the same time each year [CICA 3062.41]. However, sometimes it will be obvious that there has been no impairment and a test is not necessary. To skip testing, *all* of three criteria must be satisfied [CICA 3062.39]:

1. the reporting unit's assets and liabilities have not changed significantly since acquisition; and

2. the most recent fair-value estimate exceeded the carrying amount of the unit by a substantial amount; and

3. events and circumstances since the most recent fair-value estimation indicate that the probability of impairment is remote.

The basic requirement is that an impairment test should be made at about the same time each year. However, sometimes unforeseen events occur between annual tests that suggest goodwill has become impaired. For example, a regulator may change rules or regulations in such a way that the potential future earnings stream of a regulated reporting unit (e.g., a telephone company or cable company) is reduced significantly. In such cases, an impairment test should be made between annual dates [CICA 3062.42].

The point of making a test between annual dates is for quarterly reporting. An impairment should, in theory, be reported as soon as it happens. However, given the uncertainties involved in any impairment test, it is questionable whether much is accomplished by an intermediate test except giving management a way to affect reported quarterly earnings.

Differential reporting

A private corporation that is not otherwise publicly accountable may choose to use any or all of the differential reporting options approved by the AcSB. The goodwill impairment test is the latest addition to the list of permitted optional accounting.

If a corporation chooses differential reporting for goodwill impairment, the company does not have to perform an annual impairment test. An impairment test is necessary only when an event, transaction, or new circumstance indicates that impairment may have taken place. If there is possible impairment, then the test is applied by following the recommendations of *CICA Handbook* Section 3062, as explained above.

Wholly-Owned
Subsidiaries:
Reporting
Subsequent to
Acquisition

193

Appendix 4B

Income Tax Allocation Subsequent to Acquisition

Introduction and review

Appendix 3A discussed the issue of income allocation as it applies in a business combination, and illustrated the calculation of future income tax (FIT) at acquisition. The essence of income tax allocation for business combinations is that the buyer, *on its consolidated balance sheet*, must calculate future income tax as part of the purchase equation. The future income tax for each asset and liability is based on its temporary difference. The temporary difference is the difference between (1) the tax basis of the asset to the *subsidiary* and (2) the fair value of the asset as it is included on the *parent's* consolidated statement. For the purchase transaction in Chapter 3, which also pertains to this chapter, the amounts are as follows:

	Target Ltd's book value (1)	Tax basis for Target (2)	Fair value to Purchase (3)	Temporary difference (3) – (2)
Land	$300,000	$300,000	$400,000	$100,000
Buildings and equipment	350,000	250,000	550,000	300,000
Total	$650,000	$550,000	$950,000	$400,000

Target Ltd.'s book values are included as column (1), but they really are irrelevant for determining the amount of future income tax. They are irrelevant because we need to compare the fair values with the assets' *tax bases*, not with their carrying values on the subsidiary's books. We have put them in the table to emphasize that the tax bases of Target Ltd.'s assets may be different from their carrying values. For income tax allocation, the relevant figures are those in columns (2) and (3).

The temporary differences are shown in the last column. The tax basis for each asset is subtracted from its fair value. If we assume that Purchase Ltd.'s income tax rate is 40%, we must include $400,000 \times 40\% = \$160,000$ as a future income tax liability when we allocate the purchase price. As we explained in Appendix 3A, the effect of including the future income tax liability is to increase the amount of the purchase price that is allocated to goodwill.

Post-acquisition tax accounting for fair-value increments

The balance in the future income tax account is a function of the temporary differences at each balance sheet date. In a business combination, the temporary difference is the difference between the tax basis of an asset to the tax-paying entity (that is, to the *subsidiary* that legally owns the asset and that deducts the CCA) and its value as reported *on the parent company's consolidated balance sheet* [CICA 3465.17].

In a business combination, we must focus on the fair-value increments relating to amortizable capital assets, both tangible and intangible. Residual goodwill in a purchase of shares is not a capital asset, and it is not deductible for tax purposes.

For amortizable capital assets, in years subsequent to the acquisition, (1) the fair-value increments are amortized and flow into expense, thereby reducing their carrying value, and (2) the assets' tax bases change as the assets are recognized in taxable income (e.g., through CCA). Therefore, the temporary differences change. The change in temporary differences arising from fair-value increment (FVI) amortization must be recognized on the consolidated balance sheet.

In this chapter, we amortized the fair-value increment relating to buildings and equipment. The amortization for each of 2006 and 2007 was $20,000. Therefore, the fair-value increment declined from $200,000 at the date of acquisition to $180,000 at the end of 2006 and $160,000 at the end of 2007.

The change in the FVI is only half of the situation. The other half is the tax basis. The tax basis changes because Target Ltd. continues taking CCA on its buildings and equipment. The overall temporary difference depends on both the FVI amortization and the change in the tax basis. Fortunately, however, we really don't need to know the tax basis of all of the subsidiary's assets in order to adjust for the change in temporary differences during each year.

Remember that the starting point for consolidation is the companies' separate-entity financial statements (or trial balances). The subsidiary will be using tax allocation procedures on its own books. Therefore, the subsidiary will already have recorded the future income tax that relates to temporary differences between its assets' tax bases and their carrying values. All we have to do for consolidation is to supplement that already-reported future income tax amount by recognizing the additional change to the temporary difference that relates to the FVI:

Wholly-Owned
Subsidiaries:
Reporting
Subsequent to
Acquisition

195

Tax basis of Target assets } *Recorded* on Target's books

Carrying value on Target's books }

Consolidation value = carrying value + FVI } Added as a consolidation *adjustment*

In essence, therefore, we only have to make a future income tax (FIT) adjustment for the change in the temporary difference that is caused by the FVI amortization. In each of 2006 and 2007, the amortization is $20,000. At an assumed income tax rate of 40%, each year's worksheet adjustment for the additional change in consolidated FIT will be:

Future income tax liability—long term	8,000	
Income tax expense ($20,000 ×40%)		8,000

The adjustment always will be to *reduce* the future income tax liability because FVIs will never increase—they will only decrease. This does not mean that the *overall* temporary difference may not increase. Instead, it means that an increase that might have been recorded on Target Ltd.'s books will be reduced by the additional adjustment in consolidation.

For example, suppose that in 2006, Target Ltd. recorded depreciation of $35,000 on its buildings and equipment and took CCA of $65,000. The carrying value of buildings and equipment *on Target Ltd.'s books* will be $350,000 − $35,000 = $315,000. The tax basis will be $250,000 − $65,000 = $185,000. The changes can be summarized as follows:

	2005	2006
Tax basis	$250,000	$185,000
Target's carrying value	350,000	315,000
Temporary difference	$100,000	$130,000

From 2005 to 2006, Target Ltd.'s temporary difference for the buildings and equipment increased by $30,000. Target Ltd. will have *recorded* the appropriate increase in the FIT liability of $12,000 (that is, $30,000 × 40% = $12,000) resulting from the increase in the temporary difference.

Looking now at Purchase Ltd.'s consolidated amounts (i.e., including FVI), the consolidated temporary difference is as follows:

	2005	2006
Tax basis	$250,000	$185,000
Purchase's consolidated value	550,000	495,000
Temporary difference	$300,000	$310,000

The consolidated value of the buildings and equipment acquired in the business combination was initially a Target Ltd. book value of $350,000 plus FVI of $200,000, for a total fair value of $550,000. One year later, the Target Ltd. book value has been depreciated to $315,000 and the FVI has been amortized to $180,000—the sum of these two amounts equals the $495,000 shown above.

Overall, the temporary difference relating to the fair values shown on Purchase Ltd.'s consolidated balance sheet is increased by $10,000. The related increase in the consolidated FIT liability is $10,000 × 40% = $4,000. The change in consolidated FIT liability relating to Target Ltd.'s buildings and equipment can be summarized as follows:

	Temporary Difference	Future Income Tax Liability
Increase recorded on Target Ltd.'s books	$30,000	$12,000 Cr
Decrease from FVI amortization upon consolidation	20,000	8,000 Dr
Net change in consolidated amounts	$10,000	$ 4,000 Cr

Therefore, when we make the consolidation adjustments relating to future income tax, we need concern ourselves only with the changes in the fair-value increments. We can safely assume that the subsidiary has already recorded the FIT arising from the timing differences between the tax basis and the carrying value of its assets and liabilities.

Unrealized profit

The only other income tax aspect that we need to worry about is that relating to unrealized profit. At the end of 2006, there is unrealized upstream profit of $8,000 in inventory. This profit is unrealized only from the viewpoint of the consolidated entity. So far as the Canada Revenue Agency is concerned, Target Ltd. has earned this profit and will be taxed on it in 2006. The tax, at 40%, will amount to $3,200.

On consolidation, the unrealized profit is eliminated. Since the profit is removed from net income, tax allocation requires that the related taxes also be removed from net income. The adjustment to achieve this is quite straight-forward:

Future income tax—current	3,200	
Income tax expense ($8,000 × 40%)		3,200

All unrealized profit eliminations must be accompanied by an adjustment for income tax, deferring recognition of the income taxes paid by the selling company to the period in which the profit is realized.

A reminder: future income tax balances must be segregated between current and long-term. If the unrealized profit relates to a current asset such as inventory (or to a current liability), the *current* FIT balance is affected. If the unrealized profit relates to a non-current asset (such as in an intercompany sale of a capital asset), the *long-term* FIT balance is affected. The classification has nothing to do with the expected timing of the reversal of the temporary difference.

In 2007, the beginning-of-year unrealized profit is recognized in consolidated net income, and therefore the income tax expense also is recognized:

Income tax expense ($8,000 × 40%)	3,200	
Future income tax—current		3,200

Of course, the year-end 2007 unrealized profit must be eliminated, and those eliminations must be accompanied by adjustments to defer recognition of the related income tax expense.

Summary

Income tax allocation affects consolidation in two ways:

1. Amortization of the fair-value increments changes the consolidated reporting values of tangible and intangible capital assets (except land), and therefore the temporary differences are affected.

2. The tax relating to unrealized profits must be removed from consolidated net income and deferred as part of the future income tax balance(s) on the balance sheet.

Fortunately, we need not worry about making the full adjustment for the changes in consolidated temporary differences for capital assets. The subsidiary company will have recorded the effects of changes in temporary differences between their carrying values and the tax bases. On consolidation, we need only to adjust for the income tax effect of the FVI amortization.

Wholly-Owned
Subsidiaries:
Reporting
Subsequent to
Acquisition

197

Consolidation of Non-Wholly Owned Subsidiaries

The previous two chapters dealt with the preparation of consolidated statements when the parent company owns 100% of the shares of the subsidiary. However, some subsidiaries have other shareholders in addition to the parent. Such subsidiaries are known simply as *non-wholly owned subsidiaries*, a designation that is rather obvious, although somewhat cumbersome.

In this chapter, we will examine consolidation of non-wholly owned subsidiaries. The following sections will discuss:

- the reasons that some subsidiaries are not wholly owned
- the conceptual alternatives for consolidating non-wholly owned subsidiaries
- the process of consolidation at the date of acquisition
- consolidation one year following acquisition, and
- consolidation two years after acquisition.

The illustration in this chapter will exactly parallel the illustration in Chapters 3 and 4, except that we assume the parent buys less than 100% of the subsidiary's shares.

Why Own Less Than 100%?

It is most common for a parent corporation to own all of a subsidiary's shares. There are two reasons for full ownership.

1. Most subsidiaries are established by the parent in order to carry out part of the parent's business. These subsidiaries are integral parts of the parent's operations and are established for tax, regulatory, or risk-isolation purposes.

2. When one corporation buys another one (that is, in a business combination), it is most common for the buying company to acquire 100% of the outstanding shares. Indeed, if the acquired company is a private company, there usually is little alternative to buying the entire ownership.

Nevertheless, a parent's ownership interest may be less than 100% for either of two reasons:

- in a business combination, the acquiring company (the parent) may buy a majority of the shares, but less than 100%, or
- a parent may form a new subsidiary with the involvement of a non-controlling partner who is providing specialized expertise, management ability, market access, governmental support, etc.

Some parent corporations prefer to purchase significantly less than 100% of the shares in a business combination. The parent then need not invest the full value of the subsidiary's net assets. A less-than-100% investment conserves the parent's liquid resources (if the purchase was for cash) or reduces its share dilution (if the purchase was an exchange of shares). In addition, the maintenance of a significant non-controlling interest in the subsidiary can spread the ownership risk, can provide valuable links with other corporate shareholders, and can maintain a market for the subsidiary's shares.

Non-controlling interests may also exist if the parent initially establishes the subsidiary, but subsequently sells shares in the subsidiary to others. The sale may be of shares originally owned by the parent (i.e., a secondary offering by the parent) or may be of new shares (i.e., a direct or primary offering by the subsidiary). In either case, the parent ends up holding less than 100% of the subsidiary. Subsequent changes in ownership interest will be discussed in Appendices 5A and 5B.

Conceptual Alternatives

As is the case with most aspects of accounting, there is no single theoretical approach to accounting for subsidiaries when a non-controlling interest exists. Two consecutive questions arise.

1. Should the non-controlling interest's share of net assets be included in the consolidated balance sheet?

2. If included, should they be shown at their book value on the subsidiary's books or at their fair value as of the date of acquisition?

The answers to these two questions are, to some extent, dependent upon the basic theory of consolidation that is applied to business combinations, as we discussed in Chapter 3. For example, the pooling-of-interests approach assumes that two previously independent businesses combine on equal terms and both carry on jointly and equally. It would be mechanically possible to exclude the non-controlling interest's share of assets from the consolidated balance sheet. But excluding the non-controlling interest's share is inconsistent with the underlying philosophy of the pooling approach, which is that the two companies are combining to jointly and equally carry on the previously separate businesses.

Similarly, the new-entity approach to consolidations would seem to call for inclusion of the non-controlling interest at fair value. To exclude the non-controlling interest or to include it at book value is inconsistent with the underlying conceptual basis of the new-entity method, which is that the newly combined entity is getting a "fresh start" and revaluing all of its assets and liabilities at fair value.

The only really viable alternatives exist under the fair-value purchase method. There are three alternatives.

1. Include only the parent's share of the fair value of the subsidiary's assets and liabilities, and revenues and expenses (excluding the non-controlling interest entirely). This is known as the **proportionate consolidation method**.

2. Include the parent's share of the fair values of the subsidiary's assets and liabilities, plus the book value of the non-controlling interest's share. This approach is most commonly called the **parent-company method**. The consolidated income statement would include 100% of the subsidiary's revenues and expenses.

3. Include 100% of the *fair value* of the subsidiary's assets and liabilities, and 100% of all revenues and expenses. This is usually called the **entity** method, or the **new-entity** method to consolidations, as was discussed in Chapter 3.

If we include all of the subsidiary's net assets in the parent company's consolidated balance sheet (using either the entity or the parent-company approaches), the combined net assets will exceed the parent's investment in the subsidiary. Therefore, we must balance the *non-controlling interest's* share of assets and liabilities with an amount for non-controlling interest on the liabilities/equity side of the parent company's consolidated balance sheet.

Similarly, if we include 100% of the subsidiary's revenues and expenses in the consolidated income statement, the result will be the combined earnings attributable to *both* the parent's shareholders and the non-controlling interest in the subsidiary. The consolidated statements are reports to the parent's shareholders, not to the outside shareholders in the subsidiary. Therefore, we must subtract the non-controlling interest's share of the earnings of the subsidiary in order to determine the net income attibutable to the parent corporation's shareholders.

Exhibit 5–1 summarizes the alternative approaches to the treatment of the non-controlling interest's share of net assets under the fair-value purchase method of consolidation. As described above, exclusion of the non-controlling interest is known as *proportionate consolidation*, inclusion at book value is known as the *parent-company approach*, and inclusion at fair value is known as the *new-entity approach*.

As we pointed out in Chapter 2, the general term for shareholdings that do not enable the shareholder to control the enterprise is "non-controlling interest," which is the term used in Sections 1600.14 and 1600.15 of the *CICA Handbook*. In the vast majority of cases, the non-controlling interest will in fact be a *minority interest*, i.e., less than 50%. Many corporations continue to use the term "minority interests" in their financial statements rather than the more general term. The reader must be aware that minority interests are a narrower category of non-controlling interests, just as depreciation is a specific form of amortization.

Illustration of the alternative methods

In order to clarify the conceptual issues underlying the three different methods to non-controlling interest, we will apply the three alternatives to a simple example. The example uses the same facts as the illustration in Chapter 3, except that less than 100% of the shares are purchased.

Assume that instead of buying 100%, Purchase Ltd. buys only 70% of the outstanding shares of Target Ltd. on December 31, 2005, giving 28,000 Purchase Ltd. shares in exchange. If we assume that the market value of Purchase Ltd.'s shares is $30 per share, then the total cost of the acquisition is $840,000. The post-acquisition balance sheets of Purchase Ltd. and Target Ltd., and the fair values of Target Ltd.'s assets and liabilities, are shown in Exhibit 5–2.

EXHIBIT 5–1	THE FAIR-VALUE PURCHASE METHOD APPROACHES TO REPORTING NON-CONTROLLING INTEREST (NCI)		
Consolidation Method	**Include NCI Net Assets?**	**Book Value or Fair Value?**	**Name of Approach**
Fair value purchase	**a.** no	—	Proportionate consolidation
	b. yes	Book value	Parent-company
	c. yes	Fair value	Entity

EXHIBIT 5–2   BUSINESS COMBINATION—PURCHASE OF 70% OF TARGET

Post-acquisition asset positions, December 31, 2005

	Balance sheets		Target
	Purchase Ltd.	Target Ltd.	fair values
Cash	$1,000,000	$ 50,000	$ 50,000
Accounts receivable	2,000,000	150,000	150,000
Inventory	200,000	50,000	50,000
Land	1,000,000	300,000	400,000
Buildings and equipment	3,000,000	500,000	550,000
Accumulated depreciation	(1,200,000)	(150,000)	
Investment in Target Ltd.	840,000		
	$6,840,000	$900,000	
Current accounts payable	$1,000,000	$100,000	(100,000)
Long-term notes payable	400,000	—	
Common shares	3,440,000	200,000	
Retained earnings	2,000,000	600,000	
	$6,840,000	$900,000	$1,100,000

Exhibit 5–3 shows the allocation of the purchase price and derivation of the goodwill. Note that in this case, the goodwill is 70% of the goodwill of $100,000 that resulted from Purchase Ltd.'s 100% purchase of Target Ltd. in Chapter 3. Note also that the nature of the calculations in Exhibit 5–3 is exactly the same as in Chapters 3 and 4 (Exhibit 4–1), except that only 70% of Target Ltd.'s assets and liabilities are included in the analysis instead of 100%.

Exhibit 5–4 shows the Purchase Ltd. consolidated balance sheet immediately after the business combination, prepared (by the direct approach) under each of the three alternatives, each of which will be discussed in turn.

EXHIBIT 5–3   ALLOCATION OF PURCHASE PRICE

70% Purchase of Target Ltd., December 31, 2005

Purchase price						$840,000
	Book value	Fair value	Fair value increment	% share	FVI acquired	
Cash	$ 50,000	$ 50,000	—			
Accounts receivable	150,000	150,000	—			
Inventory	50,000	50,000	—			
Land	300,000	400,000	$100,000 × 70% =		$ 70,000	
Buildings and equipment	500,000	550,000	50,000 × 70% =		35,000	
Accumulated depreciation	(150,000)	—	150,000 × 70% =		105,000	
Accounts payable	(100,000)	(100,000)	—			
Total fair value increment					210,000	
Net asset book value	$ 800,000			× 70% =	560,000	
Fair value of assets acquired						770,000
Goodwill						$ 70,000

Purchase Ltd. Acquires 70% of Target Ltd.
Purchase Ltd. Post-Acquisition Consolidated Balance Sheets
December 31, 2005

	(1) Proportionate consolidation	(2) Parent company	(3) New Entity
Assets			
Cash	$1,035,000	$1,050,000	$1,050,000
Accounts receivable	2,105,000	2,150,000	2,150,000
Inventory	235,000	250,000	250,000
Land	1,280,000	1,370,000	1,400,000
Buildings and equipment	3,385,000	3,490,000	3,550,000
Accumulated depreciation	(1,200,000)	(1,200,000)	(1,200,000)
Goodwill	70,000	70,000	100,000
Total assets	$6,910,000	$7,180,000	$7,300,000
Liabilities			
Accounts payable	$1,070,000	$1,100,000	$1,100,000
Long-term notes payable	400,000	400,000	400,000
	1,470,000	1,500,000	1,500,000
Non-controlling interest	—	240,000	360,000
Shareholders' equity			
Common shares	3,440,000	3,440,000	3,440,000
Retained earnings	2,000,000	2,000,000	2,000,000
	5,440,000	5,440,000	5,440,000
Total liabilities and shareholders' equity	$6,910,000	$7,180,000	$7,300,000

Proportionate consolidation The first column of Exhibit 5–4 shows the Purchase Ltd. consolidated balance sheet as it would appear using proportionate consolidation. Under this method, the Purchase Ltd. balance sheet includes only Purchase Ltd.'s share of Target Ltd.'s assets and liabilities. Since Purchase Ltd. does *not* own the remaining 30% of the Target Ltd. shares, the assets and liabilities that are represented by the *non-owned* shares are *excluded* from Purchase Ltd.'s consolidated statements. The investment account balance of $840,000 is disaggregated and the purchased portion (i.e., 70%) of the fair values is distributed to the appropriate assets and liabilities and to goodwill.

Under proportionate consolidation, the only subsidiary assets and liabilities that are shown on the parent's balance sheet are those in which the shareholders of the parent have an ownership interest. Because of the strict identification of consolidated assets and liabilities as only those owned by parent shareholders, this approach is sometimes called the *proprietary* method.

Proportionate consolidation focuses on *ownership* interest rather than on *control*. When a parent controls a subsidiary, the parent controls *all* of the net assets of the subsidiary, not just the proportion represented by the parent's ownership interest. Users of proportionately consolidated statements do not get a complete picture of the resources, obligations, and revenue-generating activities of the combined entity. Users have no way of compensating for the deficiency, unless they also are given separate-entity financial statements for the subsidiary, thus enabling the users to fill in the missing information. As a result, proportionate consolidation has not been accepted in practice for accounting for *controlled* subsidiaries.[1]

However, proportionate consolidation is the prescribed method in Canada for reporting investments in *joint ventures*. **Joint ventures**, as we noted in Chapter 2, are business ventures entered into by two or more co-venturers to be operated jointly. In a joint venture, no one investor or co-venturer has control over the activities of the venture. Instead, all of the co-venturers must agree on any course of action.

Consolidation normally is based on the concept of *control*; that is, that the reporting entity can control the assets and liabilities of the investee corporation *without the co-operation of others* and can determine the strategic policies of the investee. In contrast, the very nature of a joint venture is that no investor can unilaterally determine the strategic direction or operating policies of a joint venture. Co-operation of the other investors is absolutely essential in a joint venture.

Canada is the *only* country that requires proportionate consolidation for joint ventures. In contrast, international standards call for use of the equity method only. A 1999 international study on joint venture accounting argues that "the conceptual basis for the proportionate consolidation of joint ventures is weak" because the method requires recognition of portions of assets and liabilities that are not under the control of the co-venturer. The study concludes that:

> The equity method of accounting is the most appropriate method for presenting an interest in a joint venture enterprise in the financial statements of the venturer.[2]

Since Canada is harmonizing its accounting standards with those of the IASB, it is quite possible that we will see the AcSB propose a change in joint venture accounting in the future.

Parent-company method The second column of Exhibit 5–4 shows the Purchase Ltd. consolidated balance sheet under the parent-company method. *All* of Target Ltd.'s assets and liabilities are reflected in Purchase Ltd.'s consolidated statements, recognizing that Purchase Ltd. controls all of the Target Ltd. assets.

The parent-company method is a strict application of the historical cost basis of accounting. The parent consolidated assets include:

1. the historical cost of parent's separate-entity assets

2. the historical cost to Purchase Ltd. of Purchase Ltd.'s share of Target Ltd. assets (i.e., the purchase price of Target Ltd. shares acquired), and

3. the historical cost to *Target Ltd.* of the 30% portion of the net assets *not* acquired by Purchase Ltd.

Since the non-controlled share of net assets has been included, these net assets must be balanced by the amount of Target Ltd.'s shareholders' equity that relates

1. However, empirical research studies have found that proportional consolidation is actually more useful than the alternative (equity-basis reporting) because proportional consolidation conveys more information about off-balance-sheet liabilities that are "concealed" under equity reporting. Also, "financial statements under proportionate consolidation better predict one-year-ahead return on common equity" [Mark P. Baumann, "The Impact and Valuation of Off-Balance-Sheet Activities Concealed by Equity Method Accounting," *Accounting Horizons* (December 2003), pp. 303–314.]

2. J. Alex Milburn and Peter D. Chant, *Reporting Interests in Joint Ventures and Similar Arrangements*, (Financial Accounting Standards Board, 1999), p. 25. This was a study for the accounting standards boards of Australia, Canada, New Zealand, the U.K., the U.S.A., and the IASB.

to the non-controlling interest (in this example, a minority interest). The consolidated balance sheet includes the 30% of the book value of the Target Ltd. net assets that relates to minority interest, and therefore the offset is 30% of Target Ltd.'s unconsolidated shareholders' equity (or net assets), which is $240,000.

A curious outcome of the parent-company method is that the same assets (of Target Ltd.) are reported on two different bases: (1) fair value for the parent's percentage of each asset, and (2) book value for the percentage of each asset that relates to non-controlling interest. If the purpose of consolidated statements is to give the user a view of the total resources controlled by the parent, then it is difficult to rationalize the parent-company method; Purchase Ltd. controls the fair value of 100% of Target Ltd.'s assets, not just 70%. Nevertheless, the parent-company method is recommended in the *CICA Handbook* [CICA 1600.15]. It also is the method in general use around the world.

Entity method The third column of Exhibit 5–4 shows the Purchase Ltd. consolidated balance sheet as it would appear using the entity method. The entity method includes the full fair value of Target Ltd.'s assets and liabilities in the Purchase Ltd. consolidated balance sheet, rather than just the fair-value increments that relate to Purchase Ltd.'s 70% share.

The total fair value of Target Ltd.'s identifiable net assets is $1,100,000, as shown in Exhibit 5–2. The total amount of Purchase Ltd.'s identifiable net assets is increased by that amount upon consolidation. Purchase Ltd. paid $70,000 for goodwill; therefore the total Target Ltd. goodwill, based on the price that Purchase Ltd. paid for its 70% interest, could be calculated at $100,000. Since 30% of the goodwill pertains to the Target Ltd. minority shareholders, minority interest is shown as $360,000, that is: (30% × $1,100,000) + (30% × $100,000).

Assigning goodwill to the minority shareholders' interest can be defended since if 70% of Target Ltd. is worth $840,000, then 30% must be worth 3/7 of that amount, or $360,000. Securities laws give some support to this approach. When there has been a block purchase of shares in certain publicly traded companies,[3] an offer to buy non-controlling shareholders' shares must be at least as attractive as the price paid for the majority shares.

However, an acquiring company may be willing to pay a bonus in order to gain control, and it may be *control* of the assets that gives rise to goodwill, not just a non-controlling interest in the assets. That control gives rise to goodwill is shown by the fact that many takeover bids propose a high price, but offer to buy only enough of the outstanding shares (e.g., 51%) to gain control.

Therefore, the entity method can be modified so that only the goodwill actually purchased by the parent is shown on the consolidated balance sheet—no goodwill is assigned to the non-controlling interest. In that case, the last column of Exhibit 5–4 will differ in two respects: (1) the amount shown for goodwill will be $70,000, and (2) the amount for non-controlling interest will be only $330,000, or 30% of the fair value of Target Ltd.'s identifiable net assets. This approach is called the *parent-company extension method*.

Recommended method The recommended method around the world is essentially the parent-company approach to the fair-value purchase method. We will use that approach in all of the following consolidation illustrations.

Consolidation under the entity method is very similar; the only difference is that the consolidated assets and liabilities and the non-controlling interest will include the non-controlling interest's share of the subsidiary's fair-value incre-

---

3. For example, those covered by the *Ontario Securities Act* (Section 91).

ments. Amortization of the non-controlling interest's fair-value increments is charged against non-controlling interest on the consolidated balance sheet.

Consolidation at Date of Acquisition

Direct method

The Purchase Ltd. consolidated balance sheet at date of acquisition (December 31, 2005—parent-company method) is illustrated in the second column of Exhibit 5–4. In order to clarify the procedure, the process of consolidation is presented in Exhibit 5–5, using two different approaches to using the direct method.

EXHIBIT 5–5   CONSOLIDATION AT DATE OF ACQUISITION, NON-WHOLLY OWNED SUBSIDIARY

Purchase Ltd. Acquires 70% of Target Ltd.
(Direct Approaches)

Approach A

	Purchase Ltd. unconsolidated net assets	+ 70% of fair value	+ 30% of book value	= Purchase Ltd. consolidated net assets
Cash	$ 1,000,000	$ 35,000	$ 15,000	$ 1,050,000
Accounts receivable	2,000,000	105,000	45,000	2,150,000
Inventory	200,000	35,000	15,000	250,000
Land	1,000,000	280,000	90,000	1,370,000
Buildings and equipment	3,000,000	385,000	105,000	3,490,000
Accumulated depreciation	(1,200,000)			(1,200,000)
Goodwill		70,000		70,000
Accounts payable	(1,000,000)	(70,000)	(30,000)	(1,100,000)
Long-term notes payable	(400,000)			(400,000)
Non-controlling interest in Target Ltd.			$240,000	(240,000)
Purchase Ltd. net assets	$ 4,600,000	$ 840,000		$ 5,440,000

Approach B

	Purchase Ltd. unconsolidated net assets	+ 100% of book value	+ 70% of FVI	= Purchase Ltd. consolidated net assets
Cash	$ 1,000,000	$ 50,000		$ 1,050,000
Accounts receivable	2,000,000	150,000		2,150,000
Inventory	200,000	50,000		250,000
Land	1,000,000	300,000	$ 70,000	1,370,000
Buildings and equipment	3,000,000	350,000	140,000	3,490,000
Accumulated depreciation	(1,200,000)			(1,200,000)
Goodwill			70,000	70,000
Accounts payable	(1,000,000)	(100,000)		(1,100,000)
Long-term notes payable	(400,000)			(400,000)
Non-controlling interest in Target Ltd.		(240,000)		(240,000)
Purchase Ltd. net assets	$ 4,600,000	$ 560,000	$280,000	$5,440,000

In Approach A, we can directly obtain the consolidated amount for the assets and liabilities by starting with Purchase Ltd.'s book values and adding 70% of the fair values and 30% of the book values for Target Ltd.'s assets and liabilities. The sum of the amounts in the 30% book value column represents the minority interest, which is extended into the consolidated column. The resultant consolidated net asset balance of $5,440,000 is balanced by Purchase Ltd.'s shareholders' equity: $3,440,000 in common shares and $2,000,000 in retained earnings. Thus the consolidated balance sheet can be prepared from the figures in the last column, plus Purchase Ltd.'s shareholders' equity account balances.

When calculating the consolidated amount of buildings and equipment in Exhibit 5–4, Purchase Ltd.'s accumulated depreciation is carried forward. The accumulated depreciation for Target Ltd., however, is netted against the asset account and only the net book value is carried forward. Therefore, the consolidated accumulated depreciation at the date of acquisition is only the amount relating to Purchase Ltd.'s own assets. In future periods, the consolidated accumulated depreciation will include both depreciation on Purchase Ltd.'s own assets and depreciation on Target Ltd.'s assets *since the date of acquisition* only, including amortization of the fair-value increments.

Approach A is a literal representation of the derivation of the consolidated assets and liabilities at the date of acquisition. Target Ltd.'s assets and liabilities are consolidated at 70% of their fair values plus 30% of their book values.

A somewhat different approach that yields the same result is presented as Approach B in Exhibit 5–5. In this approach, the Target Ltd. assets are consolidated at 100% of book value plus the *fair-value increment* relating to the 70% of the net assets acquired. Since the net assets' fair value is equivalent to the book value plus the fair-value increment, the two approaches are mathematically equivalent. If **BV** denotes book value, and **FV** denotes fair value:

$$70\% \text{ FV} + 30\% \text{ BV} = 70\% [\text{BV} + (\text{FV} - \text{BV})] + 30\% \text{ BV}$$
$$= (70\% + 30\%) \text{ BV} + 70\% (\text{FV} - \text{BV})$$
$$= 100\% \text{ of book value} + 70\% \text{ of fair-value increments}$$

The minority interest, calculated at 30% of Target Ltd.'s net book value, is included in the second column of Approach B as a credit. The sum of the second and third columns is $840,000, which is the purchase price paid by Purchase Ltd. for 70% of Target Ltd.'s shares. The sums of each of these two columns can be reconciled directly with the analysis of the purchase as was shown in Exhibit 5–3.

Since both approaches give the same result, it makes no difference which one is used. Approach B, however, is a more useful way of looking at consolidation subsequent to the date of acquisition. In Approach B we can consolidate the total book value of the assets existing at each balance sheet date without trying to separate the amounts into those existing at the date of acquisition (for fair values) and those acquired thereafter.

Worksheet approach

Exhibit 5–6 illustrates the worksheet that can be used to prepare the balance sheet at the date of acquisition. We get the consolidated balance sheet by adding together the separate-entity balances for Purchase Ltd. and Target Ltd. in the first and second columns, plus and minus the eliminations and adjustments shown in the third column. The eliminations and adjustments pertain to the original acquisition and consist of two components:

1. elimination of Target Ltd.'s shareholders' equity, and

Purchase Ltd. Acquires 70% of Target Ltd., December 31, 2005

| | Trial balances | | Adjustments | Purchase Ltd. |
	Purchase	Target	& eliminations	Consolidated
Cash	$ 1,000,000	$ 50,000		$ 1,050,000
Accounts receivable	2,000,000	150,000		2,150,000
Inventory	200,000	50,000		250,000
Land	1,000,000	300,000	$ 70,000 **a2**	1,370,000
Buildings and equipment	3,000,000	500,000	(10,000) **a2**	3,490,000
Accumulated depreciation	(1,200,000)	(150,000)	150,000 **a2**	(1,200,000)
Investments (at cost)	840,000	—	{ (560,000) **a1** (280,000) **a2** }	—
Goodwill	—	—	70,000 **a2**	70,000
Accounts payable	(1,000,000)	(100,000)		(1,100,000)
Long-term notes payable	(400,000)	—		(400,000)
Non-controlling interest in Target Ltd.			(240,000) **a1**	(240,000)
Common shares	(3,440,000)	(200,000)	200,000 **a1**	(3,440,000)
Retained earnings	(2,000,000)	(600,000)	600,000 **a1**	(2,000,000)
	$ —	$ —	$ —	$ —

2. adjustment of Target Ltd.'s net assets by the amount of the fair-value increment for which Purchase Ltd. has paid.

In general journal format, the worksheet adjustments are:

a1	Common shares	200,000	
	Retained earnings	600,000	
	Investment in Target Ltd.		560,000
	Non-controlling interest in Target Ltd. (B/S)		240,000
a2	Land	70,000	
	Accumulated depreciation	150,000	
	Goodwill	70,000	
	Buildings and equipment		10,000
	Investment in Target Ltd.		280,000

Entry **a1** allocates Target Ltd.'s net asset book value of $800,000 to the non-controlling interest (for 30%) and Purchase Ltd.'s controlling interest (to eliminate the investment account). The recording of non-controlling interest is the only substantive difference between the eliminations for wholly owned subsidiaries and for non-wholly owned subsidiaries when we consolidate at the date of acquisition.

The credit to buildings and equipment in **a2** for $10,000 is the net result of eliminating Target Ltd.'s accumulated depreciation of $150,000 at the date of acquisition and recording the fair-value increment of $140,000. The total impact of the adjustment on the net of buildings and equipment less accumulated depreciation is to increase net buildings and equipment on the balance sheet by $140,000.

Consolidation One Year After Acquisition

Basic information

For the year ended December 31, 2006 (i.e., one year following the business combination), the following occurred:

1. Target Ltd.'s buildings and equipment will be depreciated over 10 years after the date of acquisition, using straight-line depreciation.

2. During 2006, Target sold goods of $55,000 to Purchase Ltd. Target Ltd.'s gross margin is 40% of sales.

3. On December 31, 2006, $20,000 of the goods acquired by Purchase Ltd. from Target Ltd. are still in Purchase Ltd.'s inventory. Unrealized profit is $20,000 × 40% = $8,000.

4. During 2006, Target Ltd. paid dividends totalling $30,000. Of this amount, 70% (i.e., $21,000) were received by Purchase Ltd. Purchase Ltd. maintains its investment in Target Ltd. on the cost basis, therefore, the dividends were recorded as dividend income.

Direct method

Exhibit 5–7 shows the separate-entity financial statements for 2006. These statements are very similar to those shown in Exhibit 4–2. The differences are due to two factors:

1. Purchase Ltd. acquired 70% instead of 100%, and therefore:

   - investment in Target Ltd. is smaller by $360,000 (i.e., $1,200,000 – $840,000), and

   - Purchase Ltd.'s common share account is less by $360,000 due to the lower value of the shares issued in the acquisition.

2. Although Target declared and paid $30,000 in dividends (just as in 2006 in Chapter 4), Purchase Ltd. received only 70% of Target Ltd.'s dividends. Therefore, Purchase Ltd.'s dividend income, closing retained earnings, and cash balance are all less by 30% × $30,000 = $9,000.

Purchase Ltd.'s 2006 consolidated statement of income and retained earnings and consolidated balance sheet are shown in Exhibit 5–8 as prepared by the direct method. As usual, we assume that Purchase Ltd. is using the cost basis of *recording* its investment in Target Ltd.

Many of the adjustments to the combined Purchase + Target amounts are logical extensions of the adjustments already described in Chapter 4. One important new wrinkle is added, however—the appearance of an amount for *non-controlling interest* in the income statement. We will discuss this adjustment in general terms first, and then we will explain the detailed adjustments.

Non-controlling interest in earnings In every consolidation of a controlled subsidiary, 100% of the subsidiary's revenues and expenses are added to those of the parent. The income statement shows the total combined revenues and expenses for the entire economic entity.

EXHIBIT 5–7   SEPARATE-ENTITY FINANCIAL STATEMENTS FOR 2006

Income Statements
Year Ended December 31, 2006

	Purchase Ltd.	Target Ltd.
Revenue:		
Sales	$2,400,000	$ 300,000
Dividend income	21,000	—
	2,421,000	300,000
Expenses:		
Cost of sales	1,750,000	180,000
Depreciation expense	100,000	35,000
Other expenses	250,000	20,000
	2,100,000	235,000
Net income	$ 321,000	$ 65,000
Retained earnings, December 31, 2005	2,000,000	600,000
Dividends declared	—	(30,000)
Retained earnings, December 31, 2006	$2,321,000	$ 635,000

Balance Sheets
December 31, 2006

	Purchase Ltd.	Target Ltd.
Assets		
Current assets:		
Cash	$ 971,000	$ 100,000
Accounts receivable	2,200,000	250,000
Inventory	250,000	70,000
	3,421,000	420,000
Property, plant, and equipment:		
Land	1,000,000	300,000
Buildings and equipment	3,000,000	500,000
Accumulated depreciation	(1,300,000)	(185,000)
	2,700,000	615,000
Other assets:		
Investments (at cost)	840,000	—
Total assets	$6,961,000	$1,035,000
Liabilities and shareholders' equity		
Liabilities:		
Accounts payable	$ 800,000	$ 200,000
Long-term notes payable	400,000	—
	1,200,000	200,000
Shareholders' equity:		
Common shares	3,440,000	200,000
Retained earnings	2,321,000	635,000
	5,761,000	835,000
Total liabilities and shareholders' equity	$6,961,000	$1,035,000

Consolidation of
Non-Wholly Owned
Subsidiaries

209

EXHIBIT 5–8	PURCHASE LTD. CONSOLIDATED FINANCIAL STATEMENTS

[Purchase owns 70% of Target Ltd.—Direct Method]
Statement of Income and Retained Earnings
Year Ended December 31, 2006

Sales revenue [2,400,000 + 300,000 − **55,000**]	$ 2,645,000
Dividend income [21,000 + 0 − **21,000**]	
Operating expenses:	
Cost of sales [1,750,000 + 180,000 − **55,000 + 8,000**]	1,883,000
Depreciation expense [100,000 + 35,000 **+ 14,000**]	149,000
Other expenses [250,000 + 20,000]	270,000
Non-controlling interest in earnings of Target Ltd. [**(65,000 − 8,000)** × **30%**]	17,100
	2,319,100
Net income	$ 325,900
Retained earnings, December 31, 2005 [2,000,000 + 600,000 − **600,000**]	2,000,000
Dividends declared [0 + 30,000 − 30,000]	—
Retained earnings, December 31, 2006	$ 2,325,900

Balance Sheet
December 31, 2006

Assets

Current assets:	
Cash [971,000 + 100,000]	$ 1,071,000
Accounts receivable [2,200,000 + 250,000]	2,450,000
Inventory [250,000 + 70,000 − **8,000**]	312,000
	3,833,000
Property, plant, and equipment:	
Land [1,000,000 + 300,000 **+ 70,000**]	1,370,000
Buildings and equipment [3,000,000 + 500,000 − **10,000**]	3,490,000
Accumulated depreciation [1,300,000 + 185,000 − **150,000 + 14,000**]	(1,349,000)
	3,511,000
Other assets:	
Investments [840,000 + 0 − **840,000**]	—
Goodwill	70,000
Total assets	$ 7,414,000

Liabilities and shareholders' equity

Liabilities:	
Current accounts payable [800,000 + 200,000]	$ 1,000,000
Long-term notes payable [400,000 + 0]	400,000
	1,400,000
Non-controlling interest in net assets of Target Ltd. [**(835,000 − 8,000)** × **30%**]	248,100
Shareholders' equity:	
Common shares [**Purchase Ltd. shares only**]	3,440,000
Retained earnings [2,321,000 + 635,000 − **600,000 − 10,500**	
− (8,000 × 70%) − 14,000]	2,325,900
	5,765,900
Total liabilities and shareholders' equity	$ 7,414,000

However, if all of the subsidiary's earnings were distributed to the shareholders as dividends, the parent would receive only the proportion relating to its ownership interest in the subsidiary—the remainder would go to the people or institutions that hold the remaining (or non-controlling) shares. Therefore, we say that the non-controlling proportion of earnings **accrues** to the minority or non-controlling interest.

Be careful here—*accrue* in this sense does not mean that the earnings are recorded on anyone's books the way we usually use the word. The term is used simply to indicate that the parent corporation does not have the right to receive the benefits of shares it does not own.

Because all of the revenues and expenses of the subsidiary are included in the parent's consolidated statements, we must deduct the proportion of the subsidiary's net income that accrues to the benefit of the non-controlling shareholders. This amount is an expense from the viewpoint of the parent company's shareholders. Therefore, an amount for *non-controlling interest in subsidiary's earnings* will appear on the consolidated income statement whenever the parent does not own 100% of the shares.[4]

The amount of the deduction for the non-controlling share of earnings is based on the subsidiary's separate-entity net income, *adjusted for unrealized profits*. We will explain the calculation below.

Statement of income and retained earnings

- *Sales.* The upstream intercompany sales of $55,000 are eliminated.
- *Dividend income.* The dividends paid by Target Ltd. to Purchase Ltd. are eliminated: $30,000 \times 70\% = $21,000$.
- *Cost of sales.* Cost of sales is reduced by $55,000 to avoid counting the intercompany sales in cost of goods sold twice. However, this elimination is partially offset by the unrealized profit in Purchase Ltd.'s ending inventory: $20,000 \times 40\% = $8,000$.
- *Depreciation expense.* As usual, the FVI for buildings and equipment must be amortized. But the amortization is based on the ownership proportion, which is now 70% of the full FVI of $200,000. The FVI amortization therefore is $140,000 \div 10 = $14,000$.
- *Non-controlling interest in earnings.* Target Ltd. reported separate-entity earnings of $65,000. However, this amount includes the unrealized profit on the upstream inventory that is in Purchase Ltd.'s ending inventory. The unrealized profit is $20,000 \times 40\% = $8,000$. Before calculating the non-controlling interest in Target Ltd.'s earnings, the unrealized profit must be deducted. The non-controlling interest is:

$$30\% \times (\$65,000 - \$8,000) = 30\% \times \$57,000 = \textbf{\$17,100}$$

Why do the earnings of the non-controlling interest get reduced just because Purchase Ltd. failed to sell all of its inventory? They don't! The deduction for non-controlling interest has nothing to do with the non-controlling interest's real entitlement to the subsidiary's earnings and dividends. The non-controlling shareholders look at the *subsidiary's* financial statement and receive the *subsidiary's* dividends.

---

4. If the amount is immaterial, it may not be separately disclosed but instead may be included in other expenses. If the amount is material, then it should be shown separately.

The calculation of non-controlling interest is only an adjustment to the *parent's* consolidated statements, not to the subsidiary's separate-entity statements. In effect, the reduction in the non-controlling interest deduction (by 30% of the unrealized upstream profit) is to make up for the fact that consolidated cost of sales was adjusted for 100% of the unrealized profit.

Balance sheet

- *Inventory*. Inventory is adjusted for the $8,000 unrealized profit on upstream sales. Notice that the full amount of unrealized profit is eliminated, not just 70%. This is because Purchase Ltd. controls Target Ltd. If only 70% of the unrealized profit were eliminated, Purchase Ltd. could inflate its consolidated inventory by buying a lot of merchandise from Target Ltd. and retaining 30% of the unrealized profit in its reported inventory.

- *Land*. The FVI of $70,000 is added (that is, 70% of the full FVI of $100,000).

- *Buildings and equipment*. Buildings and equipment is *reduced* by $10,000 to reflect the fair value at the date of acquisition, as was the case for consolidation at the date of acquisition.

- *Accumulated depreciation*. Target Ltd.'s date-of-acquisition accumulated depreciation is not carried forward on the consolidated balance sheet. The elimination is for the full amount of the date-of-acquisition accumulated depreciation of $150,000. There are two effects to this adjustment:

- The net date-of-acquisition value assigned to Target Ltd.'s buildings and equipment is increased by $140,000: (1) the elimination of accumulated depreciation, less (2) the decrease in value assigned to the asset account.

- The amount remaining in Target Ltd.'s accumulated depreciation is only the depreciation taken *since the date of acquisition*. In addition, we must add one year's amortization of the FVI: $140,000 ÷ 10 = $14,000.

- *Investment in Target Ltd.* This account is eliminated completely, of course.

- *Non-controlling interest*. The minority interest in Target Ltd.'s net assets is 30%. Net assets must be adjusted for the unrealized upstream inventory profit of $8,000. Target Ltd.'s adjusted net assets at the end of 2006 is $835,000 − $8,000 = $827,000; 30% of the adjusted net assets is $248,100.

- *Common shares*. Only Purchase Ltd.'s shares are included.

- *Retained earnings*. The starting point is to add the end-of-year balances together. Then several adjustments are necessary:

  - Target Ltd.'s retained earnings balance at the date of acquisition ($600,000) is eliminated.

  - The non-controlling interest's share of the change in Target Ltd.'s retained earnings *since the date of acquisition* is subtracted. Target Ltd.'s retained earnings increased by $35,000, from $600,000 at the date of acquisition to $635,000 at the end of 2006. The adjustment is for $35,000 × 30% = $10,500.

  - Purchase Ltd.'s share of the unrealized inventory profit of $8,000 is deducted: $8,000 × 70% = $5,600.

  - Accumulated amortization of fair-value increments is deducted. By the end of 2006, there is one year's amortization, $14,000.

In summary, the year-end 2006 consolidated retained earnings is:

Purchase separate-entity retained earnings	$2,321,000
Target separate-entity retained earnings	635,000
Target's date-of-acquisition retained earnings	−600,000
Non-controlling interest's portion of Target's share equity	−10,500
Purchase share of unrealized upstream profit	−5,600
2006 amortization of FVI on buildings and equipment	−14,000
Consolidated retained earnings, December 31, 2006	$2,325,900

Classification of non-controlling interest on the balance sheet

Throughout this book, non-controlling interest will be shown on the balance sheet as a separate item between liabilities and shareholders' equity [CICA 1600.69].

In the accounting profession worldwide, there has always been some unease about the presentation of non-controlling interest on the consolidated balance sheet. Theoretically, items on the equities side of the balance sheet should be a part of either creditors' equity (i.e., liabilities) or shareholders' equity. Having an unidentified floating object between liabilities and shareholders' equity seems contrary to the basic concept of the balance sheet.

IAS 27, which deals with consolidated statements, recommends that minority (i.e., non-controlling) interests "be presented in the consolidated balance sheet within equity, separately from the parent shareholder's equity" [IAS27, ¶33].

However, national differences are prevalent. Germany, for example, requires that non-controlling interests "must be disclosed within the equity section of the group [i.e., consolidated] balance sheet".[5]

In Australia, the preferred term for non-controlling interests is outside equity interest:

> Outside equity interests must be disclosed in the consolidated balance sheet as an item of equity indicating the separate components of capital, retained profits or accumulated losses and reserves.[6]

Yet another alternative comes from the U.K. FRS 4, Capital Instruments (1994), requires minority interest to be analyzed between the aggregate amount attributable to equity interest and the amounts attributable to non-equity interest.[7]

In the U.S., the FASB tentatively decided in early 2000 that non-controlling interest should be shown as a separate component within the shareholders' equity section of the consolidated balance sheet instead of as a separate item between liabilities and shareholders' equity. As this book goes to press, there is no final decision.

The implication of a change in U.S. classification is that the AcSB may consider adopting the U.S. classification approach. It is quite possible that there will be a future change in the recommended balance sheet classification of non-controlling interest.

5. *TRANSACC:Transnational Accounting*, (London: KPMG and The Macmillan Press, 1995), edited by Professor D. Ordelheide, University of Frankfurt, page 2007.

6. *Ibid.*, page 2890.

7. *Ibid.*, page 2789.

Worksheet approach

Exhibit 5–9 shows the 2006 separate-entity trial balances for Purchase Ltd. and Target Ltd. in the first two columns. The trial balances are almost identical to those shown in Exhibit 4–4 for 100% ownership. The differences are:

1. The investment account is for the cost of 70% of the shares, or $840,000, instead of $1,200,000.

2. The Purchase Ltd. common shares are $3,440,000 instead of $3,800,000, reflecting the fact that 28,000 shares were issued to accomplish the business combination instead of 40,000 shares.

3. Purchase Ltd.'s dividend income is only 70% of the $30,000 paid by Target Ltd., or $21,000.

EXHIBIT 5–9 PURCHASE LTD. CONSOLIDATION WORKSHEET—PURCHASE LTD. OWNS 70% OF TARGET LTD.

December 31, 2006

	Trial balances		Adjustments		Purchase
	Purchase Dr/(Cr)	Target Dr/(Cr)	Adjustments Dr/(Cr) [a]	Operations Dr/(Cr) [c]	consolidated trial balance
Cash	$ 971,000	$ 100,000			$1,071,000
Accounts receivable	2,200,000	250,000			2,450,000
Inventories	250,000	70,000		$ (8,000) c2	312,000
Land	1,000,000	300,000	$ 70,000 a2		1,370,000
Buildings and equipment	3,000,000	500,000	(10,000) a2		3,490,000
Accumulated depreciation	(1,300,000)	(185,000)	150,000 a2	(14,000) c3	(1,349,000)
Investments (at cost)	840,000	—	(560,000) a1		
			(280,000) a2		
Goodwill			70,000 a2		70,000
Accounts payable	(800,000)	(200,000)			(1,000,000)
Long-term notes payable	(400,000)	—			(400,000)
Non-controlling interest in Target Ltd.			(240,000) a1	(17,100) c4	
				9,000 c5	(248,100)
Common shares	(3,440,000)	(200,000)	200,000 a1		(3,440,000)
Dividends declared	—	30,000		(30,000) c5	
Retained earnings, December 31, 2005	(2,000,000)	(600,000)	600,000 a1		(2,000,000)
Sales	(2,400,000)	(300,000)		55,000 c1	(2,645,000)
Dividend income	(21,000)	—		21,000 c5	—
Cost of sales	1,750,000	180,000		(55,000) c1	
				8,000 c2	1,883,000
Depreciation expense	100,000	35,000		14,000 c3	149,000
Non-controlling interest in earnings				17,100 c4	17,100
Other expenses	250,000	20,000			270,000
	$ —	$ —	$ —	$ —	$ —

4. The cash is less by $9,000 owing to the smaller amount of dividends received by Purchase Ltd. from Target Ltd.: $21,000 instead of $30,000.

Acquisition adjustments The two adjustments for the acquisition are shown in the third numerical column. Entry **a1** eliminates Target Ltd.'s shareholders' equity accounts and establishes the non-controlling interest's share of Target Ltd.'s net assets at the date-of-acquisition. Entry **a2** adds the fair-value increments for Purchase Ltd.'s share of Target Ltd.'s net assets and recognizes the purchased goodwill. Together, these two entries eliminate Purchase's investment account.

Current operations The fourth numerical column shows the adjustments that are necessary as a result of operations for 2006. These adjustments are similar to those illustrated in Chapter 4 (Exhibit 4–4), except that in this chapter we are assuming 70% ownership rather than 100%. Therefore the non-controlling interest must be accounted for.

The first two adjustments are to eliminate the intercompany sales and to reduce the inventory by the total amount of unrealized intercompany profit:

c1	Sales	55,000	
	Cost of sales		55,000
c2	Cost of sales	8,000	
	Inventory		8,000

Adjustment **c2** is exactly the same adjustment as we made in Chapter 4. The existence of non-controlling interest does not affect this adjustment. The entire inventory will be included in the consolidated balance sheet, and therefore the entire unrealized profit must be eliminated. Similarly, since 100% of Target Ltd.'s revenues and expenses are included in the consolidated income statement, the full amount of the intercompany transactions must be eliminated, not just 70%.

The next two adjustments amortize the fair-value increment relating to buildings and equipment:

c3	Depreciation expense	14,000	
	Accumulated depreciation		14,000

The amortization is only for the fair-value increment relating to the 70% share acquired by Purchase Ltd. Since the minority interest's share of assets and liabilities is being reported at book value, there is no additional amortization relating to the other 30%.

Non-controlling interest in earnings is next. The Purchase Ltd. consolidated income statement will show the total revenues and the total expenses for the two companies. The consolidated income from operations will reflect the entire operations for both companies. However, the shareholders of Purchase Ltd. will benefit from only 70% of Target Ltd.'s earnings. The 30% share of Target Ltd.'s earnings that increases the equity of Target Ltd.'s non-controlling shareholders must be subtracted to determine consolidated net income from the point of view of Purchase Ltd.'s shareholders.

Target Ltd.'s separate-entity net income must first be adjusted by subtracting any unrealized profits that are included in Target Ltd.'s separate-entity net income. The $8,000 unrealized inventory profit is subtracted from Target Ltd.'s reported net income of $65,000. Then, we take 30% of the adjusted Target Ltd. net income of $57,000, which is $17,100. The adjustment is:

c4 Non-controlling interest in earnings of Target Ltd. (**I/S**)   17,100
      Non-controlling interest in Target Ltd. (**B/S**)   17,100

This adjustment may be a bit confusing since the account titles are very similar. The account debited in adjustment **c4** is the *income statement* account. The account credited is the *balance sheet* account.

As for all consolidation adjustments, entry **c4** is a worksheet entry only. *The financial statements of Target Ltd. as a separate legal entity are in no way affected by the adjustments made in Exhibit 5–9.* Target Ltd. will still report to its non-controlling shareholders a net income of $65,000 for 2006 and net assets of $850,000 at year-end. Adjustment **c4** is a necessary part of the consolidation process *for Purchase Ltd.*, but it does not affect the income or financial position of Target Ltd. itself or the rights of non-controlling shareholders in the earnings of Target Ltd.

The final adjustment eliminates the dividends paid by Target Ltd. Since 30% of the dividends were paid to Target Ltd.'s minority shareholders, the entry reduces the non-controlling interest to reflect the fact that Target Ltd.'s net assets have been reduced by the payment of dividends:

c5 Dividend income   21,000
      Non-controlling interest (B/S)   9,000
          Dividends declared   30,000

The consolidated statements are for the parent company's shareholders, and therefore 100% of the subsidiary's dividend payments must be eliminated when consolidated statements are being prepared, regardless of the ownership percentage held by the parent company.

After the foregoing adjustments, the balance sheet non-controlling interest is $248,100. This amount is 30% of the book value of the net assets of Target Ltd. that will be reported in Purchase Ltd.'s consolidated financial statements on December 31, 2006. The amount of non-controlling interest can be verified as follows:

	100%	30%
Target net assets, December 31, 2005	$800,000	$240,000
Target 2006 net income, as reported	65,000	19,500
Target 2006 dividends	−30,000	−9,000
Unrealized profit in inventory	−8,000	−2,400
Target adjusted net assets, December 31, 2006	$827,000	$248,100

All of Target Ltd.'s net assets of $827,000 are included in the consolidated balance sheet, but the non-controlling interest reduces the interest of the Purchase Ltd. shareholders to their 70% ownership of Target Ltd.

Consolidation in Second Subsequent Year

The separate-entity financial statements for the two companies are shown in Exhibit 5–10. Assume that during 2007, the following occurred:

1. Target Ltd. had sales of $60,000 to Purchase Ltd.; Target Ltd.'s 2007 gross margin was 45%; $10,000 (sales price) of the goods are in Purchase Ltd.'s inventory on December 31, 2007. Unrealized upstream profit therefore is $10,000 × 45% = $4,500.

EXHIBIT 5-10 SEPARATE-ENTITY FINANCIAL STATEMENTS FOR 2007

Statements of Income and Retained Earnings
Year Ended December 31, 2007

	Purchase Ltd.	Target Ltd.
Revenue:		
Sales	$3,000,000	$ 400,000
Dividend income	14,000	—
Gain on sale of land	—	150,000
	3,014,000	550,000
Expenses:		
Cost of sales	2,100,000	220,000
Depreciation expense	100,000	35,000
Other expenses	440,000	75,000
	2,640,000	330,000
Net income	$374,000	$ 220,000
Retained earnings, December 31, 2006	2,321,000	635,000
Dividends declared	(135,000)	(20,000)
Retained earnings, December 31, 2007	$2,560,000	$ 835,000

Balance Sheets
December 31, 2007

	Purchase Ltd.	Target Ltd.
Assets		
Current assets:		
Cash	$ 475,000	$ 70,000
Accounts receivable	1,900,000	775,000
Inventory	300,000	60,000
	2,675,000	905,000
Property, plant, and equipment:		
Land	1,450,000	—
Buildings and equipment	3,800,000	500,000
Accumulated depreciation	(1,400,000)	(220,000)
	3,850,000	280,000
Other assets:		
Investments (at cost)	840,000	—
Total assets	$7,365,000	$1,185,000
Liabilities and shareholders' equity		
Liabilities:		
Accounts payable	$ 865,000	$ 150,000
Long-term notes payable	500,000	—
	1,365,000	150,000
Shareholders' equity:		
Common shares	3,440,000	200,000
Retained earnings	2,560,000	835,000
	6,000,000	1,035,000
Total liabilities and shareholders' equity	$7,365,000	$1,185,000

2. Purchase Ltd. had sales of $20,000 to Target Ltd.; Purchase Ltd.'s 2007 gross margin was 30%; $6,000 (sales price) of the goods sold to Target Ltd. are in Target Ltd.'s 2007 ending inventory. Unrealized downstream profit is $6,000 × 30% = $1,800.

3. Purchase Ltd. borrowed $500,000 from Target Ltd. on December 29, 2007. Both companies have reported this as a current item on their separate-entity balance sheets.

4. Target Ltd. sold its land to Purchase Ltd. for $450,000. The land originally cost Target Ltd. $300,000, and its fair value at the date of Purchase Ltd.'s acquisition of Target Ltd. was $400,000. The gain on the sale ($150,000) is separately disclosed on Target Ltd.'s income statement as an unusual item.

These facts are exactly the same as those used in Chapter 4; they are repeated here for convenience.

Direct method

Statement of income and retained earnings The consolidated statement of income and retained earnings is shown in Exhibit 5–11. The amounts that require adjustment are as follows:

- *Sales*. The two companies' combined sales of $3,400,000 are adjusted for the $80,000 in intercompany sales.
- *Dividend income*. The intercompany dividends are eliminated.
- *Gain on sale of land*. The $150,000 unrealized gain is eliminated.

EXHIBIT 5–11 PURCHASE LTD. CONSOLIDATED INCOME STATEMENT (DIRECT METHOD)

Statement of Income and Retained Earnings
Year Ended December 31, 2007

Revenue:	
Sales revenue [3,000,000 + 400,000 – **60,000** – **20,000**]	$3,320,000
Dividend income [14,000 + 0 – **14,000**]	—
Gain on sale of land [0 + 150,000 – **150,000**]	—
	3,320,000
Operating expenses:	
Cost of sales [2,100,000 + 220,000 – **60,000** – **20,000** – **8,000** **+ 4,500 + 1,800**]	2,238,300
Depreciation expense [100,000 + 35,000 **+ 14,000**]	149,000
Other expenses [440,000 + 75,000]	515,000
Non-controlling interest in earnings [(**220,000 + 8,000 – 4,500 – 150,000**) × 30%]	22,050
	2,924,350
Net income	$ 395,650
Retained earnings, December 31, 2006 [2,321,000 + 635,000 – **600,000** – (35,000 × .30) – (8,000 × .70) **– 14,000**]	2,325,900
Dividends declared [135,000 + 20,000 – **20,000**]	(135,000)
Retained earnings, December 31, 2007	$2,586,550

- *Cost of sales.* The unrealized profit adjustments to cost of sales are identical to those shown in Chapter 4 for 2007. The non-controlling interest does not affect the adjustments—the entire unrealized profit in opening inventory ($8,000) must be subtracted from cost of sales (thereby increasing net income), and the unrealized profits in the ending inventory ($4,500 and $1,800) must be added.

- *Depreciation expense.* Amortization of the fair-value increment on Target Ltd.'s buildings and equipment is added to the book amount of depreciation. As in 2006, the amortization is $140,000 ÷ 10 years, or $14,000.

- *Non-controlling interest in earnings.* Target Ltd.'s book net income of $220,000 is increased by the $8,000 of unrealized profit in the *opening* inventory, and reduced by the unrealized upstream profit in the *closing* inventory ($4,500) and in land ($150,000). Then, we take 30% of that adjusted net income to get the non-controlling interest's share of Target Ltd.'s earnings.

- *Opening retained earnings.* The 2007 opening retained earnings is, obviously, the same as the year-end 2006 retained earnings. The sum of the book balances is reduced by Target Ltd.'s date-of-acquisition retained earnings, by the non-controlling interest's share of earnings since acquisition, by Purchase Ltd.'s share of unrealized upstream profits, and by pre-2007 amortization of FVI.

- *Dividends declared.* Target Ltd.'s $20,000 in dividends are eliminated. Only Purchase Ltd.'s dividends are shown on Purchase Ltd.'s retained earnings statement.

Balance sheet The consolidated balance sheet is shown in Exhibit 5–12. Adjustments are as follows:

- *Accounts receivable.* The intercompany receivable of $500,000 that is included on Target Ltd.'s books is eliminated.

- *Inventory.* The unrealized profits from both the upstream and downstream sales are eliminated: $4,500 upstream and $1,800 downstream.

- *Land.* We add the FVI for land, and then subtract the $150,000 unrealized gain on the intercompany sale.

- *Buildings and equipment.* The balance is reduced by $10,000, to reflect fair value.

- *Accumulated depreciation.* Target Ltd.'s date-of-acquisition accumulated depreciation of $150,000 is eliminated; two years' worth of FVI amortization of $14,000 per year is added.

- *Investments.* Purchase Ltd.'s $840,000 investment in Target Ltd. is eliminated.

- *Current accounts payable.* The intercompany balance of $500,000 is eliminated.

- *Non-controlling interest.* The non-controlling interest is determined by starting with the total shareholders' equity as reported on Target Ltd.'s separate-entity balance sheet, Exhibit 5–10: $1,035,000. From this amount we must deduct any and all year-end 2007 unrealized upstream profits. There are two unrealized profit amounts, $4,500 in Purchase Ltd.'s inventory and $150,000 from Target Ltd.'s sale of land to Purchase Ltd.:

EXHIBIT 5–12 PURCHASE LTD. CONSOLIDATED BALANCE SHEET (DIRECT METHOD)

Balance Sheet
December 31, 2007

Assets

Current assets:

Cash [475,000 + 70,000]	$ 545,000
Accounts receivable [1,900,000 + 775,000 − **500,000**]	2,175,000
Inventory [300,000 + 60,000 − **4,500** − **1,800**]	353,700
	3,073,700

Property, plant, and equipment:

Land [1,450,000 + 0 **+ 70,000 − 150,000**]	1,370,000
Buildings and equipment [3,800,000 + 500,000 − **10,000**]	4,290,000
Accumulated depreciation [1,400,000 + 220,000 − **150,000 + 28,000**]	(1,498,000)
	4,162,000

Other assets:

Investments [840,000 + 0 − **840,000**]	—
Goodwill	70,000
Total assets	$7,305,700

Liabilities and shareholders' equity

Liabilities:

Current accounts payable [865,000 + 150,000 − **500,000**]	$ 515,000
Long-term notes payable [500,000 + 0]	500,000
	1,015,000
Non-controlling interest [(**1,035,000 − 4,500 − 150,000**) × **30%**]	264,150

Shareholders' equity:

Common shares [**Purchase Ltd. shares only**]	3,440,000
Retained earnings [2,560,000 + 835,000 − **600,000 − (235,000 × .30)** − **(150,000 × .70) − (4,500 × .70) − 1,800 − (14,000 × 2)**]	2,586,550
	6,026,550
Total liabilities and shareholders' equity	$7,305,700

Target Ltd.'s shareholders' equity, December 31, 2007	$1,035,000
Unrealized year-end 2007 upstream profits:	
Inventory	−4,500
Land	−150,000
Target's adjusted shareholders' equity	$ 880,500
Non-controlling interest's proportion	× 30%
Non-controlling interest, December 31, 2007	**$ 264,150**

- *Retained earnings.* We start with the book balances of the two companies, and then:

  (1) subtract Target Ltd.'s date-of-acquisition retained earnings

  (2) subtract the non-controlling interest's share of the change in retained earnings since the date of acquisition: ($835,000 − $600,000) × 30% = $70,500

  (3) subtract Purchase Ltd.'s 70% share of upstream unrealized profits in land and in ending inventory

(4) subtract 100% of unrealized downstream profits

(5) subtract the cumulative amount of FVI amortization since the date of acquisition (i.e., $14,000 × 2 years)

The calculation for Purchase Ltd.'s consolidated retained earnings for December 31, 2007, is as follows:

Purchase separate-entity retained earnings	$2,560,000
Target separate-entity retained earnings	+ 835,000
Target's date-of-acquisition retained earnings	− 600,000
Non-controlling interest's share of Target Ltd.'s post-acquisition retained earnings	− 70,500
Purchase Ltd.'s share of unrealized profit on sale of land	− 105,000
Purchase Ltd.'s share of unrealized upstream profit in ending inventory	− 3,150
Unrealized downstream profit in ending inventory	− 1,800
2 years' amortization of FVI in buildings and equipment	− 28,000
Purchase's consolidated retained earnings	**$2,586,550**

Worksheet approach

To construct the consolidated financial statements for 2007, we must make the same three types of worksheet adjustments and eliminations as we did for 2006 in Chapter 4:

a Adjust for the acquisition.

b Adjust for the amortization of fair-value increments and goodwill and for Target Ltd.'s earnings between the date of acquisition and the *beginning* of 2007.

c Adjust for 2007 unrealized profits and amortization, and eliminate 2007 intercompany transactions and balances.

In addition, we must recognize the non-controlling interest when we make the worksheet adjustments and eliminations for non-wholly owned subsidiaries. The consolidation worksheet is shown in Exhibit 5–13.

Acquisition and cumulative adjustments The first adjustment column, **a**, contains the two adjustments for the acquisition. Nothing new there.

The second adjustment column, **b**, contains the balance sheet changes that have occurred since acquisition, but prior to the current year. There are three adjustments in this column, all of which involve a charge against retained earnings:

b1 recognizes the prior years' amortization of the FVI on buildings and equipment. Since only one year has elapsed, this adjustment includes only 2006's amortization. More generally, however, this adjustment will include all FVI amortization from the date of acquisition to the *beginning* of the current year.

b2 recognizes the beginning-of-year unrealized upstream profit by reducing cost of sales, thereby increasing consolidated net income.

b3 allocates to non-controlling interests their share of the cumulative change in Target Ltd.'s retained earnings from the date of acquisition to the *beginning* of the current year, adjusted for unrealized upstream profit: ($35,000 − $8,000) × 30% = $8,100.

EXHIBIT 5–13 PURCHASE LTD. CONSOLIDATION WORKSHEET

December 31, 2007

	Trial balances		Acquisition [a]	Cumulative [b]	Current [c]	Purchase Ltd. consolidated trial balance
	Purchase	Target				
Cash	$ 475,000	$ 70,000				$ 545,000
Accounts receivable	1,900,000	775,000			$(500,000) c6	2,175,000
Inventories	300,000	60,000			{ (4,500) c2 (1,800) c4	353,700
Land	1,450,000	—	$ 70,000 a2		(150,000) c3	1,370,000
Buildings and equipment	3,800,000	500,000	(10,000) a2			4,290,000
Accumulated depreciation	(1,400,000)	(220,000)	150,000 a2	$(14,000) b1	(14,000) c5	(1,498,000)
Investments (at cost)	840,000	—	{ (560,000) a1 (280,000) a2	—	}	—
Goodwill			70,000 a2			70,000
Accounts payable	(865,000)	(150,000)			500,000 c6	(515,000)
Long-term notes payable	(500,000)					(500,000)
Non-controlling interest in Target			(240,000) a1	{ (8,100) b3	{ (22,050) c7 6,000 c8	(264,150)
Common shares	(3,440,000)	(200,000)	200,000 a1			(3,440,000)
Dividends declared	135,000	20,000			(20,000) c8	135,000
Retained earnings, December 31, 2006	(2,321,000)	(635,000)	600,000 a1	{ 14,000 b1 8,000 b2 8,100 b3		(2,325,900)
Sales	(3,000,000)	(400,000)			80,000 c1	(3,320,000)
Dividend income	(14,000)	—			14,000 c8	—
Gain on sale of land	—	(150,000)			150,000 c3	—
Cost of sales	2,100,000	220,000		{ (8,000) b2	{ (80,000) c1 4,500 c2 1,800 c4	2,238,300
Depreciation expense	100,000	35,000			14,000 c5	149,000
Non-controlling interest in earnings					22,050 c7	22,050
Other expenses	440,000	75,000				515,000
	$ —	$ —	$ —	$ —	$ —	$ —

Current operations Many of these adjustments are identical to or very similar to those that we have made repeatedly, and we will not repeat all of the adjustments in general journal form. The adjustments can be summarized as follows:

c1 Eliminate the intercompany sales.

c2 Eliminate Target Ltd.'s unrealized profit on upstream sales in Purchase Ltd.'s ending inventory.

c3 Eliminate Target Ltd.'s unrealized profit on upstream sale of land to Purchase Ltd.

c4 Eliminate Purchase Ltd.'s unrealized profit on downstream sales in Target Ltd.'s ending inventory.

c5 Adjust for 2007 amortization of FVI on buildings and equipment.

c6 Eliminate intercompany receivable and payable balances.

c7 Adjust for the non-controlling interest's share of Target Ltd.'s earnings, as adjusted for unrealized profits. The calculation is as follows:

	100%	30%
Target Ltd.'s book net income (Exhibit 5–10)	$ 220,000	$ 66,000
Plus unrealized upstream profit in opening inventory	+ 8,000	+ 2,400
Minus unrealized upstream profit in ending inventory	− 4,500	− 1,350
Minus unrealized profit on upstream sale of land	−150,000	−45,000
Target adjusted 2007 net income	$ 73,500	$ 22,050

This calculation shows both a 100% column and a 30% column, but that is not necessary. Any calculation that gets you to the correct answer (and that you feel most comfortable with) is okay.

c8 Eliminate Target Ltd.'s dividends. Of the $20,000, 70% (i.e., $14,000) is eliminated against Purchase Ltd.'s dividend income and 30% ($6,000) is charged to non-controlling interest on the balance sheet.

The Next Steps

Chapters 4 and 5 have worked methodically through the consolidation process at three points in time: the date of acquisition, one year after acquisition, and two years after acquisition. Chapter 4 assumed that the parent owned 100% of the subsidiary shares. Chapter 5 relaxed that assumption and illustrated consolidation when the subsidiary is *not* wholly owned. Through the course of these two chapters, most of the major aspects of consolidation have been illustrated.

The next chapter covers the one remaining major aspect of consolidations—intercompany sale of depreciable or amortizable assets. Then, it presents a general approach to consolidation that can be used at any point in time, freeing us from the methodical process of year-by-year consolidations. We also will take a third and final look at the equity basis of reporting. We'll bet you can hardly wait!

SUMMARY OF KEY POINTS

1. When a parent company purchases control of a subsidiary but acquires less than 100% of the subsidiary's shares, the *parent-company* approach to consolidation is used. The subsidiary's assets and liabilities are consolidated with those of the parent (1) at fair value for the parent's share of the subsidiary's net assets and (2) at carrying value for the non-controlling interest's share. The parent-company approach is the widely accepted international practice for controlled subsidiaries.

2. *Proportionate consolidation* is the required consolidation method in Canada for joint ventures, and *only* for joint ventures. Under proportionate consolidation, only the reporting enterprise's proportionate share of the joint venture's assets and liabilities is included on the investor's consolidated balance

sheet. Canada is the only country to require proportionate consolidation for joint ventures. All other countries require equity-basis reporting.

3. All of the subsidiary's assets and liabilities are consolidated on the parent's balance sheet, but part of those net assets represents the equity of the non-controlling interests. On the parent's balance sheet, there must be an amount shown for the non-controlling interest's share of the subsidiary's net assets. In Canada, this amount is shown after liabilities but before shareholders' equity.

4. All of the subsidiary's revenues and expenses are included in the parent's income statement, but part of the subsidiary's earnings accrues to the non-controlling interests. Therefore, the parent must deduct an amount for the non-controlling interest's share of earnings. The non-controlling interest's share of earnings is reduced by its proportionate share of any upstream unrealized profits.

SELF-STUDY PROBLEM 5–1

On January 10, 2005, Regina Ltd. acquired 60% of the shares of Dakota Ltd. by issuing common shares valued at $150,000. Prior to the acquisition of Dakota, Regina's balance sheet appeared as shown in Exhibit 5–14. The balance sheet of Dakota Ltd. at the date of acquisition is shown in Exhibit 5–15.

Required:

Prepare a consolidated balance sheet for Regina Ltd., as it would appear immediately following the acquisition of Dakota.

EXHIBIT 5–14 REGINA LTD.	
Balance Sheet **December 31, 2004**	
Current assets:	
Cash	$ 50,000
Accounts and other receivables	70,000
Inventory	80,000
	200,000
Capital assets:	
Building	260,000
Accumulated depreciation	(40,000)
Equipment	175,000
Accumulated depreciation	(70,000)
	325,000
Total assets	$525,000
Liabilities:	
Current accounts payable and accrued liabilities	$ 80,000
Shareholders' equity:	
Common shares	220,000
Retained earnings	225,000
	445,000
Total liabilities and shareholders' equity	$525,000

EXHIBIT 5–15 DAKOTA LTD.

Balance Sheet
January 10, 2005

	Book value	Fair value
Current assets:		
Cash	$ 10,000	$ 10,000
Accounts and other receivables	20,000	20,000
Inventory	30,000	30,000
	60,000	
Capital assets:		
Land	45,000	80,000
Building	150,000	130,000
Accumulated depreciation	(50,000)	
Equipment	130,000	10,000
Accumulated depreciation	(80,000)	
	195,000	
Total assets	$255,000	
Liabilities:		
Current accounts payable	$ 40,000	40,000
Long-term debenture payable	50,000	50,000
	90,000	
Shareholders' equity:		
Common shares	100,000	
Retained earnings	65,000	
	165,000	
Total liabilities and shareholders' equity	$255,000	

SELF-STUDY PROBLEM 5–2

During 2005, the following transactions occurred between Regina Ltd. and Dakota Ltd. (see SSP5–1):

a. Regina lent $50,000 at 10% interest to Dakota Ltd. on July 1, 2005, for one year. The interest was unpaid at December 31, 2005.

b. During 2005, Regina purchased inventory from Dakota at a cost of $400,000; $100,000 of that amount was still in Regina's inventory at the end of 2005. [Hint: look at Dakota's income statement to compute Dakota's gross profit percentage.]

c. During 2005, Dakota purchased inventory of $200,000 from Regina; $40,000 of that amount was still in Dakota's inventory at the end of 2005.

Other Information:

d. Dakota's building and equipment were estimated to have remaining useful lives from January 10, 2005, of 10 and 5 years, respectively. Straight-line depreciation is being used.

e. There has been no impairment of goodwill.

f. No fixed assets were sold or written off during 2005.

The December 31, 2005, separate-entity financial statements for both companies are shown in Exhibit 5–16.

Required:

Prepare the consolidated statement of income and retained earnings and the consolidated balance sheet for Regina Ltd. for the year ended December 31, 2005.

EXHIBIT 5–16	REGINA LTD. AND DAKOTA LTD.

Balance Sheets
December 31, 2005

	Regina Ltd.	Dakota Ltd.
Current assets:		
Cash	$ 28,000	$ 10,000
Accounts and other receivables	110,000	30,000
Inventories	160,000	60,000
	298,000	100,000
Capital assets:		
Land	—	135,000
Buildings	300,000	150,000
Accumulated depreciation	(45,000)	(60,000)
Equipment	200,000	130,000
Accumulated depreciation	(80,000)	(90,000)
	375,000	265,000
Other assets:		
Investment in Dakota Ltd. (at cost)	150,000	—
Total assets	$823,000	$365,000
Liabilities:		
Current accounts payable and accrued liabilities	$ 40,000	$ 80,000
Long-term liabilities	65,000	50,000
	105,000	130,000
Shareholders' equity:		
Common shares	370,000	100,000
Retained earnings	348,000	135,000
	718,000	235,000
	$ 823,000	$ 365,000

Statements of Income and Retained Earnings
Year Ended December 31, 2005

	Regina Ltd.	Dakota Ltd.
Sales	$2,000,000	$1,000,000
Dividend income	24,000	—
Other income	7,000	—
	2,031,000	1,000,000
Cost of sales	1,000,000	600,000
Other operating expenses	886,000	280,000
Interest expense	2,000	10,000
	1,888,000	890,000
Net income	143,000	110,000
Retained earnings, December 31, 2004	225,000	65,000
Dividends declared	(20,000)	(40,000)
Retained earnings, December 31, 2005	$ 348,000	$ 135,000

SELF-STUDY PROBLEM 5–3

Regina Ltd. owns 60% of the common shares of Dakota Ltd., acquired on January 10, 2005. The details of the purchase are given in SSP 5–1, and the trial balances for December 31, 2005, and selected transactions for 2005 are shown in SSP 5–2. The financial statements of both companies (unconsolidated) at December 31, 2006, are shown in Exhibit 5–17.

EXHIBIT 5–17	REGINA LTD. AND DAKOTA LTD.

Balance Sheets
December 31, 2006

	Regina Ltd.	Dakota Ltd.
Current assets:		
Cash	$ 63,800	$ 52,500
Accounts and other receivables	120,000	77,000
Inventories	130,000	55,000
	313,800	184,500
Capital assets:		
Land	—	135,000
Buildings	380,000	150,000
Accumulated depreciation	(56,200)	(70,000)
Equipment	230,000	170,000
Accumulated depreciation	(68,000)	(47,000)
	485,800	338,000
Other assets:		
Investment in Dakota Ltd. (at cost)	150,000	—
Total assets	$949,600	$522,500
Liabilities:		
Current accounts payable and accrued liabilities	$ 51,600	$ 97,500
Long-term liabilities	180,000	120,000
	231,600	217,500
Shareholders' equity:		
Common shares	370,000	100,000
Retained earnings	348,000	205,000
	718,000	305,000
	$949,600	$522,500

Statements of Income and Retained Earnings
Year Ended December 31, 2006

	Regina Ltd.	Dakota Ltd.
Sales	$2,200,000	$1,100,000
Dividend income	36,000	—
Gain on sale of equipment	10,000	—
Other income	12,000	—
	2,258,000	1,100,000
Cost of sales	1,300,000	660,000
Other operating expenses	864,000	292,000
Interest expense	20,000	18,000
	2,184,000	970,000
Net income	74,000	130,000
Retained earnings, December 31, 2005	348,000	135,000
Dividends declared	(74,000)	(60,000)
Retained earnings, December 31, 2006	$ 348,000	$ 205,000

Additional Information:

1. At the beginning of 2006, unrealized upstream profits in inventory amounted to $40,000 held in Regina's inventory (i.e., from upstream sales) and $20,000 in Dakota's inventory (i.e., downstream).

2. During 2006, Dakota sold inventory to Regina for $160,000 at the normal gross margin. One-half of that amount is still in Regina's inventory at year-end.

3. Late in 2006, Regina sold inventory to Dakota at a special price of $40,000. All of these goods are still in Dakota's inventory on December 31, 2006. The cost to Regina of the goods sold to Dakota was $20,000, a 50% gross margin on the selling price.

4. The one-year, $50,000 loan that Regina extended to Dakota on July 1, 2005, was extended for two more years (to July 1, 2008). Simple interest (at 10%) has been accrued by both companies, but no interest will be paid until the principal is repaid.

Required:

Calculate the following amounts for the year ended December 31, 2006:

a. Non-controlling interest in earnings (i.e., on Regina's consolidated income statement).

b. Non-controlling interest (on Regina's consolidated balance sheet), December 31, 2006.

c. Regina's year-end consolidated retained earnings.

REVIEW QUESTIONS

5–1 Define the following terms:
   a. Non-controlling interest
   b. Minority interest
   c. Proportionate consolidation
   d. Parent-company approach

5–2 Why do some corporations prefer to control their subsidiaries with less than full ownership?

5–3 How can the inclusion of 100% of a subsidiary's assets on the consolidated balance sheet be justified when the parent owns less than 100% of the subsidiary's shares?

5–4 When all of a non-wholly owned subsidiary's revenues and expenses are consolidated, what recognition is given to the fact that the parent's share of the subsidiary's earnings is less than 100%?

5–5 Under a pure application of the new-entity approach of reporting minority interest, what value is assigned to goodwill?

5–6 How does the parent-company method modify the new-entity approach? What is the rationale for this modification?

5-7 Using generally accepted accounting principles, explain why a subsidiary's assets and liabilities are consolidated using two different valuations under the parent-company method.

5-8 At the date of acquisition, how is the amount of minority interest measured?

5-9 One year after the date of acquisition, how is the amount of minority interest on the balance sheet measured?

5-10 How do unrealized profits on upstream sales affect the minority interest's share of a subsidiary's earnings?

5-11 How do unrealized profits on downstream sales affect the minority interest's share of a subsidiary's earnings?

5-12 How are minority shareholders likely to react to the reduction of their share of the subsidiary's earnings as a result of unrealized profits?

5-13 What is the impact on minority interest of unrealized profits in *beginning* inventories?

5-14 Why are a non-wholly owned subsidiary's dividend payments completely eliminated even though the parent does not receive all of the dividends?

5-15 In Canada, all of a subsidiary's assets and liabilities are consolidated regardless of the ownership percentage of the parent. Nevertheless, the ownership percentage may affect the amount of the reported (consolidated) assets. Explain.

CASES

CASE 5–1   McIntosh Investments Ltd.

McIntosh Investments, Ltd., (MIL) is a diversified public company. Loraine McIntosh, the president, owns 40% of the common shares of MIL. Another 30% are owned jointly by Loraine's brothers, Blair and Bill. The 70% ownership by Loraine and her brothers gives her control of the company. The remaining 30% of the shares are widely distributed.

On April 1, 2006, the first day of MIL's fiscal year, Loraine succeeded in negotiating the acquisition by MIL of 30% of the outstanding common shares of Efrim Auto Parts, Inc. (EAPI). EAPI was an important supplier of parts to Candide Cars Corporation (CCC), a maker of specialty automobiles ("the best of all possible cars"), which was 40% owned by MIL. Loraine was particularly pleased at being able to arrange the purchase of the shares of EAPI because she was certain that great efficiency could be obtained by having the operations of EAPI and CCC more closely coordinated.

The EAPI shares were purchased from a descendant of the founder of EAPI, Jeffrey Efrim. The shares were purchased for a consideration of $600,000 cash and the issuance of 10,000 shares of MIL common stock. MIL shares were currently being traded on the TSX at $40 per share. Exhibit A presents the balance sheet of EAPI as of March 31, 2006, the end of EAPI's fiscal year.

During the following year, Loraine and her fellow managers took an active interest in the affairs of both CCC and EAPI. CCC became EAPI's major customer, and purchased $2,000,000 of parts from EAPI during fiscal 2007. At the end of fiscal 2007, CCC had parts in inventory that were purchased from EAPI at a cost (to CCC) of $300,000, as compared to only $100,000 of such parts in inventory a year earlier. The attentions of MIL management had increased EAPI's efficiency so that average gross profit on sales rose to 35% in fiscal 2007. EAPI's net income after tax in fiscal 2007 reached a record high of $300,000 after tax, enabling EAPI to declare a dividend of $1.50 per common share on March 31, 2007.

Required:

Determine what impact MIL's investment in EAPI shares and EAPI's fiscal 2007 activities will have on the financial statements of MIL. Where alternatives are possible, state them and briefly explain the alternatives you choose. State any assumptions that you find it necessary to make.

EXHIBIT A

EAPI Balance Sheet
March 31, 2006

	Book value	Fair value
Cash	$ 200,000	$ 200,000
Accounts receivable	300,000	300,000
Inventories	400,000	440,000
Equipment (net)	2,100,000	2,400,000
Long-term investment (cost)	300,000	360,000
	$3,300,000	
Accounts payable and accrued liabilities	600,000	600,000
Debentures outstanding	700,000	600,000
Common shares (60,000 shares)	500,000	—
Retained earnings	1,500,000	—
	$3,300,000	

CASE 5–2   Simpson Ltd.

Simpson Ltd. is a private Ontario corporation controlled by Ted Simpson. The company owns a series of chocolate chip cookie stores throughout Ontario, and also has a wholly owned Quebec subsidiary that operates stores in Montreal and Quebec City. Because of its lack of stores in Western Canada and its managers' lack of knowledge about that part of the country, Simpson Ltd. has just acquired 70% of the outstanding class A voting shares of Ong Inc. for $6,000,000 cash. Ong Inc. is another cookie store chain that is headquartered in Vancouver and has stores throughout Vancouver and Victoria, as well as in Edmonton, Saskatoon, and Winnipeg.

Ted expects that the acquisition will greatly help the Simpson Ltd. "bottom line," which in turn will help Simpson Ltd. to obtain expanded debt financing because of the greater net income and cash flow. The management of Ong Inc. will not change as a result of the purchase; the former sole owner, John Ong, retains the remaining 30% of the Ong Inc. shares and has agreed to continue as CEO of Ong Inc. for at least five years after the change in control. The president and chief operating officer, Travis Hubner, will also stay on, so there is no reason that the acquired company should not continue to be highly profitable. The condensed balance sheet of Ong Inc. at the date of acquisition is shown in Exhibit B.

EXHIBIT B

Ong Inc.
Condensed Balance Sheet
May 8, 2005

Assets

Cash		$ 200,000
Accounts receivable		100,000
Inventories—raw materials and supplies		1,200,000
Buildings	$ 7,000,000	
Accumulated depreciation	(1,400,000)	5,600,000
Equipment	$ 3,000,000	
Accumulated depreciation	(1,200,000)	1,800,000
Total assets		$8,900,000

Liabilities and shareholders' equity

Liabilities:		
Accounts payable	$ 350,000	
Accrued expenses	50,000	
Total current liabilities		$ 400,000
Bank loan payable, due May 3, 2007		2,700,000
Future income taxes		1,100,000
Total liabilities		4,200,000
Shareholders' equity:		
Common shares—Class A voting	$ 1,000,000	
Retained earnings	3,700,000	4,700,000
Total liabilities and share equity		$8,900,000

The acquisition was financed mainly by debt; $4,500,000 was borrowed by Simpson Ltd. from the Western Bank of British Columbia, secured by the assets of both Simpson Ltd. and Ong Inc. The bank has requested audited financial statements of both companies on an annual basis, supplemented by unaudited quarterly statements.

Ong Inc. owns the buildings in which some of its stores are located, but most are leased. None of the land is owned. The buildings are being depreciated over 30 years. John has obtained two separate appraisals of the owned buildings; one appraisal firm has placed the aggregate current value at $9,500,000, while the second firm arrived at a value of $8,400,000. Ong Inc. owns all of the equipment in its stores; the equipment is being depreciated over 10 years, and is, on average, 40% depreciated. It would cost $3,300,000 to replace the existing equipment with new equipment of similar capacity. Inventories are generally worth their book values, except that the replacement cost of the stock of imported Belgian chocolate in the Vancouver warehouse is $20,000 less than book value because of the strengthening Canadian dollar. On the other hand, the accounts payable shown in Exhibit B includes an unrealized gain of $10,000 because much of the liability is denominated in Belgian francs.

Required:

Determine, on a line-by-line basis, the impact on Simpson Ltd.'s consolidated assets and liabilities as a result of the acquisition, in accordance with Ted Simpson's objectives in acquiring Ong. Where alternative values could be used, explain the reasons for your selection.

[ICAO]

CASE 5–3   Proctor Industries

You, CA, are the senior in charge of an audit of Proctor Industries (PI), a public company in the business of selling plumbing parts wholesale. It is now November 3, 2005—five weeks after PI's year-end of September 30, 2005, and one week before your firm has been asked to discuss the financial statements for PI, including any significant accounting issues, with PI's audit committee.

PI's unconsolidated annual sales approximate $36 million. It operates through six regional branches with approximately equal sales volumes at each branch.

PI has a 60% interest in Minor Inc., a company located in the United Kingdom. It also has a September 30 year-end and is audited by a firm of chartered accountants in the United Kingdom.

You are at the client's premises reviewing the year-end working papers for Proctor Industries, and you note the following items:

1. PI's unconsolidated net income before income taxes is normally about $2 million.

2. The allowance for doubtful accounts in PI is $200,000. Based on the work performed in this section of the audit, the audit assistant concluded that the allowance should be at least $250,000, and could be as high as $350,000.

3. You have contacted the auditors for Minor Inc. (MI) to obtain its financial statements. However, they are unable to provide you with the audited financial statements since the president of MI refused to sign the management representation letter. He disagrees with the revenue recognition policy insisted on by the auditors of MI and intends to obtain opinions from other audit firms on this issue. The financial statements, under the policy supported by the auditors, show a net loss of $320,000 for the year. MI's current policy for revenue recognition is when items are produced, based on the support that there is a ready market for MI's supplies, which are currently in short supply. PI's revenue recognition policy is when goods are shipped to the customer.

4. There is a new item on PI's balance sheet called "Investments." The working papers indicate that this represents a cash payment in June 2005 for $100,000 for all the common shares of Chemicals Inc. (CI). This company has an August 31 year-end. Although CI has previously never been audited, PI requested, and you have completed, an audit of CI for its August 31, 2005 year-end. The audited financial statements for CI appear in Exhibit C. CI manufactures household cleaning products. The equipment used in the manufacturing process is not complex and is inexpensive to replace. CI has earned large profits in the past, mainly from government contracts. This year, the financial statements show an after-tax profit of $100,000.

5. An extract of the agreement to purchase CI states that if the company earns more than $1 million per year in any of the next five years, the vendor may buy back the common shares for a price to be determined.

6. One of the legal letters for PI was returned with the following comment:

> Chemicals may be liable for damages arising from the alleged dumping of hazardous chemicals from its Bedford plant into the nearby Black River. As of the current date, a statement of claim has been filed. CI denies these allegations.

The partner has asked you to prepare a memo on the above items for his use in discussions with the audit committee.

Required:

Prepare the memo requested by the partner.

[CICA, adapted]

EXHIBIT C

Chemicals Inc.
Extracts from Audited Balance Sheet
As at August 31, 2005

Assets

Accounts receivable	$ 900,000
Prepaid expenses	100,000
Inventory	400,000
Capital assets, net	400,000
	$1,800,000

Liabilities and shareholders' equity

Accounts payable	$ 500,000
Common shares (100 issued)	50,000
Retained earnings	1,250,000
	$1,800,000

CASE 5–4   Floral Impressions Ltd.

You, CA, are employed at Beaulieu & Beauregard, Chartered Accountants. On November 20, 2005, Domenic Jones, a partner in your firm, sent you the following e-mail:

"Our firm has been reappointed auditors of Floral Impressions Ltd. (FIL) for the year ending December 31, 2005. I met with the president and major shareholder of FIL, Liz Holtby, last week. I have prepared some background information on FIL for you to review, including the company's October 31, 2005, internal non-consolidated financial statements (Exhibit D). FIL is increasing the amount of business it does on the Internet, and Liz would like us to provide comments on the direction in which FIL is moving. I made notes on her plans for FIL's increasing use of the Internet (Exhibit E). I also met with Craig Albertson, the controller, and I made notes from that meeting (Exhibit F)."

"Once you have reviewed the material, I would like you to draft an audit planning memo identifying the new accounting and audit issues for the 2005 audit. I would also like the memo to address Liz's specific requests."

"I'd like to receive something by next week. Let me know if you have any questions."

Required:

Prepare the memo requested by the partner.

EXHIBIT D

BACKGROUND INFORMATION

Floral Impressions Ltd. (FIL), a small public company listed on a Canadian stock exchange, is a wholesaler of silk plants with three warehouses located in Ontario, Alberta, and British Columbia. It imports its inventory of silk flowers and accessories from Indonesia. FIL employees arrange bouquets, trees, wreaths, and decorative floral products for sale in Canada to flower shops, grocery stores, and other retailers.

The silk plant concept was novel when FIL was incorporated in 1994. For the first three fiscal years, sales grew at approximately 40% per year, and FIL expanded to meet the demand. However, increased competition resulted in declining sales and operating losses over the next six years. Liz inherited the shares of the company in 2003. She had just completed a marketing course and was very excited about becoming involved in the business and applying her new skills. The fiscal year ended December 31, 2004, brought a return to higher sales levels and a modest net income. Liz's management contract, which was negotiated in 2004, provides for stock options to be granted to her each year based on the percentage increase of FIL's revenue from one year to the next. On October 31, 2005, Liz was granted stock options for the first time. She received 4,500 stock options at $2.50 each, the market price at that date.

On January 15, 2005, when shares were trading at $4 each, FIL announced an agreement with the shareholders of Rest-EZE Wreath Corporation (RWC) whereby FIL would acquire 100% of the voting shares of RWC by issuing 200,000 FIL common shares. The acquisition of RWC was completed on October 31, 2005. The market value of FIL's shares has declined significantly since the announcement. RWC, a small private Canadian corporation, sells funeral wreaths, made with fresh flowers, on the Internet. The suppliers, florists throughout Canada, advertise their wreath models on RWC's website, which is targeted at funeral homes and their customers. These clients order their flowers through RWC's website. RWC records 100% of the sales, invoices the client for the same amount, and remits 85% of the proceeds to the supplier. RWC absorbs any bad debts. RWC is in the process of installing a billing system on its website that would allow customers to pay by credit card, but is still working out some bugs. RWC's assets (mainly accounts receivable and office equipment) less the liabilities have a fair market value of $150,000, as established by an independent evaluator. RWC has never been audited and its year-end is November 30.

Floral Impressions Ltd.
Non-Consolidated Balance Sheet
(in thousands of dollars)

	October 31, 2005 (unaudited)	December 31, 2004 (audited)
Assets		
Current assets		
Accounts receivable	$2,003	$1,610
Inventory	610	420
	2,613	2,030
Property, plant and equipment	216	239
Computer development costs	32	22
Intangibles—customer list	20	0
	$2,881	$2,291
Liabilities		
Current liabilities		
Bank indebtedness	$1,850	$1,520
Accounts payable	1,253	1,199
	3,103	2,719
Shareholders' deficiency		
Common shares (2005: 600,000; 2004: 400,000)	400	400
Deficit	(622)	(828)
	(222)	(428)
	$2,881	$2,291

Floral Impressions Ltd.
Non-Consolidated Income Statement
(in thousands of dollars)

	Ten months ended October 31, 2005 (unaudited)	Year ended December 31, 2004 (audited)
Sales	$24,950	$22,119
Cost of goods sold	20,630	18,801
Gross margin	4,320	3,318
General and administrative expenses	4,114	3,229
Income before income taxes	206	89
Income taxes	0	0
Net income	$ 206	$ 89

EXHIBIT E

NOTES FROM DOMENIC JONES' CONVERSATION WITH LIZ HOLTBY

Liz believes the acquisition of RWC provides an opportunity to expand into a less cyclical market and to sell on the Internet. RWC has well-established relationships with two major funeral home chains. Liz is excited about benefiting from

RWC's website because the site fits perfectly with FIL's new direction and allows FIL to gain access to the Internet immediately. So far, the site has not generated significant new business for FIL, but Liz is confident that, with time, sales will increase. As soon as RWC's billing system allows payments by credit card, FIL also intends to link directly into RWC's accounting system to invoice its own clients. Liz anticipates that RWC will account for about 40% of FIL's consolidated revenue this year. Liz plans to exercise her stock options and sell the shares acquired as soon as the share price reaches $9 or more.

To gain greater exposure on the Internet, FIL is also developing its own website. FIL will pay for the costs of running the site by selling advertising spots on the site to home decorating companies. Liz believes she can generate $80,000 in advertising revenue over a 12-month period once the site is up and running. So far, FIL has pre-sold 10 spots for $200 each. The advertisements are to run for one month. Unfortunately, the site delays have caused some advertisers to cancel their contracts. Others are threatening to cancel their contracts unless FIL gets the site up and running within the next month. The controller has recorded the advertising revenue as sales.

FIL has two technicians working in its computer department. Most of their time is spent keeping the network up and running. Since developing an intranet two months ago to give all employees access to the Internet, the network has been bombarded with junk mail and has slowed down or crashed regularly. As a result, the two technicians have not had time to develop the website or to upgrade the firewall as planned. Liz wants the website up and running right away and has threatened to hire RWC's programmers to develop the website if FIL's technicians don't do it quickly enough.

Very recently, Liz spoke to a representative from a company offering to perform all of FIL's accounting over the Internet. Now Liz's vision for FIL is to do everything on the Internet. The representative says that a company will maintain, on its own website, the latest version of whatever standard accounting package FIL uses. FIL would access the site and post the transactions (accounts receivable, accounts payable, and payroll). His company would generate the accounting books and records and would generate FIL's monthly financial statements. Liz likes the plan because she could reduce both administrative staffing costs and the amount of time she spends managing the administration group. It would allow Liz to better focus her efforts on developing FIL's Internet site and related sales.

EXHIBIT F

NOTES FROM DOMENIC JONES' CONVERSATION WITH CRAIG ALBERTSON

Craig Albertson was hired by FIL in September 2005 as the controller. FIL's previous controller resigned in June 2005 due to illness and the position was temporarily filled by the accounts payable clerk. Craig anticipates that he will have all year-end information ready for our audit team by March 15, 2006.

In February 2005, Liz outsourced FIL's payroll function to a service bureau that offered an exceptional price if FIL signed a five-year contract. The payroll consists of 50 employees. Craig has heard rumours that the service bureau is experiencing financial difficulties.

Historically, FIL's sales are highest during February and March, and August to October. Accounts receivable consist of a large number of small dollar value accounts, with the exception of five large chain store customers that account for approximately 40% of the total accounts receivable. The allowance returns typically have been 1% of fourth-quarter sales.

Management counts inventory at the end of each quarter and cost of goods sold is adjusted accordingly. At September 30, 2005, the inventories held at each location were as follows: 55% of the total dollar value in British Columbia, 35% in Alberta, and 10% in Ontario. By year-end, Craig expects inventory at all sites to be at much lower levels. While visiting the warehouse, I observed that the physical security over inventory was tight. Craig commented that FIL has never written down inventory in the past and that he estimates about 2% of the current inventory is obsolete because it is out of style.

During the year, management negotiated an operating line of credit with a new financial institution. The amount authorized is limited to 75% of accounts receivable under 90 days old and 50% of inventory, to a maximum of $2 million. The loans bear interest at prime plus 3%. Under this agreement, FIL is required to provide audited financial statements within 90 days of the fiscal year-end.

Craig did not record the investment in RWC, since the only change was in the number of common shares issued.

On October 1, 2005, FIL purchased a customer list for $20,000 from a former competitor that was going out of business. FIL has not yet determined an amortization policy for this purchase.

Some employees and board members have questioned FIL's sudden focus on the Internet when other companies seem to be moving away from it and back to traditional sales methods. Craig raised the same concern. He doesn't understand why FIL is changing direction when the new management's marketing changes produced such good results in 2004.

CASE 5–5   Major Developments Corporation

John "Calc" Gossling is one of Canada's foremost real estate investment analysts. He works for the firm of Bouchard Wiener Securities Inc. (BWS). His job is to do research and make recommendations on the stock of publicly traded companies, independent of any interest his employer may have in the companies. The research gets published and is used by investors in making their investment decisions. He is noted for his superb number-crunching ability, scathing comments, and accurate analysis. In late 1994, he correctly predicted the end of the real estate bubble, which occurred about two years later. His writing style is in marked contrast to the traditional dry prose of most investment analysts.

Major Developments Corporation (Major) is a publicly traded company operating primarily in the real estate sector. Major has a March 31 year-end and in 2005 reported revenues of $704 million and after-tax income of $118 million. The company buys and sells commercial real estate properties and manufactures commercial elevator components (its original business before it got into real estate). Major survived the recession of the 1990s, and during that time purchased a number of commercial "jewels" at bargain prices. In 2004, Major ventured overseas, acquiring properties in three Asian countries.

Major's share price climbed steadily from 1999 until July 11, 2005. On that date BWS released a stunning research report by Gossling on Major (see extracts in Exhibit G). The report caused an uproar, as it claimed that many of Major's accounting policies in 2005 were misleading and therefore not in accordance with Canadian generally accepted accounting principles. It further claimed that the company was overvalued and had poor prospects because of its real estate portfolio mix.

The stock had been trading in the $15–16 range but immediately dropped to around $9. BWS profited from the decline in the stock price because it held a significant short position in Major's stock. Within four days, lawyers working for

Major launched a legal suit against BWS, claiming damages plus a full retraction of all statements made to be published in a national newspaper.

BWS's legal counsel is now examining various courses of action. To help prepare for the case, counsel has hired Brick & Mortar, Chartered Accountants, to provide a report on the validity of the positions of each of the parties on the disagreements over accounting policies as well as any other relevant advice. You, CA, work for Brick & Mortar. You have obtained a copy of Major's 2005 annual report (see extracts in Exhibit H). Major's lawyers have provided the information in Exhibit I.

Required:

Prepare a draft report to legal counsel for the partner to review.

EXHIBIT G

EXTRACTS FROM JOHN GOSSLING'S RESEARCH REPORT

—I have done a detailed review of Major's 2005 annual report. I approached management of the company with a detailed list of further questions, but management did not respond in the four days that I gave them.

—It is my contention that in 2005, Major clearly violated Canadian generally accepted accounting principles (GAAP), as set out in the *Handbook of the Canadian Institute of Chartered Accountants*, on a number of issues. I am saying that the accounting is wrong, not just aggressive.

—Major's accounting for its real estate loans really takes the cake for non-compliance. The company consolidates the assets and results of two corporations to whom it has granted loans when it does not own any shares in either of the two companies.

—I don't like the accounting in Major's non-real estate business. There is no question it is misleading. Starting in 2005, the company specifically states in the financial statement notes that revenue (and profit, I might add) is recognized on product that is still sitting in the company's warehouse.

—How can Rely Holdings—a company that lost $750,000, in which Major had acquired an additional 25% interest for $5 million—be valued at over $29 million? The valuation of Rely Holdings makes no sense.

—How can a company capitalize costs incurred for properties that were never acquired? Clearly these costs cannot be considered assets, and it is misleading to do so.

—It is absurd that Major continues to recognize the revenue from properties in certain economically unstable Asian countries. It is unlikely that the money will be collected. Major should write off these buildings immediately instead of recognizing revenue from them.

Recommendation on Major Developments Corp.

Price earnings multiplier based last fiscal year	12.7
Overall rating on their stock	underperform
Recommendation	sell

EXHIBIT H

EXTRACTS FROM MAJOR DEVELOPMENTS CORPORATION'S 2005 ANNUAL REPORT

Note 1: Accounting Policies

The company incurs significant costs in investigating new properties for purchase. Costs incurred in investigating any and all properties, whether or not these properties are ultimately purchased by the company, are capitalized as part of the cost of properties actually acquired. These costs are amortized over the useful lives of the properties acquired.

Economic problems in certain Asian countries where the company owns properties have made collection of rental revenues from these properties difficult at this time. The company expects that, once the difficulties in these countries have been resolved, amounts owed will be collected in full. It is the company's policy to accrue the revenue from these properties.

Revenue on product sales is recognized when the goods are shipped to the customer. In the case of "bill and hold" sales, revenue is recognized when the goods are placed in the company's designated storage area.

The consolidated financial statements include the accounts of Major and its majority-owned subsidiaries and, commencing prospectively in fiscal 2005, the accounts of companies in which Major has no common share ownership but to which it has advanced loans that are currently in default. The equity method is used for investments in which there is significant influence, considered to be voting ownership of 20% to 50%.

Note 14: Investments

	2005	2004
Rely Holdings	$29,640,000	$25,000,000

In 2000, Major purchased an additional 25% interest in Rely Holdings Inc. for $5 million. Major now owns 48% of Rely Holdings Inc. Major accounts for its investment on an equity basis. In 2005, Major recorded a loss of $750,000 from Rely Holdings Inc.

EXHIBIT I

EXTRACTS FROM INFORMATION PROVIDED BY MAJOR'S LAWYERS

1. Major's auditor has always provided an unqualified report on the audited financial statements of Major, including the 2005 financial statements.

2. Major has a legal opinion that the two loans are in default (Item A), and a third party opinion (Item B) that the default permits consolidation of these companies.

Item A " . . . In my opinion, loan 323 to Skyscraper Inc. and loan 324 to Wenon Corporation are in default as of February 1, 2004, under the aforesaid terms of default of the respective loan agreements, dated the 12th day of August, 2001. The lender has the right under law and contract to repossess said aforementioned properties, for the purposes of realization on the loans, subject to restrictions of right under clause 43.(b) . . . " [Matthew Krebs, Q.C.]

Item B "Based on facts set out in the attached document, we concur that it is acceptable, under Canadian generally accepted accounting principles, for Major to consolidate Skyscraper Inc. and Wenon Corporation." [Jesse & Mitchell, Chartered Accountants]

3. "Bill and hold" refers to a practice whereby a customer purchases goods but the seller retains physical possession until the customer requests shipment. Delivery is delayed at the purchaser's request, but the purchaser accepts both the title to the goods and the related billing.

[CICA]

CASE 5–6   Brand Drug Limited

In the course of the audit of Brand Drug Limited (BDL), CA, while reviewing the draft financial statements for the year ended August 31, 2006, noticed that BDL's investment in National Pharmaceuticals Limited (NPL) was valued on the cost basis. In 2005, it had been valued on the equity basis. Representing a 22% interest in NPL, this investment had been made 10 years ago to infuse fresh equity, with a view to protecting BDL's source of supply for drugs.

BDL's controller informed CA that NPL had suffered a large loss in 2006, as shown by the May interim financial statements. BDL's representative on NPL's board of directors had resigned because BDL's purchases from NPL now constituted less than 5% of its total purchases. In addition, NPL had been uncooperative in providing profit data in time to make the year-end equity adjustment. Consequently, BDL's controller had revised the method of accounting for the investment in NPL.

CA then found out that BDL's managers are planning a share issue in 2007 and do not want their earnings impaired by NPL's poor performance. However, they are reluctant to divest themselves of NPL in case the rumoured development by NPL of a new drug to reduce the impact of colitis materializes.

When CA approached NPL's managers, they refused to disclose any information on NPL's operations. CA then learned from a stockbroker friend that NPL's poor results were due to its market being undercut by generic drug manufacturers. The loss had been increased when NPL's management wrote off most of NPL's intangible assets. CA summarized the relevant information on the treatment of the investment for his audit file (Exhibit J).

Required:

Discuss the matters raised above.

[CICA, adapted]

EXHIBIT J

CA'S NOTES ON INVESTMENT IN NPL'S SHARES

Extracts from BDL's draft financial statements for the year ended August 31, 2006, in thousands of dollars:

	2006 (Draft)		2005 (Actual)	
Investment in NPL (Note 3)	$25,000	(1)	$27,400	(2)
Retained earnings:				
Opening balance	$ 6,500		$ 2,350	
plus: net earnings	4,500		7,300	
	11,000		9,650	
less: prior period adjustment (Note 1)	(2,400)		—	
dividends	(2,250)		(3,150)	
Closing balance	$ 6,350		$ 6,500	

Note 1: Represents original cost. The 2005 balance has been reduced by the amount of previously recorded equity interest of $2.4 million. In the nine months ended May 31, 2006, NPL reported a net loss of $140 million after writing off development and patent costs as extraordinary items.

Note 2: Valued on equity basis. Equity adjustment for 2005 involved the elimination of $5.5 million unrealized profit included in ending inventory, on sales from NPL to BDL. The unrealized profit in BDL's ending inventory for 2006 amounts to $1.5 million.

Note 3: Stock market trading in NPL's common shares has been heavy in 2006. Prices for the year are as follows:

August 31, 2005:	$22.00
February 28, 2006:	$ 4.00
August 31, 2006:	$12.00

BDL owns 2,000,000 common shares of NPL; in neither 2005 nor 2006 did NPL declare or pay any dividends.

PROBLEMS

P5–1

On December 30, 2005, the balance sheets of the Perk Company and the Scent Company are as follows:

	Perk Company	Scent Company
Cash	$ 7,000,000	$ 200,000
Accounts receivable	1,000,000	600,000
Inventory	1,300,000	800,000
Capital assets, net	6,700,000	3,400,000
	$16,000,000	$5,000,000
Current liabilities	$ 3,000,000	$ 200,000
Long-term liabilities	4,000,000	800,000
Common shares	5,000,000	1,000,000
Contributed surplus	—	1,000,000
Retained earnings	4,000,000	2,000,000
	$16,000,000	$5,000,000

For both companies, the fair values of their identifiable assets and liabilities are equal to their carrying values except for the following fair values:

	Perk	Scent
Inventories	$1,000,000	$ 600,000
Capital assets (net)	7,000,000	5,000,000
Long-term liabilities	3,800,000	1,100,000

The following cases are *independent*:

1. On December 31, 2005, the Perk Company purchases the net assets of the Scent Company for $5.5 million in cash. The Scent Company distributes the proceeds to its shareholders in return for their shares, cancels the shares, and ceases to exist as a separate legal entity.

2. On December 31, 2005, the Perk Company purchases 75% of the outstanding voting shares of the Scent Company for $4.5 million in cash. The Scent Company continues to operate as a separate legal entity.

Required:

For each of the two independent cases, prepare a consolidated balance sheet for Perk Company at December 31, 2005, subsequent to the business combination. For the second case, prepare a consolidated balance sheet using *each* of the following four approaches.

a. Fair-value purchase:
   1. Proportionate consolidation
   2. Parent-company
   3. Entity

b. New entity

[SMA, adapted]

P5–2

Zoe Ltd. has the following balance sheet at December 31, 2005:

Zoe Ltd.
Balance Sheet
December 31, 2005

Current assets		$ 80,000
Capital assets		
Land	$ 30,000	
Building, net	100,000	
Equipment, net	50,000	180,000
Goodwill		20,000
		$280,000
Current liabilities		$ 55,000
Bonds payable		80,000
Common shares		100,000
Retained earnings, Jan. 1, 2005		60,000
Net loss for 2005		(15,000)
		$280,000

On December 31, 2005, Halifax Ltd. bought 70% of the outstanding shares of Zoe Ltd. and paid $190,000. The current fair values of the net assets of Zoe Ltd. on December 31, 2005, are:

Current assets	$ 80,000	Current liabilities	$55,000
Land	180,000	Bonds payable	$70,000
Building	160,000		
Equipment	20,000		

Halifax Ltd. is an investment company that has assets composed only of cash and short-term marketable investments.

Required:

Calculate the following items, as they would appear on the Halifax Ltd. consolidated balance sheet at December 31, 2005:

a. Land

b. Goodwill

c. Non-controlling interest

[CGA–Canada]

P5–3

Calgary Ltd. acquired a subsidiary, Ottawa Ltd., on July 1, 2005, by paying $200,000 for 70% of the outstanding shares. The fiscal year-end for both companies is December 31. The balance sheets of Ottawa Ltd. and Calgary Ltd. are shown below.

Required:

Prepare the consolidated balance sheet as at July 1, 2005, for Calgary Ltd., following *CICA Handbook* recommendations.

[CGA–Canada]

Ottawa Ltd.
Balance Sheet
July 1, 2005

	Book values	Fair market values
Current assets	$140,000	$140,000
Capital assets		
Land	90,000	150,000
Building, net	215,000	200,000
Equipment, net	60,000	90,000
	$505,000	
Current liabilities	$ 70,000	70,000
Bonds payable	210,000	225,000
Common shares	100,000	
Retained earnings, Jan 1, 2005	70,000	
Net income (Jan. 1–July 1)	55,000	
	$505,000	

Calgary Ltd.
Balance Sheet
July 1, 2005

	Book values	Fair market values
Current assets	$ 150,000	$100,000
Capital assets		
Land	400,000	700,000
Building, net	550,000	400,000
Equipment, net	360,000	200,000
Investment in Ottawa Ltd.	200,000	
Goodwill	400,000	
	$2,060,000	
Current liabilities	$ 60,000	60,000
Bonds payable	200,000	170,000
Common shares	1,000,000	
Retained earnings, July 1, 2005	800,000	
	$2,060,000	

P5–4

Qorp Ltd. has the following balance sheet at December 31, 2005.

Qorp Ltd.
Balance Sheet
December 31, 2005

Current assets		$ 85,000
Capital assets		
Land	$ 30,000	
Building, net	120,000	
Equipment, net	50,000	200,000
Goodwill		50,000
		$335,000
Current liabilities		$ 65,000
Bonds payable, due 2023		70,000
Common shares		120,000
Retained earnings, Jan. 1, 2005		140,000
Net loss for 2005		(60,000)
		$335,000

On January 1, 2006, Zip Ltd., whose assets are composed entirely of share investments and cash, paid $185,000 for 70% of the outstanding shares of Qorp Ltd. The current fair values of the net assets of Qorp Ltd. on January 1, 2006, were:

Current assets	$ 85,000	Current liabilities	$65,000
Land	75,000	Bonds payable	70,000
Building (net)	180,000		
Equipment (net)	30,000		

Zip Ltd. had the following shareholders' equity on January 1, 2006:

Common shares	$ 480,000
Retained earnings	710,000
	$1,190,000

Required:

a. Assume a consolidated balance sheet is prepared on January 1, 2006. Calculate the dollar amounts for the following items as they would appear on that consolidated balance sheet:

1. Goodwill
2. Land
3. Equipment
4. Common shares
5. Retained earnings
6. Non-controlling interest

b. What does non-controlling interest represent on the consolidated balance sheet?

[CGA–Canada]

P5–5

On January 1, 2005, Big Ltd. purchased 80% of the shares of Small Ltd. for $1,400,000 and, on the same day, Small Ltd. purchased 60% of the shares of Smaller Ltd. for $930,000. Any excess of the purchase price was allocated to goodwill.

At January 1, 2005			
	Big Ltd.	**Small Ltd.**	**Smaller Ltd.**
Shares	$1,950,000	$1,600,000	$ 500,000
Retained earnings	2,300,000	1,910,000	730,000
	$4,250,000	$3,510,000	$1,230,000

During 2005			
Net income (cost basis)	$ 800,000	$ 600,000	$ 300,000
Dividends paid	120,000	100,000	40,000

There were no intercompany transactions.

Required:

Calculate the balance of minority interest as it would be shown on the consolidated balance sheet of Big Ltd., at December 31, 2005.

[CGA–Canada]

P5–6

Parent Ltd. pays $550,000 cash for 70% of the outstanding voting shares of Sub Ltd. on January 1, 2005. The following information was available:

$580,000 for 70%.

Sub Ltd.
Trial Balance
January 1, 2005

	Book value	Fair value
Cash	$ 40,000	$ 40,000
Inventory	40,000	30,000
Equipment, net	120,000	100,000
Building, net	300,000	360,000
Land	50,000	160,000
	$550,000	
Liabilities	10,000	14,000
Common shares	250,000	—
Retained earnings	290,000	—
	$550,000	

During 2005, Sub Ltd. earned $180,000 and paid no dividends. The inventory on hand at January 1, 2005, was sold during 2005. The equipment will be depreciated over 10 years straight-line, the building will be depreciated over 20 years straight-line. The liabilities were paid during 2005. Parent Ltd. uses the cost method of accounting for its investment.

Required:

Prepare the eliminating entries that would appear on the consolidated working papers at December 31, 2005, based on the above information.

[CGA-Canada]

P5–7

On January 1, 2005, Par Ltd. purchased 80% of the voting shares of Sub Ltd. for $906,400. The balance sheet of Sub Ltd. on that date was as follows:

Sub Ltd.
Balance Sheet
January 1, 2005

	Net book value	Fair value
Cash	$ 160,000	$160,000
Accounts receivable	200,000	240,000
Inventory	300,000	380,000
Capital assets, net	900,000	750,000
	$1,560,000	
Current liabilities	$ 150,000	130,000
Bonds payable	362,000	362,000
Common shares	200,000	—
Retained earnings	848,000	—
	$1,560,000	

The accounts receivable, inventory, and current liabilities have "turned over" by December 31, 2005, and the net capital assets will be amortized over 10 years, on a straight-line basis.

Additional Information:

1. During 2005, Par Ltd. sold goods costing $100,000 to Sub Ltd. for $140,000. At December 31, 2005, 20% of these goods were still in the inventory of Sub Ltd.

2. In 2005, Sub Ltd. sold goods costing $200,000 to Par Ltd. for $250,000. At December 31, 2005, 30% of these goods were still in the inventory of Par Ltd.

3. In 2005, Sub Ltd. sold land to Par Ltd. for $300,000. The land had cost Sub $240,000.

4. Both companies pay income taxes at the rate of 40%.

The balance sheets and income statements for Par Ltd. and Sub Ltd. at December 31, 2005, are presented below.

Required:

a. Prepare the consolidated income statement for the year ended December 31, 2005.

b. Present the following as they would appear on the consolidated balance sheet at December 31, 2005:

   1. Net capital assets
   2. Goodwill
   3. Retained earnings

[CGA–Canada]

Balance Sheets
December 31, 2005

	Par Ltd.	Sub Ltd.
Cash	$ 200,000	$ 140,000
Accounts receivable	300,000	190,000
Inventories	500,000	460,000
Buildings and equipment (net)	1,200,000	900,000
Investment in Sub Ltd.	906,400	—
Other investments	417,600	—
Total assets	$3,524,000	$1,690,000
Current liabilities	$ 300,000	$ 206,000
Bonds payable	513,000	362,000
Common shares	500,000	200,000
Retained earnings	2,211,000	922,000
Total liabilities and share equity	$3,524,000	$1,690,000

Income Statements
Year Ended December 31, 2005

	Par Ltd.	Sub Ltd.
Sales	$2,000,000	$2,000,000
Cost of sales	1,400,000	1,700,000
Gross margin	600,000	300,000
Depreciation expense	100,000	90,000
Interest expense	63,000	44,000
Income tax expense	140,000	74,000
Other expenses	124,000	78,000
Investment income	(37,000)	(60,000)
Net income	$ 210,000	$ 74,000

P5–8

On January 1, 2004, Parent Ltd. purchased 90% of the shares of Sub Ltd. for $975,000. At that time Sub Ltd. had the following balance sheet:

Sub Ltd.
Balance Sheet
January 1, 2004

	Net book value	Fair value
Cash	$ 60,000	$ 60,000
Accounts receivable	120,000	150,000
Inventory—FIFO	180,000	230,000
Capital assets, net	1,500,000	1,350,000
Goodwill	100,000	—
	$1,960,000	
Current liabilities	$ 140,000	140,000
Bonds payable (Note)	800,000	850,000
Common shares	400,000	—
Retained earnings	620,000	—
	$1,960,000	

The bonds were issued at par and will mature in 10 years. Sub Ltd. has a receivables and inventory turnover of greater than six times per year. The capital assets have an average of 10 years of remaining life and are being amortized straight-line. The subsidiary's goodwill has not been amortized. Any goodwill on acquisition has not been amortized. Furthermore, the annual tests for goodwill impairment have indicated no impairment of goodwill since the date of acquisition.

In 2004, Sub Ltd. sold inventory to Parent Ltd. for $320,000; the inventory had cost $260,000. At the end of 2004, 25% was still in Parent's inventory but it was all sold in 2005.

In 2005, Parent Ltd. sold inventory to Sub Ltd. for $275,000; the inventory had cost $200,000. At the end of 2005, 35% was left in Sub's inventory.

During 2004, the subsidiary earned $875,000 and paid dividends of $50,000. During 2005, the subsidiary incurred a loss of $180,000 and paid dividends of $60,000.

The parent company used the cost method for the investment in subsidiary and netted almost everything to "Other expenses."

At December 31, 2005, the following financial statements were available:

Balance Sheet
December 31, 2005

	Parent Ltd.	Sub Ltd.
Cash	$ 400,000	$ 75,000
Accounts receivable	850,000	179,000
Inventory	970,000	245,000
Capital assets, net	2,631,000	1,863,000
Goodwill	0	100,000
Investment in Sub Ltd.	975,000	0
	$5,826,000	$2,462,000
Current liabilities	$ 450,000	$ 49,000
Bonds payable	0	800,000
Common shares	1,000,000	400,000
Retained earnings	3,026,000	1,385,000
Net income (loss)	1,350,000	(172,000)
	$5,826,000	$2,462,000

Income Statement
Year Ended December 31, 2005

	Parent Ltd.	Sub Ltd.
Sales	$9,865,000	$1,650,000
Cost of sales	8,040,000	1,140,000
Gross profit	1,825,000	510,000
Depreciation	(106,000)	(104,000)
Other expenses	(369,000)	(808,000)
Gain on sale of building	0	230,000
Net Income	$1,350,000	$ (172,000)

Required:

a. Prepare a consolidated income statement for 2005.

b. Calculate the amounts that would appear on the consolidated balance sheet at December 31, 2005, for:

1. Goodwill
2. Capital assets, net
3. Bonds payable
4. Non-controlling interest

[CGA–Canada]

P5–9

The consolidated income statement of Top Corporation (TOP) and its subsidiary Bottom Company (BTM) was prepared incorrectly by an inexperienced accounting clerk. You have now been hired by TOP and you are asked to prepare a corrected consolidated income statement for an upcoming meeting. TOP owns 80% of the outstanding shares of BTM, and BTM declared and paid a dividend of

$25,000 on December 15, 2005. The following is the preliminary consolidated income statement of TOP, as prepared by the accounting clerk, for the year ended December 31, 2005.

Income Statement
Year ended December 31, 2005

	TOP Corporation	Bottom Company	Consolidated
Sales	$900,000	$400,000	$1,300,000
Gain on sale of capital assets	0	50,000	50,000
Investment income	20,000	0	20,000
	920,000	450,000	1,370,000
Cost of goods sold	600,000	200,000	800,000
Gross profit	320,000	250,000	570,000
Expenses			
Selling and administrative	120,000	90,000	210,000
Amortization	50,000	40,000	90,000
Income taxes	60,000	48,000	108,000
Net income	$ 90,000	$ 72,000	$ 162,000

Additional Information:

Your discussions with other management personnel provided you with the following additional information:

1. The gain on sale of capital assets resulted from BTM selling equipment to TOP on January 1, 2005. At the time of the sale, the equipment was recorded on BTM's books with a cost of $120,000 and net book value of $60,000. The equipment was purchased on January 1, 1999, and has been amortized on a straight-line basis over its estimated useful life of 12 years. There was no change in the estimated useful life of the equipment upon acquisition by TOP. Amortization in the year of acquisition/sale is based on the number of months owned, for both companies.

2. TOP and BTM had never had any intercompany sales prior to January 1, 2005. However, on October 31, 2005, TOP sold BTM inventory for $60,000, which originally cost TOP $40,000. By December 31, 2005, 50% of this inventory was resold by BTM to its retail customers.

3. TOP and BTM both pay income taxes at a rate of 40%, including taxes for gains on sales of capital assets.

4. TOP uses the cost method of accounting to record its investment in BTM.

5. At the date of acquisition of the common shares of BTM, there was no purchase price discrepancy.

Required:

Prepare a corrected consolidated income statement for the year ended December 31, 2005.

[CGA]

Appendix 5A

Step Purchases

Introduction

So far, we have assumed that one corporation acquires control of (or significant influence over) another corporation by a single purchase of the acquiree's shares. However, corporations sometimes make strategic investments via a series or sequence of purchases. Sequential purchases are known as **step purchases** or **step acquisitions**.

Step purchases can have three types of accounting significance:

Effect of Step Purchase	Accounting Implication
1. Increase strategic ownership without changing reporting method	No change in reporting method, but add a new layer of FVIs and goodwill
2. Increase ownership from significant influence to control	Change financial reporting method from equity basis to consolidation; add a new layer of FVIs and goodwill
3. Increase ownership from portfolio investment to significant influence	Change financial reporting method from cost basis to equity basis; establish fair values

In the rest of this appendix, we will illustrate the reporting consequences of step purchases. Our numerical example will examine the reporting effects of the first type of change—an increase in a parent company's control percentage. This example illustrates all of the financial reporting implications of step purchases. Following the numerical example, we will discuss the implications of the second and third types of change.

Example: Increase in controlling interest

Assume that on December 31, 2006, Parent Corporation (PC) acquires 60% of the shares of Subsidiary Corporation (SC) for $600,000. The condensed balance sheets for PC and SC are shown in Part 1 of Exhibit 5–18, together with the fair values for SC.

Part 2 of Exhibit 5–18 shows the allocation of the purchase price. PC paid a price that was $270,000 above the book value of the 60% share of net assets acquired; of this amount, $180,000 is estimated to be the FVI on capital assets and the remainder ($90,000) is goodwill.

The consolidated balance sheet for PC on the date of the acquisition is shown in Exhibit 5–19. PC's consolidated assets include 100% of the book values plus 60% of the FVIs of SC's assets. Non-controlling interest is 40% of the net book value of SC's net assets.

For the next step, assume the following additional information:

- In 2007, SC reported net income of $70,000 and paid $20,000 in dividends.
- The remaining useful life of SC's capital assets is 10 years from December 31, 2006.
- There were no intercompany transactions during 2003.

EXHIBIT 5–18   PARENT CORPORATION ACQUISITION OF SUBSIDIARY CORPORATION

December 31, 2006

1. Net asset positions subsequent to acquisition

	Parent book values	Subsidiary Book values	Subsidiary Fair values
Current assets	$1,000,000	$ 400,000	$ 400,000
Capital assets (net)	1,900,000	1,100,000	1,400,000
Investment in Subsidiary Corporation	600,000	0	
Total assets	$3,500,000	$1,500,000	
Liabilities	$1,500,000	$ 950,000	− 950,000
Common shares	400,000	100,000	
Retained earnings	1,600,000	450,000	
Total liabilities and shareholders' equity	$3,500,000	$1,500,000	
Net asset fair value for Subsidiary Corporation			$ 850,000

2. Allocation of purchase price

	Subsidiary Corporation Book values	Subsidiary Corporation Fair values	Subsidiary Corporation Fair value increments
Current assets	$ 400,000	$ 400,000	0
Capital assets (net)	1,100,000	1,400,000	$ 300,000
Liabilities	(950,000)	(950,000)	0
	$ 550,000	850,000	$ 300,000
Parent's ownership share		× 60%	× 60%
FV of net assets acquired		510,000	**180,000**
Purchase price		600,000	
Goodwill		$ 90,000	90,000
Total purchase price discrepancy			$ 270,000

The separate-entity balance sheets for PC and SC at December 31, 2007, are shown in Part 1 of Exhibit 5–20.

So far, there has been nothing new in this analysis. But now, assume that PC buys an additional 10% of the shares of SC for $140,000 cash on the next business day, January 2, 2008. The additional 10% increases PC's ownership interest in SC to 70%.

PC has made two purchases. The fair value of the net assets will be different at each purchase date. Therefore, we must consolidate SC using two different sets of FVIs: one set for the 2006 purchase (as above) and a second set for the 2008 purchase. PC's consolidated balance sheet will include SC's assets and liabilities on the following basis:

- 100% of the book value of SC's assets and liabilities at the date of consolidation, January 2, 2008;
- 60% of the FVIs at December 31, 2006 (the date of the first purchase); and
- 10% of the FVIs at January 2, 2008 (the date of the second purchase).

EXHIBIT 5–19   PARENT CORPORATION CONSOLIDATED BALANCE SHEET

December 31, 2007

Current assets (1,000,000 + 400,000)	$1,400,000
Capital assets (1,900,000 + 1,100,000 + **180,000**)	3,180,000
Goodwill	90,000
Total assets	$4,670,000
Liabilities (1,500,000 + 950,000)	$2,450,000
Non-controlling interest **(550,000 × 40%)**	220,000
Common shares, Parent Corporation	400,000
Retained earnings	1,600,000
Total liabilities and shareholders' equity	$4,670,000

EXHIBIT 5–20   PARENT AND SUBSIDIARY

1. Condensed separate-entity balance sheets, December 31, 2007

	Parent	Subsidiary
Current assets	$1,000,000	$ 500,000
Capital assets (net)	1,900,000	1,000,000
Investment in Subsidiary (at cost)	600,000	0
Total assets	$3,500,000	$1,500,000
Liabilities	$1,300,000	$ 900,000
Common shares	400,000	100,000
Retained earnings	1,800,000	500,000
Total liabilities and shareholders' equity	$3,500,000	$1,500,000

2. Parent Corporation consolidated balance sheet, December 31, 2007

Current assets (1,000,000 + 500,000)	$1,500,000
Capital assets [1,900,000 + 1,000,000 + **(180,000 × 9/10)**]	3,062,000
Investment in Subsidiary (600,000 – **600,000**)	0
Goodwill	90,000
Total assets	$4,652,000
Liabilities (1,300,000 + 900,000)	$2,200,000
Non-controlling interest **(600,000 × 40%)**	240,000
Common shares	400,000
Retained earnings (see below)	1,812,000
Total liabilities and shareholders' equity	$4,652,000

Consolidated shareholder's equity, December 31, 2007

Separate entity retained earnings, December 31, 2007:	
Parent	$1,800,000
Subsidiary	500,000
Less Subsidiary's share equity at date of acquisition	– 450,000
Less non-controlling interest's share of S's earnings since date of acquisition [**(600,000 – 550,000) × 40%**]	– 20,000
Less amortization:	
FVI on capital assets **(180,000 × 1/10)**	– 18,000
Consolidated shareholders' equity, Parent Corporation	$1,812,000

The assigned valuations for the first purchase are left untouched by the second purchase. The cost of the second purchase ($140,000 for 10%) is allocated to fair-value increments and goodwill at the date of the purchase as a separate investment. This allocation is shown in Exhibit 5–21. FVI of $50,000 is allocated to capital assets on the 10% share acquired. The remaining $30,000 purchase price discrepancy is goodwill.

The pro-forma consolidated balance sheet is shown in Exhibit 5–22. Current assets are reduced (compared to Exhibit 5–20) by $140,000, the amount expended to buy the additional 10%.

Consolidated capital assets are increased by $50,000 as compared to the day before (December 31, 2007; Exhibit 5–20). The increase in capital assets is due solely to the FVI on the additional 10% of SC's net assets. Goodwill is increased by $30,000 (to $120,000). From 2008 onward, the two FVIs will be amortized, and the larger goodwill amount will be subjected to the annual impairment test.

EXHIBIT 5–21　PARENT ACQUIRES AN ADDITIONAL 10% OF SUBSIDIARY

January 2, 2008

Allocation of purchase price

	Subsidiary Corporation		
	Book values	Fair values	Fair value increments
Current assets	$ 500,000	$ 500,000	0
Capital assets (net)	1,000,000	1,500,000	$500,000
Liabilities	(900,000)	(900,000)	0
	$ 600,000	1,100,000	$500,000
Parent's new ownership share acquired		× 10%	× 10%
FV of net assets acquired		110,000	50,000
Purchase price		140,000	
Goodwill		$ 30,000	30,000
Total purchase price discrepancy			$ 80,000

EXHIBIT 5–22　PARENT CORPORATION PRO-FORMA CONSOLIDATED BALANCE SHEET

January 2, 2008

Current assets (1,000,000 + 500,000 − **140,000 purchase price**)	$1,360,000
Capital assets [1,900,000 + 1,000,000 + **(180,000 × 9/10) + 50,000**]	3,112,000
Goodwill **(90,000 + 30,000)**	120,000
Total assets	$4,592,000
Liabilities (1,300,000 + 900,000)	$2,200,000
Non-controlling interest **(600,000 × 30%)**	180,000
Common shares	400,000
Retained earnings	1,812,000
Total liabilities and shareholders' equity	$4,592,000

Increases in equity-basis investments

Equity-method accounting is intended to yield the same net income and investor-corporation retained earnings as would consolidation. Therefore, when an investment is being reported on the equity basis, the same principles apply for step acquisitions as were discussed above in accounting for consolidated subsidiaries. In general, each significant purchase of shares is accounted for separately, with separate estimates of fair values and goodwill at each date of purchase. For practical purposes, numerous small purchases can be grouped together and treated as a single purchase [CICA 1600.11].

An investor corporation may increase its ownership in a significantly influenced company to the point where the investor becomes the majority shareholder and consequently controls the investee. Once control is achieved, consolidation becomes appropriate, rather than equity-basis reporting. Since the equity method is completely consistent with the parent-company approach to consolidation, shifting from equity reporting to consolidation poses no additional problems.

Acquisition of significant influence

One further situation that should briefly be considered is where the initial purchase (or purchases) is reported on the cost basis because significant influence does not exist, but an additional purchase does give significant influence to the investor corporation.

For example, suppose that an investor buys an initial stake of 18% in an investee corporation. The initial purchase of 18% does not give significant influence to the investor, and the investment is reported on the cost basis.

Subsequently, the investor buys an additional 12%, resulting in a 30% ownership interest. The additional acquisition gives the investor significant influence. A change in the reporting basis from the cost basis to the equity basis therefore is required. Any purchase price discrepancy must be allocated to fair-value increments and goodwill.

To be consistent with the methodology described above for increases in control, it may seem logical to go back and revalue the first acquisition of 12%, and then add the FVIs and goodwill arising from the 18% purchase. As a practical matter, this approach is impossible. The fair values that may have existed at the first purchase cannot be known in retrospect. Therefore, the *CICA Handbook* states:

> Where the investment position has been reached as the result of two or more purchases, the assigned costs of the subsidiary's identifiable assets and liabilities should reflect this fact. For practical purposes, *assignable costs will normally be determined as at the time the first use of equity accounting becomes appropriate* (or as at the time the first use of consolidation becomes appropriate, if equity accounting has not previously been appropriate) and at each further major purchase. [CICA 1600.11; italics added]

Equity-basis accounting is applied when the investor corporation first achieves significant influence. FVIs and goodwill are measured at that date, not in retrospect.

REVIEW QUESTIONS

5–16 What is meant by a *step purchase*?

5–17 P Ltd. acquired 51% of S Inc. by means of a tender offer on April 1, 2005. On February 14, 2007, P increased its ownership of S by an additional 19% through additional purchases. How would P determine the total goodwill pertaining to its 70% interest in S?

5–18 When a step acquisition has occurred, why are the fair-value increments of the subsidiary's net assets not measured entirely at the date of the last purchase?

5–19 P Corp. owned 40% of the voting shares of S Ltd. and exercised significant influence over the affairs of S. Subsequently, P acquired an additional 20% of S's shares. How would the additional acquisition affect the nature of P's reporting of its investment in S?

5–20 P Inc. owned 22% of S Corp. and reported the investment on the cost basis. Subsequently, P acquired an additional 20% interest; the additional shares gave P the ability to significantly influence the affairs of S. How would the fair-value increments and goodwill be determined for the 42% total interest?

PROBLEMS

P5–A1

Pine Ltd. had the following transactions in the shares of Sap Ltd.:

Year	Date	%*	Cost	Equity Jan. 1	Equity Dec. 31	Goodwill
2003	January 1	30%	$ 70,000	$150,000	$220,000	$25,000
2004	January 1	35%	110,000	220,000	300,000	33,000

*Of Sap Ltd.'s shares.

The income of Sap Ltd. is earned evenly over the year.

Any excess of purchase price over book value is attributable solely to goodwill. The annual tests for goodwill impairment have indicated no impairment of goodwill since the date of acquisition.

Sap Ltd. has 100,000 shares outstanding.

Required:

Prepare the journal entries for Pine Ltd. for 2003 and 2004, assuming no dividend, and using both the cost and equity methods.

[CGA–Canada, adapted]

P5-A2

On December 31, 2003, PC Company acquired 60% of the 10,000 outstanding voting shares of SL Limited for $295,000. The balance sheet and fair market values for SL Limited were:

SL Limited
Balance Sheet
At December 31, 2003

	Book value	Fair market value
Cash	$ 100,000	$100,000
Accounts receivable	250,000	250,000
Inventory	300,000	250,000
Capital assets (net)	800,000	900,000
	$1,450,000	
Accounts payable	$ 300,000	325,000
Bonds payable	800,000	800,000
Common shares	100,000	
Retained earnings	250,000	
	$1,450,000	

The capital assets have a remaining useful life of 10 years. The bonds mature on December 31, 2007.

On December 31, 2004, SL issued an additional 6,000 shares to PC for $130,000. The variance between the purchase price and the fair market values of $400,000 is to be allocated to goodwill. The annual tests for goodwill impairment have indicated no impairment of goodwill since the date of acquisition.

SL had a net income of $60,000 for the year ended December 31, 2004, and $70,000 for the year ended December 31, 2005. SL declared and paid $5,000 in dividends in 2004, and $10,000 in 2005.

Required:

Calculate the balance in the investment in SL Limited account on December 31, 2005, assuming PC uses the equity method.

[CGA]

P5-A3

On January 1, 2000, Hoola Company (Hoola) purchased 60,000 shares of Soop Ltd. (Soop) for $560,000. On January 1, 2003, Hoola purchased another 30,000 shares of Soop for $400,000. During the entire period, Soop had a total of 100,000 shares outstanding. Hoola accounts for its investment in Soop using the equity method. The following information was extracted from the financial records of Soop:

	January 1, 2000	January 1, 2003	December 31, 2004
Net book value of patent	$110,000	$80,000	$60,000
Fair value of patent	$165,000	$240,000	$240,000
Remaining useful life of patent in years	11	8	6
Common shares	$100,000	$100,000	$100,000
Retained earnings	$400,000	$550,000	$710,000

All net identifiable assets had a fair value equal to book value on the date of acquisition except for the patent. The annual tests for goodwill impairment have indicated no impairment of goodwill since the dates of acquisition. Hoola and Soop do not have any goodwill recorded on their separate entity balance sheets. Hoola does not have any patents on its own balance sheet.

There have not been any intercompany transactions between Hoola and Soop.

Required:

a. Calculate the balances of the following accounts on the consolidated balance sheet at December 31, 2004:

   i.   patents

   ii. goodwill

   iii. non-controlling interest

b. Calculate the balance in the Investment in Soop account at December 31, 2004.

[CGA]

Appendix 5B

Decreases in Ownership Interest

Introduction

On occasion, an investor corporation may reduce its ownership share in a subsidiary or a significantly influenced affiliate. A reduction may occur because:

- the investor may sell part of its holdings, thereby directly reducing its ownership percentage, or
- the investee may issue new shares, thereby indirectly reducing the investor's ownership interest, assuming that the investor does not buy a proportionate part of the new offering.

The financial reporting impact is similar whether applied to parent–subsidiary relationships or to equity-basis investments. Therefore, we will explicitly discuss only reductions in interest experienced by a parent corporation. The same principles apply to significantly influenced investees.

Sale of part of an investment

When a parent corporation sells part of its investment in a subsidiary, the accounting *on the parent's books* is quite straightforward: (1) the investment account is reduced by the proportionate part of the carrying value of the investment, and (2) the difference between the carrying value of the investment and the proceeds from the sale is a gain or loss on the sale. The difficulty is in measuring the carrying value of the investment.

Since investments normally are recorded on the cost basis, it is tempting to view the carrying value as being simply the proportionate part of the cost of the investment. However, the *recorded* carrying value is not the same as the *reported* carrying value. The reported carrying value is the net asset value of the subsidiary as reported in the parent's consolidated balance sheet.

For example, assume that on December 31, 2006, Parent Corporation acquired 30,000 of the 50,000 outstanding shares (i.e., 60%) of Subsidiary Corporation for $20 per share, or $600,000 total. The net book value of the shares on the date of acquisition is $11 per share, or a total of $330,000 for the acquired shares. The purchase price discrepancy of $270,000 is allocated $180,000 to FVI on capital assets and $90,000 to goodwill. (Note that these are the same amounts that we used previously, in Exhibit 5–18.)

On January 1, 2008, Parent's management decides to reduce Parent's share of Sub to the minimum of 51% needed to retain control. Therefore, Parent sells 4,500 of its Sub shares (15% of its 60% ownership interest) for $30 per share: 4,500 shares × $30 = $135,000. The effect on PC's consolidated balances is to reduce Parent's equity in Sub's net assets by 15%. Note that the key word is *equity*. The assets and liabilities for Sub that are included in Parent's 2007 consolidated balance sheet (Exhibit 5–20) are as follows:

Current assets	$ 500,000
Capital assets [1,000,000 + (**180,000** × **9/10**)]	1,162,000
Goodwill	90,000
Liabilities	−900,000
Non-controlling interest (**600,000** × **40%**)	−240,000
Parent's consolidated equity in Subsidiary's net assets	$ 612,000

15% of Parent's consolidation equity in Sub's net assets is $612,000 × 15% = $91,800. The gain on the sale is the difference between the sale proceeds and the surrendered 15% equity in Sub's net assets: $135,000 − $91,800 = $43,200. The difference between the surrendered equity and the recorded cost of the 15% interest represents Parent's equity in Sub's increase in net asset value since acquisition, which must be credited to Parent's retained earnings.

The entry to record the sale *on Parent's books* is as follows (assuming that Parent carries its investment in Sub at cost on its books):

Cash	135,000	
Investment in SC (cost basis: 600,000 × 15%)		90,000
Retained earnings (91,800 − 90,000)		1,800
Gain on sale of investment (135,000 − 91,800)		43,200

The credit to retained earnings simply records 15% of the unremitted adjusted earnings of Sub that Parent has already recognized in its consolidated financial statements for 2007 but that has not been recorded on Parent's books. The unremitted earnings can be verified as follows:

Increase in Sub's shareholders' equity since acquisition (600,000 − 550,000)	$ 50,000
Less non-controlling interest's share (50,000 × 40%)	−20,000
Less amortization of FVI on capital assets (180,000 × 1/10)	−18,000
Parent's equity in unremitted earnings of Sub	$ 12,000
Proportion of Parent's ownership interest being sold	× 15%
Unremitted earnings related to sold portion of investment	$ 1,800

These entries are no different in substance from any entry to record the sale of part of any investment. However, the sale of part of Parent's interest in Sub has implications that a sale of a portfolio investment does not have. The sale will affect consolidated net assets, non-controlling interest (which has now risen to 49%), and Parent's equity in the earnings of Sub.

Issuance of shares by subsidiary

At first glance, it may appear that issuance of new shares by the subsidiary to outside parties should not affect the parent. The parent corporation still holds the same number of shares, and the cost of acquiring those shares is not directly affected by the new issue of the subsidiary.

However, it is not quite so simple. While it is true that the number of shares held by the parent is not changed, the percentage of ownership *is* changed. After the issuance, the parent owns a smaller percentage of the subsidiary and the non-controlling interest is larger.

Under the purchase method of accounting for business combinations, the parent is considered to have purchased a proportionate share of the fair value of the subsidiary's net assets. If a subsidiary issues additional shares to outsiders, then new capital is brought into the subsidiary, thereby increasing its net asset value. But the parent's *proportionate* interest in the increased net asset value is *decreased*. The parent's equity in the subsidiary is affected by both factors: the increase in the subsidiary's net assets and the decrease in the parent's proportionate interest.

To illustrate the impact of a new issue, assume that on January 1, 2008, Subsidiary Corporation issues 8,824 new shares to outside interests for net proceeds of $264,706 (about $30 per share). The new issue will increase Sub's total outstanding shares to 58,824, and will thereby reduce Parent's holdings of 30,000 shares to 51% of the total, the same level of ownership that we used in the example in the previous section. Before the new issue, Sub had total shareholders' equity of $600,000 (including common shares of $100,000). The new issue increases the total to $864,706 by raising the amount in the common share equity account to $364,706. Parent formerly owned 60% of $600,000 book value; now Parent owns 51% of the $864,706 book value.

The change in the net assets of Sub and Parent's share thereof is illustrated in Exhibit 5–23. As a result of Sub's new issue of shares, Parent's equity in the book value of Sub's net assets has increased from $360,000 to $441,000 (that is, $864,706 × 51% = $441,000). But the change in book value is not the only impact that Sub's new issue has on Parent's equity in Sub. Parent now has an interest in only 51% of the date-of-acquisition fair-value increment on Sub's net assets and only 51% of the goodwill. Parent will include in consolidated net income only 51% of Sub's future net income. If Parent continues to amortize 60% of the fair-value increment, Parent will be understating its share of Sub's earnings.

Therefore, the fair-value increment and the goodwill must be adjusted to reflect Parent's lessened interest. Parent's ownership interest has declined from 60% to 51%, a decline of nine percentage points, or 15% of the original 60% interest. The unamortized fair-value increment attributable to Parent's equity declines by 15%, from $162,000 (i.e., $180,000 × 9/10) to $137,700 (that is, $180,000 × 9/10 × 85%). The goodwill declines by 15% from $90,000 to $76,000 (that is, $90,000 × 85%). These decreases in Parent's equity partially offset the increase in Parent's share of the net book value, with the result that the equity underlying Parent's investment in Sub increases from $612,000 to $655,200 as shown at the bottom of Exhibit 5–23.

EXHIBIT 5–23 CHANGE IN PARENT'S SHARE OF SUBSIDIARY'S NET ASSETS AFTER NEW SHARE ISSUE

	Before new share issue		After new share issue	
	100%	60%	100%	51%
Current assets	$ 500,000	$300,000	$ 764,706	$390,000
Capital assets (net)	1,000,000	600,000	1,000,000	510,000
Total assets	$1,500,000		$1,764,706	
Liabilities	$ 900,000	(540,000)	$ 900,000	(459,000)
Common shares	100,000		364,706	
Retained earnings	500,000		500,000	
Total liabilities and share equity	$1,500,000		$1,764,706	
Parent's equity in NBV of Sub		$360,000		$441,000
Parent's share of FVI:				
$180,000 x 9/10		162,000		
$180,000 x 9/10 x 85%				137,700
Goodwill				
$90,000		90,000		
$90,000 x 85%				76,500
Parent's equity in FV of Sub's net assets		**$612,000**		**$655,200**

The net change in Parent's equity in Sub amounts to $43,200. This amount is exactly the same as the profit that was recognized in the previous section when Parent sold part of its holdings. Thus the general impact of a reduction in the parent's proportionate interest in the subsidiary is the same regardless of whether the reduction is the result of a sale by the parent or a new issue by the subsidiary. The gain is reported in consolidated net income [CICA 1600.45].

Nevertheless, there is some unease in the professional accounting community about taking the gain into the income statement. It can be argued that capital for a parent and its subsidiary can be raised by issuing shares in either corporation, and that the accounting results for the consolidated entity should be the same regardless of whether the parent or the subsidiary issued the shares. When the parent issues shares, there is no gain or loss recognized on the capital transaction. But when the subsidiary issues shares, a gain may be recognized.

In the example used above, the new share issue resulted in a gain to Parent and an equivalent increase in Parent's equity in Sub. However, it also is possible for a loss to occur. The break-even point between a gain and a loss will be the price that is equal to the average consolidation carrying value of Sub's net assets per share.

Before the change in ownership interest, the consolidation carrying value of Parent's ownership interest was $612,000 (see Exhibit 5–23). Dividing this amount by the number of shares held by Parent yields $612,000 ÷ 30,000 = $20.40 per share. Any sale of shares by Parent *or* an issuance of new shares by Sub at a price higher than $20.40 will result in Parent's reporting a gain. Any price lower than $20.40 will result in a loss.

SELF-STUDY PROBLEM 5-4

The balance sheet for Subco Ltd. at July 1, 2007, is shown in Exhibit 5–24. On that date, Parco Ltd. purchased 6,000 common shares of Subco for $312,500 and thereby attained significant influence over the affairs of Subco.

Subco amortizes its tangible capital assets over 10 years straight-line. The inventory is expected to turn over six times per year and is on a FIFO cost allocation system.

On September 1, 2008, Parco purchased 3,000 more shares of Subco for $183,500. The balance sheet of Subco and the related fair values are shown in Exhibit 5–25.

Between September 1 and December 31, 2008, Subco had net income of $30,000 and paid no dividends.

On January 1, 2009, Parco sold 4,000 of its shares in Subco for $300,000.

EXHIBIT 5–24   SUBCO LTD.

Balance Sheet
July 1, 2007

	Book Value	Fair Value
Cash	$ 75,000	$ 75,000
Inventory	200,000	250,000
Tangible capital assets, net	800,000	750,000
	$1,075,000	
Current liabilities	$ 50,000	50,000
Long-term liabilities	150,000	150,000
Common shares, 20,000 issued and outstanding	200,000	
Retained earnings at January 1, 2007	575,000	
Net income, 2007 to date	100,000	
	$1,075,000	

EXHIBIT 5–25   SUBCO LTD.

Balance Sheet
September 1, 2008

	Book Value	Fair Value
Cash	$ 80,000	$ 80,000
Inventory	190,000	200,000
Tangible capital assets, net	1,020,000	1,200,000
	$1,290,000	
Current liabilities	$ 40,000	40,000
Long-term liabilities	150,000	150,000
Common shares, 20,000 issued and outstanding	200,000	
Retained earnings at January 1, 2008	775,000	
Net income, 2008 to date	125,000	
	$1,290,000	

Required:

Calculate Parco's gain or loss on disposal of the Subco shares on January 1, 2009. [CGA–Canada, adapted]

REVIEW QUESTIONS

5–21 What are two basic ways in which a parent company can decrease its ownership interest in a subsidiary?

5–22 Why would a parent company want to decrease its share of a subsidiary?

5–23 When a parent company sells part of its investment in a subsidiary, how is the gain or loss on the sale determined?

5–24 Why does the issuance by the subsidiary of new shares to outsiders affect the parent's consolidated assets?

5–25 Why does the parent corporation recognize a gain or loss when the subsidiary issues new shares to third parties?

5–26 How can one determine whether the issuance by a subsidiary of new shares to outsiders will result in a gain or a loss to the parent company?

PROBLEMS

P5–B1

On October 1, 2005, XYZ Ltd. sold its 80% interest in the subsidiary, Sub Ltd., for $2,430,000. Prior to the date of sale, XYZ Ltd. had recorded the investment in a subsidiary account on the *cost* basis, which showed $1,100,000. At the date of sale, the consolidated entity had a residual unamortized revaluation of the capital assets (from the original purchase price discrepancy) of $260,000 and goodwill arising from the acquisition of the subsidiary of $148,500. Annual tests have indicated no impairment of goodwill since the date of acquisition. There were no intercompany transactions between the parent and the subsidiary.

At the date of the sale, October 1, 2005, the balance sheet of Sub Ltd. was:

Sub Ltd.
October 1, 2005

	Net Book Value	Fair Market Value
Cash	$ 110,000	$ 110,000
Receivables	180,000	180,000
Inventory	510,000	570,000
Capital assets, net	950,000	880,000
	$1,750,000	
Current liabilities	$ 124,000	124,000
Common shares	300,000	
Retained earnings	1,006,000	
Income: Jan.1–Oct. 31, 2005	320,000	
	$1,750,000	

XYZ Ltd.'s 2004 and 2005 consolidated balance sheets were as follows:

XYZ Ltd.
Consolidated Balance Sheet
December 31

	2004	2005
Cash	$ 256,000	$1,420,000
Receivables	368,000	246,000
Inventory	742,000	538,000
Capital assets, net	1,720,000	845,000
Goodwill	160,000	—
	$3,246,000	$3,049,000
Current liabilities	$ 422,000	$ 115,000
Minority interest	261,200	—
Common shares	500,000	500,000
Retained earnings	2,062,800	2,434,000
	$3,246,000	$3,049,000

The net income for the year for the consolidated entity was $371,200, but this was after the extraordinary item for the gain on the sale of the subsidiary. No dividends were paid. The consolidated depreciation expense was $104,000, which included the depreciation of the capital asset revaluation. Ignore the impact of income taxes on the sale.

Required:

Calculate the gain or loss on the sale of the subsidiary.

[CGA–Canada, adapted]

P5–B2

On December 31, 2003, Plummer Company acquired 70% (7,000 common shares) of Summer Company for $950,000. On the acquisition date, all of the identifiable assets and liabilities of Summer had fair values that were equal to their carrying values except for the equipment, which had a fair value of $200,000 more than its carrying value and a remaining useful life of 10 years. The only other purchase price discrepancy adjustment relates to consolidated goodwill of $40,000. There has been no impairment of goodwill since the date of acquisition. Plummer uses the cost method to record its investment in Summer. The following financial information is available about the two companies.

	Plummer	Summer
Retained earnings, Dec. 31, 2003	$333,000	$ 72,000
Net income, 2004	137,000	26,000
Dividends declared, 2004	(60,000)	(10,000)
Retained earnings, Dec. 31, 2004	410,000	88,000
Net income, 2005	110,000	30,000
Dividends declared, 2005	(50,000)	(15,000)
Retained earnings	$470,000	$103,000

During 2004, Plummer sold merchandise inventory to Summer for $72,000. On December 31, 2004, a portion of inventory remained unsold. An unrealized profit of $15,000 remained in this ending inventory.

On January 1, 2005, Plummer sold 1,000 of its shares of Summer for $150,000.

Required:

a. Determine consolidated net income for the year ended December 31, 2004.

b. Determine the gain or loss on the sale of the 1,000 shares of Summer sold by Plummer in 2005.

c. Determine consolidated retained earnings at December 31, 2005.

[CGA]

P5–B3

On January 1, 2003, Pumpkin Company acquired 70% of the 10,000 outstanding voting shares of Squash Limited for $769,000. The balance sheet and fair values for Squash Limited were:

**Squash Limited
Balance Sheet
At December 31, 2003**

	Book value	Fair market value
Cash	$ 120,000	$120,000
Accounts receivable	190,000	180,000
Inventory	240,000	270,000
Capital assets (net)	700,000	820,000
	$1,250,000	
Accounts payable	$ 330,000	330,000
Common shares	500,000	
Retained earnings	420,000	
	$1,250,000	

The capital assets had a remaining useful life of 20 years. There has been no impairment of goodwill since the date of acquisition. Squash had a net income of $50,000 for the year ended December 31, 2003, and $80,000 for the year ended December 31, 2004. Squash paid dividends of $5,000 in 2003 and paid dividends of $10,000 in 2004.

On January 1, 2005, Pumpkin sold 1,000 of the Squash shares for $130,000.

Required:

a. Calculate the balance in the investment in the Squash account before and after the sale of the 1,000 shares, assuming Pumpkin uses the equity method.

b. Calculate the gain/loss on the sale of the 1,000 shares.

P5–B4

Big Limited has three subsidiaries, all 80% owned, and, at December 31, 2005, they have the following balance sheets:

	Sub 1 Limited	Sub 2 Limited	Sub 3 Limited
Cash	$ 200,000	$ 120,000	$ 140,000
Receivables	400,000	230,000	250,000
Inventory	1,040,000	590,000	610,000
Capital assets, net	1,320,000	890,000	920,000
	$2,960,000	$1,830,000	$1,920,000
Current liabilities	$ 260,000	$ 140,000	$ 150,000
Common shares	600,000	400,000	500,000
Retained earnings	2,100,000	1,290,000	1,270,000
	$2,960,000	$1,830,000	$1,920,000

Selected balance sheet information of Big Limited as at December 31, 2005, with respect to each subsidiary is as follows:

	Sub 1 Limited	Sub 2 Limited	Sub 3 Limited
Investment in Sub	$2,470,000	$1,252,000	$1,536,000
Capital asset, unamortized revaluation	300,000	(100,000)	—
Goodwill	280,000	—	120,000
Number of shares outstanding	100,000	100,000	10,000

The "Investment in Sub" account for each subsidiary is kept on the equity basis and includes all entries for 2005, with the exception of the following.

On the last day of the year, after all the accounts had been brought up to date but before the closing entries had been made, the subsidiaries had the following transactions:

1. Sub 1 Limited issued a 100% stock dividend to all common shareholders.

2. Sub 2 Limited issued shares equal to 10%, or 10,000 shares of the present outstanding amount, to the minority interest shareholders for $38 per share.

3. Sub 3 Limited purchased and retired 10% or 1,000 shares of the outstanding shares from the minority interest for a price of $150 per share.

Big Limited will consolidate the subsidiaries but has kept the investment in subsidiary accounts on the equity basis.

Required:

Considering that the parent company is using the equity method for its investment in subsidiary accounts, prepare a separate journal entry(ies) to record the above events for each subsidiary on the parent company's books. If no journal entry on the parent's books is needed, then explain why. Indicate any gain or loss that would appear on the consolidated financial statements. If no gain or loss is present, explain why. Support your answer fully.

[CGA–Canada, adapted]

6

Subsequent-Year Consolidations: General Approach

In this chapter, we reach the end of our exploration of the major facets of consolidated financial statements. We do not intend to be exhaustive (even though you may feel exhausted!). There are many additional complications to preparing consolidated statements. It is easy to imagine "what if...?" scenarios. But additional complications are rare and should not be your focus. Once you understand Chapters 3 through 6, you will understand all of the significant issues in consolidation.

The following sections will discuss:

- adjustments for intercompany sale of long-term assets
- the general approach to consolidation in the years after founding or buying a subsidiary
- equity-basis reporting, and consolidation when the parent uses equity-basis *reporting* in its separate-entity financial statements, and
- consolidated reporting of discontinued operations and extraordinary items.

In addition, we provide two appendices for issues that do not generally arise:

- Throughout this book, we have discussed only investments in another company's voting common shares. However, parent corporations may also invest in non-voting shares. Appendix 6A will briefly discuss the impact that such investments have on control and on consolidation.
- Intercompany bond holdings also are possible. In the vast majority of cases, intercompany debt can be eliminated by a simple adjustment, as we have shown in earlier chapters. In rare instances (very rare in Canada), there may be intercompany bond holdings involving premiums and discounts. Appendix 6B illustrates the adjustments for bond premium or discount.

Readers who are not interested in some of the more arcane aspects of consolidation are encouraged to skip over Appendices 6A and 6B and proceed directly to Chapter 7.

Intercompany Sale of Long-Term Assets

General concept

We have repeatedly illustrated that unrealized profits on intercompany sales must be removed from the consolidated net income. The concept of eliminating unrealized intercorporate profits or gains is applicable to *any* sale between members of a group of controlled or significantly influenced companies. The sale need not involve the parent or investor corporation; sales from one subsidiary to another or from one significantly influenced investee corporation to another require elimination of unrealized profit.

Downstream sales of amortizable assets

For example, suppose that at the end of 2006, Company P buys a piece of equipment for $200,000 and sells it to its subsidiary, Company S, for $250,000. S will depreciate the asset over 10 years on a straight-line basis, beginning in 2007 (and assuming zero salvage value).

When consolidating the financial statements for 2006, we must reduce the reported value of the equipment from its carrying value on S's books of $250,000 to the actual cost to the consolidated entity (that is, to P) of $200,000. To prepare the consolidated statements, we must:

- eliminate the $50,000 gain on the intercompany sale from P's revenue, and
- reduce the equipment account by $50,000.

On a consolidation worksheet, the adjustment at the end of 2006 (assuming that amortization will begin in 2007) will be:

Gain on sale of equipment	50,000	
Equipment		50,000

In 2007, S will begin to depreciate the equipment at the rate of $25,000 per year. Depreciation expense is overstated from the viewpoint of the consolidated entity because S's carrying value of the equipment includes unrealized profit. Based on the actual cost of the equipment of $200,000, depreciation expense should only be $20,000 per year. Thus, the year-end 2007 consolidation adjustments must:

1. reduce the cost of the equipment on the balance sheet from $250,000 to $200,000

2. eliminate the unrealized profit from the opening retained earnings

3. decrease depreciation expense by $5,000, and

4. reduce accumulated depreciation by $5,000.

In worksheet terms, the adjustments are:

(1)	Retained earnings (opening)	50,000	
	Equipment		50,000
(2)	Accumulated depreciation	5,000	
	Depreciation expense		5,000

On intercompany *inventory* sales, the profit is realized when the inventory is eventually sold to an outside party. On depreciable assets, the profit is realized not by direct sale to outsiders, but rather by using the asset to produce goods or services to be sold to outsiders. The $5,000 depreciation adjustment in 2007 recognizes the realization of one-tenth of the 2006 unrealized profit.

In 2008, the *previously unrealized profit* must be eliminated. So far, there has been only one year's depreciation recognized (i.e., in 2007), which accounts for one-tenth of the unrealized profit. Therefore, the unrealized profit at the *beginning* of 2008 is $50,000 \times 9/10 = \$45,000$. The $5,000 that has been realized is now in the accumulated depreciation account, which must also be adjusted by:

- reducing retained earnings by $45,000, which is $50,000 \times 9/10$
- reducing accumulated depreciation by the $5,000 depreciation in previous years (one for 2007, so far), and
- reducing the equipment account by the full intercompany profit of $50,000.

As a worksheet adjustment:

(1)	Retained earnings	45,000	
	Accumulated depreciation	5,000	
	Equipment		50,000

In 2008, S will amortize another $5,000 of the intercompany profit in its equipment account. When we prepare the year-end 2008 consolidated statements, we will make exactly the same additional adjustment for 2008 as we made for 2007's depreciation:

- decrease depreciation expense by $5,000, and
- reduce accumulated depreciation by $5,000.

(2)	Accumulated depreciation	5,000	
	Depreciation expense		5,000

In subsequent years, the adjustment for the remaining unrealized gain will reflect the depreciation taken to date. For example, in 2013 we will recognize the fact that the equipment has already been depreciated for six years (2007 through 2012, inclusive). Using the direct approach to consolidation, the line-by-line adjustments will be as follows:

- Equipment—reduce by the full unrealized profit of $50,000
- Accumulated depreciation—multiply the unrealized profit by the fraction of years elapsed since the intercompany sale (i.e., $50,000 \times 7/10 = \$35,000$), and subtract that amount from accumulated depreciation balance
- Depreciation expense—reduce by the current year's depreciation on the unrealized profit ($50,000 \times 1/10$)
- *Opening* retained earnings (on the retained earnings statement)—reduce by the four years' unrealized profit on the transaction that remains at the start of the year: $50,000 \times 4/10 = \$20,000$
- *Closing* retained earnings—reduce by the remaining three years' unrealized profit on the transaction: $50,000 \times 3/10 = \$15,000$

The 2013 worksheet adjustments will be as follows:

(1)	Retained earnings ($50,000 \times 4/10$)	20,000	
	Accumulated depreciation ($50,000 \times 6/10$)	30,000	
	Equipment		50,000
(2)	Accumulated depreciation	5,000	
	Depreciation expense		5,000

Keeping the two adjustments separate may keep the process clearer and help avoid confusion. However, these can be combined into a single adjusting entry under the worksheet approach:

Retained earnings (opening)	20,000	
Accumulated depreciation ($50,000 × 7/10)	35,000	
Equipment		50,000
Depreciation expense		5,000

By the end of 2016, the asset is fully depreciated and there will be no depreciation expense in subsequent years. The only consolidation adjustment that will be made in 2017 and thereafter (until the asset is retired and written off) will be a cumulative adjustment that has no impact on either consolidated net income or consolidated retained earnings:

Accumulated depreciation	50,000	
Equipment		50,000

Upstream sales of amortizable assets

When the intercompany sale of an amortizable asset is upstream or is horizontal (i.e., between two subsidiaries), the consolidation eliminations are exactly the same as those shown above *if* the selling subsidiary is 100% owned by the parent.

If the selling subsidiary is not wholly owned, then the adjustments are complicated somewhat by the presence of non-controlling interest.

For example, assume the same situation as above except that S sells the equipment to P, and P owns 75% of the shares of S. The non-controlling interest will have a 25% interest in the $50,000 gain.

The full $50,000 will be eliminated from consolidated net income in 2006, and the annual amortization of $5,000 also will be eliminated in each of the following 10 years. However, the non-controlling interest will also have to be adjusted for elimination of the unrealized profit.

When non-controlling interest is computed for the consolidated balance sheet, the unrealized profit *at the end of the year* must be deducted from the subsidiary's net book value before we multiply by the non-controlling interest's share. The impact on the year-end 2006 balance sheet can be shown as follows:

Non-controlling interest (B/S) ($50,000 × 25%)	12,500	
Retained earnings ($50,000 × 75%)	37,500	
Equipment		50,000

Notice that the retained earnings and the non-controlling interest (B/S) are on the same side of the adjustment. That will always be the case, because they are simply the allocated proportions of the unrealized profit.

In 2007, we make the same unrealized profit adjustment again, since none of the unrealized profit had been recognized by the beginning of the year. In addition, we also must make the income statement adjustment, including the portion allocated to non-controlling interest. The two adjustments for 2007 are as follows:

Non-controlling interest (B/S) ($50,000 × 25%)	12,500	
Retained earnings ($50,000 × 75%)	37,500	
Equipment		50,000
Accumulated depreciation	5,000	
Non-controlling interest in earnings (I/S)	1,250	
Depreciation expense		5,000
Non-controlling interest (B/S) ($5,000 × 25%)		1,250

At the beginning of 2008, one-tenth of the unrealized profit will have been recognized, and therefore the profit eliminations are for only nine-tenths of the intercompany profit:

(1)	Non-controlling interest (B/S) ($50,000 × 25% × 9/10)	11,250	
	Retained earnings ($50,000 × 75% × 9/10)	33,750	
	Accumulated depreciation	5,000	
	Equipment		50,000
(2)	Accumulated depreciation	5,000	
	Non-controlling interest in earnings (I/S)	1,250	
	Depreciation expense		5,000
	Non-controlling interest (B/S)		1,250

Jumping ahead to 2013, the adjustments will be:

(1)	Non-controlling interest (B/S) ($50,000 × 25% × 4/10)	5,000	
	Retained earnings ($50,000 × 75% × 4/10)	15,000	
	Accumulated depreciation ($50,000 × 6/10)	30,000	
	Equipment		50,000
(2)	Accumulated depreciation	5,000	
	Non-controlling interest in earnings (I/S)	1,250	
	Depreciation expense		5,000
	Non-controlling interest (B/S)		1,250

Each year, the current operations adjustment is the same as long as depreciation is being charged. The cumulative adjustment, however, gradually shifts the total net gain from unrealized (as deductions from retained earnings and non-controlling interest) to realized (as a reduction in accumulated depreciation).

Direct amortization

For depreciable tangible capital assets, normal practice is to maintain the asset account at the original cost of the asset and to record depreciation in a separate accumulated depreciation account. However, many companies do not maintain a separate accumulation account for intangible capital assets. The annual amortization may be credited directly to the asset account instead.

When the amortization is credited directly to the asset account, the consolidation adjusting entries are a little different. In each entry above, the two amounts for the asset account (equipment) and the accumulated depreciation will be netted together, simplifying the adjustment somewhat. Otherwise, the process is exactly as illustrated above.

For example, suppose that S sells a *patent* to P at the end of 2006. The remaining unamortized cost of the patent on S's books is $200,000, and the selling price to P is $250,000. Assume that S is 75% owned by P. The adjustment for 2006, the year of the sale, will be the same as above in the previous section:

Non-controlling interest (B/S) ($50,000 × 25%)	12,500	
Retained earnings	37,500	
Patent		50,000

If the patent will be amortized over 10 remaining years, P will record amortization of $25,000 each year (the $250,000 purchase price for 10 years) by crediting the patent account directly. Remember, however, that the $25,000 annual amortization is overstated by $5,000 due to the $50,000 upstream profit. The 2007 consolidation adjustment to correct for the overamortization is:

(1)	Non-controlling interest (B/S) ($50,000 × 25%)	12,500	
	Retained earnings ($50,000 × 75%)	37,500	
	Patent		50,000
(2)	Patent	5,000	
	Non-controlling interest in earnings (I/S)	1,250	
	Amortization expense		5,000
	Non-controlling interest (B/S)		1,250

This adjustment may appear slightly baffling, because it *increases* the patent account, whereas adjustments for unrealized profit usually *decrease* the asset account. The explanation is that P already credited the patent account for $25,000 in amortization, which includes amortization on the unrealized profit. The first adjustment removed the remaining unrealized profit, and the second adjustment restores the $5,000 overamortization taken by P.

In 2008, (1) the remaining $45,000 of unrealized profit is removed from the asset account, and (2) the annual amortization is corrected:

(1)	Non-controlling interest (B/S)	11,250	
	Retained earnings	33,750	
	Patent ($50,000 × 9/10)		45,000
(2)	Patent	5,000	
	Non-controlling interest in earnings (I/S)	1,250	
	Amortization expense		5,000
	Non-controlling interest (B/S)		1,250

By the *beginning* of 2013, the balance in the patent account will be reduced to $20,000 after six years of amortization. The year-end 2013 adjustments are similar to those in the previous section, where there is a separate accumulated depreciation account:

(1)	Non-controlling interest (B/S) ($50,000 × 25% × 4/10)	5,000	
	Retained earnings ($50,000 × 75% × 4/10)	15,000	
	Patent		20,000
(2)	Patent	5,000	
	Non-controlling interest in earnings (I/S)	1,250	
	Amortization expense		5,000
	Non-controlling interest (B/S)		1,250

We have been explaining intercompany sales of depreciable assets outside of the broader context of the consolidation process. To isolate and highlight the effects of the unrealized profit elimination, we have shown the impact on *non-controlling interest in earnings*. In practice, this adjustment is included in the overall adjustment for non-controlling interest, just as we did in earlier chapters for unrealized profits in intercompany inventory transactions. The next major section of this chapter will illustrate the broader approach to calculating the non-controlling interest in earnings.

Losses on intercompany sales

Losses on intercompany sales may or may not be eliminated [CICA 1600.27]. The key question is whether or not the loss reflects a real decline in the value of the asset sold. If there is no evidence of impairment of the value of the asset sold, then the intercompany loss on the sale should be eliminated. But if the sale price reflects a new, lower value-in-use for the asset, then the asset should have been written down even without the sale, because the loss on the sale simply reflects a decline in the value of the asset that should have been reflected by a reduction in the carrying value of the asset anyway. Thus, the crucial question in deciding whether or not to eliminate a loss is whether the item that was sold should have been written down had it *not* been sold.

For capital assets, market or resale value may not be relevant for answering this question. An intercompany sale may occur at a fair market price that results in a loss. But a decline in market value (or net realizable value) of productive assets is not normally recognized, as long as the productive usefulness of the asset is not impaired. Book value of a productive capital asset represents its unrecovered cost, not its realizable value. Therefore, a loss on an intercompany sale of a productive asset will normally be eliminated unless the loss reflects a decline in the recoverable cost of the asset.

Subsequent sale of capital assets acquired intercompany

One company may buy a depreciable asset from another in the consolidated group, and then later sell that asset to a third party in an arm's-length transaction.

For example, suppose P sells the equipment that it acquired from S for $220,000 at the beginning of 2010. P will recognize a gain of $45,000, the $220,000 proceeds from sale minus the remaining net book value to P of $175,000 (i.e., $250,000 cost to P × 70% remaining useful life).

At the beginning of 2010, there will be 70% of the original gain from the intercompany sale still unrealized. Once the asset has been sold to a third party, the entire remaining unrealized gain must be recognized and added to the gain (or deducted from the loss) on the third-party sale:

Retained earnings	35,000	
Gain on sale of equipment		35,000

Thus the gain on P's sale will be increased by the remaining unrealized profit on S's sale, reflecting the fact that for the consolidated entity as a whole, a profit of $80,000 was realized on the sale of the equipment to an unrelated party:

Sales price		$220,000
Consolidated carrying value:		
Cost to S	$200,000	
Depreciation (3 years @ $20,000)	60,000	140,000
Gain to consolidated entity		$ 80,000

Subsequent-Year Consolidations—General Approach

So far, we have discussed the process of preparing consolidated financial statements (1) at the date of acquisition, (2) one year subsequent to acquisition, and (3) two years subsequent to acquisition. We have explored the basic concepts underlying consolidation and the treatment of non-controlling interest. The major procedural aspects of consolidation have also been presented. In this section, we discuss the general approach to preparing consolidated financial statements at any reporting date subsequent to acquisition, regardless of how long ago the business combination occurred.

Basic conceptual approach

Previous chapters have emphasized that consolidated financial statements must reflect adjustments for three types of events: (1) the acquisition transaction, (2) the cumulative effects of amortization and transactions to the beginning of the current reporting period, and (3) the effects of amortization and transactions in the current period. It doesn't matter whether the three types of adjustments are kept separate or combined.

The general nature of these adjustments is portrayed in Exhibit 6–1 with a time line. The first point of interest on the time line is point A, the date of acquisition of the parent's controlling interest in the subsidiary. The consolidation worksheet entry for this event is a constant, and has been thoroughly discussed.

Point C on the time line is the most recent point, which is the current balance sheet date. The worksheet adjustments for point C and for the year then ended (the time between point B and point C) have been reviewed several times in the previous chapters and should be reasonably clear by now.

The more problematic adjustment is apt to be that for the time between acquisition (point A) and the beginning of the current year (point B). We have pointed out that the consolidation adjustments for the intervening period (points A to B) are *cumulative* adjustments. We can simply accumulate the effects of each year's current operations adjustments, bearing in mind that the net effect of all adjustments to income statement accounts and to previous years' current non-monetary accounts (e.g., inventories) will usually be reflected in retained earnings. The result will then be the point A-to-B adjustment when we prepare the consolidated statements for the next accounting period (point B to C).

If we have the task of preparing only a year-end consolidated balance sheet, then we don't have to worry about point B but can adjust the balance sheet amounts directly to year-end balances. For example, there would be no reason to distinguish between fair-value amortizations in the current year and those relating to prior years. Although balance-sheet-only consolidations may be encountered in student examination situations, actual accounting practice calls for preparing a full set of financial statements and not just a non-comparative year-end balance sheet. In preparing a full set of financial statements, we need to iso-

EXHIBIT 6–1   OVERVIEW OF CONSOLIDATION ADJUSTMENTS

1. Acquisition adjustments

    a. Eliminate subsidiary's share equity accounts; establish non-controlling interest

    b. Add fair value increments and goodwill

    c. Offset subsidiary's accumulated depreciation against the asset account(s)

2. Cumulative operations adjustments to start of the current year (i.e., affecting current year's *beginning*-of-year balance sheet amounts)

    a. Recognize the non-controlling interest's share of subsidiary retained earnings from date of acquisition to *start* of the current year.

    b. Recognize the cumulative amortization of fair value increments (or decrements) and goodwill.

    c. Eliminate the impact of intercompany transactions that affect carrying values:

        i. Gains and losses from intercompany transactions that are still unrealized at the start of the year.

        ii. Flow-through to retained earnings of fair-valued assets and liabilities that have since been sold to third parties.

3. Current year operations adjustments

    a. Amortize fair value increments (decrements) and goodwill.

    b. Eliminate the current year's intercompany transactions.

    c. If equity-basis reporting is used, eliminate the subsidiary earnings and dividends that were recorded by the parent.

    d. Realize previously unrealized profits (losses), if they are realized or partially realized in the current year.

    e. Eliminate unrealized profits (losses) arising from intercompany transactions in the current year.

    f. Recognize the non-controlling interest in earnings.

    g. Eliminate year-end intercompany balances.

| A | Date of acquisition | | B | Start of current year | C | End of current year |

late the adjustments relating to the current period so that we can prepare the income statement as well as the comparative balance sheet.

To illustrate the preparation of consolidated financial statements in *any* year, we will use a different example than the one used in previous chapters. This example will include an intercompany sale of capital assets to illustrate the adjustments described in the first part of this chapter.

Basic information

On December 31, 2004, Parent Corp. acquired 80% of the outstanding common shares of Sub Ltd. by issuing Parent shares worth $800,000. At the date of acquisition, Sub's shareholders' equity totalled $855,000, consisting of $300,000 in the common share account and $555,000 in retained earnings. Parent acquired 80% of the book value of the net assets, $855,000 × 80% = $684,000.

Some of Sub's assets had a fair value that differed from carrying value as shown in Exhibit 6–2. Parent's 80% share of the fair-value increments is a total of $76,000. Goodwill is $40,000, as shown in Exhibit 6–2.

Exhibit 6–3 shows the separate-entity financial statements for Parent and Sub at December 31, 2010, six years after Parent's acquisition of its 80% interest in Sub. Other relevant information is as follows:

1. Sub's machinery had an estimated remaining useful life of 10 years from December 31, 2004. At the date of acquisition, the balance in Sub's accumulated depreciation (on machinery) account was $575,000. Machinery is depreciated on a straight-line basis, assuming no salvage value.

2. In 2007, Sub sold its investments for a profit of $45,000 over book value.

3. During 2010, intercompany sales were as follows:

   a. Parent had sales totalling $100,000 to Sub at a gross margin of 40% of selling price. On December 31, 2010, $40,000 of the amount sold was still in Sub's inventory.

   b. Sub had sales of $700,000 to Parent at a gross margin of 40% of sales. At year-end, $70,000 was still in Parent's inventory.

   Both companies had a gross margin of 40% of the sales price during 2010.

4. The inventories on January 1, 2010, contained intercompany purchases as follows:

   a. Sub held goods purchased from Parent for $20,000.
   b. Parent held goods purchased from Sub for $100,000.

EXHIBIT 6–2   PARENT CORP. BUYS 80% OF SUB LTD.

December 31, 2004

Fair-value increments, date of acquisition:

	Excess of Fair Value Over Book Value [Dr/(Cr)]	
	100%	**80%**
Inventories	$ 10,000	$ 8,000
Machinery	75,000	60,000
Investments	10,000	8,000
Total	$ 95,000	$ 76,000

Goodwill calculation:

Purchase price		$800,000
Book value of net assets acquired		
($855,000 × 80%)	$684,000	
Fair-value increments (above)	76,000	760,000
Goodwill		$ 40,000

EXHIBIT 6–3   PARENT CORP. AND SUB LTD. CONDENSED SEPARATE-ENTITY FINANCIAL STATEMENTS

Balance Sheets
December 31, 2010

	Parent	Sub
Assets		
Cash	$ 50,000	$ 20,000
Accounts receivable	150,000	160,000
Inventories	180,000	100,000
Machinery	5,000,000	2,700,000
Accumulated depreciation	(1,770,000)	(1,240,000)
Investment in Sub Ltd. (at cost)	800,000	—
Other investments	100,000	—
Total assets	$ 4,510,000	$ 1,740,000
Liabilities and shareholders' equity		
Accounts payable	$ 450,000	$ 200,000
Bonds payable	300,000	500,000
Total liabilities	750,000	700,000
Common shares	1,200,000	300,000
Retained earnings	2,560,000	740,000
Total shareholders' equity	3,760,000	1,040,000
Total liabilities and shareholders' equity	$ 4,510,000	$ 1,740,000

Income Statements
Year Ended December 31, 2010

	Parent	Sub
Sales revenue	$ 2,000,000	$ 1,500,000
Royalty revenue	150,000	—
Dividend income	75,000	—
Total revenue	2,225,000	1,500,000
Cost of sales	1,200,000	900,000
Other expenses	560,000	411,000
Total expenses	1,760,000	1,311,000
Net income	465,000	189,000
Dividends declared	(300,000)	(90,000)
Retained earnings, beginning of year	2,395,000	641,000
Retained earnings, end of year	$ 2,560,000	$ 740,000

The gross margin on intercompany sales held in the beginning inventories was 40% of selling price for both companies. All of the beginning inventories were sold to third parties during 2010.

5. Parent collects royalties from Sub (as well as from other companies). Between January 1, 2005, and December 31, 2009 (that is, prior to the current year), Sub paid a total of $500,000 in royalties to Parent. During 2010, Sub paid $90,000 to Parent for royalties.

6. In 2008, Sub sold machinery to Parent for $91,000. The machinery had originally been acquired by Sub in 2005 for $100,000. Sub had been depreciating the machinery on a straight-line basis over 10 years (i.e., at $10,000 per year), with a full year's depreciation in the year of acquisition and no depreciation in the year of disposal. Thus, the net book value of the machine to Sub was $70,000 at the time of the sale to Parent. After the sale from Sub to Parent, Parent continued to depreciate the machinery over the seven remaining years of its original useful life (i.e., at $13,000 per year beginning in 2008).

A caution for students

Before we launch into an illustration of consolidation techniques, we would like to caution students about their problem-solving approach to complex consolidation problems.

When we prepare financial statements for a real enterprise, it is rather obvious that balance sheets must balance, and that the full set of four financial statements must *articulate* or tie in to each other. However, when we are attempting consolidations for learning and practice, it may well be beneficial not to worry too much if our balance sheets don't balance! It is possible to spend many hours in an attempt to find the error (or errors) that keep our statements from balancing or from articulating properly. This particularly is a problem when we are using the direct approach, in which the ad hoc nature of the adjustment process denies us the self-balancing feature of the worksheet approach.

Often, the error is very minor—sometimes only a simple arithmetic error. We generally recommend, therefore, that students not get too stressed when their problem solutions don't quite work. This is especially true in examination situations, where time wasted looking for small mistakes will consume valuable time that could be used to answer other questions and problems.

Therefore, we urge all users of this book not to get too upset if your statements don't balance. Even the authors of this book sometimes have trouble getting their solutions to balance!

Direct approach

Statement of income and retained earnings The consolidated income statement for Parent Corp. is shown in Exhibit 6–4. The calculation of each item of revenue and expense is shown in brackets.

- *Sales revenue.* The consolidated sales are reduced by the intercompany sales during 2010 of $100,000 (downstream) plus $700,000 (upstream).
- *Royalty revenue.* Royalties are reduced by the intercompany royalties of $90,000 paid by Sub to Parent during 2010.
- *Dividend income.* Sub paid dividends of $90,000 during 2010. Of this amount, Parent received $90,000 × 80% = $72,000. The dividend income of Parent is reduced by the amount of the intercompany dividends of $72,000.
- *Cost of sales.* The cost of sales of the two companies is adjusted for (1) the intercompany sales, (2) the unrealized profits in the ending inventories, and (3) the realization of the previously unrealized profits in the beginning inventories:
  - The intercompany sales are $100,000 and $700,000, which are deducted from cost of sales as the offset to the deduction from sales, above.

EXHIBIT 6–4   PARENT CORP.

Condensed Consolidated Statement of Income and Retained Earnings
Year Ended December 31, 2010

Revenues

Sales revenue [2,000,000 + 1,500,000 – **100,000** – **700,000**]	$2,700,000
Royalty revenue [150,000 – **90,000**]	60,000
Dividend income [75,000 – **72,000**]	3,000
	2,763,000

Expenses

Cost of sales [1,200,000 + 900,000 – **100,000** – **700,000** + **16,000** + **28,000** – **8,000** – **40,000**]	1,296,000
Other expenses [560,000 + 411,000 – **90,000** + **6,000** – **3,000**]	884,000
Non-controlling interest in earnings of Sub Ltd.	
[(189,000 **+ 40,000 – 28,000 + 3,000**) × **20%**]	40,800
	2,220,800

Net income	$ 542,200
Retained earnings, December 31, 2009 [2,395,000 + 641,000 – **555,000** – **20% × (641,000 – 555,000) – 8,000 – 8,000 – (100,000 × 40% × 80%)** – **(20,000 × 40%) – (6,000 × 5) – (21,000 × 5/7 × 80%)**]	2,365,800
Dividends declared [300,000 + 90,000 – **90,000**]	(300,000)
Retained earnings, December 31, 2010	$2,608,000

- The unrealized profits in the ending inventories are $16,000 for the down-stream sales ($40,000 × 40%) and $28,000 for the upstream sales ($70,000 × 40%). These amounts are added to cost of sales.

- The now-realized profits from the beginning inventory are $20,000 × 40% = $8,000 for downstream sales (in Sub's inventory) and are $100,000 × 40% = $40,000 for upstream sales (in Parent's inventory). These now-realized amounts are subtracted from cost of sales, thereby increasing consolidated net income.

- *Other expenses.* Operating expenses are adjusted for (1) the intercompany royalty expense, (2) the amortization of the fair-value increments, and (3) for the overdepreciation of the machinery that was sold by Sub to Parent.

  (1) Intercompany royalty payments of $90,000 are eliminated.

  (2) On a straight-line basis, the $60,000 fair-value increment on the machinery is amortized over 10 years at $6,000 per year.

  (3) The depreciation expense relating to the machinery sold intercompany must be adjusted. Parent recorded $13,000 of depreciation on the asset during 2010, but the depreciation based on the cost of the machinery to Sub is only $10,000. Therefore, depreciation expense must be reduced by $3,000.

- *Non-controlling interest in earnings of Sub Ltd.* Exhibit 6–3 shows that Sub's separate-entity net income is $189,000. Parent has equity in only 80% of this amount. The remaining 20% is equity of the non-controlling interest. Before taking the 20%, we must adjust Sub's separate-entity earnings for the realized and unrealized profits from upstream sales. There are three adjustments.

Parent's *opening* inventory contains $100,000 of goods that had been purchased from Sub. The gross profit percentage was 40%, which yields an unrealized gross profit at the beginning of the year of $100,000 × 40% = $40,000. This amount has been sold to outsiders, and therefore has now been realized. We must add the $40,000 in now-realized profit to Sub's nominal earnings.

Parent's *ending* inventory contains unrealized profit of $70,000 × 40% = $28,000. We must subtract this amount from Sub's separate-entity net income.

Parent also is depreciating the machinery that had been purchased from Sub in 2004. Parent's depreciation is $91,000 ÷ 7 = $13,000. Depreciation based on the historical cost of the asset to Sub would have been $100,000 ÷ 10 = $10,000. Parent has charged an extra $3,000 in depreciation. Remember that amortization or depreciation constitutes recognition of the benefits of using a capital asset. Therefore, the extra $3,000 represents the realization of part of the previously unrealized intercompany profit. This $3,000 is added to Sub's nominal net income.

After these three adjustments are made, we can simply multiply the result by 20% to find the non-controlling interest's share of the Sub earnings that are included in Parent's consolidated net income.

- *Retained earnings*. Once the net income for the year has been determined, the ending retained earnings can be calculated. First, however, we must determine the consolidated retained earnings at the beginning of the current year, January 1, 2010. The opening balance of retained earnings will include Parent's separate-entity retained earnings, plus Parent's share of Sub's retained earnings *since the date of acquisition*, plus and minus adjustments for amortization, unrealized profits, and sale of fair-valued assets. Taking the subtractions and additions to the beginning retained earnings in the order in which they appear in Exhibit 6–4:

  - Sub's retained earnings of $555,000 at the date of acquisition is subtracted.
  - 20% of the increase in Sub's retained earnings since the date of acquisition is subtracted. This is the non-controlling interest's share of the increase in Sub's retained earnings.
  - The $8,000 fair-value increment on inventories has flowed through cost of goods sold and into retained earnings. This FVI is subtracted from retained earnings.
  - The $8,000 FVI on investments is subtracted. Item 4 in *basic information* tells us that Sub sold its investments prior to 2010 (in 2007, actually, but the exact date is irrelevant). The profit recognized by Sub on this transaction must be reduced by the amount of the fair-value increment *purchased* by Parent. In effect, the gain on the sale *to the consolidated entity* is the difference between the sales proceeds and the cost to the consolidated entity, which is the cost of the investments on Sub's books plus the $8,000 FVI.

In general, when fair-valued assets are sold to unrelated purchasers, the fair-value increment must be charged against the profit (or added to the loss) on the transaction. Note that the non-controlling interest is unaffected, because the fair-value increment related only to the investor's share.

- Unrealized profits at the *beginning* of the year are subtracted:
  - *Upstream*: 80% of the 40% gross margin on $100,000 in Parent's inventory.
  - *Downstream*: 40% gross margin on $20,000 in Sub's inventory.

- We add the accumulated amortization on fair-value increments up to the *beginning* of the year. Five years have elapsed between the acquisition date of December 31, 2004, and the end of the prior year, December 31, 2009.

    - *FVI on machinery*: $60,000 FVI at 10% per year for five years equals $60,000 × 5/10 = $30,000 debit to retained earnings.

Sub sold machinery to Parent in 2008 at a gain over book value of $21,000. The machinery is being amortized over seven years from the date of acquisition. Therefore, Parent is recording depreciation that is $3,000 higher than it should be for the consolidated entity (that is, $21,000 ÷ 7 years = $3,000 per year). Two adjustments are necessary for the beginning retained earnings:

    - Two years' (2008 and 2009) excess depreciation must be added back to retained earnings: $21,000 × 2/7 = $6,000.

    - Parent's share of the remaining unrealized profit must be removed from consolidated retained earnings: $21,000 × 5/7 × 80% = $12,000.

Notice that the total intercompany profit of $21,000 is divided between the 2/7 that has been realized (through use of the asset) and the 5/7 that remains unrealized at the end of 2009 and the beginning of 2010.

- *Dividends declared*. Parent's consolidated statements show only the dividends paid by Parent Corp.

Note that there is no need to adjust for the royalties paid by Sub to Parent prior to the beginning of 2010. The $500,000 in prior-year royalties has reduced Sub's retained earnings, but has increased Parent's retained earnings by the same amount. On consolidation, the effects are directly offsetting. No adjustment needs to be made for intercompany expenses in prior years, only for unrealized profits.

Balance sheet Exhibit 6–5 shows the consolidated balance sheet for Parent Corp. at December 31, 2010. Cash, accounts receivable, investments, and accounts payable are simply the sum of the two companies' balances. The common share amount is for Parent only, since this is Parent's balance sheet. The calculations of the other amounts are summarized below:

- *Inventories*. The inventories are reduced by the full amount of the unrealized earnings in the ending inventories, both downstream ($16,000) and upstream ($28,000).

- *Machinery*. First, Sub's accumulated depreciation at the date of acquisition ($575,000) must be offset against the asset account. Then we add the fair-value increment of $60,000. This adjustment assumes that all of the machinery to which the fair-value increment applies is still held by Sub.

Next, we must adjust for the intercompany sale of machinery. The total upstream unrealized profit of $21,000 is deducted in order to reduce the carrying value of the machinery from the $91,000 reflected on Parent's books to the $70,000 net carrying value that had been on Sub's books. However, the machinery should not be shown in the consolidated machinery account at its net book value to Sub at the time of the intercompany sale, but rather at the full historical cost ($100,000) to Sub. Therefore, the $30,000 accumulated depreciation that existed on Sub's books at the time of the sale must be restored; $30,000 is added to the machinery account and is also added to the accumulated depreciation account, below.

EXHIBIT 6–5   PARENT CORP.

Condensed Consolidated Balance Sheet
December 31, 2010

Assets

Current assets:

Cash [50,000 + 20,000]	$ 70,000
Accounts receivable [150,000 + 160,000]	310,000
Inventories [180,000 + 100,000 **−16,000 − 28,000**]	236,000
	616,000

Capital assets:

Machinery [5,000,000 + 2,700,000 − **575,000 + 60,000 − 21,000 + 30,000**]	7,194,000
Accumulated depreciation [1,770,000 + 1,240,000 − **575,000 + (6,000 × 6)**	
+ 30,000 − (3,000 × 3)]	(2,492,000)
	4,702,000

Other assets:

Investments [800,000 + 100,000 + 0 − **800,000**]	100,000
Goodwill	40,000
	140,000
Total assets	$ 5,458,000

Liabilities and shareholders' equity

Liabilities:

Current: accounts payable [450,000 + 200,000]	$ 650,000
Long-term: bonds payable [300,000 + 500,000]	800,000
Total liabilities	1,450,000
Non-controlling interest in Sub Ltd. **[1,040,000 − (70,000 × 40%) −**	
(21,000 × 4/7)] × 20%	200,000

Shareholders' equity:

Common shares	1,200,000
Retained earnings [see Exhibit 6-6]	2,608,000
Total shareholders' equity	4,008,000
Total liabilities and shareholders' equity	$ 5,458,000

- *Accumulated depreciation.* First, Sub's accumulated depreciation at the date of Parent's acquisition ($575,000) is eliminated. Next, the amortization of the fair-value increment over the six years between the date of acquisition and the current balance sheet date is added ($6,000 × 6 = $36,000). In addition, the accumulated depreciation of $30,000 that existed on the machinery sold intercompany is restored, as explained in the preceding paragraph. Deducted from accumulated depreciation is three years' annual depreciation adjustment on the intercompany machinery sale (3 years @ $3,000 per year = $9,000).

- *Non-controlling interest.* The non-controlling interest starts out as 20% of Sub's net assets (i.e., shareholders' equity) at the balance sheet date. On December 31, 2010, Sub's net assets amount to $1,040,000. The non-controlling interest's share of the net asset value is 20%. From that amount must be subtracted the non-controlling interest's share of the unrealized profit from the upstream sales at the end of the year: $70,000 × 40% × 20% = $5,600.

Also, we must deduct the non-controlling interest's share of the remaining unrealized profit (after tax) from the upstream sale of machinery.

Three years have elapsed since the sale, leaving 4/7 of the profit unrealized: $21,000 × 4/7 × 20% = $2,400.

- *Retained earnings.* The year-end retained earnings could be obtained from Exhibit 6–4, but that would take all the fun out of our consolidation. Instead, we should attempt to derive the year-end consolidated retained earnings directly. The year-end consolidated retained earnings consists of:

  1. the parent's year-end separate-entity retained earnings
  2. plus the subsidiary's year-end separate-entity retained earnings
  3. minus the subsidiary's date-of-acquisition retained earnings
  4. minus the non-controlling interests' share of the subsidiary's retained earnings *since the date of acquisition*
  5. less the cumulative amortization on fair-value increments from the date of acquisition to the current year-end, and
  6. less unrealized profits (net of non-controlling interest, where appropriate) at the *end* of the year.

The starting point is Parent's separate-entity retained earnings. To that we add 80% of the increase in Sub's retained earnings. Next we deduct the fair-value increments relating to inventory at the date of acquisition ($8,000) and investments ($8,000), both of which have been sold prior to this year's balance sheet dates and have flowed through to retained earnings in prior years. Then we deduct the six years' amortization of the fair-value increment on machinery.

There are three unrealized profit adjustments, two for year-end inventory and one for the machinery:

- The adjustment for the upstream inventory is $70,000 × 40% × 80% = $22,400.
- The adjustment for the downstream inventory is $40,000 × 40% = $16,000.
- The adjustment for Parent's share of the remaining unrealized machinery profit is $21,000 × 80% × 4/7 = $9,600.

The calculation of year-end consolidated retained earnings is summarized in Exhibit 6–6.

Worksheet approach

The consolidation worksheet for Parent Corp. at December 31, 2010, is shown in Exhibit 6–7. The first two columns contain the separate-entity financial statements for Parent and Sub. The adjustments are explained below:

Acquisition adjustments

The acquisition adjustments are to:

- eliminate Sub's shareholders' equity and establish the date-of-acquisition non-controlling interest,
- recognize the fair-value increments (that is, Parent's 80% share thereof) and goodwill, and
- eliminate Sub's accumulated depreciation at the date of acquisition.

EXHIBIT 6–6   CALCULATION OF PARENT CORP. RETAINED EARNINGS

December 31, 2010

1	Parent's separate-entity retained earnings (Exhibit 6-3)	$2,560,000
2	Sub's separate-entity retained earnings (Exhibit 6-3)	740,000
3	Less Sub's retained earnings at the date of acquisition	(555,000)
4	Less non-controlling interests' share of retained earnings since the date of acquisition (740,000 – 555,000) × 20%	(37,000)
5	Less (plus) the cumulative amortization of FVIs and goodwill since the date of acquisition:	
	Less FVI on inventories (sold to third parties)	(8,000)
	Less FVI on investments (sold to third parties)	(8,000)
	Less six years' amortization of FVI on machinery (60,000 × 6/10)	(36,000)
6	Less year-end unrealized profit on intercompany sales:	
	Less unrealized profit on upstream inventory sales [(70,000 × 40%) × 80%]	(22,400)
	Less unrealized profit on downstream inventory sales (40,000 × 40%)	(16,000)
	Less remaining unrealized profit on machinery sold intercompany [(21,000 × 4/7) × 80%]	(9,600)
		$2,608,000

Sub's shareholders' equity at the date of acquisition was $855,000, comprising $300,000 in common shares and $555,000 in retained earnings. The non-controlling interest's share is $855,000 × 20% = $171,000. The adjustment to eliminate Sub's shareholders' equity accounts and to establish the non-controlling interest is as follows:

a1	Common shares	300,000	
	Retained earnings	555,000	
	Investment in Sub Ltd.		684,000
	Non-controlling interest in Sub Ltd.		171,000

Adjustment **a1** eliminates $684,000 of the $800,000 purchase price. The remaining $116,000 purchase price discrepancy pertains to the fair-value increments and goodwill. The fair-value increments (and Parent's 80% share) and the calculation of goodwill are shown in Exhibit 6–2. The consolidation adjustment to record the FVI and goodwill, and to eliminate the remainder of the purchase price, is as follows:

a2	Inventory	8,000	
	Machinery	60,000	
	Investments	8,000	
	Goodwill	40,000	
	Investment in Sub Ltd.		116,000

The final acquisition adjustment is to offset Sub's accumulated depreciation at the date of acquisition against the machinery account, since the subsidiary's date-of-acquisition accumulated depreciation should not be carried forward in the consolidated balance sheet:

a3	Accumulated depreciation	575,000	
	Machinery		575,000

EXHIBIT 6–7   PARENT CORP. CONSOLIDATION WORKSHEET

December 31, 2010

| | Trial balances | | Adjustments | | | Parent Corp. consolidated trial balance |
	Parent	Sub	Acquisition [a]	Operations Cumulative [b]	Current [c]	
Cash	$ 50,000	$ 20,000				$ 70,000
Accounts receivable	150,000	160,000				310,000
Inventories	180,000	100,000	8,000 **a2**	(8,000) **b1**	(16,000) **c3** (28,000) **c4**	236,000
Machinery	5,000,000	2,700,000	60,000 **a2** (575,000) **a3**	(21,000) **b5** 30,000 **b6**		7,194,000
Accumulated depreciation	(1,770,000)	(1,240,000)	575,000 **a3**	(30,000) **b6** (30,000) **b1** 6,000 **b5**	(6,000) **c1** 3,000 **c6**	(2,492,000)
Investment in Sub Ltd. (at cost)	800,000		(684,000) **a1** (116,000) **a2**			—
Other investments (at cost)	100,000		8,000 **a2**	(8,000) **b1**		100,000
Goodwill			40,000 **a2**			40,000
Accounts payable	(450,000)	(200,000)				(650,000)
Bonds payable	(300,000)	(500,000)				(800,000)
Non-controlling interest in Sub Ltd.			(171,000) **a1**	(17,200) **b2** 8,000 **b3** 3,000 **b5**	18,000 **c7** (40,800) **c8**	(200,000)
Common shares	(1,200,000)	(300,000)	300,000 **a1**			(1,200,000)
Dividends declared	300,000	90,000			(90,000) **c7**	300,000
Retained earnings, December 31, 2009	(2,395,000)	(641,000)	555,000 **a1**	46,000 **b1** 17,200 **b2** 32,000 **b3** 8,000 **b4** 12,000 **b5**		(2,365,800)
Sales revenue	(2,000,000)	(1,500,000)			800,000 **c2**	(2,700,000)
Royalty revenue	(150,000)				90,000 **c5**	(60,000)
Dividend income	(75,000)				72,000 **c7**	(3,000)
Cost of sales	1,200,000	900,000		(40,000) **b3** (8,000) **b4**	(800,000) **c2** 16,000 **c3** 28,000 **c4**	1,296,000
Other operating expenses	560,000	411,000			6,000 **c1** (90,000) **c5** (3,000) **c6**	884,000
Non-controlling interest in earnings					40,800 **c8**	40,800
	$ —	$ —	$ —	$ —	$ —	$ —

The acquisition adjustment shown here can be simplified somewhat. The fair-value increment relating to inventories has long since flowed through to retained earnings. Similarly, the fair-value increment relating to Sub's investments was realized through sale in 2008. Both of these fair-value increments can be debited directly to the opening retained earnings. Since we did not take that approach in Exhibit 6–7, it will be necessary to make that transfer to retained earnings as part of the cumulative operations adjustment.

Cumulative operations adjustment As noted just above, the cumulative operations adjustment will eliminate the fair-value increments for inventories and investments by charging them to retained earnings.

Five years have elapsed between the date of acquisition and the *beginning* of the current fiscal year, and therefore five years' amortization will have occurred. The *annual* amortization for the machinery FVI is $60,000 FVI ÷ 10-year life = $6,000 depreciation per year.

Cumulatively, the machinery FVI amortization from the date of acquisition to the *beginning* of the current year amounts to $6,000 × 5 = $30,000 credited to accumulated depreciation.

The cumulative adjustment for the FVIs therefore is:

b1	Retained earnings (beginning)	46,000	
	Inventories		8,000
	Accumulated depreciation		30,000
	Other investments		8,000

The second adjustment is to credit non-controlling interest for their share of the increase in Sub's retained earnings since the date of acquisition. Non-controlling interest is credited for 20% of the increase in Sub's retained earnings between January 1, 2005, and December 31, 2009. Retained earnings increased from $555,000 to $641,000, or $86,000; 20% of that amount is $17,200:

b2	Retained earnings (beginning)	17,200	
	Non-controlling interest (B/S)		17,200

The third adjustment is to recognize the unrealized profits in the *beginning* inventories. Parent's opening inventory included $100,000 in goods acquired from Sub. Sub's gross margin was 40%; the unrealized upstream profit was $40,000. Of that amount, 20% pertains to the non-controlling interest:

b3	Retained earnings (beginning)	32,000	
	Non-controlling interest (B/S)	8,000	
	Cost of sales		40,000

Sub's opening inventories included $20,000 of goods purchased from Parent. At 40% gross margin, the unrealized profit was $8,000:

b4	Retained earnings (beginning)	8,000	
	Cost of sales		8,000

The adjustment relating to machinery that was sold intercompany from Sub to Parent is a little more complicated. The *remaining unrealized* intercompany profit must be eliminated, as follows:

- The unrealized profit at the time of the intercompany sale (in 2008) was $21,000. This full amount is in Parent's machinery account, and it must be eliminated from the consolidated machinery account.
- Two-sevenths of the $21,000 has been realized through depreciation of $3,000 per year (that is, $21,000 ÷ 7 years) in 2008 and 2009. That "excess" depreciation of $6,000 must be eliminated from the consolidated accumulated depreciation account.
- The remaining five-sevenths of the $21,000 is unrealized at the beginning of 2010. The unrealized amount is $15,000 (i.e., $21,000 ÷ 7 × 5). Of that amount, 20% (or $3,000) pertains to the non-controlling interest.

Putting that all together gives us a compound adjustment:

b5	Accumulated depreciation	6,000	
	Retained earnings	12,000	
	Non-controlling interest (B/S)	3,000	
	Machinery		21,000

Adjustment **b5** reduces the machinery from its carrying value on Parent's books ($91,000) to the date-of-sale carrying value on Sub's books ($70,000).

However, on Sub's books, the carrying value was not just in the asset account. Instead, there was $100,000 in the asset account and $30,000 in the accumulated depreciation account. Therefore, the second step is to reinstate the date-of-sale accumulated depreciation:

b6	Machinery	30,000	
	Accumulated depreciation		30,000

Current operations adjustments The first of the current operations adjustments is the 2010 amortization of the fair-value increment on machinery:

c1	Other expenses	6,000	
	Accumulated depreciation		6,000

Second is the elimination of intercompany sales. In Exhibit 6–7, we have combined the upstream and downstream intercompany sales transactions into a single amount:

c2	Sales revenue	800,000	
	Cost of sales		800,000

Sub's inventory contains goods purchased from Parent (i.e., downstream) amounting to $40,000. The unrealized profit is $40,000 × 40% = $16,000:

c3	Cost of sales	16,000	
	Inventories		16,000

Upstream sales of $70,000 are still in Parent's inventory. The unrealized profit is $70,000 \times 40\% = \$28,000$:

c4	Cost of sales	28,000	
	Inventories		28,000

The royalties that Sub paid to Parent during the year must be eliminated:

c5	Royalty revenue	90,000	
	Other expenses		90,000

No adjustment is needed for the $500,000 royalties paid in prior years. That is an extraneous or irrelevant piece of information!

The depreciation that Parent is charging on the machinery purchased from Sub must be reduced to the amount that Sub would have charged had the inter-company sale not taken place. Parent is charging $13,000 per year (i.e., $91,000 \div 7$), but depreciation on the original cost to Sub would have been $10,000. The "excess" depreciation of $3,000 must be eliminated:

c6	Accumulated depreciation	3,000	
	Other operating expenses		3,000

The next step is to eliminate Sub's dividends of $90,000; 80% of the dividends were received by Parent and are offset against Parent's dividend income. The other 20% of the dividends went to the non-controlling interest, and therefore they are offset against the non-controlling interest on the balance sheet:

c7	Dividend income ($90,000 \times 80\%$)	72,000	
	Non-controlling interest (B/S) ($90,000 \times 20\%$)	18,000	
	Dividends paid		90,000

Notice that this adjustment does not completely eliminate the dividend income on Parent's income statement. Parent has other investments as well as its investment in Sub. Parent apparently earned $3,000 in dividends from these other investments.

Finally, we must calculate the non-controlling interest's share of Sub's 2010 net income, *net of unrealized profits*. The starting point is Sub's separate-entity net income of $189,000 (from Exhibit 6–3). To this, we must add the now-realized upstream profit in the opening inventory and deduct the unrealized downstream profit in the ending inventory. In addition, we must add this year's realized profit on the upstream sale of machinery, which is represented by the "excess" depreciation charged by Parent on the machinery:

Sub's separate-entity net income	$189,000
Plus now-realized upstream profit in opening inventory, $100,000 \times 40\%$	+ 40,000
Less unrealized upstream profit in ending inventory, $70,000 \times 40\%$	− 28,000
Plus now-realized profit on upstream sale of machinery, $21,000 \times 1/7$	+ 3,000
Sub's separate-entity net income adjusted for unrealized profits	$204,000

The non-controlling interest's share of Sub's adjusted earnings, as reported on Parent's consolidated income statement, is $204,000 × 20% = $40,800:

c8	Non-controlling interest in earnings of Sub (I/S)	40,800	
	Non-controlling interest in Sub (B/S)		40,800

The result of these adjustments is consolidated net income of $542,200 and consolidated retained earnings of $2,592,000. We can verify these amounts via a separate calculation of Parent's equity in the 2010 earnings of Sub plus a calculation of Parent's year-end 2010 investment based on the equity method. Since equity-basis reporting constitutes one-line consolidation, we should get the same net income and the same retained earnings under the equity method as by consolidation.

Equity-Basis Reporting

To determine Parent's equity in Sub's 2010 earnings, we start with Parent's 80% share of Sub's reported net income of $189,000, or $151,200. This amount must then be adjusted for (1) amortization of fair-value increments, (2) previously unrealized profits now realized in 2010, and (3) unrealized profits at the end of 2010. The top section of Exhibit 6–8 illustrates the necessary calculations.

After making all the necessary adjustments, including the adjustment relating to the "excess" depreciation taken on the machinery that had been sold intercompany, Parent's equity in Sub's earnings amounts to $149,200. If we take this amount and add it to Parent's net income less the dividends received from Sub, we obtain $542,200, which is exactly the same as the consolidated net income derived on Exhibit 6–4:

Parent separate-entity net income (Exhibit 6–3)	$465,000
Less dividends received from Sub	(72,000)
Plus equity in earnings of Sub (Exhibit 6–8)	149,200
Consolidated net income	$542,200

At the end of 2010, Parent's investment in Sub should amount to:

(1) the original purchase price to acquire the 80% share

(2) plus 80% of the increase in Sub's retained earnings since the date of acquisition

(3) less amortization and realization of fair-value increments and goodwill between the date of acquisition and year-end 2010, and

(4) less any unrealized profits at year-end 2010.

The lower section of Exhibit 6–8 illustrates this calculation.

The increase in the balance of the investment account since acquisition (that is, $848,000 − $800,000 = $48,000), plus Parent's separate-entity retained earnings of $2,560,000 at the end of 2010, equals the consolidated retained earnings of $2,608,000. Thus the equity method can be used to double-check the results of the consolidation process.

EXHIBIT 6-8   PARENT CORP.'S EQUITY IN SUB LTD.

December 31, 2010

Parent Corp.'s equity in the earnings of Sub Ltd.:

Parent's share of Sub's reported net income: $189,000 × 80%		$151,200
Adjustments:		
Amortization of fair value increment:		
Machinery		$ (6,000)
Unrealized profit in opening inventories:		
Downstream	8,000	
Upstream: $40,000 × 80%	32,000	40,000
Unrealized profit in ending inventories:		
Downstream	(16,000)	
Upstream: $28,000 × 80%	(22,400)	(38,400)
Profit realized through depreciation on machinery sold intercompany: $3,000 × 80%		2,400
Parent's equity in the 2010 earnings of Sub		**$149,200**

Parent Corp.'s investment in Sub Ltd.

Initial investment (cost)		$800,000
Equity in unremitted earnings (net of dividends received from Sub):		
Parent's share of the change in Sub's retained earnings since the date of acquisition: ($740,000 − $555,000) × 80%		148,000
Less amortization of fair value increment through 2010:		
Inventories (full amount realized)	$ (8,000)	
Investments (full amount realized)	(8,000)	
Machinery: $60,000 × 6/10	(36,000)	(52,000)
Less remaining unrealized profits, December 31, 2010:		
Inventory, downstream	(16,000)	
Inventory, upstream: $28,000 × 80%	(22,400)	
Machinery: $21,000 × 80% × 4/7	(9,600)	(48,000)
Investment in Sub Ltd. (equity basis), December 31, 2010		**$848,000**

Consolidation with Equity-Basis Recording

Throughout this book, we have focused on consolidation when the parent company records its investment in the subsidiary at cost. This is the customary practice, since the cost method simplifies both parent-company bookkeeping and consolidation.

If the parent *records* its investment on the equity basis instead of the cost basis, the consolidation process must be modified accordingly. This is not a big problem. The only differences in the parent's separate-entity accounts between cost-basis and equity-basis reporting are that:

- the investment account includes the parent's share of the subsidiary's unremitted earnings to date (that is, the subsidiary's accumulated net incomes since the date of acquisition minus the dividends paid), in addition to the cost of the acquisition

- the parent's opening retained earnings includes the cumulative amount of unremitted earnings to the beginning of the year
- "Equity in earnings of subsidiary" will appear on the parent's separate-entity income statement, and
- the parent will show no dividend income from the subsidiary.

To prepare consolidated statements when the parent uses the equity basis of recording the investment, we must first remove the effects of the equity basis from the parent's accounts or trial balance. Once that is done, we can consolidate the accounts exactly as we have above.

Exhibit 6–9 shows Parent Corp.'s separate entity financial statements for 2010 using both the cost method and the equity method. The accounts that show a difference are highlighted. All other accounts are the same regardless of which recording method is used.

The first step in consolidation when Parent uses the equity basis of recording its investment is simply to reverse the differences between the two bases by undoing the equity recording. Using the amounts in the "difference" column of Exhibit 6–9, we debit for the credit difference (in the equity in earnings account) and credit for the debit differences:

Equity in earnings of Sub Ltd.	149,200	
Investment in Sub Ltd.		32,000
Dividend income		72,000
Retained earnings (opening)		45,200

A slight variation is to leave the subsidiary's dividends received in the equity in earnings account, since they will be eliminated in the consolidation process anyway:

Equity in earnings of Sub Ltd.	77,200	
Investment in Sub Ltd.		32,000
Retained earnings (opening)		45,200

Either adjustment will work equally well. The equity-reversal entry can be made either before starting the consolidation process by adjusting the parent's separate-entity accounts, or by entering the reversing amounts in the consolidation working papers—either direct method or worksheet approach—as the first step after entering the separate entity amounts.

Extraordinary Items and Discontinued Operations

In Chapter 4, we pointed out that subsidiaries' extraordinary items and discontinued operations normally maintain their reporting status in the parent's financial statements, under both equity-basis reporting and consolidated financial statements.

A parent will report a subsidiary's extraordinary item as extraordinary in its own equity-basis or consolidated income statement if the required conditions still are present within the broader economic entity. An extraordinary gain or loss in a subsidiary may become immaterial in the context of the parent's financial report-

EXHIBIT 6–9   COMPARISON OF COST-BASIS VS. EQUITY-BASIS RECORDING OF INVESTMENT

Parent Corp.
Balance Sheet
December 31, 2010

	Cost	Equity	Difference Debit/(Credit)
Assets			
Cash	$ 50,000	$ 50,000	
Accounts receivable	150,000	150,000	
Inventories	180,000	180,000	
Machinery	5,000,000	5,000,000	
Accumulated depreciation	(1,770,000)	(1,770,000)	
Investment in Sub Ltd.	**800,000**	**848,000**	**$ 48,000**
Other investments	100,000	100,000	
Total assets	$4,510,000	$4,558,000	
Liabilities and shareholders' equity			
Accounts payable	$ 450,000	$ 450,000	
Bonds payable	300,000	300,000	
Total liabilities	750,000	750,000	
Common shares	1,200,000	1,200,000	
Retained earnings	2,560,000	2,608,000	
Total shareholders' equity	3,760,000	3,792,000	
Total liabilities and shareholders' equity	$4,510,000	$4,558,000	

Income Statement
Year Ended December 31, 2010

	Cost	Equity	
Sales revenue	$2,000,000	$2,000,000	
Royalty revenue	150,000	150,000	
Dividend income	**75,000**	**3,000**	**72,000**
Equity in earnings of Sub Ltd.	**—**	**149,200**	**(149,200)**
Total revenue	2,225,000	2,302,200	
Cost of sales	1,200,000	1,200,000	
Other expenses	560,000	560,000	
Total expenses	1,760,000	1,760,000	
Net income	465,000	542,200	
Dividends declared	(300,000)	(300,000)	
Retained earnings, beginning of year	**2,395,000**	**2,365,800**	**29,200**
Retained earnings, end of year	$2,560,000	$2,608,000	

ing, or it may become merely an unusual item that merits separate disclosure but not treatment as an extraordinary item.

Similarly, a subsidiary may decide to discontinue a separable line of business and thus report a discontinued operation. But if that type of discontinued business still remains within the broader economic entity, then it will not qualify for reporting as a discontinued operation in a consolidated (or equity-basis) income statement.

The parent will report only its proportionate share of a subsidiary's extraordinary items and discontinued operations. In consolidation, the non-controlling interest absorbs its share of these gains or losses.

As is always the case with these items, they are reported net of any related income tax. If an item loses its special status and becomes an operating item in the consolidated statements, the tax effect must be added back (to *gross up* the item) and the tax effect is included in operating income tax expense.

SUMMARY OF KEY POINTS

1. When amortizable capital assets are sold between related companies, any unrealized profit must be eliminated. Intercompany *losses* on unrealized sales may or may not be eliminated, depending on whether the loss reflects a true decline in the recoverable benefit of the asset. The amount of *unrealized* profit declines as the asset is amortized because amortization reflects the use of the asset and thus the realization of its benefits. For downstream sales, the full amount of unrealized profit is eliminated. For upstream sales (or lateral sales between subsidiaries), the non-controlling interest absorbs its share of unrealized profit.

    An asset that was acquired via an intercompany sale may be sold to outside third parties. When that happens, any remaining unrealized gain must be combined with the recorded gain or loss on the sale.

2. In general, consolidation adjustments fall into three categories: (1) acquisition adjustments, (2) cumulative operations adjustments, and (3) current operations adjustments. For problems that are to be solved by a student, these three may be combined to arrive at a year-end balance sheet or for a single-year income statement. In practice, however, comparative statements are always required and the distinction between beginning and ending balance sheet amounts must be preserved.

    The acquisition adjustments stay the same over time. There is no need to alter them, although they may be modified to reflect changes in asset structure, such as the disposition of fair-valued assets that were acquired but no longer held. In effect, this is a combination of acquisition and cumulative adjustments.

    The theory underlying the cumulative operations adjustments is that date-of-acquisition balances must be updated to reflect amortizations and intercompany transactions to the *beginning* of the reporting year. Amounts such as opening inventories and opening retained earnings must be correctly stated.

    Current operations adjustments have two basic functions: (1) to correctly state consolidated end-of-period balances, and (2) to adjust the year's earnings to reflect only transactions with non-related entities.

3. Equity-basis reporting will result in the same parent-company net income and retained earnings as does consolidation. Calculations for equity-basis earnings therefore can provide a useful check on the accuracy of consolidated results.

    If the parent company records its investment on the equity basis, the first step in consolidation is to reverse the impact of the entity-basis adjustments.

Then, consolidation can proceed as has been described throughout this textbook.

4. A parent company normally will report a subsidiary's extraordinary gains and losses and discontinued operations as such in its consolidated (or equity-basis) income statement. Only the parent's proportionate part of these items is included; the non-controlling interest absorbs its portion of any such items.

SELF-STUDY PROBLEM 6–1

Sorrow Limited is an 80%-owned subsidiary of Parks Corporation, a manufacturer of industrial equipment. In 2007, Sorrow purchased a grummling machine from Parks for $100,000. Parks had manufactured the machine at a cost of $60,000. Sorrow uses straight-line depreciation over a 10-year period for its grummling machines, and follows the practice of depreciating its assets by one-half year in both the year of acquisition and the year of disposal. No salvage value is assumed. Single assets accounting (that is, not group depreciation) is used. Sorrow used the machine in its productive operations from 2007 to 2020, in which year it was sold for scrap for $1,000.

Required:

Prepare the adjustments that would be necessary in each of 2007, 2008, 2012, 2019, and 2020 for the grummling machine when preparing Parks Corporation's consolidated financial statements.

SELF-STUDY PROBLEM 6–2

On January 1, 2005, Power Corporation purchased 80% of the outstanding shares of Spencer Corporation for $2,500,000 in cash. On that date, Spencer Corporation's common shares had a carrying value of $2,000,000 and retained earnings of $1,000,000. On January 1, 2005, all of Spencer's identifiable assets and liabilities had fair values that were equal to their carrying values except for:

1. A building that had an estimated fair value of $600,000 less than its carrying value; its remaining useful life was estimated to be 10 years.

2. A long-term liability with a fair value of $500,000 less than its carrying value; the liability matures on December 31, 2012.

The income statements of Power Corporation and Spencer Corporation for the year ended December 31, 2009, are shown in Exhibit 6–10. Additional information is as follows:

1. On January 1, 2006, Spencer sold a machine to Power for $210,000. Spencer originally paid $400,000 for the machine on January 2, 2001. At the original date of purchase by Spencer, the machine had an estimated useful life of 20 years with no estimated salvage value. There has been no change in these estimates—the machine still retains its value in use.

2. Both companies use the straight-line method for all depreciation and amortization.

EXHIBIT 6–10   SEPARATE-ENTITY INCOME STATEMENTS

Year Ended December 31, 2009

	Power	Spencer
Sales	$2,000,000	$ 900,000
Investment income	1,000,000	100,000
Gain on sale of land	—	68,000
Total revenue	3,000,000	1,068,000
Cost of goods sold	1,300,000	500,000
Other operating expenses	960,000	320,000
Total expenses	2,260,000	820,000
Net income	$ 740,000	$ 248,000

3. During 2008, the following intercompany inventory sales occurred:

- Power sold $500,000 of merchandise to Spencer, $100,000 of which is in Spencer's inventory at 2008 year-end.

- Spencer sold $300,000 of merchandise to Power, $70,000 of which is in Power's inventory at the end of 2008.

4. During 2009, the following intercompany inventory sales occurred:

- Power sold $400,000 of merchandise to Spencer, $90,000 of which is in Spencer's inventory at 2009 year-end.

- Spencer sold $250,000 of merchandise to Power, $60,000 of which is in Power's inventory at the end of 2009.

5. Intercompany inventory transactions are priced to provide Power with 30% gross margin (on sales price) and Spencer with 40% gross profit (on sales). Both companies use the first-in first-out inventory cost flow assumption.

6. On September 1, 2009, Spencer sold a parcel of land to Power Company for $133,000 that it had originally purchased for $65,000.

7. During 2009, Power declared and paid $250,000 in dividends, while Spencer declared and paid $40,000 in dividends.

8. Power accounts for its investment in Spencer on the cost basis.

9. There was no impairment of goodwill at the end of 2009.

Required:

a. Prepare a consolidated income statement for Power Corporation for the year ending December 31, 2009. Show supporting calculations for each amount in the consolidated income statement.

b. Independently, calculate Power Corporation's net income using equity-basis reporting.

[SMA, adapted]

6–1 Under what conditions is a profit on an intercompany sale considered to be *unrealized*?

6–2 A capital asset is sold by a subsidiary to its parent company at the asset's fair market value, which is less than the asset's carrying value on the subsidiary's books. Would the unrealized loss on the sale be eliminated upon consolidation? Explain.

6–3 Company P owns 60% of Company S1 and 90% of Company S2. S1 sells inventory to S2 at a profit of $20,000. All the goods are still in S2's inventory at year-end. By what amount should consolidated net income be adjusted to eliminate the unrealized profit?

6–4 Company IR owns 30% of Company IE1 and 40% of Company IE2. IE1 sells inventory to IE2 at a profit of $20,000. All the goods are still in IE2's inventory at year-end. By what amount should IR's equity-basis investment income be adjusted to eliminate the unrealized profit?

6–5 In what way is the profit on intercompany sales of depreciable assets *realized*?

6–6 What happens if a company sells a capital asset that is part of its *inventory* to another company in the consolidated group instead of one that is shown as a *capital asset* on the books of the selling company?

6–7 How does the adjustment differ when there is sale of an intangible asset; e.g., patent with limited life instead of a capital asset from the subsidiary to the parent?

6–8 Explain the composition of consolidated retained earnings in terms of the parent's and subsidiary's separate-entity retained earnings.

6–9 When a fair-valued asset is sold by a subsidiary to its parent, how does the amount of the fair-value increment affect the unrealized profit elimination?

6–10 When a fair-valued asset is sold to outsiders, what is the disposition of the fair-value increment when the statements are consolidated in the year of the sale? What is the disposition of the increment in years following the sale?

6–11 Explain briefly how the process of consolidation differs when the equity method is used by the parent for recording the investment account as compared to the cost method.

6–12 What does the equity-basis balance of the investment account for a subsidiary represent (e.g., cost of the investment, market value of the investment, etc.)?

6–13 Under equity reporting, why are unrealized profits from *downstream* sales deducted from the investor's equity in the earnings of the investee, instead of from the parent's own earnings?

CASES

CASE 6–1   Alright Beverages Ltd.

Alright Beverages Ltd. (AB) was federally incorporated in 1990. In the initial years, the company produced a cranberry drink for sale at sporting and entertainment events in eastern Canada. In 1997, operations were expanded to include sales to bars, restaurants, and fast-food outlets. To penetrate additional markets, AB started manufacturing a wide variety of fruit beverages and acquired the distributorship of another company's fruit concentrate. Sold under the brand name "Fruit Brite," the fruit beverage sales were only moderately successful.

In 2000, a management review indicated that while sales of the new fruit beverage line had increased, AB's cost to manufacture was also greater than that of its competitors. Much of the profit was being made on the distribution of the fruit concentrate.

In an attempt to improve profitability, the company entered the retail market in 2001. To finance the expansion, AB obtained funds from two sources, bank loans and its first public issue of shares. The funds were used to purchase a bottling plant in Toronto and to provide working capital during the first year of operation. The retail operation was administered by a newly incorporated, wholly owned subsidiary, Fruitbrite Flavours Ltd. (FF). In the first year the company incurred a loss on its retail operations, but subsequent years were profitable.

FF continued to expand until it had a nationwide bottling and distribution network. In major cities, the bottlers were wholly owned subsidiaries of FF; in smaller cities, the bottlers were independents who bottled other products as well. In all cases, AB sold its fruit concentrate to the bottlers.

In 2004, AB acquired 70% of the shares of Concentrated Vending Ltd. (CV), a manufacturer of fruit beverage vending machines, located in Windsor, Ontario. AB purchased CV at a price well below its proportionate book value, since CV had encountered financial difficulties. AB lent CV funds to finance a plant modernization program. AB contracted with the founders of CV to continue as senior management since AB had no experience in the equipment manufacturing industry. The management contract stipulated that a bonus would be paid, amounting to 20% of CV's income before taxes, in each of the next five consecutive years. Although the plant modernization was successful, CV had difficulty selling enough machines to achieve a break-even point.

Sales of fruit beverages through vending machines were growing rapidly with the increased awareness of the importance of a healthier lifestyle. This was a segment of the market in which the AB group did not participate. Therefore, early in 2006, AB created a wholly owned subsidiary, VendSell Ltd. (VS). VS buys the machines from CV at regular retail price and then sells them to local operators with the condition that only AB products be sold in the machines. The intent was to place machines in as many locations as possible.

VS sells the majority of machines under conditional sales contracts, in which the buyer agrees to make an initial payment of $500 and payments of $75 per month for the next 48 months, for a total of $4,100. Machine maintenance is the responsibility of the operator. The payment plan was devised with three objectives in mind:

1. to place the maximum number of machines by the use of an easy payment plan

2. to defer payment of income tax by deducting the full cost of the machines when sold and deferring recognition of the revenue until the cash was collected, and

3. to ensure that only AB products were used during the payment period, since title to the machine would not transfer until all payments had been made.

The fruit concentrate for the machines is purchased by the local operators from the bottler in the particular area, who in turn had purchased the fruit concentrate from AB. The operator is charged an amount equal to the cost to the bottler plus 20%.

During 2006, VS expects to buy 8,000 machines from CV at a price of $5,000 each. The machines currently cost CV $3,000 each to manufacture. This cost to CV is significantly lower than in previous years. In order to supply VS, the volume of production in 2007 is expected to be twice that of 2005. As a result, CV expects to show a profit in 2006.

By the end of 2006, VS expects to sell 6,800 machines. The revenue from initial payments will amount to $3,400,000 and VS expects to receive total revenues of $5,100,000 from initial payments and installments in 2006.

In its annual report for 2005, AB reported after-tax earnings of $4,575,000 on consolidated revenue of $77,970,000. Since CV accounted for less than 10% of AB's consolidated assets, revenues, and income, no segmented information was presented in the 2005 annual report.

Within the management of AB there is disagreement over the proper accounting treatment for the activities of AB, VS, FF, and CV for 2006 and the effect on consolidation and reporting.

Required:

In August 2006, you were engaged as an independent advisor. Prepare a report in which you:

a. Outline the major accounting and reporting issues faced by the company and its subsidiaries.
b. Identify alternative policies to deal with the issues outlined.
c. Provide recommendations on the preferred policies.

[CICA, adapted]

CASE 6–2   Le Gourmand

Le Gourmand is one of Canada's most famous French restaurants. Located 20 kilometres north of Toronto, it draws diners from all over the province to enjoy its fare. One of the attractions at the restaurant is its private-label brand of wines—produced, bottled, and aged by Ombre Wines Ltd., located in the Niagara Peninsula.

The owner of Le Gourmand, Francois LeClerc, decided on New Year's Eve to increase the ties between Ombre Wines Ltd. and Le Gourmand Inc.; Le Gourmand is Ombre Wines' largest customer. On January 2, 2005, Le Gourmand Inc. purchased 3,000 common shares of Ombre Wines Ltd. on the open market for $207,000. This left very few common shares still available to the public. The preferred shares were owned by the founders of Ombre Wines, but their children owned many of the common shares and were gradually selling them because none of them wished to take over the business.

Ombre Wines Ltd.'s owners' equity at January 2, 2005, was:

Preferred shares:

Cumulative, 6%, non-voting;

2,000 authorized, 1,000 issued $ 20,000

Common shares:

7,000 authorized, 6,000 issued   137,000

Retained earnings   170,000

                                                             $327,000

At January 1, 2005, the book values of Ombre Wines Ltd.'s assets approximated fair values except as follows:

	Book Value	Fair Value
Two identical parcels of land, purchased in January 1993 as an investment; each parcel cost $20,000 and the fair value of each parcel was identical	$40,000	$60,000
The land on which Ombre Wines' factory was located	$70,000	$85,000
Grape press, purchased in January 2000 (useful life when the press was purchased was 10 years, no salvage value)	$20,000	$24,000

In September 2005, Ombre Wines sold one of the parcels of land that it had been holding as an investment (both lots had been put on the market but only one had sold). The proceeds were $18,000. The real estate market had declined badly in 2005. The purchaser, however, had also discovered that Ombre Wines had been using the vacant lots to dump some residue from the wine processing; the land would not be ready to produce crops for at least five years. The purchaser had originally been willing to offer $24,000, but reduced this to $18,000 when the land use was confirmed by his lawyer.

Sales from Ombre Wines to Le Gourmand totalled $100,000 and $120,000 in 2004 and 2005, respectively. At December 31, 2004, Le Gourmand's inventory contained $45,000 of Ombre Wines' wine. A year later, the inventory included $60,000 of Ombre Wines' wine. Of the ending inventory acquired from Ombre Wines, $20,000 had not been paid for as at December 31, 2005. In settlement of part of this payable, Le Gourmand sent some old office equipment to Ombre Wines. The equipment had cost $10,000 and had a net book value at December 31, 2005, of $1,000. Ombre Wines agreed to accept the equipment and to forgive $5,000 of the receivable from Le Gourmand, leaving a balance of $15,000 due from the restaurant. Ombre Wines did not depreciate this office equipment during 2005.

Ombre Wines' most recent dividend declaration was December 31, 2003.

The amortization policy for all capital assets is straight-line.

Francois LeClerc is looking forward to the cash flow from dividends that he hopes his company will receive from Ombre Wines Ltd. each year.

The balance sheets of the two companies at December 31, 2005, and the income statements for the year then ended are presented in Exhibit A below.

EXHIBIT A
TWO COMPANIES' BALANCE SHEETS

Balance Sheet
December 31, 2005

	Le Gourmand Inc.	Ombre Wines Ltd.
Assets		
Cash	$ 1,750	$ 16,400
Accounts receivable	—	66,000
Inventory	85,500	134,000
Investment in Ombre Wines	207,000	—
Land	30,000	90,000
Building	40,000	60,000
Equipment	25,000	75,000
	$389,250	$441,400
Liabilities and owners' equity		
Accounts payable	$ 34,000	$ 13,000
Taxes payable	2,150	15,000
Long-term debt	—	10,000
Future income taxes	1,600	—
Preferred shares	—	20,000
Common shares	155,000	137,000
Retained earnings	196,500	246,400
	$389,250	$441,400

Income Statement
For the Year Ended December 31, 2005

	Le Gourmand Inc.	Ombre Wines Ltd.
Sales	$400,000	$300,000
Gain on transfer of office equipment	4,000	—
Loss on sale of land	—	(2,000)
Cost of goods sold	(275,000)	(100,000)
Salaries	(78,000)	(55,000)
General & administration	(4,500)	(3,000)
Depreciation, building	(2,500)	(3,600)
Depreciation, equipment	(3,000)	(8,000)
Interest expense	—	(1,000)
Tax expense (40%)	(16,000)	(51,000)
Net income	$ 25,000	$ 76,400

Required:

Describe the alternative accounting treatments available to Le Gourmand Inc. for its investment in Ombre Wines Ltd. Describe why each alternative is an option and conclude which treatment is appropriate based on your description. Calculate Le Gourmand Inc.'s net income for the year ended December 31, 2005. Show details of all calculations.

[ICAO]

PROBLEMS

P6–1

Dudes Outfitters, Ltd., is a 70%-owned subsidiary of Trail Ltd. On January 10, 2002, Dudes sold some display cases to Trail Ltd. for $95,000, recognizing a gain of $45,000 before-tax on the transaction. Trail Ltd. depreciated the cases on a straight-line basis over six years, taking a full year's depreciation in 2002.

On February 12, 2005, Trail sold the display cases to an unaffiliated company for $55,000.

Required:

Prepare the appropriate consolidated adjustments relating to the display cases for each year ending December 31, 2002 through 2005.

P6–2

On January 1, 2003, Sub Ltd., 80% owned by Par Ltd., sold a building to Par Ltd. for $1,800,000. The building cost Sub $800,000 and was 70% depreciated (at 5% per year). Par will depreciate the building over the six remaining years, straight-line.

Required:

Give the consolidation eliminating entries relating to this transaction for the years ended:

a. 2003

b. 2005

[CGA–Canada, adapted]

P6–3

Parent Ltd. owns 70% of the voting shares of Sub Ltd. During 2004, Sub Ltd. sold inventory costing $640,000 to Parent Ltd. for $800,000. At December 31, 2004, Parent Ltd. still had $300,000 of these goods in its inventory, and had not yet paid for $480,000 of the goods. All of the remaining goods were sold in 2005.

Sub Ltd. also sold a piece of land (cost of $188,000) to Parent Ltd. on July 1, 2004, for $260,000, for which Parent Ltd. had issued Sub Ltd. a five-year, 10% per annum note. The interest will be paid on July 1, 2005.

Required:

a. Prepare the eliminating entries as they would appear on the consolidated worksheet for 2004 and 2005, as related to the foregoing information.

b. Assuming that Sub Ltd. earned $680,000 during 2004 and $880,000 during 2005, calculate the non-controlling interest in the earnings of Sub Ltd.

[CGA–Canada, adapted]

P6–4

Adam Ltd. owns 80% of the outstanding shares of Bob Ltd. Adam Ltd. also owns 70% of the shares of Xena Ltd. During the year 2005, Adam sold $500,000 (cost) of goods (widgets) to Bob at a 30% markup. Xena sold $400,000 (cost) of goods to Adam at a 25% markup.

Adam sold a piece of land (cost $100,000) to Bob for $50,000.

On October 1, 2005, Xena sold land (cost $80,000) and a building (cost $110,000) to Adam for $400,000; 40% of the price was allocated to land and 60% of the price was allocated to building. The building had five years of expected life at October 1, 2005, and was 30% depreciated at that time.

The $400,000 was unpaid at year-end and Adam had agreed to pay $10,000 interest on the unpaid amount.

An inventory count showed that 20% of the widgets that Bob had purchased from Adam were unsold at December 31, 2005; 70% of the gadgets that Adam had purchased from Xena were also unsold.

Required:

Assume that Adam Ltd. uses the cost method of keeping its accounts.

a. Prepare the eliminating entries on the working papers that would be required at December 31, 2005, to prepare the consolidated financial statements.

b. Calculate the effect on the minority interest; by how much would the income to each non-controlling interest be changed? Keep the two subsidiaries separate.

[CGA–Canada, adapted]

P6–5

On January 1, 2002, Peter Limited purchased 70% of the outstanding voting common shares of Susan Limited at a cost of $139,200. At acquisition date, the book value of Susan Limited was $161,000, inventory was undervalued by $2,500, and depreciable capital assets were undervalued by $7,500. Relevant information for 2005 is shown below.

Required:

a. Calculate non-controlling interest in net income for 2005 assuming consolidation is appropriate.

b. Calculate non-controlling interest in the consolidated balance sheet as of the end of 2005.

c. Calculate consolidated net income for 2005, assuming a 10-year remaining life at acquisition date for capital assets and straight-line depreciation. Note that Peter Limited uses the cost method and that Susan Limited paid dividends during the year.

Reported at End of 2005

	Peter	Susan
Net income	$ 44,000	$ 11,000
Dividends paid	4,000	1,000
Current assets	170,800	40,000
Investment in S (at cost)	139,200	—
Capital assets (net)	330,000	160,000
	$640,000	$200,000
Liabilities	$140,000	$ 30,000
Common shares	400,000	150,000
Retained earnings (end)	100,000	20,000
	$640,000	$200,000

[CGA–Canada, adapted]

P6–6

Anita Company owns a controlling interest in Brian Company and Gabriel Company. Anita purchased an 80% interest in Brian at a time when Brian reported retained earnings of $450,000. Anita purchased a 60% interest in Gabriel at a time when Gabriel reported retained earnings of $100,000. In each acquisition, the purchase price was equal to the proportionate net book value of the acquired company's shares, and the fair values of the assets and liabilities approximated their book values.

An analysis of the changes in retained earnings of the three companies during the year 2005 gives the following results:

	Anita Company	Brian Company	Gabriel Company
Retained earnings, Jan. 1, 2005	$ 742,000	$ 686,000	$ 475,000
Net income for the year	550,000	348,000	310,000
Dividends paid	(250,000)	(200,000)	(150,000)
Retained earnings, Dec. 31, 2005	$1,042,000	$ 834,000	$ 635,000

Gabriel sells some raw materials to Anita. After further processing and assembly, these parts are sold by Anita to Brian where they become a part of the finished products sold by Brian. Intercompany profits included in inventories at the beginning and end of the current year are estimated as follows:

	Jan. 1, 2005 Inventory	Dec. 31, 2005 Inventory
Intercompany profit included on sales from Gabriel to Anita	$70,000	$50,000
On sales from Anita to Brian	60,000	80,000

Brian also rents a building to Gabriel. Gabriel is paying $5,000 per month according to the lease contract. Anita carries its investments on a cost basis. Ignore the impact of income taxes.

Required:

a. Compute the consolidated net income for 2005.

b. Prepare a statement of consolidated retained earnings for 2005.

c. What change would there be in consolidated net income if the three companies had engaged in the same transactions, but all purchases, sales, and lending had been with firms outside the affiliated group? Give the amount of the difference and explain how it is derived.

[SMA, adapted]

P6–7

On June 30, 2001, Punt Corporation acquired 70% of the outstanding common shares of Slide Ltd. for $3,326,000 in cash plus Punt Corporation common shares estimated to have a fair market value of $1,200,000. On the date of acquisition, the fair market value and book value of each of Slide Ltd.'s assets were generally equal, except for inventory, which was undervalued by $225,000, and capital assets (net), which was overvalued by $1,000,000. The shareholders' equity of Slide at that time was $3,440,000, consisting of:

Common shares	$2,900,000
Retained earnings	540,000
	$3,440,000

Balance sheets at June 30, 2005, are as follows:

	Punt Corp.	Slide Ltd.
Assets		
Cash and marketable securities	$ 4,432,000	$ 321,000
Accounts and other receivables	2,153,000	950,000
Inventory	2,940,000	1,206,000
Capital assets (net)	17,064,000	7,161,000
Other long-term investments	3,038,000	2,240,000
Investment in Slide Ltd.	4,526,000	—
Total assets	$34,153,000	$11,878,000
Liabilities		
Current liabilities	$ 3,025,000	$ 2,090,000
Mortgage note payable	12,135,000	4,000,000
Total liabilities	15,160,000	6,090,000
Shareholders' equity		
Common shares	10,000,000	2,900,000
Retained earnings	8,993,000	2,888,000
Total shareholders' equity	18,993,000	5,788,000
Total liabilities and shareholders' equity	$34,153,000	$11,878,000

Additional Information:

1. Slide Ltd. had income of $1,460,000 for the year ended June 30, 2005. Dividends of $480,000 were declared during the fiscal year but were not paid until August 12, 2005.

2. Slide Ltd. has had an average inventory turnover of four times per year over the last decade.

3. The capital assets that were overvalued on the date of acquisition had a remaining useful life of 20 years.

4. Slide sold goods to Punt during the year ended June 30, 2004, at a gross profit margin of 25%. The opening inventory of Punt at July 1, 2004, included items purchased from Slide in the amount of $160,000. There were no sales from Slide to Punt during the year ended June 30, 2005.

5. Punt sold goods to Slide Ltd. during the current fiscal year at a gross profit margin of 30%. Of the $750,000 of sales, goods worth $200,000 were in Slide's closing inventory at June 30, 2005. None of these intercompany sales still in inventory had been paid for at the fiscal year-end.

6. Both companies follow the straight-line method for depreciating capital assets.

7. The controller of Punt has informed you that to date, there has been no impairment in goodwill.

Required:

Prepare the consolidated balance sheet for Punt Corporation and its subsidiary, Slide Ltd., at June 30, 2005.

[SMA, adapted]

P6–8

On January 1, 2001 ABC Limited purchased 90% of the outstanding common shares of XYZ Limited for $150,000. At that date, XYZ Limited's condensed balance sheet and fair values were as follows:

	Book Value	Fair Value
Cash	$20,000	$20,000
Land	40,000	60,000
Building (net)	40,000	50,000
	$100,000	
Liabilities	$20,000	20,000
Common shares	20,000	
Retained earnings	60,000	
	$100,000	

Assume a 10-year amortization period for any capital assets.

Required:

a. Assume the following information regarding net income and dividends for XYZ Limited:

Year	Net Income	Dividends
2001	$ 20,000	$ 4,000
2002	24,000	4,000
2003	18,000	4,000
2004	(20,000)	4,000*
2005	20,000	52,000

*The 2004 dividend was a stock dividend.

Calculate the balance in the investment account in ABC's books at the end of 2005 assuming that ABC uses the equity method of accounting in its books.

b. Assume that ABC uses the cost method of accounting for its investment. Prepare a journal entry or entries to reflect the information previously provided for 2004 and 2005.

[CGA–Canada]

P6–9

On April 2, 2004, Curry Ltd. acquired 40% of the outstanding common shares of Jasmine Ltd. by issuing one share of Curry plus $5 cash for each of Jasmine's shares acquired. At the time of purchase, Curry's shares were trading at $25 per share and Jasmine's shares were trading at $28. Jasmine had a total of 1 million shares outstanding.

At the date of acquistion, the shareholders' equity of Jasmine totalled $18,000,000. The fair values of Jasmine's assets and liabilities were the same as their net book values except for the following capital assets:

	Book Value	Fair Value
Land	$5,000,000	$8,000,000
Building	6,000,000	5,000,000
Equipment	5,000,000	7,000,000

The building and equipment have estimated remaining useful lives of ten years and five years respectively. Jasmine uses straight-line amortization.

For the year ended March 31, 2005, Jasmine reported net income of $1,500,000. Jasmine's dividend payout was 60% for fiscal 2005.

Required:

For the year ended March 31, 2005, compute: (1) Curry's equity in the earnings of Jasmine and (2) the balance of the investment account at the fiscal year-end, using the equity method. Provide supporting calculations.

P6–10

At the 2005 annual meeting for Jasmine's shareholders, Curry nominated seven directors for Jasmine's 12-person board of directors. After some negotiation, five of Curry's nominees were accepted onto the board. During fiscal year 2006 the following occurred:

1. Curry shifted a substantial amount of business to Jasmine. Jasmine became the major supplier of one of Curry's raw materials and had sales totalling $7,000,000 to Curry. Of that total $1,000,000 was in Curry's raw materials inventory at year-end. The other $6,000,000 had been utilized in finished goods, of which one-third was still in inventory on March 31, 2006.

2. Curry began selling some products to Cinnamon Corp. a wholly owned subsidiary of Jasmine. Fiscal 2006 sales totalled $2,500,000, all within the last two months of the year. At year-end, 60% of the sales were still in Cinnamon's inventory.

3. Operating results for fiscal 2006 were reported as follows:

	Curry	Jasmine
Sales	$ 80,000,000	$ 20,000,000
Cost of sales	(56,000,000)	(12,000,000)
	24,000,000	8,000,000
Operating expenses	(6,000,000)	(4,000,000)
Income tax expense	(7,200,000)	(1,600,000)
Net income	$ 10,800,000	$ 2,400,000

Required:

Using the information above and in **P6–9**, prepare a schedule(s) in which you:

a. Compute the amount of investment income that Curry should recognize in fiscal 2006 from its investment in Jasmine.

b. Compute the balance of Curry's investment account for its investment in Jasmine at March 31, 2006.

P6–11

On January 1, 2002, Porter Inc. purchased 80% of the outstanding voting shares of Sloan Ltd. for $3,000,000 in cash. On this date, Sloan had common shares outstanding in the amount of $2,200,000 and retained earnings of $1,100,000. The identifiable assets and liabilities of Sloan had fair values that were equal to their carrying values except for the following:

i. Capital assets (net) had a fair value $200,000 greater than its carrying value. The remaining useful life on January 1, 2002, was 20 years with no anticipated salvage value.

ii. Accounts receivable had a fair value $75,000 less than carrying value.

iii.Long-term liabilities had a fair value $62,500 less than carrying value. These liabilities mature on June 30, 2010.

It is the policy of Porter to test all goodwill balances for impairment on an annual basis. To date, there has been no impairment in goodwill. Both Porter and Sloan use the straight-line method for depreciation. Porter Inc. is a public company.

Additional Information:

1. Between January 1, 2002, and December 31, 2004, Sloan earned $345,000 and paid dividends of $115,000.

2. On January 1, 2004, Sloan sold a patent to Porter for $165,000. On this date, the patent had a carrying value on the books of Sloan of $185,000, and a remaining useful life of five years.

3. On September 1, 2004, Porter sold land to Sloan for $103,000. The land had a carrying value on the books of Porter of $82,000. Sloan still owned this land on December 31, 2005.

4. For the year ending December 31, 2005, the income statements revealed the following:

	Porter	Sloan
Total revenues	$2,576,000	$973,000
Cost of goods sold	1,373,000	467,000
Depreciation expense	483,000	176,000
Other expenses	352,000	153,000
Total expenses	2,208,000	796,000
Net income	$ 368,000	$177,000

Porter records its investment in Sloan using the cost method and includes dividend income from Sloan in its total revenues.

5. Porter and Sloan paid dividends of $125,000 and $98,000 respectively in 2005.

6. Sloan issued no common shares subsequent to January 1, 2002. Selected balance sheet accounts for the two companies at December 31, 2005, were:

	Porter	Sloan
Accounts receivable (net)	$ 987,000	$ 133,000
Inventories	1,436,000	787,000
Capital assets (net)	3,467,000	1,234,000
Patents (net)	263,000	—
Land	872,000	342,000
Long-term liabilities	1,876,000	745,000
Retained earnings	4,833,000	1,409,000

7. During 2005, Porter's merchandise sales to Sloan were $150,000. The unrealized profits in Sloan's inventory on January 1, and December 31, 2005, were $14,000 and $10,000, respectively. At December 31, 2005, Sloan still owed Porter $5,000 for merchandise purchases.

8. During 2005, Sloan's merchandise sales to Porter were $55,000. The unrealized profits in Porter's inventory on January 1, and December 31, 2005, were $1,500 and $2,500 respectively. At December 31, 2005, Porter still owed Sloan $2,000 for merchandise purchases.

Required:

a. Compute the balances that would appear in the consolidated balance sheet of Porter and Sloan as at December 31, 2005, for the following:

1. Patent (net)

2. Non-controlling interest

3. Retained earnings

b. Porter has decided not to prepare consolidated financial statements and will report its investment in Sloan by the equity method. Calculate the investment income that would be disclosed in the income statement of Porter for the year ended December 31, 2005.

[SMA]

P6–12

On January 1, 1998, the Partial Company acquired 80% of the outstanding voting shares of the Sum Company for $3,900,000 in cash. On this date, the Sum Company had $2,000,000 in common shares outstanding and $2,000,000 in retained earnings. Any excess of cost over book value is to be recorded in the consolidated financial statements as goodwill and is tested annually for impairment. On December 31, 2005, the balance sheets of the two companies are as follows:

Balance Sheets
December 31, 2005

	Partial Company	Sum Company
Cash	$ 3,000,000	$ 1,000,000
Accounts receivable	7,000,000	2,000,000
Inventories	4,100,000	3,000,000
Investment in Sum	3,900,000	—
Capital assets (net)	7,000,000	5,000,000
Total assets	$25,000,000	$11,000,000
Liabilities	$ 5,000,000	$ 3,000,000
Common shares	7,000,000	2,000,000
Retained earnings	13,000,000	6,000,000
Total equities	$25,000,000	$11,000,000

Additional Information:

1. Sum Company sells merchandise to the Partial Company at a price that provides Sum with a gross margin of 50% of the sales price. During 2005, these sales amounted to $1,000,000. The December 31, 2005, inventories of the Partial Company contain $200,000 of these purchases while the December 31, 2004, inventories of Partial contained $100,000 in merchandise purchased from Sum.

2. At the end of 2005, Partial owes Sum $60,000 for merchandise purchased on account. The account is non-interest-bearing.

3. On December 31, 2002, the Partial Company sold equipment to the Sum Company for $550,000. At the time of the sale, the equipment had a net book value in Partial's records of $450,000. The remaining useful life of the asset on this date was 10 years.

4. No impairment in goodwill since January 1, 1998.

Required:

Prepare a consolidated balance sheet for the Partial Company and its subsidiary, Sum Company, at December 31, 2005. Ignore the impact of income taxes.

[SMA, adapted]

P6–13

In January 2003, Paris Ink Company (Paris) purchased 80% of the common shares of Slade Paper Ltd. (Slade) by issuing common shares worth $800,000. At that date, Slade's common shares and retained earnings totalled $250,000 and $340,000 respectively. The net book values and fair values of the net identifiable assets of Slade were the same except for the following:

1. the fair market value (FMV) of inventory was greater than book value by $50,000

2. the FMV of capital assets had replacement cost that exceeded net book value (NBV) by $120,000, although net realizable value exceeded NBV by only $60,000 (management planned to retain the capital assets throughout their remaining useful life of 12 years), and

3. although the NBV of Slade's bonds payable was $400,000, the FMV was $460,000, due to a decline in the interest rates since the bonds were originally

issued. The bonds payable mature on December 31, 2008, and have a nominal rate of interest of 12%. The companies use straight-line amortization for bond premiums and discounts.

The financial statements for Paris and Slade for the year ended December 31, 2005 are presented in Exhibit B. Additional information on transactions between Paris and Slade is presented in Exhibit C.

EXHIBIT B	FINANCIAL STATEMENTS

Income Statements
For the Year Ended December 31, 2005

	Paris	Slade
Sales	$3,850,000	$1,650,000
Cost of goods sold	2,550,000	1,120,000
Gross profit	1,300,000	530,000
Expenses		
Administration & selling	550,000	384,000
Amortization	136,000	74,000
Interest	—	56,000
	686,000	514,000
Other income		
Interest & dividends	76,000	4,000
Gain on sale of land	—	100,000
	76,000	104,000
Income before income taxes	690,000	120,000
Income tax expense	260,000	30,000
Net income	$ 430,000	$ 90,000

Balance Sheets
As at December 31, 2005

	Paris	Slade
Assets		
Current assets		
Cash	$ 45,000	$ 80,000
Accounts receivable	655,000	455,000
Inventory	420,000	350,000
Marketable securities	380,000	45,000
Due from Slade	200,000	—
	1,700,000	930,000
Capital assets—net	1,450,000	690,000
Investment in Slade	800,000	—
	$3,950,000	$1,620,000
Liabilities		
Current liabilities		
Accounts payable	$ 665,000	$ 280,000
Note payable to Paris	—	200,000
	665,000	480,000
Bonds payable	—	400,000
Shareholders' Equity		
Common shares	2,500,000	250,000
Retained earnings	785,000	490,000
	$3,950,000	$1,620,000

EXHIBIT C

Additional Information:

1. On July 1, 2005, Paris advanced Slade $200,000, due on July 1, 2006. Interest of 8% is due at maturity.

2. Intercompany sales from Slade to Paris were as follows for 2003–2005:

	2003	2004	2005
Sales	$200,000	$240,000	$250,000
Gross profit margin	32.00%	33.33%	30.00%
Amount remaining in inventory at year-end	$ 60,000	$ 75,000	$100,000

All amounts in closing inventory at the end of each year were sold during the first four months of the following year. Round to the nearest five dollars if necessary.

3. On March 1, 2005, Slade sold land to Paris for $300,000. The original cost of the land was $200,000. Assume this transaction was taxed at the company's normal tax rate.

4. During 2005, Paris sold inventory to Slade for $108,000, which represented a markup of 35% above cost. At December 31, 2005, 20% of these goods remained in inventory.

5. During 2005, Paris paid dividends of $250,000 and Slade paid dividends of $50,000.

6. Paris and Slade pay taxes at 40% and 25% rates, respectively.

[ICAO, adapted]

Required:

a. Calculate the carrying value of the goodwill on the consolidated financial statements of Paris Ink Company at December 31, 2005. Paris tests goodwill for impairment on an annual basis.

b. Prepare a consolidated income statement for Paris Ink Company for the year ended December 31, 2005.

c. Calculate the following balances for Paris Ink Company's consolidated balance sheet as at December 31, 2005:

i. inventory

ii. non-controlling interest

P6–14

Pop Company acquired 70% of Son Limited on January 1, 2004, for $345,000. On the acquisition date, common shares and retained earnings of Son Limited were $100,000 and $200,000 respectively. The fair market values of Son's identifiable net assets were equivalent to their book value except for capital assets, which were undervalued by $50,000, and long-term debt, which was overvalued by $100,000. The undervalued capital assets have a remaining life of 10 years. The long-term debt matures on December 31, 2008. Any goodwill is tested for impairment on an annual basis. Both companies use the straight-line method of amortization.

Intercompany transactions include the downstream sale of a capital asset in 2004, which included an unrealized profit of $30,000 to be amortized over five years. During 2005, there was an intercompany upstream sale of land for $120,000. The original cost of the land was $95,000.

For the year ended December 31, 2005, Pop Company had net income of $244,000 and declared dividends of $10,000. Son Limited had 2005 net income of $85,000 and paid dividends of $10,000. All dividends have been declared and paid on December 31. Pop Company uses the cost method to account for its investment in Son Limited. Shown below are the balance sheets for the parent company and its subsidiary on December 31, 2005.

Balance Sheets
At December 31, 2005

	Pop Company	Son Limited
Current assets	$1,200,000	$250,000
Investment in Son Limited	345,000	—
Capital assets—net	900,000	450,000
Goodwill	—	—
Total assets	$2,445,000	$700,000
Current liabilities	$1,045,000	$ 75,000
Long-term debt	500,000	200,000
Minority interest	—	—
Common shares	500,000	100,000
Retained earnings	400,000	325,000
Total liabilities and equities	$2,445,000	$700,000

Required:

a. Determine consolidated net income for the year ended December 31, 2005. Show all your calculations.

b. Calculate the balances of the following accounts as they would appear in the consolidated balance sheet on December 31, 2005:

1. Capital assets, net

2. Non-controlling interest

3. Retained earnings

c. Prepare the required December 31, 2005, journal entry to eliminate the Investment in Son Limited account.

[CGA–Canada]

P6–15

Note: All dollar amounts in the question are in 000s.

On December 31, 1999, Handy Company (Handy) purchased 70% of the outstanding common shares of Dandy Limited (Dandy) for $7,000. On that date, Dandy's shareholders' equity consisted of common shares of $250 and retained earnings of $4,500. The financial statements for Handy and Dandy for 2005 were as follows:

Balance Sheet
December 31, 2005

	Handy	Dandy
Cash	$ 1,340	$ 780
Accounts receivable	2,800	1,050
Inventory	3,400	2,580
Capital assets—net	4,340	3,010
Investment in Dandy	7,000	0
Total	$18,880	$ 7,420
Current liabilities	$ 4,200	$ 540
Long-term liabilities	3,100	1,230
Common shares	1,000	250
Retained earnings	10,580	5,400
Total	$18,880	$ 7,420

Statement of Income and Retained Earnings
Year ended December 31, 2005

	Handy	Dandy
Sales	$21,900	$ 7,440
Cost of sales	14,800	3,280
Gross profit	7,100	4,160
Other revenue	1,620	0
Amortization expense	(840)	(420)
Other expenses	(5,320)	(2,040)
Income before income taxes	2,560	1,700
Income tax expense	800	680
Net income	1,760	1,020
Retained earnings, beg. year	10,420	5,180
Dividends paid	(1,600)	(800)
Retained earnings, end year	$10,580	$ 5,400

Other Information:

1. In negotiating the purchase price at the date of acquisition, it was agreed that the fair values of all of Dandy's assets and liabilities were equal to their book values, except for the following:

Asset	Book Value	Fair Value
Inventory	$2,100	$2,200
Equipment	2,500	3,000

2. Both companies use FIFO to account for their inventory and the straight-line method for amortizing their capital assets. Dandy's capital assets had a remaining useful life of ten years at the acquisition date.

3. Each year, goodwill is evaluated to determine if there has been permanent impairment. It was determined that goodwill on the consolidated balance sheet should be reported at $1,100 on December 31, 2004, and at $1,030 on December 31, 2005.

4. During 2005, inventory sales from Dandy to Handy were $10,000. Handy's inventories contained merchandise purchased from Dandy for $2,000 on

December 31, 2004 and $2,500 at December 31, 2005. Dandy earns a gross margin of 40% on its intercompany sales.

5. On January 1, 2001, Handy sold some equipment to Dandy for $1,000 and recorded a gain of $200 before taxes. This equipment had a remaining useful life of eight years at the time of the purchase by Dandy.

6. Handy charges $50 per month to Dandy for consulting services.

7. Handy uses the cost method in accounting for its long-term investment.

8. Both companies pay taxes at the rate of 40%. Ignore future taxes when allocating and amortizing the purchase price.

Required:

a. Prepare a consolidated statement of income for the year ended December 31, 2005.

b. Calculate consolidated retained earnings at January 1, 2005, and then prepare a consolidated statement of retained earnings for the year ended December 31, 2005.

c. Explain how the historical cost principle supports the adjustments made on consolidation when there has been an intercompany sale of equipment.

[CGA]

P6–16

On January 1, 2000, Pastel Corporation acquired 70% of the outstanding shares of Summer Company for $85,000 cash. On that date, Summer Company had $35,000 of common shares outstanding and $25,000 of retained earnings. On January 1, 2000, the book values of each of Summer Company's identifiable assets and liabilities were equal to their fair value except for the following:

	Book Value	Fair Value
Inventory	$25,000	$35,000
Equipment	10,000	30,000

The equipment had a useful life of 10 years as at January 1, 2000, and all inventory was sold during 2000. The following are the separate entity financial statements for Pastel and Summer at December 31, 2005:

Balance Sheet
December 31, 2005

	Pastel	Summer
Cash	$120,000	$20,000
Accounts receivable	90,000	65,000
Inventory	250,000	90,000
Capital assets—net	225,000	150,000
Investment in Summer	85,000	0
Total	$770,000	$325,000
Accounts payable	$230,000	$180,000
Future income taxes	70,000	60,000
	300,000	240,000
Common shares	200,000	35,000
Retained earnings	270,000	50,000
Total	$770,000	$325,000

Statement of Income and Retained Earnings
Year ended December 31, 2005

	Pastel	Summer
Sales	$750,000	$600,000
Cost of goods sold	(500,000)	(450,000)
Gross margin	250,000	150,000
Dividend income	21,000	0
Gain on sale of trademark	0	12,000
Amortization expense	(35,000)	(20,000)
Other expenses	(86,000)	(62,000)
Income tax expense	(60,000)	(32,000)
Net income	90,000	48,000
Retained earnings, beg. year	180,000	32,000
Dividends paid	(0)	(30,000)
Retained earnings, end year	$270,000	$ 50,000

Additional Information:

1. On January 1, 2002, Pastel sold Summer a trademark with a net book value of $20,000 for cash consideration of $28,000. The trademark has an indefinite useful life. On July 1, 2005, Summer sold the trademark to an unrelated company for cash consideration of $40,000.

2. Summer sells goods to Pastel at 25% above cost. Total sales from Summer to Pastel during 2005 were $50,000, of which $20,000 remained in Pastel's inventory at year end. Pastel still owed Summer $18,000 for this inventory at December 31, 2005. In 2004, total sales from Summer to Pastel were $40,000, of which $10,000 remained in Pastel's inventory at year end.

3. Pastel uses the cost method to account for its investment in Summer. Both companies pay taxes at a rate of 40%, and have done so since 1999. None of the transactions detailed above are considered capital gains for tax purposes. Ignore future taxes when calculating the purchase price discrepancy.

4. Each year, goodwill is evaluated to determine if there has been permanent impairment. To date there has been no impairment in value.

Required:

a. Prepare a calculation for the purchase price discrepancy and goodwill as at January 1, 2000.

b. Prepare a consolidated statement of income for the year ended December 31, 2005.

c. What would the balance be for each of the consolidated balance sheet accounts as at December 31, 2005?
   i. accounts receivable
   ii. inventory
   iii. equipment
   iv. non-controlling interest

[CGA]

P6–17

Paper Corporation purchased 70% of the outstanding shares of Sand Limited on January 1, 2002, at a cost of $80,000. Paper has always used the cost method to account for its investments. On January 1, 2002, Sand had common shares of $50,000 and retained earnings of $30,000, and fair values were equal to carrying value for all of its net assets except for inventory (fair value was $9,000 less than book value) and equipment (fair value was $24,000 greater than book value). The equipment had an estimated remaining life of six years on January 1, 2002.

The following are the separate-entity financial statements of Paper and Sand at December 31, 2005:

Balance Sheet
December 31, 2005

	Paper	Sand
Cash	$ 0	$ 10,000
Accounts receivable	40,000	30,000
Note receivable	0	40,000
Inventory	66,000	44,000
Capital assets—net	220,000	76,000
Land	150,000	30,000
Investment in Sand	80,000	0
Total	$556,000	$230,000
Accounts payable	$140,000	$ 60,000
Notes payable	40,000	0
Common shares	150,000	50,000
Retained earnings	226,000	120,000
Total	$556,000	$230,000

Statement of Income and Retained Earnings
Year ended December 31, 2005

	Paper	Sand
Sales	$798,000	$300,000
Management fee revenue	24,000	0
Investment income	14,000	3,600
Gain on sale of land	0	20,000
	836,000	323,600
Cost of sales	480,000	200,000
Amortization expense	40,000	12,000
Interest expense	10,000	0
Other expenses	106,000	31,600
Income tax expense	80,000	32,000
	716,000	275,600
Net income	$120,000	$ 48,000
Retained earnings, beg. year	106,000	92,000
Dividends paid	(0)	(20,000)
Retained earnings, end year	$226,000	$120,000

Additional Information:

1. During 2005, Sand made a cash payment of $2,000 per month to Paper for management fees, which is included in Sand's "other expenses."

2. During 2005, Paper made intercompany sales of $100,000 to Sand. The December 31, 2005, inventory of Sand contained goods purchased from Paper amounting to $30,000. These sales had a gross profit of 35%.

3. On April 1, 2005, Paper acquired land from Sand for $40,000. This land had been recorded on Sand's books at a net book value of $20,000. Paper paid for the land by signing a $40,000 note payable to Sand, bearing interest at 8%. Interest for 2005 was paid by Paper in cash on December 31, 2005. This land was still being held by Paper on December 31, 2005.

4. The fair value of the consolidated goodwill remained unchanged from January 1, 2002, to July 1, 2005. On July 1, 2005, a valuation was performed, indicating that the fair value of consolidated goodwill was $3,500.

5. Sand and Paper pay taxes at a 40% rate. Assume that none of the gains or losses were capital gains or losses. Ignore the impact of future taxes for all transactions.

Required:

a. Prepare a calculation of goodwill and any unamortized purchase price discrepancy as at December 31, 2005.

b. Prepare Paper's consolidated income statement for the year ended December 31, 2005.

c. Calculate the following balances that would appear on Paper's consolidated balance sheet as at December 31, 2005:

   i. inventory
   ii. land
   iii. notes payable
   iv. non-controlling interest
   v. common shares

[CGA]

P6–18

On January 1, 1999, Pen Company purchased 80% of the outstanding voting shares of Silk Company for $300,000. Silk's assets and liabilities all had fair values that were equal to their carrying values. The $80,000 excess of purchase price over 80% of the book values of Silk Company's net assets was allocated to goodwill. Goodwill is tested for impairment on an annual basis. Between January 1, 1999, and January 1, 2005, Silk Company earned $200,000 and paid dividends of $40,000. Both companies use the straight-line method to calculate depreciation and amortization.

Additional Information:

1. On January 1, 1995, Silk Company purchased a machine for $100,000 that had an estimated useful life of 20 years; on January 1, 2000, Silk Company sold the machine to Pen Company for $60,000. The estimated useful life of the machine remains unchanged at a total of 20 years (15 years from January 1, 2000).

2. During 2005, Silk Company had sales of merchandise in the amount of $400,000 to Pen Company, of which $60,000 remains in the December 31, 2005, inventories of Pen Company. Pen Company had no sales to Silk Company during 2005, but had sales of $200,000 to Silk Company in 2004. Of these sales, $40,000 remained in the December 31, 2004, inventories of Silk Company. Intercompany sales are priced to provide the selling company with a 40% gross profit on sales prices.

3. On September 1, 2005, Silk Company sold a piece of land to Pen Company for $50,000. The land had been purchased for $35,000. The gain on this land is not considered extraordinary for reporting purposes.

4. During 2005, Silk Company declared dividends of $6,000 and Pen Company declared dividends of $35,000.

5. During 2005, Silk Company paid Pen Company $10,000 in management fees.

6. On July 1, 2005, Pen Company lent Silk Company $100,000 for five years at an annual interest rate of 10%. Interest is paid on July 1 of each year for which the loan is outstanding.

7. To date, there has been no impairment in the value of goodwill.

Pen Company carries its investment in Silk Company by the cost method. On this date, the income statements of Pen Company and Silk Company for the year ending December 31, 2005, are as follows:

	Pen	Silk
Merchandise sales	$3,000,000	$2,000,000
Investment income	60,000	—
Other revenue	50,000	70,000
Total revenues	3,110,000	2,070,000
Cost of goods sold	1,800,000	1,400,000
Depreciation expense	400,000	400,000
Selling and administrative	500,000	200,000
Total expenses	2,700,000	2,000,000
Income before extraordinary items	410,000	70,000
Loss on sales of investments	—	(26,000)
Net income (loss)	$ 410,000	$ 44,000

Required:

a. Prepare the consolidated income statement for Pen Company and its subsidiary, Silk Company, for the year ending December 31, 2005.

b. Assume that Pen Company prepares separate-entity statements for its bank and uses the equity method of reporting its investment in Silk. Provide a detailed calculation of Pen Company's investment income for the year ending December 31, 2005.

[SMA, adapted]

P6–19

On April 1, 2005, Marsh Ltd. purchased 25% of the outstanding common shares of King Corp. for $2,000,000. The book value of King's net assets was $16,000,000, an amount that also approximated their fair value. For the year ended December 31, 2005, King reported net income of $800,000 and Marsh reported net income of $10,200,000. King paid dividends of $50,000 in each of the first two quarters of 2005, and $75,000 in each of the last two quarters. There were no intercompany transactions during the year. Both companies generate their incomes fairly evenly throughout the year. Assume no goodwill impairment.

Required:

Compute the amounts that would appear on Marsh's 2005 income statement as income from investment in King, and the balance of the investment account on the December 31, 2005, balance sheet, assuming that Marsh uses:

a. the cost method

b. the equity method

P6–20

[Copyright © 1984 by the American Institute of Certified Public Accountants Inc. Reprinted with permission.]

North Company has supplied you with information regarding two investments that were made during 2005 as follows:

1. On January 1, 2005, North purchased for cash 40% of the 500,000 shares of voting common shares of Young Company for $2,800,000, representing 40% of the net worth of Young. The book value of Young's net assets was $6,000,000 on January 1, 2005, and this amount approximated the fair value of the net assets. Young's net income for the year ended December 31, 2005, was $900,000. Young paid dividends of $0.80 per share in 2005. The market value of Young's common shares was $15 per share on December 31, 2005. North exercised significant influence over the operating and financial policies of Young.

2. On July 1, 2005, North purchased for cash 20,000 shares representing 5% of the voting common shares of the Mak Company for $500,000. Mak's net income for the six months ended December 31, 2005, was $400,000, and for the year ended December 31, 2005, it was $650,000. Mak paid dividends of $0.40 per share each quarter during 2005 to shareholders of record on the last day of each quarter. The market value of Mak's common shares was $30 per share on January 1, 2005, and $35 per share on December 31, 2005.

Required:

As a result of these two investments, determine the following:

a. What should be the balance in the investment account for North at December 31, 2005?

b. What should be the investment income reported by North for the year ended December 31, 2005?

Show all supporting calculations. The equity method of recording investments is used when appropriate for reporting purposes.

[AICPA, adapted]

P6–21

King Oil Company, to maintain closer ties with associated companies in the oil business, decided to purchase holdings of common shares in several companies. The following is a list of activities associated with these acquisitions during 2005.

February 15	Acquired 80,000 shares of Lub Oil Co. at $8 per share representing 70% of the outstanding shares. At date of acquisition, book value of the Lub Oil Co.'s net assets was $800,000. Assets were considered to be valued at market.
April 13	Acquired 140,000 shares of Richman Refineries at $11 per share representing 60% of the outstanding shares. The purchase price corresponds to the underlying book value.
May 17	Acquired 50,000 shares of Discovery Co. Ltd. at $5 per share representing 2% of the outstanding shares.
June 30	Lub Oil Co. announced a loss of $50,000 for the first six months of 2005.
	Richman Refineries announced earnings of $120,000 for the first six months of 2005 and declared a dividend of $0.10 per share.
August 15	Dividend received from Richman Refineries.
October 11	Dividend of $0.05 per share received from Discovery Co. Ltd. with a statement of earnings for the six months ending September 30 indicating net earnings of $60,000.
December 31	Lub Oil Co. announced a loss of $40,000 for the year.
	Richman Refineries announced earnings of $200,000 for the year, including an extraordinary gain of $40,000.
	Discovery Co. Ltd. announced earnings of $90,000 for the nine months ending December 31.

Additional Information:

To date, there has been no goodwill impairment.

Required:

a. Investments in shares could be recorded and/or reported using either the equity method or the cost method. Distinguish between the two methods, indicating under what circumstances each method should be used.

b. Prepare journal entries to record the above transactions in the books of King Oil Company, assuming the use of the equity method of accounting where appropriate for reporting purposes.

[SMA, adapted]

P6–22

Slater Company purchased 30% of the outstanding voting shares of Rogan Company for $1,500,000 in cash on January 1, 2003. On that date, Rogan Company's shareholders' equity was made up of common shares of $3 million and retained earnings of $1 million. There were no differences between the carrying values and the fair values of any of its net identifiable assets or liabilities. The net income and dividends declared and paid by Rogan Company for the two years subsequent to its acquisition were as follows:

	2003	2004
Net income (loss)	$(200,000)	$180,000
Dividends	50,000	60,000

The income statements for the year ending December 31, 2005, prior to the recognition of any investment income, for Slater and Rogan Companies are as follows:

	Slater	Rogan
Sales	$3,000,000	$550,000
Other revenues	200,000	—
Total revenues	3,200,000	550,000
Cost of goods sold	1,500,000	300,000
Other expenses	300,000	50,000
Total expenses	1,800,000	350,000
Income before extraordinary items	1,400,000	200,000
Extraordinary loss	—	30,000
Net income	$1,400,000	$170,000

During 2005, Slater Company declared and paid dividends of $120,000, while Rogan Company declared and paid dividends of $80,000. Rogan Company declares and pays its dividends on December 31 of each year.

Required:

a. Assume that Slater can exercise significant influence over the affairs of Rogan. Provide the following:

1. The income statement of Slater Company, including recognition of any investment income or loss, for the year ending December 31, 2005.

2. The balance in the investment in Rogan Company account as it would appear on the December 31, 2005, balance sheet of Slater Company.

Assume no impairment in the value of goodwill.

b. Assume that Slater cannot exercise significant influence over the affairs of Rogan. Provide the journal entry of Slater Company related to its investment in Rogan Company for 2005.

[SMA, adapted]

Appendix 6A

Preferred and Restricted Shares of Investee Corporations

Introduction

Throughout our discussion of intercorporate investments, we have dealt entirely with voting common shares. In all of the examples in the previous chapters, none of the investments was in senior or preferred shares, and none of the investee corporations (either subsidiaries or significantly influenced companies) had preferred shares in their capital structure.

The percentage of ownership interest affects the consolidation process in several ways, including:

- the proportion of the fair-value increments of Sub's assets that is included on Parent's balance sheet
- the amount assigned to non-controlling interest
- the amount of the purchase price assigned to goodwill, and
- the amount of consolidated net income.

Consolidated net income (and equity-basis net income) is affected because the allocation of the purchase price to fair-value increments and goodwill affects annual amortization expense.

This section discusses the effect of preferred and restricted shares on the investor's reporting of intercorporate investments. First, we will examine the effect that investee preferred shares have on the investor's ownership interest. Then we will briefly look at the accounting for an investment in preferred shares. After discussing preferred shares, we will look at *restricted common shares*—those that have reduced (or non-existent) voting rights.

Effect of preferred shares on investor's ownership interest

It is not unusual for a subsidiary or a significantly influenced investee corporation to have preferred shares outstanding. The parent or investor corporation may not own all or any of the preferred shares. For example, one company may acquire 100% of the common shares of another, while third parties continue to own the subsidiary's preferred shares. How does the existence of the subsidiary's preferred shares affect the parent company's ownership interest? Can the parent be said to own 100% of the subsidiary even though the parent does not own the preferred shares?

A simple example will help to demonstrate the issue. Suppose that Sub has total shareholders' equity of $1,000,000, consisting of $400,000 in preferred shares (redemption value) and $600,000 in common shares and retained earnings. Assume further that Parent buys all of Sub's common shares for $1,200,000. What is Parent's ownership interest in Sub?

Two alternatives seem to exist. First, Parent can be said to own 100% of Sub because Parent owns 100% of the voting shares and can presumably elect most or all of the board of directors. Alternatively, it might be argued that Parent owns shares representing only $600,000 of the $1,000,000 total shareholders' equity, or 60%.

However, the non-controlling interest in preferred shares is not a residual interest. Instead, it is a fixed amount determined by call or redemption value of the preferred shares, plus any dividends in arrears.

Increases in the value of Sub's assets increase only the common share equity—preferred shareholders do not benefit, except perhaps by the reduced risk of dividend non-payment. Therefore, Parent's purchase of 100% of the Sub common shares should be viewed as an acquisition of 100% of the Sub net assets, less the claim on those assets represented by the preferred shares.

Exhibit 6–11 shows the assignment of the purchase price, assuming that the fair value of Sub's net assets is $1,350,000. The preferred share equity is subtracted in order to find the net asset value for common equity. The fair value of the preferred equity is determined by the preferred shareholders' claim on assets. This claim is measured by the shares' call price or redemption value plus dividends in arrears, if any. Call prices are usually higher than par values or issue prices, and thus fair value is likely to be higher than book value.

In Exhibit 6–11, the preferred equity fair value of $440,000 is subtracted from the net asset fair value of $1,350,000. The result, $910,000, is the fair value of the net assets *acquired through purchase of the common shares*. The residual purchase price is allocated to goodwill: $1,200,000 − $910,000 = $290,000.

Investment in preferred shares

In the preceding section, we assumed that outsiders owned all the preferred shares. However, the parent may own some of the subsidiary's preferred shares as well as its common shares.

On the books of the parent, the cost of the shares will be debited to an investment account. When consolidated statements are prepared, the parent's investment account for the preferred shares must be eliminated, as must the portion of the subsidiary preferred share equity that is owned by the parent.

Similarly, preferred dividends paid by a subsidiary to its parent are intercompany transfers and will be eliminated on consolidation. Consolidated earnings (or the equity-basis earnings) must include the parent's share of the subsidiary's net income after provision only for the portion of preferred dividends paid or payable to outside shareholders.

Any premium on the shares that was paid by the parent will be included in the investment account. However, that premium will not be a part of preferred

---

EXHIBIT 6–11 ALLOCATION OF PURCHASE PRICE—PARENT BUYS 100% OF SUB COMMON SHARES BUT NO PREFERRED

	Sub		Fair value increment
	Book value	Fair value	
Purchase price	$1,200,000	$1,200,000	
Net assets	$1,000,000	1,350,000	$ 350,000
Less preferred share equity	400,000	440,000	40,000
Common share equity acquired	600,000	910,000	310,000
Goodwill		$ 290,000	290,000
Purchase price discrepancy	$ 600,000		$ 600,000

shareholders' equity in the subsidiary's accounts because the preferred shareholders have an equity in the subsidiary only to the extent of their redemption value.

Intercompany holdings of preferred shares must be eliminated upon consolidation. When there is a difference in the preferred share carrying value, the worksheet elimination entry must be balanced by a debit or credit for the difference.

Any difference between (1) the parent's cost of the investment and (2) the redemption value of the preferred shares is charged or credited to the shareholders' equity on the consolidated balance sheet, generally to a contributed surplus account for that class of shares, if one exists. Otherwise, the charge or credit is to retained earnings. In effect, the shares are treated as having been retired.

Restricted shares

Much of Canadian enterprise is conducted by family controlled corporations. As these corporations grow, it frequently becomes impossible to finance them adequately without going to the public equity markets. If shares are sold to the public, however, the controlling shareholders risk losing control of "their" companies.

To raise equity capital without losing control, family corporations issue **restricted shares** to the public. A restricted share is just like a regular common share, except that it either has no voting rights or has sharply reduced voting rights. Restricted shares usually share equally with regular shares in dividends and in assets upon dissolution, although they can be subordinated in those regards as well.

There are well over 200 listings of restricted shares on the Toronto Stock Exchange. A prime example is Canadian Tire Corporation, whose 77 million Class A non-voting shares comprise about 96% of the outstanding shares but are permitted to elect a maximum of 20% of the Canadian Tire directors.

As we described above, a prime motivation for issuing restricted shares is to raise equity capital while maintaining control in the hands of the original group of shareholders. Earnings usually accrue to all shareholders equally, but the voting power resides wholly or mainly in the hands of a few. This situation raises the question as to how to treat restricted shares in consolidated financial statements when a parent controls the voting shares but does not own the restricted shares. There are two separate issues: (1) control and (2) allocation of consolidated earnings.

Control Control exists when the investor has sufficient votes (or a combination of votes and convertible securities that can be converted into voting shares) to elect a majority of the board of directors and thereby determine the strategic policies of the corporation. If an investee has restricted shares, control exists when the investor has more than half the votes, regardless of the proportion of shares owned.

For example, suppose that The Odyssey Inc. has 1,000 shares of regular common shares outstanding and 10,000 restricted shares. The regular shares have ten votes each, while the restricted shares have one vote each. The total number of votes available is 20,000: 10,000 for the regular shares plus 10,000 for the restricted shares. A takeover could occur when a buyer acquires 10,001 of the available 20,000 votes. It doesn't matter whether the buyer acquires all of the regular shares plus one restricted share, or 10,000 restricted shares plus one regular share, or any linear combination thereof.

Restricted shares sometimes have a **coattail provision**, which is a provision that comes into effect when a buyer attempts to buy control of a company. If a control block is about to change hands, then the restricted shares may become fully voting shares for limited purposes. For example, Bombardier Inc. has Class A shares that have ten votes per share and Class B shares that have one vote per share. Class B shares are convertible to Class A on a one-for-one basis at the option of the holder in the event that the controlling shareholders (the Bombardier family) accept an offer to acquire substantially all of the Class A shares. In such an event, therefore, the Class B shareholders can participate equally with the Class A shareholders if control of the company changes.

The nature of coattail provisions differs significantly between companies, and they do not exist at all for many (if not most) companies. But when coattail provisions exist, the number of shares that must be *held* in order to maintain control is quite different from the number of shares that must be *purchased* in order to acquire control.

Allocation of earnings The second issue is what proportion of earnings is attributable to the non-controlling interest. If the restricted shares participate equally with the regular shares in dividends, then the non-controlling interest's share of the subsidiary's earnings is simply the proportion of shares owned relative to the total number of shares outstanding, regular and restricted.

For example, The Odyssey Inc. has a total of 11,000 shares outstanding in the two classes. If the common shares are equal in dividend participation and an acquirer obtains 1,000 regular shares plus one restricted share, then the ownership percentage for consolidation purposes is 1,001/11,000 or about 9%. If, on the other hand, control was obtained by buying all 10,000 restricted shares plus one regular share, then the ownership percentage is 10,001/11,000, or about 91%. It is obvious, therefore, that it is quite possible to have control of a subsidiary while still having a non-controlling interest of over 90%!

In summary, the key points to remember are that (1) when determining control, count *votes*, but (2) when determining non-controlling interest, look at *participation in earnings and dividends*. The two measures are not the same when restricted shares exist in an investee corporation.

SELF-STUDY PROBLEM 6–3

The capital structure of 212°F Corporation contains the following amounts of share capital:

Preferred shares—1,000,000 issued and outstanding	
$8 dividend per year, cumulative, non-participating, non-voting	$ 10,000,000
Class A common shares—600,000 issued and outstanding	30,000,000
Class B common shares—50,000 issued and outstanding	50,000
Retained earnings	84,950,000
Total shareholders' equity	$125,000,000

The preferred shares do not participate in dividends beyond their designated $8 per share. The call price for the preferred is $12 per share. The Class A common shares have one vote per share. The Class B common shares carry 15 votes per share. The two classes of common shares participate equally in dividends on a share-per-share basis.

Numbers Incorporated holds the following quantities of 212°F shares:

- 40,000 Class A common shares, purchased at $75 per share, and

- 44,000 Class B common shares, purchased at $85 per share.

Required:

a. What proportion of votes is held by Numbers? Does Numbers control 212°F?

b. When Numbers reports its investment in 212°F by consolidation or on the equity basis, as appropriate, what is Numbers' total ownership share?

c. What is the amount of the non-controlling interest in 212°F?

REVIEW QUESTIONS

6–14 Corporation S has 100,000 shares of common stock and 100,000 shares of non-voting preferred stock outstanding. Corporation P owns 60,000 of S's common shares and 45,000 of S's preferred shares. When P prepares its financial statements, what proportion of S's earnings will be reflected in P's net income?

6–15 S Corporation has 10,000 shares of common stock and 10,000 shares of non-voting preferred stock outstanding. The preferred stock carries a cumulative dividend of $10 per share per year. S reported net income of $600,000 for the year just ended. If P Corporation owns 7,000 of S's common shares and 2,000 of S's preferred shares, how much of S's net income will be included in P's net income for the year just ended?

6–16 When a subsidiary has both common and preferred shares outstanding, how is the parent's proportionate ownership interest determined?

6–17 If a parent company has purchased some of its subsidiary's preferred shares at a price higher than the carrying value of the shares on the subsidiary's books, how is the difference treated when the parent prepares consolidated financial statements?

6–18 What is a *restricted share*?

6–19 Irene Ltd. has 500,000 common shares outstanding, consisting of 100,000 regular shares with ten votes each and 400,000 restricted shares with one vote each. The shares participate equally in dividends on a share-for-share basis. Gordon Inc. owns 165,000 of the 500,000 shares, 65,000 regular plus 100,000 restricted.

  a. Does Gordon control Irene?

  b. What proportion of Irene's earnings would be included in Gordon's equity-basis earnings?

6–20 What is a *coattail provision*?

CASES

CASE 6–A1   A La Mode Inc.

A La Mode Inc. (ALM) is a retailer of women and children's clothing with stores all across Canada. ALM has been in operation for the last 35 years and is a public company with a year-end of January 31.

Currently, Mr. Jones and Mr. Grenier each own approximately 35% of the voting shares of ALM; the remaining outstanding shares are widely held. They founded ALM in the 1970s, when they were both in their late twenties. Their first store sold clothing for the working woman. It took only a few years until this first store became one of many successful stores. In 1995, they launched a new children's clothing chain.

Mr. Jones is always looking for new challenges. ALM is nearing completion in acquiring an American chain of women's apparel, USA Chic Inc. (CI), to give ALM a gateway to the U.S. market.

ALM has almost completed the acquisition of CI. Mr. Jones and Mr. Grenier already personally own some shares in CI. Mr. Jones estimates that if ALM acquires an additional 3,500,000 Class B common shares of CI, ALM could gain control of CI. ALM intends to finance the acquisition of CI shares by issuing convertible debt to a pension fund. The pension fund has agreed to advance $20,055,000 of convertible debt, bearing interest at 8%. The debt will be convertible at the option of the pension fund into multiple-voting shares on May 1, 2005. The exercise price on conversion is to be determined using the average of the 2004 and 2005 consolidated earnings per share (EPS) before discontinued operations and extraordinary items, as reported in ALM's audited financial statements, multiplied by the price–earnings ratio. The average EPS is $0.4228 and the average price–earnings multiplier is 12. Further information on the purchase of CI is included in Exhibit D.

EXHIBIT D
NOTES FROM DISCUSSION OF USA CHIC WITH MR. JONES

1. Mr. Grenier and Mr. Jones each own 1,128,600 multiple-voting shares of ALM.

2. ALM proposes to acquire 3,500,000 Class B common shares of CI from the largest shareholder, BCG Inc., an unrelated corporation, for $5.73 per share. BCG Inc. is experiencing serious cash-flow problems and therefore wants to sell its investment in CI. BCG needs to sell at least 3,500,000 shares, which it has agreed to sell to ALM. BCG is also contemplating selling the rest of its investment on the public market. If ALM buys the 3,500,000 shares from BCG Inc., it will be entitled to two seats on the board of directors of CI. The other members of the board include the CEO of CI, a lawyer, and a businesswoman.

3. The shareholdings of CI are as follows:

BCG Inc.	5,998,000	Class B common shares
Mr. Jones and Mr. Grenier	2,869,000	Class B common shares
Public	8,399,000	Class A common shares

4. The CI Class B common shares currently outstanding give the right to two votes per share and are convertible into Class A shares at the holder's option. In all other respects the Class B shares are the same as the Class A shares. A side agreement between ALM and BCG provides that BCG will convert any of its remaining shares in CI to Class A shares before selling to the public.

5. CI is a specialty retailer of moderately priced fashion apparel for women and is well established in the U.S. market. If ALM acquires voting control of this company, ALM will gain a presence in the U.S. market and obtain valuable experience, and will eventually get to open a chain of its clothing stores there. The current CI auditors will remain the auditors for the 2005 year-end.

6. ALM has completed the due diligence process related to the purchase of CI and did not find anything that would alter its decision to go ahead with the acquisition on May 1, 2004. ALM has concluded that the fair value of the assets of CI is approximately the same as their book value.

7. The total shareholders' equity for USA Chic (in Canadian dollars) for January 31, 2004, is $63,046,000. Net income for the first three months of operations (Jan. 31 to May 1, 2004) is anticipated to be $3,076,000.

Mr. Jones and Mr. Grenier would like an analysis of the number of ALM shares that need to be issued to complete the purchase of CI and any implications from the proposed financing arrangement. Mr. Jones is not sure whether ALM can consolidate the results of CI operations in ALM's 2005 financial statements. Mr. Jones was quoted as saying, "If possible, ALM would show better EPS, which is of utmost importance to the board."

You work for a CA firm that will be completing the audit of ALM. Your partner has asked you to write a memo addressing the concerns raised by Mr. Jones and Mr. Grenier. In addition, your partner wants you to identify, in a separate memo, audit concerns relating to the purchase of CI.

Required:

Write the report to Mr. Jones and Mr. Grenier and the separate memo requested by the partner.

[CICA, adapted]

CASE 6–A2 Voice Limited

National Computers (NC) and Hightech Ltd. (HT), two unrelated companies, agreed to share the latest technology in allowing visually impaired individuals to use voice recognition software to complete their banking over the phone (e.g., transferring funds from one account to another, verifying bank balances, paying bills). Eventually they hope to expand the program to allow enquiries about stock market quotes.

On January 1, 2005, NC and HT incorporated a new company, Voice Ltd. (VL). Two classes of VL common shares were issued. Each share in both classes participates equally in the company's earnings. Class A shares are nonvoting, whereas Class B shares are voting. In return for 59 Class A shares and 1 Class B share, NC contributed land with a fair market value of $1,600,000 (NC's book value for the land was $800,000). In return for 39 Class A shares and 1 Class B share, HT contributed cash of $1,000,000.

Of the five-member board of directors of VL, three are nominees of NC and two are nominees of HT. Initially, it was decided that VL would conserve its cash by paying no dividends. Under a written agreement, any change in the dividend policy of VL, and any transactions between VL and either NC or HT, must be approved in advance by both NC and HT. NC has retained the right to select VL's chief executive officer. The primary activity of NC is the manufacturing of personal computers.

Extracts from the income statements and the balance sheets for NC and VL are as follows, ignoring the impact of income taxes:

Income Statements
For the Year Ended Dec 31, 2005

	NC	VL
Sales	$3,300,000	$1,200,000
Cost of goods sold	1,600,000	600,000
	1,700,000	600,000
Depreciation	600,000	200,000
Other operating expenses	700,000	300,000
	1,300,000	500,000
Income before gain	400,000	100,000
Gain on sale of land	800,000	300,000
Net income	$1,200,000	$ 400,000

Balance Sheets
December 31, 2005

	NC	VL
Cash	$1,800,000	$1,100,000
Accounts receivable	400,000	300,000
Inventory	1,500,000	500,000
Investment in VL, at cost	1,600,000	—
Building and equipment, net	1,800,000	600,000
Land	800,000	800,000
	$7,900,000	$3,300,000
Accounts payable	$ 200,000	$ 300,000
Common shares	5,000,000	2,600,000
Retained earnings	2,700,000	400,000
	$7,900,000	$3,300,000

Additional Information:

1. During 2005, VL sold one-half of the land transferred from NC for proceeds of $1,100,000, and recorded a gain of $300,000.

2. A management fee of $150,000, paid to NC by VL during 2005, is included in other operating expenses of VL and sales of NC in the above 2005 income statements.

3. VL's ending inventory includes goods purchased from NC for $400,000. NC's cost for these goods was $275,000. NC's ending inventory includes goods purchased from VL for $250,000. VL's cost for these goods was $150,000.

Required:

The following are four possible alternatives for accounting for NC's investment in VL:

1. cost

2. equity

3. proportionate consolidation

4. consolidation

Discuss the appropriateness of using each of these four alternatives.
[SMA, adapted]

PROBLEMS

P6–A1

On July 1, 2003, Super Corp. purchased 80% of the common shares and 40% of the preferred shares of Paltry Corp. by issuing Super Corp. shares that had a total market value of $4,900,000. On that date, Paltry's shareholders' equity accounts appear as follows:

Common shares, no par (300,000 shares)	$3,000,000
Preferred shares, no par (10,000 shares)	1,100,000
Other contributed capital	400,000
Retained earnings	1,500,000
	$6,000,000

Paltry's preferred shares are cumulative and non-participating and carry a dividend rate of $15 per year per share. The dividends are paid at the end of each calendar quarter. The redemption price of the preferred shares is $100 per share. At the time of Super's purchase, the Paltry preferred shares were selling on the market at $95.

The fair values of Paltry's net assets were identical to their book values on July 1, 2003.

During 2003 and 2004, Paltry's net income and dividends declared (common and preferred) were as follows:

Years Ended December 31

	Net Income	Dividends
2003	$600,000	$400,000
2004	$800,000	$450,000

All preferred dividends were declared and paid quarterly, as due. Paltry earns its income evenly throughout the year.

Required:

a. Determine the amounts at which each of Super's investments in the common and preferred shares of Paltry should appear in Super's balance sheet on December 31, 2003, and on December 31, 2004, assuming that Super does not consolidate Paltry. Show all calculations clearly.

b. Assume that on January 2, 2005, Super Corp sells 1,000 of its Paltry preferred shares. Determine the balance remaining in the investment account for the preferred shares after the sale.

P6–A2

On January 2, 2005, Playful Inc. purchased 60% of the outstanding common shares of Serious Ltd. for $7,000,000.

Serious's condensed balance sheet at that time was as follows:

Current assets		$ 8,000,000
Capital assets		19,000,000
		$27,000,000
Current liabilities		$ 5,000,000
Long-term liabilities		10,000,000
Shareholders' equity:		
Common shares (100,000, no par)	$2,500,000	
Preferred shares (100,000, no par, $4 dividend, callable at $45; cumulative and non-voting)	4,200,000	
Retained earnings	5,300,000	
		12,000,000
		$27,000,000

The fair value of Serious's assets was the same as their book value except for capital assets, which had a fair value of $22,000,000. The capital assets have a remaining useful life of 15 years. Goodwill on the purchase is tested for impairment on an annual basis.

On October 1, 2005, Playful purchased 20,000 of Serious's preferred shares at $35 per share. There were no dividend arrearages. Serious declared the fourth-quarter preferred dividend on December 15, 2005, payable on January 15, 2006, to holders of record on December 30, 2005.

The condensed balance sheets for both Playful and Serious were as follows on December 31, 2005:

	Playful Inc.	Serious Ltd.
Current assets	$12,000,000	$ 7,000,000
Capital assets	20,000,000	22,000,000
Investments (at cost)	7,700,000	—
	$39,700,000	$29,000,000
Current liabilities	$10,000,000	$ 6,000,000
Long-term liabilities	5,000,000	10,000,000
Shareholders' equity:		
Common shares	8,000,000	2,500,000
Preferred shares	—	4,200,000
Retained earnings	16,700,000	6,300,000
	$39,700,000	$29,000,000

Required:

Prepare a consolidated balance sheet for Playful Inc. at December 31, 2005.

P6–A3

On January 1, 2005, Purple Inc. purchased 80% of the common shares of Yellow Corp. for $1,200,000. On the date of acquisition, Yellow's shareholders' equity was as follows:

Preferred shares, 8% non-cumulative, callable at $100, 2,000 shares outstanding	$ 200,000
Common shares, no par value, 20,000 shares outstanding	400,000
Retained earnings	608,000
Total	$1,208,000

Any purchase price discrepancy is allocated to goodwill. During 2005, Yellow earned a net income of $400,000 and paid dividends of $300,000.

Required:

a. What is the amount of non-controlling interest on the consolidated balance sheet at January 1, 2005?

b. What is the amount of non-controlling interest on the consolidated balance sheet at December 31, 2005?

[CGA]

Appendix 6B

Intercompany Bond Holdings

Intercompany bond transactions

On occasion, one company in an affiliated group of companies will buy bonds issued by another company of the group. When the purchase is directly from the issuing company, the transaction is clearly an intercompany transaction. When consolidated financial statements are prepared, the intercompany transaction must be eliminated in order to prevent the intercompany receivable and payable from appearing on the consolidated balance sheet. Only bonds that are held by bondholders who are outside the affiliated group can be shown as a liability of the consolidated entity. As long as the bonds are held within the group, intercompany interest expense (to the issuer) and interest revenue (to the holder) must be eliminated, as well as any amortization of related discount or premium.

When the bonds are retired, the indebtedness and the investment will both be removed from the books. However, if the retirement occurs prior to the maturity date of the bonds, a gain or loss may result on the separate company books. Any such gain or loss must also be eliminated upon consolidation.

In general, intercompany transactions in bonds pose no particular reporting problems for consolidation or for the equity method. Adjustments and eliminations for bond transactions are similar to those that are required for asset transactions. Both offsetting transactions and offsetting balances must be eliminated when consolidated statements are prepared.

Indirect acquisitions of bonds

What if one company within the economic entity buys bonds in an affiliated company not directly from the issuer, but rather from an outside holder of the bonds? In this case, the buying company still ends up holding bonds that are an indebtedness of an affiliated company and that must be eliminated upon consolidation, but the buying price and the issuer's carrying value are likely not to be the same.

While an open-market purchase of an affiliate's bonds is possible, we must point out that *it is very rare in Canadian business practice*. Its rarity is the reason that we have relegated this discussion to an appendix instead of including it in the main body of the chapter. For the sake of completeness, however, we will explain the ramifications of such a transaction.

Suppose that SubCorp has a bond issue outstanding that has a face value of $1,000,000, an unamortized premium of $50,000, a nominal interest rate of 12%, and five years remaining to maturity. Non-affiliated investors hold all of the bonds. Market rates of interest have risen above the nominal rate on the bonds, and have caused the market price of SubCorp's bonds to fall. SubCorp's parent, ParCorp, then buys $100,000 face value of the SubCorp bonds on the open market for $90,000.

When consolidated statements are prepared, the intercompany interest must be eliminated, and the amount of the bonds held by ParCorp must be eliminated against the proportionate part of the indebtedness of SubCorp. On ParCorp's books, the bond investment is carried at $90,000; while on SubCorp's books, the bond indebtedness is carried at $105,000 (10% of the $1,000,000 face value and of the $50,000 premium). The problem is how to dispose of the $15,000 difference in carrying values.

To solve this problem, we must look at the substance of the transaction. SubCorp could have used its own cash to purchase the bonds itself. If SubCorp had done so, it would have recognized a gain on the retirement of debt of $15,000. Alternatively, SubCorp could have borrowed $90,000 from ParCorp and used that cash to buy the bonds. SubCorp still would have recognized a gain of $15,000, and an intercompany payable (and receivable) for $90,000 would exist—that payable (and receivable) would be eliminated upon consolidation.

However, instead of lending SubCorp the money, ParCorp simply bought the bonds directly. SubCorp still has a legal liability (to ParCorp) for the bonds, but the substance is that for the consolidated entity, the indebtedness no longer exists. From the viewpoint of the readers of the consolidated statements, the bonds have been retired. Therefore, the $15,000 difference between SubCorp's carrying value and ParCorp's acquisition cost must be treated as a gain when the statements are consolidated and the intercompany bond holdings are eliminated. The Year 1 adjustment will appear as follows, assuming that the bonds were acquired at the end of Year 1 without accrued interest, and that *SubCorp is wholly owned by ParCorp*:

Bonds payable	100,000	
Premium on bonds payable	5,000	
Bond investment		90,000
Gain on retirement of bonds		15,000

In subsequent years, the carrying value of the bonds on SubCorp's books will decrease due to the continuing amortization of the premium. If we assume straight-line amortization, the carrying value to SubCorp will decline by $1,000 per year. This decline is offset by a decrease in SubCorp's interest expense (assuming that the premium amortization is credited directly thereto). Therefore, the Year 2 elimination, including the intercorporate payment of interest, will appear as follows:

Bonds payable	100,000	
Premium on bonds payable	4,000	
Interest income (paid to ParCorp)	12,000	
Bond investment		90,000
Interest expense (for SubCorp)		11,000
Retained earnings		15,000

Each year that ParCorp holds the bonds, the above entry will change only by the decreasing balance of the premium—the decrease in the premium will be offset by a decrease in the credit to retained earnings, reflecting the continuing amortization of the premium. The Year 3 elimination will be:

Bonds payable	100,000	
Premium on bonds payable	3,000	
Interest income (paid to ParCorp)	12,000	
Bond investment		90,000
Interest expense (for SubCorp)		11,000
Retained earnings		14,000

The above example assumes that ParCorp does not amortize the bond purchase discount. If, instead, ParCorp accounts for the bonds as an investment held to maturity, then each year ParCorp will amortize one-fifth of its $10,000 purchase discount by charging $2,000 to the bond investment account and crediting it to interest income. In that case, the elimination entry in years subsequent to acquisition will have to reflect the difference in both the investment and the interest income account, as follows:

Year 2

Bonds payable	100,000	
Premium on bonds payable	4,000	
Interest income	14,000	
Bond investment		92,000
Interest expense		11,000
Retained earnings		15,000

Year 3

Bonds payable	100,000	
Premium on bonds payable	3,000	
Interest income (paid to ParCorp)	14,000	
Bond investment		94,000
Interest expense (for SubCorp)		11,000
Retained earnings		12,000

In each of Years 4 and 5, the balance in SubCorp's premium account will decline by $1,000, while the balance of ParCorp's bond investment will rise by $2,000. The combined effect is to reduce the credit to retained earnings in the elimination entry by $3,000 per year, which represents the gradual recognition (through amortization) on both companies' books of the issue premium and purchase discount.

At the end of Year 6, SubCorp will officially retire the bonds, transferring $100,000 to ParCorp for its amount held. The bonds payable and bond investment accounts will disappear from both companies' books, and the only remnant of the bonds that will remain on the pre-consolidation financial statements will be the interest income and expense accounts. These will be eliminated in Year 6 as follows:

Interest income	14,000	
Interest expense		11,000
Retained earnings		3,000

Non-wholly owned subsidiaries

If SubCorp is not wholly owned by ParCorp, then a question arises as to whether the gain on elimination of the intercompany bond holdings is a gain to SubCorp, to ParCorp, or partially to each. The significance of this question lies in the fact that if all or part of the gain is attributable to SubCorp, then the non-controlling interest will be assigned its proportionate share of the gain.

There are two views of the gain. One is that it is attributable to each corporation based on the difference between the bond's carrying value on the books of the company and the face value of the bonds. This is known as the **par-value approach**. Under this approach, the $15,000 total gain would be attributed as $5,000 to SubCorp and $10,000 to ParCorp. The result is what would have happened if SubCorp had redeemed the bonds at face value. Indeed, if ParCorp holds the bonds until maturity, SubCorp will in fact amortize the $5,000 premium and ParCorp will amortize the purchase discount as a credit to income over the five years. Thus the par-value approach attributes the gain to the two parties in relation to their respective roles as debtor and creditor, as though they were unaffiliated companies.

If SubCorp is 80% owned by ParCorp, then 20% of the $5,000 gain attributed to SubCorp under the par-value approach will be allocated to the non-controlling interest. The Year 1 worksheet elimination entry is:

Bonds payable	100,000	
Premium on bonds payable	5,000	
Non-controlling interest in earnings (I/S)	1,000	
Bond investment		90,000
Gain on retirement of bonds		15,000
Non-controlling interest (B/S)		1,000

However, SubCorp could easily have borrowed $90,000 from ParCorp and retired the bonds itself. In that case, the par-value method would have assigned the entire $15,000 gain to SubCorp. Since there is no difference in substance between ParCorp buying the bonds or lending SubCorp the money to buy the bonds, the second approach to allocating the $15,000 total gain is to attribute it entirely to the issuing corporation—SubCorp in this example. This method is called the **agency approach** because ParCorp is effectively acting as agent for SubCorp when it buys the bonds. The Year 1 elimination entry will appear as follows.

Bonds payable	100,000	
Premium on bonds payable	5,000	
Non-controlling interest in earnings (I/S)	3,000	
Bond investment		90,000
Gain on retirement of bonds		15,000
Non-controlling interest (B/S)		3,000

The non-controlling interest is increased by 20% of the full $15,000 gain.

Unlike the par-value method, the agency method yields the same results regardless of the way in which the bond repurchase transaction was structured. Since the agency method stresses substance over form, many accountants prefer it. Either approach may be encountered in practice, however. The difference between the two is likely to be immaterial, and then the easiest treatment should be used.

In years following ParCorp's purchase of SubCorp's bonds, the eliminating entries will differ from those shown above for Year 1 as a result of the amortization of the issue premium and the purchase discount. Assuming that both are amortized on a straight-line basis over the five years to maturity, SubCorp's premium account will decrease by $1,000 per year and ParCorp's carrying value of the bond investment will increase by $2,000 per year. The resulting combined recognition of $3,000 per year of the spread between the issue and repurchase prices causes the *unrecognized* portion of the spread (i.e., gain) to decline by $3,000 per year, exactly as described in the previous section.

If SubCorp were wholly owned by ParCorp, the $3,000 decline will be reflected in the year-by-year eliminations as a reduction in the amount added (credited) to retained earnings. When SubCorp is not wholly owned, then the change in the unrecognized gain is allocated to retained earnings and non-controlling interest—the relative proportions depend on whether the par-value or the agency approach is being used.

The annual adjustment to eliminate intercompany interest income and expense (assuming that *both* the premium and the discount are being amortized) will be as follows if SubCorp is wholly owned:

Interest income	14,000	
Interest expense		11,000
Retained earnings		3,000

Since the full amount of the gain was recognized on the consolidated statements in Year 1, the separate-entity recognition of the gain through amortization must not be permitted to flow through to the consolidated income statement again. Therefore, the balancing credit is to retained earnings rather than to a gain account.

When SubCorp is only 80% owned, then part of the balancing credit of $3,000 must be allocated to non-controlling interest. The portion allocated depends on the approach used. Under the par-value approach:

Interest income	14,000	
Interest expense		11,000
Non-controlling interest (B/S)		200
Retained earnings		2,800

The $200 represents 20% of the SubCorp $1,000 discount amortization for each year.

Using the agency approach:

Interest income	14,000	
Interest expense		11,000
Non-controlling interest (B/S)		600
Retained earnings		2,400

The $600 represents 20% of the combined amortizations of $3,000 per year. The eliminating entries for the principal amount (and the related issue premium and purchase discount) are shown in Exhibit 6–12. Under both methods, the combined credits to non-controlling interest and retained earnings are $12,000 at the end of Year 2, down from $15,000 at the bond acquisition in Year 1. The combined credit declines by $3,000 each year as the carrying values of the bonds on both companies' books merge towards the maturity value of $100,000. In Year 6, the bonds mature and are retired; therefore, the only consolidation adjustment relating to the bonds in Year 6 will be for the intercompany interest.

Subsidiary purchase of parent's bonds

The foregoing example dealt solely with the purchase of a subsidiary's bonds by the parent. When the situation is reversed, how do the consolidation adjustments differ?

If the par-value method is used, the non-controlling interest is allocated its share of the difference between the bond's face value and its carrying value on the subsidiary's books. The adjustment is exactly the same as shown above, regardless of whether the subsidiary is the issuer of the bonds or the buyer.

EXHIBIT 6–12   BOND ELIMINATION ENTRIES, SUBSEQUENT TO ACQUISITION

(amounts in thousands of dollars)

	Year 2	Year 3	Year 4	Year 5
Par-value approach				
Bonds payable	100.0	100.0	100.0	100.0
Premium on bonds	4.0	3.0	2.0	1.0
Bond investment	92.0	94.0	96.0	98.0
Non-controlling interest	0.8	0.6	0.4	0.2
Retained earnings (end)	11.2	8.4	5.6	2.8
Agency approach				
Bonds payable	100.0	100.0	100.0	100.0
Premium on bonds	4.0	3.0	2.0	1.0
Bond investment	92.0	94.0	96.0	98.0
Non-controlling interest	2.4	1.8	1.2	0.6
Retained earnings (end)	9.6	7.2	4.8	2.4

If the agency approach is used, the full gain or loss is attributed to the issuing company. When the issuing company is the parent, there obviously will be no non-controlling interest; the consolidation eliminations will be exactly the same as those illustrated above for wholly owned subsidiaries.

Summary

Direct intercompany bond transactions are treated no differently than other intercompany indebtedness when consolidated statements are prepared. The offsetting liability and investment must be eliminated, as well as all intercompany interest payments and any premium and discount amortizations.

When bonds of an affiliated company are purchased from an unaffiliated holder subsequent to their original issuance, the carrying value of the bonds on the books of the issuer may be different from the cost to the acquirer. The difference in carrying values can be assigned wholly to the issuer of the bonds (the agency approach) or allocated to both the issuer and the buyer on the basis of the face value of the bonds (the par-value approach). The method of allocation will affect the non-controlling interest and the consolidated net income.

The essence of consolidated reporting is to show the assets *and liabilities* that are under the control of the parent company. Since the parent can structure the liability position of the affiliated companies in a number of ways with the same substantive result, the reporting of an in-substance debt retirement should not be affected by the technical manner by which it is accomplished. Only the agency approach achieves substance over form; the par-value approach will yield different consolidated net income depending on the technical structure of the repurchase.

Indeed, the par-value approach can lead to some odd results. For example, if the parent has bonds outstanding that were issued at a premium, then the parent can trigger recognition of a gain in its consolidated income statement by having a non-wholly owned subsidiary buy the bonds, regardless of the price paid by the subsidiary. The subsidiary could pay a price that is even higher than the carrying value of the bonds on the parent's books, and an overall economic loss to the combined entity would clearly result. But the par-value approach would still attribute a gain to the parent and a loss to the subsidiary, with part of the loss allocated to non-controlling shareholders. Thus the agency approach seems more consistent with the overall objectives of consolidated reporting and with the basic qualitative characteristic of reporting substance over form; as well, it is easier to apply. Nevertheless, both methods can be found in practice.

When part of a bond issue is retired at a gain, GAAP permits the gain to be recognized either in a lump sum or amortized over the remaining life of the bond issue. In this chapter, we have assumed for the sake of simplicity that the gain is recognized in the year of the repurchase.

SELF-STUDY PROBLEM 6–4

Sweetness Corporation is 70% owned by Passion Limited. At the beginning of 2005, Sweetness issued $1,000,000 in 12%, 10-year bonds for $958,000. On December 31, 2008, Passion purchased 50% of the bonds from their original buyer for $479,000. Passion reports the bond investment as a long-term investment. Both companies calculate amortization on a straight-line basis.

Required:

Construct the eliminating entry for the bonds (including interest) at the following dates, first using the agency approach and then using the par-value method:

a. December 31, 2008

b. December 31, 2010

c. December 31, 2014

REVIEW QUESTIONS

6-21 Parent Company holds debentures of Sub Company that were purchased by Parent as a part of the original issuance by Sub. What eliminations are necessary in preparing Parent's consolidated financial statements?

6-22 Parent Company holds bonds of its subsidiary, Sub Company, that were purchased on the open market at a substantial discount. Upon consolidation of Parent's financial statements, how should the difference in carrying values of the bonds on the two companies' books be reported?

6-23 Explain the difference in concept between the par-value and the agency approaches to eliminating intercorporate bond holdings.

6-24 "Substance over form" is an important qualitative criterion for external financial reporting. Which method of intercompany bond elimination better satisfies this criterion? Explain why.

PROBLEMS

P6–B1

Beluga Ltd. is a wholly owned subsidiary of Orcas Ltd. On January 1, 1998, Beluga issued $200,000 of 5%, 10-year bonds payable for $240,000. The interest is paid annually, on December 31. On January 1, 2005, Orcas Ltd. purchased $50,000 face value of the Beluga bonds for $41,000.

Required:

a. Give the eliminating entries relating to the bonds as they would appear on the consolidated worksheet at December 31, 2005.

b. Assume instead that Beluga is 75% owned by Orcas. Give the eliminating entries for the bonds at December 31, 2005, using:

1. Agency method

2. Par-value method

[CGA–Canada, adapted]

P6–B2

Poseidon Ltd. (P Ltd.) bought 80% of the voting shares of Submarine Ltd. (S Ltd.) for $470,000 at January 1, 2005. S Ltd. had the following balance sheet at that date:

Submarine Ltd.
Balance Sheet
January 1, 2005

Cash	$ 10,000
Accounts receivable	30,000
Inventory	50,000
Land	150,000
Capital assets, net	200,000
	$440,000
Current liabilities	$ 20,000
Bonds—20-year, 15% interest	100,000
Common shares	100,000
Retained earnings	220,000
	$440,000

The fair values, on January 1, 2005, of S Ltd.'s assets were:

Inventory	$ 90,000
Land	$220,000
Capital assets, net	$170,000

The bonds on S Ltd.'s balance sheet were issued on January 1, 2005, at face value; interest is paid July 1 and December 31.

All inventory on the books of S at January 1, 2005, was sold during the year. P sold $400,000 (cost of goods) to S for $500,000 during 2005, and 20% of the inventory was on hand at the end of the year. P sold land to S (cost $30,000) for $90,000. P purchased $60,000 face value of S's bonds on July 2, 2005, for $64,000. The premium will be amortized straight-line over the remaining life of the bonds. Any goodwill will be tested on an annual basis for impairment. S's plant and equipment have 10 years (straight-line amortization) remaining.

S had a net income of $100,000 for 2005 and paid no dividends.

The balance sheets for the two companies at December 31, 2005, are:

	P Ltd.	S Ltd.
Cash	$ 70,000	$ 15,000
Accounts receivable	100,000	45,000
Inventory	240,000	80,000
Land	600,000	240,000
Capital assets, net	800,000	250,000
Investment in subsidiary equity*	550,000	—
Investment in bonds of subsidiary	63,898	—
	$2,423,898	$630,000
Current liabilities	$ 80,000	$110,000
Bonds	—	100,000
Common shares	1,000,000	100,000
Retained earnings	1,343,898	320,000
	$2,423,898	$630,000

*Includes only the parent's share of subsidiary net income.

Required:

Calculate the balances of the following selected accounts, at December 31, 2005, that would appear on the consolidated balance sheet. Ignore income taxes for this problem.

a. Inventory

b. Land

c. Capital assets

d. Bonds payable

e. Retained earnings

[CGA–Canada]

P6–B3

Your assistant is preparing consolidated financial statements at December 31, 2005, for your company and has come to you with the following problems:

1. Subone Ltd., a 70%-owned subsidiary, sold land and buildings to Parent Ltd. for $1,180,000 ($300,000 was allocated to the land). The land cost Subone Ltd. $200,000; the building cost $1,400,000 and was 45% (i.e., nine years) depreciated at the date of sale. Parent Ltd. took a full year's depreciation on the building and will depreciate it over the original remaining life. Subone Ltd. took no depreciation on the building in 2005.

2. Subtwo Ltd., a 90%-owned subsidiary, purchased $600,000 of Parent Ltd.'s bonds on July 1, 2005, in the open market for $680,000. The bonds have a 12% interest rate; the interest will be paid on January 5, 2006, and the bonds will be due on January 1, 2009. All consolidated income statement adjustments arising from intercompany bond transactions are to be allocated between the two parties.

3. On December 1, 2005, Subthree Ltd. split its shares four to one. Prior to the split, Parent Ltd. owned 90% of the shares (90,000 shares) of Subthree Ltd. and had the account "Investment in Subthree Ltd." on the books at $2,400,000 cost basis.

Additional Information:

| | At December 31, 2004 | | At December 31, 2005 | |
	Subone Ltd.	Parent Ltd.	Subone Ltd.	Parent Ltd.
Land	$4,000,000	$8,100,000	$4,200,000	$8,400,000
Buildings, net	5,200,000	9,320,000	4,982,000	9,178,000
Depreciation expense	460,000	530,000	420,000	570,000

			Subtwo Ltd.	
Investment in bonds	—	—	668,571	—
Interest income (total from all sources)	—	—	111,000	—
Bonds payable	—	$2,000,000	—	$2,000,000
Discount on bonds	—	(130,000)	—	(97,500)
Interest expense (total on all debt)	—	368,070	—	392,462

During 2005		
	Subone Ltd.	Subtwo Ltd.
Net income	($421,000)	$400,000
Dividends	—	20,000

Required:

a. For each item in problems 1 and 2 above, calculate the amounts that would appear on the consolidated financial statements for 2005.

b. For problem 3, calculate the amounts that would be in the investment in subsidiary account and the journal entries that would appear on the books of Parent Ltd. If no journal entries are needed, explain why.

c. Calculate for Subone Ltd. and Subtwo Ltd. the amount for non-controlling interest that would appear on the consolidated income statement for 2005.

[CGA–Canada]

P6–B4

On January 1, 2005, Paco Ltd. purchased 70% of the common shares of Scot Ltd. for $506,100.

Financial data for Scot Ltd. are as follows:

Scot Ltd.
Balance Sheet
January 1, 2005

	Book value	Fair market value
Cash	$ 56,000	$ 56,000
Accounts receivable	102,000	108,000
Inventory	197,000	180,000
Capital assets, net	750,000	700,000
	$1,105,000	
Current liabilities	$ 140,000	140,000
Long-term liabilities		
Bonds payable at 12% interest	300,000	300,000
Bond discount	(60,000)	(60,000)
Preferred shares	175,000	—
Common shares	200,000	—
Retained earnings	350,000	—
	$1,105,000	

Additional Information:

1. Accounts receivable will be collected within the year.

2. Inventory is on the FIFO method and has a turnover of two times per year.

3. The capital assets are being written off over 10 years on a straight-line basis.

4. Any goodwill on the purchase will be tested for impairment on an annual basis.

5. The bond discount is being amortized over the remaining 10 years on a straight-line basis. Interest is payable semiannually.

6. The preferred shares are non-cumulative, non-participating, and redeemable at par ($100) plus a $2 premium.

During the year the consolidated entity had the following intercompany transactions:

1. Scot Ltd. sold a building, which had a cost of $300,000 and had accumulated depreciation of $180,000 at the date of sale, to Paco Ltd. for $195,000 cash. (This building was being depreciated over 10 years straight-line with no residual value, but no depreciation had been recorded for the year 2005 to the date of sale.) It is company policy that assets receive a full year's depreciation in the year of acquisition and none in the year of disposal. It is also company policy that the acquiring company amortize the asset over the remaining life of the asset.

2. On July 1, 2005, Paco Ltd. purchased one-half of the bonds payable of Scot Ltd. for $107,250. It is company policy that the purchaser be allocated any gain or loss on an intercompany transaction of this nature.

3. On September 1, 2005, Paco Ltd. sold land costing $135,000 to Scot Ltd. for $175,000.

4. To date, there has been no impairment to value of goodwill.

Financial statements of Paco Ltd. and Scot Ltd. as at December 31, 2005 are:

Balance Sheets
December 31, 2005

	Paco Ltd.	Scot Ltd.
Cash	$ 145,500	$ 85,000
Accounts receivable	300,000	200,000
Inventory	500,000	400,000
Bond investment	109,500	—
Capital assets, net	1,000,000	800,000
Investment in subsidiary (cost)	506,100	—
	$2,561,100	$1,485,000
Current liabilities	$ 100,000	$ 331,000
Long-term liabilities		
Bonds payable at 12% interest	—	300,000
Bond discount	—	(54,000)
Preferred shares	—	175,000
Common shares	400,000	200,000
Retained earnings	2,061,100	533,000
	$2,561,100	$1,485,000

Income Statements
Year Ended December 31, 2005

	Paco Ltd.	Scot Ltd.
Sales	$ 900,000	$ 800,000
Cost of goods sold	500,000	500,000
	400,000	300,000
Less:		
Depreciation	(80,000)	(70,000)
Interest expense	—	(42,000)
Other expenses	(100,000)	(80,000)
Plus:		
Interest income on bonds	11,250	—
Gain on sale of land	40,000	—
Gain on sale of building	—	75,000
Net income	$ 271,250	$ 183,000

Required:

a. Prepare the consolidated income statement for the year 2005.

b. Calculate the following, as they would appear on the consolidated balance sheet at December 31, 2005:

  1. Inventory
  2. Capital assets, net
  3. Bond discount
  4. Non-controlling interest

[CGA–Canada]

7

Segmented and Interim Reporting

The previous five chapters developed the concepts and procedures underlying consolidated financial statements. In our discussion, we pointed out that consolidated statements give the reader a broad view of the complete economic entity and of the aggregate resources under the control of the parent corporation. The focus of consolidated statements is *aggregation*—combining business activities across all lines of business and all separate legal entities within the consolidated group and reporting on an annual basis.

In contrast, this chapter looks at two types of information that a public company provides to its shareholders that are intended to remedy some of the shortcomings of annual consolidated information:

- disaggregated reporting for *segments* of the enterprise, as supplementary information, and

- reporting for shorter, *interim* periods of time, normally quarterly for public reporting in U.S. and Canada (semiannually in most other countries).

GAAP requires segment reporting and interim reporting only for *public* companies. There are only three sections of the *CICA Handbook* that apply exclusively to public companies; segment reporting and interim reporting are two of the three sections. Earnings per share is the third, which is a topic in intermediate accounting books and courses.

Segmented Reporting

Introduction

Consolidated statements conceal the financial position and results of operations for the separate entities and business lines comprising the consolidated whole. A financial statement user cannot discern the relative importance and profitability of the different lines of business that the consolidated entity may be engaged in. Nor can a user ascertain the company's risk exposure in its various types of activities.

Each type of business will be affected by different factors relating to markets, supply, competition, etc. An analyst can make reasonable predictions of cash flow and earnings only on the basis of information *not* included in the consolidated financial statements.

The response of accounting standard setters to the problems posed by consolidated reporting has been to require **segmented reporting**, which is the disaggregation of consolidated results into the major different types of businesses in which a consolidated entity engages. Also known as "line of business" reporting, segmented reporting helps analysts to understand how the risks and rewards inherent in different lines of business are affecting and will affect the corporation.

Line of business reporting is intended to enable financial-statement readers to evaluate the risk that a company is exposed to in its various types of activities. As well, however, there is risk inherent in operating in different parts of the world. Therefore, segment reporting also extends to reporting on operations by geographic area.

Segmented reporting addresses the problems cited above for consolidated statements, but it does not directly address the need of some users for reporting by a separate legal entity. Only if there is a correspondence between segments and corporate entities is the shareholder or creditor able to gain some insight into the viability of the individual corporation in which she or he has a stake.

Over 30 countries have some form of segmented reporting requirements. Some requirements provide minimal guidance. Others require disaggregated disclosures through adoption of IAS 14, "Reporting Financial Information by Segment" (revised 1997). While segmented reporting is widespread, Canada and the U.S. generally provide the most guidance in defining segments and designating the reporting requirements.

In Canada, the recommendations on segmented reporting are contained in Section 1701 of the *CICA Handbook*. The recommendations are quite broad, and permit substantial flexibility in reporting. The AcSB worked in conjunction with the FASB in the U.S. in developing a single standard for the two countries. The current segment reporting recommendations became effective in 1998.

Applicability

Unlike almost all other sections of the *CICA Handbook*, Section 1701 applies only to *public* companies—those that have either shares or bonds traded in the public capital markets, either on an exchange or over the counter.[1] This section of the *CICA Handbook* therefore does not apply to most companies in Canada, although the recommendations can be used as a guideline for private companies.

Banks or other holders of privately placed debt can also require the borrower to provide segmented results. More commonly, however, banks require borrowers to supply separate-entity statements rather than segmented breakdowns of consolidated results.

In formulating the recommendations in Section 1701, the AcSB was cognizant of the benefit–cost relationship in presenting segmented information. In general, the AcSB preferred to recommend disclosure only of information that was already readily available within the reporting enterprise, mainly from the management accounting system. Thus, some of the variability that exists in practice is the result of differing management accounting systems.

The focus of the segment disclosure recommendations is on reportable operating segments. There are two key words here—*operating* and *reportable*. Not all operating segments are reportable. We will clarify the distinction in the following discussion.

In addition to reporting on their definable operating segments, enterprises should report additional companywide information about:

- products and services
- geographic areas, and
- major customers.

---

1. The requirements also apply to co-operative business enterprises, deposit-taking institutions (e.g., banks and credit unions), and life insurance companies.

Operating segments

Identifying operating segments The first step is to identify the segments to be reported. In some instances, identifying operating segments is no problem. If a telephone company buys a gas pipeline company, it is clear that those are two distinct segments; they share no resources, market, management expertise, or common costs, except at the top corporate level. Operationally, there is no similarity.

In other instances, however, it is more difficult to identify operating segments than one perhaps might expect. The *CICA Handbook* cites three aspects to defining an operating segment [CICA 1701.10–1701.12]:

1. It is a component of the enterprise that is expected to generate revenues and incur expenses. A segment need not be generating revenues currently, but should be expected to do so in the normal future course of its activity.

2. Discrete financial information on the business component is regularly available through the company's internal financial reporting system.

3. The business component's operating results are reviewed regularly by the enterprise's "chief operating decision maker," which normally will be the COO (chief operating officer), the CEO (chief executive officer), or the president. This officer will use the various business components' financial information to make resource allocation decisions within the enterprise.

Clearly, the guidelines focus on the decision-making process within the enterprise. The accounting system must provide the information as a matter of routine, and that information must be used by senior management for allocating resources within the company.

Normally there will be a manager in charge of the business component, and that manager will interact and negotiate directly with the chief operating decision maker about the segment's plans, results, and resources. In a matrix organization, where one manager is responsible for geographic areas and another is responsible for products or services across the entire enterprise, the *CICA Handbook* recommends that the operating segments be defined on the basis of products and services [CICA 1701.15].

Some operating segments may be quite separate when defined by the criteria described above, and yet can be combined for segment reporting. For example, the business components may serve the same general market, although not necessarily the same customers. If the products are complementary, or are substitutes for each other, then the enterprise may simply be horizontally integrated in the same market rather than being in two different segments. For example, wineries may be owned by beer companies. Beer and wine are likely to have different segment managers and distinct financial reporting, and may be viewed by senior management as two different segments. But since both beer and wine serve the same general market, it may make sense to report only one alcoholic beverages segment rather than two segments.

The degree of vertical integration can also be used as a criterion for segmentation. A company may produce a raw material, refine it, convert it into manufactured products, and sell the products through its own chain of stores. Is the company in three segments (resources, manufacturing, and retailing) or in one vertically integrated segment? The answer depends on the relative independence of the various levels of the business and the degree of reliance by each on the others. If substantially all of the raw material goes into the enterprise's own manufacturing plants, and the output of the plants is sold mainly through the company's stores, then the high level of interdivisional product flows suggests that there is only one integrated segment.

On the other hand, if the three levels of business operate fairly autonomously, buying materials from external suppliers and selling intermediate outputs on the open market, then the enterprise would seem to be in separate segments rather than in just one.

Different companies with seemingly comparable operations could quite legitimately segment their results differently. One company may report several related operating segments, while another company with seemingly similar segments may choose to report the segments together as a single, dominant, integrated segment. The second company's lack of segmented reporting may suggest that the sales between divisions account for the bulk of each division's revenues, and that sales to third parties may not be sufficiently important to justify segmentation.

Reportable segments There is a difference between an *identifiable* segment and a *reportable* segment. To be reportable, a segment must be separately identifiable, but in addition must satisfy at least one of three quantitative criteria or guidelines [CICA 1701.19]. The general guidelines for reporting an operating segment are that a segment is considered reportable if it comprises 10% or more of the enterprise's:

- total revenues, including sales between segments
- operating profits, *or*
- combined assets of all operating segments.

Only one of the 10% tests needs to be met. If an operating segment does not meet any of these criteria, it can be combined with another related segment or lumped into an "other" category. In general, at least 75% of the enterprise's consolidated revenues should be disclosed by operating segment.

Management can choose to report segments that do not meet any of the 10% criteria. However, the *CICA Handbook* suggests that 10 segments may be a reasonable upper limit for disclosure [CICA 1701.27].

In applying the 10% guideline for profits, a problem arises when some of the operating segments operate at a loss while others are profitable. The offsetting effect of profits and losses reduces the size of the company's total profit (or loss), and thereby would reduce the level of segment profit or loss that would satisfy the 10% criterion. The approach taken by the AcSB to dealing with the offsetting effect is that the 10% profit guideline should be applied to the *larger* of:

1. 10% of the combined profits of all of the segments that reported profits, *or*

2. 10% of the combined losses of all of the segments that operated at a loss for the period.

For example, suppose that a company has six operating segments:

Segment	Operating Profit (Loss)
A	$ 25,000
B	(10,000)
C	15,000
D	30,000
E	(35,000)
F	40,000
Total	$ 65,000

The total profit is $65,000, and all of the segments have profits or losses that are higher than 10% of that amount. However, the sum of the profitable segments is $110,000 while the sum of the losses is $45,000. The basis for applying the 10% guideline is the larger of those two amounts, or $110,000. Any segment that has a profit or a loss larger than $11,000 is reportable. Under that criterion, segment B ceases to be a reportable segment (although it still may meet one of the other criteria).

The definition of "profit" is intentionally ambiguous. The recommendations make no reference as to how the profit is measured. It may be pre-tax or after-tax, and it may or may not include costs such as interest expense, allocated head office expenses, etc. The profit measure is defined simply as "the measure reported to the chief operating decision maker for purposes of making decisions about allocating resources to the segment and assessing its performance" [CICA 1701.32]. In other words, segment profit is measured on the same basis the company measures it in its internal reporting system. Therefore, a financial statement reader must be extremely cautious in trying to compare segment profits between different enterprises.

It is quite possible for an identifiable segment to satisfy one of the 10% criteria in one year and not the next, or vice versa. Therefore, the determination of reportable segments must be based on more than a one-year view. If a segment is likely to exceed a 10% guideline more often than not, then it probably should be reported *each* year even if it may not meet the guideline every year.

The qualitative criterion of *consistency* suggests that the same segment breakdown should be reported each year until a significant shift in relative importance of lines of business causes a segment to drop below the 10% guidelines more or less permanently. The guidelines should also be used to identify emerging segments, those that are increasing in importance in the consolidated enterprise.

Information to be reported The two basic pieces of information that should be reported for each segment are:

- total assets, and
- a measure of profit or loss.

Remember that the requirement is specifically for "a" measure of profit— there is no suggestion as to how profit should be measured. The profit measure is whatever the company's senior management uses to evaluate the segment.

The *CICA Handbook* lists the items to be disclosed for each reportable segment. However, these items are reported only *if* they are reviewed regularly by the chief operating decision maker. Regular review can be either (1) by their inclusion in the measure of segment profit that is used by senior management or (2) by being separately reported and reviewed. The information to be disclosed is as follows [CICA 1701.30–31]:

- revenues, separately disclosed by:
  - sales to external customers
  - intersegment sales
  - interest revenue and interest expense, normally disclosed separately

- revenues, expenses, gains, or losses arising from unusual non-recurring transactions
- income tax expense or benefit
- extraordinary items

- amortization of capital assets
- total expenditures for additions to capital assets and goodwill
- significant non-cash items other than amortization
- information about investees that are subject to significant influence:
  - equity in earnings
  - amount of investment

The *CICA Handbook* recommends that the reporting enterprise explain the basis for determining reportable segments. Also, the company should present a general description of the products and services from which each segment derives its revenues [CICA 1701.29].

The basis for reporting segment information to the chief operating decision maker will often be based on non-consolidated data. Therefore, a reconciliation of the segmented sales, profits, and assets to the amounts in the consolidated financial statements is recommended [CICA 1701.35].

Enterprisewide disclosures

Products and services We stated above that the company should disclose the nature of each segment's products and services. However, a company may not have separate reportable segments but still may have a series of different product types or services. In that case, the company should disclose the revenues from each group of similar products and services.

Geographic areas One of the primary tasks of a financial statement reader is to assess the potential business risks that are facing an enterprise. Several aspects of business risk are related to the countries or geographic areas in which the company does business. Risks relate to both revenue potential and asset exposure.

If a Canadian company generates significant amounts of revenue in Europe, for example, European revenues (and profits) will be threatened if the euro weakens in relation to the Canadian dollar. As the euro declines, Canadian services and products become more expensive in terms of euros. Or, if the company maintains its prices in euros, the Canadian-dollar profit margin will decline as the euro declines. Similarly, assets located in certain geographic areas may be a source of risk. The risk can arise either politically (e.g., political instability) or economically (e.g., high inflation).

To help investors assess risk, the *CICA Handbook* recommends that companies disclose the extent to which their sales are to foreign vs. domestic customers, and also the breakdown between domestic and foreign assets. The specific recommended disclosures *for each geographic area* are as follows [CICA 1701.40]:

- revenues from external customers in foreign countries
- revenue from sales to external customers in the company's home country
- assets and goodwill that are located in foreign countries, and
- amount of capital assets and goodwill that are located in the company's home country.

In many cases, the domestic–foreign breakdown is provided as part of the segment disclosure. If the segment disclosures contain all of the appropriate information, then no additional reporting is necessary. Otherwise, the company should disclose these four pieces of information for the consolidated enterprise as a whole.

Major customers Another major risk factor is the extent to which a corporation is dependent upon one or a few major customers. What will happen to the company if 45% of its services are provided to a customer that goes bankrupt?

Because of the risk inherent in relying on major customers, a reporting enterprise should disclose "information about the extent of its reliance on its major customers." [CICA 1701.42] Not too surprisingly, the guideline is 10%. If the company relies on a single customer for 10% or more of its revenue, the company should disclose the total amount of revenues from each such customer and the segment or segments that generate those total revenues. Customers under common control are considered to be a single customer.

Note that there is no requirement to disclose the *name* of the important customer or customers. This may be viewed as a shortcoming. If one or more companies in the retail clothing business is in financial jeopardy, it may not be terribly helpful to a financial-statement reader to know that a significant part of a clothing manufacturer's revenue comes from a retail clothing chain without knowing the name of the chain.

Examples of segmented reporting

There is no prescribed format for the reporting of information by segments; the method of presentation is left entirely up to the preparers. In the following paragraphs, we will discuss two quite different examples of segment disclosure.

Our first example of segmented financial reporting is shown in Exhibit 7–1, for George Weston Limited, Canada's largest public company (by revenue). George Weston has three reportable business segments: Weston Foods, Food Distribution, and Fisheries. The company gives a brief description of its segments, and then reports each of the pieces of information required by the *CICA Handbook*, including a summary to reconcile each item to the consolidated amounts. Actually, the only piece of information that really needs reconciliation in this example is the amount for sales, to provide for intersegment sales. The other reported items simply total to the consolidated amount. For the "profit" measure, the company uses operating income.

In addition to the information on operating segments, the company provides a one-line statement that no segment is reliant on a single customer. As well, the company presents a brief geographic summary for its two countries of operation—Canada and the United States.

A more extensive example of geographic segment disclosure is that of Creo Inc. Creo is a Vancouver-based company that provides imaging technology and software for companies in the publishing and printing industries. The company operates worldwide; only 3% of its revenue comes from Canada. The segmented reporting note for Creo is shown in Exhibit 7–2, slightly shortened from the original. You should observe several points in this note.

- The company reports three geographic regions. OEM (which means "original equipment manufacturing") is a corporate or headquarters function, not a region. Canada is included in the "Americas" region in the first table. Canada is listed separately in the second table even though Canada revenue is well below the 10% threshold. Canada's separate disclosure is due to the fact that 55% of the assets are in Canada, which is where the OEM research takes place.

- At the beginning, the note states that the company changed its operating performance evaluation in 2002, and that therefore the segment disclosure was

EXHIBIT 7–1 GEORGE WESTON LIMITED

Segmented Financial Reporting
December 31, 2002

20. Segment Information

The Company has three reportable operating segments: Weston Foods, Food Distribution and Fisheries. The Weston Foods segment is primarily engaged in the baking and dairy industries within North America. The Food Distribution segment focuses on food retailing and is increasing its offering of non-food products and services in Canada and is operated by Loblaw. The Fisheries segment is primarily engaged in the hatching, growing and processing of fresh farmed salmon in North America and Chile. The results for Fisheries include the Fisheries operations which were disposed of prior to 2002. In prior years, the Company reported Weston Foods and Fisheries as one segment, Food Processing.

The accounting policies of the reportable operating segments are the same as those described in the Company's summary of significant accounting policies. The Company measures each reportable operating segment's performance based on operating income. No reportable operating segment is reliant on any single external customer.

	2002	2001
Sales		
Weston Foods	$ 4,792	$ 3,412
Food Distribution	23,082	21,486
Fisheries	219	396
Intersegment	(647)	(633)
Consolidated	$27,446	$24,661
Operating Income		
Weston Foods	$ 409	$ 313
Food Distribution	1,295	1,128
Fisheries	(26)	(1)
Consolidated	$ 1,678	$ 1,440
Depreciation and Goodwill Charges		
Weston Foods	$ 144	$ 115
Food Distribution	354	359
Fisheries	9	14
Consolidated	$ 507	$ 488
Total Assets		
Weston Foods	$ 4,837	$ 5,627
Food Distribution	11,167	9,972
Fisheries	292	320
Consolidated	$16,296	$15,919
Fixed Assets and Goodwill Purchases		
Weston Foods	$ 311	$ 1,527
Food Distribution	1,087	1,110
Fisheries	7	34
Consolidated	$ 1,405	$ 2,671

The Company operates primarily in Canada and the United States.

	2002	2001
Sales (excluding intersegment)		
Canada	$23,650	$22,071
United States	3,796	2,590
Consolidated	$27,446	$24,661
Fixed Assets and Goodwill		
Canada	$ 7,635	$ 6,891
United States	2,765	2,697
Consolidated	$10,400	$ 9,588

EXHIBIT 7–2   CREO INC.

Segmented Financial Information (excerpts)
September 30, 2003

17. Segmented Financial Information

During the year ended September 30, 2002, the Company changed its segmented reporting to reflect the way management evaluates operating performance .... This change resulted from the restructuring of the Company's business during 2002 .... As of September 30, 2002, the Company operates in three reportable economic segments: Americas, the European region, and Asia–Pacific (including Japan). OEM and Other includes OEM businesses, research and development, other business activities and corporate functions. In fiscal 2003, the financial results from the Middle East and Africa, which were previously included in OEM and Other, were included in the European region. This change has been reflected in the prior year segmented disclosure and the European region has been renamed Europe, Middle East and Africa ("EMEA"). Segments are determined based on the regions where products are marketed.

The Company evaluates performance based on segment contribution, which includes net income from operations excluding financial income, taxes, and other items. Other items excluded from the performance evaluation are business integration and restructuring costs, royalty arrangement, equity losses, and intangible asset amortization for the years ended September 30, 2003 and 2002.

The Company accounts for intersegment sales, cost of sales and transfers as if the sales or transfers were to third parties; however, intersegment sales and cost of sales are excluded from segment contribution in evaluating segment performance. The Company does not evaluate segment performance based on capital expenditures or assets employed.

The following tables set forth information by segments:

Year ended September 30, 2003	Americas	EMEA	Asia–Pacific	OEM & Other	Total
External revenues	$218,207	$221,054	$72,662	$66,115	$578,038
Segment contribution	45,355	48,414	11,018	(96,612)	8,175
Reconciliation to net earnings:					
Segment contribution					$ 8,175
Financial income					7,997
Other					(9,122)
Income tax expense					(1,541)
Net earnings					$ 5,509

The Company generated revenue from the development and sale of digital prepress equipment to customers in the following geographic regions:

Years ended September 30	2003	2002	2001
Canada	$ 18,260	$ 17,802	$ 13,965
U.S	225,088	232,643	297,539
Europe	237,891	205,019	247,941
Asia–Pacific	75,539	66,714	77,169
Israel	7,793	7,877	12,136
Other	13,467	9,797	7,777
	$578,038	$539,852	$656,527

The Company has capital assets, goodwill and other intangible assets located in:

September 30	2003	2002
Canada	$ 68,106	$63,247
U.S	19,282	7,184
Europe	4,979	7,103
Asia–Pacific	4,965	4,250
Israel	28,542	30,916
Other	—	1,210
	$125,874	$113,910

changed. This reflects the approach of Section 1701—that segment reporting should reflect the evaluation methods used by management.

- The company explains the measure it uses for evaluating segment performance—segment contribution. This is the "profit" measure required by Section 1701. The measure does not include income taxes, financial income, and "other" items relating to the corporation as a whole.

- The company reports all segment revenue as being from external sales, even if the sales were to another segment. However, it is not clear why the segment revenues shown in the second table differ from those shown in the first table. Intersegment sales are excluded from the *profit* measure.

- Each of the five regions shown in the second and third tables qualifies as a reportable region because each has more than either 10% of revenue (U.S.; Asia–Pacific; Europe) or 10% of assets (Canada; Israel).

Interim Reporting

Introduction

All enterprises issue financial reports at least once a year. One of the basic postulates of accounting is *periodicity*—it is feasible to break the life of an organization into discrete time periods and to report meaningfully on financial performance during that period. However, periodicity is usually applied within the context of an annual reporting cycle.

When general purpose financial statements are issued for any period of time of *less* than one year, they are called *interim statements*. Interim statements may be prepared for external use or for management's internal use only. Public companies are required to submit quarterly reports to their shareholders. Interim reports need not be audited.

Another common use of interim statements is for internal management use. Internal interim reports may be monthly rather than quarterly, and may be more detailed than those prepared for external release. Although interim reports may be prepared in less detail than annual statements and will include more estimates, it would be a rude shock to managers and shareholders alike if the annual statements were not consonant with the operations as described by the interim statements. Thus interim statements should be prepared in a manner that is consistent with the annual statements.

General principles of application

Section 1751 of the *CICA Handbook* contains explicit recommendations for the preparation of interim statements. This section was revised in 2000 (effective for 2001) to conform more closely with International Accounting Standard (IAS) 34 and to harmonize the Canadian standard with interim reporting standards in the United States. To a large extent, the revision merely caught up with existing practice. For example, the prior Canadian standard did not require an interim balance sheet, but the vast majority of companies already provided one in their interim reports.

Section 1751 applies to companies that are required by law or regulation to prepare interim reports [CICA 1751.02]. In effect, however, the section applies almost exclusively to *public* companies, as private companies are not required to issue interim statements unless required to do so by regulation. But regulators (e.g., for financial institutions) usually have their own specific requirements about the information to be reported. Of course, companies that voluntarily prepare consolidated statements are encouraged to follow the recommendations also.

Public companies do not issue a full set of financial statements and notes as their interim results. Interim financial statements are briefer than annual financial statements and more of an *exception reporting* principle is used for note disclosure—only new or changed accounting policies are disclosed.

The period covered by the interim statements varies somewhat depending on the type of statement. Interim income statements should report on both the individual interim period and on the year to date [CICA 1751.16(b)]. For example, the third-quarter income statement will show operating results both for the third quarter and for the year-to-date cumulative amounts for the first three quarters.

The retained earnings statement and the cash flow statements, in contrast, report only on a year-to-date basis [CICA 1751.16(c) and (d)]. The balance sheet will be as of the reporting date, of course; there is no such thing as a year-to-date balance sheet, since that statement reports on financial condition at a point in time.

All financial statements need a basis for comparison. Interim statements produced for external users are normally prepared on a comparative basis. In most statements, the comparison is with the same period of the preceding year. For the balance sheet, however, the comparison is with the previous year-end balance sheet [CICA 1751.16(a)]. For internal reports, budgeted figures for the period may provide a more relevant basis for comparison.

A company normally will use the same accounting policies for interim statements as it uses for the annual financial statements. If there are exceptions, those are to be disclosed [CICA 1751.14(a)]. The interim statements should indicate that they should be read in conjunction with the company's previous annual financial statements, since fuller information is available in the annual statements than in the interim statement.

Segment information should also be presented in the interim statements [CICA 1751.14(e)]. Segment information should include at least the following:

- segment revenues, segregated between intersegment revenues and those to external customers
- segment profit (loss)
- segment assets if there has been a significant change from the amounts reported in the previous annual statements
- any changes in the basis of segmentation or the method of reporting segment profit, and
- reconciliation of segment earnings to consolidated earnings for the interim period.

The interim segment information is essentially the same as that required in the annual financial statements.

The periodicity problem

At first glance, it may appear that the preparation of interim statements poses no special problems. After all, interim reports use the same accounting policies that are used for the annual statements, so what's the problem? Just use the same policies, and interim reporting is a no-brainer, right? Wrong! Interim reporting is not quite so simple.

When we prepare annual financial statements, we face many challenges of estimation and interperiod allocation. Revenue recognition can present significant difficulties, the costs of tangible and intangible capital assets must be allocated, and future costs must be estimated in order to achieve matching. When these accounting problems are confronted for a period shorter than a year, their significance increases proportionately.

Estimation errors will have a much larger impact on the operating income for a month or a quarter than they will on the operating income for a year. Cut-off procedures will not be as stringent for the unaudited interim statements, and interim inventories are most likely to be estimated or to be taken from perpetual inventory records whose accuracy has not been verified by a physical count.

Not only will estimation errors have a greater impact, but also the materiality threshold will be lower because the amounts on the quarterly income statement and cash flow statement will be only about one-fourth of the annual amounts. Estimation variances that might be ignored in the annual statements (with the higher materiality threshold) become significant in the quarterly statements. The result is that interim statements will intrinsically be significantly less reliable than annual statements.

Additional estimation and allocation problems arise because of the shorter accounting period. Some costs and revenues are seasonal or annual in nature, and interim statements require allocations that are not necessary for annual statements.

For example, annual insurance costs pose no problems if the accounting period is a year, but how should the cost be allocated if the period is a month? An easy answer would be to allocate one-twelfth of the cost to each month. However, suppose that the insurance is an expensive public liability policy for an amusement park that is open all year, but that does the bulk of its business in the summer months. Should the cost be allocated by time or by volume of activity in order to match the cost with the revenue?

Another example is a factory that shuts down in the month of August for a vacation for all production employees. The fixed costs of the factory during August could be viewed as a cost to be allocated to all of the interim periods, or as a cost of the individual period in which August falls. Similarly, annual costs such as retooling costs or once-a-year major maintenance costs could either be allocated, or could be allowed to fall into the interim period in which they occur.

Some costs are determined not only on an annual basis, but also *after* the end of the year. Customer rebates, sales bonuses, and income taxes are examples of these costs. Should an attempt be made to estimate and allocate these costs, or should they be allowed to fall into the last interim period?

As the preceding examples suggest, there are two basic approaches to the preparation of interim statements. The interim period can be viewed either as a distinct and separate accounting period of its own (the **discrete approach**), or as a part of a year (the **integral approach**).

Discrete approach

Under the discrete or *separate-period* approach, each interim period is accounted for by using the company's normal accounting policies applied to the interim period as though it were a year. A company's policy may be to expense immediately all costs that may have future benefits that are difficult to measure, such as development costs or factory retooling costs. Under this accounting policy, deferred charges and credits are normally not carried on the balance sheet. A company that follows this policy will also apply it to the interim periods under the discrete approach. Costs will be permitted to fall into the period in which they are incurred, even though they may be annual costs that benefit other interim periods.

This approach implicitly recognizes that since revenues and expenses are likely to be "lumpy," the interim earnings are also going to be lumpy, and are not just a proportionate part of the annual earnings. This approach treats the insurance costs, vacation costs, or retooling and maintenance costs as period costs for the quarter rather than allocating them to the other periods.

On the other hand, a company could follow a general accounting policy of capitalization and amortization of costs that benefit future periods. If this policy is followed, then there could be an attempt to allocate costs that are incurred in early periods to later periods, and to accrue costs in early periods that will not be incurred until later periods. There still would be no attempt to normalize costs and revenues, however, by spreading out seasonal costs such as heating, seasonal maintenance, annual bonuses, etc., or by spreading out seasonal revenues.

Under the discrete approach, income taxes are viewed as cumulative. Income taxes are accrued for the first period based on the net operating income for the period. Income taxes for the second period will be based on the *additional* taxes payable as a result of the operations for the second period, and so forth. If a loss occurred in the first period, no benefit will be recognized. Future income taxes would be provided for all temporary differences arising during the interim period, even if the temporary difference is expected to reverse within the taxation year.

Integral approach

Under this approach, the interim period is viewed simply as a part of the longer period of a year. Expenses are allocated across the interim periods in such a way as to portray the company's likely annualized operating results. Theoretically, if a company is heading for a year in which the operating margin (net income divided by sales) is 10%, then the interim statements should reflect that fact. Under this view, the interim statements should be the best predictor available of the company's operating results for the year.

For the examples cited above, the integral approach will allocate the insurance costs proportionately to the volume of business, and will allocate the costs of the plant closing, the annual retooling and maintenance costs, and the estimated bonuses and rebates to all of the interim periods.

Income taxes are viewed as an annual expense to be allocated to interim periods in proportion to the pre-tax interim net income. There will be no separate computation of income taxes for the interim period as though it were a separate taxation period. Temporary differences will be determined on an annual basis and allocated to the interim periods. An income tax benefit will be recognized for a first-quarter loss if the company expects to earn a profit for the tax year as a whole.

Application in practice

For internal interim reports, the discrete approach will almost always be used. The comparative amounts for internal users are likely to be budgeted figures for the period (perhaps supplemented by the previous year's figures), and budgets generally include major costs as expenses of the period in which they occur. Controllability is a concern in budgeting, and costs allocated from previous periods are not controllable in the later periods to which they are allocated. Also, internal reports frequently do not include any income tax estimates, thereby removing one major estimation problem.

For public interim statements, reporting is guided by Section 1751 of the *CICA Handbook*. Interim statements should include the same headings and subtotals that appear in annual financial statements. All of the line-item disclosures that are required by the *CICA Handbook* for annual statements should also be disclosed (e.g., interest expense, income tax expense, and amortization) [CICA 1751.11]. As well, basic and diluted earnings per share should be presented on the face of the interim income statement.

Note disclosure in interim statements is very limited. A statement reader is presumed to have access to the previous year-end financial statements, and much of the information in the notes thereto will not be significantly different for the interim periods. As mentioned previously, the exception principle comes into play here—to the extent that there are significant changes, the company should provide note disclosure. Such changes include changes in accounting policy, changes in strategic investments, restructurings, extraordinary items, and discontinued operations. Subsequent event disclosure is also required.

For measuring interim period operating results, Section 1751 generally favours the discrete approach, "each interim period standing alone as an independent reporting period" [CICA 1751.19]. Generally, costs and revenues should be accrued or deferred at the end of interim periods only if those same costs or revenues would normally be accrued or deferred at the end of the fiscal year.

However, the recommendations also contain some aspects of the part-of-year approach, as described in the following paragraphs. Therefore, the *CICA Handbook* approach might better be characterized as a "modified discrete" approach.

Two specific exceptions pertain to inventories [CICA 1751.26]. Certain types of standard cost variances may be deferred if those variances are expected to be offset by the end of the year. Also, under LIFO inventory procedures, a dip into the base stock (i.e., "old" prices) should not be recognized if the inventory is expected to be replaced by the end of the year.

Another general exception arises for costs that are determined only on an annual basis. The section specifically discusses year-end bonuses, contingent lease payments, and income taxes. The section uses the terminology of "constructive obligation" to rationalize these exceptions, but the basic point is simply that companies can estimate or project the determining factors for the entire year and accrue the costs in the interim statements. For example, contingent rents may be based on annual sales in excess of a contractual minimum. In a strict application of the discrete approach, no accrual for contingent rent is made until the threshold level of sales is achieved. Section 1751, however, permits this type of cost to be spread out over the several interim periods—an application of the integral approach.

When purchases are made under an annual volume rebate or discount scheme, the section suggests different approaches for the buyer and seller [CICA 1751.26(G)]. If attainment of the required level of sales to qualify for the rebate is likely, the seller should recognize the contingent liability. The buyer, on the other hand, recognizes the contingent benefit only when the required level of sales has been achieved—the integral approach is used for the seller and the discrete approach for the buyer. Although these are conflicting treatments from the viewpoint of interim reporting, these treatments are consistent with the recommendations for contingencies, in which contingent liabilities are recognized when they are likely and measurable [CICA 3290.12], but contingent gains are recognized only when they are realized [CICA 3290.20].

Income tax expense presents a special problem. Under the discrete approach, income tax for each quarter would be calculated on the year-to-date taxable income. The increase (or decrease) in income tax from the previous quarter would be that quarter's tax expense. This is consistent with the general approach espoused in Section 1751:

> Amounts of income and expenses reported in the current interim period will reflect any changes in estimates of amounts reported in prior interim periods of the fiscal year. The amounts reported in prior interim periods are not retroactively adjusted [CICA 1751.25].

However, the AcSB recommends that interim income tax expense be estimated by using the estimated average annual effective income tax rate [CICA 1751.B13]. The average rate will differ from the marginal rate only under a two-rate tax system or a progressive tax system, in which higher levels of income are taxed at a different rate than lower levels. Instead of accruing income tax at the lower rate in the early quarters, the average rate applicable to management's estimate of the full year's earnings should be used. The average rate should be used even if the early quarters show a loss and even if the overall earnings for the year are expected to be zero.

The benefits of an income tax loss in an interim period are recognized in that period if:

- the loss will be offset by taxable income in the other interim periods of that year
- the loss can be used as a tax loss carryback to a prior year, or
- it is more likely than not that the benefit of the loss will be realized as a tax loss carryforward.

For example, suppose that a company has a loss of $50,000 in the first quarter but expects to earn $120,000 over the following three quarters. If the expected average tax rate is 30%, the first quarter interim income statement will show an income tax *benefit* or recovery (i.e., a negative tax expense, or a credit) of $50,000 × 30% = $15,000. The following quarters will show a positive income tax expense totalling $120,000 × 30% = $36,000. The total income tax expense for the year will be $36,000 − $15,000 = $21,000, based on cumulative net income of $70,000 for the year (i.e., $120,000 − $50,000).

If an income tax loss is not expected to be offset by taxable profits in the other interim periods of the current year, the benefit is recognized only if it is more likely than not that the benefit will be realized in future years.

Illustrative interim statement

Exhibit 7–3 shows interim statements for eNGENUITY Technologies Inc. These are the second-quarter statements for fiscal year 2004. eNGENUITY is based in Montreal. The company's customers are mainly in the U.S.A. and Europe. Its annual report explains that the company:

> . . . develops, markets and supports software and ready-to-use components for the development of advanced visual applications. Our solutions allow our customers to develop human–machine interfaces, simulation and training systems, as well as to create graphical representations of their strategic information. eNGENUITY's products provide the means to significantly shorten development cycles while improving software performance reliability for complex software applications, which include:

cockpit display systems, car dashboard instrumentation, network management systems, geographic information systems and aircraft behaviour modeling.

The company's interim statements appear to comply with the *CICA Handbook* recommendations. In Exhibit 7–3, we have omitted the lengthy note on Capital Stock, as well as the quantitative detail for geographic segments.

Note 1 points out that the interim statements should be read in conjunction with the annual statements. The annual statements contain extensive note

EXHIBIT 7–3 INTERIM FINANCIAL STATEMENTS

eNGENUITY TECHNOLOGIES INC.
Consolidated balance sheets

(amounts in '000s)	as at December 31, 2003 (unaudited) $	as at June 30, 2003 (audited) $
Assets		
Current assets		
Cash and cash equivalents	1,400	2,081
Accounts receivable	5,460	4,130
Investment tax credits and income taxes receivable	588	485
Prepaid expenses and deposits	324	362
Inventory	14	14
	7,786	7,072
Investment tax credits	1,789	1,789
Future income taxes	1,426	1,426
Capital assets	1,265	1,321
Goodwill	4,194	4,194
	16,460	15,802
Liabilities		
Current liabilities		
Bank loan	—	360
Accounts payable and accrued liabilities	3,058	3,609
Deferred revenue	2,683	2,198
Current portion of obligations under capital leases	112	206
Due to shareholders	421	463
	6,274	6,836
Bank loan (Note 4)	1,000	—
Obligations under capital leases	115	122
Deferred lease inducements	13	20
	7,402	6,978
Shareholders' equity		
Capital stock (Note 2)	28,105	28,105
Deficit	(19,042)	(19,276)
Cumulative translation adjustment	(5)	(5)
	9,058	8,824
	16,460	15,802

eNGENUITY TECHNOLOGIES INC.
Consolidated statements of operations

	three months ended December 31 (unaudited)		six months ended December 31 (unaudited)	
	2003	2002	2003	2002
(amounts in '000s, except per share amounts)	$	$	$	$
Revenue				
License fees	2,159	2,577	3,889	4,451
Services and maintenance	1,861	1,489	3,408	3,300
Third-party products	14	15	53	15
	4,034	4,081	7,350	7,766
Cost and expenses				
Cost of revenue	414	533	805	1,101
Sales and marketing	1,677	1,426	2,986	2,756
General and administration	1,107	1,225	2,281	2,578
Research and development	678	648	1,421	1,334
Investment tax credits and government assistance	(348)	(298)	(800)	(834)
Amortization of capital assets	89	130	180	252
	3,617	3,664	6,873	7,187
Income from operations	417	417	477	579
Financial income (expense)	(193)	(12)	(243)	321
Net income	224	405	234	900
Net income per share (Note 2)				
Basic and diluted	0.02	0.04	0.02	0.08
Weighted average number of shares				
Basic	11,530,840	11,530,840	11,530,840	11,530,840
Diluted	11,539,664	11,541,951	11,534,744	11,536,396

eNGENUITY TECHNOLOGIES INC.
Consolidated statements of deficit

	three months ended December 31 (unaudited)		six months ended December 31 (unaudited)	
	2003	2002	2003	2002
(amounts in '000s)	$	$	$	$
Deficit, beginning of period	(19,266)	(17,500)	(19,276)	(17,995)
Net income	224	405	234	900
Deficit, end of period	(19,042)	(17,095)	(19,042)	(17,095)

eNGENUITY TECHNOLOGIES INC.
Consolidated statements of cash flows

(amounts in '000s)	three months ended December 31 (unaudited)		six months ended December 31 (unaudited)	
	2003 $	2002 $	2003 $	2002 $
Operating activities				
Net income	224	405	234	900
Items not affecting cash				
Amortization of capital assets	89	130	180	252
Deferred lease inducements	(4)	(5)	(7)	(8)
	309	530	407	1,144
Changes in non-cash working capital items	(200)	(1,024)	(1,503)	(2,363)
	109	(494)	(1,096)	(1,219)
Financing activities				
Repayment of bank loan	(910)	—	(360)	—
Proceeds from issuance of long-term bank loan	1,000	—	1,000	—
Repayment of long-term debt	—	—	—	(96)
Repayment of obligations under capital leases	(24)	(77)	(101)	(162)
	66	(77)	539	(258)
Investing activities				
Purchase of capital assets	(96)	(99)	(124)	(99)
	(96)	(99)	(124)	(99)
Cash and cash equivalents increase/(decrease)	79	(670)	(681)	(1,576)
Balance, beginning of period	1,321	2,113	2,081	3,019
Balance, end of period	1,400	1,443	1,400	1,443

eNGENUITY TECHNOLOGIES INC.
Notes to the consolidated financial statements

Three and six month periods ended December 31, 2003 and 2002 (unaudited)
(all tabular amounts are in thousands of dollars, except for share information)

Note 1: Basis of presentation and significant accounting policies

In the opinion of the Company, the unaudited interim consolidated financial statements have been prepared on a basis consistent with the annual financial statements and contain all adjustments necessary for a fair presentation of the financial position as at December 31, 2003 and the results of operations and cash flows for the three and six-month periods ended December 31, 2003 and 2002. The interim consolidated financial statements should be read in conjunction with the audited consolidated financial statements and notes thereto included in the Company's annual report for fiscal year 2003.

The preparation of financial statements in conformity with Canadian generally accepted accounting principles requires management to make estimates and assumptions that affect the reported amounts of assets, liabilities, revenues and expenses, and disclosure of contingent liabilities in these financial statements. Actual results could differ from those estimates.

Note 2: Capital stock

(note omitted)

Note 3: Restructuring charges

During the third quarter of 2003, the Company recorded a restructuring charge of $1,120,000 following a review of its operations, which resulted in the restructuring of its organizational and corporate structure, the closing of certain offices and a reduction in work force.

As at December 31, 2003, the remaining balance of the restructuring charges provision is $249,000.

Note 4: Long-term loan

On November 3, 2003, the Company signed an agreement with a Canadian chartered bank to provide a long-term loan of up to $2,000,000 of which $1,000,000 has been drawn at December 31, 2003. The loan is disbursed in tranches conditional upon the Company achieving certain financial milestones.

The loan is guaranteed by Investissement Québec up to 70% and a mortgage of $2,000,000 on tangible and intangible capital assets present and future of the Company. The loan bears interest at prime rate plus 3.0%. The loan is repayable in monthly installments of $41,667, maturing in October 2008, the first repayment beginning in October 2004.

Note 5: Segmented information

The Company considers that its operations fall principally into one industry segment, the development, manufacturing, marketing and support of software development and simulation tools.

(geographic detail omitted)

coverage, while the interim statements contain only changes or events that happened during the interim period.

For example, Note 3 discloses the end-of-quarter restructuring charge provision balance that was originally recorded during the third quarter of the previous fiscal year (2003). Similarly, Note 4 describes a new term loan agreement that was negotiated during the current quarter.

One final thing to notice: the balance sheet shows a "cumulative translation adjustment" of $5,000 (debit) under shareholders' equity. We will explain the meaning of this amount in Chapter 9 – something to look forward to!

SUMMARY OF KEY POINTS

1. Segmented reporting is intended to provide information to enable financial statement readers to assess the risk and return that a company generates in its different lines of business. Segment information reveals performance aspects that are concealed by the aggregated nature of consolidated statements.

2. The recommendations for segment reporting apply only to public companies, with a few exceptions. Basically, segment information is provided for reportable operating segments. An *operating* segment is one that has a separate responsibility reporting line directly to the company's chief operating officer for evaluation and resource allocation. A *reportable* segment is an operating segment that accounts for at least 10% of the consolidated company's revenues, profits, or assets.

3. The corporation should report the total assets and a measure of profit or loss for each reportable segment. Detail, as prescribed by the *CICA Handbook*, should be provided for specific income statement line items *if* those items are reviewed regularly by the chief operating decision maker. As well, the corporation should report certain enterprisewide information on products and services, on the geographic distribution of revenues and assets, and on customers that account for 10% or more of the company's revenues.

4. Interim financial statements are those that are issued for any period less than a year. Public companies are required to issue interim statements—quarterly in the United States and Canada, semiannually in most other countries. The *CICA Handbook* recommendations on interim reporting apply only to companies that are required to prepare interim statements by law or regulation.

5. Interim statements should consist of a balance sheet, income statement, cash flow statement, retained earnings statement, and notes that explain deviations from or exceptions to the accounting policies and major estimates that are used for the annual statements. The statements can be condensed, but should include all of the subtotals and totals that the company uses in its annual statements, and should include those line items specifically required by the *CICA Handbook*. The company should disclose extraordinary items, discontinued operations, restructurings, and acquisitions and other changes in strategic investments.

6. The *CICA Handbook* approach to interim statements is very similar to that taken in the U.S. and by international accounting standards. The underlying philosophy is the *discrete* approach, in which each interim period is treated as a distinct time period. Exceptions exist, however, for certain types of expense that are calculated only on an annual basis, such as bonuses, contingent rent, income tax, and quantity discounts (for the seller). For these items, the *integral* or *part-of-year* approach is used. The annual amount is estimated and apportioned to the interim periods.

REVIEW QUESTIONS

7–1 What are the objectives of segmented reporting?

7–2 When a corporation reports financial information by segments, do the segments correspond to specific subsidiaries?

7–3 What type of company is required to provide segmented reporting?

7–4 How does the AcSB consider benefit–cost relationships for segmented reporting?

7–5 How can an operating segment be identified?

7–6 What are the guidelines for determining whether an operating segment is *reportable*?

7–7 Companies L and D both operate food processing plants, and both operate a chain of retail food stores. Company L transfers all of the output from its processing plants to its stores, while Company D's processing plants produce private-label products for other retailers. How might the segment reporting of the two companies differ?

7–8 What does the *CICA Handbook* consider a reasonable upper limit for the number of segments to disclose?

7–9 How is profit defined for determining operating segments?

7–10 How much of the consolidated enterprise's business activity must be reported in operating segments in order to satisfy the requirements of the *CICA Handbook*?

7–11 Where some operating segments operate at a loss and others are profitable, how is the problem of offsetting considered in applying the 10% guidelines for reporting?

7–12 What is the reason for requiring companies to report geographic segments?

7–13 What data must be reported for each geographic segment? How do these data differ from the data reported for industry segments?

7–14 How is the risk of relying on major customers considered in segmented reporting?

7–15 Explain briefly why interim reporting poses problems different from those of annual reporting.

7–16 What types of companies does Section 1751 of the *CICA Handbook* apply to for interim reporting?

7–17 What does the *exception reporting* principle mean for note disclosure in interim reporting?

7–18 What basis of comparison is used for interim financial statements?

7–19 What are the two basic approaches to the preparation of interim statements?

7–20 Which approach to interim statements is recommended by the *CICA Handbook*?

7–21 Under the discrete or separate-period approach to interim statements, how would an annual, one-time expenditure such as retooling cost be reported? How would the reporting differ under the integral or part-of-a-year approach?

7–22 How does the measurement of income tax expense differ between the two approaches to interim reporting?

7–23 When the quarterly statements of a public Canadian company are reported, are the same financial statements prepared as for annual reporting?

CASES

CASE 7–1   Ermine Oil Limited

Ermine Oil Limited (Ermine) is a fully integrated Canadian oil company. Ermine commenced as a petroleum exploration company and was very successful in its oil field discoveries. In order to attain market security and improve profits, Ermine was forced to embark on a program of vertical integration. It first acquired a refining division and then marketing and transportation divisions. From the beginning, management appreciated the integrated nature of the business, and production was transferred between divisions at standard cost. The management control system recognized the exploration, refining, and transportation divisions as cost centres and the marketing division as a revenue centre. While the exploration, refining, and transportation divisions did make external sales, historically, none of these divisions' external sales accounted for 10% of Ermine's total sales. However, in the last fiscal year, due to unusual world market conditions, the transportation division's sales accounted for 11% of Ermine's total sales. Over 90% of Ermine's sales were within Canada, with the balance spread over many countries worldwide. Ermine did not feel it was necessary to disclose segmented information in its annual financial statements.

Beluga Petroleum Limited (Beluga) was similar to Ermine in size and also in scope of operations except that, in addition, it had a chemical division. However, Beluga was a subsidiary of a foreign oil company and its divisions were each organized as profit centres with products transferred between divisions at world market prices. Each division purchased and sold products extensively to outside companies. In addition, about 15% of Beluga's sales were export, almost exclusively to the U.S. In its annual financial statements, Beluga showed segmented information by the five divisions (exploration, refining, transportation, chemical, and marketing) and sales were divided between domestic and export operations.

Required:

Discuss how both Ermine and Beluga could report differently with respect to disclosure of segmented information, and yet be in accordance with generally accepted accounting principles.

[SMA]

CASE 7–2   Interim Reporting

In today's rapidly changing financial markets, financial statement users are demanding more information, released more promptly than in the past. To respond to these needs, the *CICA Handbook* has recently issued a revised Section 1751 for Interim Reporting.

At a professional update session to outline the accounting changes to the *CICA Handbook*, two members engaged in a lively discussion. One member is a controller of an international public company, while the other member is a senior financial analyst in a securities firm.

Financial Analyst: My review of the *CICA Handbook* leads me to conclude that the objectives of interim reporting should be the same as those of annual reporting.

Controller: I disagree. Interim reports are aimed at different users, serve different purposes, and must be published more quickly than annual reports. It follows that the underlying objectives should also differ.

Financial Analyst: Regardless of the content of interim reports, the interim operating results should be measured on the same basis as the annual results because the interim period is an integral part of the annual period.

Controller: I agree that there is a measurement problem for interim reporting, but I don't see that there is a simple solution. For example, I find it difficult to make interim estimates for various expenses given the cyclical nature of our business. After all, the interim period is only a portion of the annual period.

Required:

Prepare a memo discussing the main issues raised in the preceding conversation.
[CICA, adapted]

CASE 7–3 Shaw Navigational Company

The Shaw Navigational Company is a public Canadian corporation that operates a fleet of ships on the Great Lakes. In common with other Great Lakes shipping companies, rates are quoted and revenues are collected in U.S. dollars, regardless of the location or nationality of the shipper. Over 90% of Shaw's consolidated gross revenues, operating profits, and identifiable capital assets relate to the shipping business, and thus Shaw's management claims exemption from segmented reporting requirements on the grounds that shipping represents its only operating segment. In 2006, Shaw's consolidated net income was $1,200,000.

Shaw does have two subsidiaries that are not in the shipping business. One is a bus company that operates on intercity routes in Manitoba, and that is consolidated with the shipping operation. The bus fleet has recently been modernized, and the new buses have been acquired by means of leases rather than by an outright purchase.

The other subsidiary, which is reported on the equity basis, is a casualty insurance company located in Michigan. About 20% of the insurance company's business involves Great Lakes shipping, although mainly for shipping companies other than Shaw. Shaw's equity in the earnings of the insurance company amounted to $180,000 in 2006.

Required:

Comment on management's assertion that Shaw is exempt from segment reporting because it operates in one line of business.

PROBLEMS

P7–1

Tech Company sells personal computers, mainframes, and software in more than seven countries. The company is required to file financial statements annually with a securities commission. The controller has just compiled the following information on last year's revenues:

Revenues (in millions)

Personal computers	$94
Mainframes	52
Software	6
	$152
United States	$36
Canada	44
Europe	30
Asia	18
Africa	12
South America	12
	$152

Required:

Which of the above should be reported as an operating segment and which as a geographical segment in a note to the financial statements?

[CICA, adapted]

P7–2

The Fellows Corporation has internal reporting for four divisions. The following data have been gathered for the year just ended.

	Div. A	Div. B	Div. C	Div. D
Interdivisional sales	$50,000	$ 10,000	—	—
External sales	5,000	100,000	$75,000	$200,000
Direct divisional expenses	25,000	60,000	15,000	50,000
Allocated joint costs	—	—	35,000	55,000
Depreciation	17,500	20,000	12,500	22,500
Capital expenditures	10,000	30,000	40,000	80,000
Identifiable assets	92,500	107,500	62,500	122,500

1. Division A sells over 90% of its output to Division B on a cost-plus basis.

2. Divisions C and D share production facilities. Joint product costs, depreciation, capital expenditures, and much of the identifiable assets are allocated one-third to Division C and the remainder to Division D.

3. Unallocated corporate expenses not included above amount to $57,500.

Required:

a. From the preceding information, what are the operating segments that should be reported by the Fellows Corporation? Explain your recommendation fully.

b. Prepare a schedule of supplementary financial information by segments, in accordance with the *CICA Handbook* recommendations based on the information provided above, together with a condensed consolidated income statement.

P7–3

The following information is available for World Wide Corporation's operating subsidiaries throughout the world, in thousands of Canadian dollars:

	External Sales	Sales to Operating Regions	Identifiable Assets	After-Tax Profit
Canada	$ 40,000	$200,000	$ 20,000	$ 5,000
United States	190,000	40,000	80,000	4,500
Europe	150,000	20,000	70,000	9,000
Asia	30,000	—	15,000	3,500
South America	40,000	—	20,000	5,000
General Corporate	—	—	30,000	3,000*
Consolidated	$450,000		$235,000	$30,000

*Investment income, less general corporate expenses.

Required:

Determine which regions you would suggest reporting as geographic segments, as defined by the *CICA Handbook*. Identify the characteristics that led to your choices.

P7–4

This year, for the first time, Samson Corporation must report supplementary information by operating segment. The controller has prepared the following note for inclusion in the annual report.

Segmented Data

Your company operates in several different operating segments. Selected financial data by division are provided below, in thousands of Canadian dollars.

	Men's Wear	Tires	Other	Consolidated
Sales to outsiders	$ 800	$ 400	$ 600	$1,800
Sales between divisions	100	20	120	240
Total sales	$ 900	$ 420	$ 720	$2,040
Operating profit	$ 30	$ 80	$ 40	$ 124
Capital expenditures	$ 10	$ 50	$ 60	$ 140
Assets	$130	$480	$180	$ 910

During the year, your company had export sales that resulted in gross profit of $100,000.

Required:

Criticize the note as prepared by the controller. Identify any missing information, either numerical or verbal, and indicate errors in presentation.

P7–5

The High End Company is a retail department store chain. The company's fiscal year ends on the Saturday closest to January 31 of each year. The company is publicly held and submits quarterly financial statements to the shareholders.

Like most retail establishments, High End operates at a loss for most of the year, but generally recovers the losses in the fourth quarter to finish the year with a profit. In fiscal year 2005, the company reported pre-tax net income of $2,000,000, and paid taxes at a rate of 45%.

In the first quarter of 2006, the company suffered a loss of $1,500,000 before taxes. In the second quarter, economic conditions improved slightly, but the cumulative six-month loss was $2,600,000, the worst in the company's history. Nevertheless, management predicted that the losses would be recovered as the economy improved, and forecast a break-even performance for the year as a whole.

The loss did decline in the third quarter, to a cumulative loss of $1,300,000; the fourth quarter almost completely wiped out the loss, ending the year with a fiscal pre-tax loss of only $100,000.

Required:

Assume that tax losses can be carried back for only one year. Determine the provision for income taxes that should be reported on High End's interim income statements for fiscal year 2006, assuming that each quarter is reported:

a. separately, not cumulatively

b. cumulatively

P7–6

Smith and Quarter Ltd. experienced the following events during the first quarter of 2006:

1. The annual sales catalogue was developed and provided on-line, at a cost of $1,000,000.

2. Programming and consulting fees were incurred for annual updates of the Internet site, at a cost of $500,000.

3. Owing to a strike at the principal supplier's factory, Smith and Quarter's inventory fell to the lowest level in 14 years. Smith and Quarter uses the LIFO method for financial reporting.

4. A notice of assessed value for property taxes was received. The tax assessment will be received and be due in the second quarter. Taxes for 2006 are estimated at $400,000.

5. Smith and Quarter uses the declining-balance method for depreciation. The total depreciation for 2006 on assets held at the start of the year will be $1,600,000.

6. The company's top management receives annual bonuses based on 10% of annual net income after taxes.

Required:

For each event reported above, indicate what impact it would have on the first-quarter interim report under each approach to interim statements:

a. the integral or part-of-year approach

b. the discrete or separate-period approach

Chapter 8

Foreign Currency Transactions and Hedges

Many corporations engage in some form of international activity. The range of possible activities is vast. At one extreme is the company that has only an occasional transaction in a foreign currency. At the opposite extreme is the corporation with a network of foreign subsidiaries that operates on a global basis.

We find most Canadian companies between these two extremes. Transborder transactions are very common, accounting for about 40% of Canada's GDP. Over 80% of those transactions are with the United States.

A smaller number of companies establish (or buy) manufacturing or direct service subsidiaries outside Canada. The Canadian population base and GDP are small, in world terms. Therefore, a Canadian company cannot become a significant international player until most of its activity is outside of Canada.

This chapter will address two major accounting issues: (1) accounting for foreign currency transactions, and (2) accounting for currency hedging activities. More specifically, the chapter will focus on the following:

- foreign currency transactions
  - the general approach to accounting for transactions that are conducted in a foreign currency
  - the carrying value for non-monetary assets and liabilities that arise from transactions in foreign currencies
  - accounting for exchange gains and losses that arise when monetary balances, both financial assets and financial liabilities, are translated at different rates at different points in time
  - the accounting approaches for the different types of financial assets: those held to maturity, those available for sale, and those held for trading
  - accounting for financial liabilities—trading liabilities and other financial liabilities

- hedging activities
  - the general nature of hedging
  - hedging an existing financial asset or financial liability
  - hedging an *anticipated* transaction
  - the requirements for using hedge accounting
  - measuring the effectiveness of a hedge

In Chapter 9, we will develop the foreign currency theme further by explaining the accounting for subsidiaries that operate in foreign countries and foreign currencies.

Foreign Currency Transactions

Definitions

Transactions that are denominated in a foreign currency are called **foreign currency transactions**. A transaction is **denominated** in a foreign currency whenever the monetary value of the transaction is specified in a currency that is *not* the company's reporting currency. Most Canadian companies prepare their financial statements in Canadian dollars; any transaction that is stated in a different currency is a foreign currency transaction. Such transactions include (1) borrowing or lending money and (2) buying or selling products at an amount stated in a foreign currency (e.g., U.S. dollars, Japanese yen, or euros). All foreign currency transactions must be translated into the reporting currency for accounting purposes. For the vast majority of Canadian companies, the reporting currency is the Canadian dollar.

On the other hand, if a Canadian company uses the U.S. dollar as its reporting currency, all transactions in Canadian dollars automatically become foreign currency transactions for that company's financial reporting. The Canadian dollar transactions must be converted to U.S. dollars.

Foreign currency transactions are a major accounting problem because exchange rates fluctuate. For example, Telus Corporation has outstanding long-term notes of US$2.0 billion maturing in 2011. At the end of 2002, those notes were shown in Telus's balance sheet at C$3.0 billion, reflecting the year-end 2002 exchange rate. During 2003, the exchange rate changed significantly, with the result that the same US$2 billion was reported at C$2.5 billion in the 2003 balance sheet. Telus's actual liability had not changed – it still was US$2.0 billion. The accounting challenge is to figure out how to account for the "extra" half-billion dollars.

Causes of exchange rate changes

Before launching into a discussion of accounting for foreign currencies, we will pause and consider briefly the reasons that exchange rates change. Near the end of the Second World War (i.e., in 1944), the world's major trading countries established fixed exchange rates among the major currencies. This was known as the Bretton Woods Agreement, named after the place where the international agreement was negotiated and signed. These fixed exchange rates were intended to facilitate international commerce by eliminating the exchange rate fluctuations that made international financial transactions so risky.

Fixed exchange rates remained in effect for over 25 years, but there was increasing strain on the system as national economies developed at different rates and in different ways. The fixed rate system did not permit natural economic adjustments in response to the flow of funds and balance of payments. Finally, in 1971, the Bretton Woods Agreement was abandoned and exchange rates were permitted to fluctuate freely in the economic marketplace.

Why do exchange rates fluctuate? Some short-run changes in exchange rates are the result of speculation in the money markets. Over the longer run, however, exchange rates are related to two economic phenomena: (1) differential inflation rates and (2) relative interest rates.

If Country A experiences inflation that is in excess of inflation in Country B, then the currency in Country A will decline in value relative to Country B's currency. The relative change in exchange rates will be approximately equal to the relative change in purchasing power of the currency; a fixed nominal amount of

Country A's currency will buy less after a period of inflation than the equivalent nominal amount of Country B's currency, and therefore the relative values of the two currencies will be adjusted through the money markets to recognize the fact that Country A's currency will not buy as much any more. This is known as the **purchasing power parity (PPP)** concept.

An alternative concept for explaining changes in exchange rates is that changes in rates are a reflection of a difference in interest rates between countries; this is known as the **Fisher Effect**, after the eminent economist who developed the theory.

Inflation rates and interest rates are related. A country that has a higher inflation rate will have higher interest rates. Both differentials will have an impact on the exchange rate, and the net result will be a currency that declines in value relative to the currency of countries with lower inflation (and lower interest rates). It is difficult (and perhaps pointless, for accounting purposes) to unravel the impact of PPP and the Fisher Effect empirically.[1]

Transactions

Example Suppose that on December 5, 2005, Domestic Corporation sells 100 units of its product in Germany for €100,000. To record this sale on its books, Domestic Corporation must translate the euro-denominated sale into the equivalent amount in Canadian dollars. If we assume that the exchange rate on the date of sale was €1 = C$1.25 (that is, that each euro is worth $1.25, or that one dollar is worth €0.80), then the Canadian equivalent is $125,000. The sale can be recorded as follows, assuming that it was a sale on account:

Accounts receivable	125,000	
Sales		125,000

The amount of the sale in its Canadian equivalent will then be added to the other domestic and foreign sales without further difficulties.

If the German customer pays the amount owing on December 21, Domestic Corporation will receive €100,000. If the exchange rate is €1 = $1.27 on the payment date, Domestic will receive $127,000 when the euros are converted to Canadian dollars. Domestic will debit cash for $127,000 and credit accounts receivable for $125,000. The $2,000 difference represents a gain that has been realized by Domestic because the value of the euro went up while Domestic was holding a receivable that was denominated in euros. If the exchange rate had gone down instead of up, Domestic would have realized a loss instead of a gain.

Alternatives The gain on the exchange rate change could be treated in either of two ways: (1) by increasing the amount of revenue recognized by $2,000, or (2) by crediting a separate gain account. The difference may seem minor, since both treatments will result in an increase in net income in the same period. The alternative treatments can have a substantive impact, however, when a company buys inventory or capital assets in a foreign currency and the exchange rate changes between the date of purchase and the date of payment. Any exchange gain or loss realized by holding the liability could either be added to the cost of the assets acquired or be treated as a gain or loss of the period.

---

1   One empirical test, for example, found that purchasing power parity is the central tendency for exchange rate movements, although "there are significant deviations from PPP theory for some years. The theory's validity increases as the length of the period is increased." Robert Z. Aliber and Clyde P. Stickney, "Accounting Measures of Foreign Exchange Exposure: The Long and Short of It," *The Accounting Review* (January 1975), pp. 44–57.

The first approach, to attach exchange gains and losses to the asset or the revenue that results from the initial transaction, is known as the **one-transaction theory** because the accrual and the cash settlement are viewed as a single economic event. The second approach is called the **two-transaction theory**; the accrual (i.e., the sale or purchase) is viewed as one economic event while the eventual cash settlement (collection of the receivable or payment of the liability) is treated as a separate financing activity. Under the two-transaction theory, exchange gains and losses normally flow through directly to the income statement in the period that they occur.

Current practice The two-transaction theory has been more widely adopted and is the one recommended in Section 1651 of the *CICA Handbook*. The financing component of a foreign currency transaction is separated from the purchase or sale itself because the cash flow is controlled by the domestic company, and the results of such essentially speculative activity should not be hidden in gross revenue or in the cost of assets. The financing component can be controlled because the company has options—purchases can be paid for by bank drafts at the time of the transaction; receivables can be sold to banks or finance companies, or can be financed by the sale of credit "paper" denominated in the same currency; the foreign currency-denominated payable or receivable can be hedged (which is the subject of the second part of this chapter); and so forth.

Under the two-transaction approach, the collection by Domestic of the €100,000 receivable will be recorded as follows:

Cash (€100,000)	127,000	
Accounts receivable		125,000
Foreign currency exchange gain		2,000

The two-transaction approach also applies to purchases. Companies frequently buy inventory or other assets at a price that is fixed in foreign currency. The cost of the asset is measured at the exchange rate in effect at the date of the purchase. If the liability is settled later at a higher or lower exchange rate, the exchange gain/loss has no impact on the carrying value of the asset.

Monetary balances Now assume instead that the receivable is not collected until January 25, 2006, and that the fiscal year of Domestic Corporation ends on December 31. The receivable was initially recorded on Domestic's books at $125,000, but actually the receivable is for €100,000. If the euro is worth $1.28 on December 31, then the value of the €100,000 receivable is $128,000, a $3,000 gain over the original recorded amount of the transaction. How should the $3,000 gain be reported?

Well, the quick answer is that the $3,000 foreign currency gain must be reported in income in 2005. Any further gain or loss between December 31, 2005, and January 25, 2006, must be taken into income in 2006. However, this leads us to a much broader issue: accounting for the full range of financial assets and liabilities that are denominated in a foreign currency.

First, however, we will examine two other issues: (1) accounting for non-monetary balances and (2) practical ways of dealing with a large volume of foreign currency transactions.

Non-monetary balances The foregoing discussion has focused on the translation of current *monetary* balances. If the foreign currency transaction was not a sale but was, for example, a purchase of inventory, then the transaction will result in *two* balance sheet amounts—(1) an account payable and (2) inventory. The account payable is a monetary balance and will be treated exactly as the account receivable discussed above, assuming that the two-transaction approach is used.

The inventory, however, is a *non-monetary balance*. A **non-monetary balance** is, by definition, *not* an amount that is fixed in terms of a currency and does not represent a claim against monetary resources. Therefore, non-monetary balances are not affected by changes in the exchange rate. If inventory is carried at historical cost, then the historical cost of inventory that was purchased with a foreign currency is simply the domestic currency equivalent of the foreign currency *at the date of the purchase*. Non-monetary balances are carried at historical exchange rates because that is the historical cost.

An exception arises when a non-monetary asset is reported on the balance sheet at current value rather than at historical cost. For example, suppose that Domestic Corporation purchased gold in U.S. dollars and that Domestic reports its gold inventory at current market value. If the current market value is quoted in U.S. dollars, it makes no sense to take a current value and translate it at a historical rate. In order to report the current value of the investment in Canadian dollars, the current value in U.S. dollars must be converted into Canadian dollars at the current exchange rate.

Practical expedients As a practical matter, companies that engage in a large volume of foreign currency transactions may not actually use the current rate for translating each transaction. If, for example, a company has thousands of sales transactions in U.S. dollars during a year, it is impractical to check on the current exchange rate (the *spot rate*) every time a sale occurs. Instead, the sales may be accumulated for a period of time and a single rate applied to the aggregate.

Alternatively, a company might use the rate at the beginning of each month for that month's transactions. Each of these approaches is an expedient for accounting for a large volume of transactions. Minor differences between the actual spot rate and the rate used for translation of the transactions will be adjusted for when the accounts are settled, or when the monetary account balances are adjusted to the current rate on the balance sheet date.

Some companies use a *pre-determined standard rate* for translating foreign currency transactions. If a company uses a profit-centre approach for evaluating its managers, it may be desirable to remove the effects of uncontrollable currency fluctuations from the profit centre's operating results so that the managers are not held accountable for factors beyond their control. The total amount of current monetary balances will then be adjusted to the current rate for external reporting.

Foreign Currency Balances

New Financial Instrument Standards

The AcSB has approved new standards for measuring and reporting *financial instruments*. These new standards are effective for fiscal years beginning on or after October 1, 2006. Early adoption is possible, but we won't really begin to see annual financial statements that apply these new standards until late 2007. Until then, financial statements will be based on existing standards which essentially do not use fair values for any financial instruments. However, foreign exchange gains and losses will generally flow through to net income under pre-2006 accounting standards.

The discussion that follows is based on the new standards. Primarily, we will be discussing *CICA Handbook* sections 3855 (*Financial Instruments–Recognition and*

Measurement) and 3865 (*Hedges*). The sections on *Comprehensive Income* (section 1530) and Foreign Currency Translation (1651) also come into effect at the same time. The four sections must be applied together. Companies do not have the liberty for early application of one or two, and delay application of the others.

Financial assets and liabilities

A financial instrument is defined as "any contract that gives rise to a financial asset of one party and a financial liability or equity instrument of another party" [CICA 3855.19(a)]. The general topic of accounting for financial instruments normally is covered in intermediate accounting courses. Our more specific interest here is with financial assets and financial liabilities that are denominated in a foreign currency.

The treatment of exchange gains and losses on financial assets and liabilities varies somewhat, depending on the type of asset or liability. A retail, manufacturing, or service business typically has several types of financial assets and liabilities that arise from the company's normal business activities. Examples include accounts receivable, notes receivable, loans receivable, accounts payable, and loans payable. These are known as financial assets and liabilities that are *held to maturity*.[2] The company does not buy and/or sell these items. Instead, they are held until they are realized—the liability is paid or cash is received for the asset.

There are two other classifications:

- available-for-sale financial assets, and
- financial assets and liabilities that are held for trading.

Notice that *available-for-sale* consists only of financial assets. The *trading* items can include both financial assets and financial liabilities.

By far the most common financial assets and liabilities are those arising in the normal course of business and therefore are held to maturity. We will discuss held-to-maturity financial instruments first, and then examine the other two classifications.

Payables, receivables, and other financial assets held to maturity In theory, we could report foreign currency-denominated assets and liabilities on the balance sheet at either (1) historical cost or (2) current value. Historical cost means translating the foreign currency amount into our reporting currency at the rate in effect when the monetary balance was created. If that approach were used, gains and losses from exchange rate fluctuations would be recognized only when realized—at the settlement or payment date. This approach was once used in Canada for long-term financial assets and liabilities, but no more. The historical approach ignores objectively measurable changes in the value of assets and liabilities, and enables management to manipulate earnings through the timing of cash settlement.

Instead, accounting practice has turned to current value as the only feasible approach for reporting foreign currency financial assets and liabilities. The balances of financial assets and liabilities, both current and long-term, are translated at the exchange rate at the balance sheet date. Exchange rates change over time— the change will cause a Canadian dollar translation gain or loss.

---

2 Actually, the *CICA Handbook* uses the "held to maturity" designation only for financial assets [CICA 3855.17(g)]. The regular types of financial liabilities such as accounts payable or loans payable are simply called "other financial liabilities" [CICA 3855.63A]. The treatment is the same, however, and therefore we have lumped assets and liabilities together as being held to maturity.

For example, suppose that on December 31, 2005, Canadian Ltd. issues five-year debentures of £1,000,000 at face value in the U.K. On that date, the exchange rate was £1 = C$2.60. The liability will be reported on Canadian Ltd.'s December 31, 2005, balance sheet as C$2,600,000. Suppose that one year later, on December 31, 2006, the exchange rate is £1 = C$2.50. On the year-end 2006 balance sheet, the liability will be reported as C$2,500,000. Since a liability balance has gone down, Canadian Ltd. has an unrealized exchange gain of C$100,000 during 2006. How should the gain be reported? There are two possible alternatives.

1. Defer the unrealized gain or loss until the liability is settled (that is, paid).

2. Recognize the gain in the 2006 income statement.

Proponents of deferral argue that exchange rates go up and down, and that the 2006 gain may well be cancelled out by a loss in 2007. The liability will not be settled until the end of 2010. There is no point in recognizing gains and losses that may never be realized. Furthermore, the debt may well be replaced by new debt (i.e., refinanced) at the end of the five years. If the debt is refinanced, no gain or loss needs to be recognized.

However, exchange gains and losses don't generally bounce up and down without reason. Exchange rates are subject to longer-term trends caused by changing relative economic performance between countries. Granted, exchange rates do not always behave in accordance with economic theory in the short run, but exchange rate changes are not random events.

The basic problem with the deferral approach is that it ignores the change in net assets. If the gain is not recognized in earnings, it must be shown somewhere on the equities side of the balance sheet. Clearly, a deferred gain is not a liability. If it is not a liability, it can only be share equity. But if the deferred gain is part of share equity, then it must be a part of retained earnings—it clearly isn't paid-in capital. A deferred gain does not fit any of the definitions of financial statement elements of Section 1000 of the *CICA Handbook*.

The gain reflects economic reality and therefore should be included in income. The exchange rate change is an economic event affecting the company in 2006. Canadian Ltd. owes less money (in Canadian dollars) at the end of 2006 than it did at the end of 2005. The income statement should recognize this change in Canadian Ltd.'s net assets.

Under current standards, foreign currency gains and losses on monetary balances must be recognized in earnings in the period in which they occur:

> An exchange gain or loss of the reporting enterprise that arises on translation or settlement of a foreign currency-denominated monetary item or a non-monetary item carried at market should be included in the determination of net income for the current period. [CICA 1651.20]

Financial assets held to maturity The discussion above applies to the operating receivables, payables, and loans (both receivable and payable) in a company's business. Exchange gains and losses are recognized in earnings each period.

The accounting for financial assets depends on the intent of management. When a company buys financial assets, management must designate whether its intent is to hold the assets to maturity or to hold the assets as available-for-sale.

For example, suppose that on October 1, 2006, Canadian Ltd. buys a US$5,000 face value corporate bond on the U.S. market. The bond is selling at

100 (that is, at face value), and the exchange rate is US$1.00 = C$1.30. The purchase price of the bond is US$5,000 × $1.30 = C$6,500.

If Canadian Ltd. designates the bond investment as being held-to-maturity, the bonds are accounted for at "amortized cost using the effective interest method" [CICA 3855.66(a)]. Held-to-maturity financial assets are not remeasured to fair value at each balance sheet date. However, that does not mean that a foreign currency-denominated bond can be carried on the balance sheet at the historical exchange rate. The spot exchange rate at the balance sheet date must be used. Any exchange gain or loss on a financial asset that is designated as held-to-maturity is reported in net income.

If the exchange rate on December 31, 2006, is US$1.00 = C$1.35, the bond investment will be shown on Canadian Ltd.'s year-end 2006 balance sheet at C$6,750 (i.e., US$5,000 × $1.35). The Canadian dollar carrying value of the investment has increased by $250. This gain will be reported in Canadian Ltd.'s earnings as a foreign exchange gain:

Investment in U.S. bond	250	
Foreign exchange gain		250

The new carrying value of the bond is C$6,750.

Held-to-maturity investments are not normally sold prior to their maturity. But suppose that management changes its designation of this bond and sells it at 105 in 2007. At the date of sale, the exchange rate is US$1.00 = C$1.34. The sale price is C$7,035:

US$5,000 × 1.05 × $1.34 = C$7,035

The overall gain or loss on the sale is $285, and is recorded as follows:

Cash	7,035	
Investment in U.S. bond		6,750
Gain on sale of investment		285

The gain is composed of two elements: (1) a gain from the price increase from 100 to 105, and (2) a loss from the decrease in exchange rate. Since both components are reported in earnings, it is not necessary to separate them.

Financial assets available for sale An *available-for-sale* financial asset is one that a company intends or is willing to sell before maturity. Generally, most available-for-sale financial assets are classified as temporary investments. When management designates a financial asset as being *available for sale*:

- the asset is reported at its fair value at each balance sheet date
- the unrealized gain or loss in each period is reported in *other comprehensive income* (OCI),[3] and
- at the date of sale, the accumulated unrealized gain or loss is transferred from other comprehensive income and recognized on the income statement, along with any additional gain or loss recognized for the period of the sale.

Suppose that Canadian Inc. makes the same bond investment as above—the company buys a US$5,000 bond in 2006 at face value when the exchange rate is US$1.00 = C$1.30. The purchase price is C$6,500 (that is, US$5,000 × 1.00 × $1.30). At the end of 2006, the market value of the bond is 110. The fair value of

3 *Other comprehensive income* is a classification introduced by the AcSB in 2005, effective in October 2005. A brief explanation is provided in Appendix 8A. Readers who are unfamiliar with this classification should read the appendix now.

the bond (in U.S. dollars) is $5,500. If the exchange rate on December 31, 2006, is US$1.00 = C$1.35, the bond investment will be shown on Canadian Ltd.'s balance sheet at C$7,425 (i.e., US$5,000 × 1.10 × $1.35). The increase in the fair value of the bond is $925, in Canadian dollars.

The gain of $925 has two components: (1) the gain from the increase in market price, and (2) the gain from the change in the exchange rate. Section 1650 of the *CICA Handbook* specifies that all exchange gains and losses from monetary (or fair-valued) items are to be recognized in income. If this recommendation were applied to foreign currency-denominated available-for-sale financial assets, we would need to separate the gain into its two components. The exchange gain would be reported in income, while the fair-value change would be deferred as a component of other comprehensive income until it was realized through sale.

Fortunately, the AcSB has relieved us of the need to separate the two components:

> ... the entire change in the fair value of a monetary available-for-sale financial asset, including foreign exchange gains and losses, is recognized directly in other comprehensive income. [CICA 3855.78]

The entry to increase the carrying value of the investment to $7,425 at December 31, 2006, is:

Investment in U.S. bond	925	
Other comprehensive income—Unrealized gain on available-for-sale assets		925

[(US$5,000 × 1.10 × $1.35) − $6,500 = $7,425 − $6,500 = $925]

To extend the example, assume the following:

1. Canadian Ltd. holds the bond investment throughout 2007. At the end of 2007, the bond is selling at 106 and the exchange rate is US$1.00 = C$1.37.

2. Canadian Ltd. sells the bond in the open market on March 1, 2008, at 108. The exchange rate is US$1.00 = C$1.38. The entries to record these events are as follows:

December 31, 2007:

Other comprehensive income —Unrealized gain on available-for-sale assets	164	
Investment in bond		164

[(US$5,000 × 1.06 × $1.37) − $7,425 = $7,261 − $7,425 = $(164)]

This entry decreases the carrying value of the bond from $7,425 at the end of 2006 to $7,261 at the end of 2007.

March 1, 2008:

Cash (US$5,000 × 1.08 × $1.38)	7,452	
Other comprehensive income—Unrealized gain on available-for-sale assets ($925 − $164)	761	
Investment in bond		7,261
Gain on sale of investment ($7,452 − $6,500)		952

In this entry, the full gain on the bond is recognized as the difference between the final selling price of $7,452 and the original purchase price of $6,500.

Available-for-sale financial assets often are investments, such as we have described above. However, available-for-sale assets can also be financial assets that arise in the normal course of business. For example, a company may make most of its sales on an installment basis. When the company sells its product, the installment notes receivable are a financial asset. Rather than hold these install-ment notes until maturity, the company may sell the notes to another company at their discounted present value. Since the notes are intended for sale, they are available-for-sale assets. Their fair value will change in response to interest rate changes and in response to economic conditions that will affect the default risk.

An important point to remember is that the classification of "available for sale" applies only to financial *assets*—liabilities cannot be included in this classification.

Financial assets and liabilities held for trading The final classification of financial assets *and liabilities* is that of "held-for-trading." A held-for-trading asset or liability is defined [CICA 3855.19(f)] as one that is:

- acquired or incurred principally for the purpose of selling or repurchasing in the near term; or
- part of a portfolio of identified financial instruments that are managed together and for which there is evidence of a recent actual pattern of short-term profit-taking; or
- a derivative, except for a derivative that is a designated and effective hedging instrument.

Examples of trading instruments include (1) the investment portfolio of a securities dealer and (2) the loan portfolio of a financial institution.

Trading generally reflects active and frequent buying and selling, and financial instruments held for trading generally are used with the objective of generating a profit from short-term fluctuations in the price or dealer's margin [CICA 3855.20].

Financial assets and liabilities that are held for trading are reported at fair value at the balance sheet date. The change in fair value is recognized in income, regardless of whether the change has been realized or not [CICA 3855.76(a)]. When the asset or liability is denominated in a foreign currency, the exchange gains and losses are included in the overall fair-value gain or loss and are recognized in income. There is no "detour" through other comprehensive income for gains and losses on trading instruments.

Since trading instruments are used mainly in specialized industries, we will not discuss or illustrate them further here. In any event, the accounting for them is quite straightforward.

Summary Accounting for financial assets and liabilities may seem complex and confusing, especially when they are denominated in a foreign currency. In practice, however, the complexities are not really so daunting. There are four types of financial assets:

- assets held to maturity
- loans and receivables
- assets available for sale
- trading assets

and two types of financial liabilities:

- trading liabilities
- all others.

There are two alternatives for reporting the carrying value at the balance sheet date—(1) cost or (2) fair value. There also are two alternatives for reporting the gain/loss from changes in fair value—(1) recognize it in income immediately, or (2) defer it in other comprehensive income until realized. Foreign currency gains and losses are recognized in net income when they occur, whether realized or unrealized, with only one exception—unrealized foreign currency gains/losses on available-for-sale financial assets are placed in other comprehensive income until realized, at which time the cumulative gain or loss is recognized in net income.

Exhibit 8–1 summarizes the accounting for the different types of foreign currency-denominated financial assets and liabilities. The exhibit cites the disposition of both the fair-value gain/loss and the exchange gain/loss.

EXHIBIT 8–1	ACCOUNTING FOR FOREIGN CURRENCY-DENOMINATED FINANCIAL ASSETS AND LIABILITIES		
Type of financial asset or liability	Carrying value on balance sheet	Disposition of each period's unrealized gains and losses	Disposition of each period's foreign currency gains and losses
Available-for-sale financial assets	Fair value	Other comprehensive income	Other comprehensive income
Trading assets/liabilities	Fair value	Net income	Net income
Receivables and other financial liabilities	Historical cost	Not applicable	Net income*
Held-to-maturity financial assets	Amortized cost	Not applicable	Net income*

* Except for hedged items; gains and losses on hedged items go into other comprehensive income.

Accounting for Cash Flow Hedges

Nature of hedging

When a company holds a receivable denominated in a foreign currency, there will be a loss if the foreign currency falls in value relative to the Canadian dollar. Conversely, a loss on a foreign currency-denominated liability will occur if the foreign currency strengthens or increases in value relative to the Canadian dollar. To protect against foreign currency losses, companies frequently *hedge* their monetary foreign currency balances.

Hedging is the creation of an offsetting balance in the same foreign currency. If a company is holding a receivable of 1 million Japanese yen, the risk of gain or loss can be neutralized by incurring a liability of ¥1,000,000 for an equal term.

There are several ways of hedging. The most common is to enter into a *forward contract* with a bank or currency dealer. If a receivable is being hedged, then the company will contract to pay a bank an equivalent amount of foreign currency in exchange for Canadian dollars at a specified rate at a specified time in the future.

Some major currencies are also traded in a *futures* market. Futures markets for agricultural products are well known. Wheat, oats, and corn are traded on the commodities exchanges, as are cattle, cotton, copper, coffee, orange juice, plywood, and heating oil. The commodity that is of immediate concern here is money. On the Chicago Mercantile Exchange, for example, one can buy a futures contract for Canadian dollars, U.S. dollars, euros, British pounds, or Japanese yen, among others. Futures contracts are for standard terms (e.g., 30, 60, 90, and 180 days) and for limited denominations and currencies.

In this chapter, we focus on forward contracts rather than on futures contracts, since forward contracts are the most common form of hedge in Canada. Forward contracts are individually negotiated and thus can be tailored to suit the needs of the hedger in terms of currency type and contract duration.

Forward contracts and futures contracts are examples of *secondary* or *derivative instruments*. **Derivative instruments** are those that do not themselves represent financial contracts but that derive their value from transferring one or more of the financial risks inherent in an underlying primary financial instrument.

Another example of a derivative instrument is a **currency swap**, wherein corporations in two different countries agree to guarantee the payment of each other's interest and principal on foreign currency-denominated long-term debt. A Canadian company with outstanding British pound sterling debt may enter into a currency swap agreement with a British company that has outstanding Canadian-dollar debt.[4] Each party to the agreement thereby converts its foreign currency exposure to a fixed domestic equivalent, effectively eliminating exchange rate risk.

For example, Nortel Networks Corporation has the following statement in the notes to its annual financial statements:

> Nortel Networks' net earnings (loss) and cash flows may be negatively impacted by fluctuating interest rates, foreign exchange rates and equity prices. To effectively manage these market risks, Nortel Networks enters into foreign currency forwards, foreign currency swaps, foreign currency option contracts, [and] interest rate swaps.

As this note implies, there are many different types of hedging instruments. In this book, we will focus on forward contracts because they are the most common and generally the most effective form of foreign currency cash flow hedge.

Hedging an existing monetary position

To illustrate the use of hedging, suppose that on October 20, 2005, Domestic Corporation sells some of its product in Germany for €100,000. At the date of the sale, the euro is selling at a current or **spot rate** of $1.2717 in Canadian funds. As a result of the sale, Domestic has acquired a foreign currency monetary balance (account receivable) of $127,170. If Domestic wishes to protect itself against a possible exchange loss caused by a fall in the value of the euro, Domestic can buy a forward contract for an equivalent amount of euros. Assuming that the receivable will be collected in 90 days (on January 18, 2006), Domestic can buy a contract for the *payment* of €100,000 90 days hence. The commitment to pay €100,000 will offset the commitment to receive €100,000 from the German customer.

In October 2005, a 90-day forward contract for euros is available for $1.2740. Domestic contracts to deliver or pay €100,000 in 90 days, and the contract will be for $127,400. The $230 difference between the current value of €100,000 ($127,170) and the price of the forward contract ($127,400) reflects the anticipated change in the exchange rate over the next month. In effect, Domestic is selling the euros that it will receive from the German customer. But since Domestic will not receive the euros for 90 days, the contract to deliver the euros will not be executed until then.

---

4 In practice, swaps are usually more complicated than this example and may involve more than two companies. Swaps normally are arranged through financial intermediaries, usually banks.

As a result, Domestic will have a *receivable* (from the customer) that is denominated in euros, but will also have a *payable* that is denominated in euros. The euro receivable and the euro payable are due at the same time. The two financial instruments will fluctuate in tandem as the euro exchange rate changes—a gain on one instrument will be exactly offset by a loss on the other.

The entries to record **1(a)** the sale of the merchandise and **1(b)** the sale of the euros for delivery in the future will be as follows:

October 20, 2005:

1(a)	Accounts receivable (€100,000)	127,170	
	Sales		127,170
	[sale of merchandise for €100,000 on account]		
1(b)	Forward contract receivable (in C$)	127,400	
	Forward contract payable (€100,000)		127,400
	[purchase of a forward contract to deliver €100,000]		

In the second entry, it appears that the receivable and the payable for the forward contract are offsetting. However, this is not really the case. The receivable is fixed in terms of Canadian dollars and represents the amount to be received by Domestic when Domestic delivers the euros. The payable, on the other hand, is denominated in euros; the actual dollar equivalent will change as the price of the euro changes. Thus the receivable from the customer and the payable to the purchaser of the forward contract are both denominated in a foreign currency—euros.

Assume that Domestic's fiscal year ends on January 31. On January 18, 2006, the customer pays €100,000 to Domestic, and Domestic delivers the euros in execution of the forward contract. Also assume that the spot rate for the euro is $1.2500 on the settlement date. The receipt of the €100,000 from the customer **(c)** will be recorded as follows:

January 18, 2006:

1(c)	Cash (€100,000 @ 1.2500)	125,000	
	Exchange gains and losses	2,170	
	Accounts receivable (€100,000 @ 1.2717)		127,170
	[receipt of €100,000 from customer, on account]		

There is a loss of $2,170 due to the fact that the exchange rate fell during the 90-day period.

To execute the forward contract that is now due, Domestic will **(d)** deliver €100,000 and **(e)** receive the contracted amount of $127,400 in return. The entries to record this transaction will appear as follows:

January 18, 2006:

1(d)	Cash	127,400	
	Forward contract receivable (in C$)		127,400
	[receipt of cash from the buyer of the forward contract]		
1(e)	Forward contract payable	127,400	
	Exchange gains and losses		2,400
	Cash (€100,000 @ 1.2500)		125,000
	[payment of €100,000 to fulfill the forward contract obligation]		

Domestic recognizes a *loss* of $2,170 on the receivable and a *gain* of $2,400 on the forward contract. The net amount is a gain of $230. The existence of this net gain may suggest that the forward contract was not completely successful at eliminating risk, but that is not the case. The $230 gain is the difference between the spot rate on the date of the original sale and the forward rate, multiplied by the amount of the foreign currency balance being hedged: €100,000 × ($1.2717 − $1.2740).

What the hedge really does is limit any possible gain or loss to a known amount, the spread between the spot rate and the forward rate. The same net gain will exist in our example regardless of the actual exchange rate at the settlement date.

For example, suppose that instead of a rate of $1.2500, the actual spot rate on the settlement date was $1.2850. The three entries to record the receipt from the customer and the settlement of the forward contract will then be as follows:

1(c2)	Cash (€100,000 @ 1.2850)	128,500	
	Accounts receivable		127,170
	Exchange gains and losses		1,330
	[receipt of €100,000 from customer, on account]		
1(d2)	Cash	127,400	
	Forward contract receivable (in C$)		127,400
	[receipt of cash from the buyer of the forward contract]		
1(e2)	Forward contract payable	127,400	
	Exchange gains and losses	1,100	
	Cash (€100,000 @ 1.2850)		128,500
	[payment of €100,000 to fulfill the forward contract obligation]		

Settlement of **1(c2)** the customer receivable and **1(e2)** the forward contract results in a gain of $1,330 and a loss of $1,100 respectively, for a net gain of $230, exactly as when the spot rate was $1.2500.

In the example that we have used above, the forward rate happened to be *higher* than the spot rate, resulting in a net *gain*. Forward rates may be either higher or lower than the spot rate. The spread between the spot and forward rates depends on (1) the interest rate differential between the two countries and (2) how the market predicts the rate will move.

If the forward rate is *lower* than the spot rate, the hedge of a receivable would lock the hedger into a *loss*. But the loss would be quite minor in comparison to the potential loss from an unprotected position. The day-to-day change in the spot rate can easily be larger than the spread between the spot and forward rates. Thus the small certain loss can be viewed as the cost of insurance against a possibly substantial speculative loss. Of course, hedging also eliminates the possibility of realizing a gain as well.

When the forward rate is higher than the spot rate, the contract has a premium. When the forward rate is less, then a discount exists. If the hedge is of a foreign currency *receivable*, as above, a premium results in a gain while a discount results in a loss.

Conversely, if the hedge is of a foreign currency *liability*, a premium results in a loss while a discount causes a gain. The following table summarizes this relationship:

	Net result if a forward contract is priced at a:	
Item being hedged	**Premium**	**Discount**
Monetary assets	gain	loss
Monetary liability	loss	gain

In the example above, the forward contract was recorded by means of a journal entry that assigned equal values to the receivable and the payable. In addition to this first method of recording, there are two other methods of recording the hedge that yield the same result and that may be more appropriate if the transaction spans a year-end.

Recording premium/discount at inception The second method is to record the receivable at the Canadian dollar value that is established by the forward contract at $1.2740. The liability is recorded at the euro spot rate of $1.2717, which is the amount of the hedge—that is, the amount of the receivable as recorded at the date-of-sale spot rate. The difference between the receivable of $127,400 and the payable of $127,170 is the premium on the forward contract. Since the premium will not be realized until the settlement date, it should be treated as a deferred gain. Under this approach, the initial entry to record the purchase of the forward contract will be as follows:

October 20, 2005:

2(b)	Forward contract receivable (€100,000 × $1.2740)	127,400	
	Forward contract payable		127,170
	Deferred exchange gains/losses		230
	[purchase of forward contract]		

When the account receivable is collected and the forward contract is settled, the entries will appear as follows (assuming a spot rate at settlement date of $1.25):

January 18, 2006:

2(c)	Cash (€100,000 × $1.25)	125,000	
	Exchange gains and losses	2,170	
	Accounts receivable		127,170
	[receipt of €100,000 cash from the customer @ $1.25]		
2(d)	Cash	127,400	
	Forward contract receivable		127,400
	[receipt of payment on forward contract, as established in Cdn $]		
2(e)	Forward contract payable	127,170	
	Deferred exchange gain	230	
	Exchange gains and losses		2,400
	Cash (€100,000 @ $1.25)		125,000
	[payment of obligation of €100,000 on forward contract]		

The net result will be the same as in the earlier example, a net exchange gain of $230.

Recording the premium or discount on the forward contract at the date of entering into it may seem to complicate the recording of the transaction. However, the purpose is to identify the gain or loss in order to facilitate its appropriate treatment between the contract date and the settlement date. As is discussed in the next two sections, the premium or discount is not always recognized solely at the settlement date. When the contract spans two fiscal periods, part of the premium or discount is recognized in the income statement or as part of the cost of an asset at the end of the reporting period.

Memorandum entry The third method of accounting for the forward contract is to use only a memorandum entry. That is, the forward contract is not recorded at all. The contract enters the accounting records only when it is settled. There is no cost at the beginning of the contract, and therefore there is no explicit cost to record. Indeed, part of the *CICA Handbook* definition of a derivative instrument is that "it requires no initial net investment..." [CICA 3855.19(e)].

A forward contract is an **executory contract**, a contract that represents an agreement by two parties to perform in the future. For accounting purposes, no liability or receivable is normally deemed to exist for an executory contract until one of the parties has actually performed, or *executed*, the contract. Under a forward contract, neither party will perform until the settlement date, and thus no accounting recognition is necessary for the contract. The liability and the receivable relating to the contract will not be recorded, and on the settlement date, the net gain or loss will flow out of the cash transactions:

January 18, 2006:

3(c)	Cash (€100,000 @ $1.25)	125,000	
	Exchange gains and losses	2,170	
	Accounts receivable (book balance)		127,170
	[receipt of €100,000 from customer, on account]		

3(d)	Cash (Cdn. dollar forward contract receivable)	127,400	
	Exchange gains and losses		2,400
	Cash (€100,000 forward contract payable)		125,000
	[settlement of forward contract @ $1.25 spot rate]		

The disadvantage of this approach is that since the premium or discount has not been explicitly recognized on the books, it is easy to overlook when adjustments are made at year-end.

This example described an asset exposure. A liability exposure (e.g., a foreign-currency account payable) is treated similarly. However, the company will then enter into a forward contract to receive instead of deliver the foreign currency.

The three methods of recording the hedge are shown in Exhibit 8-2. The two entries for the sale and the collection of the customer receivable are identical under all three methods. The accounting for the hedge does not affect the transactions for the primary instrument.

The third method – treating the forward contract as an executory contract and thus not formally recording it – is the most common in practice. We will use this method in the remainder of this chapter.

It is important to note that this is another example of recording vs. reporting. We do not record the hedge because it has no cost. In the financial statements, however, we must report all outstanding hedges at fair value in the disclosure notes.

Intervening year-end The foregoing illustration dealt with the simplest situation, in which all of the related events occurred within the same accounting period. More commonly, a hedging relationship spans more than one accounting period, especially if the reporting enterprise is a public company that must report quarterly. When a foreign currency hedge spans two or more accounting periods:

1. the discount or premium on the hedge is allocated to the periods, much like an insurance premium

EXHIBIT 8–2 ALTERNATIVE RECORDING METHODS FOR HEDGING CONTRACTS

(Assuming January 31 fiscal year-end)

	Method 1*		Method 2*		Method 3*	
October 20, 2005:						
a Accounts receivable	127,170		127,170		127,170	
Sales		127,170		127,170		127,170
b Forward contract receivable	127,400		127,400			
Forward contract payable		127,400		127,170		
Deferred exchange gains/losses				230		
January 18, 2006						
c Cash	125,000		125,000		125,000	
Exchange gains and losses	2,170		2,170		2,170	
Accounts receivable		127,170		127,170		127,170
d Cash (Canadian dollar contract)	127,400		127,400		127,400	
Exchange gains and losses						2,400
Forward contract receivable		127,400		127,400		
Cash (€100,000)						125,000
e Forward contract payable (as recorded)	127,400		127,170			
Deferred exchange gains/losses			230			
Exchange gains and losses		2,400		2,400		
Cash (€100,000)		125,000		125,000		

* Methods:

  1. Recording forward contracts at contract and spot rates, with no deferral of premium or discount.

  2. Recording forward contracts at contract rates, with recognition of future (deferred) premium or discount.

  3. No recording of forward contract until settlement.

2. the primary instrument (that is, whatever is being hedged) is revalued on the balance sheet to Canadian dollars, using the spot rate on the balance sheet date

3. the foreign exchange gain/loss on the primary instrument is recorded in other comprehensive income (OCI) instead of net income, and

4. the fair value of the hedge is disclosed in the notes to the financial statements.

Since the premium or discount is the benefit or cost of limiting the risk exposure of the company over the period of time in which the monetary asset or liability being hedged is outstanding, the premium or discount is allocated to net income over all the periods affected.

To illustrate, we can slightly modify the previous example by assuming that Domestic's fiscal year ends on *December 31* instead of January 31. There will be a financial statement reporting date between the October 20 sale and the January 18 settlement date. Assume also that the spot rate for the euro on December 31 is $1.2600.

If the receivable were *not* hedged, the entries relating to (a) the sale at a rate of $127,170, (b) the year-end adjustment of the account receivable balance to $126,000 at the December 31 spot rate of $1.2600, and (c) the settlement at $1.2500 would be as follows:

October 20, 2005:

(a) Account receivable (€100,000 @ 1.2717) 127,170
    Sales 127,170
[sale for €100,000 when the spot rate = $1.2717]

December 31, 2005:

(b) Exchange gains and losses 1,170
    Account receivable 1,170
[reduce receivable to year-end spot rate: €100,000 × ($1.2600 − $1.2717)]

January 18, 2006:

(c) Cash (€100,000 @ $1.25) 125,000
    Exchange gains and losses 1,000
      Account receivable 126,000
[receipt of cash to settle the €100,000 receivable at the January 18 spot rate of $1.25]

In the absence of a hedge, the exchange gain/loss is recognized in the period in which it occurred. Of the total $2,170 exchange loss, $1,170 occurred in 2005 and $1,000 occurred in 2006.

If the receivable is hedged, however, no gain/loss is recognized because it will be offset by a loss/gain on the forward contract liability on the settlement date. Since the receivable balance must be adjusted to the current rate on the balance sheet date (December 31), any gain or loss on exchange rate changes is deferred.

When the receivable is hedged, the year-end adjustment to the customer receivable is as follows:

December 31, 2005:

OCI foreign-exchange gains and losses 1,170
    Account receivable 1,170
[reduce receivable to year-end spot rate: €100,000 × ($1.2600 − $1.2717)]

In addition, a proportionate part of the premium will be recognized as a benefit for the year ended December 31, 2005. The elapsed time between the sale (and hedge) and the end of the fiscal year is 72 days. Therefore, 72/90ths of the premium is allocated to 2005:

December 31, 2005:

Unrealized forward premium 184
    Exchange gains and losses 184
[premium recognized = $230 × 72/90 days = $184]

When the customer's account is settled, the entry to record the receipt of €100,000 (at the January spot rate of $1.2500) will be:

January 18, 2006:

Cash (€100,000 × $1.25) 125,000
Exchange gains or losses 2,170
    Account receivable 126,000
    OCI foreign-exchange gains and losses 1,170

The settlement of the forward contract will be recorded as follows:

January 18, 2006:

Cash	127,400	
Exchange gains and losses		2,216
Unrealized forward premium		184
Cash (€100,000 × $1.25)		125,000

The exchange loss of $2,170 recognized from settlement of the customer's account is offset against the $2,216 exchange gain from settlement of the forward contract. The net result is a gain of $46, the remaining 18/90ths of the discount that is allocable to 2006.

The premium or discount on a forward contract is allocated to the periods during which the contract is outstanding because the cost of the contract is thereby assigned to the periods that receive the benefit of the protection.

Hedging anticipated transactions

So far, we have discussed only hedges of recognized financial assets or liabilities. However, companies often have a foreign currency risk exposure for anticipated transactions. For example, a Canadian airline is exposed to risk on its anticipated purchases of aircraft fuel. The risk takes two forms: (1) a *fair-value risk* that the U.S. dollar price will increase, and (2) a *currency risk* that the U.S.–Canada exchange rate will go down. Both types of risk can be hedged against. The airline can hedge the fair-value risk on fuel prices by buying futures options for oil. But the fair-value hedge won't solve the currency risk because the options are in U.S. dollars. Therefore, the airline may also hedge against adverse exchange rate changes through a currency hedge.

An anticipated transaction is "any transaction expected to occur in the future that has not yet given rise to a recognized asset or liability" [CICA 3865.07(h)]. Once a firm commitment for a purchase or sale has been made, the fair-value risk disappears but the currency risk remains. The *CICA Handbook* hedging recommendations apply to currency hedges for anticipated transactions, including commitments.

Anticipated transactions, including commitments, do not immediately cause any financial assets or liabilities to be recorded, because by definition the transactions are *anticipated* future transactions. Nevertheless, a company has a currency exposure for any foreign currency-denominated transactions that it expects to occur.

To offset the currency risk, companies often hedge the anticipated cash flow. The terms of the hedge establish the cost of the anticipated goods or services. When a purchase or sale of goods or services in a foreign currency is hedged before the transaction, the Canadian dollar price of such goods or services is *established by the terms of the hedge*.

For example, assume that Domestic Corporation issues a purchase order to Français Ltée. on October 31, 2005, to purchase a machine for €200,000. The machine is delivered on November 30, and payment is made on January 31, 2006. Domestic has a December 31 fiscal year-end.

Domestic Corp. finalized the decision to purchase the machine on October 31, based on the Canadian-dollar equivalent cost of the machine at that time. If the euro appreciates significantly in value between October 31 and the payment date, Domestic will incur substantial additional cost for the machine. Therefore, it is common for a purchaser to hedge a commitment as soon as the purchase contract is signed and the foreign-currency cost of the asset or service is established. Of course, Domestic will not recognize a liability on the balance sheet until the machine has been delivered.

Suppose that on October 31, 2005, the spot rate for the euro is €1 = C$1.25. The €200,000 initial commitment is equivalent to C$250,000. Domestic Corp. hedges its euro commitment by entering into a forward contract to *receive* €200,000 on January 31, 2006. Assume that the three-month forward rate for the euro is $1.22 on October 31. The cost of the machine is established at the forward rate: €200,000 × $1.22 = $244,000.

By November 30, 2005, the spot rate declines to $1.24 per euro. On that date, the machine is delivered and the monetary liability is recorded at $248,000 (€200,000 × $1.24). The cost of the machine is recorded at the forward rate of $1.22. The difference between the liability and the asset cost is the discount on the forward contract. At the settlement date, whatever gain or loss has arisen *since the date of the commitment* on the liability to Français Ltée. will be offset by an equal loss or gain on the forward contract. Therefore, *the value of the forward contract establishes the cost of the machine.*

Using the more common *executory contract method* of accounting for the hedge (i.e., the third method presented in Exhibit 8–2), the hedge itself is not explicitly recognized in the accounts. The entry to record the liability is:

November 30, 2005:

Machinery (€200,000 × $1.22)	244,000	
OCI–foreign exchange gains and losses [€200,000 × ($1.24 – $1.22)]	**4,000**	
Accounts payable (€200,000 × $1.24)		248,000

The discount reduces the cost of the machine. However, in order to balance the entry, we must temporarily charge the discount to other comprehensive income (OCI) (which we have highlighted in this series of entries). This deferral will be eliminated at settlement date, as we shall illustrate shortly.

On December 31, 2005, the liability must be adjusted to the year-end spot rate for balance sheet purposes. If we assume that the year-end spot rate is $1.20, the adjustment is as follows:

December 31, 2005:

Accounts payable [€200,000 × ($1.24 – $1.20)]	8,000	
OCI–foreign exchange gains and losses		**8,000**

The gain arising from the decrease in the exchange rate from $1.24 to $1.20 will be offset against a corresponding loss on the forward contract. Therefore, the loss is deferred until the settlement date by crediting the amount of the adjustment to an OCI exchange gains and losses account.

On January 31, 2006, Domestic pays €200,000 to Français Ltée. when the spot rate is $1.26. Simultaneously, the forward contract is settled. The two entries to record these events are as follows:

January 31, 2006:

Accounts payable (€200,000 × $1.20)	240,000	
OCI–foreign exchange gains and losses	**12,000**	
Cash (€200,000 × $1.26)		252,000
[payment of €200,000 to the supplier]		
Cash (€200,000 × $1.26)	252,000	
Cash (Cdn. dollar forward contract liability)		244,000
OCI–foreign exchange gains and losses		**8,000**
[settlement of forward contract]		

The debit to accounts payable is for the balance in that account as adjusted to the spot rate on the last balance sheet date, December 31, 2006. In both entries, the foreign currency amount of €200,000 is translated at the January 31 spot rate of $1.26. The credit to cash in the second entry is for the Canadian dollar liability that was established by the forward contract, at the forward rate of $1.22.

After the transaction is complete, the foreign currency gains and losses all cancel out:

- A deferred *debit* of $4,000 (relating to the discount on the forward contract) is recorded when the machine is received and the initial supplier liability is recognized.

- A deferred *credit* of $8,000 is recorded when the account payable is adjusted to the year-end spot rate on December 31, 2005.

- Payment of the euro-denominated account payable results in an additional *debit* of $12,000.

- Settlement of the forward contract establishes a *credit* of $8,000.

In total, the OCI exchange gains and losses account has $16,000 in debits and $16,000 in credits—the foreign exchange gains and losses successfully balance out, and the discount is reflected in the capitalized cost of the asset.

In this example, the foreign currency gains and losses offset each other perfectly. Such a perfect hedge often is not possible. As well, transaction costs often add an additional expense to the transaction that emerges when the exchange gains and losses are offset against each other.

When a company is acquiring a non-financial asset and the cash flow hedge gains and losses do not offset completely, the residual exchange gain or loss in OCI is recognized in net income in the periods in which the asset affects net income. This can be done most easily by simply combining the residual gain/loss with the acquisition cost of the asset. The cost of the asset is then charged to expense or amortized according to the company's normal accounting policy for that type of asset.

This example illustrated the purchase of an asset. The same principles apply if the purchase is of services rather than of an asset.

If the company were *selling* assets or services priced in a foreign currency, the same procedures also would apply, except that the recognized monetary item would be a receivable instead of a payable; any discount or premium on the forward contract would be reflected in sales revenue.

Requirements for hedge accounting Within the meaning of the *CICA Handbook, hedge accounting* is a formal accounting designation and not simply a net result. For example, a Canadian company may have a substantial amount of receivables that are denominated in euros and may also have a large amount of payables in the same currency. Effectively, the currency risks from the receivables and the payables offset each other. This sort of offsetting position is sometimes called an *implicit* or *natural* hedge—any gain or loss from the receivables will be offset by the loss or gain from the payables. The foreign exchange gains and losses will flow through to net income and naturally tend to offset each other. While this is a form of hedge in substance, it is not hedge accounting!

Cash flow hedge accounting means that:

- a specific currency risk is identified and designated as a hedged item
- a specific hedging item is designated, and

- the hedging relationship is formally documented, within the company's overall risk management strategy.

Other points that underlie the concept of hedge accounting are as follows.

- A *hedged item* is a recognized asset, recognized liability, or anticipated transaction. A derivative instrument cannot be a hedged item. The hedged item is the currency exposure that is being hedged.
- A *hedging item* (that is, the offsetting risk) is normally a derivative. For currency hedges only, it also can be a recognized financial asset or liability.
- A *non-financial* asset (or liability) can be neither a hedged item nor a hedging item because its carrying value is not subject to foreign currency fluctuations.
- There must be reasonable assurance that the hedging relationship will be effective at negating or substantially reducing the currency risk.

Hedge accounting gives companies the ability to put certain unrealized foreign currency gains and losses into other comprehensive income rather than net income. Hedge accounting may not be applied until and unless the company has made a formal designation of a hedging relationship. The objective of the formal declaration is to keep companies from loosely defining their hedging relationships and thereby exercising choice of reporting options at reporting dates—net income versus OCI.

Effective hedges and tandem currencies A perfect currency hedge has three characteristics:

- the amount of the hedge is exactly the same as the amount of the risk exposure
- the timing of the cash flows from the hedge exactly corresponds with the timing of the cash flows from the hedged item, and
- the hedge is in the same currency as the hedged item.

To the extent that the first two characteristics are not met, the hedge is ineffective. For example, if Canadian Ltd. enters into a forward contract for €80,000 instead of the full exposure of €100,000, only the hedged portion is effectively hedged, and the exchange gain or loss pertaining to only €80,000 of the receivable can be recognized in OCI. Translation gains and losses on the unhedged €20,000 must flow through to net income.

Sometimes, a forward contract is not available for a currency. Prior to the adoption of Section 3865, it was common for companies to hedge in a currency that was deemed to be closely related to the currency of risk. Under Section 3865, however, the burden of proof of effectiveness is on management if it hedges in a different currency. The only reliably effective hedge is in a *tandem currency*. A tandem currency exists when "a formal arrangement exists in one or both of the countries to maintain the exchange rate between the currencies" [CICA 3865.41].

For example, suppose that Canadian Ltd. buys a substantial amount of inventory from a supplier in China, and agrees to pay Canadian dollars in an amount that is equivalent to the invoice price in Chinese currency, the renminbi (RMB). The renminbi is not a freely traded currency, and therefore it would be difficult to acquire an effective hedge in renminbi. However, the value of the renminbi is fixed against the U.S. dollar. Canadian Ltd. can hedge the renminbi obligation effectively by hedging in U.S. dollars, since the renminbi is pegged to the U.S. dollar.

After Canadian Ltd. establishes a hedge in U.S. dollars, China might decide to revalue its currency. The "peg" will be set at a different level. At that point, part of the hedge ceases to be effective. Only the portion covered by the new U.S. dollar-to-renminbi ratio can now be treated as an effective currency hedge.

Revenue hedges Companies that have substantial foreign currency revenue may wish to view that revenue as a hedge of foreign currency liabilities.

For example, Air Canada has debt that is denominated in U.S. dollars. The airline also has substantial revenue flows in U.S. dollars. Can the revenue be designated as a hedge against foreign currency changes in the interest and principal payments of the debt?

If future revenue is designated as a hedging item, the anticipated revenue is intended as a hedging item for a recognized foreign currency financial liability. However, Section 3865 specifies that:

> ... an anticipated transaction may be a hedged item. However, it cannot be a hedging item. [CICA 3865.42]

The relationship can be reversed. The debt obligation (a hedging item) could be used to hedge the revenue stream (a hedged item). That arrangement would satisfy Section 3865...

> only when it is probable that the anticipated transaction will occur at a time and in the amount expected, so that the relationship may be specifically identified and its effectiveness measured and assessed. [CICA 3865.42]

The timing and amount of cash outflows from the debt obligation (interest and principal) must coincide with cash inflows from U.S. dollar revenue. But if the flows coincide, there is no reason to use hedge accounting – the gains/losses on the debt will offset the losses/gains on the revenue, and nothing is recognized in OCI.

International standards The IASB view of hedging is contained in IAS 39, *Financial Instruments: Recognition and Measurement*. The position of the IASB on hedging is essentially the same as that contained in *CICA Handbook* Section 3865. IAS 39 is somewhat simpler than Section 3865 because the AcSB was striving to harmonize with U.S. GAAP. IAS 39 defines a hedging instrument for foreign currency risk to be a derivative (e.g., a forward contract) or a non-derivative financial asset or liability. As in Section 3865, there is no provision for using anticipated transactions as a hedge.

The IASB permits designation of a hedge only if "the hedge is expected to be highly effective" [IAS 39.88(b)]. A hedge is highly effective only if:

> At the inception of the hedge and in subsequent periods, the hedge is expected to be highly effective in achieving offsetting changes in fair value or cash flows attributable to the hedged risk during the period for which the hedge is designated. [IAS 39.AG105(a)]

IAS 39 sets a numerical range for measuring effectiveness:

> A hedge is regarded as highly effective only if... the actual results of the hedge are within a range of 80-125 per cent. [IAS 39.AG105(b)]

SUMMARY OF KEY POINTS

1. Exchange rates change for several reasons. Some changes, especially short-term fluctuations, are the result of the speculative activities of money market traders. The more fundamental causes for changes in exchange rates are (1) differential inflation rates between countries and (2) differences in interest rates. Differential inflation rates cause exchange rates to change to compensate for the changing purchasing power between currencies. Exchange rates also change in response to investment opportunities that are caused by international interest rate differentials.

2. Many, if not most, Canadian corporations engage in international activities to some extent. Foreign currency transactions are very common; the value of the transaction is fixed in a currency other than the enterprise's reporting currency. Foreign currency transactions must be recorded on the corporation's books at their equivalent in Canadian dollars at the time of the transaction. For revenues, expenses, and non-monetary balances, the amounts that are established by the initial transaction are not changed at subsequent reporting dates.

3. Monetary balances arising from foreign currency transactions must be translated at the spot rate at the balance sheet date. Monetary balances are reported at their Canadian dollar equivalent at the balance sheet date. The Canadian dollar equivalent of a foreign currency-denominated financial asset or financial liability will change over time. The change in exchange rates causes a foreign currency exchange gain or loss. If the exposure to currency fluctuations is not hedged, currency gains and losses are reported in net income.

4. Financial assets and liabilities that are denominated in a foreign currency may be hedged. Hedging involves incurring a foreign currency liability to offset a foreign currency financial asset, or an asset to offset a liability. Derivative instruments are most commonly used for hedging. In Canada, the most common derivative instrument for foreign currency hedges is a forward contract. Futures options and currency swaps are other types of derivatives for hedging a foreign currency risk exposure.

5. When a foreign currency exposure has been hedged, the exchange gains/losses on the primary instrument (i.e., the financial asset or financial liability) are deferred as a component of *other comprehensive income.* When the asset or liability is settled, the accumulated exchange gain/loss is removed from accumulated other comprehensive income and recognized in net income. The offsetting loss/gain from the hedging instrument is also recognized in net income.

6. A hedging relationship must be specifically designated and documented by management within the company's risk management strategy. Hedge accounting may not be used prior to explicit designation and documentation of the hedge.

7. Once the hedging relationship has been established, management must evaluate the effectiveness of the hedge. Hedge accounting can continue to be used only if the hedge continues to be effective. Canadian standards have no quantitative criteria for effectiveness, but the IASB specifies 80% to 125% offset as a reasonable measure of effectiveness. To the extent that a hedging relationship is not effective, gains and losses arising from the portion of the exposure that is not effectively hedged must be recognized in net income.

8. A hedged item cannot be a derivative instrument. Only recognized financial assets and financial liabilities can be hedged. However, a hedging item can be either a recognized financial asset or liability, or a derivative instrument.

SELF-STUDY PROBLEM 8–1

On December 31, 2005, Debtor Limited issued €5,000,000 in debentures to a private investment company located in Frankfurt, Germany. The debentures are due on December 31, 2008. Debtor Limited is a privately held Alberta company that reports to its shareholders and creditors in Canadian dollars using Canadian GAAP. Debtor did not hedge its euro-denominated debt. Over the life of the bonds, the exchange rates for the euro were as follows:

Date	Canadian dollar equivalent
December 31, 2005	$1.27
December 31, 2006	$1.30
December 31, 2007	$1.34
December 31, 2008	$1.35

Required:

Calculate the amount of gain or loss that will appear on Debtor Limited's income statement for each of 2006, 2007, and 2008, following the recommendations of Section 1651 of the *CICA Handbook*.

SELF-STUDY PROBLEM 8–2

On December 2, 2006, Domestic Corporation sold merchandise to a Taiwanese customer for 1 million New Taiwan Dollars (NTD). The NTD was worth C$0.0500 on the date of the sale. On December 3, 2006, Domestic entered into a forward contract with its bank to deliver NTD1,000,000 in 60 days at a rate of $0.0520.

Domestic's fiscal year ended on December 31, 2006. The NTD was worth $0.0510 at year-end. On February 1, 2007, the customer paid the balance owing, and Domestic also settled the forward contract. The exchange rate on the settlement date was $0.0525.

Required:

a. In general journal form, record the entries in 2006 and 2007 relating to the account receivable and to the forward contract, assuming the hedge is recorded as an executory contract.

b. How would the entries relating to the account receivable differ if Domestic had not hedged the receivable?

SELF-STUDY PROBLEM 8-3

On October 14, 2007, Buycorp signed a contract with Sellco, a U.S. company, to purchase a piece of equipment for US$200,000. The equipment was to be delivered on December 1, 2007, with payment to be made (in U.S. dollars) no later than January 30, 2008.

Having signed the contract, Buycorp immediately arranged a forward contract through the company's bank for US$200,000 as a hedge against the commitment. The spot rate for the U.S. dollar was $1.20 on October 14; the forward rate was $1.22.

Sellco delivered the equipment to Buycorp on December 7, 2007, slightly late owing to customs delays at the border. The spot rate on that date was $1.18, as compared to $1.19 on December 1. On December 31, 2007, the spot rate was $1.19. Despite the late delivery, Buycorp paid the amount due on January 30, 2008, per the contract. The spot rate was $1.24 on January 30.

Required:

Prepare journal entries to record the acquisition of the equipment and the related hedge on Buycorp's books through January 30, 2008. Buycorp's fiscal year ends on December 31.

REVIEW QUESTIONS

8-1 What is a foreign currency transaction?

8-2 What are the primary causes of changes in exchange rates over the long run?

8-3 CarpCorp, a Canadian company, bought a machine from the United States for US$100,000 when the exchange rate was C$1.20. The liability for the machine was paid when the exchange rate was C$1.25. At what cost should the machine be recorded in the accounts, assuming (1) the one-transaction theory and (2) the two-transaction theory?

8-4 CarpCorp bought inventory from the United Kingdom when the pound was worth C$1.80. When the year-end balance sheet was prepared, the pound was worth C$1.70. If the account payable for the inventory was unpaid at year-end, and the amount of the purchase was £5,000, how should the liability be reported on the balance sheet? How should the change in the value of the pound be reported (if at all)?

8-5 Explain the difference between a *monetary balance* and a *non-monetary balance*.

8-6 Why would some companies decide to use a *pre-determined standard rate* for translating foreign currency transactions?

8-7 Explain the difference between a held-to-maturity financial instrument, available-for-sale financial asset, and financial assets and liabilities held for trading.

8-8 What is the appropriate carrying value on the balance sheet for a held-to-maturity financial instrument, available-for-sale financial asset, and financial assets and liabilities held for trading?

8–9 What is the appropriate method of accounting for a foreign currency gain or loss related to a financial asset classified as held-to-maturity?

8–10 Where are available-for-sale financial assets usually classified?

8–11 What is *other comprehensive income*?

8–12 What is the appropriate method of accounting for an unrealized gain or loss for an available-for-sale financial asset?

8–13 What is the appropriate method of accounting for a foreign currency gain or loss related to an available-for-sale financial asset?

8–14 How are financial assets and liabilities held for trading reported on the balance sheet?

8–15 What is the appropriate method of accounting for a foreign currency gain or loss related to a held-for-trading financial asset or liability?

8–16 What is the purpose of *hedging*?

8–17 CarpCorp has a liability of €400,000. If CarpCorp wants to hedge the liability, should the company enter into a forward contract to *buy* euros or to *sell* euros?

8–18 Does hedging eliminate all gains and losses arising from a foreign currency exposure? Explain.

8–19 Why is a forward contract viewed as an executory contract?

8–20 Why is the discount or premium on a forward contract allocated to the periods during which the monetary balance and the hedge are outstanding, rather than being recognized in the period of settlement?

8–21 How does hedging an *anticipated transaction* differ from hedging a liability?

8–22 CharCo signs a contract to buy a special-order machine from a Swiss manufacturer. CharCo then hedges the commitment. How will the Canadian-dollar cost of the machine be determined?

8–23 Explain the term "cash flow hedge accounting."

8–24 What is the difference between a hedged item and a hedging item?

8–25 Where are the unrealized foreign currency gains and losses put in a hedging relationship?

8–26 What must a company do for hedge accounting to be applied?

8–27 What are the three characteristics for a perfect currency hedge?

8–28 What is a tandem currency?

CASES

CASE 8–1 Graham Enterprises Limited

Graham Enterprises Limited (Graham) has just negotiated the purchase of an office building for £20 million in London, England, to be used as the head office of its newly incorporated wholly owned European operating subsidiary, Graham Overseas Limited (GOL). Transfer of ownership to GOL is to be made on January 1, 2006. Graham has arranged a loan for £20 million to finance the purchase through its bankers. The loan, to be dated January 1, 2006, is at 12% and is repayable in 20 equal annual installments commencing January 1, 2007. The loan would be made to GOL, which would make all interest and principal payments in pounds sterling.

The building will be depreciated on a straight-line basis over 20 years. Assume the following exchange rates: January 1, 2006, £1 = $2.50; December 31, 2006, £1 = $2.00.

Required:

Discuss fully the options available to Graham in structuring its relationship to GOL, and evaluate the impact of each alternative on the consolidated financial statements. Show all supporting calculations.

[SMA]

CASE 8–2 Video Displays, Inc.

Video Displays, Inc. (VDI) is a privately held corporation chartered under the *Canada Business Corporations Act*. The corporation was formed in 1998 by four engineers who found themselves jobless after their previous employer (Argo Corporation) discontinued the production of television sets in Canada.

One of the sidelines of Argo had been the assembly of video display units (VDUs). A VDU is the basic chassis containing the cathode ray tube and related components that are used in video-display computer terminals and in computer game sets. When Argo discontinued production, the four engineers purchased some of Argo's assembly and testing equipment and formed VDI.

VDI has been fairly successful because it is the only Canadian producer of VDUs. Some computer terminal manufacturers have a policy of obtaining their components in the country in which they manufacture the terminals and thus VDI has enjoyed the benefits of local-sourcing policies since it is the only Canadian producer.

In 2004, VDI needed additional debt financing. After being refused by several Canadian banks, the executives of VDI went to New York, where on March 1, they quickly obtained a five-year, 12% term loan of $3,000,000 (U.S.) from Citibank, with interest payable annually on the anniversary date of the loan. The U.S. dollar was worth C$1.20 on March 1, 2004. By the end of 2004, the exchange rate had slipped to $1.18.

In 2005, VDI extended its operations into the United States by contracting with an electronics component distributor in Cambridge, Massachusetts. The U.S. distributor supplies component assemblies to small manufacturers, and saw an opportunity to sell VDI's VDUs to independent manufacturers of computer terminals. The December 31, 2005, VDI unadjusted trial balance showed a balance due from the U.S. distributor of $500,000. The 2005 shipments to and payments from the distributor are shown in Exhibit A. VDI gave the distributor US$60,000 on April 4 as an accountable advance for financing promotional expenses. By

December 31, 2005, the distributor had spent and accounted for $40,000 of this advance. At the end of 2005, the exchange rate was C$1.25 to US$1.00.

Required:

Explain the impact of the transactions described above on VDI's financial statements on December 31, 2005.

EXHIBIT A

CURRENT ACCOUNT WITH U.S. DISTRIBUTOR 2005*

		Dr	Cr	Balance
Feb. 1: Shipment	(US$100,000)		$115,000	$115,000
April 1: Shipment	(US$180,000)		207,000	322,000
May 1: Payment	(US$100,000)	$118,000		204,000
July 1: Shipment	(US$200,000)		240,000	444,000
Aug. 30: Payment	(US$150,000)	186,000		258,000
Nov. 15: Shipment	(US$200,000)		242,000	500,000

* In Canadian dollars.

CASE 8–3 Canada Cola Inc.

Canada Cola Inc. (CCI) is a public company engaged in the manufacture and distribution of soft drinks across Canada. Its primary product is CanaCola ("Fresh as a Canadian stream"), which is a top seller in Canada and generates large export sales.

You, CA, met with Jim MacNamara, the partner in charge of the CCI engagement, to commence planning for the upcoming audit of CCI.

During this meeting, the partner informed you that early this year CCI entered into an agreement with the government of Russia and has commenced the manufacture and sale of CanaCola in Russia. A short summary of the agreement is contained in Exhibit B. The partner would like you to prepare a detailed report that discusses the accounting and auditing implications of this new division of CCI for this engagement.

EXHIBIT B

SUMMARY OF AGREEMENT

1. The Russian government will provide the land and the building for the plant. It will make no further investment.

2. CCI will install bottling machinery costing $5 million in the Russian plant. Once installed, the machinery may not be removed from Russia.

3. CCI will be required to provide the funds for the initial working capital. CCI will sell U.S. dollars to the Russian government in exchange for local currency (rubles).

4. CCI will be wholly responsible for the management and daily operations of the plant. Canadian managers will be transferred to Russia.

5. CCI will be permitted to export its cola syrup to Russia at CCI's Canadian cost.

6. CCI and the Russian government will share equally in the profits from the sale of CanaCola in Russia.

7. Although foreign currency can be converted into rubles, rubles cannot be converted back into any foreign currency. Therefore, the Russian government will sell vodka to CCI (at the prevailing export price in Russia) in exchange for the rubles CCI earns in profits. CCI will be permitted to export this vodka to Canada, where it may be sold in the Canadian domestic market only.

Required:

a. Prepare the report for the partner.
b. Explain how your recommendations would differ for accounting if CCI formed a separate subsidiary, compared to a division, to run the operations in Russia.

[CICA]

PROBLEMS

P8–1

On January 1, 2004, a Canadian company, Canuck Enterprises Ltd., borrowed US$200,000 from a bank in Seattle, Washington. Interest of 7% per annum is to be paid on December 31 of each year during the four-year term of the loan. Principal is to be repaid on the maturity date of December 31, 2007. The foreign exchange rates for the first two years were as follows:

January 1, 2004	C$1.38 = US$1.00
December 31, 2004	C$1.41 = US$1.00
December 31, 2005	C$1.35 = US$1.00

Required:

Determine the exchange gain/loss on the loan to be disclosed in the financial statements of Canuck Enterprises Ltd. for the years ended December 31, 2004 and 2005.

[CGA]

P8–2

Domestic Corp., a Canadian company, sells its products to customers in the United Kingdom at prices quoted in pounds sterling. On November 14, 2004, Domestic sold and shipped goods that had cost $160,000 to produce to an English company for £200,000. On December 20, Domestic received an international draft for part of the amount due, £80,000. At year-end (December 31), the remaining £120,000 was unpaid.

On February 12, 2005, Domestic received payment of the remaining £120,000.

Required:

In general journal form, prepare journal entries to record the above events, and any adjustments necessary at year-end. Exchange rates (Canadian-dollar equivalent to £1) are as follows:

November 14	$1.80
December 20	$1.85
December 31	$1.87
February 12	$1.84

P8–3

At the end of the fiscal year, December 31, 2004, Export Ltd. finds itself with two accounts receivable in pesos:

1. From a sale on July 1, 2004, and due to be collected on December 1, 2005, for 2,000,000 pesos.

2. From a sale on September 1, 2004, and due to be collected on December 1, 2007, for 4,000,000 pesos.

Exchange rates (spot):

$1 = 160 pesos	July 1, 2004
$1 = 174 pesos	September 1, 2004
$1 = 180 pesos	December 31, 2004
$1 = 110 pesos	December 1, 2005
$1 = 90 pesos	December 31, 2005

Required:

Prepare the journal entries for December 31, 2004, and December 1 and December 31, 2005, assuming that the foreign exchange risk is *not* hedged.
[CGA–Canada]

P8–4

Pear Limited is a Canadian company that recently completed two large transactions with companies based in France:

1. On July 1, 2004, Pear acquired equipment at a cost of €250,000 from Pomme Ltd. Pear received reasonable terms regarding this purchase acquisition. The €250,000 was in the form of a notes payable to be paid on June 30, 2007, at an interest rate of 8% per year, the interest to be paid semiannually on December 31 and June 30.

2. On October 1, 2004, Pear also sold inventory that cost C$50,000 to another French company, Fromage Ltd., for €87,500. Payment is due from Fromage on March 1, 2005. Pear uses a perpetual inventory system. The spot rates for the euro were as follows:

July 1, 2004	C$1.00 = €1.250
October 1, 2004	C$1.00 = €1.125
December 31, 2004	C$1.00 = €1.000
Average rate July 1 – December 31, 2004	C$1.00 = €1.075
Average rate 2004	C$1.00 = €1.200
March 1, 2005	C$1.00 = €0.875

Required:

a. Prepare all journal entries regarding Pear's notes payable and interest-related transactions on July 1, 2004, and December 31, 2004.

b. Prepare all journal entries regarding Pear's sales, cost of sales, and accounts receivable transactions on October 1, 2004, December 31, 2004, and March 1, 2005.

[CGA]

P8–5

PL Corporation has a December 31, 2005, year-end. The company submitted a purchase order for US$30,000 of equipment on July 1, 2005, when the exchange rate was C$1.00 = US$0.6500. It received the equipment on September 30, 2005, when the exchange rate was C$1.00 = US$0.6667. The company paid US$20,000 to the supplier on December 1, 2005, when the exchange rate was US$0.6900. On December 31, 2005, the exchange rate was US$0.7000. The company uses straight-line amortization commencing in the month following the acquisition. The equipment is expected to last five years.

Required:

a. What would be the net book value of PL's equipment on its December 31, 2005, balance sheet?

b. What will be the balance of the account payable on PL's December 31, 2005, balance sheet?

[CGA]

P8–6

Using the information in P8–5, assume that on December 1, 2005, PL entered into a forward contract to buy US$10,000 on January 1, 2006 – the expected date of payment to the equipment manufacturer. The forward contract is designated as a hedge of the remaining amount due. The forward contract rate on December 1, 2005, was C$1 = US$0.6750.

Required:

Give the journal entries to record all aspects of the purchase and the hedge for 2005 and 2006.

[CGA, adapted]

P8–7

On September 7, 2005, Biran Limited signed a contract to buy equipment from a U.S. manufacturer. The price of the equipment was US$500,000. On the same date, Biran entered into a forward contract with the bank to buy US$400,000 on February 1, 2006. Biran designated the forward contract as a hedge of the outstanding purchase commitment on the equipment.

The equipment is to be delivered no later than December 1, 2005. Biran made a 20% down payment on September 7, 2005, and signed a promise to pay the balance on or before February 1, 2006. The exchange rates are:

September 7, 2005	C$1.00 = US$0.72
December 1, 2005	C$1.00 = US$0.70
December 31, 2005	C$1.00 = US$0.65
February 1, 2006	C$1.00 = US$0.68

The forward contract rate on September 7, 2005, was C$1.00 = US$0.71.

The equipment was delivered on schedule. Biran paid the manufacturer and closed out the forward contract on February 1, 2006.

Required:

Record the journal entries to record the purchase and the related hedge for 2005 and 2006. Biran's fiscal year ends on December 31. Ignore amortization of the equipment.

P8–8

PT Limited began purchasing parts from China. The Chinese currency is the renminbi (RMB). PT entered into the following transactions in 2004 and 2005:

November 1, 2004	Ordered machine parts from the Chinese supplier for RMB2,000,000. The supplier promised to deliver the machine parts at the beginning of December, and payment is expected on January 15, 2005.
December 1, 2004	Received shipment of the machine parts.
December 31, 2004	Acquired a forward contract to receive RMB2,000,000 on January 15, 2006, as a hedge of the account payable to the Chinese supplier. The forward contract rate was RMB1 = C$0.16. PT treats all forward contracts as executory contracts.
January 15, 2005	Received RMB2,000,000 on the forward contract; paid RMB2,000,000 to the Chinese supplier in settlement of the payable.

Spot rates were as follows:

November 1, 2004	RMB1 = C$0.15
December 1, 2004	RMB1 = C$0.18
December 31, 2004	RMB1 = C$0.17
January 15, 2005	RMB1 = C$0.19

Required:

Prepare the journal entries for these transactions, including any adjusting entries needed at the December 31, 2004, fiscal year-end. Specify if no entry is required on any specific date(s).

[CGA]

P8–9

At the beginning of 2004, Domo Industries Ltd. obtained a four-year loan of US$200,000 from a bank in New York City. At the time of the loan, the U.S. dollar was worth C$1.20. At the end of 2004, the exchange rate had changed to US$1.00 = C$1.24. By the end of 2005, the U.S. dollar was worth C$1.30.

During 2005, Domo Industries Ltd. sold goods to a German customer for €400,000. At the time of the sale, the euro was worth C$1.50. The customer paid one-fourth of the amount due later in the year, when the euro was worth C$1.41. By the end of 2005, the euro had declined in value to C$1.35.

Required:

Determine the impact of the transactions described above on Domo Industries' financial statements for the year ended December 31, 2005.

P8–10

Wayne Limited purchased a capital asset from France for €500,000. The asset was delivered to Wayne Limited on November 1, 2005. Wayne Limited agreed to pay the supplier in full on February 1, 2006. The payment was made as agreed. The exchange rates were as follows:

November 1, 2005	C$1.00 = €0.70
December 31, 2005	C$1.00 = €0.60
February 1, 2006	C$1.00 = €0.62

Required:

a. Prepare journal entries for 2005 and 2006 to record the above information.

b. Assume that Wayne Limited hedged the obligation on November 1, 2005. The forward rate was C$1.00 = €0.64. Prepare the appropriate journal entries for 2005 and 2006.

P8–11

On May 5, 2005, Roy Corp. purchased inventory from a Japanese supplier, and gave the supplier a 90-day note for ¥20,000,000. On the same date, Roy entered a forward contract with its bank to receive ¥20,000,000 in 90 days. The spot rate for the yen was $0.0095. The forward rate was $0.0100.

Required:

Prepare general journal entries to record the purchase, the hedge, and final settlement of both the note and the hedge, assuming each of the following spot rates at the settlement date:

a. $0.0095

b. $0.0100

c. $0.0093

d. $0.0102

P8–12

On October 15, 2004, Zap Limited sold merchandise to two companies in Portugal. In the first transaction, the price was 3,000,000 escudos and was to be paid in 90 days. Worried about the exposure to the exchange risk, the company hedged the receivable for a 90-day period with a forward contract.

In the second transaction, the price was 3,600,000 escudos and the date of payment was November 15, 2007. Due to the difficulty of getting a forward contract to match the date payment is due, the company decided to remain in an "unhedged" position on this receivable.

Exchange rates (for purposes of this question, all months have 30 days):

October 15, 2004, spot rate	$1 = 800 escudos
December 31, 2004, spot rate	$1 = 910 escudos
January 13, 2005, spot rate	$1 = 945 escudos
October 15, 2004, forward 90-day rate	$1 = 926 escudos
December 31, 2005, spot rate	$1 = 775 escudos

Required:

Ignoring closing entries:

a. Prepare all the related journal entries required for the first sale for 2004 *and* 2005.

b. Assuming instead that the company had not hedged the receivable from the first sale in any way, prepare the appropriate journal entries for 2004 *and* 2005 to record this situation.

c. Prepare all the related journal entries for the *second* sale for 2004 *and* 2005.

[CGA–Canada, adapted]

P8–13

Quality Wholesalers Inc. (Quality) imports goods from countries around the world for sale to retailers in Canada. On May 1, 2005, Quality purchased Swiss watches from a supplier in Switzerland for 200,000 Swiss francs (SF). The invoice called for payment to be made on August 31, 2005. On May 2, 2005, Quality entered into a forward contract with a bank to hedge the existing monetary position by agreeing to purchase SF200,000 on August 31, 2005, at a rate of SF1 = C$0.945. Quality's year-end is June 30. On August 31, 2005, the forward contract was settled and the Swiss supplier was paid.

Spot rates were as follows:

May 1, 2005	SF1 = C$0.930
May 2, 2005	SF1 = C$0.930
June 30, 2005	SF1 = C$0.920
August 31, 2005	SF1 = C$0.915

Required:

Prepare journal entries to record all of the transactions, including any adjustments required on June 30, 2005. Show your supporting calculations.

[CGA]

P8–14

Following are transactions of Import Ltd., a company engaged in importing products into Canada.

September 1, 2005:	Incurred a liability for 1,000,000 pesos, due February 1, 2006, for purchasing inventory.
October 1, 2005:	Incurred a liability for 6,000,000 yen, due November 1, 2006, for purchasing inventory.
November 1, 2005:	Incurred a liability for 22,000 Russian rubles, due March 1, 2007, for purchasing inventory.

Exchange Rates:

September 1, 2005
$1 = 150 pesos   Spot rate
$1 = 120 pesos   Forward contract rate

October 1, 2005
$1 = 800 yen   Spot rate
$1 = 950 yen   Forward contract rate

November 1, 2005
$1 = 1.80 rubles   Spot rate
$1 = 1.60 rubles   Forward contract rate

December 31, 2005
$1 = 100 pesos
$1 = 1,000 yen
$1 = 1.50 rubles

Required:

Parts a and b, below, are based on different policies regarding hedging. Answer each part as an independent problem.

a. Import Ltd. did not hedge or cover its exchange risk position. Prepare the journal entries for 2005. The company has a December 31 year-end.

b. At the time of each transaction, Import Ltd. paid $100 for a forward contract, which was a perfect and complete hedge against the foreign exchange risk. Prepare the journal entries for 2005. The company has a December 31 year-end.

[CGA–Canada, adapted]

P8–15

Orange Furniture Inc. (Orange) imports pine furniture from factories around the world for sale to retailers in Canada. On October 31, 2004, Orange bought a bedroom furniture set from a supplier in the U.S. for US$2,000. The invoice called for payment to be made on February 28, 2005. On November 1, 2004, Orange entered into a forward contract with a bank to hedge the existing monetary position by agreeing to buy US$2,000 on February 28, 2005, at a rate of US$1 = C$1.65. Orange's year-end is December 31. On February 28, 2005, Orange settled the forward contract with the bank and the US supplier was paid.

Spot rates were as follows:

October 31, 2004	US$1 = C$1.64
November 1, 2004	US$1 = C$1.64
December 31, 2004	US$1 = C$1.66
February 28, 2005	US$1 = C$1.69

Required:

Prepare journal entries to record all of the transactions, including any adjustments required on June 30, 2005. Show your supporting calculations.

[CGA, adapted]

P8–16

Harley Ltd., a manufacturer of motorcycles located in Burnaby, B.C., successfully negotiated a contract to sell 100 small motorcycles to the police department of Fairbanks, Alaska. The contract price for the cycles was US$10,000 each. The contract was signed on May 12, 2005, with payment to be made by October 1. Harley then entered into a forward contract to hedge against changes in the U.S. dollar exchange rate.

Delivery of the motorcycles began on June 11 and continued in 20-cycle lots at two-week intervals until the last delivery on August 30, 2005. The buyer then paid the US$1,000,000 contract price when due, and Harley settled with the bank.

The exchange rates were as follows:

Canadian equivalent of US$1.00:	Spot rate	Forward rate
May 12, 2005	$1.15	$1.18
June 11–August 30, 2005	1.10	1.08
October 1, 2005	1.12	1.14

Required:

a. What amounts relating to the sale and the hedge would appear on Harley's income statement and balance sheet for the year ended December 31, 2005?

b. Assume instead that Harley's year-end was August 30. What amounts would appear on Harley's financial statements at August 30, 2005?

P8–17

Chan Can Corporation (CCC), a Canadian corporation, engaged in the following transactions in late 2004 and early 2005:

December 2	Purchased sheet aluminum from a U.S. subsidiary of a Canadian aluminum company for US$160,000, payable in 60 days.
December 2	Acquired a forward contract to receive US$160,000 in 60 days, as a hedge of the account payable. The forward contract rate was C$1.40.
December 20	Sold large cans to a Buffalo canner for US$200,000, due in 60 days.
January 31	Received US$160,000 on the forward contract; paid US$160,000 to the aluminum company.
February 18	Received US$200,000 from the Buffalo canner.

Spot rates for the U.S. dollar were as follows:

December 2	$1.37
December 20	$1.42
December 31	$1.44
January 31	$1.50
February 18	$1.47

Required:

Prepare journal entries for these transactions, including any adjusting entries needed at the December 31, 2004, year-end.

Appendix 8A

Comprehensive Income

The AcSB has introduced a new *CICA Handbook* section on comprehensive income, Section 1530. This section is effective for fiscal years beginning on or after October 1, 2006.

Comprehensive income is a concept that has been required in U.S. public companies for several years and is also (under a different name) included in international standards. Section 1530 harmonizes Canadian standards with U.S. standards.

Comprehensive income is defined as follows:

> **Comprehensive income** is the change in equity (net assets) of an enterprise during a period from transactions and other events and circumstances from non-owner sources. It includes all changes in equity except those resulting from investments by owners and distributions to owners. [CICA 1530.03(a)]

Companies are required to prepare a statement of comprehensive income. Comprehensive income has two components:

- net income, and
- other comprehensive income.

Other comprehensive income:

> . . . comprises revenues, expenses, gains and losses that, in accordance with primary sources of GAAP, are recognized in comprehensive income, but excluded from net income. [CICA 1530.03(b)]

Although the definition of comprehensive income includes all non-owner changes in equity, the definition of other comprehensive income (OCI) specifically limits OCI to items that the AcSB has specifically identified. The only items that AcSB currently permits or requires in OCI are:

- exchange gains and losses on foreign currency hedges
- gains and losses on available-for-sale financial assets
- foreign currency translation of self-sustaining foreign operations (discussed in the next chapter), and
- appraisal increase credits.

The cumulative effects of changes in accounting policy are not the result of transactions with owners and would seem to fit within the OCI framework, but they will continue to be treated as direct adjustments to retained earnings.

In effect, the Canadian version of OCI is to serve as a temporary holding place for unrealized gains and losses. As we illustrated in the chapter, unrealized exchange gains and losses are placed in OCI until the hedged item and the hedge are settled, at which time the cumulative net gain or loss on the hedge is transferred to net income.

There is no requirement in either U.S. or Canadian GAAP that requires the use of the term "other comprehensive income." The IASB requires a statement that is similar to a statement of comprehensive income, but calls it a "statement of changes in equity." Many companies in the U.S. do not use the OCI label, preferring to call that classification "other changes in shareholders' equity."

Exhibit 8–3 shows the statement of comprehensive income for the Royal Bank of Canada. Royal Bank reports in U.S. GAAP and therefore shows "additional pension obligation" as one item. There is no equivalent in Canadian GAAP. Otherwise, the elements of the Royal Bank statement are identical to those that would be shown under Canadian GAAP.

The Royal Bank statement contains four items of unrealized foreign currency gains and losses relating to hedged items and to hedging instruments. The last of the four, "Reclassification to earnings of gains and losses on cash flow hedges," is the transfer of the net cumulative exchange gains and losses to net income as a result of settlements on hedged items and their related hedging items.

In addition to an annual statement of comprehensive income, a company presents a statement of accumulated other comprehensive income as a part of its shareholders' equity.

EXHIBIT 8–3 ROYAL BANK OF CANADA		
Statement of Comprehensive Income **Years Ended October 31**		
Comprehensive income, net of related income taxes	**2003**	**2002**
Net income	$3,036	$2,898
Other comprehensive income:		
Change in unrealized gains and losses on available for sale securities	(89)	12
Change in unrealized foreign currency translation gains and losses	(2,988)	(59)
Impact of hedging unrealized foreign currency translation gains and losses	2,149	43
Change in gains and losses on derivatives designated as cash flow hedges	(57)	(50)
Reclassification to earnings of gains and losses on cash flow hedges	80	113
Additional pension obligation	(197)	(276)
Total comprehensive income	$1,934	$2,681

CASE 8–A1 Accounting Conversation

The following conversation took place between an accounting policy analyst and an accounting student:

Accounting student: "Thanks for agreeing to meet me for lunch today. I am having some difficulty understanding Section 3855 and the impact of certain types of financial instruments on the accounting for foreign currency transactions. I am going to school part-time and took Intermediate Accounting a couple of years ago. So what I need from you is a little accounting update."

Accounting policy analyst: "I am happy to help you out. Why don't you ask me your questions and then I can write out the answers to your questions for you and e-mail you tomorrow."

Accounting student: "That would be great. First, I am a little confused about the difference between a financial asset or liability held-to-maturity, an available-for-sale financial asset or liability, and a financial asset or liability held for trading. How do we decide which classification a financial asset or liability belongs in and could you provide me a specific example of each one?"

Accounting policy analyst: "That is a good starting point since that classification will determine the appropriate accounting policy."

Accounting student: "All of these items are recorded on the balance sheet. Is that statement correct? Does historical cost accounting apply for each item?"

Accounting policy analyst: "Other than the valuation of these items, do you have any other questions?"

Accounting student: "This is the part that I am having real difficulty in understanding. Since I took my Intermediate Accounting course, I've come to understand that there is this new statement called "comprehensive income." What exactly is this statement?"

Accounting policy analyst: "Comprehensive income is new in Canada but has been in the U.S. for awhile. I will provide you with a couple of examples for when it would be used."

Accounting student: "My last question relates to gains and losses related to changes in the market value of financial instruments as well as gains and losses related to foreign currency transactions. Is there a difference in how these are accounted for in the different types of financial assets and liabilities based on their classification discussed above?"

Accounting policy analyst: "The quick answer is 'yes, there is a difference.' I will explain this in my e-mail. There is also an impact if an item is hedged or not. I am going to exclude that from this week's e-mail. Why don't we plan to have lunch again in two weeks? That way I can answer any additional questions that you have and we can discuss the impact of hedging."

Required:

Prepare the e-mail to the student.

Chapter 9

Reporting Foreign Operations

The previous chapter illustrated the accounting for foreign-currency transactions. Foreign-currency transactions affect a large proportion of Canadian corporations because Canadian companies so often have transactions with companies in other countries, especially in the U.S.A.

A somewhat different problem arises when a Canadian corporation actually has one or more active, self-contained, operations located in a foreign country. In that case, the company is not merely selling its products in U.S. dollars and/or buying inventory in Japanese yen; instead the foreign operation will actually have to prepare financial statements, usually in the subsidiary's host-country currency.

This chapter examines the problems of accounting for foreign operations. We begin with a brief discussion of the possible forms of organization for a foreign operation. Then, we discuss:

- the reasons for preparing separate financial statements for foreign operations and why that presents a problem for the parent corporation
- the two methods that can be used for translating foreign operations—(1) the temporal method and (2) the current-rate method—and their relationship with foreign-currency transaction accounting
- the competing concepts of foreign exchange risk exposure—(1) accounting exposure and (2) economic exposure
- the alternative treatments of gains and losses that arise from translating a foreign operation
- the necessary conditions for the use of each method, and
- a final summary comparison of the two translation methods.

Of course, we will provide illustrations as we proceed through the discussion.

Forms of Organization for Foreign Operations

In theory, a Canadian parent company could organize its foreign operations in any way that it wants. In increasing order of likelihood, the options are:

- branch office of the parent
- unincorporated partnership involving officers or directors of the parent corporation
- unincorporated partnership with an unrelated partner

- incorporated joint venture with one or more unrelated corporate co-venturers
- incorporated subsidiary, with minority shareholdings by unrelated shareholders, or
- wholly owned incorporated subsidiary.

A corporation is most likely to incorporate its foreign operations as a wholly owned subsidiary to conduct its operations in the foreign country. When a corporation operates in a host country, the foreign operation is subject to the laws of the host country, including its tax laws. An incorporated subsidiary is most suitable for abiding by local business law and for tax assessment. Unincorporated branches, partnerships, and joint ventures may leave the parent company vulnerable to adverse situations in the host country. For example, if the foreign subsidiary gets into financial difficulty, it can be kept separate from the parent and can be sold or liquidated without endangering the health of the parent.

Sometimes the foreign subsidiary is not wholly owned by the parent. This may be either by choice or by law. It often is useful to have a local shareholder who can provide local knowledge, political contacts, access to capital, or other intellectual capital. It can be foolish for a company to venture into a market that it does not understand, and a local "partner" can be very valuable. In some host countries, foreign companies are required to have local participation in their affairs. Until quite recently, both Mexico and China required local "partners." These mandatory legal arrangements are often called "joint ventures," but be careful here; the arrangement often is not a joint venture in an accounting sense.

Generally speaking, unincorporated foreign operations are not practical. An exception that occasionally arises is an unincorporated joint venture between two corporations—one foreign and one Canadian. These are often either marketing or production arrangements. The two companies pool their resources to operate in either or both countries.

An example is Molson Canada, which was formed as a partnership between Molson Inc. and Foster's Brewing Group Limited. The objective was "to merge and rationalize the North American brewing operations" of both companies. Each company owned 50% of the partnership, which made it an unincorporated joint venture.

The accounting for foreign operations is not affected by the form of organization. The accounting standards that we discuss in the remainder of this chapter are applicable regardless of the form of organization.

Translation Methods

To illustrate the nature of the problem, assume that Domestic Corporation decides to establish a sales subsidiary in the country of Pantania. Domestic's legal representatives in Pantania draw up the papers for a corporation in that country, to be named Forsub Ltd. The founding board of directors of Forsub is nominated (by Domestic) and Forsub begins operating. One hundred common shares of Forsub are issued to Domestic Corporation for 500 pants per share, the pant being the local currency of Pantania. Forsub will record the investment *in Pantanian pants* (P) as follows:

Cash	P50,000	
Common shares		P50,000

If the pant is worth C$2 at the time of the transaction, P50,000 will be worth C$100,000. Domestic will record the investment on its books at cost, as it would any initial investment:

Investment in Forsub Ltd.	$100,000	
Cash		$100,000

Now, suppose that after receiving the cash, Forsub buys inventory for P20,000 (P5,000 on account) and land for P40,000. To finance this purchase, Forsub issues five-year bonds amounting to P25,000. The transactions will be recorded as follows on Forsub's books:

Cash	P25,000	
Bonds payable		P25,000
Inventory	P20,000	
Cash		P15,000
Accounts payable		5,000
Land	P40,000	
Cash		P40,000

At the time of these transactions, the exchange rate is still P1 = C$2. Forsub's balance sheet will then appear as follows:

Cash	P20,000	Accounts payable	P 5,000
Inventory	20,000	Bonds payable	25,000
Land	40,000	Common shares	50,000
		Total liabilities and share-	
Total assets	P80,000	holders' equity	P80,000

A short while later, Domestic Corporation's fiscal year-end occurs. Since Forsub is a subsidiary of Domestic, Domestic will consolidate Forsub. As with any subsidiary that is consolidated, the investment account is eliminated and Forsub's assets and liabilities are added to those of the parent company in Domestic's balance sheet.

However, Forsub's assets and liabilities are expressed in pants, not dollars. We can't add pants to dollars, and therefore we must translate all of Forsub's financial statement elements from pants to Canadian dollars.

In the previous chapter, we translated individual foreign-currency *transactions*. When we are trying to consolidate a foreign *operation*, however, we need to translate the whole set of foreign-currency financial statements before we can consolidate. There are at least four possible translation methods, but only two methods are now reflected in accounting standards by the AcSB, FASB, and IASB:

- temporal method, and
- current rate method.

The following discussion will focus on these two methods.

Temporal method

Temporal means "related to time." The temporal method uses multiple rates for translating a foreign operation's financial statement elements:

- All *monetary* assets and liabilities (and any assets or liabilities reported at current value) are translated at the current rate.

- All *non-monetary* assets and liabilities are translated at the exchange rate that existed when the element was first recognized.

On the balance sheet, the year-end spot rate is used to translate cash, accounts receivable, accounts payable, long-term debt, and all other monetary items. The current spot rate is also used for assets or liabilities that are reported on the balance sheet at current value. For example, some inventories (such as precious metals) and some held-for-sale assets may be reported on the subsidiary's balance sheet at fair value rather than at historical cost. These balances are reported at the current rate because their carrying value represents an amount that can be converted to cash.

On Forsub's balance sheet, the monetary items are cash, accounts payable, and long-term debentures. These three elements are translated at the current spot rate. If the spot rate at the balance sheet date is P1 = C$2.30, the P20,000 cash balance is translated to C$46,000 for consolidation purposes.

Non-monetary items that are reported at historical cost are translated at the exchange rate in effect at the date of the transaction that created the non-monetary items. The rate on the date of the transaction is known as the **historical rate**. In essence, the temporal approach uses the same translation rules as we described in the previous chapter for monetary and non-monetary balances arising from foreign-currency transactions.

For Forsub Ltd., the non-monetary items are inventory and land, both purchased when the rate was P1 = C$2.00. Thus, these two assets will be translated at the $2.00 historical rate, while the cash and bonds will be translated at the $2.30 current rate.

Note that the historical rate is $2.00 because that was the rate existing at the time that the inventory and land were purchased. The fact that the rate was also $2.00 when the original investment in Forsub was made by Domestic is coincidental. If the land had been purchased when the rate was $2.10 and the inventory bought when the rate was $2.15, then those would be the historical rates used for translating each account balance.

The only account on the Forsub balance sheet that we have not yet discussed is the common shares. Since this is a non-monetary item, it is logical that it should be translated at the historical rate of $2.00. This account will be eliminated when Forsub is consolidated. Since the offsetting account in Domestic's balance sheet is the investment in Forsub account, the subsidiary's common share account should be translated at the historical rate in order to facilitate the elimination on consolidation.

In summary, the accounts on Forsub's balance sheet will be translated as follows under the temporal method:

Item	Rate
Cash	Current
Inventory	Historical
Land	Historical
Accounts payable	Current
Bonds payable	Current
Common shares	Historical

Since the accounts are being translated at two different rates, the translated balance sheet will not balance until we allow for a *translation gain or loss*. The total gain or loss will be the amount needed to balance the translated balance sheet, and it is a loss of $3,000 in this example. With this addition to the balance sheet, the translated balance sheet of Forsub Ltd. will appear as shown in the last column of Exhibit 9–1.

Composition of translation loss The $3,000 translation loss can be derived directly from the information given about Forsub's transactions. There are three components to the loss:

1. The first is a gain of $6,000 on the balance of cash. Forsub originally received P50,000 in cash when the exchange rate was $2.00, and obtained another P25,000 from the issuance of bonds. While the rate was still $2.00, the company purchased land and inventory, thereby reducing the cash balance to P20,000. The company then held this balance of cash while the exchange rate rose to $2.30. The increase in the exchange rate meant that the P20,000 balance was worth $46,000 at the end of the fiscal year (P20,000 × $2.30) as compared to only $40,000 (P20,000 × $2.00) when the cash was received. Thus, holding a cash balance when the exchange rate rose resulted in an increase in the equivalent amount in Canadian dollars, a gain of $46,000 −$40,000 = $6,000.

2. The second component of the $3,000 translation loss is a loss of $1,500 on the accounts payable. Forsub still owes P5,000 to its trade creditors, but the dollar equivalent of this amount has changed from $10,000 (P5,000 × $2.00) to $11,500 (P5,000 × $2.30). In Canadian dollar terms, the value of the debt has risen, thereby resulting in a loss.

EXHIBIT 9–1   TRANSLATION OF BALANCE SHEET, TEMPORAL METHOD

Forsub Ltd.
December 31, 2005

Exchange rate, December 31, 2005: P1.00 = Cdn$2.30

	Balance on Forsub's books	Exchange rate	Translated amount
Cash	P20,000	$2.30	$ 46,000
Inventory	20,000	2.00	40,000
Land	40,000	2.00	80,000
Total assets	P80,000		$166,000
Accounts payable, current	P 5,000	$2.30	$ 11,500
Bonds payable, long term	25,000	2.30	57,500
Common shares	50,000	2.00	100,000
Translation gain (loss)	—		(3,000)
	P80,000		$166,000

Calculation of net translation loss:

Cash	P 20,000	asset	× ($2.30 – $2.00) =	$ 6,000	gain
Accounts payable	(5,000)	liability	× ($2.30 – $2.00) =	(1,500)	loss
Bonds payable	(25,000)	liability	× ($2.30 – $2.00) =	(7,500)	loss
Net	P(10,000)	liability	× ($2.30 – $2.00) =	$(3,000)	loss

3. The final component of the overall translation loss arises from the bonds payable. The P25,000 in bonds were issued when the exchange rate was $2.00, or a Canadian equivalent of $50,000. At year-end, the Canadian equivalent of the bond indebtedness is $57,500, at the year-end exchange rate of $2.30. Therefore, a loss of $7,500 ($50,000 − $57,500) has arisen as a result of holding a liability that is denominated in pants as the Canadian equivalent increased because of changes in the exchange rate.

By breaking the translation loss down into its component amounts, we can see that the loss of $3,000 is really a net amount arising from a loss of $9,000 ($1,500 + $7,500) on monetary liabilities less a gain of $6,000 on holding cash. This information is summarized at the bottom of Exhibit 9–1. We will examine the nature of this loss and its accounting implications more extensively later in the chapter. For the moment, however, note that the only items that give rise to translation gains or losses are those account balances that are translated at the *current* rate.

The net amount of balances that are translated at the current rate is the measure of the foreign operation's **accounting exposure** to currency rate fluctuations. In Exhibit 9–1, the accounting exposure is a net monetary liability balance of P10,000: (P20,000 − P5,000 − P25,000). The translation loss is

P10,000 × ($2.30 − $2.00) = $3,000

Balances that are translated at historical rates do not give rise to translation gains or losses because the rate at which they are translated does not change. The net amount of the exchange gain or loss can be calculated by looking only at the net changes in those balances that are translated at the current rate.

Different methods of translation will yield different accounting exposures and different amounts of gain or loss. Indeed, as we will demonstrate shortly, a translation loss that arises under one method often becomes a gain under the other method. These accounting gains and losses usually do not adequately reflect the economic impacts on the company of exchange rate fluctuations. This issue will be addressed after our discussion of the alternative methods, in the subsection entitled "Accounting Exposure vs. Economic Exposure."

Relationship of temporal method to transaction accounting

In Exhibit 9–1, we translated Forsub's year-end balances by using the temporal method, and we calculated a gain on the balance of cash and a loss on the balance of bonds and accounts payable. An important characteristic to note about the temporal method is that *it yields exactly the same results in terms of the translated amounts as would have resulted from translating each transaction separately.* In substance, the temporal method views the operations of the foreign company as though the transactions had been carried out directly by Domestic Corporation operating from its home base in Canada.

Exhibit 9–2 illustrates the individual transactions as they would have been recorded by Domestic if they had been direct transactions. The first transaction shows the depositing of $100,000 in the Bank of Pantania—this amount is translated to P50,000 by the bank. The remaining transactions record the issuance of the bonds and the purchase of the inventory and land, recorded in the equivalent amount of Canadian dollars.

At year-end, it is necessary to record the monetary foreign currency-denominated balances at their current equivalents. These adjustments (for cash,

EXHIBIT 9–2   DIRECT TRANSACTIONS EQUIVALENT TO FORSUB'S TRANSACTIONS

If the parent company had engaged in the transactions directly instead of through Forsub, the transactions would have been recorded on Domestic's books as follows:

a Cash (in Bank of Pantania)	100,000	
Cash (in Canadian bank)		100,000
[to record transfer of cash for Pantanian bank account]		
b Cash (in Pantania)	50,000	
Bonds payable		50,000
[to record issuance of bonds in Pantania]		
c Inventory (cost = P20,000)	40,000	
Cash (in Pantania)		30,000
Accounts payable (P5,000)		10,000
[to record purchase of inventory in Pantania, paid in pants]		
d Land (cost = P40,000)	80,000	
Cash (in Pantania: P40,000)		80,000
[to record purchase of land in Pantania, paid in pants]		

Year-end adjusting entries, December 31, 2005:

e Cash [P20,000 × (2.30 − 2.00)]	6,000	
Foreign currency gains/losses		6,000
[to adjust the cash balance to the year-end current rate]		
f Foreign currency gains/losses	1,500	
Accounts payable [P5,000 × (2.30 − 2.00)]		1,500
[to adjust the accounts payable balance to the year-end current rate]		
g Foreign currency gains/losses	7,500	
Bonds payable [P25,000 × (2.30 − 2.00)]		7,500
[to adjust the bonds payable balance to the year-end current rate]		

accounts payable, and bonds payable) result in a net foreign-currency loss of $3,000. The impact of these individual transactions on Domestic Corporation's balance sheet would be exactly the same as translating Forsub's balance sheet by the temporal method and consolidating.

Current-rate method

An alternative approach to the translation of the results of foreign operations is to translate *all* of the asset and liability balances at the current rate. The historical rate is used only for the shareholders' equity accounts. The current-rate balance sheet is shown in Exhibit 9–3.

Under the current-rate method, the total assets of Forsub translate to $184,000 as compared to $166,000 under the temporal method. The much larger amount is due to the fact that under the temporal method, the large non-monetary assets were translated at the lower historical rate. Conversely, if the

EXHIBIT 9–3   TRANSLATION OF BALANCE SHEET, CURRENT-RATE METHOD

Forsub Ltd.
December 31, 2005

Exchange rate, December 31, 2001: P1.00 = Cdn$2.30

	Balance on Forsub's books	Exchange rate	Translated amount
Cash	P20,000	$2.30	$ 46,000
Inventory	20,000	2.30	46,000
Land	40,000	2.30	92,000
Total assets	P80,000		$184,000
Accounts payable, current	P 5,000	$2.30	$ 11,500
Bonds payable, long term	25,000	2.30	57,500
Shareholders' equity	50,000	2.00	100,000
Translation gain (loss)*	—		15,000
	P80,000		$184,000

* *Calculation of net translation gain:*

Translation gain = net asset position × change in exchange rate
= P50,000 × ($2.30 − $2.00)
= $15,000 gain

exchange rate had declined during the period, the translated total assets would be less under the current-rate method than under the temporal method.

Every solvent corporation has more assets than liabilities. When all the assets and liabilities are translated at the current rate, the translated assets will always exceed the translated liabilities. As a result, the translated net assets will always be positive—the excess of assets over liabilities. Thus, when the current-rate method is used, the net balance of those balance sheet accounts that are translated at the current rate will always be a net *asset* balance.

The accounting exposure to foreign-currency fluctuations under the two methods can be summarized as follows:

- Under the current-rate method, the accounting exposure to currency fluctuations is always measurable as the net assets of the foreign subsidiary—almost always a positive net asset value.

- Using the temporal method, the accounting exposure can be either a net asset or net liability balance, depending on whether monetary assets exceed monetary liabilities (for net asset exposure) or vice versa (for a net liability exposure).

A distinct characteristic of the current-rate method is that the proportionate amounts of the various asset and liability accounts do not change when the balance sheet is translated. For example, bonds are 31% of Forsub's total assets in pants (P25,000 ÷ P80,000), and they continue to be 31% of total assets in dollars ($57,500 ÷ $184,000). Under the temporal method, however, the proportion changes from 31% to 35% ($57,500 ÷ $166,000).

Many people feel that this characteristic is an advantage of the current-rate method—the "true" financial position of Forsub is that shown by the balance sheet in pants, and the process of currency translation should not change this picture of the foreign operation. As one eminent author puts it, "It is analogous to painting a stone wall; the colour may change, but the bumps remain; the wall is the same as before, just a different colour."[1]

Summary of translation methods

The two translation methods can be summarized as follows:

1. Temporal method

   a. translates all monetary and current-value items at the current exchange rate; translates all non-monetary historical cost items at their individual historical rate

   b. yields an accounting exposure to exchange rate fluctuations of the net balance of monetary and current-value assets and liabilities, depending on the financial structure of the company

   c. does not give effect to implicit hedges of monetary items by offsetting non-monetary items.

2. Current-rate method

   a. translates all assets and liabilities at the current rate, whether current or non-current and whether monetary or non-monetary

   b. yields an exposure to exchange rate changes that is always a net asset position, equivalent to the owners' equity in the foreign operation[2]

   c. preserves the proportionate relationships between the various balance sheet items; does not "distort" the statement compared to the way it would appear in local currency.

So far, we have been treating the net translation gain or loss under each of the methods as a balance sheet item. However, there actually are various treatments possible *under each method* of translation. Before we consider these alternative treatments of the translation gain or loss, however, we should further address the issue of *exposure*.

Accounting Exposure vs. Economic Exposure

Throughout the foregoing discussion, we have pointed out that under each translation method, we can anticipate the nature of the translation gain or loss. We know which items will be translated at the current exchange rate, and only those amounts will give rise to a translation gain or loss. If we know which way the exchange rate is moving, then we can predict whether the translation will result in a gain or a loss for the current period.

We have also observed that since the different methods translate different accounts at the current exchange rate, a given movement in the exchange rate may cause a gain under one method but may cause a loss under another method.

---

1. Dr. Pierre Vezina, *Foreign-currency Translation: An Analysis of Section 1650 of the CICA Handbook* (Toronto: CICA, 1985), p. 6.

2. This is true unless the foreign operation has more liabilities than assets, in which case the owner's equity will be a deficit and there will be a net liability position rather than a net asset position.

In the case of Forsub, above, we calculated a loss of $3,000 under the temporal method and a gain of $15,000 under the current-rate method.

The net balance of those balance sheet amounts that we translated at the current exchange rate is the *accounting exposure* to fluctuations in the foreign exchange rate. This exposure arises as the result of the accounting method of translation that we are using at the time. If a translation gain or loss is to be reported on the financial statements of the parent corporation, then the qualitative characteristic of "representational faithfulness" (in the FASB and *CICA Handbook* sets of criteria) should be present. In other words, is there really an *economic* gain to the parent when an accounting gain is reported?

It might seem that when a Canadian company holds an asset that is denominated in a foreign currency and that currency rises in value against the Canadian dollar, the company experiences an economic gain because the asset increases in value as measured in dollars. Since a Canadian company's equity in a foreign operation is almost always a net asset position, one could argue that an increase in the exchange rate will result in a gain to the parent because that net investment will be worth more as a result of the change in the rate.

Such an argument, however, does not take into consideration the impact of changes in the relative values of the currencies on the earnings ability of the foreign subsidiary. In most instances, the foreign operation exists as a going concern that is expected to contribute favourably to the profits of the parent. Therefore, it makes sense to evaluate the impact of currency realignments on the earnings ability of the foreign operation. This impact is known as the **economic exposure** of the foreign operation. The economic exposure is much more complicated than the accounting exposure because many more factors are involved than simply the mechanical aspects of the translation method and the direction of change in the exchange rates.

Example of economic exposure

Suppose, for example, that the business of Forsub Ltd. is to import a product from Canada and to sell it in Pantania. The cost to produce the product is $10.00, and it is sold in Pantania at P6. When the exchange rate is P1 = $2.00, the value of the sale is $12.00 (P6 × $2), resulting in a gross profit of $2.00 ($12 – $10) to Domestic Corporation.

If the exchange rate goes up to P1 = $2.30, the value of each sale will then be $13.80, for an increased gross profit of $3.80. In such a situation, the increase in the value of the pant is a real gain in economic terms. Forsub will either have a larger profit on its sales (if it maintains the same selling price in pants), or it may decrease its price and increase its volume of sales in Pantania (owing to the price elasticity of demand). Either way, Domestic may be better off as a result of the increase in the value of the pant.

Now, suppose instead that the business of Forsub is to produce a product from materials in Pantania and then to transfer the product to Domestic Corporation for sale in Canada. The product costs P10 to produce in Pantania, and sells for $25 in Canada. When the exchange rate is P1 = $2.00, the cost of production is the equivalent of $20, yielding a gross margin of $5. An increase in the value of the pant to $2.30 will cause the production cost to rise to $23 in Canadian dollars, thereby lowering the gross margin to $2.00. In this situation, an increase in the value of the pant can be disadvantageous to Forsub and Domestic Corporation. Instead of being a gain, a rise in the value of the pant is actually a loss in earnings ability.

Of course, things are not really all that simple. Exchange rates do not change autonomously, but are the result of other economic factors, such as relative rates of inflation and interest rate differentials in the various countries. If the value of the pant increased because of high inflation in Canada, then Domestic may be able to charge a higher price for the product and maintain or possibly even increase the relative gross margin on it.

The economic impact of changes in exchange rates is quite complex and will vary from company to company and situation to situation.

Past vs. future

Economic exposure is a result of the economic characteristics of the foreign operation, such as the sources of its raw materials, the sources of its debt financing, the market in which its products are sold, the price elasticity of demand for its products, and much more. Economic exposure is forward-looking. *Economic exposure is the impact of an exchange rate change on the present value of future cash flows.*

Accounting exposure, like many other accounting measurements, is historically oriented. It measures the mechanical impact of translating the results of past transactions. The economic exposure is not determinable from the accounting exposure, since the accounting exposure is mechanical in origin and is not necessarily indicative of the earnings impact of a change in exchange rates.

However, application of the concept of representational faithfulness leads to the conclusion that, in any situation, the preferred accounting translation method is the one that yields an accounting exposure that best reflects the economic exposure. If an increase in the exchange rate is likely to have a beneficial economic impact on the foreign operation and the consolidated subsidiary, then the accounting translation method should yield a translation gain when the exchange rate goes up, rather than a loss.

Alternatives for Reporting Translation Gains and Losses

So far in this chapter, we have treated the gain or loss arising from the translation of the balance sheet of a foreign operation simply as a balancing figure on the subsidiary's translated balance sheet. However, several alternatives are available for the disposition of these gains or losses. All but one of the alternatives have already been discussed in Chapter 8. The broad alternatives are:

1. Recognize the net gain or loss immediately in the consolidated income statement.

2. Disaggregate the net gain or loss and recognize each component in accordance with the treatment of similar types of *transaction* gains or losses.

3. Defer until realized, as a balancing amount in the consolidated balance sheet (e.g., as a separate component of shareholders' equity).

Each of these alternatives can be applied under either method of translation. However, some of the alternatives are more logical under certain methods, as we shall see later.

Immediate recognition

Immediate recognition of all exchange gains and losses was the alternative adopted by the FASB in 1975, SFAS 8, which caused a considerable furor. The FASB considered the various alternatives and found them all lacking. The Board concluded, however, that current recognition was the least misleading or artificial treatment: "...Rate changes are historical facts, and the Board believes that users of financial statements are best served by accounting for the changes as they occur. It is the deferring or spreading of those effects, not their recognition and disclosure, that is the artificial process" [SFAS 8, ¶198].

Since the Board works on the premise that the users of financial statements are sophisticated, it felt that users would understand that the translation gains and losses were unrealized and would not be misled by recognizing the net gains or losses in income.

While the Board was probably correct in assessing the reaction of an efficient market, they failed to anticipate the reactions of managers to the prospect of showing possibly substantial unrealized gains or losses on their companies' income statements. The market as a whole could no doubt properly evaluate the translation gains and losses, but managers were concerned about individuals' reactions to reported amounts, especially losses. The losses would affect net income from operations and therefore would affect earnings per share, dividend payout ratios, and profit-sharing and bonus calculations, as well as certain debt-covenant calculations such as times-interest-earned.

Furthermore, the translation gains and losses were a product of the accounting exposure and were not necessarily an indication of the economic exposure of the company. Empirical research following the implementation of SFAS 8 indicated that many managers with no economic exposure were taking actions to minimize the accounting exposure of their companies, even though those actions might be dysfunctional or represent a misallocation of resources. Some managers were engaging in massive hedging operations in order to offset possible losses from an accounting exposure in a foreign operation. The point of hedging, however, is to offset one economic exposure with another economic exposure in the opposite direction. If hedging is used to offset an artificial accounting exposure, then a real economic exposure is created by the hedge in order to offset a mechanical translation-method "paper" loss.

Other managers were reorganizing the financial affairs of their foreign subsidiaries in order to reduce the accounting exposure. If we assume that the managers made the best decisions in the financial structure of the subsidiaries in the first place, then changes in those decisions as the result of an accounting exposure must be changes that are less than optimal in economic terms.

An additional problem perceived by researchers was that the actions of managers to cover their accounting exposures were placing considerable pressure on the U.S. dollar. Ironically, the foreign-currency fluctuations that were causing managers to take possibly dysfunctional actions were themselves causing greater fluctuations in the value of the U.S. dollar.

In response to the objections of many people and to the research findings, the FASB reconsidered its position on the disposition of translation gains and losses and issued SFAS 52 in 1981, only six years after SFAS 8 had been issued. The FASB concluded that, in certain circumstances, the translation gains and losses should not be recognized in income, but should instead be reported on a cumulative basis as a separate component of shareholders' equity.

The experience in the United States with SFAS 8 clearly indicated the practical inadvisability of mandating the current recognition of translation gains and losses in all cases. Those instances in which current recognition seems particularly inappropriate are when the foreign operation is substantially autonomous in its activities.

If a foreign operation functions as a separate business unit, then recognition of a translation gain or loss is apt to be misleading because the accounting exposure is not indicative of the economic exposure. The FASB concluded that current recognition "produces results that are not compatible with the expected economic effects of changes in exchange rates" [SFAS 52, ¶88].

Disaggregation

The second of the broad approaches to the disposition of translation gains and losses is that of disaggregating the net gain or loss and treating each component individually. Under this alternative, gains and losses arising from monetary items would be treated in the same manner as foreign-currency *transactions*, as described in the preceding chapter.

Some foreign operations are extensions of the parent's domestic business. Examples include foreign sales offices and foreign production centres that have no real economic autonomy. Since the parent is directly involved in the foreign operation, the parent is, in effect, using the subsidiary as a facilitating mechanism for a series of foreign-currency transactions. Therefore, it is logical to apply the same recognition principles to foreign operations that are interdependent with the parent as would be applied to foreign-currency transactions.

The disaggregation alternative is inappropriate for relatively autonomous operations. Disaggregation implies that the parent has direct involvement with the subsidiary, and that the assets and liabilities of the subsidiary should be viewed as directly controlled assets and obligations of the parent. But if the foreign operation is engaged in its own day-to-day activities with little direct interaction from the parent, perhaps arranging its own financing and using the foreign profits to retire the debt, then the parent does not have direct control of the subsidiary's assets and liabilities.

Deferral

The third alternative is to indefinitely defer income statement recognition of the translation gain or loss. The cumulative translation gain or loss will be reported as a balance sheet item. A gain or loss is recognized in income only when the foreign operation is liquidated or significantly wound down. Therefore, the gain or loss would be recognized only when realized by liquidating the investment or a significant portion thereof.

This alternative seems to be appropriate for autonomous operations. There are two possible arguments for deferral of cumulative translation gains and losses:

1. the gain or loss is the result of a mechanical process of translating from a foreign currency into the reporting currency, and thus has no real economic impact on the reporting entity, or

2. the gain or loss is real, but it has not been realized and is not likely to be realized by the parent corporation.

When translation gains and losses are accumulated directly on the balance sheet, they could be treated as a deferred credit or debit, or they could be placed directly in shareholders' equity. Treatment of the cumulative gain or loss as a deferred credit or charge would imply that the translation gain or loss is a liability or an asset. Since there is no logic to support this view, the cumulative foreign-currency adjustment is treated as a component of consolidated shareholders' equity. The adjustment is shown in *other comprehensive income*, which is part of shareholders' equity.

The Two Solitudes: Integrated vs. Self-Sustaining Operations

We discussed above the three general alternatives for reporting translation gains and losses for foreign operations. In practice, not only in Canada but also in international accounting standards and in the U.S., two of the three alternatives are applied. The one alternative that is *not* used is the first one—recognizing all gains and losses immediately in the income statement. As we saw above, that alternative has been tried and found inadequate.

The other two approaches are used in practice, not only in Canada, but around the world. Practice is quite consistent, worldwide. To apply two different approaches, we must define the circumstances under which each can be used. The distinction essentially is on the basis of whether the foreign operation is in part an extension of the parent's operation (i.e., operates as a branch) or is quite autonomous in its operations. In Canada, the distinction is between (1) integrated and (2) self-sustaining foreign operations. Essentially, integrated operations are those that are interdependent with the parent, while self-sustaining operations are those that are relatively autonomous.

The *CICA Handbook* definition of an **integrated operation** is that it is:

> ...a foreign operation which is financially or operationally interdependent with the reporting enterprise such that the exposure to exchange rate changes is similar to the exposure which would exist had the transactions and activities of the foreign operation been undertaken by the reporting enterprise [CICA 1651.03].

Such operations usually are treated as revenue centres or cost centres from a management accounting standpoint. Integrated operations are largely or entirely dependent on the parent, either for a source of product or for disposition of production. Interdependent foreign operations are a direct arm of the parent and the parent controls the assets and liabilities of the subsidiary. The IASB calls such operations "foreign operations that are integral to the operations of the reporting enterprise."

The *CICA Handbook* calls independent or autonomous foreign operations *self-sustaining*. The definition of a **self-sustaining foreign operation** is:

> ...a foreign operation which is financially and operationally independent of the reporting enterprise such that the exposure to exchange rate changes is limited to the reporting enterprise's net investment in the foreign operation. [CICA 1651.03]

Unfortunately, this definition combines elements of independence with aspects of assumed economic exposure. As the previous section pointed out, economic circumstances seldom are so simple as to permit a company to declare that its economic exposure is limited to its net investment in the foreign operation.

Section 1651 provides a set of six criteria to aid preparers in deciding whether a foreign operation is self-sustaining. In essence, they are as follows:

a. Are the cash flows of the operation independent of the parent?

b. Are prices responsive to local market conditions?

c. Are the sales made primarily in foreign markets?

d. Are operating costs, products, and services obtained primarily in the foreign country?

e. Are the day-to-day operations financed from its own operations?

f. Does the foreign operation function without day-to-day transactions with the parent?

The U.S. FASB and the international accounting standards have similar guidelines.

It must be emphasized that these are only *guidelines*, not *rules*. Applying the guidelines is not a matter of score-keeping (e.g., four "yes" versus two "no") but is an exercise of professional judgment in determining the substance of the relationship between the domestic parent and its foreign operation(s).

An implicit assumption is that foreign operations can be categorized as *integrated* or *self-sustaining* with little ambiguity. Integrated and self-sustaining are really the two ends of a continuum, and many foreign operations fall in between the two extremes, with some aspects of each type of operation. In particular, the operations of worldwide corporations tend to be neither integrated nor self-sustaining, but to display aspects of both. The selection of translation method from among the limited alternatives currently offered in the *CICA Handbook* therefore becomes a matter of professional judgment.

In the U.S., the FASB defines the accounting treatment on the basis of the foreign operation's *functional currency*. The **functional currency** is the currency in which the bulk of the foreign operation's transactions are carried out. For example, if the foreign operation is financed by its parent, acquires its product from the parent, and remits payment for the product (and perhaps also for licence fees and management fees) in U.S. dollars, then the functional currency is the U.S. dollar rather than the local currency. The means of defining the basis for translation is different in the U.S. than in Canada, but the net result is essentially the same.

Integrated foreign operations

By definition, integrated operations operate as extensions of the parent company in a foreign country. Therefore, their operations are viewed simply as a series of foreign-currency *transactions*. The results obtained by translating the financial statements of the foreign operation should appear as though the parent had engaged in the foreign-currency transactions directly, rather than through a foreign subsidiary.

The method used for translating integrated operations should be compatible with that used for reporting the results of foreign-currency transactions. The method that accomplishes this objective is the *temporal method*. Therefore, the *CICA Handbook* recommends the temporal method for translating integrated foreign operations [CICA 1651.22].

Since the objective of translating integrated operations is to achieve the same results as for foreign-currency transactions, the disposition of the translation gains and losses that arise from translating integrated foreign operations is treated in the same manner as for transactions [CICA 1651.24]. That is, under the recommendations of Section 1651, the cumulative gain or loss is disaggregated and reported as follows:

1. in the current year's net income, to the extent that the gain or loss relates to monetary transactions and balances

2. as a part of retained earnings, to the extent that the gain or loss has been recognized in previous years' income.

We will demonstrate the application of this disaggregation in the following sections.

Specific assets or liabilities in an integrated foreign operation could be hedged by the parent. In that case, any gain or loss arising from the hedge would be offset against the exchange loss or gain on the hedged balance.

Self-sustaining foreign operations

A self-sustaining foreign operation is viewed as being an individual, autonomous foreign business entity. The parent company's accounting exposure to exchange rate changes is limited to the net investment of the parent in the foreign subsidiary. Therefore, the AcSB recommends the use of the *current-rate method* for translating the financial statements of self-sustaining operations [CICA 1651.26].

The net gain or loss that arises from translating self-sustaining operations is not recognized on the income statement, but is reported as a component of accumulated other comprehensive income (in shareholders' equity) [CICA 1651.29]. As we explained above, this treatment is recommended because:

1. the accounting exposure may not be indicative of the economic exposure, and

2. this exchange gain or loss has no direct effect on the activities of the reporting enterprise.

For fiscal years beginning on or after October 1, 2006, the annual change in the translation gain/loss must be reported as part of *other comprehensive income* on the statement of comprehensive income. The cumulative gain or loss will be reported as part of *cumulative other comprehensive income* in the shareholders' equity section of the balance sheet.

The translation gains or losses from self-sustaining foreign operations will continue to accumulate in the accumulated other comprehensive income account. Section 1651 recommends that companies disclose "the significant elements that give rise to changes" in the amount in this component of accumulated other comprehensive income [CICA 1651.32], but many companies simply summarize the changes in the balance without any attempt to disclose "significant elements," presumably because it is difficult (if not irrational) to try to segregate the components of a net investment.

If the parent's net investment in the subsidiary is decreased, a proportionate part of the accumulated amount will be transferred from accumulated other comprehensive income to net income [CICA 1651.31]. Thus, as long as dividends declared by a self-sustaining subsidiary do not exceed current earnings, and as long as the parent does not sell part of its investment in the subsidiary, none of the translation gain will be recognized in income.

The parent may choose to hedge its net investment in a self-sustaining subsidiary. Any gains or losses from the hedge will be offset against the cumulative translation loss or gain in other comprehensive income [CICA 3865.58].

Operations in hyper-inflationary economies

An exception to the general recommendation to use the current-rate method for self-sustaining operations arises when the self-sustaining operation is in a country that has a high inflation rate. Some countries historically have had very high rates of inflation, sometimes well over 100% per year. Historical-cost financial statements will show long-term non-monetary assets at a cost that is expressed in currency of a far different purchasing power than the current exchange rate suggests. One solution is to adjust the foreign operation's financial statements for changes in the price level in the foreign country, and then to translate the adjusted statements. But since price level adjustments are not normally included in primary financial statements in Canada, the AcSB has rejected this approach.

Instead, the recommendation is to use the *temporal method* for translating the statements of operations in highly inflationary economies [CICA 1651.26]. In substance, the effects of inflation are removed from the foreign accounts by restating the accounts using the historical exchange rates for non-monetary items. Of course, the effects of Canadian inflation are still present in the accounts, but the relative difference in inflation rates between Canada and the foreign country is adjusted for by using the temporal method. The AcSB does not provide guidelines as to what constitutes a "highly inflationary" economy, but the similar recommendations in the FASB's SFAS 52 suggest that an inflation rate of 100% over a three-year period (that is, averaging 26% per year, compounded) would be highly inflationary. However, the FASB guideline is absolute, whereas the *CICA Handbook* criterion is relative to the Canadian inflation rate.

Application of Section 1651 Recommendations

Integrated operations

Let us return to the introductory example of Domestic Corporation and its Pantanian subsidiary, Forsub Ltd. We determined earlier in the chapter that under the temporal method of translation, there was a net translation loss of $3,000 in the first year. If Forsub is an integrated subsidiary, the temporal method is used, and the net translation loss of $3,000 will be disaggregated *on Domestic Corporation's statements.*

Exhibit 9–1 shows that the $3,000 loss is composed of three components:

- a $6,000 gain from holding cash
- a $1,500 loss from the accounts payable, and
- a $7,500 loss from the bonds payable.

Self-sustaining operations

Instead, suppose that Forsub Ltd. is treated as a *self-sustaining* foreign operation. Then the current-rate method is appropriate—the entire translation gain or loss will be reported as a separate component of Domestic Corporation's shareholders' equity. Exhibit 9–3 shows that the current-rate method yields a net translation gain of $15,000, none of which is included in net income.

Obviously, a key facet of applying the AcSB recommendations is the determination of whether a foreign operation is integrated or is self-sufficient. Bear in mind, however, that if the foreign operations are relatively minor or if the parent is not otherwise constrained to follow the *CICA Handbook* recommendations, it may be simpler and no less informative to apply the current-rate method across the board to all foreign subsidiaries and to report the translation gains or losses either in the parent's consolidated shareholders' equity or in income.

Extending the example

Earlier in this chapter, we described the initial transactions for the establishment of Forsub Ltd. by Domestic Corporation. After Forsub was established, the subsidiary purchased land and inventory and issued bonds. Exhibits 9–1 and 9–3 illustrate translation of Forsub's balance sheet accounts under three different translation methods. For simplicity, we assumed that Forsub had no operating revenues or expenses for the first year, 2005 (even though, strictly speaking, there should have been some bond interest accrued). While we did point out that the translation gain or loss may be taken into income in 2005, it is taken into income by the *parent* company and reported on the consolidated income statement.

Now let us make the example more realistic by looking at Forsub's financial statements for the next year, 2006. Forsub Ltd.'s separate-entity balance sheet and income statement are shown in Exhibit 9–4. Additional information is as follows:

EXHIBIT 9–4   FORSUB LTD. FINANCIAL STATEMENTS, 2006

Balance Sheet
December 31, 2006

Assets		Liabilities and shareholders' equity	
Cash	P 15,000	Accounts payable, current	P 22,000
Accounts receivable	15,000	Bonds payable, long term	25,000
Inventory	10,000		47,000
Land	40,000	Common shares	50,000
Equipment	30,000	Retained earnings*	8,000
Accumulated depreciation	(5,000)		58,000
Total assets	P105,000		P105,000

* No revenues or expenses were recognized in 2005, the only previous year.

Income Statement
Year Ended December 31, 2006

Sales revenue		P 60,000
Cost of sales:		
Beginning inventory	P20,000	
Purchases	30,000	
Ending inventory	(10,000)	40,000
Gross margin		20,000
Operating expenses:		
Depreciation	5,000	
Interest expense	3,000	
Other expenses	4,000	12,000
Net income		P 8,000

1. At the beginning of 2006, Forsub purchased some equipment for P30,000; the equipment has an expected useful life of six years.

2. The ending inventory was purchased in the last quarter of the year, when the exchange rate was $2.45.

3. The exchange rate at December 31, 2006, was $2.50; the average rate during the year was $2.40.

Current-rate method The translation of Forsub's account balances by using the current-rate method is shown in Exhibit 9–5. All of the assets and liabilities are translated at the year-end exchange rate of $2.50. The shareholders' equity accounts are translated at the historical rates:

- common shares at the rate that existed at the time of the initial investment, and

- retained earnings at the rate that existed at the time the earnings were recognized.

In this example, the only amount in retained earnings is the current earnings for 2006, and thus the translated amount is the same as that shown on the translated income statement. The balancing figure for the balance sheet is the cumulative translation gain of $25,800.

Under a pure application of the current-rate method, the income statement would also be translated at the year-end rate. However, Exhibit 9–5 shows the income statement being translated at the average rate for the year rather than at the year-end rate. This is known as the **average-rate approach** to the current-rate method, and is used primarily in order to ensure additivity of the interim earnings figures of the parent company. Section 1650, SFAS 52, and IAS 21 all recommend the use of the average rate rather than the year-end rate for income statement amounts.

On the income statement, all items are translated at the current (average) rate, regardless of the type of revenue or expense, assuming that the revenue and expense accrued evenly through the year. Allocations of past costs, such as depreciation, are translated the same as are current costs, such as interest expense. As a result, the translated amount of net income is also equal to the current (average) rate times the net income as expressed in pants.

The cumulative translation gain of $25,800 that arises under the current-rate method can be broken down into three components:

1. the $15,000 gain arising from the first year's change in the exchange rate from $2.00 to $2.30 (Exhibit 9–3)

2. an additional $10,000 gain in the current year, 2006, caused by a further increase in the exchange rate from $2.30 to $2.50, and

3. an $800 gain on the retained earnings from the period of their generation (mid-2006) to the end of 2006, during which period the exchange rate changed from $2.40 to $2.50.

These components of the cumulative gain are summarized at the bottom of Exhibit 9–5.

EXHIBIT 9–5   TRANSLATION BY CURRENT-RATE METHOD, 2006

Exchange rate, December 31, 2006: P1.00 = Cdn$2.50
Average exchange rate for 2006: P1.00 = Cdn$2.40

Balance Sheet
December 31, 2006

	Local currency (pants)	Exchange rate	Translated amounts (C$)
Assets			
Cash	P 15,000	$2.50	$ 37,500
Accounts receivable	15,000	2.50	37,500
Inventory	10,000	2.50	25,000
Land	40,000	2.50	100,000
Equipment	30,000	2.50	75,000
Accumulated depreciation	(5,000)	2.50	(12,500)
Total assets	P105,000		$262,500
Liabilities and shareholders' equity			
Accounts payable, current	P 22,000	2.50	$ 55,000
Bonds payable, long term	25,000	2.50	62,500
	47,000		117,500
Common shares	50,000	2.00	100,000
Retained earnings	8,000	(below)	19,200
Cumulative translation gain (loss)*	—		**25,800**
	58,000		145,000
Total liabilities and shareholders' equity	P105,000		$262,500

Income Statement
Year Ended December 31, 2006

	Local currency (pants)	Exchange rate	Translated amounts (C$)
Sales	P 60,000	$ 2.40	$144,000
Cost of sales:			
Beginning inventory	20,000		
Purchases	30,000		
Ending inventory	(10,000)		
	40,000	2.40	96,000
Gross margin	20,000		48,000
Operating expenses:			
Depreciation	5,000	2.40	12,000
Interest expense	3,000	2.40	7,200
Other expenses	4,000	2.40	9,600
	12,000		28,800
Net income	P 8,000		$ 19,200

* *Cumulative exchange gain:*
  2005 gain on P50,000 net investment: P50,000 × ($2.30 – $2.00) = $15,000
  2006 gain on P50,000 net investment: P50,000 × ($2.50 – $2.30) = 10,000
  2006 gain on retained earnings: P8,000 × ($2.50 – $2.40) = 800
  Cumulative translation gain $25,800

Temporal method If, instead, the accounts of Forsub Ltd. are translated by using the temporal method, then the procedure is somewhat more complicated. Exhibit 9–6 illustrates the application of the temporal method for 2006.

The monetary assets and liabilities are translated by using the current rate. The non-monetary assets are translated at their historical rates. It is assumed that the ending inventory was purchased when the exchange rate was $2.45, and thus that is the historical rate for inventory. The specific historical rate for land is $2.00 and for the equipment is $2.30. The accumulated depreciation must be translated at the same rate as was used for the gross asset cost.

On the income statement, the revenues and expenses are translated at the rates that were in effect at the time that the revenues were realized or the costs incurred. For many revenue and expense items, realization coincides with recognition, so that the historical rate is essentially the same as the average rate for the period as was used in the current-rate method. Although the result is the same for some income statement items, the concept is quite different.

Under the current-rate method, cost of sales could be translated simply by taking the cost of sales in pants and multiplying it by the average exchange rate for the period. Under the temporal method, however, the cost of sales amount must be derived by multiplying the beginning inventory by its historical rate of $2.00, adding the purchases at the historical/average rate of $2.40, and subtracting the ending inventory at its historical rate of $2.45. The resulting figure for cost of sales, $87,500, *cannot be derived directly by multiplying any exchange rate by the cost of sales in pants, P40,000.*

Similarly, any depreciation or amortization expense must be translated at the exchange rates that existed at the time the original costs were incurred. In this example, the only such expense is the depreciation of the equipment. Since the equipment was purchased when the rate was $2.30, the depreciation expense must be translated at $2.30. Other expenses are translated at the rate that existed when they were *accrued*. It does not matter whether they have been paid in cash or not. Thus interest expense and other expenses have been translated at the average rate for the year.

The net income that results from using the temporal method amounts to $28,200 before considering any components of the translation loss. This amount cannot be derived directly from the original net income of P8,000—it must be obtained by working through the income statement and translating all of its individual components by the appropriate historical rates. Note that the temporal method net income of $28,200 is quite different from the current-rate method net income of $19,200. This difference is due to the lags in expense recognition of two types of costs: inventory and depreciable capital assets.

Translation of Forsub Ltd.'s accounts to dollars results in total assets of $237,000, as compared to total equities of $245,700. The cumulative translation loss therefore is $8,700. In Exhibit 9–6, the cumulative translation loss is shown as a single amount pending disposition, rather than being distributed to the income statement, the balance sheet, or both. The reason is that when the foreign operation's statements are translated, the translation gain or loss is not part of the statements of the subsidiary, but is an amount that must be allocated or assigned *on the parent's consolidated statements.*

Allocating the translation loss—temporal method We know from Exhibit 9–1 that $3,000 of the $8,700 cumulative translation loss arose in 2005, and therefore that the loss arising in 2006 must be the remainder, or $5,700. The $5,700 loss for 2006 has two components:

EXHIBIT 9–6   TRANSLATION BY TEMPORAL METHOD, 2006

Exchange rate, December 31, 2006: P1.00 = Cdn$2.50
Average exchange rate for 2006: P1.00 = Cdn$2.40

Balance Sheet
December 31, 2006

	Local currency (pants)	Exchange rate Type	Exchange rate Amount	Translated amounts (Cdn$)
Assets				
Cash	P 15,000	C	$ 2.50	$ 37,500
Accounts receivable	15,000	C	2.50	37,500
Inventory	10,000	H	2.45	24,500
Land	40,000	H	2.00	80,000
Equipment	30,000	H	2.30	69,000
Accumulated depreciation	(5,000)	H	2.30	(11,500)
Total assets	P105,000			$237,000
Liabilities and shareholders' equity				
Accounts payable, current	P 22,000	C	2.50	$ 55,000
Bonds payable, long term	25,000	C	2.50	62,500
	47,000			117,500
Common shares	50,000	H	2.00	100,000
Retained earnings	8,000			28,200
	58,000			128,200
Total liabilities and shareholders' equity	P105,000			$245,700
Cumulative translation gain (loss) [Exhibit 9-7]				$ (8,700)

Income Statement
Year Ended December 31, 2006

	Local currency (pants)	Exchange rate Type	Exchange rate Amount	Translated amounts (Cdn$)
Sales	P 60,000	H/A	$2.40	$144,000
Cost of sales:				
Beginning inventory	20,000	H	2.00	40,000
Purchases	30,000	H/A	2.40	72,000
Ending inventory	(10,000)	H	2.45	(24,500)
	40,000			87,500
Gross margin	20,000			56,500
Operating expenses:				
Depreciation	5,000	H	2.30	11,500
Interest expense	3,000	A	2.40	7,200
Other expenses	4,000	H/A	2.40	9,600
	12,000			28,300
Net income	P 8,000			$ 28,200

Exchange rate types:
    C = current, year-end rate
    A = average rate for the year
    H = historical rate for the individual item
    H/A= historical rate, assumed to be the average for the year

1. a loss arising from the long-term liability of the bonds payable, and

2. a loss from the net current items.

The loss on the bonds payable is the P25,000 balance times the exchange rate *change* during the period, $2.30 to $2.50: P25,000 × ($2.50 − $2.30) = $5,000 for 2006. The remainder of $700 is attributable to the current items.

The gain or loss from holding current monetary assets and liabilities can be computed by analyzing the flow of these items. Unlike the bonds payable in this example, the current assets and liabilities are not constant throughout the year. The impact of the exchange gains and losses must be measured only for the period of time that the current monetary items are in the enterprise.

For example, sales revenue increased current monetary assets, either as cash or as accounts receivable, by P60,000. Assuming that the sales were even throughout the year, we can measure the gain from holding monetary assets resulting from the sales by multiplying the P60,000 by the change in the exchange rate from the average for the year ($2.40) to the end of the year ($2.50). Similarly, the current expenses (or expenditures) that caused either a decline in monetary assets or an increase in monetary liabilities must be taken into account.

The easiest way to measure the net gain or loss from the current monetary assets and liabilities is to construct a funds-flow statement, with funds defined as net current monetary assets. Starting with the beginning-of-year balance of these net assets, we can add the inflows and subtract the outflows, to arrive at the year-end balance of net current monetary assets expressed in pants. We then need only to convert each balance or flow at the exchange rate in effect at the time of the balance or flow, and find the difference at year-end between the balance in foreign currency and the derived amount in domestic currency.

Such a funds-flow statement is shown at the top of Exhibit 9–7. The ending balance in pants is P8,000, as can be verified by referring to Exhibit 9–4. The year-end balance is equivalent to $20,000 at the balance sheet date. The sum of the inflows and outflows, however, when translated at the rates in effect during the year, amounts to $20,700.

In effect, the $20,700 shows what the ending balance of the net current monetary assets would have been if Domestic Corporation had maintained all of its Pantanian balances in dollars rather than in pants, and had converted to and from dollars only on the transaction dates. Since the actual dollar-equivalent balance of the accounts in pants is only $20,000, Domestic Corporation has suffered a loss of $700 by having Forsub Ltd. hold balances in pants.

The remainder of Exhibit 9–7 summarizes the remaining amounts included in the $8,700 cumulative translation loss at December 31, 2006. As we stated above, a total of $3,000 of the loss pertains to 2005, while the remaining loss of $5,700 pertains to 2006.

When Domestic Corporation consolidates Forsub Ltd., the total cumulative translation loss of $8,700 must be included somewhere in Domestic's consolidated financial statements. The temporal method is intended to yield the same result as if Domestic had carried out the foreign transactions directly. Therefore, the *translation* loss must be reported in Domestic's consolidated statements in a way that duplicates the treatment of gains and losses from foreign-currency *transactions*.

The consolidation process is quite straightforward:

- The portion of the cumulative translation gain or loss that relates to *prior years* is included in opening consolidated retained earnings.

EXHIBIT 9–7   TEMPORAL METHOD—ANALYSIS OF CUMULATIVE TRANSLATION LOSS, 2006

	Local currency (pants)	Exchange rate	Translated amounts (Cdn$)
Amounts arising in 2006:			
Current monetary items:			
Balance, January 1, 2006	P15,000	$2.30	$ 34,500
Changes during 2006:			
Sales revenue	60,000	2.40	144,000
Inventory purchases	(30,000)	2.40	(72,000)
Interest expense	(3,000)	2.40	(7,200)
Other expenses	(4,000)	2.40	(9,600)
Purchase of equipment	(30,000)	2.30	(69,000)
Derived balance, December 31, 2006			20,700
Actual balance, December 31, 2006	P 8,000	2.50	20,000
Net exchange loss from current monetary items, 2006			700
Long-term debt:			
2006 loss due to change in exchange rate:			
P25,000 × ($2.50 − $2.30)			5,000
Total exchange loss for 2006			5,700
Amounts relating to previous periods (Exhibit 9-1):			
Current monetary items (gain)	$ (4,500)		
Long-term debt	7,500		
Loss from previous years			3,000
Cumulative translation loss, December 31, 2006			**$ 8,700**

- The portion of the gain or loss that relates to the *current year* is reported in the consolidated income statement, along with any foreign-currency gains and losses of the parent.

For Domestic, the $8,700 year-end 2006 cumulative translation loss will be reported as follows:

- The $3,000 loss that arose in 2005 will be included in consolidated retained earnings for January 1, 2006.
- The $5,700 loss pertaining to 2006 will be reported as an expense (i.e., foreign exchange loss) in Domestic's consolidated income statement for the year ending December 31, 2006.

Comparison of accounting implications

Exhibit 9–8 compares the reporting implications of judging a foreign operation to be either *self-sustaining* or *integrated.* The decision to report a foreign subsidiary as one type or the other will determine the translation method to be used,

EXHIBIT 9–8　COMPARISON OF ACCOUNTING FOR FOREIGN OPERATIONS

Accounting issue	Self-sustaining	Integrated
Translation method	Current-rate method	Temporal method
Basis of accounting exposure	Net investment in subsidiary (usually a net asset position)	Net monetary items (most often a net liability position)
Most likely translation gain/loss:		
If foreign currency is strengthening	Exchange gain	Exchange loss
If foreign currency is weakening	Exchange loss	Exchange gain
Accounting treatment of gain/loss:		
Arising from previous years	Report in accumulated other comprehensive income	Include in opening consolidated retained earnings
Arising in the current year	Report in other comprehensive income	Report in consolidated income statement
Indication of true economic exchange risk exposure?	No relationship	No relationship

which in turn will decide (1) whether the translation effect will be a gain or a loss and (2) how that gain or loss will be reported in the parent's consolidated financial statements.

Remember, however, that the accounting exposure does not reflect the economic exposure. There is no necessary relationship between the direction of change in a foreign-currency and its impact on the economic contribution of the foreign operation to its parent's welfare.

SUMMARY OF KEY POINTS

1. A domestic Canadian corporation may establish a subsidiary in another country. When that happens, the parent has a foreign operation. The separate-entity financial statements of the foreign operation will be stated in terms of the host country's local currency. In order to prepare consolidated financial statements, the parent must translate the foreign-currency statements of the subsidiary into the parent's reporting currency (normally Canadian dollars, but sometimes U.S. dollars).

2. There are two methods for translating foreign operations: the temporal method and the current-rate method.

3. The temporal method translates all monetary assets and liabilities at the exchange rate at the balance sheet date, known as the *current rate*. Non-monetary assets and liabilities are translated at historical rates, except for those that are carried at current value. For current-valued non-monetary assets, the current rate is used.

The temporal method achieves the same translated amounts as would have arisen if the parent corporation had carried out all of the foreign operations directly, as a series of foreign-currency transactions, instead of through a foreign subsidiary.

4. The current-rate method translates all balance sheet amounts at the current rate as of the balance sheet date. Income statement amounts usually are translated at the average rate for the year.

5. In a world of fluctuating exchange rates, all translation methods will yield a translation gain or loss. The apparent foreign-currency gain or loss is not a real economic gain or loss, however. Accounting gains and losses are the result of the *accounting exposure* to foreign-currency fluctuations, and are a mechanical result of the translation method used. Economic exposure to foreign-currency fluctuations is the result of real economic impacts on the foreign subsidiary's operations, and cannot be measured by accounting methodologies. Any correspondence between accounting exposure and economic exposure is purely coincidental.

6. Translation gains and losses can be (1) recognized in income immediately, (2) disaggregated in accordance with the treatment given to *transaction* gains and losses, or (3) deferred. Immediate recognition has been tried (in the U.S.) and subsequently rejected. The two remaining methods are both in use, even though they give diametrically opposed results. Disaggregation is the approach applied to foreign operations that are integral to the parent's operations. These are called *integrated foreign operations*. Deferral, as a separate component of the parent's shareholders' equity, is the approach used for foreign operations that operate autonomously, known as *self-sustaining foreign operations*.

7. The translation gain or loss that arises from translating the statements of an integrated foreign operation must be disaggregated and reported in a manner that is consistent with reporting foreign-currency transactions. Under Section 1651, this requires allocation of the total translation gain or loss to (1) retained earnings, to the extent that gains and losses relate to previous periods and (2) current earnings, for the current year's gain or loss relating to monetary or current-valued assets and liabilities.

SELF-STUDY PROBLEM 9–1

Early in 2005, Irene Corporation established a subsidiary in Simonia. The subsidiary was named Gordon Limited, and Irene's investment was $1,250,000. When this investment was translated into Simonian frasers (SF), the currency of Simonia, the initial capitalization amounted to SF500,000.

Gordon Limited negotiated a three-year bank loan of SF200,000 from a Simonian bank when the exchange rate was $2.40. The company purchased depreciable capital assets for SF600,000 (exchange rate = $2.30).

The company then began operations. Due to an accumulation of cash through operations, Gordon invested SF200,000 in *non-monetary* temporary investments during 2006. The exchange rate at the time of the investments was $1.90. At the end of 2006, Gordon's comparative balance sheet and income statement are as shown in Exhibit 9–9.

Other exchange rate information for the Simonian fraser is as follows:

2005 average	$2.20
2005 year-end	$2.00
2006 average	$1.70
2006 year-end	$1.50

Required:

Assume that Gordon Limited is a self-sustaining subsidiary. Determine how the financial statement amounts shown in Gordon's balance sheet and income statement will affect Irene Corporation's consolidated statements for *each* of 2005 and 2006, including disposition of the cumulative translation gain or loss.

EXHIBIT 9–9   GORDON LIMITED

Income Statement
Years Ending December 31

	2006	2005
Revenue	SF300,000	SF220,000
Depreciation expense	60,000	60,000
Interest expense	40,000	40,000
Other expenses	120,000	80,000
	220,000	180,000
Net income	SF 80,000	SF 40,000

Balance Sheet
December 31

	2006	2005
Assets		
Cash	SF 30,000	SF160,000
Accounts receivable	40,000	30,000
Temporary investments (at cost)	200,000	—
Tangible capital assets	600,000	600,000
Accumulated depreciation	(120,000)	(60,000)
Total assets	SF750,000	SF730,000
Liabilities and shareholders' equity		
Accounts payable, current	SF 10,000	SF 20,000
Notes payable, due January 1, 2008	200,000	200,000
	210,000	220,000
Common shares	500,000	500,000
Retained earnings	40,000	10,000
	540,000	510,000
Total liabilities and shareholders' equity	SF750,000	SF730,000

SELF-STUDY PROBLEM 9–2

Refer to the information in SSP9–1 and Exhibit 9–9. Assume instead that Gordon Limited is an integrated foreign operation, as defined by Section 1650 of the *CICA Handbook*.

Required:

a. Translate Gordon's 2005 financial statements.

b. Disaggregate the 2005 translation gain or loss. Prove the amount of gain or loss relating to current monetary items. Indicate how the translation gains or losses would appear on Irene Corporation's consolidated statements.

c. Translate Gordon's 2006 financial statements.

d. Determine the amount of translation gain or loss on the current monetary items for 2006.

REVIEW QUESTIONS

9–1 Distinguish between foreign-currency *transactions* and foreign-currency *operations*.

9–2 Explain the differences between these two translation methods:
  a. Temporal
  b. Current-rate

9–3 Which translation method views the foreign subsidiary's operations as though they were foreign-currency transactions of the parent?

9–4 Why is the common share account of a foreign subsidiary translated at the historical rate under both translation methods?

9–5 What is meant by the *accounting exposure* of a foreign operation? How is the accounting exposure measured?

9–6 How does the accounting exposure under the temporal method differ from the accounting exposure under the current-rate method?

9–7 For a given foreign operation for a given accounting period, is it possible for the accounting exposure under the temporal method to result in a translation loss, while the accounting exposure under the current-rate method results in a translation gain? Explain.

9–8 Define *economic exposure*. Distinguish between economic exposure and accounting exposure.

9–9 Forop Ltd. is a foreign subsidiary of Domop Inc. Domop's accounting exposure to exchange rate changes when translating the accounts of Forop is a substantial net liability exposure. Domop's management expects the foreign currency in which Forop operates to increase in value relative to the Canadian dollar; such an increase will result in a large translation loss. The management of Domop proposes to enter into a forward contract to receive an equivalent amount of foreign currency in order to hedge against the potential translation loss. Would you recommend that Domop's management follow their proposed course of action? Explain.

9–10 Distinguish between *self-sustaining* foreign operations and *integrated* foreign operations.

9–11 What translation method is recommended by the *CICA Handbook* for *integrated* foreign operations? Why is this method recommended?

9–12 What recommendation does the *CICA Handbook* make regarding the financial statement disposition of translation gains or losses for integrated foreign operations? Why?

9–13 How can management decide whether a foreign operation is integrated or self-sustaining?

9–14 Mammoth Corporation has subsidiaries in 13 different countries, operating in 10 different currencies. Do all 13 have to be viewed the same way, or can some be considered integrated operations while others are considered self-sustaining?

9–15 What translation method is recommended in the *CICA Handbook* for *self-sustaining* foreign operations?

9–16 Under the current-rate method, why are the revenue and expense accounts translated at average exchange rates, rather than at the current rate at the balance sheet date?

9–17 How does the translation of cost of goods sold differ between the current-rate method and the temporal method?

9–18 How does the translation of depreciation and amortization differ under the current-rate method as opposed to the temporal method?

9–19 Explain how the translation gain or loss on current monetary items can be computed. Is the amount of gain or loss affected by the translation method used?

9–20 What is the impact of hyper-inflation on the translation method for a self-sustaining operation?

CASES

CASE 9–1   Elite Distributors Limited

Elite Distributors Limited is a Canadian public company that has been undergoing rapid expansion. The company is based in a major Canadian seaport, and several years ago found it necessary to open a sales office in the United States, in order to transact business directly in that country.

Elite also has a wholly owned subsidiary, located in Singapore, that manufactures one of the main products that Elite sells in Canada. Substantially all of the Singapore subsidiary's sales are to Elite. There is a second (80% owned) subsidiary, located in the Republic of Ireland, that was acquired in an attempt to diversify. This company sells exclusively through its own sales offices throughout Northern Europe, and has very few transactions with Elite, except for the regular payment of dividends.

Required:

Recommend the appropriate accounting policies for Elite to follow with respect to each of these foreign operations. Support your recommendations.

[SMA]

CASE 9–2   Care Inc.

Care Inc. (CI), a national manufacturer and retailer of women's shoes, purchased 100% of the common shares of ShoeCo, a footwear manufacturing company located in a foreign country. CI financed the purchase of ShoeCo's shares through a loan from a Canadian bank. To obtain this financing, CI had to offer one of its Canadian manufacturing plants as security. ShoeCo will continue to be managed and operated by locals and be responsible for obtaining operational loans.

ShoeCo sells most of its production to its domestic market. Previously a supplier of CI's, ShoeCo will continue to supply about 10% of its production to CI. CI has established a contract with ShoeCo fixing the quantity and the price in Canadian dollars.

Required:

a. State whether ShoeCo is an integrated or a self-sustaining operation of CI, and explain how you reached your conclusion.
b. Describe both the temporal and current-rate translation methods. Which method would CI use?

[CICA]

CASE 9–3   Multi-Communications Ltd.

Multi-Communications Ltd. (MCL) is a Canadian-owned public company operating throughout North America. Its core business is communications media, including newspapers, radio, television, and cable. The company's year-end is December 31.

You, CA, have recently joined MCL's reporting office as a finance director, reporting to the chief financial officer, Robert Allen. It is October 2005. Mr. Allen has asked you to prepare a report discussing the accounting and auditing issues that may arise with the auditors during their visit in November.

MCL's growth in 2005 was achieved through expansion into the United States by acquiring a number of newspaper, television, and cable operations. Since the U.S. side of MCL's operations is now significant, management will be reporting its financial statements in U.S. dollars. Shareholders' equity at the beginning of the period was $220 million, including a separately disclosed cumulative foreign exchange gain of $45 million. Management merged this balance with retained earnings because "the operations it relates to are no longer considered foreign for accounting purposes, and as a result no foreign-currency exposure will arise."

With recent trends to international free trade, MCL decided to position itself for future expansion into the South American market. Therefore, in 2005 MCL bought a company that owns a radio network in a country in South America that has high inflation. MCL was willing to incur losses in the start-up since it was confident that in the long run it would be profitable. The South American country has had a democratic government for the last two years. Its government's objectives are to open the country's borders to trade and lower its inflation rate. The government was rather reluctant to let a foreign company purchase such a powerful communication tool. In exchange for the right to buy the network MCL agreed, among other conditions, not to promote any political party, to broadcast only pre-approved public messages, and to let the government examine its books at the government's convenience. Management has recorded its investment in the books using the cost method.

In 2005, MCL acquired a conglomerate, Peter Holdings (PH), which held substantial assets in the communications business. Over the past three months, MCL has sold off 80% of PH's non–communication-related businesses. In the current month, MCL sold PH's hotel and recreational property business for $175 million, realizing a gain of $22 million ($14.5 million after tax). The assets related to the non-communications businesses were scattered throughout the U.S. and MCL lacked the industry expertise to value them accurately. Management therefore found it difficult to determine the net realizable value of each of these assets at the time PH was acquired.

Newspaper readership has peaked, leaving no room for expansion. In 2004, to increase its share of the market, MCL bought all the assets of a competing newspaper for $10 million. In 2005, MCL ceased publication of the competing newspaper and liquidated the assets for $4.5 million.

In 2005, MCL decided to rationalize its television operations. Many of PH's acquisitions in the television business included stations in areas already being served by other stations operated by MCL. MCL systematically identified stations that were duplicating services and did not fit with MCL's long-range objectives. These assets have been segregated on the balance sheet and classified as current. The company anticipates generating a gain on the disposal of the entire pool of assets, although losses are anticipated on some of the individual stations. Operating results are capitalized in the pool. Once a particular station is sold, the resulting gain or loss is reflected in income.

Nine stations are in the pool at the present time. In 2005, three were sold, resulting in gains of $65,000 after tax. Losses are expected to occur on several of the remaining stations. Although serious negotiations with prospective buyers are not underway at present, the company hopes to have disposed of them in early 2006. In order to facilitate the sale of these assets, MCL is considering taking back mortgages.

In 2005, MCL estimated the fair market value of its intangible assets at $250 million. Included as intangibles are newspaper and magazine circulation lists, cable subscriber lists, and broadcast licences. Some of these assets have been acquired through the purchase of existing businesses; others have been generated internally by operations that have been part of MCL for decades.

Amounts paid for intangibles are not difficult to determine; however, it has taken MCL staff some time to determine the costs of internally generated intangibles. In order to increase subscriptions for print and electronic media, MCL spends heavily on subscription drives by way of advertisements, cold calls, and free products. For the non-acquired intangibles, MCL staff have examined the accounting records for the past 10 years and have identified expenditures totalling $35 million that were expensed in prior years. These costs relate to efforts to expand customer bases. In addition, independent appraisers have determined the fair market value of these internally generated intangibles to be in the range of $60 to $80 million. In order to be conservative, management has decided to reflect these intangibles on the December 31, 2005, balance sheet at $60 million.

The market values of companies in the communications industry have been escalating in the past few years, indicating that the value of the underlying assets (largely intangibles) is increasing over time. MCL management stated that these licences do not lose any value, and in this industry, actually increase in value over time.

One of the items included in the intangible category is MCL's patented converter, which was an unplanned by-product of work being done on satellite communications devices a few years ago.

To combat the arrival of a direct broadcast satellite that transmits multiple TV signals to antennas, the communication industry has been developing its own interactive communication services at a cost of over $6 billion. This service will allow viewers to interact with banks, shops, and other viewers through the television. MCL hopes this will maintain its market share of viewers.

MCL has invested in the installation of fibre optic cable, which can transmit far more, far faster than conventional cable. The cost of the cable itself is negligible. MCL will be using it for transmission between its stations in two major Canadian cities. MCL needed only six cables to link all its television and radio stations between the two cities, but it decided to put in 36 cables since it was doing the digging anyway. To date, MCL has sold six cables and charges a monthly fee to new owners to cover their share of maintenance expenses. MCL is leasing 10 other cables for 15-year periods.

Required:

Prepare the report.

[CICA]

CASE 9–4   Johnston Co. Ltd.

Johnston Co. Ltd. is a medium-sized Canadian company, incorporated in 1980, whose shares are traded on the Toronto Stock Exchange. It began its operations as a processor and distributor of frozen herbs, but quickly branched out until it provided a full line of Canadian specialty foods. Some of these products were processed by Johnston itself, while others were processed by Johnston under contract with other Canadian companies.

The company's strategic plan calls for steady growth in sales and earnings. Accordingly, expansion into the lucrative United States market in 2006 is under serious consideration. A major concern is changes in the exchange rate of the Canadian and American dollar because the company has received very different predictions from various analysts with respect to this.

Johnston is considering the following proposals. The first proposal involves setting up sales offices in the United States with orders filled from Johnston's Canadian warehouses. The sales offices would be responsible for sales, billing, and collections. All transactions would be in U.S. dollars.

Alternatively, Johnston is considering establishing a wholly owned subsidiary in the United States to process and distribute a full line of specialty foods. It has not yet decided how to finance the purchase of the plant and equipment for this subsidiary.

The president has asked you, the controller, to prepare a report for possible use at a meeting of the board of directors. Specifically, he wants you to recommend which of the above proposals is preferable with respect to the impact of each on current and future income. He wants you to fully support your recommendation and to limit your discussion to foreign-currency translation issues, ignoring hedging and income tax considerations.

Required:

Prepare the report for the president.

[SMA, adapted]

CASE 9–5   Transpar Transportation Ltd.

Transpar Transportation Ltd. (TTL) is a Canadian public company that operates primarily in the commercial and recreational transportation sector. The commercial transportation business worldwide is growing strongly, fueled in part by rapid rates of urbanization. Traffic congestion, pollution and commuting times are rising in major cities. Rail transportation represents an efficient, cost effective solution to these problems. Analysts expect that the global passenger rail equipment market will grow at a compounded annual rate of more than 5%. Constraints on government ability to finance new transportation systems have resulted in the contracting of services to private companies such as TTL.

TTL has three divisions. The rail and transit operation offers a full range of urban, suburban, and intercity vehicles as well as complete rail transit systems. The recreational products division designs, builds, and distributes personal recreational transportation vehicles such as snowmobiles and watercraft. The capital services division oversees the financing activities for the company and provides secured financing for customer purchases of recreational product inventories and railcar leasing and management services for commercial customers.

Despite an uneasy economy, TTL has expanded its operations considerably in fiscal year 2005. This expansion is consistent with management's published objective to double the corporation's revenues, profits, and earnings per share over the next five years.

It is now June 2005 and TTL's fiscal year ends on September 30. You, CA, have recently accepted the position as assistant to the chief financial officer of TTL, Dave Butler. Your duties at TTL include overseeing the external reporting process and coordinating the external audit function.

TTL is an audit client of Rankin & Rankin (R&R), your previous employer. Mr. Butler has scheduled a meeting with the R&R audit partner and manager. In preparation for this meeting, Mr. Butler has asked you to prepare a report that discusses the major accounting and audit issues that might arise during the meeting. Mr. Butler has provided you with information about new developments in the company's three divisions (Exhibits A, B, and C). Mr. Butler would also like to know what information should be gathered to help the audit go as smoothly as possible. He is hopeful that your previous experience as an auditor at R&R will help reduce disagreements (that have been a problem between management and the auditors) and the current year's audit fee.

Required:

Prepare your report for Mr. Butler.

EXHIBIT A

CURRENT ACTIVITIES IN RECREATIONAL DIVISION

1. Sale of recreational watercraft products peaked in the late 1990s, leaving little room for expansion. In addition, several provincial governments now require users of watercraft to have a licence, and therefore the sale of these products to

rental companies has declined. To increase its share of the market, TTL bought all of the net assets of Wavemaker Ltd., a competitor, in 2004 for $9 million. In 2005, TTL ceased the manufacturing operations and liquidated the net assets for $6.2 million.

2. To ensure that its recreational products remain on the cutting edge from the design, safety, and environmental perspectives, TTL established a Design and Innovation Centre. The centre's mandate is to study emerging trends, analyze potential market opportunities, and conceptualize and create exciting new products. The centre is also looking to exploit the considerable upside potential for overseas sales of the products. To date the centre has incurred and capitalized costs of approximately $3 million.

3. Partially as a result of the centre's activities, TTL received a major contract with the government of Russia to design a snowmobile that would be suitable for Russia's rugged northern terrain. The design contract is for $2 million, which is not expected to cover all costs; however, TTL management believes that the Russian government will order several hundred snowmobiles from TTL once a proven product is available.

EXHIBIT B

CURRENT ACTIVITIES IN CAPITAL SERVICES DIVISION

1. In order to finance expansion activities, TTL completed a public share offering of 50 million Class A non-voting shares at an offering price of $9.00 per share in January 2005. Underwriter's fees amounting to $18 million have been deferred. In May 2005, TTL considered another public offering; however, the board of directors decided to defer the issue until fiscal year 2006 and to issue the new securities through a U.S. exchange. Fees of approximately $1 million related to the deferred offering have been incurred and capitalized to current assets.

2. TTL has $100 million of outstanding 6% convertible bonds that mature on September 30, 2007. The equity component associated with these bonds is approximately $7.5 million. In light of declining interest rates, management intends to repurchase the bonds in the market with proceeds from a fixed-term loan arranged with a large bank. It is expected that the repurchase will be completed prior to the current fiscal year-end.

3. In connection with the sale of rail and transit equipment, the company may provide financial support to its customers in the form of guarantees of financing. Currently, the company has guaranteed $30 million of debt related to prior purchases. The net resale value of equipment under guarantee is estimated to be $22 million.

EXHIBIT C

CURRENT ACTIVITIES IN RAIL AND TRANSIT DIVISION

1. On May 1, 2005, TTL announced that it had signed an agreement to purchase all of the shares of Alltrans Rail Systems Inc., a U.S. transportation company, for US$300 million (approximately C$500 million), A summary of the balance sheet items of Alltrans at April 30, 2005, (in thousands of US$) is as follows:

Assets

Receivables	$ 80,500
Inventories	100,200
Capital assets	500,100
Goodwill	20,000
Other assets	50,000
	$750,800

Liabilities

Short-term borrowings	$20,500
Accounts payable and accrued liabilities	62,300
Long-term debt	330,000
Future income taxes	80,200
	$493,000

Alltrans has a contract with a U.S. city to provide inter-city bus transit until December 1, 2009. To ensure adequate continuation of services, key members of Alltrans have been retained under management contracts, which provide bonuses for the next two years based on Alltrans' operating results. The fiscal year-end of Alltrans is June 30. Management of Alltrans does not want to change the year-end and wishes to retain its current auditors, Patterson & Cole.

The Alltrans purchase is the single largest acquisition in TTL's history. As a result of this acquisition, U.S. operations are now the largest part of TTL's global operations. Management has decided to report its financial statements in U.S. dollars. The existing cumulative foreign exchange gain on other U.S. operations of $16 million was transferred to retained earnings because reporting in U.S. dollars means there is no longer any exposure to the Canadian/U.S. dollar exchange rate.

2. In accordance with its intention to position itself in the growing international markets, TTL incorporated a company in Peru, South America, Transcom SA. The intent is to develop a citywide transit system in the country's capital city, Lima. In order to secure government approval and licences for the system, TTL agreed to invest C$50 million in the company. The government has agreed to provide subsidies for the purchase of the transit vehicles. These subsidies will become repayable if Transcom SA does not meet government-imposed quotas for hiring local employees to service the rail system.

TTL engineers will design the transit system and TTL will provide the transit vehicles. TTL engineers have been seconded to oversee the design stage of the project. The engineers are working with local government officials and construction of the rail system and manufacture of the transit vehicles is expected to commence in February 2006. The local government must approve all stages of the rail system design and will also approve the design of the transit vehicles. Once the system is complete, Transcom SA will operate it; however, the services provided would be rate-regulated by local government. The local government will also approve transit schedules. TTL agreed to allow government officials to review all books and records of Transcom SA at the convenience of the government. TTL expects that Transcom SA will incur losses in the start-up of the operations. Management of TTL has recorded its $50 million investment in Transcom SA using the cost method.

[ICAO]

PROBLEMS

P9–1

Efren Ltd. is a foreign subsidiary of a Canadian parent located in the country of Matos. The balance sheet accounts of Efren are as follows, stated in mats (M):

Cash	M 20,000
Accounts receivable	10,000
Inventory (at market)	60,000
Capital assets	200,000
Accumulated depreciation	(80,000)
Long-term note receivable	50,000
Total assets	M260,000
Accounts and notes payable	M 40,000
Bonds payable	150,000
Common shares	70,000
Total equities	M260,000

Additional Information:

1. Efren Ltd. is wholly owned by Hialea Corp. Hialea established Efren when the mat was worth $2.00.

2. The capital assets were purchased when the mat was worth $2.40.

3. The bonds payable were issued when the exchange rate for the mat was $2.30.

4. The long-term note receivable arose when the mat was worth $2.60.

5. The inventory was purchased when the mat was worth $2.80.

6. The current exchange rate for the mat is $3.00.

Required:

a. Translate the balance sheet accounts of Efren Ltd. into Canadian dollars, using each of the following methods:

   1. Current-rate
   2. Temporal

   In each case, treat the translation gain or loss as a single, balancing figure.

b. For each method, calculate:

   1. The accounting exposure
   2. The additional gain or loss that would result if the exchange rate one year hence were $3.50, assuming no change in the balance sheet accounts in mats.

P9–2

The income statement for 2005 for Hilary Co., expressed in Coker francs (CF), is as follows:

Sales revenue	CF3,000,000
Cost of goods sold:	
Beginning inventory	CF 200,000
Purchases	1,000,000
	CF1,200,000
Ending inventory	400,000
	CF 800,000
Depreciation	300,000
Other operating expenses	900,000
Interest expense	200,000
Total expenses	CF2,200,000
Net income	CF 800,000

Hilary Co. is 100% owned by Bryan Inc., a Canadian corporation.

Sales revenue, purchases of inventory, and operating expenses (except depreciation) all occurred evenly through the year. Interest expense accrued throughout the year, but was all paid at the end of the year. The beginning inventory was purchased on October 1, 2004, when the exchange rate was $0.82; the ending inventory was purchased on November 1, 2005, when the exchange rate was $0.93. The capital assets were acquired when the exchange rate was $0.70. Other exchange rate information is as follows:

December 31, 2004	$0.85
Average for 2005	$0.90
December 31, 2005	$0.95

Required:

Translate the income statement into Canadian dollars, using:

a. The current-rate method

b. The temporal method

P9–3

Investco Ltd. is a Canadian real estate and property developer that decided to hold a parcel of land in downtown Munich, Germany for speculative purposes. The land, costing €12,000,000, was financed by a five-year bond (€9,000,000), which is repayable in euros, and an initial equity injection by Investco of €3,000,000. These transactions took place on January 1, 2005, at which time a German subsidiary company was created to hold the investment. Investco plans to sell the land at the end of five years and use the euro proceeds to pay off the bond. In the interim, rent is being collected from another company, which is using the land as a parking lot.

The 2005 year-end draft financial statements of the German subsidiary company are shown below (assume that rental revenue is collected and interest and other expenses are paid at the end of each month).

Required:

a. Prepare the translated 2005 income statements and balance sheets at December 31, 2005, following Canadian generally accepted accounting principles and assuming
   1. the German subsidiary is an integrated foreign operation as defined in Section 1651 of the *CICA Handbook*; and
   2. the German subsidiary is a self-sustaining foreign operation as defined in Section 1651.

b. Which translation method better reflects Investco's *economic exposure* to exchange rate movements? Explain.

c. Which translation method would Investco be required to use? Explain.

[SMA, adapted]

German Subsidiary
Income Statement
For the Year Ended December 31, 2005

Rental revenue		€ 1,000,000
Interest expense	€ 990,000	
Other expenses	10,000	1,000,000
Net income		€ 0

Balance Sheet
December 31, 2005

Cash	—
Land	€ 12,000,000
	€ 12,000,000
Bond (due December 31, 2009)	€ 9,000,000
Common shares	3,000,000
	€12,000,000

Assume the following exchange rates:

January 1, 2005	€1 = $1.30
December 31, 2005	€1 = $1.75
Average, 2005	€1 = $1.50

P9–4

Birch Limited is a 100% owned foreign subsidiary with operations in England. Birch was acquired by its Canadian parent on January 1, 2004. The financial records of Birch are maintained in pounds sterling (£) and provide the following information related to its equipment:

Date of Purchase	Cost of Purchase
January 1, 2004	£1,000
January 1, 2005	£1,500

The equipment is being amortized on a straight-line basis over its estimated useful life of 10 years.

Foreign exchange rates were as follows:

January 1, 2003	£1 = C$2.50
Average for 2003	£1 = C$2.51
January 1, 2004	£1 = C$2.55
Average for 2004	£1 = C$2.58
January 1, 2005	£1 = C$2.63
Average for 2005	£1 = C$2.47
December 31, 2005	£1 = C$2.40

Birch's financial statements must be translated into Canadian dollars so that they can be consolidated with the financial statements of the Canadian parent.

Required:

a. Assume that Birch is a self-sustaining foreign subsidiary. Calculate the translated Canadian-dollar balances for the following accounts for 2005:

1. Equipment

2. Accumulated amortization—equipment

3. Amortization expense

b. Assume that Birch is an integrated foreign subsidiary. Calculate the translated Canadian-dollar balances for the following accounts for 2005:

1. Equipment

2. Accumulated amortization—equipment

[CGA]

P9–5

On December 31, 1999, Oak Company (Oak), a Canadian corporation purchased 100% of the outstanding common shares of Maple Limited (Maple). Maple was incorporated on January 2, 1996, and began operations immediately in the southwestern United States. Common shares were issued on the date of incorporation and no more common shares have been issued since then. The balance sheet for Maple at December 31, 2005, was as follows:

Maple Limited
Balance Sheet
December 31, 2005

Cash	US$ 100,000
Accounts receivable (note 1)	200,000
Inventory (note 2)	300,000
Equipment-net (note 3)	1,100,000
	US$1,700,000
Accounts payable	US$ 250,000
Bonds payable (note 4)	700,000
Common shares	100,000
Retained earnings	650,000
	US$1,700,000

Other Information:

1. The accounts receivable relating to sales occurred evenly throughout the month of December 31, 2005.

2. Maple uses the FIFO method to account for its inventory. The inventory available for sale during the year was purchased as follows:

Date of Purchase	Cost of Purchase	Exchange Rate
December 31, 2004	US$ 100,000	US$1.00 = C$1.55
March 1, 2005	1,000,000	US$1.00 = C$1.60
November 1. 2005	180,000	US$1.00 = C$1.63

3. The equipment was purchased on May 26, 1999.

4. Bonds of US$700,000 were issued on May 26, 1999, to finance the purchase of the equipment.

5. Maple reported net income of US$200,000, which was earned evenly throughout the year, and paid dividends of US$160,000 on July 1, 2005.

6. Foreign exchange rates were as follows:

January 2, 1996	US$1.00 = C$1.30
May 26, 1999	US$1.00 = C$1.40
December 31, 1999	US$1.00 = C$1.42
December 31, 2005	US$1.00 = C$1.56
July 1, 2004	US$1.00 = C$1.61
December 31, 2005	US$1.00 = C$1.65
Average for December 2005	US$1.00 = C$1.64
Average for 2005	US$1.00 = C$1.59

Required:

a. Translate the balance sheet of Maple at December 31, 2005, into Canadian dollars using the temporal method. Assume the translated balance sheet will be consolidated with Oak's balance sheet. For retained earnings, simply use the amount required to balance your balance sheet.

b. Calculate the foreign exchange gain or loss on the bonds payable for the year ended December 31, 2005.

c. Prepare an independent calculation of the change in the cumulative translation adjustment for 2005, assuming that Maple is a self-sustaining operation.

d. "Since the current-rate method uses the current rate to translate capital assets, the translated amount should represent the current value of the capital assets in Canadian dollars." Is this a valid statement? Briefly explain.

[CGA]

P9–6

On January 1, 2005, Pop Company of Regina, Saskatchewan, purchased 80% of the outstanding shares of Soda Limited of Switzerland. Soda's balance sheets as at December 31, 2004 and December 31, 2005, and Soda's 2005 statement of income and retained earnings follow:

Soda Ltd.
Balance Sheet
at December 31

Assets	2005	2004
Cash	SF120,000	SF 50,000
Accounts receivable	85,000	75,000
Inventory	80,000	60,000
Equipment, net	250,000	300,000
	SF535,000	SF485,000
Liabilities and shareholders' equity		
Accounts payable	SF 60,000	SF 90,000
Bonds payable	200,000	200,000
Common shares	100,000	100,000
Retained earnings	175,000	95,000
	SF535,000	SF485,000

Soda Ltd.
Statement of Income and Retained Earnings
Year ended December 31, 2005

Sales	SF500,000
Cost of sales	280,000
Amortization	50,000
Other expenses	20,000
Net income	150,000
Retained earnings, January 1, 2005	95,000
	245,000
Dividends paid	70,000
Retained earnings, December 31, 2005	SF175,000

Additional Information:

1. Soda was incorporated on January 1, 2002, at which time it acquired all of its equipment and issued its 10-year bonds.

2. Soda's purchases and sales occurred evenly during 2005. Soda's December 31, 2004, and December 31, 2005, inventory was acquired evenly over the final six months of 2004 and 2005, respectively.

3. Dividends were paid on July 1, 2005. Ignore income taxes.

4. Foreign exchange rates were as follows:

January 1, 2002	SF1 = C$0.80
Average for July–December 2004	SF1 = C$0.82
December 31, 2004/January 1, 2005	SF1 = C$0.84
July 1, 2005	SF1 = C$0.88
December 31, 2005	SF1 = C$0.92
Average for July–December 2005	SF1 = C$0.90
Average for 2005	SF1 = C$0.89

Required:

a. Translate the liabilities and shareholders' equity of Soda as at December 31, 2005, assuming that Soda is a self-sustaining subsidiary. Include a calculation of the cumulative translation adjustment in good form, including an analysis of changes in the cumulative translation adjustment from January 1, 2005, to December 31, 2005.

b. Translate the following accounts from the financial statements of Soda for the year ended December 31, 2005, assuming that Soda is an integrated subsidiary:

1. Cost of sales

2. Amortization expense

3. Bonds payable

[CGA]

P9–7

On December 31, 2004, Pepper Company of Winnipeg acquired 100% of the outstanding shares of Salt Company of Switzerland. On this date, the fair values of Salt's identifiable assets and liabilities were equal to their carrying value. Salt's balance sheets as at December 31, 2004, and December 31, 2005, and Salt's 2005 statement of income and retained earnings follow:

Salt Co.
Balance Sheet
December 31

	2005	2004
Assets		
Cash	SF 80,000	SF 60,000
Accounts receivable	140,000	80,000
Inventory	110,000	80,000
Equipment, net	250,000	280,000
	SF580,000	SF500,000
Liabilities and shareholders' equity		
Accounts payable	SF 150,000	SF115,000
Bonds payable	120,000	120,000
Common shares	140,000	140,000
Retained earnings	170,000	125,000
	SF580,000	SF500,000

Salt Co.
Statement of Income and Retained Earnings
Year ended December 31, 2005

Sales	SF 850,000
Cost of sales	(500,000)
Gross margin	350,000
Amortization expense	(30,000)
Other expenses	(245,000)
Net income	75,000
Retained earnings, January 1, 2005	125,000
	200,000
Dividends paid	(30,000)
Retained earnings, December 31, 2005	SF 170,000

Additional Information:

1. Inventory on hand as at December 31, 2004, and December 31, 2005, was purchased evenly over the final three months of 2004 and 2005, respectively, from suppliers in Switzerland. Sales and purchases occurred evenly throughout the year.

2. The plant and equipment on hand at December 31, 2004, was originally acquired for SF450,000 on January 1, 1998, the date of Salt's incorporation. No plant and equipment was acquired or sold during fiscal 2005.

3. Dividends were declared and paid on September 30, 2005.

4. The bonds were issued on January 1, 2000, and mature on December 31, 2009. The Swiss franc has changed over time relative to the Canadian dollar, but the foreign exchange trend has little effect on Salt's sales prices, which are largely determined by local competition. Foreign exchange rates were as follows:

January 1, 1998	SF1 = C$0.60
January 1, 2000	SF1 = C$0.70
December 31, 2004/January 1, 2005	SF1 = C$0.80
July 1, 2005	SF1 = C$0.86
September 30, 2005	SF1 = C$0.88
December 31, 2005	SF1 = C$0.90
Average for October–December 2004	SF1 = C$0.78
Average for October–December 2005	SF1 = C$0.89
Average for 2005	SF1 = C$0.85

Required:

a. Indicate whether Salt's operations should be considered self-sustaining or integrated. State three facts from the problem to support your conclusion.

b. Ignore your answer in part a and assume that Salt is an integrated subsidiary. Translate the statements of income and retained earnings for the year ended December 31, 2005, to Canadian dollars. Include an independent calculation of any exchange gains/losses.

c. Ignore your answers to parts a and b and assume that Salt is a self-sustaining subsidiary. Calculate the cumulative translation adjustment on its December 31, 2005, translated balance sheet.

[CGA]

P9–8

On December 31, 2004, KTR Corporation acquired 80% of the outstanding shares of SJC Limited for $5,000,000. KTR is a Vancouver-based company, while SJC is based in Las Vegas, U.S.A. SJC's financial statements follow:

SJC Ltd.
Balance Sheet
as of December 31

Assets	2005	2004
Cash	US$ 300,000	US$ 250,000
Accounts receivable	1,350,000	1,100,000
Inventory	2,100,000	1,800,000
Equipment, net	3,250,000	3,000,000
	US$7,000,000	US$6,150,000
Liabilities and shareholders' equity		
Accounts payable	US$ 560,000	US$ 400,000
Bonds payable	3,000,000	3,000,000
Common shares	1,500,000	1,500,000
Retained earnings	1,940,000	1,250,000
	US$7,000,000	US$6,150,000

SJC Ltd.
Statement of Income and Retained Earnings
Year ended December 31, 2005

Sales	US$5,000,000
Cost of sales	(3,200,000)
Amortization expense	(350,000)
Bond interest expense	(240,000)
Other expenses	(470,000)
Net income	740,000
Retained earnings, January 1, 2005	1,250,000
	1,990,000
Dividends paid	(50,000)
Retained earnings, December 31, 2005	US$1,940,000

Additional Information:

1. Inventory on hand as at December 31, 2004, and December 31, 2005, was purchased when the exchange rates were US$1.00 = C$1.40 and US$1.00 = C$1.58, respectively. Sales and purchases occurred evenly throughout 2005.

2. Of the $3,000,000 plant and equipment (net) recorded on the December 31, 2004, balance sheet, $2,000,000 (net) was purchased on December 31, 2000, and $1,000,000 (net) was purchased on December 31, 2004. Plant and equipment costing an additional $600,000 was purchased on December 31, 2005. The plant and equipment purchased in 2000 and 2004 is being amortized at $250,000 per year and $100,000 per year respectively.

3. Dividends were declared and paid on October 31, 2005.

4. The bonds were issued at par on December 31, 2000, with an 8% interest rate, and they mature on December 31, 2010. They pay interest semiannually.

5. Ignore the impact of income taxes in the question.

6. Foreign exchange rates were as follows:

December 31, 2000	US$1.00 = C$1.30
December 31, 2004	US$1.00 = C$1.50
October 31, 2005	US$1.00 = C$1.57
December 31, 2005	US$1.00 = C$1.60
Average for 2005	US$1.00 = C$1.55

Required:

a. You are the controller of KTR. Assuming that SJC is an integrated subsidiary, translate the statement of income for the year ended December 31, 2005, into Canadian dollars. Include an independent calculation of any foreign exchange gains/losses.

b. Assuming that SJC is an integrated subsidiary, translate the following balance sheet accounts for SJC into Canadian dollars as at December 31, 2005:

1. Accounts receivable
2. Plant and equipment (net)
3. Bonds payable

c. Assuming that SJC is a self-sustaining subsidiary, translate the following balance sheet accounts for SJC into Canadian dollars as at December 31, 2005:

1. Plant and equipment (net)
2. Common shares
3. Retained earnings

d. Assume that you have just been hired at KTR and you are discussing the operations of SJC with the chief executive officer. List two questions about the operations of SJC that you could ask the CEO to help you establish whether SJC should be considered a self-sustaining or an integrated subsidiary.

[CGA]

P9–9

On December 31, 2003, CL Limited, a Canadian company, acquired 100% ownership of British Company, a company based in London, England. Information for the translation of the foreign subsidiary is presented below. Sales, purchases, operating expenses, and interest expense all occurred evenly throughout the year. The 2005 beginning inventory was acquired when the exchange rate was £1.00 = $2.15. The 2005 ending inventory was acquired on October 1, 2005, when the exchange rate was £1.00 = $2.25. The land was acquired on December 31, 2005. Dividends are declared and paid on December 31. The bonds mature on December 31, 2008.

Required:

Using the information provided, calculate the following amounts:

a. Using the current-rate method, determine British Company's:
   1. Cost of goods sold
   2. Amortization expense

3. Equipment (net)—December 31, 2004
4. Equipment (net)—December 31, 2005
5. Common shares
6. Dividends—2005

b. Using the temporal method, determine British Company's:

1. Cost of goods sold
2. Amortization expense
3. Equipment (net)—December 31, 2005
4. Bonds payable—December 31, 2005
5. Gain on current monetary items

Data Table

Dates	Exchange Rate: No. of C$ = £1
December 31, 2003	2.00
October 1, 2004	2.10
December 31, 2004	2.20
October 1, 2005	2.25
Average rate 2005	2.30
December 31, 2005	2.40

Other Relevant Information:

Issue of common shares	2.00
Acquisition of capital assets	2.25
2004 retained earnings rate	2.10

British Company
Income Statement
Year Ended December 31, 2005

(Dr) Cr	£
Sales	4,500,000
Cost of goods sold	
Beginning inventory	(400,000)
Purchases	(1,500,000)
Ending inventory	600,000
	(1,300,000)
Amortization expense	(300,000)
Other operating expenses	(1,000,000)
Interest expense	(300,000)
Total expenses	(2,900,000)
Net income	1,600,000

British Company
Balance Sheet
Year Ended December 31, 2004

	£
Cash	200,000
Accounts receivable	700,000
Inventory	400,000
Equipment (net)	3,200,000
Total assets	4,500,000
Accounts payable	600,000
Bonds payable	2,000,000
Common shares	1,500,000
Retained earnings	400,000
Total liabilities & equities	4,500,000

British Company
Balance Sheet
Year Ended December 31, 2005

	£
Cash	100,000
Accounts receivable	100,000
Inventory	600,000
Land	1,300,000
Equipment (net)	2,900,000
Total assets	5,000,000
Accounts payable	100,000
Bonds payable	2,000,000
Common shares	1,500,000
Retained earnings, 2004	400,000
Income, 2005	1,600,000
Dividends	(600,000)
Total liabilities & equities	5,000,000

[CGA]

P9–10

On January 2, 2005, EL Limited established a subsidiary in Mexico City, Mexico. The subsidiary was named GC Company and the cost of EL's investment was C$1,000,000. When this investment was translated into Mexican pesos, the cost of the investment was p5,000,000. On January 2, 2005, GC obtained long-term debt of p1,000,000 from a bank in Mexico City when the exchange rate was p1.00 = C$0.20. The long-term debt must be repaid at the end of four years. The opening balance sheet for GC on January 2, 2005, is shown below:

GC Company
Balance Sheet
January 2, 2005

Current monetary assets	p6,000,000
Long-term debt	1,000,000
Common shares	5,000,000
	p6,000,000

The December 31, 2005, balance sheet and income statement for GC are shown below:

GC Company
Income Statement
December 31, 2005

Revenues	p3,200,000
Amortization expense	300,000
Operating expenses	2,200,000
Total expenses	2,500,000
Net income	p 700,000

GC Company
Balance Sheet
December 31, 2005

Current monetary assets	p2,800,000
Capital assets	4,900,000
Accumulated amortization	(300,000)
	p7,400,000
Current monetary liabilities	p 900,000
Long-term debt	1,000,000
Common shares	5,000,000
Retained earnings	500,000
	p7,400,000

The relevant exchange rates for the Mexican peso were as follows:

January 2, 2005	p1.00 = C$0.20
Average for 2005	p1.00 = C$0.22
December 31, 2005	p1.00 = C$0.24

During 2005, GC purchased capital assets when the exchange rate was p1.00 = C$0.21. Dividends were declared and paid when the exchange rate was p1.00 = C$0.23. Revenues and other expenses were incurred evenly throughout the year.

Required:

a. Calculate the exchange gains/losses for the temporal and current methods to be disclosed on the December 31, 2005, balance sheet and income statement.

b. Translate the 2005 balance sheet and income statement for GC assuming:

1. GC is a self-sustaining foreign operation
2. GC is an integrated foreign operation

[CGA]

P9–11

On January 1, 2004, Woods Ltd. formed a foreign subsidiary that issued all of its currently outstanding common shares on that date. Selected captions from the balance sheets, all of which are shown in local currency units (LCU), are as follows:

	2005	2004
Accounts receivable, net of allowance for uncollectable accounts of 2,200 LCU at December 31, 2005, and 2,000 LCU at December 31, 2004	40,000	35,000
Inventories, at cost	80,000	75,000
Capital assets, net of accumulated depreciation of 31,000 LCU at December 31, 2005, and 14,000 LCU at December 31, 2004	163,000	150,000
Long-term debt	100,000	120,000
Common stock, authorized shares par value 10 LCU per share, issued and outstanding 5,000 shares at December 31, 2005, and December 31, 2004	50,000	50,000

Additional Information:

Exchange Rates

January 1, 2004 to July 31, 2004	2.1 LCU to $1
August 1, 2004 to October 31, 2004	1.9 LCU to $1
November 1, 2004 to June 30, 2005	1.8 LCU to $1
July 1, 2005 to December 31, 2005	1.6 LCU to $1
Average rate for 2004	2.0 LCU to $1
Average rate for 2005	1.7 LCU to $1

Accounts Receivable—Analysis

	2005	2004
	(in LCUs)	
Balance beginning of year	37,000	—
Sales (36,000 LCU per month in 2005 and 31,000 per month in 2004)	432,000	372,000
Collections	423,600	334,000
Write-offs (May 2005 and December 2004)	3,200	1,000
	42,200	37,000

Allowance for Uncollectable Accounts

	2005	2004
	(in LCUs)	
Balance beginning of year	2,000	—
Provision for uncollectables	3,400	3,000
Write-offs	3,200	1,000
	2,200	2,000

Inventory, FIFO Basis

	2005	2004
	(in LCUs)	
Balance beginning of year	75,000	—
Purchases (June 2005 and June 2004)	335,000	375,000
Less: Inventory at year-end	80,000	75,000
Cost of goods sold	330,000	300,000

On January 1, 2004, Woods' foreign subsidiary purchased land for 24,000 LCU and capital assets for 140,000 LCU. On July 1, 2005, additional equipment was purchased for 30,000 LCU. Capital assets are being depreciated on a straight-line basis over a 10-year period with no salvage value. A full year's depreciation is taken in the year of purchase.

On January 15, 2004, 7% bonds with a face value of 120,000 LCU were sold. The bonds pay interest on July 15 and January 15 each year. The first payment was made on July 15, 2004.

Required:

Prepare a schedule translating the selected captions above into Canadian dollars at December 31, 2004, and December 31, 2005, using the temporal method. Show supporting computations in good form.

[CGA–Canada, adapted]

P9–12

Refer to **P9–2**. The comparative year-end balance sheets for Hilary Co. were as follows:

	2005	2004
Cash	CF 200,000	CF 500,000
Accounts receivable	400,000	300,000
Inventory	400,000	200,000
Land	500,000	—
Equipment (net)	1,700,000	2,000,000
Total assets	CF3,200,000	CF3,000,000
Accounts payable	CF 500,000	CF 400,000
Bonds payable	1,800,000	1,800,000
Common shares	500,000	500,000
Retained earnings	400,000	300,000
Total equities	CF3,200,000	CF3,000,000

The common shares were issued when the exchange rate was $0.60.

The land was purchased at the end of 2005. The bonds were issued at the end of 2003, and mature at the end of 2009. The exchange rate at the end of 2003 was $0.70. Dividends are declared and paid at the end of each year. The retained earnings at the end of 2004 were earned at an average rate of $0.75.

Required:

a. Translate the 2004 and 2005 balance sheets, using the current-rate method. (Note that each year's balance sheet is translated at the current rate *at that year's balance sheet date.*)

b. Translate the 2004 and 2005 balance sheets, using the temporal method.

c. Calculate the net change in the cumulative translation gain or loss for 2005, under each translation method.

10 Financial Reporting for Non-Profit Organizations

Most study of accounting focuses on business enterprises. However, there are many organizations in Canada that are not businesses. Schools, universities, hospitals, social service agencies, performing arts organizations, museums, trade associations, unions, political parties, and philanthropic foundations are a few examples of the *non-profit organizations* that have an important place in our society. In addition, governments themselves, the entire public sector of the economy, are organizations that are not businesses.

Overall, close to 20% of all Canadian employment is in non-profit organizations or governments. The larger segments are health care, education, and the various levels of government and government services. Indeed, *non-business organizations* comprise a larger component of the economy than manufacturing.

Given the importance of non-business organizations, not only in Canada but worldwide, it is somewhat surprising that so little attention is given to this important segment of the economy in accounting courses. Generally, it is only when students reach the advanced level that they are introduced to the particular problems faced by non-profit organizations and by governments.

Well, better late than never! In this chapter, we discuss non-profit organizations. We discuss governmental accounting in Chapter 11, "Public Sector Financial Reporting."

In this chapter we will discuss:

- the characteristics of non-profit organizations (NPOs) and how NPOs differ from business enterprises
- the primary reporting issues that arise from the special characteristics of NPOs, and
- GAAP for NPOs and the various reporting methods that are available.

Finally, we will illustrate the possible reporting models.

Overview of Non-Business Organizations

As a first step, we must make a distinction between *non-business* and *non-profit* organizations. A **non-business organization** is any organization except a private enterprise operating for profit. The general category of non-business organizations can be roughly divided into three groups: (1) governments, (2) governmental units, and (3) non-profit organizations.

Governmental accounting is the body of principles and practices that has been developed for recordkeeping and reporting by the various levels of government: municipal, regional, provincial, territorial, and federal. Governmental accounting is usually regulated by law. The accounting and reporting principles on which the law is based were developed by governments and by professional organizations. In Canada, the pronouncements of the CICA's Public Sector Accounting Board influence financial reporting by governments.

Governmental units are organizations that are set up by governments to carry out some aspect of their policy. Governmental units include school boards, public housing authorities, parking authorities, public cemeteries, water systems, and electric utilities. Such units may be incorporated, but they are **corporations without share capital** and must be distinguished from **Crown corporations**, such as VIA Rail Canada or the Liquor Control Board of Ontario, which are business corporations having the government as the only shareholder. Some governmental units do carry on some type of business (e.g., local transportation systems), but they are public sector organizations rather than private enterprises. Therefore, they fall within the general classification of non-business organizations.

Non-profit organizations are non-business and non-governmental organizations that function as educational, scientific, charitable, artistic, or social agencies. The term "social agency" covers a lot of ground, since a social agency can range anywhere from an amateur baseball club to a hospital, with the Salvation Army, the Liberal Party of Canada, and the Kiwanis in between.

Terms other than "non-profit organization" (or "not-for-profit organization") are often used to describe the widely diverse types of organizations that are in this sector of the economy. One alternative is "third sector" (as distinguished from the other two sectors, public and private). Another alternative is "volunteer organizations," because they frequently use the services of volunteers for delivering the organization's services. Also the directors of non-profit organizations are generally prohibited from being paid, and thus are volunteer directors. "Public service sector" is also used, although this phrase can be too easily confused with the "public sector." In this book we will use the term *non-profit organization*.[1]

It is neither possible nor necessary to draw a clear line between governmental units and non-profit organizations. Canadian universities, for example, usually are established as independent corporate entities. But they are dependent on governments for most of their funding and they carry out part of government's educational policy. Similarly, hospitals and public utilities are semi-independent corporations that have some characteristics of governmental units. For accounting purposes, the distinction between non-profit organizations and governmental units is not crucial. The objectives of both are similar, and there is more variation within the broad group of non-profit organizations than there is between non-profit and governmental units.

Governments, on the other hand, have quite different financial statement objectives because of the sources of their funds, their ability to tax, and their legal reporting obligations. In this chapter, we focus on non-profit organizations, including governmental units. Our discussion of governmental financial reporting is in Chapter 11.

---

1   Robert Anthony, somewhat annoyed by the use of "not-for-profit," analyzed the relative use of "non-profit" and "not-for-profit" in the NPO literature. He found that "non-profit organization" was used in 90% of article abstracts and book titles, 81% of U.S. federal court documents, and 77% of U.S. state laws [Anthony, *Should Business and Nonbusiness Accounting Be Different?*, p. 102]. The term "not-for-profit" seems to have evolved from a concern that people will be overly literal in taking "non-profit" to mean business corporations that are operating at a loss, which is rather like fearing that naive users will think an asset is a small donkey.

Characteristics of Non-Profit Organizations

There are four very fundamental ways in which non-profit organizations (NPOs) differ from business enterprises:

1. NPOs have *members* instead of owners; there are no residual economic interests.

2. The organization has a different "bottom line." The organization's objectives may be to serve the common good rather than to maximize net income or generate a return on investment.

3. The nature of revenues and their relationship to costs differs significantly from those of businesses. As well, the sources of revenue often sharply restrict the flexibility of the organization to use that revenue.

4. The suppliers of funds (who are the primary users of the financial statements) are not providing capital in order to earn a return on their investment. Therefore, financial reporting objectives often differ significantly from the profit sector.

These four characteristics profoundly affect the nature of NPO financial reporting. We will expand upon each of these characteristics in the following sections.

No owners

Non-profit organizations have no owners. Regardless of whether an NPO is incorporated or unincorporated, no one has a right to the residual earnings of the organization. Legally, incorporated NPOs are *corporations without share capital*. Since NPOs have no owners, they have no transferable ownership interest.

Although NPOs have no shareholders, they do have *members* who elect the board of directors.[2] The constitution of the organization specifies the conditions for membership. Membership may either be *open* or *closed*.

In an **open membership**, the conditions for membership are clearly specified in the constitution or bylaws of the organization, and membership is available to anyone who is able to fulfill the membership requirements. A **closed membership** exists when the members are designated by the board of directors. Membership is *closed* because it is not automatically open to all qualified individuals who apply, and because the board has the power to change the requirements for membership at any board meeting. In some non-profit organizations, the directors are the *only* members of the organization—in effect, the board elects itself.

A different "bottom line"

NPOs exist in order to perform a service. Since there are no residual economic interests, financial performance on its own is not a primary objective. Obviously, an NPO must remain financially viable in order to continue to operate and to fulfill its service objectives, but financial viability is a *means to an end* rather than being the end itself as is the case with business enterprises.

---

2 In some NPOs, the members elect only some of the directors, while other directors are appointed by stakeholder groups, such as government or constituency groups.

Businesses provide goods and services to individuals (or to organized groups such as other businesses) at a price. Price is the rationing mechanism, but it also provides the revenue that finances the cost of providing the goods and services. Goods and services that are consumed by individuals and that are rationed are referred to as **private goods and services**.

Non-profit organizations may also provide private goods and services. This is particularly true in NPOs such as sports or social clubs, wherein the primary objective of the organization is to provide services to its members. Private goods are also provided by organizations such as trade unions and professional organizations.

However, an NPO may provide goods and services that are not intended to benefit specific individuals but rather to benefit groups within society at large, or the common welfare. Greenpeace, for example, is engaged in environmental awareness activities that benefit society as a whole. The Canadian Cancer Society is engaged not in helping individuals, but rather in supporting cancer research and in increasing public awareness of cancer (and understanding for those who are afflicted with it). The benefits of the activities of organizations such as Greenpeace and the Canadian Cancer Society are available to all individuals within the "target" group either free or at a nominal charge—these benefits are known as **collective goods and services**. Other examples of collective goods include accounting standard-setting, AIDS awareness programs, anti-racism campaigns, and art and museum exhibitions.

Collective goods are not provided by business enterprises; collective goods are provided only by governments and by non-profit organizations. Because there is no parallel in the private sector, proprietary accounting is of little help in designing financial reports for providers of collective goods. Accounting standard setters have implicitly acknowledged this fact in providing for different accounting principles for governments (as we will discuss in Chapter 11).

The accounting policies of an NPO are not driven foremost by a need to determine residual interest, as is the case with shareholders in a business corporation. NPOs do, of course, have a residual of net assets. NPOs also have recognized costs, but the residual "bottom line" of revenues minus recognized costs is more of a true *residual, what is left over*, rather than a business-type net income measure.

Relationship between revenue and costs

In business enterprises, the providers of revenue are the beneficiaries of the business's goods and services. There is a direct link between the service performed, the beneficiary of the service, and the generation of revenue. Therefore, much of business accounting focuses on *matching* of revenue with the costs incurred to generate that revenue.

In some NPOs, there is a similar link. Clubs, private societies, and religious organizations generate revenue primarily from their members and spend that revenue primarily on activities and services that benefit their members. For convenience, we can refer to those organizations wherein the members are the primary (or only) beneficiary of the organization's goods and services as being **self-beneficial organizations**. The members provide the primary revenues, and they receive the benefits of the goods and services.

However, many other types of NPOs do not derive their primary revenues from the beneficiaries of their services. Instead, most social service agencies and arts organizations obtain the bulk of their revenue from governments or private donors, or both. When the beneficiaries of the goods and services are different from the providers of the resources, the NPO is a **public-beneficial organization**.[3]

A key aspect of public-beneficial NPOs is that their revenue is largely independent of the costs. The revenue comes from one group, but the money is spent on serving a different group. This is very different from businesses, where the costs are incurred to earn the revenue. Therefore, non-profit organizations (and governments) need expenditure controls that are markedly different from those normally encountered in private enterprise.

Businesses measure their expenses in relation to revenue, thereby using the cost/revenue relationship as a control device. When revenues are received by an NPO as a block grant, the relationship between costs and revenues is broken and costs must be controlled directly. The budgetary and management reporting system is designed to prevent managers from exceeding their *spending* authority; *expenditures* become more a focus than *expenses*.

Some or all of the donations or grants received by a non-profit organization may be restricted for particular uses or programs. The donor wants assurance that the funds were used for the intended purpose. The accounting and reporting system must be able to match expenditures to specific programs or purposes. Funds are not transferable from one program to another; therefore, it may not be meaningful to combine revenues and expenditures relating to different programs into a single operating statement for the NPO as a whole.

For example, a school or university will have a large amount of operating funds (grants from government and fees received from students) that are specifically designated for operating the educational programs. The operating funds cannot be used for buildings or for ancillary activities such as providing free parking for faculty or low-cost meals for students. The school will receive separate capital grants that can be used only for capital projects such as new buildings or substantial renovations, and there will also be scholarship funds that must be used only for student aid. Therefore, the accounting and financial reporting system of many NPOs must be able to distinguish between the various funds and be able to show that the various restrictions have been observed.

Objectives of Financial Reporting

The primary users of the financial statements of a non-profit organization are the suppliers of its funds. Funds are derived from (1) members, (2) granting agencies, (3) the general public, and (4) creditors. The objective of financial statements for non-profit organizations "focuses primarily on information needs of members, contributors and creditors" [CICA 1000.11]. In general, the financial reporting objectives for non-profit organizations are:

- stewardship
- measuring the cost of services rendered
- cash flow prediction, and
- management evaluation.

The first two are the primary objectives; the others tend to flow from satisfying the first two objectives. The relevance and priority of the primary objectives depends on the characteristics of the non-profit organization.

---

3 Charitable organizations are sometimes called "beneficial organizations," which is the same idea.

If a public-beneficial organization provides collective goods and services using funds donated by the public, *stewardship reporting* of the resources provided by the contributors is most likely to be the primary objective. Greenpeace is a good example. Measurement of the cost of Greenpeace's environmental protection activities is of limited usefulness; there is no meaningful measure of output and thus no useful cost of providing services can be determined. The emphasis in NPO reporting often is on disposition of the resources provided for specific purposes or programs rather than on the costs of services provided. This is an *input* base of reporting rather than the *output* basis that we are accustomed to in business reporting.

On the other hand, a public-beneficial organization may provide private goods and services on a *cost recovery basis*. An overnight hostel for homeless people may be supported by reimbursement on a fee-for-service basis from the city government. The city is the source of funds, and the city will want to know the cost per bed per night; the city may support several such programs and will want to compare the efficiency of the services provided. In such a case, measuring the cost of service becomes the primary reporting objective, and an output base of reporting similar to that used by business enterprises is appropriate.

A distinctive feature of NPO financial reporting is a strong commonality of interest amongst the various users of the statements. Members, managers, directors, and creditors need to see the organization and its programs in the same light as do the major providers of the resources. Managers and directors are accountable to the resource providers for the disposition of resources entrusted to their care. Creditors are also aware that future cash flows may be coming from the suppliers of resources (e.g., government ministries) rather than from the sale of goods and services.

Therefore, there often is a strong dominant influence by the providers of the resources in shaping financial reporting objectives and thereby determining accounting policies. This is particularly true of public-beneficial organizations that are providing goods and services (either private or collective) with a fixed revenue base.

Primary Reporting Issues

There are several important reporting issues that shape the financial reporting of non-profit organizations. The primary reporting issues for an NPO are:

1. expense versus expenditure reporting

2. capital assets

3. segregation of resources

4. donated goods and services

5. accounting for pledges

6. accounting for a collection (e.g., museums)

7. defining the reporting entity, and

8. consolidated reporting.

We will discuss these issues first, and then we will examine the basic reporting options that are available to NPOs. An NPO should choose the option that best meets its users' needs.

Expense versus expenditure reporting

There are three different bases on which the resource outflows of any organization can be recognized in the statement of operations:

- *Disbursement* basis: outflows are recognized only when the cash is paid out or disbursed (i.e., a strict cash basis of reporting).
- *Expenditure* basis: outflows are recognized when liabilities are incurred or cash is paid out (i.e., accrual accounting applied to liabilities).
- *Expense* basis: outflows are recognized when goods and services are used in the operations (i.e., a "full accrual" basis of reporting).

Non-profit organizations must decide whether they are going to recognize their costs on the basis of disbursements, expenditures, or expenses. *If* they have a GAAP constraint, the *CICA Handbook* requires the expense basis.

A disbursement basis may be suitable for small organizations with minimal accrued expenses or payables. The use of a strict cash basis, however, may result in reported expenditures that do not properly reflect the commitments made by the organization during the reporting period. Strict cash basis reporting can cause an organization to lose control of its resource management and to lose track of what it owes.

The real choice therefore is between recognizing costs in the statement of operations on the basis of *expenditures* or of *expenses*. The expenditure basis has little equivalency in the private sector, where we normally think in terms of expenses. But the notion of expenses is related to the concept of profit, which generally does not exist in the non-profit sector.

The CICA's *Terminology for Accountants* defines **expenditure** as "a disbursement, a liability incurred, or the transfer of property for the purpose of obtaining goods or services...."[4] Note that the emphasis is on *obtaining* goods and services instead of on *using* goods and services, which is the focus of expense.

The expenditure basis means that costs are recorded in operations when incurred, either by disbursing cash or by incurring a liability. Supplies, for example, would be recognized in the statement of operations when acquired rather than when used—no supplies inventory would appear on the balance sheet. In contrast, the expense basis means that goods and services are recognized in the statement of operations when they are used in performing the organization's service.

An expenditure basis is most appropriate when service and program outputs are difficult to measure and therefore there is no clear basis for allocating expenses or measuring efficiency. A clear example would be any form of public or collective good wherein there is no specific beneficiary and no revenue derived from the costs incurred. Specific activities may be clearly defined but the general operations of the organization cannot be specifically related to programmatic goals with measurable outputs. An expenditure basis is also appropriate for programs wherein fixed-grant revenues are intended to finance variable-cost services, as in public-beneficial organizations that derive their primary revenues from block grants by government ministries or foundations.

4 *Terminology for Accountants*, Fourth Edition (Toronto: CICA, 1992), p. 88.

In contrast, the expense basis is likely to be most appropriate when the NPO is delivering goods or services to individuals and needs to measure the cost of providing those goods or services. For example, hospitals may use an expense basis so that they know the cost of specific services. Revenue providers, such as the provincial governments, often use comparative cost information (that is, from many different hospitals) to evaluate the efficiency of individual hospitals.

On the other hand, it may be useful to exclude certain costs from the cost-of-services calculation when those costs fall outside of the funding guidelines that have been established by the funding agency (i.e., the provincial Ministry of Health). The most notable such cost is the cost of capital assets, which leads us directly to our next major reporting issue—capital assets.

Capital assets

Capital asset accounting is controversial largely because of the various methods that NPOs use to finance asset acquisitions. Some NPOs must fund their asset acquisitions through operating revenue (including non-restricted donations), while others may acquire major long-term assets only by special grants or donations. As a result, three different approaches used for accounting for capital assets have developed:

1. charge to operations immediately (an expenditure basis)

2. capitalize and depreciate (an expense basis), or

3. capitalize but *not* depreciate.

Charging to operations immediately is the expenditure basis as applied to capital assets. It is possible to use an expenditure basis for capital assets while using an expense basis for other costs. The main reason for the popularity of this approach in the past relates to the nature of the revenue used to acquire the assets.

Many funding organizations (especially government granting agencies and ministries) restrict NPOs' use of operating revenues to operating expenditures, *excluding* capital asset acquisition. Separate grants are given as capital grants for the acquisition of capital assets, and the funding organizations usually prohibit the inclusion of depreciation in the operating accounts. When a capital grant is given, the revenue from the grant is matched to the cost of acquiring the asset in the period of acquisition, and no capitalization or depreciation occurs.

Sometimes capital grants are given only for major assets such as buildings, while smaller acquisitions (such as furniture or computers) must be financed through the operating grants. In that case, different accounting policies sometimes have been used for the two types of assets due to the differing relationship to revenues.

It has been argued that depreciation is a cost of providing services and that depreciation should therefore be recorded regardless of the way in which the assets were financed. For example, the FASB has argued that "using up assets in providing services... has a cost whether those assets have been acquired in prior periods or in the current period and whether acquired by paying cash, incurring liabilities, or by contribution."[5] Similarly, the *CICA Handbook* recommends that capital assets of limited life should be amortized, and that amortization should be included in the NPO's operating statement as an expense [CICA 4430.16].

---

5 Statement of Financial Accounting Standard No. 93, *Recognition of Depreciation by Not-for-Profit Organizations* (FASB, 1987), ¶20.

Even in organizations where revenue comes from general donations rather than from government grants, expenditures for major depreciating capital assets may be financed by means of special capital fund-raising campaigns. There is no intent on the part of either the organization or the donors that part of the cost of assets be charged against operations. If depreciation is taken in periods following the acquisition, then the organization will show a deficit in those periods even if fund-raising activities are sufficient to cover the expenditures for the period (or, conversely, if expenditures are held to the level of the revenue raised).

Depreciation accounting makes sense under either of two circumstances:

1. the cost of replacing capital assets must be recovered from general revenues, or

2. evaluation of efficiency requires that the cost of *all* inputs, including capital assets, be included in the measurement of outputs.

An expense basis that includes depreciation seems appropriate for self-beneficial organizations and for private goods that are paid for on a fee-for-service basis, regardless of whether the payer is the direct beneficiary or is an outside funder (e.g., a hostel that receives reimbursement from a city for overnight accommodation of homeless people).

The third approach to reporting capital assets is to capitalize the assets and never charge the cost to operations. This approach makes sense when (1) asset replacement or renewal is separately funded or (2) the assets do not decline in value or in usefulness.

When an organization receives separate funding for its capital acquisitions and replacements, it is a form of double-counting to deduct depreciation from operating funds. The usual approach in such circumstances is to charge the full cost of the acquisition against the capital grant when it is received; this approach achieves matching of the revenues and related expenditures. However, the disadvantage of immediate write-off is that the assets do not appear on the balance sheet.

The *CICA Handbook* recommends that NPOs capitalize and amortize all capital assets (except that land is not amortized, of course). Smaller NPOs need not comply with this recommendation. The exemption applies to any organization with gross annual consolidated revenues of less than $500,000 [CICA 4430.03].

A related issue is the capitalization of *collections*. Museum and gallery collections are worth a great deal of money, and they were acquired through the use of donors' funds. Since the AcSB requires the capitalization of capital assets, they also would like to see collections capitalized. However, the Board realizes that this is impractical in most situations. The Board takes an ambivalent position:

> The cost of capitalizing collections often would exceed the incremental benefit of the information gained, especially for organizations that have been in existence for several decades. Accordingly, although the capitalization of collections is not precluded, it is not required [CICA 4440.06].

In other words, capitalizing the cost of collections is *permissible* but not *required*.

Segregation of resources

NPOs often receive revenue grants that are earmarked for specific purposes. When the use of the revenue is specified by the donor, the revenue is called an **external restricted fund**. If the resources are earmarked by the NPO's board, they are called a **board-designated (internal restricted) fund**. The distinction is important because a board can change its mind and remove its own designation. A restriction imposed by an external donor cannot be reversed or changed by the board.

When restricted funds exist, they generally are reported separately for two reasons:

- the donor and other external users need to see that the funds are being used for the proper purposes, and
- the NPO needs to show that restricted funds are not available for general purposes and cannot be transferred to general operations.

One way of accomplishing segregated reporting of restricted funds is through the use of *fund accounting*. **Fund accounting** has been defined as follows:

> Accounting procedures resulting in a self-balancing set of accounts for each fund established by legal, contractual or voluntary actions of an organization [CICA 4400.02(c)].

The focus of fund accounting is on keeping track of resources that are designated for specific purposes. The purpose is to avoid mixing up resources that are intended for diverse purposes and to ensure that management fulfills its stewardship responsibility for proper disposition of the resources. A single non-business organization can have several (or many) such accounting entities. The extent to which funds need to be segregated in an organization is largely a matter of common sense, based on the types of contributions they receive and the users' needs.

Appendix 10A describes the basic principles of fund accounting.

Donated goods and services

It is not unusual for people and businesses to donate goods and services instead of (or in addition to) money. Indeed, the very nature of most NPOs and volunteer organizations means that much of the work is being carried out by volunteers through contributed services. As well, companies often choose to donate goods or services, such as an airline that provides free transportation to a sports organization to fly athletes to major competitions. An accounting issue arises from non-monetary donations—should the donated goods and services be assigned a value and reported in the statements?

In some cases, goods or services are donated as a way of helping the organization raise money. The goods or services are sold or auctioned off, and the organization ultimately receives cash in exchange for the donated goods or services. In such instances, the inflow of cash determines the value of the donation, and the amount of cash received must be recorded as a donation by the non-profit organization.

More commonly, however, the goods and services are donated in order to help the organization to achieve its objectives. The United Way, for example, receives substantial donations of executive time from businesses to help manage its campaigns. Should the United Way assign a value to the donated time?

When donated goods or services are assigned a value and recorded by the organization, the credit to revenues offsets the debit to expenditures and there is no impact on the net operating results. However, the absolute values of the revenues and expenses are affected, and it is possible that management's performance could be evaluated differently.

For example, one measure of the performance of a fund-raising organization is the proportion of funds raised that are consumed as fund-raising expenses. An organization that spends only 10% of the donations to obtain those donations is perceived as doing a better job than one that spends 40% of the funds it raises. But if the 40% organization is paying for all of the services it receives, while the 10% organization is using enormous amounts of volunteer effort, are the financial results of the two organizations really comparable? If the 10% organization were to record the value of its donated effort, its cost ratio may rise to 60%. Thus the recording of donated goods and services can have an impact on the perceptions of the readers of the statements, at least in terms of performance evaluation.

For stewardship reporting, the advantages of reporting the value of donated goods and services are not so clear. If the primary objective of the statements is to report on how management used the funds at its disposal, then reporting donated services on the statements may only impair the reporting objective, because it will appear that management had more funds at its disposal than was actually the case.

Practice has varied considerably. Recording and reporting the value of donated goods and services seems to have been the exception rather than the rule in the past. The *CICA Handbook* states that:

> An organization may choose to recognize contributions of materials and services, but should do so only when a fair value can be reasonably estimated and when the materials and services are used in the normal course of the organization's operations and would otherwise have been purchased [CICA 4410.16].

While the general recommendation for donated goods and services is permissive (i.e., "may"), the suggested recommendation for donated capital assets is stronger. The *CICA Handbook* recommends that donated capital assets "should" be recorded at fair value. When the fair value cannot be reasonably determined, the capital asset should be recorded at nominal value [CICA 4430.06].

Some capital assets may be partially contributed or donated. For example, a builder may construct a new addition to a building at cost rather than fair market value. In this situation, the capital asset would still be recorded at fair value with the donated portion being recognized as a contribution.

Other *CICA Handbook* recommendations call for disclosure of the accounting policies used and the nature and amount of any donated goods or services recorded.

Accounting for pledges

A **pledge** is "a promise to contribute cash or other assets" [CICA 4420.05]. A promise to pay could be viewed as a receivable. However, a donor may give a pledge, but may subsequently decide not to actually give the money. In business, accounts receivable are routinely recognized because there has been an *exchange*—the customer or client has received goods or services and therefore has an obligation to pay. For an NPO donor, there is no exchange, but only a one-way promise that can be rescinded, retracted, or ignored by the donor.

An NPO can recognize a pledge as a receivable on its balance sheet if both of two criteria are met: (1) the amount can be reasonably estimated, and (2) ultimate collection is reasonably assured.

The amount is not usually in doubt. Most pledges are for cash, and are payable within a fairly short period of time. Even cash pledges may be uncertain in amount, however, if they depend on future events. For example, a business may promise to contribute 1% of its revenue from sales of a certain product. Even though the contribution will be in cash, the amount will not be known until the sales results are known.

The estimation criterion may also not be met when the pledge is not in cash but is in the form of a non-cash asset. It may be impossible to get a reasonable estimate of the value of the asset until it is in the NPO's hands and can be reliably assessed. As well, the donation may be contingent on some future event, such as the donor's death, which makes both the timing *and* value of the donation uncertain.

The dual criteria of measurability and collectibility often are difficult to achieve for many non-profit organizations. Most NPOs prefer not to count their cash before it has been received. Therefore, revenue is usually recognized only when the amount is collected. For example, the accounting policies note of the Canadian Cancer Society states:

> Revenues from campaign and in-memoriam donations are recognized on a cash basis, with no accrual being made for amounts pledged but not received.

Accounting for a collection

Some non-profit organizations (e.g., museums and art galleries) are dedicated to building and maintaining a *collection*. A **collection** is defined as "works of art, historical treasures or similar assets" [CICA 4440.03] that meet *all* three of the following criteria.

1. The asset(s) must be available to be seen or used (e.g., for education or research) by the public.

2. The collection needs to be maintained and protected.

3. If an asset from the collection is sold, the proceeds from its sale cannot be used for the operations of the NPO. The funds must be used to acquire new pieces for the collection or to help in meeting the second criterion—to care for the collection.

Classification as a *collection* is important because the *CICA Handbook* recommendation to capitalize capital assets does not apply to collections. Instead, the NPO has three options:

- capitalize with no depreciation
- capitalize and depreciate, or
- disclose only.

The most common alternative is simply to disclose the *existence* of a collection. Although reporting or disclosing the *value* of a collection may be desirable, the practice is not generally followed. Estimates of the value of assets inevitably are unreliable, difficult to verify, and may not be free from bias. In addition, there is a cost associated with having independent appraisals made, and most institutions would prefer not to incur that cost.

Defining the reporting entity

There are many types of relationships that may exist between legally distinct but operationally similar NPOs that are under common control. As a result, the definition of the reporting entity is not as simple as it is for business enterprises.

For example, some arts organizations and social service organizations have a *foundation* that serves primarily to raise money for the main organization. The foundation usually has a board of trustees that is drawn directly from the board of directors of the principal operating arts or social service organization that it controls. Therefore, both the foundation and the operating agency are under common control.

Since the foundation is a legally separate organization, it could report separately from the operating agency. If reporting were done on this basis it would be difficult to evaluate the operations of the operating agency because a large part of the revenues (or the expenses) would be "hidden" in the foundation's statements. Unless the reader of the operating agency knows that the foundation exists, he or she will have difficulty evaluating the agency's financial position or the results of its operations.

To reduce this problem, the *CICA Handbook* recommends that an organization report each controlled organization either by consolidating that entity or by providing specific disclosure [CICA 4450.14]. The obvious issue is what constitutes "*control.*"

The most common indicator that control exists is when one organization has the right to appoint the majority of another NPO's board of directors. However, there may be other factors that indicate control for an NPO, including (1) significant economic interest, (2) provisions in the organization's charter or bylaws, (3) or common or complementary objectives [CICA 4450.06]. Clearly, professional judgment is required for determining whether control exists.

Consolidated or combined statements

The previous section discussed the issue of consolidation of related entities, which is the usual connotation of consolidation, as we have seen in Chapters 2 through 7 of this book. However, there is another aspect of consolidation that is unique to non-business organizations: to what extent should separate funds and restricted resources be *consolidated* or *combined* on the organization's financial statements?

If there is a large number of separate funds under control of management, separate reporting of the operations and balance sheet of each fund would result in quite a voluminous report, even though columnar formats could be used for conciseness. Separate reporting by funds may clarify the status of each individual fund for stewardship reporting purposes, but may obscure the overall financial position of the organization and the results of its operations.

On the other hand, consolidation of the various funds may hide important characteristics of individual funds, and may impede stewardship reporting. In a research report for the FASB, Professor Robert Anthony observed that:

> Although reports on a funds basis are more difficult to understand than reports on an aggregated basis, especially by users who are accustomed to reading financial statements of business organizations, the complexity is necessary in order to report the realities of a complex situation.[6]

The AcSB supports consolidated reporting. The *CICA Handbook* recommends that the *statement of financial position* show "totals for the organization as a whole . . . to give a complete understanding of the total resources available to the organization" [CICA 4400.09]. The recommendation for a consolidated total

---

6 Robert Anthony, *Financial Reporting in Nonbusiness Organizations: An Exploratory Study of Conceptual Issues* (Stamford, Connecticut: Financial Accounting Standards Board, 1978), p. 111.

does not rule out separate reporting of funds (or of programs), but simply states that everything should be added together at the end.

Note that the requirement is only for a total for the statement of financial position. The operating statement need not have a total column under one of the two methods permitted by the *CICA Handbook*—the restricted fund approach—because to provide a total for the operating statement would suggest that the money is interchangeable between funds, which clearly is not the case for restricted funds.

While this recommendation for aggregating all of the resources on the balance sheet may seem relatively innocuous, reporting of organizationwide totals implicitly suggests that resources can be moved from fund to fund or program to program. Many NPOs oppose the recommendation for consolidated reporting for that reason.

There is a middle ground between fully detailed fund reporting and full consolidation. Similar types of funds or funds with similar objectives can be combined for reporting purposes. All of the ancillary, self-supporting activities of a university—such as the bookstore, food services, parking, and residences—can be grouped together because they are similar types of funds. Also, all the student aid funds can be combined for reporting purposes since they serve a similar objective.

The funds do not need to have the same treatment for reporting on all the financial statements. Funds (or groups of funds) can be reported separately on the statement of operations, but combined on the statement of financial position. Conversely, the funds may be combined on the statement of operations, but reported separately on the statement of financial position and the cash flow statement. As we will discuss below, an NPO may account in different ways for different funds or programs. When such is the case, it is impossible to meaningfully consolidate the various funds or programs.

GAAP for Non-Profit Organizations

In the sections above, we have briefly described the substantial differences between NPOs and businesses. These differences include the nature of the organizations, the financial reporting objectives, and the specific reporting issues. Due to these differences, it is not surprising that GAAP for NPOs developed quite differently from that for business enterprises. In recognition of these differences, NPOs had for many years been exempted from the reporting recommendations of the *CICA Handbook*.

However, the AcSB began taking an interest in NPO financial reporting in the late 1980s, and in 1996 issued a substantial set of recommendations aimed at making NPO financial statements look a lot like business enterprises'. Not only did NPOs get their own set of sections in the *CICA Handbook*, but also most of the other sections (e.g., pensions and leases) of the *CICA Handbook* were applied to NPOs for the first time. Generally speaking, the AcSB declined to acknowledge the differences between NPOs and business organizations, implying that whatever is good for business reporting must be good for NPO reporting too.

Initially, the AcSB proposed that NPO financial statements should look virtually identical to business statements, with no provision for segregation of funds. However, opposition to that proposal was sufficiently strong to prompt the AcSB to propose two different approaches that NPOs can use:

- the restricted fund method, in which funds can be segregated for financial reporting, and

- the deferral method, in which all funds are combined in the financial statements without distinction between restricted and unrestricted funds.

If an NPO has at least one externally restricted fund (that is, restricted by the *donor*), management can choose either of the two methods. If there are no restricted funds, then the deferral method must be used.

Many NPOs are not constrained by GAAP and do not need to comply with the *CICA Handbook* recommendations. These organizations may use a reporting method that is mandated by their primary funding agency, such as the Ministry of Health or the Ministry of Social Services. Alternatively, they may follow a more traditional expenditure-based reporting system.

In the following sections we will explain the various methods of reporting. The first is the expenditure-based approach, which we are calling the "traditional" method. Then we will look at the two methods recommended by the *CICA Handbook*. It is important to understand that this is not a theoretical discussion—*all of these methods are used in practice.*

Many organizations use a dual reporting approach. They may use one of the AcSB's recommended methods in order to obtain an audit opinion, and then use an expenditure-based set of statements to satisfy their primary user's needs. Such an approach is somewhat costly, since it involves extensive year-end adjustments to get from an expenditure approach to one of the *CICA Handbook* expense approaches.

Types of Financial Statements

The *CICA Handbook* recommends that NPOs prepare the following four financial statements [CICA 4400.05]:

1. statement of financial position

2. statement of operations

3. statement of changes in net assets, and

4. cash flow statement.

The second and third statements will often be combined into a single statement of operations and fund balances. A separate cash flow statement need not be prepared if the statement would contain no new information that is not apparent from the statement of operations [CICA 4400.53]. As a result, many NPOs report only two statements: (1) a statement of financial position and (2) a statement of operations and changes in net assets.

The statements should be in a comparative format, with comparisons to the previous year. There may also be comparisons to budgeted amounts. In addition to the statements themselves, there should be notes to the financial statements.

This list of statements looks deceptively simple. The statements do not look much different from those that we are accustomed to seeing for businesses. The differences can be great, however. As we will discuss shortly, the presentation will depend on whether the NPO has selected the *deferral method* or *restricted fund method* for recognizing contributions.

Reporting Options

Traditional method

In the sections above on reporting issues, we outlined the basic nature of NPO financial reporting as it developed throughout the twentieth century. Generally speaking, most NPOs used the following reporting practices.

- Revenues were recognized when received; accruals were rare.
- Resource *outflows* were recognized when the cost was incurred or when the liability was incurred. Accruals were almost never made for items such as pensions, leases, or vacation pay. The general tendency was to report on a flow-of-funds accrual basis, without interperiod allocations.
- Capital assets may or may not have been recorded on the balance sheet, but depreciation was used only for funds that conducted activities that were expected to be self-supporting on a cost-recovery or profit-making basis.
- Funds were segregated on the balance sheet, and separate statements of operations were used for different funds (or for different groups of funds of similar nature).
- Funds rarely were totalled on the statement of operations; the balance sheet more often showed a total for all funds.
- Related organizations were not consolidated.

Many NPOs still follow these practices, usually because that is what their donors or funding agencies want in order to see what the organization's managers have done with the resources placed at their disposal during the year. When audit requirements force an NPO to use an expense basis of reporting, there sometimes are interesting note disclosures that alert users to the difference between expenditure and expenses. An example is the following note from a social services agency's annual report:

> **Accounting for vacation pay** In accordance with generally accepted accounting principles, the Centre uses the accrual basis of accounting for vacation pay. As a result, the deficit in the Operating Fund amounts to $209,297 at fiscal year-end, of which $199,568 relates to the accrual for vacation pay. In accordance with the Ministry's funding policy, vacation pay is funded on a cash basis and therefore the funding related to this liability has not been reflected in these financial statements.

In other words, the deficit (and a related liability) appears in the financial statements almost entirely because the Centre is required by the *CICA Handbook* to accrue vacation pay. However, the funding agency will support those costs only on a pay-as-you-go basis. There is no doubt that the Ministry will cover those costs, but no revenue can be accrued because the Ministry doesn't owe the money yet!

The accounting policies that are used under the traditional expenditure-based method are shown in Exhibit 10–1, along with those recommended by the methods proposed in the *CICA Handbook*.

CICA Handbook methods

The *CICA Handbook* recommends two alternative methods of accounting: the *deferral method* or the *restricted fund method*. Before we discuss and demonstrate these two methods, we must first explain the three different types of contribu-

EXHIBIT 10–1 ALTERNATIVE APPROACHES TO NPO FINANCIAL REPORTING

| | | CICA Handbook recommendations* | |
Accounting practice	Traditional approach	Restricted fund method	Deferral method
Accrual of pledges	Not done	Required if recognition criteria are met	Required if recognition criteria are met
Revenue recognition	Recognize when realized	Recognize when realized	Match to expense recognition
Expense or Expenditure basis	Expenditure	Expense	Expense
Capital assets:			
Capitalize	Sometimes	Required*	Required*
Charge to operations	Seldom	Not required (may use separate fund)	Required*
Combine funds in "Total" column:			
Statement of operations	Seldom	Not required	Required
Statement of financial position	Seldom	Required	Required
Consolidation of related organizations	Not done	Required	Required
General application of *CICA Handbook* (e.g., pensions, leases, expense accruals)	Not done	Required	Required

* Not required for NPOs with consolidated gross revenue of less than $500,000 [CICA 4430.03].

tions—restricted contributions, endowment contributions, and unrestricted contributions.

External restricted contributions are contributions that are *restricted by the donor* for specific purposes or uses. They may not be used for other purposes, and the system of accounts must maintain the integrity of the donation and its purpose. External restricted contributions must be distinguished from **board-designated funds (internal restricted)**, which are funds that the board of directors has earmarked for a specific purpose. The board can decide to reverse its *internal restriction*, and therefore internal restrictions do not have the same importance for financial reporting as do true restricted funds.

An **endowment contribution** is a special type of restricted contribution. Not only is the contribution restricted in purpose, but also the principal amount of the contribution cannot be spent. The contribution must be invested in an endowment fund and only the earnings on the investment can be spent for the intended purposes. An example is a scholarship fund within a university. The principal amount to establish the scholarship is maintained and interest earned on that principal is used to provide scholarships.

An **unrestricted contribution** is provided without any restrictions on its use by the organization. Basically, it is any contribution that does not meet the definition of either a restricted contribution or an endowment contribution.

It is critical to remember the differences between these types of contributions as we discuss the NPO reporting options. The recognition and presentation of different types of contributions on the financial statement differs among these methods. Fund accounting will be discussed briefly in Appendix 10A.

The two methods can be briefly described as follows:

- The **deferral method** can be used by any NPO. Under this method, no distinction is made between different funds or groups of resources in the balance sheet or the statement of operations. A full accrual basis is used, including the accrual of pledges and full interperiod allocation of revenues and expenses in accordance with the recommendations of the *CICA Handbook* for business enterprises. Capital assets must be capitalized and amortized. Restricted revenues must be deferred and matched to the expenses that they were intended to fund.

- The **restricted fund method** may be used by any NPO that has at least one fund or resource group that is restricted by an outside donor. Under this method, the NPO presents a separate operating statement for each fund (or group of similar funds)—no totals for the organization need appear on the statement of operations because the funds are not interchangeable. The statement of financial position should present totals for the organization as a whole, however. Accrual accounting is applied and capital assets are capitalized, but amortization does not have to be charged to general operations; amortization can be charged to a separate capital fund instead. In contrast to the deferral method, however, revenue usually is recognized in the appropriate fund when it is received (or accrued) rather than when the expenses are incurred.

The choice of method depends primarily on the users and their needs. If the organization wants the simplest financial statements it may select the first alternative. If the primary purpose is to show information on specific activities or programs, or if there is a large number of external users who have imposed restrictions, the second alternative may be more appropriate.

Exhibit 10–1 compares some of the fundamental characteristics of these two methods, as well as comparing them to the traditional method.

Deferral method: business-type accounting This method is conceptually similar to that used by business enterprises, at least on the surface. The concept behind this method is to match the revenues with the associated expenses. The revenue is recognized as the related expenses are incurred.

Unrestricted contributions are recognized as revenues in the current period. They are available for any use by the organization.

The treatment of *restricted contributions* depends on the purpose for which they have been restricted by the donor. If the contribution is for expenses of the current period, the contribution should be recognized as revenue in the current period. If the contribution is for expenses of a future period, it is recorded as *deferred revenue* until the related expense is recognized.

Note that this matching process is reversed from our normal expectation in business enterprise accounting. For businesses, the usual focus is on recognizing revenue first, and then matching expenses to that revenue. If there are related costs that will be incurred in the future (e.g., warranty expense), those future costs are estimated and recognized in the period in which the revenue has been recognized to achieve matching.

Under the deferral method of NPO accounting, the matching process is reversed. First, the expenses are recognized, and then the revenue is matched. If revenue is received prior to the expense, the revenue must be deferred until the expense is recognized. Note that the deferral is until the *expense* is recognized, not the *expenditure*. If a restricted contribution is for a capital asset, the treatment depends on whether or not that asset will be depreciated. If the asset is depreciated, the revenue will be deferred and recognized on the same basis as the amortization of the specific asset that has been purchased.

For example, suppose that a donor contributes $30,000 to a social agency on December 13, 2005. The donation is restricted for the purchase of a new van. The van will be purchased in 2006. The van will be depreciated over three years, straight-line. When the contribution is received, the credit will be to deferred revenue:

December 13, 2005:

Cash	30,000	
Deferred revenue (restricted—van)		30,000

If the van is purchased on January 27, 2006, the transaction will have no immediate impact on the statement of operations:

January 27, 2006:

Capital asset—van	30,000	
Cash		30,000

At the end of 2006, the agency will record $10,000 in depreciation. Simultaneously, the same amount of revenue will be recognized:

December 31, 2006:

Depreciation expense	10,000	
Accumulated depreciation—van		10,000
Deferred revenue (restricted—van)	10,000	
Revenue		10,000

Under the deferral method, all revenues from all funds are added together in the statement of operations. If the restricted revenue were recognized when it is received or when the van is purchased, the agency would show restricted revenue that is not matched by an expense; and any unmatched revenue will lead financial statement readers to believe that the NPO has more revenue available for unrestricted purposes than it really does.

To avoid showing revenue without any related expenses, *endowment contributions* are recognized as direct increases in net assets in the current period because they will never be available to meet expenses of the organization. Remember we said that net assets *may* be shown in a separate statement or combined with the statement of operations.

Restricted fund method The second method is based on the concepts of fund accounting that have been used in non-profit organizations for many years. A number of separate funds (i.e., self-balancing sets of accounts) are used in order to segregate the three basic different types of contributions: (1) restricted funds, (2) endowment funds, and (3) the general fund (or operating fund) for unrestricted contributions.

Under the restricted fund method, the *CICA Handbook* does recommend that the resources and liabilities of the various funds be added together for a "total" column on the statement of financial position. However, there is no requirement that the various funds be added together on the statement of operations. The whole point of this method of accounting is to recognize that restricted and endowed funds are not interchangeable with unrestricted funds, and that a deficit in the operating fund cannot be remedied by transferring money from the restricted funds to the operating fund.

As a result, an NPO might show a surplus under the one-column operating statement of the deferral method, when all of the funds are added together. But under the restricted fund method of reporting, the funds are segregated and it will be apparent to the financial statement user that the restricted and endowment funds cannot be used for general operating purposes.

Another important distinction between the deferral method and the restricted fund method is that depreciation and amortization on capital assets does not need to be charged to the operating fund under the restricted fund method. Depreciation and amortization can be segregated in the capital asset fund instead. This eliminates one of the major objections that many NPOs have to the idea of business-style accounting—that depreciation is charged against operations that are not intended to recover the costs of capital assets, if the assets have been acquired through special grants or fund-raising drives.

It is the organization's option as to how many restricted funds it wishes to have on its statements. An NPO may decide not to have a separate fund for smaller restricted contributions. Instead, smaller funds can be combined into a single larger restricted fund. For example, the many different scholarship and bursary endowments in a college or university are combined into a single "financial aid endowment fund."

Even though funds may be combined, their distinct nature should be preserved. Restricted donations and endowment donations are not combined with unrestricted donations. Unrestricted contributions are recognized as revenue in the *general fund* in the current period. This is similar in treatment to the deferral method.

The accounting for restricted contributions depends on whether or not there is a separate restricted fund for that contribution. If there is a separate restricted fund, it is recognized as revenue in the current period in that fund. If there is no separate fund, it is *recognized in the general fund using the deferral method* of accounting for contributions. Therefore, restricted contributions are treated differently depending on whether or not they are shown in a separate fund.

Endowment contributions are recognized as revenues in the *endowment fund* in the current period. Note the difference here between the two reporting methods. The restricted fund method shows the contributions as *revenue* in a separate fund. In contrast, the deferral method shows endowment contributions as a direct increase in net assets—there is no revenue recognition on the statement of operations.

Notice also that under the restricted fund method, contributions in separate restricted and endowment funds are recognized currently rather than being deferred. When restricted funds are shown separately, there will be no confusion about whether excess revenue is available for general use. The use of a restricted fund makes it clear to users that those resources are not available for general operations. Matching of revenues to expenses is not of concern in this reporting framework, and therefore there is no need to defer recognition of the revenue.

The restricted fund method of accounting tends to result in a higher level of revenue than does the deferral method. The reasons are that (1) restricted revenues often are recognized earlier because there is no need to defer recognition of the revenue until the expense has been recognized, and (2) contributions to endowment funds are recognized as revenue under the restricted fund method but not under the deferral method. Therefore, the selection of accounting method may place an organization over the size test for capitalizing capital assets (i.e., average revenues of less than $500,000) if the restricted fund method is used, but not if the deferral method is used.

Illustration of Reporting Methods

Deferral method

Exhibit 10–2 gives an illustration of a simple set of NPO financial statements prepared by using the deferral method. This organization has all three types of funds—endowment, restricted, and unrestricted—but the statements do not have to be prepared on the restricted fund method. Any NPO can use the deferral method.

There are three statements: a statement of financial position, a statement of operations, and a statement of changes in net assets. In the first two statements, no distinction is made between the resources in the various funds.

However, notice that on the statement of financial position, there is not just one amount for capital, shown here as "net assets" (other often-used headings are *fund balances*, *net resources available*, or *accumulated excess of revenues over*

EXHIBIT 10–2	SAMPLE NPO FINANCIAL STATEMENTS—DEFERRAL METHOD

Statement of Financial Position
December 31, 2005
(in thousands)

	2005	2004
Assets		
Current assets		
Cash and term deposits	$ 520	$ 280
Accounts receivable	150	160
Supplies	160	60
	830	500
Investments	570	200
Capital assets, net	1,000	1,100
Total assets	$2,400	$1,800
Liabilities, deferred contributions, and net assets		
Current liabilities		
Accounts payable & accrued liabilities	$ 70	$ 10
Current portion mortgage payable	10	10
	80	20
Mortgage payable	120	130
	200	150
Deferred contributions:		
Capital	600	720
Other deferred contributions	110	—
	710	720
Net assets:		
Externally restricted	150	100
Invested in capital assets	280	250
Internally restricted	100	200
Endowments	570	200
Unrestricted	390	180
	1,490	930
Total liabilities, deferred contributions, and net assets	$2,400	$1,800

EXHIBIT 10–2   SAMPLE NPO FINANCIAL STATEMENTS—DEFERRAL METHOD (continued)

Statement of Operations
Year Ended December 31, 2005
(in thousands)

	2005	2004
Revenues		
Grants and contributions	$2,140	$2,400
Amortization of capital contributions	120	100
Other revenue	1,400	1,200
	3,660	3,700
Expenses		
Salaries	2,790	2,800
Amortization of capital assets	200	260
Other expenses	480	460
	3,470	3,520
Excess of revenues over expenses	$ 190	$ 180

expenditures). Instead, there are five different fund balances shown. This is an important option in NPO accounting. Even when the deferral method is used, the net resources that relate to each fund may be shown separately on the statement of financial position. By using this approach, users can see that, although the total fund balances amount to $1,490, only $390 of that amount is unrestricted and is available for future operations.

The third statement reconciles the beginning and ending balances of each of the fund balances shown on the balance sheet. If the statement of financial position shows more than one fund balance, then the beginning balance must be reconciled to the ending balance for each fund.

On the statement of changes in net assets, observe that the total column shows a surplus of $190 (i.e., excess of revenues over expenses). This statement reveals that:

- the surplus in the unrestricted fund actually was $220

Statement of Changes in Net Assets
Year Ended December 31, 2005
(in thousands)

Net assets	Externally restricted	Invested in capital assets	Internally restricted	Endow-ments	Unrestricted	Total
Balance, January 1	$100	$250	$ 200	$200	$ 180	$ 930
Excess (deficiency) of revenues over expenses	50	(80)			220	190
Investment in capital assets		110			(110)	—
Endowment contribution				370		370
Internally imposed restrictions			(100)		100	—
Balance, December 31	$150	$280	$ 100	$570	$ 390	$1,490

- the contributions to the endowment fund of $370 were not included in revenues on the statement of operations
- capital assets of $110 were purchased from unrestricted funds during the year, and the board reversed an internal restriction by $100, releasing those funds for general unrestricted use.

Restricted fund method

Exhibit 10–3 shows the same organization, but this time using the restricted fund method of reporting. Only two statements are presented—a statement of financial position and a combined statement of operations and changes in net assets. A cash flow statement is considered to be unnecessary because the cash flows are apparent from the other statements.

In this approach, detailed statements of financial position are presented for the operating fund, for each restricted fund (research and capital assets), and for the endowment fund. We can see, for example, that of the total current assets of $830, only $680 are for unrestricted use.

EXHIBIT 10–3 SAMPLE NPO FINANCIAL STATEMENTS—RESTRICTED FUND METHOD

Statement of Financial Position
December 31, 2005
(in thousands)

	Operating fund	Research fund	Capital asset fund	Endowment fund	2005 Total	2004 Total
Current assets						
Cash and term deposits	$370	$150			$ 520	$ 280
Accounts receivable	150				150	160
Supplies	160				160	60
	680	150			830	500
Investments				$570	570	200
Capital assets, net	200		$800		1,000	1,100
Total assets	$880	$150	$800	$570	$2,400	$1,800
Current liabilities						
Accounts payable & accrued liabilities	$ 70				$ 70	$ 10
Current portion, mortgage payable	10				10	10
	80				80	20
Mortgage payable			$120		120	130
Total liabilities	80		120		200	150
Fund balances						
Externally restricted	110	$150			260	100
Invested in capital assets	200		680		880	970
Internally restricted	100				100	200
Endowments				$570	570	200
Unrestricted	390				390	180
Total fund balances	800	150	680	570	2,200	1,650
Total liabilities and fund balances	$880	$150	$800	$570	$2,400	$1,800

EXHIBIT 10–3   SAMPLE NPO FINANCIAL STATEMENTS—RESTRICTED FUND METHOD (continued)

Statement of Operations and Changes in Net Assets
Year Ended December 31, 2005
(in thousands)

	Operating fund	Research fund	Capital asset fund	Endowment fund
Revenues				
Grants and contributions	$1,650	$640		$370
Other revenue	1,400			
	3,050	640		370
Expenses				
Salaries	2,300	490		
Amortization of capital assets	200			
Other	480			
	2,980	490		
Excess (deficiency) of revenues over expenses	70	150		370
Fund balance, January 1	640	—	$770	200
Interfund transfers	90		(90)	
Fund balance, December 31	$ 800	$150	$680	$570

Revenue recognition also is quite different between the two methods. Notice that in the balance sheet in Exhibit 10–3, there is no liability for deferred revenue. That is because revenue is recognized when realized in the restricted fund method. The endowment is in a separate fund, and therefore the contributions to the endowment fund are recognized as revenue *for that fund* in the restricted fund method. In the deferral method, the endowment contributions are not recognized as revenue.

Since revenue recognition is different, the total fund balances are different between the two methods. Notice that the total fund balances (or "net assets") shown in Exhibit 10–2 are $1,490, while in Exhibit 10–3 the total fund balances amount to $2,200.

In order to avoid complicating the presentation, we have omitted the 2004 comparative data for the statement of operations in Exhibit 10–3. In practice, comparative information would be presented either by putting more columns in the statement or by providing another statement in identical format for the prior year. The restricted fund approach tends to present a lot of numbers. But the numbers are necessary in order to try to grasp the real operating situation of the organization.

The Chore of Users: Unravelling GAAP

We pointed out earlier in the chapter that the users of NPO financial statements often are interested in the organization's use of the resources given to help the organization accomplish its mandate. There are two aspects to this interest—(1)

stewardship over the resources themselves, and (2) effectiveness in accomplishing the organization's objectives. Unfortunately, the annual financial statements of an NPO usually do not satisfy either goal very well.

Stewardship is difficult to assess because the expense basis of reporting that is recommended by the AcSB often is in conflict with users' interest in how the organization *spent* the money given to it—expenditures rather than expenses. Sometimes the organization tries to help users by pointing out the impact of major unfunded accruals, such as the vacation pay example cited earlier in the chapter.

The deferral method makes it especially difficult to unravel the financial performance of any NPO that has restricted funds. Some universities, for example, have chosen to use the deferral method, adding together unrestricted funds, restricted funds, endowment funds, and enterprise accounts into a single set of numbers. The "bottom line" in such a situation is meaningless. If there is a surplus, is it a surplus that can be used for future operations (i.e., unrestricted), or is the surplus due to restricted funds that hide a deficit in the general fund? If the university shows a deficit, is it a deficit in the operating funds or is it because the university is losing piles of money on its enterprises, such as the bookstore or food operations? It is impossible to unravel the reasons for either a surplus or a deficit when the deferral method is used in an NPO that has restricted donations.

The difficulty of evaluating *efficiency* in an NPO has led to a demand for a greater volume of non-financial data as supplementary information in non-business financial statements. Data on the level of services performed or activities accomplished, membership levels, contributors, etc., can be provided. For example, a CICA Research Study on NPOs recommends that non-profit organizations provide the following information along with their annual financial statements:[7]

- the nature and objectives of the organization
- plans for the future
- significant events during the year and their relationship to or impact on the financial results
- any unusual or important items or trends in the financial statements, and
- important non-financial information.

It would be most useful if quantitative supplementary information were audited. Sometimes the audit opinion does cover at least some such information, but normally the supplementary information is outside the scope of the audit opinion. Auditors find it difficult to independently verify most non-financial data unless it is directly tied into the accounting and reporting system. Therefore, financial statement readers have to accept supplementary information largely on trust.

Unfortunately, there have been instances of overenthusiastic managers issuing inflated performance data in order to enhance the apparent efficiency or effectiveness of the organization. For example, one Canadian film festival was alleged to have announced attendance figures that were in excess of the combined maximum seating capacities of its theatres! But this type of behaviour is undoubtedly the exception rather than the rule.

---

7   Canadian Institute of Chartered Accountants, *Financial Reporting for Non-Profit Organizations* (Toronto: CICA, 1980), pp. 41–42.

Budgetary Control and Encumbrance Accounting

By now, you will have seen that accounting for non-profit organizations is quite different from accounting for business enterprises. But we are not done yet. There are two other special aspects of NPO accounting. We will conclude this chapter with an overview of these two special accounting techniques—*budgetary control accounts* and *encumbrance accounting*.

Budgetary control accounts

A unique characteristic that is often used in fund accounting is the practice of formally incorporating budgetary accounts into the accounting system. **Budgetary accounts** enable a running comparison of budgeted with actual amounts (of revenue and expenditure) and a monitor of the level of expenditure.

It is quite possible to accomplish the same result without formally including the budget in the accounting system; many businesses routinely have budget vs. actual comparisons on their internal statements. The difference in non-business organizations, and especially in governments, is that when strict expenditure limits are in effect, a formalized system acts as an internal control so that managers are not permitted to issue purchase orders that will push the expenditure total above the budgeted limit. The comparison between the budget and the combined total of expenditures is constant and routine, rather than being occasional and special.

We will not go into the technical aspects of budgetary control accounts here. There are many books that explain the mechanics of fund accounting and budgetary accounts in exquisite detail. It will be sufficient to say simply that the nature of the budgetary accounts is to create a self-balancing set of accounts *within* the regular accounting system, normally within the general or operating fund. In general, the bookkeeping approach that is used for budgetary accounts is as follows:

- Budgeted revenues are *debited* to an account that serves as an offset to actual revenues (which are credits). The difference between the budgeted and actual revenues is automatically shown within the system by netting the actual against the budgeted amounts. A net debit balance indicates that actual revenues are falling short of the budget, while a net credit balance shows that revenues are exceeding budget.

- Budgeted *expenditures* (not *expenses*) are shown as credits. The level of detail matches the level of expenditure control that has been mandated by the board of directors (or, for governments, by the legislature). The budget balance is the upper limit of permitted expenditures. Managers and employees will not be permitted to make additional commitments once the budget limit has been met.

The budget limits on expenditure are enforced by means of an encumbrance system.

The encumbrance system

The **encumbrance system** records the estimated cost of commitments in the formal accounting system when the commitments are made rather than when a legal liability has arisen. For example, purchase orders for supplies are recorded as an *encumbrance* at the estimated cost of the supplies when the purchase order is issued, even though no liability (in either a legal or an accounting sense) exists until the supplier delivers the supplies. In theory, an encumbrance system could be used in private enterprise accounting—encumbrances are not necessarily limited to fund accounting. In practice, encumbrance accounting is unique to governments and NPOs.

The objective of using an encumbrance system is to keep track of the commitments that an organization's managers have made for the acquisition of goods and services. If there is a budgetary or legislative limit on the total amount of expenditure that a manager can make during the year, then use of the encumbrance system keeps the manager from overcommitting the organization and running up a large deficit.

Even in the absence of fixed budgetary limits, encumbrances can be used simply as an aid to planning and control. This is particularly true when commitments on the same budget amount can be made by several people within the organization. When control is decentralized, an encumbrance system improves regulation and communicates to managers and to the people making the expenditures just what the actual level of commitment is.

The encumbrance system is widely used in governmental accounting; budget amounts are legislated maxima that must not be exceeded. In NPOs, however, whether or not an encumbrance system is used depends on the nature of the organization and its operations. In fact, encumbrance accounting can be used in some parts of an organization and not in others, and for some types of expenditure (such as for supplies) and not others (such as salaries). The system is most appropriate when the following conditions are present:

1. The organization, fund, or activity is a cost centre with a maximum expenditure limit *or* has no relationship between costs and revenues.

2. Goods and services acquired discretionally are a significant part of the total budget.

3. There is a significant lag between the commitment (e.g., purchase order) and the receipt of the purchased items.

4. Levels of activity (and expenditure) within the organizational unit are not affected in the short run by an autonomous demand, either external to the organization or from other parts of the organization.

5. Reporting is on an expenditure basis rather than an expense basis.

6. Responsibility for making commitments and expenditures is decentralized throughout a large organization.

If, in contrast, a small organizational unit must vary its level of activity in response to market demand for its services, if it is able to generate revenues to cover expenses, and if externally acquired goods and services are either of little consequence or are received very shortly after ordering, then there is little reason to use an encumbrance system.

Encumbrance systems are used to control costs when expenditure limits are basically fixed and are not tied to revenue or activity levels. If these conditions do not exist, then encumbrances are of limited usefulness. Also, if only a very small part of expenditures is discretionary rather than being tied to longer-term employment or supply contracts, then there is little point to using encumbrances.

A Final Example

We will end this chapter with an example of NPO financial statements. Exhibit 10–4 shows the basic 2003 statements for the Canadian Cancer Society. As is common in NPO reporting, the Canadian Cancer Society (CCS) takes a slightly eclectic approach. The balance sheet has only one column (for each year), which might lead one to believe that the statements are prepared on the deferral method.

However, the statement of operations has two columns for each year—operations and externally restricted. There is no total column. Therefore, the CCS must be using the restricted fund method. This is confirmed in the accounting policy note (not reproduced in Exhibit 10–4), which states that "the Society follows the restricted fund method of accounting for contributions."

EXHIBIT 10–4	SAMPLE NPO FINANCIAL STATEMENTS

**Canadian Cancer Society
Consolidated Statement of Resources
(In thousands of dollars)**

January 31, 2003, with comparative figures for September 30, 2001 (note 10)

	2003	2001
Assets		
Current assets:		
Cash	$26,087	$ 6,509
Accounts receivable	4,567	2,264
Prepaid expenses	3,320	4,287
Investments	35,424	47,235
	69,398	60,295
Accrued pension benefit asset	—	1,187
Capital assets (note 2)	12,196	11,079
	$81,594	$72,561
Liabilities and Resources		
Current liabilities:		
Accounts payable	$ 4,728	$ 3,827
Research contribution payable to National Cancer		
Institute of Canada	4,930	7,964
Deferred revenue	4,884	3,905
	14,542	15,696
Accrued pension benefit liability	64	—
Obligation for post-retirement benefits other than pensions	6,855	5,701
Resources:		
Externally restricted	6,144	4,780
Invested in capital assets	12,196	11,079
Internally restricted	29,829	20,308
Unrestricted	11,964	14,997
	60,133	51,164
Commitments (note 7)		
	$81,594	$72,561

See accompanying notes to consolidated financial statements

EXHIBIT 10–4   SAMPLE NPO FINANCIAL STATEMENTS (continued)

Consolidated Statement of Financial Activities —
Operations and Externally Restricted Resources
(In thousands of dollars)

Sixteen-month period from October 1, 2001, to January 31, 2003, with comparative figures for the year ended September 30, 2001 (note 10)

	Operations		Externally Restricted	
	2003	2001	2003	2001
Revenues				
Annual giving	$51,168	$44,252	$ 313	$ 19
Special events, gross revenue	39,901	25,090	—	—
In memoriam	17,959	13,526	—	9
Major and planned gifts	41,204	29,678	1,459	584
Lotteries, net revenue (note 6)	8,376	75	1,270	609
Other income	11,027	5,982	1,253	992
Investment income	2,014	2,968	158	147
	171,649	121,571	4,453	2,360
Expenditures				
Grants and fellowships:				
Research grants — NCIC (note 3)	53,094	43,194	30	—
Research grants to other organizations	2,100	100	—	252
Fellowships and professional education	390	524	10	23
Grants to lodges and health centres	4,705	3,394	—	—
	60,289	47,212	40	275
Functional disbursements:				
Public education	22,233	13,756	1,004	604
Patient services	29,013	19,988	380	277
Fundraising — general	31,906	22,733	536	94
Fundraising — special events	10,052	5,043	—	—
Administration	10,377	7,248	52	17
	103,581	68,768	1,972	992
	163,870	115,980	2,012	1,267
Excess of revenues over expenditures before the undernoted	7,779	5,591	2,441	1,093
Pension expense	1,251	707	—	—
Increase in resources	$ 6,528	$ 4,884	$ 2,441	$ 1,093

See accompanying notes to consolidated financial statements

The statements are headed as "consolidated" statements. The notes explain that "these financial statements include the financial activities and financial position of the ten provincial Divisions and the National Operations of the Canadian Cancer Society."

The consolidated statement of changes in resources contains the reconciliation of beginning fund balances (called "resource balances" in the CCS statements) with the ending balances. In this statement, there are four columns for the

EXHIBIT 10–4   SAMPLE NPO FINANCIAL STATEMENTS (continued)

Consolidated Statement of Changes in Resources
(In thousands of dollars)

Sixteen-month period from October 1, 2001, to January 31, 2003, with comparative figures for the year ended September 30, 2001 (note 10)

	Externally Restricted	Invested in Capital Assets	Internally Restricted	Unrestricted	2003 Total	2001 Total
Resource balances, beginning of period	$ 4,780	$11,079	$20,308	$ 14,997	$51,164	$45,187
Increase (decrease) in resources	2,441	(2,352)	(310)	9,190	8,969	5,977
Additions to capital assets	(1,011)	3,469	(1,315)	(1,143)	—	—
Appropriations (note 5)	(66)	—	11,146	(11,080)	—	—
Resource balances, end of period	$ 6,144	$12,196	$29,829	$ 11,964	$60,133	$51,164

See accompanying notes to consolidated financial statements

Consolidated Statement of Cash Flows
(In thousands of dollars)

Sixteen-month period from October 1, 2001, to January 31, 2003, with comparative figures for the year ended September 30, 2001 (note 10)

	2003	2001
Cash provided by (used in):		
Operating activities:		
Increase in resources	$ 8,969	$ 5,977
Items not involving cash:		
Amortization of capital assets	2,352	2,223
Decrease in deferred pension costs	1,251	707
Increase in deferred revenue	979	1,145
Increase in obligation for post-retirement benefits other than pensions	1,154	786
Change in non-cash operating working capital	(3,469)	1,675
	11,236	12,513)
Investing activities:		
Capital asset additions	(3,469)	(1,898)
Decrease (increase) in investments	11,811	(12,957)
	8,342	(14,855)
Increase (decrease) in cash	19,578	(2,342)
Cash, beginning of period	6,509	8,851
Cash, end of period	$26,087	$ 6,509

See accompanying notes to consolidated financial statements

current year as contrasted with two columns in the operating statement. The four-column reconciliation in the statement of changes corresponds with the four balances shown under "resources" on the statement of financial position.

Finally, the CCS does present a cash flow statement. In 2003, the adjustments to operating activities increase the accrual-basis surplus of $8,969 to a cash flow surplus of $11,236.

SUMMARY OF KEY POINTS

1. Non-profit organizations are significantly different from business enterprises. The primary differences are that (1) they have members, but no owners; (2) they do not exist to generate a return on investment; (3) expenses are not usually incurred in order to generate revenue; and (4) the suppliers of funds usually do not receive the benefits of an NPO's activities.

2. The objectives of financial reporting tend to emphasize (1) stewardship and (2) measuring the cost of services. Most NPOs obtain their funding from members, external donors, and public or government granting agencies. These donors need to see how the organization used the resources that were given to it during the year. Therefore, there often is a heightened interest in stewardship reporting—what did the managers do with the funds entrusted to their care? Accounting for expenditures becomes an important reporting objective.

3. Some NPOs provide goods and services to individuals on a cost recovery basis. In such cases, a primary reporting objective is to measure the cost of providing those services. The emphasis then falls on expense accounting rather than expenditure accounting.

4. There are many reporting issues that are unique to NPOs and governments. Unlike business enterprises, NPOs often have resources that are restricted for specific uses. They also receive donated goods and services. Accounting for pledges and for capital asset acquisitions also becomes problematic. Finally, there often is a problem in simply identifying the reporting entity and implementing consolidated reporting.

5. There are three basic approaches to accounting for NPOs. One is the traditional, expenditure-based approach, using fund accounting. Restricted funds are reported separately from unrestricted funds. Capital assets seldom are capitalized and amortization is rarely charged to operations. Capital assets often are funded by special grants or by special fund-raising drives, and operating funds are not expected to bear the costs of the capital assets. This method is most commonly used by smaller NPOs—those with gross revenues of less than $500,000—who are not required to follow the AcSB's recommendation for capitalizing capital assets.

6. The *CICA Handbook* recommends two other methods of reporting: the deferral method, or the restricted fund method. The deferral method can be used by any NPO. The restricted fund method can be used only by an NPO that has at least one externally restricted fund.

7. The deferral method adds all of the various funds together into a single total column. No segregation is reported, except that separate fund balances may be reported in the statement of financial position. The individual reported fund balances then are reconciled in a statement of changes in fund balances.

8. The restricted fund method permits segregated reporting for restricted and endowment funds. The funds do not need to be added together on the statement of operations, although a total column should be provided on the statement of financial position.

9. An accounting procedure that is unique to NPOs and governments is the use of budgetary accounts within the formal set of accounts. The purpose of budgetary accounts is to control the level of expenditure, and also to permit an automatic comparison of budget versus actual amounts at every reporting date. Expenditure limits are enforced by means of encumbrance accounting. Encumbrance accounting records an obligation as soon as a purchase order is issued, thereby reducing the amount of available funds that can be committed to other purchases.

10. Fund accounting is a system of accounting that segregates an organization's resources into a series of separate, self-balancing account sets. Each fund will have its own financial statements, at least in theory. In practice, separate funds of a similar nature usually are combined for external financial reporting. Fund basis *recording* does not necessarily lead to fund basis *reporting*.

11. A desirable attribute of fund accounting is that it encompasses techniques for maintaining budgetary control over the actions of managers. Fund accounting also enables senior management to ensure that restricted funds are used only for the proper purposes.

12. There are several different types of funds. Every organization has an operating or general fund, through which the principal operating activities of the organization are conducted. In addition, an organization may have a variety of special funds, enterprise funds, capital funds, fiduciary funds, and endowment funds.

13. In addition to funds, NPOs and governments often have account groups. The two types of account groups are the capital asset group and the long-term liability group. Each of these groups is a control mechanism for assets or liabilities that are not otherwise recorded on the balance sheet. There are no liquid resources in either capital asset or liability groups.

14. Interfund transfers present a special opportunity for management to affect the "bottom line" of segregated funds. Surpluses and deficits can be "managed" by the adroit use of interfund transfers. Caveat emptor!

REVIEW QUESTIONS

10–1 What proportion of Canadian employment is in non-profit organizations?

10–2 Who owns non-profit organizations?

10–3 Why are non-profit organizations sometimes called "voluntary organizations"?

10–4 What distinguishes non-business organizations from business organizations?

10–5 What is the difference between *non-business* organizations and *non-profit* organizations?

10–6 What distinguishes non-profit organizations from governmental units?

10–7 Who elects the directors of a non-profit organization?

10–8 Distinguish between an *open membership* non-profit organization and a *closed membership* organization.

10–9 Explain what is meant by a "self-perpetuating board."

10–10 What are *collective goods and services*? What types of organizations offer collective goods and services?

10–11 What types of organizations offer *private goods and services*?

10–12 Describe the ways in which the nature of revenue in non-profit organizations can differ from the nature of revenue in business enterprises.

10–13 What is a *public-beneficial organization*? Explain how a public-beneficial organization differs from a *self-beneficial organization*.

10–14 Why might the revenues of an NPO not be derived from the recipients or beneficiaries of its goods and services?

10–15 Who are the primary users of the financial statements of non-profit organizations?

10–16 What are most likely to be the two primary objectives of financial reporting for NPOs?

10–17 What objectives of financial reporting for businesses do not exist for non-business organizations?

10–18 If the emphasis in accounting for many non-profit organizations is on the control of cash flows, why is the accrual basis recommended?

10–19 Explain the difference between the *expense basis*, the *expenditure basis*, and the *disbursements basis* of reporting.

10–20 Why in the past did many non-profit organizations not capitalize their capital assets?

10–21 What alternative approaches are there to accounting for capital assets in non-profit organizations?

10–22 What is the size test for capital assets?

10–23 What is the distinction between an *externally restricted fund* and a *board-designated (internally restricted) fund*?

10–24 Why would an organization want to report the value of donated services in its statement of operations?

10–25 What is a *pledge* and what are the criteria for recognizing pledges?

10–26 What is a *collection* and what criteria are required for something to be defined as a collection?

10–27 How could consolidation hide important characteristics of individual funds?

10–28 Why might it be possible for a non-profit organization to combine the statement of operations with the statement of changes in net assets?

10–29 Explain the distinction between the *restricted fund method* and the *deferral method*.

10–30 What types of financial statements will a non-profit organization normally issue?

10–31 How standardized are the statements of non-profit organizations, as compared to business organizations?

10–32 Explain the differences between an *externally restricted contribution*, a *board-designated (internally restricted) fund*, an *endowment contribution*, and an *unrestricted contribution*.

10–33 How are *externally restricted contributions* recognized in the deferral method compared to the restricted fund method? What is the difference if there is no separate fund in the *restricted fund method* for that contribution?

10–34 Does the restricted fund method or the deferral method of accounting tend to result in a higher level of revenues?

10–35 Why is non-financial supplementary information often needed for performance evaluation?

10–36 Explain the purpose of recording budgetary amounts in the accounts.

10–37 When budgetary accounts are used, why is the amount for estimated revenues a debit instead of a credit?

10–38 What is an *encumbrance*?

10–39 What is the purpose of an *encumbrance system*?

CASES

CASE 10–1 Reporting Objectives

You have recently been appointed auditor of three different organizations. The first organization is a mining company that was formed a year ago to develop a gold mining site in northern Ontario. The largest single part of the initial investment was provided by a major, publicly held mining company in exchange for 36% of the common shares. The remaining shares were issued publicly in the over-the-counter market, where they are very thinly traded. The company is still in the development stage and does not expect to commence production for at least another year.

The second organization is a non-profit secondary school that provides courses for students who intend to pursue a career in one of the performing arts. The school is fully recognized by the provincial Ministry of Education, which provides about 50% of the school's operating budget. Another 20% of the operating funds are provided by the Ministry of Culture and Recreation, while the remainder is derived from student fees and by fund-raising in the private sector. The school occupies an old public high school building that was no longer being used by the city; the school acquired the building on a 20-year lease from the city's board of education.

The third organization is a labour union for the graduate students at a major university. The union receives its funding from dues that are mandatorily deducted by the university from the earnings of all members of the bargaining unit, whether they are members of the union or not. A portion of the funds is sent to the union's parent national organization, and another part is set aside for the strike fund, which is held and invested by a trustee until such time as it is needed to pay striking union members.

Required:

Explain how the objectives of financial reporting would likely differ for these three organizations.

CASE 10–2   Gold Development

Gold Development (GD), a newly incorporated non-profit organization with a December 31 year-end, will offer low-rent housing services for people with low income.

GD reports to Logimex, a government agency that requires audited annual financial statements to be filed. Mr. Bilodeau, the project originator and administrator of GD, is not familiar with the preparation of financial statements.

GD received a non-repayable grant from Logimex in February 2006 for the construction of an eight-storey apartment building. Construction began in April 2006.

Residents will start to move into the apartment building between October and December 2006, although it will not be entirely completed until the end of December 2006. By December 2006 all the apartments should be rented.

GD receives donations from companies and individuals in the region. It has received pledges from large, well-known companies for the next five years, and pledges from individuals for the current and next year. Pledge amounts have been set out in writing on forms signed by the donors.

For a nominal salary, Mr. Bilodeau manages the organization with the help of his wife and the local priest, both of whom are volunteers.

Required:

a. Explain to Mr. Bilodeau what is meant by "reporting on a restricted fund accounting basis" according to the *CICA Handbook*.
b. Advise Mr. Bilodeau on the appropriate accounting for the above issues assuming that GD decides to report on a restricted fund accounting basis.

CASE 10–3   Perth Housing

Perth Housing Corporation (PHC) is a community-sponsored non-profit organization that was incorporated on September 1, 2005. Its purpose is to provide residential accommodation for physically handicapped adults in the town of Perth.

The nature of PHC's operations is described in Exhibit A. The sources of funding are described in Exhibit B.

The executive director has asked for your assistance in establishing accounting policies for PHC for its general purpose year-end financial statements. The accounting policies should comply with GAAP.

Required:

Provide recommendations for accounting policies for PHC for the year ended August 31, 2006. Assume that PHC would want to set up two funds for reporting purposes—a general fund and a capital fund—and that annual revenues exceed $700,000.

EXHIBIT A

NATURE OF OPERATIONS

In October 2005, PHC purchased a 15-unit apartment building in downtown Perth for $750,000. It then spent $250,000 in renovations to upgrade the building and make it accessible for physically handicapped adults.

PHC offers 24-hour non-medical attendant care. Support care services are provided through a combination of staff members and volunteers. The staff members receive a monthly salary. As an inducement to recruit and retain qualified support care workers, each staff member is allowed 15 sick days per year. The employee can bank the sick days not used in any one year. Upon termination or retirement, the employee is paid for banked sick days at the wage rate in effect at that time.

Rental payments are due the first day of each month and are geared to tenant income. Most of the tenants are very good about making their rent payments on time. Some rental payments are received late. On August 31, 2006, there was $13,000 of unpaid rent.

PHC plans to install central air conditioning in the building in April 2007 at an expected cost of $50,000. This expenditure is being financed by a special fund-raising drive, which, by August 31, 2006, has raised $20,000 in cash and $15,000 in pledges from citizens in the local community.

EXHIBIT B

SOURCES OF FUNDING

The cost of acquiring and renovating the apartment building was financed by a $1,000,000 cash donation received from the estate of Mr. Smith. The provincial government funds approximately 70% of non-medical and support costs. Claims are made monthly for the previous month's eligible costs. PHC depends on outside fund-raising efforts, primarily door to door canvassing and sponsored bingos, to cover the remaining non-medical care and support costs.

[CGA]

CASE 10–4 Youth Singers

Youth Singers (YS) is a non-profit organization that was formed in 2000 by Nancy, a retired professional singer. Members of the choir range in age from 8 to 20. The choir has won a number of major singing competitions across North America and is producing its first CD next month. The choir plans to record an annual CD of its Christmas concert.

Nancy is in charge of YS's daily operations. All major decisions need to be approved by the board of directors. Initial financing for YS came solely from private donations, and a fund-raising committee was recently formed to raise funds for special projects. Last year, YS qualified for two government grants that require audited financial statements to be submitted on an annual basis. YS has attached a set of financial statements to government grant applications in the past. The Canada Revenue Agency also requires financial statements in order to provide tax receipts for donors.

Your CA firm has a policy of supporting its staff in volunteering their time to NPO activities. You have recently joined YS as a member of its board of directors and have volunteered to assist with all accounting issues. Details on past accounting policies are provided in Exhibit C.

You have been asked to prepare a report identifying any changes you would make to the current accounting policies for the next board of directors' meeting.

Required:

Prepare the draft report to the board of directors.

EXHIBIT C

ACCOUNTING POLICIES AND OTHER INFORMATION

1. Donation—Original Historic Sheet Music

    A donor recently died, leaving in her will a large selection of sheet music to YS. It is impossible to verify the value of this donation due to its historical value. The music will be performed by the choir during concerts. The original sheet music will be displayed in a glassed-in case.

2. Annual Pledges

    Every Christmas, YS holds an annual benefit concert. At this time, YS holds a major fund-raising drive and asks all concert guests to provide a donation or pledge an amount. All pledges are recognized when the pledge is made by the donor.

3. Capital Assets

    All capital assets are recorded at their market value as determined by the finance director. During 2006, a local music store provided sheet music stands at manufacturer's direct costs of $20,000. Purchasing these stands at retail prices would have cost $40,000.

4. Revenues

    Individual choir members started providing singing lessons during 2006 as a source of fund-raising. The revenue during 2006 from lessons was $50,000. Annual revenue from all sources was $200,000 in 2005 and $280,000 during 2006.

5. Amortization

    Capital assets are not amortized.

CASE 10–5 Finest Art Gallery

Finest Art Gallery (Finest) is a major art gallery in Toronto. Finest has the largest collection of art in Canada and has five major exhibits a year. Finest is a non-profit organization with funding received primarily from private contributors and government grants.

The board of directors turns over its members every three years. A new board just announced for 2006 to 2008 has a number of younger members who have rejuvenated a previous idea to expand a new section of the gallery for the work of children. This would require major fund-raising over the next few years. It is anticipated that this addition would attract a wider audience to the gallery and encourage young children to become interested in art at an early age.

The new board, although energetic and ambitious, lacks knowledge of accounting. Board members were recruited for their marketing skills and love of art. They have asked you, CA, to assist them over the next few months in selecting accounting policies and provide recommendations for changes to their existing policies. They want to comply with any *CICA Handbook* recommendations for non-profit organizations, but are not familiar with the *Handbook*'s content. You have committed to preparing a report for the next board meeting outlining specific accounting policies. If you recommend any changes, they must be fully supported. The board is concerned with the costs involved with preparing financial statements and wants to minimize these costs.

After the meeting with the board of directors you sat down and reviewed the financial statements for 2006. Notes from your review are included in Exhibit D.

A set of financial statements has been provided to any donors who requested them in the past. In addition, government agencies require a set of audited financial statements as a requirement for government grants.

Required:

Prepare the report for the board of directors.

EXHIBIT D

NOTES TAKEN FROM A REVIEW OF THE 2006 FINANCIAL STATEMENTS

1. The financial statements include a statement of income and expenditures and a statement of financial position. A cash flow statement was not prepared since it was felt that it does not provide meaningful information.

2. Revenues for 2006 included the following:

Memberships	$ 600,000
Admission fees	800,000
Government grants	2,000,000
Contributions	450,000
Endowment fund revenue	950,000

3. Admission fees are recognized as money is collected. Contributions are recognized when a pledge is made by the donor. Notes to the financial statements segregate the number of restricted and unrestricted contributions. Restricted funds include any amounts donated for a specific purpose and amounts segregated by the board for future expansion or special projects.

4. All capital assets are recorded at a dollar value to have a nominal amount provided on the financial statements. No amortization is taken on these assets. A recent review of the capital assets indicated the following items. The amounts were estimated by one of the board of directors:

Office equipment	$ 500,000
Automobiles	70,000
Facilities	10,000,000
Artwork	unable to estimate

5. During 2006, the roof was replaced on the art gallery at a cost of $260,000. This amount was expensed. In addition, a new air-conditioning unit was installed to protect the artwork from damages due to temperature changes. The cost was $300,000. To finance the purchase of the new air-conditioning system, a piece of artwork was sold.

6. Volunteer services are not recorded.

CASE 10–6 TGF Care Facility

The TGF Care Facility (TGF) is a non-profit organization dedicated to providing services in the care and rehabilitation of seniors with physical or mental disabilities. The main programs are the seniors' residence program and the home care program. TGF also sponsors research activities and conducts educational activities for its clients, their relatives, and the general public.

TGF has an eight-person board of directors that sets policy and approves plans, but the day-to-day operations are left to Joe, the full-time, salaried executive director. At a recent meeting, Joe told you that he is not satisfied with the information provided in the annual financial statements. He does not see how he and the board can make useful decisions on the basis of information presented in the financial statements. He wants the financial statements to be audited as this may help improve financial reporting and provide credibility to the financial statements, which may, in turn, increase donor confidence and donations. The financial statements have never been audited in the past.

Revenues for TGF's activities exceeded $600,000 per year in 2005 and 2006. Revenues are obtained from a variety of sources. Approximately 50% of the total revenue is obtained from the residents in the form of a user fee. Approximately 30% of the total revenue is obtained from the Ministry of Social Services. Most of the remainder is obtained from bequests and from donations by foundations, corporations, and individuals.

The Ministry of Social Services provides funds on the basis of annual budgets prepared for each program. Many of the public donations are also designated for specific programs or purposes such as research. The bequests are usually given under the condition that the principal amount cannot be expended. The income from investing the bequest can be used for designated purposes. The board at its discretion can allocate unrestricted donations.

TGF has constructed several buildings over the years to house the various programs. All the buildings were paid for by a combination of specific capital grants from the municipal and provincial governments and funds raised for capital projects by public campaigns. The repair and maintenance of the furniture and equipment, as well as general maintenance of the buildings, are paid for out of operating funds as needed.

You are an accountant with a professional designation. You have been asked by Joe to prepare a memo to the board of directors. The memo should describe the changes in accounting policies necessary to ensure a clean audit opinion in accordance with GAAP for the December 31, 2006 year-end. The memo should also explain how these accounting practices will better serve the needs of the users of TGF's financial statements. A description of current accounting practices for TGF is provided in Exhibit E.

Required:

Prepare the memo to the board of directors. Revenue recognition policies should use the deferral method.

EXHIBIT E

NOTES ON ACCOUNTING SYSTEM AND PRACTICES

1. The annual financial statements consist of a balance sheet, a statement of cash receipts and disbursements, and a statement of changes in net assets. The statement of cash receipts and disbursements compares the actual results for the year against the original budget of the year.

2. The budget is prepared annually by the treasurer of the board in cooperation with the executive director. A monthly comparison of the year-to-date expenditure with the total budgeted amounts, on a line-by-line basis, is prepared by the bookkeeper and forwarded to the executive director and treasurer.

3. Grants from governments, foundations, and corporations are recorded as revenue when pledges are made or grants are announced. Donations from individuals are recorded as revenue when the cash, cheque, or credit card voucher is received, regardless of whether the cheque or voucher is current-dated or post-dated.

4. Expenditures are charged to accounts as paid, on the basis of the type of expenditure; for example, all salaries are charged to a single account, all furniture replacements and repairs are charged to a single account, and so forth.

5. The historical cost of the buildings and land is carried on the balance sheet. The buildings are not amortized. The cost of furniture and equipment is charged to operations when the expenditure is made.

[CGA]

CASE 10–7   CKER–FM Ethnic Radio

In the fall of 2005, eight wealthy businesspeople from the same ethnic background formed a committee (CKER committee) to obtain a radio licence from the Canadian Radio-Television and Telecommunications Commission (CRTC). Their goal is to start a non-profit, ethnic community radio station for their area. They plan to call the station CKER–FM Ethnic Radio (CKER). It will broadcast ethnic music, news and sports from their country of origin, cultural information, ethnic cooking, and other such programs, seven days a week.

The station's capital requirements are to be financed by memberships, donations, and various types of loans. It is expected that the on-going operations will be supported by advertising paid for by businesspeople from that ethnic community and by the larger business community targeting that ethnic audience, as well as by donations and memberships.

It is now March 2006, and the CRTC has announced that hearings will start in one month on a number of broadcasting licence applications, including the CKER committee's application. The CKER committee members are fairly confident about the viability of their proposal; however, they have decided to seek the advice of a professional accounting firm to assist with the endeavour. The CKER committee has engaged Maria & Casano, Chartered Accountants, for the assignment, as three of the five partners of the firm are from the same ethnic community. The partner in charge of the assignment has stated that the firm will donate half its fee for the work.

You, CA, work for Maria & Casano and have been put in charge of the assignment. You have met with the CKER committee and various volunteers associated with the project. Information gathered on station start-up is contained in Exhibit F. Exhibit G provides other information on the CKER committee's proposal. The partner has asked you to prepare a draft report to the committee members discussing the viability of the proposed radio station over the initial three-year period. Since the committee members are fairly confident that they will receive the licence, the partner has asked you to recommend accounting policies for the transactions that CKER is contemplating. Your report must also cover other significant issues that the station will face after it commences operations.

Required:

Prepare the draft report.

EXHIBIT F

INFORMATION ON STATION START-UP

1. Costs to date have totalled $50,000 and are mostly transportation and meeting costs, as well as postage. These costs have been paid for personally by the CKER committee members.

2. To approve the licence application, the CRTC must see written commitments to finance the station's start-up costs and operating losses in the first two years. Remaining costs to obtain the licence, excluding donated legal work, are expected to be about $8,000, and will be paid by CKER committee members.

3. If the CRTC approves the licence application, the CKER committee will immediately set up a non-profit organization and apply to the Canada Revenue Agency (CRA) for charitable status, which it will likely receive.

4. Fairly exhaustive efforts to obtain commercial financing have failed. As a result, four wealthy individuals have volunteered to provide CKER with the financing for the start-up. They will each personally borrow $25,000 from financial institutions and give the funds to the station. These individuals expect the loan to be cost-free to them, as the station will make the interest and principal payments.

5. A "Reverse Lifetime Contribution" program will be instituted. Under this program a donor will pay the station a capital sum of at least $50,000. The station can do whatever it wants with the funds, but it will repay the donor an equal annual amount calculated as the capital sum divided by 90 years less the individual's age at the time of contribution. Upon the death of the donor, the station will retain the balance of the funds. Currently, a 64-year-old station supporter has committed $78,000, and seven other individuals are considering this method of assisting the station.

6. Initially, the station is to broadcast with a 2,500-watt signal. Within three to four years it hopes to obtain commercial financing for a second transmitter that will boost the power of the signal and the broadcast range.

EXHIBIT G

OTHER INFORMATION ABOUT PLANS FOR THE STATION

1. The CKER committee has analyzed census and other data to determine the potential market for the station. Engineering studies have mapped out the area that will be covered by the broadcast signal. There are about 1.1 million people in the target listening area. The latest Canadian census shows that 14% of the population comes from the target ethnic group. By applying a conservative factor of 40% to these findings, the CKER committee has arrived at a listenership figure of about 5.6% or about 62,000 people. The CKER committee has found that about one in five of the businesses in the area are run by members of the ethnic community, many of whom would like a medium for reaching their own people through direct advertising.

2. The amount of time expected to be devoted to commercials per hour is four minutes in year one, five minutes in year two, and six minutes in year three. Advertising cost per minute, discounted to 25% below the current market rate, will be:

Prime time (6 hours a day)	$40
Regular time (10 hours a day)	$30
Off-peak (8 hours a day)	$25

Advertising time will be sold by salespeople whose remuneration will be a 15% commission.

3. Miscellaneous revenue from renting out the recording studio when not in use by CKER could approach $3,000 per month in year three, but will start out at about $2,200 per month.

4. At least 120 people have committed to pay a $125 annual membership fee. Membership carries no special privileges other than to be identified as a supporter of the station. Membership is expected to grow by 20% per year.

5. Start-up capital expenditures are as follows: transmission equipment $61,000; broadcast studio equipment $62,000; and production studio equipment $40,000. Administration and other costs, including rent, are expected to total about $1,237,000 per year and will not increase when advertising sales increase.

6. The committee believes that there are no GST implications related to running the station, since it is a non-profit venture.

7. About one-third of the person-hours needed to run the station are expected to come from volunteers.

[CICA]

CASE 10–8 Safety Net

Safety Net (SN) is a not-for-profit organization operating in Big Town, Canada. SN runs a shelter for the homeless, operates a soup kitchen, and provides counselling services to runaway teenagers and street kids. The demand for SN's services has expanded rapidly over the last few years, as has its operating budget. Exhibit H describes SN's operations.

SN's operations have changed substantially in the past year (Exhibit H). Fund-raising has been much more aggressive, two government grants have been obtained, and the "bequest on death" campaign begun several years ago yielded one large bequest during the year. In dealing with these changes, the board of directors of SN realized that they need financial advice. Accordingly, they recently approached your firm, Fortin & Larose, Chartered Accountants, to advise them on the reporting requests they should be making of management to ensure the board is making informed business decisions based on relevant information. Where appropriate, the board would like advice on the selection of accounting policies and on financial statement disclosure and other matters of importance. In the past, SN has recorded revenue and expenses on a cash basis.

The board has asked your firm to perform an audit to meet the requirements of one of the government grants and to provide the certified documentation for both grants, for the year ended March 31, 2006 (see Exhibit I).

It is now January 22, 2006. The senior partner of Fortin & Larose has asked you, CA, to draft a report to the board of directors of SN providing them with the requested information. The partner has also requested a memo highlighting the various engagement issues. He believes that there are additional service opportunities, and he wants you to note in the memo the services that the firm could perform for SN.

Required:

Prepare the report and the memo.

DESCRIPTION OF SAFETY NET'S OPERATIONS

SN has three core operations: a shelter for the homeless, a soup kitchen for the needy, and a drop-in counselling service for runaways and street kids. There are also administrative and fund-raising activities.

Shelter for the homeless

The shelter operates out of a former university residence. The residence was donated to SN several years ago when the university was closed as part of the provincial government's plan to rationalize higher education. No amount was recorded on SN's books for the donated residence. The shelter is run by a very small number of staff.

Soup kitchen

The soup kitchen operates out of leased facilities: a former church in a run-down part of town. The signing of a 20-year lease on this property resulted in the dismissal of the previous executive director of SN after the board discovered the lease costs exceeded the fair market-value rent for similar properties and that the remaining useful life of the church, at the signing of the lease, was only 15 years.

Paid staff and volunteers prepare two meals a day. Volunteers include chefs from local restaurants, university food-service providers, and students from a local university's food sciences program.

Donated food supplies are a major component of operations, and the level of donations remains relatively constant. Corporations make donations throughout the year, and individuals donate large volumes of fresh produce in the summer and fall months. None of these donated goods or services is currently recorded.

Counselling services for runaways and street kids

The drop-in centre has two paid counsellors who work closely with the kids and provide referrals to other programs, such as drug rehabilitation.

The centre has entered into several innovative arrangements to provide assistance to runaways needing transportation back home. A major airline has begun a frequent-flyer grant program whereby the members of its frequent-flyer program are asked to donate some or all of their frequent-flyer points to the drop-in centre. The centre can then use the donated points to acquire a plane ticket. Counsellors attempt to identify the kids most likely to benefit from free transportation back home.

Administration

The administrative staff consists of the executive director, a full-time fund-raiser, managers for the three operating areas, a bookkeeper, and an accounting clerk/receptionist. There is a relatively large number of volunteer fund-raisers. In the past, fund-raising consisted mainly of a door-to-door campaign by volunteers seeking donations and selling "I care" SN memberships. In SN's financial statements, the costs of the campaign are netted against total funds raised to present a single door-to-door fund-raising total.

The bookkeeper handles all accounting and banking duties except for verifying accounts payable invoices for accuracy and filing documents. The two tasks are handled by a receptionist. The bookkeeper has a microcomputer system and uses an off-the-shelf computerized accounting package.

The executive director orally promised the full-time fund-raiser a bonus of 10% of funds raised in excess of $500,000.

EXHIBIT I

CHANGES TO SAFETY NET'S OPERATIONS

Fund-raising

The full-time fund-raiser aggressively pursued fund-raising opportunities. Among the new fund-raising efforts was a Safety Net charity golf tournament put on by a local golf club. The net proceeds of the tournament received from the golf club were recorded on SN's books.

SN's annual telethon was held on a local cable television station during December 2005. Its success was greatly enhanced when a country music super-star, in town for a series of concerts, saw the broadcast and volunteered to do a one-hour personal appearance as soon as five companies pledged $20,000 each. Five local car dealers responded by making pledges, although payment has yet to be received. News of this commitment increased the number of personal pledges by viewers. Even though the number of personal pledges increased, only a small percentage of them have been honoured to date. As a result, the bookkeeper is not sure how to record the pledges.

The "bequest on death" program began several years ago. There was one large bequest during the year, which left SN with a cash fund to be used for capital acquisitions only. During the years some of the money from the fund was used to acquire furniture for the shelter, at a cost substantially below fair market value.

Two grants were negotiated during the year. The first provides for the recovery of 50% of operating costs for the shelter and soup kitchen and 30% of other operating costs. The second government grant was a lump sum contribution of $200,000 to assist with capital costs related to the shelter for the next five years. SN must provide a minimum number of beds at the shelter during that period and create at least one full-time position or 33% of the grant becomes payable. Both grants include a clause that states, "Safety Net will provide certified documentation annually to support its claim of government funds." The second grant also requires annual audited financial statements to be submitted to the government.

During the year, SN began a campaign to raise funds to build a new shelter for runaway children. The shelter is expected to begin operations in three years. Thus far, $2 million in pledges has been raised, and construction of the building is scheduled to begin sometime in July 2006. SN plans to apply most of the $200,000 grant from the government to the capital costs of the new shelter. The funds have therefore been set aside for this use.

[CICA]

CASE 10–9 European Exchange Club

On August 15, 2000, the European Exchange Club (EEC) was formed in an effort to create a united social group out of several separate regional clubs in the vicinity of the city of Decker, located in central Canada. The purpose of the group is to combine resources to meet the recreational, cultural, and social needs of their collective members. EEC was formed through the collaboration of the following clubs and their memberships:

Members	
The Canadian Russian Society	12,300
The Italian Club of Canada	10,800
Portuguese Cultural Foundation	4,100
Association of Greeks of the World	2,700
The German Groups	1,100
Other	1,700
	32,700

It is now December 2006, and EEC's executives have spent the past few years planning and preparing for the club's operation. The club's community centre is expected to be fully completed next year. Its facilities will include the following:

- a multi-purpose building to house banquets, meetings, and arts activities
- hiking trails
- indoor/outdoor tennis facilities
- bicycle trails
- baseball diamonds
- an indoor/outdoor pool, and
- a soccer field.

The multi-purpose building is 75% complete, and EEC's executives have stated that it is "approximately within budget." Estimated building costs were outlined in a 2005 feasibility study as follows:

Construction cost	$2,300,000
Site preparation costs	400,000
Furniture and fixtures	550,000
Consulting fees	120,000
Miscellaneous	80,000
	$3,450,000

The four hectares of land on which the facility is built were provided by the provincial government by way of a five-year lease at $1 a year. The Italian Club of Canada contributed the 60 hectares of adjacent land. Previously, this land had been leased to a farmer for $54,000 a year. The 64 hectares will be used for the following projects, which will incur the additional costs listed below:

Hiking trails	$ 595,000
Baseball diamonds	30,000
Soccer field	22,000
Bicycle trails	95,000
Indoor/outdoor pool	700,000
Indoor/outdoor tennis facilities	300,000
	$1,742,000

In addition to these development costs, the club faces annual operating costs of approximately $740,000, outlined in Exhibit J. John Mendez-Smith, the newly elected president of the club, has approached your firm, Young and Kerr, Chartered Accountants, to prepare a report that provides recommendations on accounting, finance, and internal control issues. You took the notes appearing in Exhibit K at a meeting with the club's president and executive committee.

Required:

Prepare the requested report for the president.

EUROPEAN EXCHANGE CLUB YEARLY BUDGET

Operating revenues	
Membership fees	$ 91,000
Social rentals	185,000
Meeting rentals	50,000
Sports rentals	23,000
Concessions	61,000
Fund-raising events	225,000
Total operating revenues	$635,000
Operating costs	
Salaries	$363,000
Administrative costs	39,000
Maintenance	126,000
Utilities	112,000
Educational scholarships	100,000
Total operating costs	$740,000

EXHIBIT K

NOTES FROM MEETING

1. Under the lease agreement with the province, EEC is responsible for maintenance and all costs of improvements. The lease agreement provides for 20 renewal terms of five years' duration each. Renewal is based on the condition that EEC makes the club's services available to all present and future EEC member clubs and their membership.

2. EEC has requested an operating grant from the provincial government. Its proposal asks the province to provide EEC with annual funds to cover 50% of "approved" operating costs incurred to provide services to all club members. The city of Decker wishes to construct an arena and a swimming pool and has opposed the provincial operating grant. The city has asked to be the first in line for available provincial funds. The province has informed EEC that if funds are granted, EEC will have to supply audited financial statements of the organization for all future fiscal year-ends.

   The committee members suspect that they will have to compromise on their proposal and are having problems determining the minimum annual funds required by the club from the province.

3. The Russian and Italian clubs have been arguing with other clubs over the equalization payments required from each club. Currently, each club makes payments to EEC based upon its proportionate membership. Payments for each calendar year are made on February 1 of the following year.

4. The accounting function is a major concern of the member club representatives. In particular, they have raised the following issues:

   a. Several fund-raising events are organized by individual member clubs.

   b. Any donations to EEC are received through the member clubs.

   c. No accounting has been made of services donated to EEC by the members of the individual clubs.

d. EEC has approached a bank to assist in future phases of the club's development. The bank has informed EEC that it is interested in asset values and EEC's ability to repay the loans.

[CICA]

CASE 10–10 Art Gallery

You have been hired to prepare a report for the board of directors of a large art gallery. The board has just reviewed the annual financial statements of the art gallery, and is dissatisfied with the financial information provided in the statements. You have been provided with the following information.

The principal activity of the art gallery is the acquisition and exhibition of modern and contemporary pieces of art. The gallery is open to the general public on a daily basis, and has special exhibits for specific interest groups. Each year the gallery has a number of fund-raising activities to help defray operating costs and make the acquisition of art possible. These activities are organized by the support staff, but rely on volunteers to staff the various functions. The major fund-raising activity is an Annual Rennaise Telethon (ART), which solicits pledges from corporations and individuals and has been very successful.

Capital assets, in addition to the pieces of artwork, include a building, maintenance equipment, office furniture, and fixtures. The building that houses the art gallery is a large Victorian mansion that was donated by a prominent local family several years ago. Because the building has been designated a heritage property, utilities are provided by the local utility companies for a nominal fee of one dollar a year. As well, the municipal government has exempted the gallery from paying property taxes. Funding for capital asset acquisitions comes from various granting agencies and from fund-raising activities of the gallery.

The gallery also operates a gift shop on a break-even basis, with the objective of attracting visitors to the gallery. The gift shop has a small staff of salaried employees, but also operates with the assistance of a number of volunteers. The gift shop has an annual inventory of $175,000, and annual sales of approximately $1 million.

The gallery has a support staff of 17 employees, a curator, and a director who is responsible for the overall operation of the gallery. The total operating budget for the gallery is $4.2 million.

Required:

Prepare a report addressing the concerns of the board of directors of the art gallery. Your report should include a brief description of the purpose and objective of a fund accounting system. As well, you have been asked to recommend the different types of funds that would be most appropriate for the gallery. A discussion of relevant accounting policies is also required.

[CGA]

PROBLEMS

P10–1

The OPI Care Centre is a not-for-profit organization funded by government grants and private donations. It prepares its annual financial statements using the deferral method of accounting for contributions, and it uses only the operations fund to account for all activities. It uses an encumbrance system as a means of controlling expenditures.

Required:

The following summarizes some of the transactions that were made during 2006. Assuming a GAAP constraint, prepare the journal entries to reflect the transactions.

a. The founding member of OPI contributed $100,000 on the condition that the principal amount be invested in marketable securities and that only the income earned from the investment be spent on operations.

b. During the year, purchase orders were issued to cover the budgeted cost of $1,400,000 for goods and contracted services.

c. During the year, a public campaign was held to raise funds for daily operations for the current year. Cash of $800,000 was collected, and pledges for an additional $100,000 were received by the end of the year. It is estimated that approximately 95% of these pledges will be collected early in the new year.

d. The provincial government pledged $600,000 for the year to cover operating costs and an additional $1,000,000 to purchase equipment and furniture. All of the grant money was received by the end of the year, except for the last $50,000 to cover operating costs for December.

e. OPI used the $1,000,000 received from the provincial government to purchase equipment and furniture for the care facility. The amortization of these assets amounted to $100,000 for the year. A purchase order has not been issued for this purchase.

f. Invoices totalling $1,450,000 were received for goods and contracted services. Of these invoices, 90% were paid by the end of the fiscal year. Purchase orders in the amount of $1,375,000 had been issued for these services.

[CGA]

P10–2

You have been appointed to the board of directors for a local non-profit organization called "Food for Friends" (FFF). This organization has been in operation for 12 months and has never prepared a set of financial statements. Operations started on July 1, 2005, and FFF's first set of financial statements is now being prepared for the year just ended (at June 30, 2006). A volunteer bookkeeper has done his best to keep track of the organization's financial affairs. Although he has taken an introductory accounting course, he has limited knowledge of reporting requirements for non-profit organizations. You have tried to explain the differences between the deferral method and the restricted fund method of accounting to him, but he still needs your help.

Required:

Prepare the journal entries in response to each of the following questions from the bookkeeper:

a. On January 1, 2006, a local business donated a van to FFF. This saved us from having to rent a van twice per week. The van has a fair market value of $10,000 but we obtained it for $1. It is expected to last four years. I want to record it and amortize it on a straight-line basis, if this is acceptable. What journal entries would I make for the year ended June 30, 2006, related to this van, using the deferral method and assuming we do not have a separate capital fund?

b. In September 2005, one of our "friends" won $5 million in a lottery. She was so grateful to have been helped in her time of need that she provided us with a $1 million endowment on September 30, 2005, with the requirement that the purchasing power of the endowment be maintained. We invested it in a government bond on October 1, 2005 (at par). The bond pays 8% interest annually with the first payment to be received on September 30, 2006. We are happy with this investment as it is quite secure and it protects us against inflation, which has been steady at 2% for years. What journal entries would I make for the year ended June 30, 2006, for these transactions using the deferral method of accounting? What journal entries would I make for these transactions using the restricted fund method, assuming FFF has both a general fund and a separate endowment fund?

[CGA]

P10–3

You have recently received an accounting designation and, to celebrate, you are out for dinner with a long-time friend, Sandy. Sandy feels that "the key to success is networking, because getting to know influential people can help your career." However, Sandy may be taking this a little too far.

Sandy recently joined the board of directors for two non-profit organizations (NPOs). Big Charity ("Big") has annual revenues of $850,000, 20 paid employees, and separate funds for its key activities (a capital fund, an endowment fund, and a general fund). Small Foundation ("Small") has average annual revenues of $75,000 and only one paid employee. It uses the deferral method of accounting. Sandy has been appointed as the treasurer at both organizations. "A great way to network!" says Sandy. Unfortunately, Sandy barely passed her high school accounting course and has not taken any accounting courses since that time. She knows that the boards of directors of both organizations want to comply with GAAP to ensure key donors will be confident about the NPOs' financial statements. However, Sandy is not sure what the specific guidelines are for NPOs under GAAP.

Required:

Address each of Sandy's concerns, making sure your advice complies with GAAP.

a. Sandy stated that "Small received a piece of equipment valued at $16,000, which was donated by a friend of the charity on January 1, 2006. We want to record the $16,000 as contribution revenue and amortize the equipment on a straight-line basis over four years."

Prepare the journal entries required for the contribution and amortization for the year ended December 31, 2006.

b. "Small also received its first pledge ever, and it is a big one," said Sandy. "A local high-technology company has promised to pay us $20,000 per year for the next three years, starting July 1, 2007. It put no restrictions on how we use the donation."

Explain how the not-for-profit organizations should account for pledges. In particular, would the accounting for pledges differ for Small since this is its "first pledge ever"?

c. "Big received a $400,000 endowment donation on January 1, 2006, to be used as follows: the principal is to remain intact but any interest earned can be used for charity for whatever purpose it chooses."

Prepare the journal entries for the $400,000 and $25,000 interest earned and received in 2006 on the endowment donation.

d. "I convinced the board of directors of Big to hold a vote next week to change our accounting for our head office building. It was acquired for $1,000,000 on January 1, 1999, and was amortized over 20 years at $50,000 per year. However, buildings similar to ours are selling for close to $2,000,000 now. Therefore, I want to stop amortizing the building. Since we are a NPO, this is acceptable isn't it?" asks Sandy.

State whether this would be acceptable and briefly explain.

[CGA]

P10–4

Forest Hill Lodge (Lodge) is a seniors' residence operated as a non-profit organization. During 2006, Lodge built a new bingo hall on its property at a cost of $1,200,000. The bingo hall was financed with $600,000 of donations from private individuals and a $600,000 grant from the provincial government. In addition, a $50,000 donation was received specifically to cover the cost of future maintenance of the bingo hall. The bingo hall commenced operations on September 1, 2006. In the last four months of the year, $15,000 was spent on maintenance of the bingo hall. The estimated useful life of the bingo hall is 40 years. Lodge amortizes its capital assets using the straight-line method.

Among other things, Lodge has an excellent reputation for its bingo nights. Most of the callers and runners for the bingo nights are unpaid volunteers.

Required:

a. Based on the information provided, prepare a partial balance sheet to capture all activities related to the bingo hall, assuming Lodge uses the deferral method and does not have a separate capital fund for the bingo hall.

b. Based on the information provided, prepare a partial statement of revenues and expenses to capture all activities related to the bingo hall, assuming Lodge uses the restricted fund method and has a separate capital fund to record the contributions for the construction and maintenance of the bingo hall.

c. Differentiate between expenditure accounting and expense accounting as they apply to the $1,200,000 cost of the bingo hall.

d. Identify the conditions that must be met in order to recognize the value of volunteers' time in the financial statements of a non-profit organization.

e. Prepare the journal entry that would be made in the general fund if volunteers' services were to be recorded at a value of $10,000.

[CGA]

P10–5

You have been recruited to act as the treasurer on the board of directors of a non-profit organization that has had difficulty in recent years in controlling expenditures. The board of directors has very limited accounting experience. The organization, Protect Purple Plants (PPP), is considering implementing an encumbrance accounting system to assist in expenditure control. PPP receives an estimated $800,000 per year in regular contributions from the federal government.

Required:

a. State two advantages and two disadvantages of implementing an encumbrance accounting system.

b. PPP uses the deferral method of accounting for contributions and has no separate fund for restricted contributions. On January 1, 2006, PPP received its first restricted cash contribution—$100,000 for the purchase and maintenance of land and a greenhouse building for its rare purple plant collection. On July 1, 2006, PPP acquired land and a building for $22,000 and $60,000 cash, respectively. The building has an estimated useful life of 20 years and zero salvage value. On December 31, 2006, the remaining $18,000 cash was paid to KJ Maintenance Ltd. for a three-year maintenance contract that requires KJ personnel to provide maintenance services four days per month until December 31, 2009.

Assuming that encumbrance accounting will not be implemented until 2007, prepare the journal entries for the following dates:

i. January 1, 2006

ii. July 1, 2006

iii. December 31, 2006

[CGA]

P10–6

Glendale College is a private girls' school and is operated as a non-profit organization. During 2006, the school received $500,000 in private donations from individuals to establish a scholarship fund for its students. The principal amount of the fund must be invested in government bonds. Only the interest on the fund can be used to provide scholarships to students. For the year ended December 31, 2006, the fund earned interest of $30,000, and scholarships totalling $20,000 were awarded to students in need. At the end of the year, the balance in the scholarship fund was $510,000.

On January 1, 2006, a local businessperson donated a small bus to the school. The bus seats 20 people and was worth approximately $40,000 at the time of the donation. It has an estimated useful life of six years with a residual value of $10,000. The school amortizes its capital assets using the straight-line method.

Required:

a. Prepare the journal entries to capture all activities related to the scholarship fund under the following assumptions:

i. The school uses the deferral method and records all entries in the operating fund because it does not have a separate endowment fund for the scholarship.

ii. The school uses the restricted fund method and records all entries in a separate endowment fund for the scholarship.

b. Assume the school wishes to record the value of the donated bus. Prepare journal entries for 2006 to capture all activities related to the donated bus, assuming the school uses the deferral method and does not have a separate fund for the donated bus.

[CGA]

P10–7

You have been hired as a consultant to provide accounting advice for a non-profit organization that wishes to improve its accounting system. In particular, the organization, Save the Ozone (STO), is considering changing its method for contributions and implementing a new budgeting and encumbrance accounting system. STO has a December 31 year-end.

Required:

a. In November 2006, STO issued a $1,000 purchase order for key chains to be provided as an incentive to donors who contribute to its Spring 2007 fundraising drive. In December 2006, the key chains were shipped to STO with an invoice price of $1,095. Prepare the journal entries for November 2006 and December 2006 using encumbrance accounting.

b. Briefly explain the difference between an encumbrance and a liability.

c. STO has always used the restricted fund method of accounting for contributions, but other similar organizations have been using the deferral method. Briefly explain how STO would account for the following restricted contributions using the deferral method:

  i. Restricted contributions for expenses of future periods

  ii. Restricted contributions for the acquisition of amortizable capital assets

  iii. Restricted contributions for expenses of the current period

[CGA]

P10–8

Zak Organization is a non-profit organization set up for famine relief. It uses fund accounting and has three funds: a general fund; a capital fund (through which it is raising cash to support the purchase of a new administrative building); and an endowment fund. Zak has been operating for 25 years and has a December 31 year-end. Zak's policy with respect to capital assets is to capitalize and amortize the capital assets over their expected useful lives.

On June 30, 2005, Zak received three donations from a former director:

i. $30,000 cash for famine relief.

ii. $50,000 to be used solely for construction of the new administrative building. Of the $50,000, 70% was received in cash, with the remainder promised in February 2006. (Note: construction is expected to commence in October 2006.)

iii. $600,000 cash, which was invested on July 1, 2005, in long-term Government of Canada bonds, with 10% interest to be paid semiannually on December 31 and June 30. The $600,000 donation was given with the stipulation that it be invested in interest-bearing securities with the principal maintained by Zak, although interest earned on the securities is not restricted.

Required:

a. Briefly explain (do not provide journal entries) how each of the three donations should be accounted for using fund accounting. In particular, should each of the donations be recognized as revenue for the year ended December 31, 2005? If yes, in which fund(s) would the revenue be recognized (including interest earned in fiscal 2005 on the bonds purchased with the $600,000 donation)?

b. If Zak used the deferral method of accounting instead of using fund accounting, how would this change the requirements for accounting for the $50,000 and $600,000 donations?

c. Despite the recent donations from its former director, Zak is increasingly faced with severe budgetary constraints. Zak is considering implementing encumbrance accounting in the coming year.

 i. Briefly describe the process of encumbrance accounting.

 ii. Briefly describe how encumbrance accounting might serve as a device to help control spending when it is used in conjunction with a formal budgeting system.

[CGA]

Appendix 10A

Fund Accounting

Introduction

In non-profit organizations and in governments, the maintenance of financial capital is not of high concern; indeed, it may not be a concern at all. Because costs are not incurred in order to generate revenue (except in certain self-sustaining or cost-recovery activities), there is not the same need to measure consumption of goods and services. Instead, the emphasis is on controlling expenditures and keeping within budget. The change in emphasis has resulted in the development of *fund accounting*, one of the three fundamentally different accounting systems that are in general use.[8]

Fund accounting has three attributes, any or all of which may be useful in accounting for specific non-business organizations. The three attributes are (1) the segregation of funds by purpose or restriction, (2) the ability to account for commitments, and (3) the capacity to incorporate budgetary controls directly into the accounts. As we discussed in the main body of Chapter 10, the restricted method of accounting for contributions has specifically designated funds. In this appendix we will discuss fund accounting as an option, even when the deferral method is used.

In fund accounting, there is a set of self-balancing accounts for each separately identified fund. Therefore, each fund will also have its own financial statements. The statements for some funds will be very simple, while those for other funds can be very complex. Interfund transfers complicate matters further,

---

8 The first system is *proprietary accounting*—the basis for all business enterprise accounting. The second is *fund accounting.* The third system is *entity accounting,* wherein economic institutions are viewed as entities generating value added. The value added is distributed to the factors of production without adopting the point of view of any particular factor (such as the suppliers of capital, as in proprietary accounting). Entity accounting is the basis for all macro-economic accounting, such as the national income accounts. It also is useful in developing countries for enterprise accounting (instead of proprietary accounting) because the enterprise accounts then fit into the framework of the macro-economic systems, which aids in guiding development.

particularly if the transfers are not clearly identified in the financial statements. To avoid a fragmented approach to financial reporting, many NPOs combine similar funds for external reporting. For example, a university will not report each scholarship fund separately, but will combine them all into a single set of accounts for financial statement purposes.

This brief appendix will outline the major characteristics of fund accounting and will describe the basic different types of funds. The bookkeeping aspects will not be presented herein, however. The technical aspects of fund accounting are dealt with in many other books, large and small, that are readily available.

Purpose of fund accounting

Fund accounting has been defined as: "Accounting procedures resulting in a self-balancing set of accounts for each fund established by legal, contractual or voluntary actions of an organization" [CICA 4400.02(c)].

The focus of fund accounting is on keeping track of resources that are designated for specific purposes, in order to avoid mixing up resources that are intended for diverse purposes and to ensure that management fulfills its stewardship responsibility for proper disposition of the resources. A single non-business organization can have several (or many) such accounting entities.

As the definition of fund accounting suggests, funds can be created as the result of legal or regulatory requirements, by contract with donors or grantors, or voluntarily by the directorate of the organization. As discussed in the chapter, the different types of fund restrictions fall into three categories: endowed funds, and externally and internally restricted funds.

Fund balances may also be *appropriated*. Appropriations in fund accounting are no different from appropriations of retained earnings in businesses; there is no segregation of funds, but simply an indication that the board or legislature intends to devote some of the resources of a particular fund to an indicated purpose.

The extent to which funds need to be segregated in an organization is largely a matter of common sense. When a donor gives a contribution that is earmarked for a specific purpose, there must be some way of ensuring that the contribution is used only as intended. If an organization operates an ancillary enterprise in order to perform a service or to raise money, it makes sense to segregate all the revenues and costs of that enterprise in order to measure the net cost of providing the service or the net revenue raised. Thus there are no hard and fast rules as to the types of funds that an organization may have.

Fund-basis *recording* does not necessarily imply fund-basis *reporting*. It is common to consolidate several or all funds when preparing the financial statements, especially the statement of operations. The statements of financial position can also be consolidated.

Types of funds

There are several different types of funds. Distinctions between types of funds generally relate to either the nature of the activity being carried out by the fund or to restrictions on the uses of monies, or both. Terminology varies somewhat, thereby adding to the confusion. We will distinguish among six basic types of funds. In addition, there are two types of *account groups*. The nature of the different types of funds and account groups is discussed below.

Operating or general funds Non-profit organizations tend to use the term *operating fund* or *general fund* for the central fund of the organization that bears the costs of conducting the organization's primary functions, and into which unrestricted funds flow. An organization can have more than one operating fund if it conducts more than one primary function, and if it is desirable for managerial purposes to keep the assets, liabilities, revenues, and expenses of the primary functions separate. But if the revenues, expenses, assets, and liabilities are not directly assignable to the various functions, then segregation is not really feasible and only a single operating fund will be maintained.

Maintaining separate *funds* should not be confused with maintaining separate *accounts* within the operating fund for different activities. In modern computerized accounting systems, it is easy to have a triple classification of each account:

- by type or object of revenue or expenditure
- by fund, and
- by program or activity.

Special or reserve funds A special fund is a fund created to record the resource flows associated with a special project or event. Special funds could be created by an NPO, for example, to carry out a specific research project, to conduct a special event such as a benefit concert, or to institute a new program using a special grant from a donor or a government grantor. Special funds (1) may generate their own revenue (as for a fund-raising event), (2) may be carried out with funds voluntarily segregated by the directorate of the organization and transferred from the operating fund, or (3) may be financed by restricted grants from outside the organization.

Separate reserve funds often are not necessary; the same result often can be obtained by appropriating or designating part of the fund balance in the general fund.

Self-sustaining or enterprise funds This type of fund accounts for those activities that generate their own revenues to recover their costs, and thus are segregated from the other funds both for control purposes and for performance appraisal. Self-sustaining funds are also known as *enterprise* funds or *revolving* funds. Self-sustaining funds may be created by money advanced from the general fund. In such instances, the amount advanced is a receivable in the general fund accounts and a liability in the self-sustaining fund accounts; the interfund obligation is eliminated if consolidated statements are prepared.

Capital funds A capital fund (or *plant* fund) is one in which the resources are intended for use for capital improvements or new capital assets. The fund may be an externally restricted fund if it contains monies given specifically for capital purposes only, as with a capital grant by a province to a hospital. Capital funds may also be board-designated funds, if the capital was appropriated by the board of directors for capital improvements rather than being externally restricted by the donor. If a capital fund contains both restricted amounts and designated amounts, then the fund balance should segregate the net resources within each category.

Capital funds may be used to account for both assets acquired and liabilities incurred, such as mortgages and bonds. The term "capital" can thereby apply to both sides of the balance sheet: to long-term assets (capital used) and to long-term liabilities (capital provided).

If capital funds are not used to keep track of assets and/or liabilities, then one of the *account groups* discussed below may be used.

Fiduciary funds A fiduciary fund is any fund that is held in trust for outside parties. An organization may hold funds in trust for other organizations or groups, and not be entitled to any of the benefits of the funds. For example, a church or university may hold cash and provide accounting services for clubs or subgroups within the organization but the funds are those of the clubs and not those of the church or university that is functioning as trustee. Similarly, employee pension funds are sometimes administered by a non-profit organization for the benefit of its employees. *Fiduciary funds* can also be called *trust*, *agency*, or *custodial* funds.

The distinction between trust funds and reserve funds is that trust funds are legally restricted for specified uses, while reserve or special funds are board-designated funds.

Endowment funds The capital in an *endowed fund* cannot be disbursed at all. The purpose of the endowed fund may also be restricted. Endowment funds, scholarship funds, and loan funds are examples. The income arising from the investment of the fund capital may or may not be disbursed. If the income can be disbursed, it may be restricted (i.e., as to purpose), depending on the conditions of the donor. Sometimes, a fund is endowed only for a designated period of time, after which the capital becomes available for use as directed by the donor.

Endowed funds are sometimes expended on a constant rate of return basis. Under this approach, a given percentage of a fund's net asset *value* may be expended each year, regardless of the actual earnings of the fund. The percentage generally reflects long-term expectations for inflation-free investment earnings, such as from 3% to 5%. The intent is to permit the organization to use a predictable amount of income each year for the fund's operating purpose, without worrying about the vagaries of the investment market in any particular year. In addition, establishing the permissible expenditure at a "real" rate of return permits the endowment to accumulate enough additional principal to offset the erosive effects of inflation on the real value of the return.

The distinction must be clear between a fund that is legally restricted by the donor and one that is voluntarily restricted by the organization's directors. Voluntary restrictions can be reversed at a later date by the directors. Only funds in which the capital is non-expendable by order of the donor should be called endowed funds.

Account groups

In addition to the types of funds explained above, non-business organizations can also have one or two *groups* of accounts. Groups differ from funds in that there are no liquid assets within the group; the group is simply a self-balancing set of accounts that is intended to keep track of assets and liabilities that may otherwise not be included within the control systems of the organization.

One type of group is the *capital asset group*. Acquisitions of new capital assets are generally treated as current expenditures of the fund making the acquisition, such as the operating fund.[9] In order to include the cost of the capital assets on the organization's balance sheet, the assets may be recorded as a debit to an asset account within a group of capital asset accounts, with an offsetting credit to a fund balance or group balance account. The offsetting credit is often to an account that identifies the source of financing for the asset. In this manner, the

---

9   The principal exceptions would be in self-sustaining or enterprise funds in which capital assets are capitalized and depreciated.

organization's long-term sources of financing for its capital assets can be identified. The group really represents a collection of memorandum entries; there are no resources or transactions relating to the group itself.

Capital asset groups are used largely for control purposes and to permit consolidated reporting that shows all of the organization's assets and liabilities. When a non-business organization chooses to capitalize its capital assets (if a GAAP constraint exists), an alternative practice is to capitalize the asset within the capital fund, the operating fund, or whichever other fund has expended the resources to acquire the capital assets.

The second type of account group is the *long-term liability group*. In government accounting, this group has traditionally been called the bonded debt group. The purpose of this group is to keep track of outstanding long-term obligations. This group is used almost exclusively by senior governments—most local governments in Canada are not permitted to issue long-term debt, and NPOs seldom have long-term debt except for property mortgages and occasional bank term loans.

The liability group is used by governments to keep track of the overall debt obligations and repayment schedules. The group also can be used to keep track of loan guarantees that the government has handed out, but few governments do bother to track their guarantees—a control weakness that various auditors general have pointed out from time to time!

Fund accounting and the segregation of funds

In theory, each fund is a separate group of accounts. In practice, however, it is not always necessary to be so formal about the individual funds. For example, suppose that an organization receives a special grant to produce its literature in French translation. Technically, this is a donation that is restricted to a specific use and would call for the establishment of a special fund. More likely, however, the organization will create a single control account in its operating fund and credit the grant to that account. All expenditures relating to the translation and production of the French materials will be charged to that account, so that the account balance corresponds to what would be the fund balance if a separate set of accounts had been established. A subsidiary set of accounts can be maintained in support of the control account, if desired.

Interfund transfers

Transfers between funds create a potential problem area for financial reporting. The problem arises from the difficulty of making the distinction between three types of transfers: (1) interfund loans, (2) redesignations of fund balances by the board of directors, and (3) expenditures by one fund that are revenues to the other. The first type of transfer results in a receivable in the lending fund and a payable in the borrowing fund; the expectation is that the loan will be repaid sometime in the foreseeable future. Interfund loans will show on the statements of financial position of the individual funds and on their statements of changes in net assets, but will not affect the statement of operations or the fund balances. Interfund loans would be eliminated in consolidated statements.

Redesignation of fund balances by the board represents a permanent shift of resources from one fund to another. These transfers should be reflected in the statement of changes in net assets for both the paying and the receiving funds, but should not result in an offsetting receivable and payable or have any impact on the statement of operations. If, on the other hand, the transfer is recognition that one fund is using the services of another fund and is paying for the services rendered, then the transaction should flow through the statement of operations of *both* funds.

A problem that exists in practice in NPOs is that the accounting treatment of the transaction may be determined more by management's desire to influence the reported operating results than by the real nature of the transaction. If the operating fund has a substantial surplus, for example, management may redesignate part of the fund balance and transfer the surplus to another fund (e.g., the capital fund). Rather than report the transfer simply as a fund balance transfer, management may list it as an expenditure in the operating fund in order to bring down the apparent surplus so that potential donors won't think that the organization doesn't really need more money.

A similar ploy is not to transfer the surplus to another fund but simply to make an appropriation within the operating fund, separating the fund balance into appropriated and unappropriated amounts, and to charge the appropriation against operations as though it were an expenditure instead of simply debiting the fund balance. Unfortunately, both ploys are common in practice, making the "bottom line" of the statement of operations even less meaningful than it already is (due to the multiplicity of alternative accounting policy choices, almost all of which affect the bottom line).

Any reader of the financial statements of a government or NPO must watch for interfund transfers, not because there is anything wrong with them per se, but because they can be used to hide a variety of sins!

Chapter 11

Public Sector Financial Reporting

This chapter continues our discussion of accounting for *non-business organizations*. The preceding chapter discussed non-profit organizations. In this chapter, we focus on *public sector reporting*—that is, the financial reporting for governments and governmental units.

"Authoritative" accounting policies for the public sector did not exist prior to 1980; accounting policies were set individually by each senior level of government, and accounting policies for municipalities were (and are) established by each provincial legislature.

In 1981, the CICA established the Public Sector Accounting Board (PSAB), which strives to improve the quality of public sector reporting by issuing accounting recommendations. One of the most pressing problems was the lack of comparability among governments. Each senior government (that is, the federal, provincial, and territorial governments) had its own individual set of accounting policies. Nevertheless, the PSAB has been able to achieve considerable progress, which culminated in 2003 with proposals for a new government accounting model, as we will discuss in this chapter.

In this chapter, we will:

- review the characteristics of governments and governmental units
- discuss the objectives of financial reporting for the public sector, and how they differ from the objectives of for-profit enterprises
- describe the types of financial statements normally prepared by governments and governmental units, and
- discuss the major reporting and measurement issues.

Unlike the CICA's Accounting Standards Board for public for-profit enterprises, the PSAB has little "clout"—no senior governments are *required* to follow PSAB recommendations, but each senior government voluntarily adopts PSAB recommendations. Progress is made by persuasion and, it is hoped, consensus among senior governments.

Contrast Between NPOs and Governments

At the beginning of Chapter 10, we drew a distinction between governments, governmental units, and non-profit organizations. All three are *non-business organizations,* and they have several distinguishing characteristics in common. All three types of non-business organization:

- have no investors
- may provide both private and collective goods and services
- may derive the bulk of their revenues from sources other than the sale of goods and services
- have funds that are restricted for specific purposes, and
- have revenues that are not responsive to the demand for services.[1]

All of these characteristics were discussed in Chapter 10. These characteristics have led to financial reporting for governments that is very similar to that for NPOs. Governments (1) use fund accounting, (2) may use different accounting policies for different funds, (3) may not report on a fully consolidated basis, and (4) cannot clearly define the reporting entity.

Despite the many similarities between non-profit organizations and governments, there are some important differences between the two types of organizations. One of the most basic differences is the nature of the financial statement user group. Each non-profit organization has clearly identifiable primary stakeholders who have specific information needs. The financial reporting objectives of NPOs must be directed towards the needs of their primary funders. In contrast, governments have a legal reporting requirement to their legislatures or city councils, and they also have a far larger potential user group.

Consequently it is quite difficult to be very specific about who the users of government financial statements really are. One can say that all Canadian citizens are interested in the financial results of the federal government, for example, but such a statement is difficult to translate to meaningful reporting objectives that will help us make a choice from amongst alternative accounting policies or families of policies.

We must make one more distinction to fully understand public sector accounting. This is the difference between a *government business organization* compared to the non-business government organizations discussed in the above section. The PSAB (PS1300.28) defines a **government business organization** as one that:

- is a separate legal entity with the power to contract in its own name and can sue and be sued
- has been delegated the financial and operational authority to carry on a business
- sells goods and services to individuals and organizations outside of the government reporting entity as its principal activity, and
- can, in the normal course of its operations, maintain its operations and meet its liabilities from revenues received from sources outside of the government reporting entity.

It is important to remember these distinctions between business and non-business organizations during the following discussion.

Public Sector Reporting Standards

Until the decade of the 1980s, not much interest was demonstrated by professional accountants in governmental reporting. Since 1980, however, there has been quite a bit of interest in developing governmental reporting, and both the

---

1   Indeed, governments have revenues that are inversely related to the demand for services in recessions; e.g., the demand for services goes up while the tax revenues fall.

CICA and the Canadian Certified General Accountants' Research Foundation have been quite active.

We pointed out in Chapter 10 that the domain of accounting standard-setting for non-profit organizations in Canada is in the hands of the CICA's Accounting Standards Board. The efforts of the AcSB to date have largely been attempts to apply business enterprise GAAP to NPOs.

In contrast, the CICA has given the responsibility for public sector reporting to a separate board. In 1981, the CICA established the Public Sector Accounting and Auditing Board (PSAAB). In 1998, the CICA created the Public Sector Accounting Board (PSAB) and transferred responsibility for assurance and related services to the Assurance Standards Board. The mandate of the Public Sector Accounting Board (PSAB) is to:

- serve the public interest by issuing recommendations and guidance with respect to matters of accounting in the public sector, and
- strengthen accountability in the public sector through developing, recommending, and gaining acceptance of accounting and financial reporting standards of good practice.[2]

In 2000, the PSAB approved a strategic plan that set out five overriding objectives for the next five years. The proposed objectives are to:

- issue recommendations and guidance that enhance the usefulness of public sector financial statement information
- issue recommendations that enhance the usefulness of public sector financial and non-financial performance information
- engage interest and debate by improving stakeholders' understanding of public finances
- efficiently coordinate activities with other accounting standard-setters and other public sector related organizations, and
- provide the PSAB's program of standard-setting and communications effectively, efficiently and economically.[3]

By early 2004, the PSAB had issued 26 public sector accounting recommendations and three accounting guidelines. The Board's accounting recommendations are "intended to apply to all governments unless specifically limited in individual statements."[4]

This is where the distinction between business and non-business government organizations becomes important. Government business organizations, government business-type organizations, and government non-profit organizations are guided by the *CICA Handbook* and *not* by the *Public Sector Accounting Handbook*.[5]

In addition, not all of the recommendations apply to all levels of government. The first four accounting recommendations apply to senior governments (i.e., the 13 federal, provincial, and territorial governments), two apply specifically to local governments, and the remaining 20 apply to specific items. There is a very strong similarity between the recommendations for senior and local governments.

---

2   PSAB "Introduction to Public Sector Accounting Recommendations," revised August 2003, ¶01.

3   PSAB "Draft Strategic Plan," issued 2000.

4   PSAB "Introduction to Public Sector Accounting Recommendations," revised August 2003, ¶05.

5   *Ibid.*, Appendix 1.

The compliance issue

PSAB recommendations are just that: *recommendations*, not *requirements* for most levels of government. Other types of organizations may have compelling reasons to comply with recommendations of the *CICA Handbook*, but such is not the case with governments and the recommendations of the PSAB.

For most levels of government, there is no mechanism to compel compliance with the PSAB recommendations. Governmental financial reporting is governed by legislation, which may be either extensive or virtually non-existent at different levels and in different provinces and territories. Senior governments are not audited by external auditors, but by the governments' auditors general. Auditors general are not required to report in accordance with the recommendations of the PSAB. Local governments usually are audited by external auditors, although some major cities have their own city auditor. Local government auditors are required to report in accordance with provincial legislation governing municipal reporting. Some local governments are now required to report in compliance with the PSAB based on provincial legislation.[6]

While there is no compliance mechanism for the PSAB accounting recommendations, the recommendations can serve as a useful guide to auditors general and city auditors. The recommendations give the auditors an authoritative lever for persuading government authorities to improve their financial reporting. Ultimately, the PSAB recommendations can guide provincial legislatures in stipulating requirements for local and provincial governmental reporting.

A standard-setting body such as the PSAB can make progress only if the initial recommendations are largely a codification of existing practices. Changes or improvements in existing practice can then be "eased" into practice with greater likelihood of acceptance, even when there is no legal compliance requirement.

One example of an accounting recommendation that was not accepted by governments is the 1997 recommendation to introduce capital asset accounting into public sector financial statements. Governments did not comply with this recommendation because it was a sharp deviation from existing practice. As we will discuss shortly, the new PSAB government reporting model has revised the general standards of statement presentation to correspond more closely to existing practice, and thereby reduce the extent of non-compliance.[7]

Objectives of Governmental Reporting

Government reporting objectives have not suffered from a lack of attention. Several research studies have examined the users and uses of financial statements and, not surprisingly, have come up with a wide variety of both.

In 1980, the CICA issued a research study entitled *Financial Reporting by Governments* (*FRG*) that focused on financial reporting by senior governments. This research study formed the basis of PS 1400, "Objectives of Financial Statements." The study classified the users of the financial reports of governments as fitting into five categories: (1) policy makers, (2) legislators, (3) program administrators, (4) investors, and (5) the general public. Each of these five groups will have advisors. The advisors or analysts for each group can be viewed as being a part of that group rather than as a separate user group.

---

6   Legislation in five provinces requires municipalities in their jurisdictions to follow the recommendations for local governments in the *Public Sector Accounting Recommendations*.

7   CICA, *Financial Reporting by Governments* (CICA, 1980), pp. 24–27.

The *FRG* study states the financial reporting objectives for senior governments as follows:[8]

1. to facilitate evaluation of economic impact

2. to facilitate evaluation of program delivery choices and their management

3. to demonstrate stewardship and compliance with legislative authority, and

4. to display the state of the government's finances.

The PSAB incorporated the information from this study in issuing PS 1100, "Objectives of Financial Statements," applicable to federal, provincial, and territorial governments. PS 1100 suggests the following four objectives for financial statements:

1. to provide accounting of financial affairs and resources

2. to demonstrate government's ability to finance activities, meet liabilities, and provide future services

3. to account for sources, allocation, and use of government resources; evaluate how activities affected net debt; and show how activities were financed and cash requirements met, and

4. to display the state of government's finances and evaluate if in accordance with legislative requirements.[9]

An extensive CGA Research Foundation study of the actual reporting practices of local governments found a lack of focus in local government reporting. Professor Beedle, the study's author, credited the lack of focus to the absence of guidance or authoritative pronouncements and to the government's attempt to use the general purpose financial statements to be all things to all people:

> Faced with this paucity of guidance and authoritative pronouncements, present Canadian practice in accounting reports of local governments seems to stab at satisfying an undefined range of users and their needs without (with exceptions) specifically defining those users, their needs, or the objectives of the reports.... The result in many cases is a complex, scarcely comprehensible set of reports requiring specialized expert accounting knowledge in the government field. There is a failure to realize that "general purpose statements are not all purpose statements, and never can be."[10]

In 1985 the CICA also published a research study, *Local Government Financial Reporting (LGFR)*. The *LGFR* study group and PS 1700, "Objectives of Financial Statements for Local Governments," consider Beedle's findings and the diverse set of potential users of government financial statements in establishing the specific objectives for local government reporting.

The study group recognized that it is necessary to make a distinction between *general purpose* and *special purpose* financial reporting. While such a distinction is hardly new, it is important in governmental reporting because it makes it clear that the general purpose reports that go to the citizenry at large may be quite different from special purpose reports that are prepared for making specific operational

---

8   *Ibid.*, pp. 27–29.

9   PSAB 1100 "Objectives of Financial Statements of Federal, Provincial and Territorial Governments," issued August 2003.

10 A. Beedle, *Accounting for Local Government in Canada: The State of the Art* (Vancouver: The Canadian Certified General Accountants' Research Foundation, 1981) p. 73.

decisions such as resource allocation or performance evaluation of major programs and activities. PS 1700.27 states that:

> Financial statements cannot be expected to fulfill all of the needs served by a local government's financial reporting system. Local governments produce various financial reports in addition to financial statements. For example, there are reports prepared by individual entities, reports to measure and report on the performance of individual programs and activities, and special purpose reports designed to meet particular needs of specific users. In addition, local governments set out their financial plan in the Budget. Thus, certain information is better provided, or can only be provided, by financial reports other than financial statements.[11]

Qualitative Characteristics

The *LGFP* study group conducted interviews with a sample of representatives from various categories of users of governmental financial reports. Not surprisingly, the users expressed a wide diversity of needs. However, the users tended to stress similar qualitative characteristics of good financial reports, and the report cites four qualities that were stressed by the interviewees: (1) comparability among governments, (2) consistency between years, (3) completeness, and (4) timeliness. The users were particularly emphatic about comparability:

> Almost above everything else, users wanted to compare the reports of various governments. This meant they wanted consistency among governments in the basis for:
> • defining the reporting entity to make clear what kinds of Crown corporations were included and excluded;
> • classifying and reporting revenues, expenditures, assets and liabilities; and
> • reporting government debt including contingent debt.
>
> They also wanted consistency, to the extent possible, between the Public Accounts and various statistical compilations of government figures (e.g., the National Accounts) and the ability to reconcile two sets of figures where differences in basis are justified by the different purposes served by the two sets of figures.[12]

The PSAB incorporated qualitative criteria into Section 1000:

> Financial statements should communicate information that is relevant to the needs of those for whom the statements are prepared, reliable, comparable, understandable and clearly presented in a manner that maximizes its usefulness. [PS 1000.24]

Characteristics of Governments

In designing the new government reporting model, the PSAB identified the unique characteristics of a government and how that differs from businesses. These characteristics have reporting implications that mean the financial statements for government should not look like those of a business.

Appendix A to Section 1100 Financial Statements, "Objectives of Financial Statements," identifies the following nine unique characteristics of governments:

---

11 PSAB 1700 "Objectives of Financial Statements for Local Governments," issued March 1995, ¶27.

12 *Financial Reporting by Governments* (CICA, 1980), p. 31.

- the goal is to provide services and redistribute resources, not to make a profit
- public tangible capital assets are different in nature from business tangible capital assets
- capital spending is *not* focused on maximizing returns
- the principal source of revenue is taxation
- all assets acquired are held in the right of the Crown
- the environment is non-competitive
- a budget shows public policy, establishes estimates and financing requirements, and is part of public accountability
- governments have huge debt capacities
- there is a higher standard of accountability.

It is interesting to note that the PSAB has taken a strong approach in identifying the distinguishing characteristics of governments. The PSAB approach is in contrast with the AcSB approach to non-profit organizations, which assumes that NPOs have no significant differences from business enterprises.

Types of Financial Statements

The new government reporting model issued in January 2003 focuses on economic rather than financial resources. The new model sends the following five messages about government finances:

- net debt/net financial assets
- accumulated surplus/deficit
- annual surplus/deficit
- change in net debt
- change in cash and cash flows that contributed to the change

Based on the new government reporting model, the PSAB recommends that federal, provincial, and territorial governments present the following four statements [PS 1200.31]:

- statement of financial position
- statement of operations
- statement of change in net debt, and
- statement of cash flow.

This model supports the current focus on the importance of net debt as an indicator of the government's finances but also recognizes the importance of providing information about the costs of providing government services. The paper recommends that the financial statements have four features.

First, the statement of financial position reports net debt, and then deducts non-financial assets from net debt to measure the government's accumulated surplus or deficit.[13] *Net debt* is the difference between financial assets and liabilities. Net debt provides an indicator of future revenues required to pay for past transactions. The *accumulated surplus/deficit* is an indication of the government's ability to provide future services.

13 CICA, "The New Government Reporting Model," January 2003, p. 1–2.

Second, the model recommends that governments issue a statement of operations that shows the excess (or deficiency) of revenues over *expenses*.[14] This recommendation moves away from the expenditure basis of reporting to full accrual accounting. In addition, this statement is easier to understand because there is a separate statement to show changes in net debt.

Third, the new statement of changes in net debt reconciles a government's total expenses for the period to its spending on operations (i.e., expenditures) for the period. The statement also reports (1) the capital spending in the period, (2) the extent to which total government spending was financed by revenues earned in the period (i.e., the change in net debt in the period), and (3) the opening and closing net debt balances.[15]

This new statement shows the importance of net debt as an indicator of the government's finances. It also focuses attention on the operating cost of government services compared to capital. Full disclosure is provided in this statement of the amount of capital spending. For that reason, the previous statement of tangible capital assets was eliminated.

Fourth is a statement of cash flow. This statement calculates the cash flow from operating activities using the direct method or the indirect method that adjusts the surplus or deficit for the accounting period to the amount of cash used or available from operations. Capital transactions are shown as a separate section.[16]

The new reporting model requires that budget and actual numbers must be reported on the statement of operations and the statement of change in net debt. This highlights the differences between the two, which provides accountability or a measure of the government's achievement of its objectives.

This new model applies to federal, provincial, and territorial governments only. Changes have not been recommended yet for local governments. Currently, the PSAB recommends that local government financial statements "should include, as a minimum, a statement of financial position, a statement of financial activities, and a statement of changes in financial position" [PS 1800.07].[17]

Note the subtle difference between the "statement that reports the surplus or deficit in the accounting period" and a "statement of financial activities." The latter expression is much less specific.

Also, with local governments there is no requirement to include a statement of tangible capital assets. This is further explained by the statement, "Many local governments do not have adequate physical information to report fully on their acquired physical assets. Therefore, they are encouraged to collect information about their physical assets" [PS 1800.30].[18]

Major Reporting Issues

The primary reporting issues for governments are quite similar to those of NPOs:

- cash versus accrual
- expenditure versus full accrual
- capital assets

14 CICA "20 Questions About Government Financial Reporting," January 2003, p. 21.

15 *Ibid.*, p. 21.

16 *Ibid.*, p. 21.

17 PSAB 1800 "General Standards of Financial Statement Presentation for Local Governments," issued August 2003, ¶07.

18 *Ibid.*, ¶30.

- consolidation and the reporting entity, and
- restricted assets and revenues.

In addition, governments have major reporting issues concerning liabilities. Liability issues do not arise for NPOs, because NPOs normally do not issue long-term debt.

Cash vs. accrual

The cash versus accrual debate in government accounting is similar to that for NPOs. The choice is between cash, modified cash or modified accrual, and full accrual. As was discussed in Chapter 10, full accrual is sometimes used to include the full range of interperiod allocations, and therefore this book uses the term *modified accrual* to mean accrual of assets and liabilities without necessarily allocating the costs on an expense basis.

Up until the new Government Reporting Model, the PSAB supported a modified accrual accounting (i.e., without necessarily including expense-basis allocations). There are two main reasons for reporting on a modified accrual basis.

1. Operations can be reported on an expenditure or expense basis rather than simply on a disbursements basis; this makes it less likely that government managers will be tempted to manipulate cash payments to suppliers and others in order to "manage" the reported surplus or deficit.

2. Accrual is essential in order to measure and report the government's liabilities. Liability reporting is a major issue in governmental accounting, and will be discussed briefly later in this chapter.

The vast majority of governments use a modified accrual basis. However, the new Government Reporting Model has moved to recommending full accrual accounting by eliminating the option of reporting expenditures.

Expenditure vs. full accrual

Initially PSAB recommendations supported the use of an expenditure basis of reporting rather than an accrual basis. The *LGFR* study group provided the following support for the expenditure basis:

> While the cost of operating may have some place in enterprises (which can be accommodated in *separate* financial reports to their constituents), the "significant" users of local government financial reports contemplated by this study have little interest in costs. They are much more interested in whether inflows of resources are adequate to meet outflows. They are not interested in when resources are used up and which periods benefited from them.[19]

An expenditure basis has been the normal reporting practice for both senior and local governments. This reality is reflected in PS 1700.90, for example, which recommends that financial statements for local governments should report *expenditures* of the accounting period by function.

The expenditure basis is consistent with the budgetary control that governmental managers must exercise. If governments report on an expense basis, then

---

19 *Ibid.,* p. 32.

they are "required" by the accounting system to raise sufficient revenues to offset the expenses, even if the expenses gave rise to no obligation for cash outflows in the current period. Alternatively, expenses can be significantly lower than expenditures; the government can break even on an expense basis while running a substantial deficit on an expenditure basis.

Gradually, there has been a shift from the expenditure basis to a full accrual basis. Particularly notable is PS 3250, in which the Board recommends pension accounting that is consistent with the recommendations of Section 3461 of the *CICA Handbook*, an expense-basis recommendation.

PS 3250 recommends that, when a defined benefit pension plan is in effect, pension costs should be determined in accordance with the accrued benefit method, and that actuarial gains and losses (i.e., from changes in assumptions or from experience) should be amortized over the expected average remaining service life of the related employee group.[20] The PSAB supports its recommendations by pointing to the importance of measuring liabilities, and an expenditure is defined as the incurrence of a liability. However, the pension recommendations seem to be substituting one actuarial measure of expense for whatever actuarial expenditure is called for by the pension agreement.

With the new government reporting model there is a further shift to a full accrual basis. The full model analyzes the characteristics of governments and reporting implications, and stresses the importance of identifying the net cost of services, net debt, and capital spending. The following comment from the study illustrates the rationale for full accrual accounting.

> A move towards full accrual accounting and reporting of the consumption of tangible assets supports the new thinking and reorganization of governments in Canada. The current model is a stepping-stone towards the target destination of a reporting model that sees the deferral of expenditures and measurement of the net cost of services as the ultimate goal.[21]

Capital assets

Historically, Canadian governments almost universally reported capital assets on an expenditure basis. There are exceptions for certain types of activities, such as for publicly-owned utilities and other enterprise activities that operate on a cost-recovery basis. There also are differences in the fund bases used, largely reflecting differences in the ways that capital assets are financed. But in general, capital assets were seldom capitalized and are almost never depreciated except in government units that are expected to recover their full cost through user fees, such as an electricity-generating utility.

One of the reasons for this method is that governments did not have or maintain systems that enabled them to report fully on acquired physical assets. The government reporting model states that "when the PASB started looking at the reporting model, many governments did not even have an inventory of their assets. And, without such an inventory, it is very difficult to plan for maintenance and replacement of capital assets in a cost-effective way."[22] PS 1800 recognizes this problem at the local government level: "many local governments do not have adequate financial information to report fully on their acquired physical assets."[23]

20 PSAB 3250 "Employee Pension Obligations," issued March 1995.

21 CICA's "Senior Government Reporting Model," July 2000, p. 19.

22 CICA "20 Questions About Government Financial Reporting," January 2003, p. 20.

LGFR recommended that all capital assets be shown on the balance sheet, regardless of whether or not the initial charge for the asset was to expenditure, and that the source of financing of those assets be shown. However, the *LGFR* study group concluded that depreciation accounting is not appropriate in the general purpose statements. Instead of reporting depreciated amounts, governments should carry their capital assets "at their initially recorded value until they reach the end of their useful economic lives, when they should be written off."[24]

The New Government Reporting Model identifies the following problem when governments use the modified accrual or expenditure basis of accounting:

> Many in the government were concerned that the existing modified accrual or "expenditure" model was creating a bias against spending on capital assets—a bias that was contributing to the "infrastructure deficit" in Canada. Governments needing to balance their budgets found that putting off capital spending was an easy way to meet this objective.

The new reporting model requires the use of "full accrual" accounting. This requires that capital assets are recorded as an asset and the annual expense of owning and using the capital asset is recognized as an expense.

One of the reasons the report cites in support of full accrual accounting is that the presentation of government financial reports on an expense basis would make the information in such reports more understandable to many potential users who are familiar with expense-based accounting as commonly applied in profit-oriented enterprises and non-profit organizations.[25] However, as discussed in Chapter 10, this is an area of disagreement for governments as well as for NPOs.

PS 1200 and 3150 include infrastructure assets (e.g., roads and water mains), heritage assets (e.g., monuments, historic buildings, and works of art), donated assets, and defence assets.

Consolidation and the reporting entity

All governments use fund accounting, wherein a separate self-balancing group of accounts is provided for each program or major operating activity. Resources are allocated by the legislature for specified purposes, and some revenues are specifically designated for special purposes. Governments sometimes issue bonds in order to finance specific capital projects; special tax assessments are levied in order to cover the costs of specified local improvements. Fund accounting therefore is ubiquitous.

Fund *accounting* need not lead to fund-basis *reporting*. Detailed reporting on individual funds causes a multiplicity of statements and an inability to get an overview of the financial condition and operations of the government. While fund-basis accounting is appropriate, financial statements can and should group together the various activities of the government into those activities and programs of similar nature, so that statement users can get some idea about the resource flows associated with the major activities of the government. This is similar to fund accounting using the deferral method of reporting in NPOs, except that the activity groupings may be larger.

23 PSAB 1800, ¶30.

24 *Local Government Financial Reporting* (Toronto: CICA, 1985), p. 24.

25 PSAB 1300 "Financial Reporting Entity," issued August 2003, ¶07.

In Chapter 10, we discussed the problem of defining the reporting entity for non-profit organizations. This problem not only exists for governments as well, but is actually much more severe. PS 1300 addresses the issue in "Financial Reporting Entity" for all levels of government and further guidance is provided in PS 2500—"Basic Principles of Consolidation." In August 2003, the PSAB provided further guidance since new activities and organizational types have arisen since PS 1300 was originally released. Further guidance is provided on applying the criteria of accountability, ownership, and control.

Government activities are carried out through a very complex set of ministries, agencies, Crown corporations, quasi-business enterprises, and non-profit organizations formed by government for the purpose of carrying out parts of government's policies. When financial statements are prepared for a government, which of the many bodies that are directly or indirectly related to the government are to be included in the statements? PS 1300 recommends that the government reporting entity include all organizations that are controlled by government.[26] The definition of the reporting entity excludes those organizations that are instruments of government or that are dependent on government but that are not directly accountable to government. As a result, hospitals and universities would be excluded from the reporting entity.

PS 1300 suggests that control may be indicated by the government:

- having the power to appoint a majority of the members of a governing body
- having access and control over the assets of the organization
- holding the majority of the voting shares, or
- having unilateral power to dissolve the organization.

For example, school boards are a part of local government, but they are usually administered by a separately elected board of trustees that has its own financial responsibility. Consolidation of the school board's financial results with those of the municipality would only decrease the usefulness of the financial statements, because it would be impossible to tell whether excessive expenditure, for example, was the responsibility of the school board or of the city council. Another example is an art gallery that has 11 of its 18 board members appointed by the provincial government. Although the gallery was created by a special act, and although a majority of the board members are appointed by government, the gallery functions completely independently of government. The directors are *appointed* by the province, but they do not *represent* the province.

PS 1300 also addresses the question of how organizations that constitute parts of the reporting entity should be reported in the financial statements. In general, the conclusions of the statement are that (1) investments in entities that are not controlled by the government (portfolio investments) should be reported on the cost basis,[27] (2) investments in business or quasi-business enterprises, such as public utilities or transportation companies, should be reported on a modified equity basis,[28] and (3) the financial statements of all other organizations or agencies that are part of the reporting entity should be consolidated with the government's own financial statements.[29]

---

26 PSAB 1300 "Financial Reporting Entity," issued August 2003, ¶07.

27 *Ibid.*, ¶37.

28 *Ibid.*, ¶35. Under the modified equity method, the net profit or loss of the business enterprise is included in the government's statement of operations (net of dividends or distributions) and is added to the investment account related to that enterprise.

29 *Ibid.*, ¶27.

Restricted assets and revenues

An issue similar to NPOs that we discussed in Chapter 10 is the reporting of restricted assets and revenues. Governments may also have restrictions by external parties or other governments that limit the use of assets or revenues. PS 3100 makes similar distinctions to NPOs between external restrictions that are imposed by an external party and internal restrictions or internally restricted entities. The recommended method for external restrictions is similar to the deferral method of recognizing contributions. PS 3100.11 states "External restrictions should be recognized as revenue in the period in which the resources are used."[30] Internal restrictions or designated assets are treated differently since the government can change its mind through changing legislation. To provide information to the users, disclosure is required of all internal restrictions and designated assets.

Liability measurement

Reporting the liabilities of government is a bigger problem than may be apparent on the surface. The problem starts with those governments that are still reporting on a cash basis; there is not even any measurement of current liabilities. Therefore, the first step is to get cash-basis governments to move to accruing their liabilities.

The second step is the recording of long-term debt. Unlike NPOs, senior governments issue debt instruments, often in very large quantities, which frequently are denominated in foreign currencies. When debt instruments are issued, the proceeds are credited to revenue. PS 1200 and 1800 both recommend that governments should report their "liabilities at the end of the accounting period, segregated by main classification."[31] The debt should be shown as a liability even when the proceeds have been reported as revenue. This is accomplished by means of a debt "group" of accounts that can be consolidated into the balance sheet when the general purpose financial statements are prepared. Further guidance on long-term debt specifying disclosure requirements is provided in PS 3230, "Long-term Debt."

A third type of liability is that of *commitments*. PS 1200 and PS 1700 require that material financial commitments should be disclosed.[32] Specific guidance on pensions is provided in PS 3250.

A fourth type of liability is that of *contingencies*. In particular, senior governments have a habit of guaranteeing others' debts, sometimes as a part of a legislated program such as small business loans or student loans. Contingencies should not be reported as liabilities on the balance sheet, but they should be disclosed.[33] Unfortunately, many governments currently have no record of how much they have guaranteed; recording systems need to be developed to keep track of such commitments and to enable the commitments made by various branches of a government to be brought together for financial reporting purposes.

A unique type of liability is one that is related to solid waste landfill closure costs. PS 3270 requires that "financial statements should recognize a liability for closure and post-closure care as the landfill site capacity is used."[34]

30 PSAB 3100 "Restricted Assets and Revenues," issued June 1997, ¶11.

31 PSAB 1200 ¶41 and PS 1800 ¶25.

32 PSAB 1200 ¶69 and PS 1700 ¶117.

33 PSAB 1200 ¶73 and PS 1700 ¶121.

34 PSAB 3270 "Solid Waste Landfill Closure and Post-Closure Liability," issued Feb. 1998, ¶13.

Other issues

A number of other government reporting issues also are of concern. One issue is the question of whether budgeted amounts should be disclosed in the statement of operations along with the actual results. Budget figures provide a basis of comparison and enable the user to see how effective the government was in controlling expenditures or in achieving anticipated revenue levels. Since the government can amend the budget during the year (thereby making the budget closer to actual), the budget figures should be "those originally planned."[35] This is further supported in the government reporting model[36] that requires "an actual to budget comparison should be provided in the financial statements."[37]

Another issue is that of interfund transfers. Interfund transfers are sometimes reported as revenues to the receiving fund and expenditures to the transferring fund. In some cases, interfund transfers are used as a way of reducing surpluses or creating deficits in general or operating funds (or, conversely, eliminating a deficit). There are many legitimate reasons for interfund transfers, but such transfers should clearly be labelled and should appear on statements of operations. PS 1200 states that revenues should segregate transfers from other governments.[38] In consolidated statements, interfund transfers should be eliminated.[39]

Accounting for loans receivable is an issue because governments often grant forgivable loans or give grants that are repayable under certain circumstances. If a grant is accounted for as a loan receivable, it will not appear as an expenditure on the government's statement of operations; therefore the issue has real impact for measuring a government's surplus or deficit for the period. PS 3050 deals with this issue explicitly, and recommends criteria for determining whether a payment constitutes a loan or an expenditure. Another issue is loans that are provided with significant concessionary terms or where part of the loan is in substance a grant. There is also guidance in establishing when a write-off needs to be made for loan receivables.

SUMMARY OF KEY POINTS

1. Governments have characteristics similar to those of non-profit organizations. The largest difference is that governments have a larger potential user group and a legal reporting requirement to legislatures or city councils.

2. The Public Sector Accounting Board sets the standards in accounting for the public sector. To date, 26 public sector accounting recommendations have been issued in the *CICA Public Sector Accounting Handbook*.

3. The objectives of financial statements for local governments are different than for federal, provincial, and territorial governments due to their diverse set of potential users. Local governments often issue various financial reports in addition to financial statements to meet the specific needs of their user groups.

---

35 PSAB 1200, ¶79.

36 PSAB 1200 "General Standards of Financial Statement Presentation," issued January 2003, ¶128.

37 *Ibid.*, p. 128.

38 PSAB 1200, ¶79.

39 PSAB 2500 "Basic Principle of Consolidation," issued January 2003, ¶06.

4. Four qualitative characteristics of good financial reports for governments are: comparability among governments, consistency between years, completeness, and timeliness.

5. Recommendations issued in the "Senior Government Reporting Model" in January 2003 require four financial statements: statement of financial position; statement of operations; statement of changes in net debt; and statement of cash flow.

6. Governments have reporting issues that are similar to those of an NPO: cash versus accrual; full accrual accounting versus expenditure; capital assets; consolidation; and restricted assets and revenues. The new government reporting model moves towards full accrual accounting. In addition, there are many issues unique to the government—e.g., forgivable loans and liabilities related to solid waste landfill closure costs.

REVIEW QUESTIONS

11–1 How does the primary user group for government financial statements differ from that for NPO financial statements?

11–2 What is the Public Sector Accounting Board? What is its role?

11–3 Are government auditors required to report in accordance with the PSAB's recommendations?

11–4 Who controls municipal government reporting practices?

11–5 What types of financial statements does the government reporting model recommend for senior governments?

11–6 What are the advantages of the government reporting on a modified accrual or accrual basis compared to a cash flow basis?

11–7 What problems are encountered by governments in capitalizing and depreciating capital assets?

11–8 How does the expenditure basis of accounting discourage reinvestment in long-lived assets?

11–9 Distinguish between fund *accounting* and fund *reporting*.

11–10 Why is it difficult to determine the governmental reporting entity?

11–11 How does the PSAB recommend the reporting entity be defined?

11–12 Explain why liability measurement is so much more of a problem for governments than it is for NPOs and businesses.

11–13 How should interfund transfers be reported?

11–14 What is a forgivable loan?

CASES

CASE 11–1   Province of Majestic Lakes

You are a staff member in the Finance department for the Province of Majestic Lakes. You have just completed a meeting with a new member of the provincial legislature. As part of the background material in preparing for this position, the member had been provided with a detailed reading on the "New Government Reporting Model." The council member came to you and asked for a quick written briefing on the following questions:

- What characteristics are unique for governments and what are the reporting implications?
- What are the five key messages in the model?
- What are the required financial statements and what are they like?
- What key information should I look for in each of the statements?
- What is the key impact of the change to "accrual" accounting?
- Why is it important to have a comparison with budgeted numbers?
- Why is it important to account for capital assets?

Required:

Provide the requested briefing for the member.

CASE 11–2   Comparison of Objectives

William Witherspoon III is executive vice-president of Marble Industries Ltd., a publicly held industrial company. Mr. Witherspoon has just been elected to the city council of Turnwater, a major industrial city. Prior to assuming office as a city councillor, he asks you, as his accountant, to explain the major differences that exist in accounting and financial reporting for a large city when compared to a large industrial corporation.

Required:

Describe the major differences that exist in the purpose of accounting and financial reporting and in the types of reports of a large city when compared to a large industrial corporation.

[CGA–Canada]

Solutions to Self-Study Problems

SSP2–1

Worksheet Method
Archie Corp. Consolidation Worksheet

| | Trial balances | | | Archie Corp. |
	Archie Corp. Dr/(Cr)	Bunker Ltd. Dr/(Cr)	Adjustments Dr/(Cr)	consolidated trial balance*
Cash and current receivables	$ 200,000	$ 400,000	$ (80,000) **b**	$ 320,000
			(200,000) **c**	
Inventories	900,000	500,000		1,400,000
Furniture, fixtures, and equipment (net)	2,000,000	1,700,000		3,700,000
Buildings under capital leases (net)	6,000,000	3,000,000		9,000,000
Investment in Bunker Ltd. (at cost)	1,000,000	—	(1,000,000) **a**	—
Current liabilities	(1,500,000)	(400,000)	80,000 **b**	(1,620,000)
			200,000 **c**	
Long-term liabilities	(4,000,000)	(2,000,000)		(6,000,000)
Common shares	(1,500,000)	(1,000,000)	1,000,000 **a**	(1,500,000)
Retained earnings, December 31, 2005	(2,100,000)	(1,600,000)		(3,700,000)
Dividends declared	2,000,000	500,000	(500,000) **d**	2,000,000
Sales revenue	(13,000,000)	(5,000,000)	4,000,000 **e**	(14,000,000)
Dividend income	(500,000)	—	500,000 **d**	—
Cost of sales	7,000,000	3,200,000	(4,000,000) **e**	6,200,000
Other expenses	3,500,000	700,000		4,200,000
	$ —	$ —	$ —	$ —

*The balance sheet and income statement must be prepared from the amounts in this column.
This worksheet does **not** constitute a set of financial statements!

Direct Method
Archie Corp. Consolidated Financial Statements

Balance Sheet
December 31, 2006

Assets

Current assets:

Cash and current receivables [200,000 + 400,000 – **80,000 – 200,000**]	$	320,000
Inventories [900,000 + 500,000]		1,400,000
		1,720,000

Property, plant, and equipment:

Furniture, fixtures, and equipment, net of accumulated depreciation [2,000,000 + 1,700,000]	3,700,000
Buildings under capital leases, net of related amortization [6,000,000 + 3,000,000]	9,000,000
	12,700,000

Other assets:

Investment in Bunker Ltd. [1,000,000 – 1,000,000]	—
Total assets	$14,420,000

Liabilities and shareholders' equity

Liabilities:

Current liabilities [1,500,000 + 400,000 – **80,000 – 200,000**]	$	1,620,000
Long-term liabilities [4,000,000 + 2,000,000]		6,000,000
		7,620,000

Shareholders' equity:

Common shares [1,500,000 + 1,000,000 – 1,000,000]	1,500,000
Retained earnings [3,100,000 + 2,200,000]	5,300,000
	6,800,000
Total liabilities and shareholders' equity	$14,420,000

Statement of Income and Retained Earnings
Year Ended December 31, 2006

Sales revenue [13,000,000 + 5,000,000 – **4,000,000**]	$14,000,000
Dividend income [500,000 – **500,000**]	—
	14,000,000

Operating expenses:

Cost of sales [7,000,000 + 3,200,000 – **4,000,000**]	6,200,000
Other operating expenses [3,500,000 + 700,000]	4,200,000
	10,400,000
Net income	$ 3,600,000
Retained earnings, December 31, 2005 [2,100,000 + 1,600,000]	3,700,000
Dividends declared [2,000,000 + 500,000 – **500,000**]	(2,000,000)
Retained earnings, December 31, 2006	$ 5,300,000

SSP 3–1

Analysis of Fair Value of Net Assets Acquired:

	Book value	Fair value	Fair value increment		% share		FVI acquired
Cash and cash equivalents	$ 1,200,000	$ 1,200,000	$ —	×	100%	=	$ —
Accounts receivable	1,800,000	1,800,000	—	×	100%	=	—
Machinery and equipment, net	8,400,000	11,000,000	2,600,000	×	100%	=	2,600,000
Deferred development costs	3,100,000	4,000,000	900,000	×	100%	=	900,000
Accounts payable	(1,100,000)	(1,100,000)	—	×	100%	=	—
Notes payable, long-term	(1,000,000)	(900,000)	100,000	×	100%	=	100,000
	$12,400,000	$16,000,000	$3,600,000				$3,600,000

1. Direct Purchase of Blue's Net Assets for $20,000,000:

	Ace's book value	+ FV of Blue assets acq'd	+ Cost of purchase =	Ace balance sheet after purchase
Cash and cash equivalents	$ 2,350,000	$ 1,200,000	$ (2,000,000)	$ 1,550,000
Accounts receivable	2,000,000	1,800,000		3,800,000
Land	5,000,000	—		5,000,000
Machinery and equipment, net	13,500,000	11,000,000		24,500,000
Deferred development costs	600,000	4,000,000		4,600,000
Goodwill*		4,000,000		4,000,000
				$43,450,000
Accounts payable	(650,000)	(1,100,000)		$ 1,750,000
Notes payable, long-term	(2,000,000)	(900,000)	(18,000,000)	20,900,000
Common shares	(15,000,000)			15,000,000
Retained earnings	(5,800,000)			5,800,000
	$ —	$20,000,000	$(20,000,000)	$43,450,000

* 20,000,000 purchase price – 16,000,000 fair value of net assets = 4,000,000 goodwill

2. Purchase of 100% of Blue's shares by issuance of Ace shares worth $20,000,000:

	Ace's book value	Blue's book value	Adjustments	Ace consolidated balance sheet
Cash and cash equivalents	$ 2,350,000	$ 1,200,000		$ 3,550,000
Accounts receivable	2,000,000	1,800,000		3,800,000
Land	5,000,000	—		5,000,000
Machinery and equipment, net	13,500,000	8,400,000	2,600,000	24,500,000
Investment in Blue*	20,000,000		(20,000,000)	—
Deferred development costs	600,000	3,100,000	900,000	4,600,000
Goodwill			4,000,000	4,000,000
				$45,450,000
Accounts payable	(650,000)	(1,100,000)		$ 1,750,000
Notes payable, long-term	(2,000,000)	(1,000,000)	100,000	2,900,000
Common shares*	(35,000,000)	(6,950,000)	6,950,000	35,000,000
Retained earnings	(5,800,000)	(5,450,000)	5,450,000	5,800,000
	$ —	$ —	$ —	$45,450,000

*These accounts are **after** recording the purchase of Blue's shares. The common shares account is increased by 400,000 × $50 = $20,000,000

3. Purchase of 100% of Blue's shares by shares and cash worth $14,500,000:

Note: In this scenario, the purchase price is less than the fair value of Blue's net assets.
Therefore, negative goodwill is $1,500,000.
Negative goodwill is offset against the intangible asset with no observable market value.

	Ace's book value*	Blue's book value	Adjustments	Ace consolidated balance sheet
Cash and cash equivalents*	$ 1,350,000	$ 1,200,000		$ 2,550,000
Accounts receivable	2,000,000	1,800,000		3,800,000
Land	5,000,000	—		5,000,000
Machinery and equipment, net	13,500,000	8,400,000	2,600,000	24,500,000
Investment in Blue*	14,500,000		(14,500,000)	—
Deferred development costs	600,000	3,100,000	{ 900,000	3,100,000
[Negative goodwill]			{ (1,500,000)	
				$38,950,000
Accounts payable	(650,000)	(1,100,000)		$ 1,750,000
Notes payable, long-term	(2,000,000)	(1,000,000)	100,000	2,900,000
Common shares*	(28,500,000)	(6,950,000)	6,950,000	28,500,000
Retained earnings	(5,800,000)	(5,450,000)	5,450,000	5,800,000
	$ —	$ —	$ —	$38,950,000

*These accounts are **after** recording the purchase of Blue's shares. Cash is reduced by $1,000,000;
Common shares is increased by $270,000 x $50 = $13,500,000; Investment in Blue is increased by $14,500,000.

SSP4–1

Analysis of the purchase transaction:

Purchase price		$10,000,000
Net assets acquired:		
Book value of Subco's net assets	7,000,000	
Fair value increment on buildings	1,400,000	
		8,400,000
Goodwill		$ 1,600,000

a. Consolidated net income:

Separate-entity net incomes:		
Parco	$ 680,000	
Subco	350,000	
		$ 1,030,000
Adjustments:		
Eliminate dividend income from Subco	(150,000)	
Unrealized profit from upstream sales [200,000 × 20%]	(40,000)	
Amortization of fair value increment [1,400,000/14]	(100,000)	
		(290,000)
Consolidated net income, year ended December 31, 2005		$ 740,000

b. Consolidated retained earnings:

	Parco	Subco	Consolidated
Separate-entity retained earnings, January 1, 2005	$3,450,000	$ 1,250,000	
Separate-entity net incomes for 2005	680,000	350,000	
Dividends declared in 2005	(200,000)	(150,000)	
Book value of retained earnings, December 31, 2005	$3,930,000	$ 1,450,000	$5,380,000
Consolidation adjustments:			
Eliminate Subco date-of-acquisition retained earnings			(1,250,000)
Unrealized profit from upstream sales [200,000 × 20%]			(40,000)
Amortization of fair value increment [1,400,000/14]			(100,000)
			(1,390,000)
Consolidated retained earnings, December 31, 2005			$3,990,000

c. Parco's equity-basis earnings in Subco

Subco's unadjusted separate-entity net income		$350,000
Equity-basis adjustments:		
Unrealized profit from upstream sales [200,000 x 20%]	$ (40,000)	
Amortization of fair value increment [1,400,000/14]	(100,000)	
		(140,000)
Subco's adjusted equity-basis earnings		$ 210,000

SSP4–2

Analysis of the purchase transaction:

Purchase price   **$1,084,000**

	Book value	Fair value	Fair value increment	% share	FVI acquired	
Cash	$ 80,000	$ 80,000	—			
Accounts receivable	99,000	99,000	—			
Inventory	178,000	195,000	$ 17,000 × 100% =		$ 17,000	
Property, plant, and equipment	800,000	740,000	140,000 × 100% =		140,000	
Accumulated depreciation	(200,000)	—				
Accounts payable	(70,000)	(70,000)	—			
Long-term liabilities	(200,000)	(200,000)				
Total fair value increment			$157,000 × 100% =		$157,000	**157,000**
Net asset book value	$687,000			× 100% =		**687,000**
Fair value of assets acquired		$844,000				**844,000**
Goodwill						**$ 240,000**

Consolidated Financial Statements (direct method)

Statement of Income and Retained Earnings
Year Ended December 31, 2009

Sales revenue [1,200,000 + 987,000 − **390,000** − **150,000**]	$1,647,000
Cost of goods sold [800,000 + 650,000 − **390,000** − **150,000** −**12,000** + **(90,000 × 20%) + (50,000 × 40%)**]	936,000
Gross profit	711,000
Other operating expenses [235,000 + 147,000 **+ 210,000 + 14,000**]	606,000
Net income	105,000
Retained earnings, December 31, 2008 [1,153,000 + 330,000 − **437,000** **−17,000 − 12,000 − (140,000/10 × 2)**]	989,000
Retained earnings, December 31, 2009	$1,094,000

Balance Sheet
December 31, 2009

Assets

Current assets:

Cash [120,000 + 110,000]	$ 230,000
Accounts receivable [150,000 + 135,000]	285,000
Inventory [240,000 + 195,000 − **(90,000 × 20%) − (50,000 × 40%)**]	397,000
	912,000
Property, plant, and equipment [1,400,000 + 910,000 − **60,000** − **210,000**]	2,040,000
Accumulated depreciation [510,000 + 320,000 − **200,000** + **(140,000/10 × 3)**]	(672,000)
	1,368,000
Goodwill [76,000 **+ 240,000**]	316,000
Total assets	$2,596,000

Liabilities and shareholders' equity

Liabilities:

Accounts payable (current) [142,000 + 60,000]	$ 202,000
Long-term notes payable [600,000 + 200,000]	800,000
	1,002,000

Shareholders' equity:

Common shares	500,000
Retained earnings [1,318,000 + 520,000 – **437,000 – 17,000 – 210,000** **–(90,000 × 20%) – (50,000 × 40%) – (140,000/10 × 3)**]	1,094,000
	1,594,000
Total liabilities and shareholders' equity	$2,596,000

Consolidation Worksheet: Dr./(Cr.)

	Trial balances		Acquisition	Adjustments Operations Cumulative	Current	Purchase Ltd. consolidated trial balance
	Parent Ltd.	Sub. Inc.				
Cash	$120,000	$110,000				$230,000
Accounts receivable	150,000	135,000				285,000
Inventories	240,000	195,000			(18,000) **c2**	397,000
					(20,000) **c4**	
Property, plant & equipment	1,400,000	910,000	(60,000) **a**		(210,000) **c5**	2,040,000
Accumulated depreciation	(510,000)	(320,000)	200,000 **a**	(28,000) **b2**	(14,000) **c6**	(672,000)
Investments (at cost)	1,084,000		(1,084,000) **a**			—
Goodwill	76,000		240,000 **a**			316,000
Accounts payable	(142,000)	(60,000)				(202,000)
Long-term notes payable	(600,000)	(200,000)				(800,000)
Common shares	(500,000)	(250,000)	250,000 **a**			(500,000)
Retained earnings, December 31, 2008	(1,153,000)	(330,000)	437,000 **a** 17,000 **a**	12,000 **b1** 28,000 **b2**		(989,000)
Sales	(1,200,000)	(987,000)			390,000 **c1** 150,000 **c3**	(1,647,000)
Cost of sales	800,000	650,000		(12,000) **b1**	(390,000) **c1** (150,000) **c3** 18,000 **c2** 20,000 **c4**	936,000
Other operating expenses	235,000	147,000			210,000 **c5** 14,000 **c6**	606,000
	$ —	$ —	$ —	$ —	$ —	$ —

Notes:

a1. The inventory on date of acquisition is assumed to have been sold. Therefore, the FVI on inventory has passed through cost of sales and is now in retained earnings.

a2. The $140,000 FVI on PP&E is recognized by eliminating Subsidiary's accumulated depreciation of $200,000 and by reducing the asset account by $60,000. The net effect is to increase net book value by $140,000.

b. The cumulative operations adjustments include two years' amortization of FV and the unrealized profit in Parent's 2009 *beginning* inventory.

SSP5–1

Analysis of the purchase transaction:

Purchase price   **$150,000**

	Book value	Fair value	Fair value increment (decrement)	% share	FVI acquired	
Cash	$ 10,000	$ 10,000	—			
Accounts & other receivables	20,000	20,000	—			
Inventories	30,000	30,000	—			
Land	45,000	80,000	$ 35,000 ×	60% =	$21,000	
Buildings	150,000	130,000	(20,000) ×	60% =	(12,000)	
Accumulated depreciation	(50,000)	—	50,000 ×	60% =	30,000	
Equipment	130,000	10,000	(120,000) ×	60% =	(72,000)	
Accumulated depreciation	(80,000)	—	80,000 ×	60% =	48,000	
Accounts payable	(40,000)	(40,000)	—			
Long-term liabilities	(50,000)	(50,000)	—			
Total fair value increment			$ 25,000 ×	60% =	$15,000	**15,000**
Net asset book value	$165,000			× 60% =		**99,000**
Fair value of net assets acquired		$190,000		× 60% =		**114,000**
Goodwill						**$ 36,000**

Notes:

1. The net fair value increment acquired for buildings works out to $18,000, as follows:

60% of buildings carrying value: $150,000 × 60%	$ 90,000
less 60% of accumulated depreciation: $50,000 × 60%	(30,000)
	60,000
60% of fair value: $130,000 × 60%	78,000
Net fair value increment of buildings acquired	$ 18,000

2. The net fair value decrement acquired for equipment is $24,000, as follows:

60% of equipment carrying value: $130,000 x 60%	$ 78,000
less 60% of accumulated depreciation: $80,000 x 60%	(48,000)
	30,000
60% of fair value: $10,000 × 60%	6,000
Net fair value (decrement) of equipment acquired	$(24,000)

These amounts are necessary for the solution, under both the direct approach and the worksheet approach.

Consolidated Balance Sheet (direct method)
January 10, 2005

Assets

Current assets:

Cash [50,000 + 10,000]	$ 60,000
Accounts and other receivables [70,000 + 20,000]	90,000
Inventories [80,000 + 30,000]	110,000
	260,000

Capital assets:

Land [0 + 45,000 **+ 21,000**]	66,000
Buildings [260,000 + 150,000 **– 50,000 + 18,000**]	378,000
Accumulated depreciation [40,000 + 50,000 **– 50,000**]	(40,000)
Equipment [175,000 + 130,000 **– 80,000 – 24,000**]	201,000
Accumulated depreciation [70,000 + 80,000 **– 80,000**]	(70,000)
	535,000
Goodwill [**150,000 – (190,000 × 40%)**]	36,000
Total assets	$831,000

Liabilities and shareholders' equity

Liabilities:

Accounts payable (current) [80,000 + 40,000]	$120,000
Long-term liabilities [0 + 50,000]	50,000
	170,000
Non-controlling interest [**165,000 × 40%**]	66,000

Shareholders' equity:

Common shares [220,000 **+ 150,000**]	370,000
Retained earnings	225,000
	595,000
Total liabilities and shareholders' equity	$831,000

Consolidation Worksheet

	Trial balances		Acquisition adjustment		Consolidated trial balance
	Regina	**Dakota**			
Cash	50,000	10,000			60,000
Accounts receivable	70,000	20,000			90,000
Inventories	80,000	30,000			110,000
Land	—	45,000	21,000	**a2**	66,000
Buildings	260,000	150,000	(32,000)	**a2**	378,000
Accumulated depreciation	(40,000)	(50,000)	50,000	**a2**	(40,000)
Equipment	175,000	130,000	(104,000)	**a2**	201,000
Accumulated depreciation	(70,000)	(80,000)	80,000	**a2**	(70,000)
Investments (at cost)	150,000		(99,000)	**a1** ⎫	—
			(51,000)	**a2** ⎭	
Goodwill			36,000	**a2**	36,000
Non-controlling interest			(66,000)	**a1**	(66,000)
Accounts payable	(80,000)	(40,000)			(120,000)
Long-term liabilities	—	(50,000)			(50,000)
Common shares	(370,000)	(100,000)	100,000	**a1**	(370,000)
Retained earnings	(225,000)	(65,000)	65,000	**a1**	(225,000)

SSP5–2

Regina Ltd.

Consolidated Statement of Income and Retained Earnings (direct method)
Year Ended December 31, 2005

Sales [2,000,000 + 1,000,000 – **600,000**]	$2,400,000
Dividend income [24,000 + 0 – **24,000**]	—
Other income [7,000 + 0 – **2,500**]	4,500
	2,404,500
Cost of sales [1,000,000 + 600,000 – **600,000** + 40,000 + 20,000]	1,060,000
Other operating expenses [886,000 + 280,000 **+ 1,800 – 4,800**]	1,163,000
Interest expense [2,000 + 10,000 – **2,500**]	9,500
Non-controlling interest in earnings [(**110,000 – 40,000**) × **40%**]	28,000
	2,260,500
Net income	144,000
Retained earnings, December 31, 2004	225,000
Dividends declared [20,000 + 40,000 – **40,000**]	(20,000)
Retained earnings, December 31, 2005	$ 349,000

Consolidated Balance Sheet
December 31, 2005

Assets

Current assets:	
Cash [28,000 + 10,000]	$ 38,000
Accounts and other receivables [110,000 + 30,000 – **50,000 – 2,500**]	87,500
Inventories [160,000 + 60,000 – **40,000 – 20,000**]	160,000
	285,500
Capital assets:	
Land [0 + 135,000 **+ 21,000**]	156,000
Buildings [300,000 + 150,000 – **50,000 + 18,000**]	418,000
Accumulated depreciation [45,000 + 60,000 – **50,000 + 1,800**]	(56,800)
Equipment [200,000 + 130,000 – **80,000 – 24,000**]	226,000
Accumulated depreciation [80,000 + 90,000 – **80,000 – 4,800**]	(85,200)
	658,000
Goodwill	36,000
Total assets	$ 979,500

Liabilities and shareholders' equity

Liabilities:	
Accounts payable (current) [40,000 + 80,000 – **50,000 – 2,500**]	$ 67,500
Long-term liabilities [65,000 + 50,000]	115,000
	182,500
Non-controlling interest [(**235,000 – 40,000**) × **40%**]	78,000
Shareholders' equity:	
Common shares	370,000
Retained earnings [348,000 + 135,000 – **65,000– (70,000 × 40%)** **– (40,000 × 60%) – 20,000 + 4,800 – 1,800**]	349,000
	719,000
Total liabilities and shareholders' equity	$ 979,500

Consolidation Worksheet—Regina Ltd.

	Regina	Dakota	Adjustments Acquisition	Adjustments Operations	Consolidated trial balance
Cash	28,000	10,000			38,000
Accounts and other receivables	110,000	30,000		(52,500) **c4**	87,500
Inventories	160,000	60,000		(40,000) **c2**	160,000
				(20,000) **c3**	
Land	—	135,000	21,000 **a2**		156,000
Buildings	300,000	150,000	(32,000) **a2**		418,000
Accumulated depreciation	(45,000)	(60,000)	50,000 **a2**	(1,800) **c6**	(56,800)
Equipment	200,000	130,000	(104,000) **a2**		226,000
Accumulated depreciation	(80,000)	(90,000)	80,000 **a2**	4,800 **c7**	(85,200)
Investments (at cost)	150,000		(99,000) **a1**		—
			(51,000) **a2**		
Goodwill			36,000 **a2**		36,000
Accounts payable	(40,000)	(80,000)		52,500 **c4**	(67,500)
Long-term liabilities	(65,000)	(50,000)			(115,000)
Non-controlling interest			(66,000) **a1**	16,000 **c8**	(78,000)
				(28,000) **c9**	
Common shares	(370,000)	(100,000)	100,000 **a1**		(370,000)
Retained earnings	(225,000)	(65,000)	65,000 **a1**		(225,000)
Dividends declared	20,000	40,000		(40,000) **c8**	20,000
Sales	(2,000,000)	(1,000,000)		600,000 **c1**	(2,400,000)
Dividend income	(24,000)	—		24,000 **c8**	—
Other income	(7,000)	—		2,500 **c5**	(4,500)
Cost of sales	1,000,000	600,000		(600,000) **c1**	1,060,000
				40,000 **c2**	
				20,000 **c3**	
Other operating expenses	886,000	280,000		1,800 **c6**	1,163,000
				(4,800) **c7**	
Interest expense	2,000	10,000		(2,500) **c5**	9,500
Non-controlling interest in earnings				28,000 **c9**	28,000
	$ —	$ —	$ —	$ —	$ —

Operations adjustments:

c1 Eliminate intercompany sales, $400,000 upstream + $200,000 downstream

c2 Upstream unrealized profit, $100,000 × 40% gross margin = $40,000

c3 Downstream unrealized profit, $40,000 × 50% gross margin = $20,000

c4 Eliminate intercompany loan receivable and payable (1 year = current) + 1/2 year accrued interest

c5 Eliminate intercompany interest revenue and expense, $50,000 × 10% × 1/2 = $2,500

c6 Amortize FVI on building, $18,000/10 = $1,800

c7 Amortize FV *decrement* on equipment, $24,000/5 = $4,800

c8 Eliminate Dakota's dividend payments

c9 Non-controlling interest's share of Dakota's earnings, ($110,000 − $40,000) × 40% = $28,000

SSP5–3

Analysis of the purchase transaction: see the solution to SSP5-1.

1. Non-controlling interest in earnings:

Dakota's separate-entity net income for 2006 (Exhibit 5-17)	$130,000
Plus unrealized upstream profit in opening inventory:	
$100,000 × 40% gross margin	40,000
Less unrealized upstream profit in ending inventory:	
$160,000 sales × 50% remaining in inventory × 40% gross margin	(32,000)
Adjusted Regina net income	138,000
Non-controlling interest share	× 40%
	$ 55,200

2. Non-controlling interest:

Dakota's shareholders' equity, December 31, 2006 (Exhibit 5-17)	$305,000
Less unrealized upstream profit at year-end:	
Ending inventory, $160,000 × 50% × 40% gross margin	(32,000)
	273,000
Non-controlling interest share	× 40%
	$109,200

3. Consolidated retained earnings:

Regina's separate-entity retained earnings,		
December 31, 2005 (Exhibit 5-17)		$348,000
Dakota's retained earnings, December 31, 2005	$205,000	
Less Dakota's retained earnings at date of acquisition	(65,000)	
Change in Dakota's retained earnings since acquisition	140,000	
Regina's ownership share	× 60%	
Regina's share of Dakota's cumulative earnings		84,000
Less unrealized profits at December 31, 2006:		
Upstream: $160,000 × 50% × 40% gross margin × 60% share		(19,200)
Downstream: $40,000 × 50% gross margin		(20,000)
Amortization of FVI:		
Less Building ($18,000 ÷ 10 × 2)	$ (3,600)	
Plus Equipment (−$24,000 ÷ 5 × 2)	9,600	6,000
Regina consolidated retained earnings		$398,800

SSP5–3 Alternate Solution

3. Consolidated retained earnings

Total retained earnings (398,000 + 205,000)	$553,000
Less Dakota's R/E at acquisition date	65,000
Regina's share of Dakota's cumulative earnings since acquisition	
(205,000 − 65,000) × 40%	56,000
Less 60% of upstream sales $160,000 × 50% × 40% gross margin	19,200
Less 100% of downstream sales $40,000 × 50% gross margin	20,000
Amortization of FVI:	
Less building ($18,000/10 × 2)	3,600
Plus equipment (−$24,000/5 × 2)	9,600
Regina's consolidated retained earnings	$398,800

SSP5–4

Essentially, this problem requires that the balance of the investment account be determined at January 1, 2009, prior to the sale of part of the investment. The FVI and goodwill (if any) must be determined at each of the two purchase dates. The fact that the purchases are in midyear is not a problem; the year-to-date net income is simply included as part of the net book value (i.e., as retained earnings on acquisition). The two purchases can be analyzed as follows:

July 1, 2007 purchase (30%):

Purchase price	$312,500
Subco net fair value acquired: $875,000 × 30%	262,500
Subco net book value acquired: $875,000 × 30%	262,500

There is no *net* fair value increment, because the inventory FVI is offset completely by the capital asset fair value decrement:

Inventory fair value increment: $50,000 × 30%	$ 15,000
Capital asset fair value decrement: $(50,000) × 30%	(15,000)
Net fair value increment (decrement)	$ 0

The entire purchase price discrepancy of $50,000 is allocated to goodwill. The FVI on inventory will flow through to earnings in two months (i.e., a "six times" inventory turnover rate) and the capital asset FVD will be amortized over 10 years at $1,500 per year (as a *reduction* in amortization expense).

September 1, 2008 (15%):

Purchase price	$183,500
Subco net fair value acquired: $1,290,000 × 15%	193,500
Subco net book value acquired: $1,100,000 × 15%	165,000

Fair value increments total to $28,500:

Inventory fair value increment: $10,000 × 15%	$ 1,500
Capital asset fair value increment: $180,000 × 15%	27,000
Net fair value increment (decrement)	$ 28,500

However, the net fair value acquired is higher than the purchase price. Negative goodwill of $10,000 exists. The fair value increments must be reduced by $10,000 to fully absorb the negative goodwill. Any one of three approaches can be used:

1. Eliminate the FVI on inventory and reduce the FVI on capital assets to $18,500.

2. Reduce the FVI on both inventory and capital assets proportionately, to 185/285 of their full fair value.

3. Leave the inventory FVI at $1,500 and reduce the capital asset FVI by $10,000, to $17,000.

Each approach will yield a different result, but all will be "correct." In practice, the choice will depend on Parco's financial reporting objectives. We will use the third approach in the remainder of this solution.

After the two purchases have been analyzed, the balance in the equity-basis investment account can be determined as of the date of the sale, January 1, 2009. The balance is $562,183, as shown in Exhibit 5–26.

When Parco sells 4,000 of its 9,000 shares, the investment account must be reduced by 4/9. The difference between the sale proceeds and the proportionate carrying value of the investment is the gain or loss to Parco:

Proceeds from selling 4,000 Subco shares	$300,000
Carrying value of portion sold: $562,183 × 4/9	249,859
Gain on sale	$ 50,141

Exhibit 5–26 Calculation of Investment Account Balance, Equity Method

July 1, 2007, acquisition purchase price	$312,500
Subco earnings for remainder of 2003: $100,000 × 30%	30,000
FVI on inventory	− 15,000
1/2 year amortization on capital asset FV decrement	750
Balance, December 31, 2007	**$328,250**
September 1, 2008, acquisition purchase price	183,500
Subco earnings for 2008:	
$125,000 × 30% for first eight months	37,500
$30,000 × 45% for last four months	13,500
Amortization:	
Inventory flow-through, second purchase	− 1,500
Capital assets, first purchase (FV decrement)	1,500
Capital assets, second purchase (FV increment)	− 567
Balance, December 31, 2008	**$562,183**

SSP6–1

Note: This is a *downstream* sale; minority interest is not affected, except by the gain from sale as scrap in 2016.

2007:

Sales	100,000	
Cost of sales		60,000
Equipment		40,000
Accumulated depreciation	2,000	
Depreciation expense (40,000 ÷ 10 × 1/2 year)		2,000

2008:

Retained earnings [40,000 − (40,000 ÷ 10 × 1/2 year)]	38,000	
Accumulated depreciation	2,000	
Equipment		40,000
Accumulated depreciation	4,000	
Depreciation expense (40,000 ÷ 10)		4,000

2012:

Retained earnings [40,000 − (40,000 ÷ 10 × 4.5 years)]	22,000	
Accumulated depreciation	18,000	
Equipment		40,000
Accumulated depreciation	4,000	
Depreciation expense		4,000

2019:

Accumulated depreciation	40,000	
Equipment		40,000

2020:

Non-controlling interest in earnings	200	
Non-controlling interest		200

SSP6–2

a. Consolidated income statement:

Power Corporation
Consolidated Income Statement
Year Ended December 31, 2009

Sales (2,000,000 + 900,000 − 400,000 − 250,000)	$2,250,000
Investment income (1,000,000 + 100,000 − 32,000)	1,068,000
Gain on sale of land (68,000 − 68,000)	—
Total revenues	3,318,000
Cost of goods sold (see below)	1,143,000
Other operating expenses (see below)	1,288,000
Non-controlling interest in earnings of Spencer Corporation	35,600
Total expenses	2,466,600
Net income	$ 851,400

Purchase transaction (January 1, 2005):

80% of net book value acquired ($3,000,000 × 80%)	$2,400,000
Fair value decrements:	
Building ($600,000 × 80%)	− 480,000
Long-term liabilities ($500,000 × 80%)	+ 400,000
Fair value of net assets acquired	2,320,000
Purchase price	2,500,000
Goodwill	$ 180,000

Cost of goods sold:

As reported:	
Power	$1,300,000
Spencer	+ 500,000
Less intercompany sales, 2009:	
Downstream	− 400,000
Upstream	− 250,000
Less realized profit, beginning inventories:	
Downstream (100,000 × 30%)	− 30,000
Upstream (70,000 × 40%)	− 28,000
Plus unrealized profit, ending inventories:	
Downstream (90,000 × 30%)	+ 27,000
Upstream (60,000 × 40%)	+ 24,000
Consolidated cost of sales	$1,143,000

Other operating expenses:

As reported:	
Power	$ 960,000
Spencer	320,000
Depreciation on unrealized loss on sale of machine	1,280,000
([210,000 − (15/20 × 400,000)] ÷ 15)	+ 6,000
Additional amortization:	
FV decrement on building (480,000 ÷ 10)	− 48,000
FV decrement on long-term liabilities (400,000 ÷ 8)	+ 50,000
Consolidated other operating expenses	$1,288,000

Non-controlling interest in earnings of Spencer:

Spencer's separate-entity net income, as reported (Exhibit 6-10)	$ 248,000
Adjustments for intercompany upstream profits:	
Unrealized profit from intercompany sale of land	– 68,000
Realized from beginning inventory (70,000 × 40%)	+ 28,000
Unrealized in ending inventory (60,000 × 40%)	– 24,000
Machine [210,000 – (15/20 × 400,000) ÷ 15]	– 6,000
Spencer net income adjusted for realized and unrealized profits	$ 178,000
Non-controlling interest's share	× 20%
Non-controlling interest in earnings of Spencer	$ 35,600

b. Check via equity-basis income:

Power Corporation separate-entity net income		$740,000
Equity in earnings of Spencer Corporation:		
Spencer separate-entity net income (248,000 × 80%)	$ 198,400	
Unrealized upstream profit from land sale (68,000 × 80%)	– 54,400	
Unrealized downstream profit, ending (90,000 × 30%)	– 27,000	
Unrealized upstream profit, ending (60,000 × 40% × 80%)	– 19,200	
Realized downstream profit, beginning (100,000 × 30%)	+ 30,000	
Realized upstream profit, beginning (70,000 × 40% × 80%)	+ 22,400	
Under-depreciation on intercompany sale of machine (6,000 × 80%)	– 4,800	
Amortization of FV decrement on building (480,000 ÷ 10)	+ 48,000	
Amortization of FVD on long-term liabilities (400,000 ÷ 8)	– 50,000	
Spencer adjusted net income		$143,400
Less dividends received from Spencer (40,000 × 80%)		– 32,000
Consolidated net income		$851,400

SSP6–3

a. The total available votes and Numbers' share thereof are as follows:

	Total available votes			Numbers Inc.'s votes		
Class	Shares outstanding	Votes per share	Total votes	Shares held	Votes per share	Total votes
A	600,000	1	600,000	40,000	1	40,000
B	50,000	15	750,000	44,000	15	660,000
	650,000		1,350,000	84,000		700,000

Numbers Incorporated owns 700,000 ÷ 1,350,000 = 51.85% of the votes, and therefore controls 212°F Corporation.

b. The ownership share for consolidation purposes (or for equity-basis earnings) is the proportion of residual earnings that accrues to Numbers. Preferred shares are a prior claim, and therefore do not participate in residual earnings. The two classes of common shareholders participate equally in earnings. Therefore, Numbers' ownership share is simply the investor's proportionate share of the total shares outstanding: 84,000 ÷ 650,000 = 12.923%.

c. The amount of the non-controlling interest is the sum of the preferred share redemption value (call price) plus 87.077% of the residual shareholders' equity after deducting the prior claim of the preferred shares:

Preferred shares:

1,000,000 shares × $12 per share call price		$ 12,000,000
Residual common equity:		
Total 212°F shareholders' equity	$125,000,000	
Less preferred share redemption value	− 12,000,000	
Residual common equity	113,000,000	
Non-controlling interest percentage	× 87.077%	98,397,010
Non-controlling interest amount		$110,397,010

SSP6–4

The $500,000 face value bonds were purchased by Passion for $479,000, a discount of $21,000. The discount will be amortized by Passion over the six years remaining to maturity at $3,500 per year. On Sweetness's books, the original issue discount (which also is $21,000) will be amortized over 10 years at $2,100 per year. Over the life of the bonds, the book value of the $500,000 bonds on the issuing (Sweetness, the subsidiary) and investing (Passion, the parent) companies' books will be as follows:

	Sweetness	Passion
Original issue price, January 1, 2005	$479,000	
4 years' accumulated amortization	8,400	
Book value, December 31, 2008	487,400	
Purchase price, December 31, 2008		$479,000
2 years' amortization	4,200	7,000
Book value, December 31, 2010	491,600	486,000
4 years' amortization	8,400	14,000
Book value, December 31, 2014	$500,000	$500,000

The consolidation adjustments must dispose of the difference between the carrying values of the bonds on the two companies' books. Assuming that the bonds are carried *net* of the discount on each company's books, the adjustments under each method are as follows:

Agency method:

December 31, 2008

Bonds payable	487,400	
Bond investment		479,000
Gain on bond retirement		8,400
Non-controlling interest in earnings	2,520	
Non-controlling interest		2,520
[30% of the gain of $8,400]		

December 31, 2010

Bonds payable	491,600	
Bond investment		486,000
Non-controlling interest (5,600 × 30%)		1,680
Retained earnings		3,920
Interest income (including $3,500 amortization)	63,500	
Interest expense (including $2,100 amortization)		62,100
Minority interest [(3,500 − 2,100) × 30%]		420
Retained earnings		980

December 31, 2014

Bonds payable	500,000	
Bond investment		500,000
Interest income (including $3,500 amortization)	63,500	
Interest expense (including $2,100 amortization)		62,100
Minority interest [(3,500 − 2,100) × 30%]		420
Retained earnings		980

Par-value method:

December 31, 2008

Bonds payable	487,400	
Bond investment		479,000
Gain on bond retirement		8,400
Non-controlling interest in earnings	3,780	
Non-controlling interest [(500,000 − 487,400) × 30%]		3,780

December 31, 2010

Bonds payable	491,600	
Bond investment		486,000
Non-controlling interest (8,400 × 30%)		2,520
Retained earnings		3,080
Interest income (including $3,500 amortization)	63,500	
Interest expense (including $2,100 amortization)		62,100
Minority interest (2,100 × 30%)		630
Retained earnings		770

December 31, 2014

Bonds payable	500,000	
Bond investment		500,000
Interest income (including $3,500 amortization)	63,500	
Interest expense (including $2,100 amortization)		62,100
Minority interest (2,100 × 30%)		630
Retained earnings		770

SSP8–1

The *CICA Handbook* recommends that at each balance sheet date, monetary items denominated in a foreign currency should be adjusted to reflect the exchange rate in effect at the balance sheet date, and that the corresponding exchange gains or losses be recognized in net income for the period.

Fiscal Year	Exchange rate at year-end	CAD$ value of bonds	Gain (loss) for period
Dec. 31/05	1.27	6,350,000	N/A—bond issuance
2006	1.30	6,500,000	(150,000)
2007	1.34	6,700,000	(200,000)
2008	1.35	6,750,000	(50,000)

SSP8–2

a. Assuming the receivable is hedged

Note: The forward contract was established at $0.0520, a premium of $0.0020 per NTD over the spot rate at the date of the hedge. The total premium is NTD1,000,000 × $0.0020 = $2,000. The premium must be allocated over the periods for which the hedge is effective.

December 2, 2006:

Accounts receivable (NTD1,000,000 × $0.05)	50,000	
Sales revenue		50,000
[to record the sale at the spot rate of $0.0500]		

December 31, 2006:

Accounts receivable [NTD1,000,000 × ($0.0500 – $0.0510)]	1,000	
OCI–exchange gains and losses		1,000
[to adjust the receivable to the year-end spot rate of $0.0510]		

December 31, 2006:

Unrealized forward premium	1,000	
Exchange gains and losses		1,000
[recognition of one-half of the premium on the forward contract]		

February 1, 2007:

Cash (NTD1,000,000 × $0.0525)	52,500	
OCI–foreign exchange gains and losses	1,000	
Exchange gains and losses		2,500
Accounts receivable		51,000
[receipt of NTD1,000,000 cash from the customer]		

February 1, 2007

Cash (Cdn. dollars received on the forward contract)	52,000	
Exchange gains and losses	1,500	
Cash (NTD1,000,000 × $0.0525)		52,500
Unrealized forward premium		1,000
[settlement of the forward contract]		

b. Assuming the receivable is not hedged

December 2, 2006:

Accounts receivable (NTD1,000,000 × $0.0500)	50,000	
Sales revenue		50,000
[to record the sale at the spot rate of $0.0500]		

December 31, 2006:

Accounts receivable [NTD1,000,000 × ($0.0500 – $0.0510)]	1,000	
Exchange gains and losses		1,000
[to adjust the receivable to the year-end spot rate of $0.0510]		

February 1, 2007:

Cash (NTD1,000,000 × $0.0525)	52,500	
Accounts receivable		51,000
Exchange gains and losses		1,500
[receipt of NTD1,000,000 cash from the customer]		

SSP8–3

October 14, 2007 (contract signed): no entries are necessary.

December 7, 2007 (delivery of equipment):

Equipment (US$200,000 × $1.22)	244,000	
Accounts payable (US$200,000 × $1.18)		236,000
OCI – foreign exchange gains and losses		8,000
[to record the receipt of equipment, the related liability, and the premium on the forward contract]		

December 31, 2007 (year end):

OCI–foreign exchange gains and losses	2,000	
Accounts payable [US$200,000 × ($1.19 – $1.18)]		2,000
[to adjust the account payable to the year-end spot rate of $1.19]		

January 30, 2008 (payment):

Accounts payable	238,000	
OCI–foreign exchange gains and losses	10,000	
Cash (US$200,000 × $1.24)		248,000
[payment of US$200,000 to supplier]		

January 30, 2008 (settlement of forward contract):

Cash (US$200,000 × $1.24)	248,000	
Cash (received in Cdn. dollars)		244,000
OCI–foreign exchange gains and loss		4,000
[payment of US$200,000 to supplier]		

SSP9-1

Income statements, translated at the average rate for the year.

	2006 @ $1.70	2005 @ $2.20
Revenue	$510,000	$484,000
Depreciation expense	102,000	132,000
Interest expense	68,000	88,000
Other expenses	204,000	176,000
	374,000	396,000
Net income	$136,000	$ 88,000

Balance sheets, translated at the year-end rate (except for shareholders' equity):

	2006 @1.50	2005 @2.00
Assets		
Cash	$ 45,000	$ 320,000
Accounts receivable	60,000	60,000
Temporary investments (at cost)	300,000	—
Tangible capital assets	900,000	1,200,000
Accumulated depreciation	(180,000)	(120,000)
	$1,125,000	$1,460,000
Liabilities and shareholders' equity		
Accounts payable, current	$ 15,000	$ 40,000
Notes payable, due January 1, 2009	300,000	400,000
	315,000	440,000
Common shares (Note 1)	1,250,000	1,250,000
Retained earnings (Note 2)	73,000	22,000
Translation loss (Note 3)	(513,000)	(252,000)
	810,000	1,020,000
	$1,125,000	$1,460,000

Notes:

1. The original investment is translated at the historical rate of $2.50.
2. The retained earnings is translated at the historical rate at which the subsidiary's earnings were included in the *parent's* net income:

	2006	2005
SF10,000 from 2005 @ $2.20	$22,000	$22,000
SF30,000 from 2006 @ $1.70	51,000	—
	$73,000	$22,000

3. The translation loss can be derived as a balancing amount in the balance sheet, but it also can be calculated independently, as follows:

Loss pertaining to 2005:

Loss on initial investment, SF500,000 × ($2.00 − $2.50)	$250,000
Loss on 2005 earnings retained, SF10,000 × ($2.00 − $2.20)	2,000
Balance, December 31, 2005	252,000

Loss pertaining to 2006:

Loss on beginning of year shareholders' equity, SF510,000 × ($1.50 − $2.00)	255,000
Loss on 2006 earnings retained, SF30,000 × ($1.50 − $1.70)	6,000
Balance, December 31, 2006	$513,000

SSP9–2

a. Translated 2005 financial statements (temporal method)

Income statement:

	Local currency	Exchange rate	Canadian dollars
Revenue	SF 220,000	2.20	$ 484,000
Depreciation expense	60,000	2.30	138,000
Interest expense	40,000	2.20	88,000
Other expenses	80,000	2.20	176,000
	180,000		402,000
Net income	SF 40,000		$ 82,000

Balance sheet:

	Local currency	Exchange rate	Canadian dollars
Assets			
Cash	SF 160,000	2.00	$ 320,000
Accounts receivable	30,000	2.00	60,000
Tangible capital assets	600,000	2.30	1,380,000
Accumulated depreciation	(60,000)	2.30	(138,000)
	SF 730,000		$1,622,000
Liabilities and shareholders' equity			
Accounts payable, current	SF 20,000	2.00	$ 40,000
Note payable, long term	200,000	2.00	400,000
	220,000		440,000
Common shares	500,000	2.50	1,250,000
Retained earnings	10,000	(Note 1)	22,000
Translation gain (loss)	—		(90,000)
	510,000		1,182,000
	SF 730,000		$1,622,000

Note 1

	Local currency	Exchange rate	Canadian dollars
Net income, per income statement	SF 40,000	(as above)	$ 82,000
Less dividends declared and paid at year-end 2005	(30,000)	2.00	(60,000)
Retained earnings	SF 10,000		$ 22,000

b. Translation loss

	Local currency	Exchange rate	Canadian dollars
(1) *Loss on current monetary items:*			
Current monetary balance, January 1, 2005	—		—
Additions:			
Investment by Irene Corporation	SF 500,000	2.50	$1,250,000
Funds from operations:			
Net income	40,000	(as above)	82,000
Depreciation	60,000	2.30	138,000
Cash provided by note payable	200,000	2.40	480,000
	800,000		1,950,000
Uses:			
Purchase of tangible capital assets	600,000	2.30	1,380,000
Dividends declared	30,000	2.00	60,000
	630,000		1,440,000
Computed balance, December 31, 2005			510,000
Actual balance, December 31, 2005	SF 170,000	2.00	340,000
Total exchange loss for 2005			170,000
(2) *Gain on long-term note payable:*			
SF200,000 × ($2.40 − $2.00)			(80,000)
Loss on current monetary items			$ 90,000

Presentation on consolidated statements:

The total exchange loss of $90,000 will be shown as an exchange loss on Irene Corporation's 2005 income statement.

c. Translated 2006 financial statements (temporal method)

Income statement:

	Local currency	Exchange rate	Canadian dollars
Revenue	SF 300,000	1.70	$ 510,000
Depreciation expense	60,000	2.30	138,000
Interest expense	40,000	1.70	68,000
Other expenses	120,000	1.70	204,000
	220,000		410,000
Net income	SF 80,000		$ 100,000

Balance sheet:

	Local currency	Exchange rate	Canadian dollars
Assets			
Cash	SF 30,000	1.50	$ 45,000
Accounts receivable	40,000	1.50	60,000
Temporary investments	200,000	1.90	380,000
Tangible capital assets	600,000	2.30	1,380,000
Accumulated depreciation	(120,000)	2.30	(276,000)
	SF 750,000		$1,589,000
Liabilities and shareholders' equity			
Accounts payable, current	SF 10,000	1.50	$ 15,000
Note payable, long term	200,000	1.50	300,000
	210,000		315,000
Common shares	500,000	2.50	1,250,000
Retained earnings	40,000	(Note 1)	47,000
Translation gain (loss)	—		(23,000)
	540,000		1,274,000
	SF 750,000		$1,589,000

Note 1

	Local currency	Exchange rate	Canadian dollars
Balance, January 1, 2006	SF 10,000		$ 22,000
Net income, per income statement	80,000	(as above)	100,000
Less dividends declared and paid at year-end 2005	(50,000)	1.50	(75,000)
Retained earnings	SF 40,000		$ 47,000

d. Translation loss on current monetary items for 2006

	Local currency	Exchange rate	Canadian dollars
Current monetary balance, January 1, 2006	SF 170,000	2.00	$ 340,000
Additions:			
Funds from operations:			
Net income	80,000	(as above)	100,000
Depreciation	60,000	2.30	138,000
	310,000		578,000
Uses:			
Purchase of nonmonetary investments	200,000	1.90	380,000
Dividends declared	50,000	1.50	75,000
	250,000		455,000
Computed balance, December 31, 2006			123,000
Actual balance, December 31, 2006	SF 60,000	1.50	90,000
Loss on current monetary items			$ 33,000

Index

Wholly-Owned
Subsidiaries:
Reorting
Subsequent to
Acquisition

565

Wholly-Owned
Subsidiaries:
Reorting
Subsequent to
Acquisition

567

Wholly-Owned
Subsidiaries:
Reorting
Subsequent to
Acquisition

569

Wholly-Owned
Subsidiaries:
Reorting
Subsequent to
Acquisition

571

"AS IS" LICENSE AGREEMENT AND LIMITED WARRANTY

READ THIS LICENSE CAREFULLY BEFORE OPENING THIS PACKAGE. BY OPENING THIS PACKAGE, YOU ARE AGREEING TO THE TERMS AND CONDITIONS OF THIS LICENSE. IF YOU DO NOT AGREE, DO NOT OPEN THE PACKAGE. PROMPTLY RETURN THE UNOPENED PACKAGE AND ALL ACCOMPANYING ITEMS TO THE PLACE YOU OBTAINED THEM. THESE TERMS APPLY TO ALL LICENSED SOFTWARE ON THE DISK EXCEPT THAT THE TERMS FOR USE OF ANY SHAREWARE OR FREEWARE ON THE DISKETTES ARE AS SET FORTH IN THE ELECTRONIC LICENSE LOCATED ON THE DISK:

1. GRANT OF LICENSE and OWNERSHIP: The enclosed computer programs <<and any data>> ("Software") are licensed, not sold, to you by Pearson Education Canada Inc. ("We" or the "Company") in consideration of your adoption of the accompanying Company textbooks and/or other materials, and your agreement to these terms. You own only the disk(s) but we and/or our licensors own the Software itself. This license allows instructors and students enrolled in the course using the Company textbook that accompanies this Software (the "Course") to use and display the enclosed copy of the Software for academic use only, so long as you comply with the terms of this Agreement. You may make one copy for back up only. We reserve any rights not granted to you.

2. USE RESTRICTIONS: You may not sell or license copies of the Software or the Documentation to others. You may not transfer, distribute or make available the Software or the Documentation, except to instructors and students in your school who are users of the adopted Company textbook that accompanies this Software in connection with the course for which the textbook was adopted. You may not reverse engineer, disassemble, decompile, modify, adapt, translate or create derivative works based on the Software or the Documentation. You may be held legally responsible for any copying or copyright infringement which is caused by your failure to abide by the terms of these restrictions.

3. TERMINATION: This license is effective until terminated. This license will terminate automatically without notice from the Company if you fail to comply with any provisions or limitations of this license. Upon termination, you shall destroy the Documentation and all copies of the Software. All provisions of this Agreement as to limitation and disclaimer of warranties, limitation of liability, remedies or damages, and our ownership rights shall survive termination.

4. DISCLAIMER OF WARRANTY: THE COMPANY AND ITS LICENSORS MAKE NO WARRANTIES ABOUT THE SOFTWARE, WHICH IS PROVIDED "AS-IS." IF THE DISK IS DEFECTIVE IN MATERIALS OR WORK-MANSHIP, YOUR ONLY REMEDY IS TO RETURN IT TO THE COMPANY WITHIN 30 DAYS FOR REPLACE-MENT UNLESS THE COMPANY DETERMINES IN GOOD FAITH THAT THE DISK HAS BEEN MISUSED OR IMPROPERLY INSTALLED, REPAIRED, ALTERED OR DAMAGED. THE COMPANY DISCLAIMS ALL WAR-RANTIES, EXPRESS OR IMPLIED, INCLUDING WITHOUT LIMITATION, THE IMPLIED WARRANTIES OF MERCHANTABILITY AND FITNESS FOR A PARTICULAR PURPOSE. THE COMPANY DOES NOT WAR-RANT, GUARANTEE OR MAKE ANY REPRESENTATION REGARDING THE ACCURACY, RELIABILITY, CURRENTNESS, USE, OR RESULTS OF USE, OF THE SOFTWARE.

5. LIMITATION OF REMEDIES AND DAMAGES:IN NO EVENT, SHALL THE COMPANY OR ITS EMPLOY-EES, AGENTS, LICENSORS OR CONTRACTORS BE LIABLE FOR ANY INCIDENTAL, INDIRECT, SPECIAL OR CONSEQUENTIAL DAMAGES ARISING OUT OF OR IN CONNECTION WITH THIS LICENSE OR THE SOFTWARE, INCLUDING, WITHOUT LIMITATION, LOSS OF USE, LOSS OF DATA, LOSS OF INCOME OR PROFIT, OR OTHER LOSSES SUSTAINED AS A RESULT OF INJURY TO ANY PERSON, OR LOSS OF OR DAMAGE TO PROPERTY, OR CLAIMS OF THIRD PARTIES, EVEN IF THE COMPANY OR AN AUTHORIZED REPRESENTATIVE OF THE COMPANY HAS BEEN ADVISED OF THE POSSIBILITY OF SUCH DAMAGES. SOME JURISDICTIONS DO NOT ALLOW THE LIMITATION OF DAMAGES IN CERTAIN CIRCUM-STANCES, SO THE ABOVE LIMITATIONS MAY NOT ALWAYS APPLY.

6. GENERAL: THIS AGREEMENT SHALL BE CONSTRUED AND INTERPRETED ACCORDING TO THE LAWS OF THE PROVINCE OF ONTARIO. This Agreement is the complete and exclusive statement of the agreement between you and the Company and supersedes all proposals, prior agreements, oral or written, and any other communications between you and the company or any of its representatives relating to the subject matter.

Should you have any questions concerning this agreement or if you wish to contact the Company for any reason, please contact in writing: Customer Service, Pearson Education Canada, 26 Prince Andrew Place, Don Mills, Ontario M3C 2T8.